Indiana
Grade 7

interactive
SCIENCE

Boston, Massachusetts
Chandler, Arizona
Glenview, Illinois
Upper Saddle River, New Jersey

AUTHORS

You're an author!

As you write in this science book, your answers and personal discoveries will be recorded for you to keep, making this book unique to you. That is why you are one of the primary authors of this book.

✎ **In the space below, print your name, school, town, and state. Then write a short autobiography that includes your interests and accomplishments.**

YOUR NAME _____

SCHOOL _____

TOWN, STATE _____

AUTOBIOGRAPHY _____

_____

_____

_____

_____

_____

_____

_____

_____

Your Photo

Acknowledgments appear on pages 615–619, which constitute an extension of this copyright page.

ISBN-13: 978-0-13-253476-5
ISBN-10: 0-13-253476-2
6 7 8 9 10 V011 17 16 15

ON THE COVER
Indiana Sand Dunes
Indiana's Mount Baldy sand dune, 55 meters above Lake Michigan, dates back to Earth's most recent Ice Age. Melting glaciers, continent-sized sheets of ice, left behind mounds of sand and the Great Lakes themselves. The beauty of this dune has been preserved at Indiana Dunes National Lakeshore.

Program Authors

DON BUCKLEY, M.Sc.
Information and Communications Technology Director,
The School at Columbia University, New York, New York
Mr. Buckley has been at the forefront of K–12 educational technology for nearly two decades. A founder of New York City Independent School Technologists (NYCIST) and long-time chair of New York Association of Independent Schools' annual IT conference, he has taught students on two continents and created multimedia and Internet-based instructional systems for schools worldwide.

ZIPPORAH MILLER, M.A.Ed.
Associate Executive Director for Professional Programs and Conferences, National Science Teachers Association, Arlington, Virginia
Associate executive director for professional programs and conferences at NSTA, Ms. Zipporah Miller is a former K–12 science supervisor and STEM coordinator for the Prince George's County Public School District in Maryland. She is a science education consultant who has overseen curriculum development and staff training for more than 150 district science coordinators.

MICHAEL J. PADILLA, Ph.D.
Associate Dean and Director, Eugene P. Moore School of Education, Clemson University, Clemson, South Carolina
A former middle school teacher and a leader in middle school science education, Dr. Michael Padilla has served as president of the National Science Teachers Association and as a writer of the National Science Education Standards. He is professor of science education at Clemson University. As lead author of the *Science Explorer* series, Dr. Padilla has inspired the team in developing a program that promotes student inquiry and meets the needs of today's students.

KATHRYN THORNTON, Ph.D.
Professor and Associate Dean, School of Engineering and Applied Science, University of Virginia, Charlottesville, Virginia
Selected by NASA in May 1984, Dr. Kathryn Thornton is a veteran of four space flights. She has logged over 975 hours in space, including more than 21 hours of extravehicular activity. As an author on the *Scott Foresman Science* series, Dr. Thornton's enthusiasm for science has inspired teachers around the globe.

MICHAEL E. WYSESSION, Ph.D.
Associate Professor of Earth and Planetary Science, Washington University, St. Louis, Missouri
An author on more than 50 scientific publications, Dr. Wysession was awarded the prestigious Packard Foundation Fellowship and Presidential Faculty Fellowship for his research in geophysics. Dr. Wysession is an expert on Earth's inner structure and has mapped various regions of Earth using seismic tomography. He is known internationally for his work in geoscience education and outreach.

Instructional Design Author

GRANT WIGGINS, Ed.D.
President, Authentic Education, Hopewell, New Jersey
Dr. Wiggins is a co-author with Jay McTighe of *Understanding by Design, 2nd Edition* (ASCD 2005). His approach to instructional design provides teachers with a disciplined way of thinking about curriculum design, assessment, and instruction that moves teaching from covering content to ensuring understanding.

UNDERSTANDING BY DESIGN® and UbD™ are trademarks of ASCD, and are used under license.

Planet Diary Author

JACK HANKIN
Science/Mathematics Teacher, The Hilldale School, Daly City, California Founder, Planet Diary Web site
Mr. Hankin is the creator and writer of Planet Diary, a science current events Web site. He is passionate about bringing science news and environmental awareness into classrooms and offers numerous Planet Diary workshops at NSTA and other events to train middle and high school teachers.

ELL Consultant

JIM CUMMINS, Ph.D.
Professor and Canada Research Chair, Curriculum, Teaching and Learning department at the University of Toronto
Dr. Cummins focuses on literacy development in multilingual schools and the role of technology in promoting student learning across the curriculum. *Interactive Science* incorporates essential research-based principles for integrating language with the teaching of academic content based on his instructional framework.

Reading Consultant

HARVEY DANIELS, Ph.D.
Professor of Secondary Education, University of New Mexico, Albuquerque, New Mexico
Dr. Daniels is an international consultant to schools, districts, and educational agencies. He has authored or coauthored 13 books on language, literacy, and education. His most recent works are *Comprehension and Collaboration: Inquiry Circles in Action* and *Subjects Matter: Every Teacher's Guide to Content-Area Reading*.

REVIEWERS

Contributing Writers

Edward Aguado, Ph.D.
Professor, Department of Geography
San Diego State University
San Diego, California

Elizabeth Coolidge-Stolz, M.D.
Medical Writer
North Reading, Massachusetts

Donald L. Cronkite, Ph.D.
Professor of Biology
Hope College
Holland, Michigan

Jan Jenner, Ph.D.
Science Writer
Talladega, Alabama

Linda Cronin Jones, Ph.D.
Associate Professor of Science and Environmental Education
University of Florida
Gainesville, Florida

T. Griffith Jones, Ph.D.
Clinical Associate Professor of Science Education
College of Education
University of Florida
Gainesville, Florida

Andrew C. Kemp, Ph.D.
Teacher
Jefferson County Public Schools
Louisville, Kentucky

Matthew Stoneking, Ph.D.
Associate Professor of Physics
Lawrence University
Appleton, Wisconsin

R. Bruce Ward, Ed.D.
Senior Research Associate
Science Education Department
Harvard-Smithsonian Center for Astrophysics
Cambridge, Massachusetts

Museum of Science.

Special thanks to the Museum of Science, Boston, Massachusetts, and Ioannis Miaoulis, the Museum's president and director, for serving as content advisors for the technology and design strand in this program.

Content Reviewers

Paul D. Beale, Ph.D.
Department of Physics
University of Colorado at Boulder
Boulder, Colorado

Jeff R. Bodart, Ph.D.
Professor of Physical Sciences
Chipola College
Marianna, Florida

Joy Branlund, Ph.D.
Department of Earth Science
Southwestern Illinois College
Granite City, Illinois

Marguerite Brickman, Ph.D.
Division of Biological Sciences
University of Georgia
Athens, Georgia

Bonnie J. Brunkhorst, Ph.D.
Science Education and Geological Sciences
California State University
San Bernardino, California

Michael Castellani, Ph.D.
Department of Chemistry
Marshall University
Huntington, West Virginia

Charles C. Curtis, Ph.D.
Research Associate Professor of Physics
University of Arizona
Tucson, Arizona

Diane I. Doser, Ph.D.
Department of Geological Sciences
University of Texas
El Paso, Texas

Rick Duhrkopf, Ph.D.
Department of Biology
Baylor University
Waco, Texas

Alice K. Hankla, Ph.D.
The Galloway School
Atlanta, Georgia

Mark Henriksen, Ph.D.
Physics Department
University of Maryland
Baltimore, Maryland

Chad Hershock, Ph.D.
Center for Research on Learning and Teaching
University of Michigan
Ann Arbor, Michigan

Jeremiah N. Jarrett, Ph.D.
Department of Biology
Central Connecticut State University
New Britain, Connecticut

Scott L. Kight, Ph.D.
Department of Biology
Montclair State University
Montclair, New Jersey

Jennifer O. Liang, Ph.D.
Department of Biology
University of Minnesota–Duluth
Duluth, Minnesota

Candace Lutzow-Felling, Ph.D.
Director of Education
The State Arboretum of Virginia
University of Virginia
Boyce, Virginia

Cortney V. Martin, Ph.D.
Virginia Polytechnic Institute
Blacksburg, Virginia

Joseph F. McCullough, Ph.D.
Physics Program Chair
Cabrillo College
Aptos, California

Heather Mernitz, Ph.D.
Department of Physical Science
Alverno College
Milwaukee, Wisconsin

Sadredin C. Moosavi, Ph.D.
Department of Earth and Environmental Sciences
Tulane University
New Orleans, Louisiana

David L. Reid, Ph.D.
Department of Biology
Blackburn College
Carlinville, Illinois

Scott M. Rochette, Ph.D.
Department of the Earth Sciences
SUNY College at Brockport
Brockport, New York

Karyn L. Rogers, Ph.D.
Department of Geological Sciences
University of Missouri
Columbia, Missouri

Laurence Rosenhein, Ph.D.
Department of Chemistry
Indiana State University
Terre Haute, Indiana

Sara Seager, Ph.D.
Department of Planetary Sciences and Physics
Massachusetts Institute of Technology
Cambridge, Massachusetts

Tom Shoberg, Ph.D.
Missouri University of Science and Technology
Rolla, Missouri

Patricia Simmons, Ph.D.
North Carolina State University
Raleigh, North Carolina

William H. Steinecker, Ph.D.
Research Scholar
Miami University
Oxford, Ohio

Paul R. Stoddard, Ph.D.
Department of Geology and Environmental Geosciences
Northern Illinois University
DeKalb, Illinois

John R. Villarreal, Ph.D.
Department of Chemistry
The University of Texas–Pan American
Edinburg, Texas

John R. Wagner, Ph.D.
Department of Geology
Clemson University
Clemson, South Carolina

Jerry Waldvogel, Ph.D.
Department of Biological Sciences
Clemson University
Clemson, South Carolina

Donna L. Witter, Ph.D.
Department of Geology
Kent State University
Kent, Ohio

Edward J. Zalisko, Ph.D.
Department of Biology
Blackburn College
Carlinville, Illinois

Indiana Content Reviewers

Sandra Davis, Ph.D.
Department of Biology
University of Indianapolis
Indianapolis, Indiana

Laurence Rosenhein, Ph.D.
Department of Chemistry
Indiana State University
Terre Haute, Indiana

Klaus Neumann, Ph.D.
Department of Geological Sciences
Ball State University
Muncie, Indiana

Janet Vaglia, Ph.D.
Department of Biology
DePauw University
Greencastle, Indiana

Built especially for
Indiana

Indiana Interactive Science covers 100% of Indiana's Academic Standards for Science without extraneous content. Built on feedback from Indiana educators, *Interactive Science* focuses on what is important to Indiana teachers and students, creating a personal, relevant, and engaging classroom experience.

Indiana K-8 Science Teacher Advisory Board

Jodi Allen
Glen Acres Elementary School
Lafayette, IN

Rick Dubbs
Monrovia Middle School
Monrovia, IN

Margaret Flack
Vincennes University-Jasper Campus
Jasper, IN

Michael Gibson
New Haven Middle School &
East Allen County School
New Haven, IN

Jill Hatcher
Spring Mill School
Indianapolis, IN

Jamie Hooten
Lincoln Elementary School, NLCS
Bedford, IN

Jamil Odom
Mary Bryan Elementary School
Indianapolis, IN

Mike Robards
Franklin Community Middle School
Franklin, IN

Richard Towle
Noblesville Middle School
Noblesville, IN

CONTENTS

Lab zone Enter the Lab zone for hands-on inquiry.

Chapter Lab Investigation:
• Directed Inquiry: Keeping Flowers Fresh
• Open Inquiry: Keeping Flowers Fresh

Inquiry Warm-Ups: • Is It Really True?
• How Keen Are Your Senses? • What's Happening?

Quick Labs: • Classifying Objects • Thinking Like a Scientist • Using Scientific Thinking • Scientific Inquiry • Theories and Laws

MY SCIENCE ONLINE.com

Go to MyScienceOnline.com to interact with this chapter's content. **Keyword: Scientific Thinking**

UNTAMED SCIENCE
• What is Science, Anyway?

PLANET DIARY
• What is Science?

INTERACTIVE ART
• Why Make a Model? • Inquiry Diagram
• Scientific Stumbling Blocks • Super Scientists

VIRTUAL LAB
• Introduction to Virtual Lab • What is Scientific Inquiry?

 Enter the Lab zone for hands-on inquiry.

Chapter Lab Investigation:
• Directed Inquiry: Density Graphs
• Open Inquiry: Density Graphs

Inquiry Warm-Ups: • History of Measurement • How Many Marbles Are There? • What's in a Picture? • Scale Models • Where Is the Safety Equipment in Your School?

Quick Labs: • How Many Shoes? • Measuring Length in Metric • For Good Measure • How Close Is It? • What's a Line Graph? • Making Models • Systems • Models in Nature • Be Prepared • Just in Case

my science online.com

Go to MyScienceOnline.com to interact with this chapter's content. **Keyword:** Using Mathematics in Science

> **UNTAMED SCIENCE**
• Measuring Up

> **PLANET DIARY**
• Using Mathematics in Science

> **INTERACTIVE ART**
• The Need for Numbers • Plotting a Line Graph • Modeling a System

> **VIRTUAL LAB**
• How Are Units Useful?

CONTENTS

Lab zone® Enter the Lab zone for hands-on inquiry.

△ **Chapter Lab Investigation:**
- Directed Inquiry: Stopping on a Dime
- Open Inquiry: Stopping on a Dime
- Directed Inquiry: Sticky Sneakers
- Open Inquiry: Sticky Sneakers

△ **Inquiry Warm-Ups:** • What Is Motion?
• How Fast and How Far? • Will You Hurry Up?
• Is the Force With You? • Observing Friction
• What Changes Motion?

△ **Quick Labs:** • Identifying Motion • Velocity
• Motion Graphs • Describing Acceleration
• Graphing Acceleration • What Is Force?
• Modeling Unbalanced Forces • Calculating
• Around and Around • Newton's Second Law

my science online.com

Go to MyScienceOnline.com to interact with this chapter's content.
Keyword: Forces and Motion

> **UNTAMED SCIENCE**
• The Adventures of Velocity Girl

> **PLANET DIARY**
• Forces and Motion

> **INTERACTIVE ART**
• Speed and Acceleration • Graphing Motion
• Balanced and Unbalanced Forces

> **ART IN MOTION**
• Relative Motion • Types of Friction

> **VIRTUAL LAB**
• How Can You Measure Acceleration?
• Investigating Newton's Laws of Motion

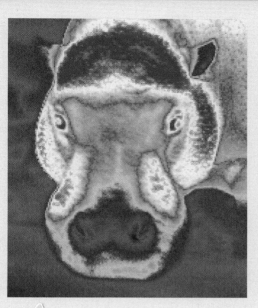

Lab zone® **Enter the Lab zone for hands-on inquiry.**

Chapter Lab Investigation:
• Directed Inquiry: Transforming Energy
• Open Inquiry: Transforming Energy

Inquiry Warm-Ups: • Pulling at an Angle
• Pendulum Swing • What Does It Mean to Heat Up?

Quick Labs: • Forms of Energy • Energy Transfer • Visualizing Convection Currents

my science online

Go to MyScienceOnline.com to interact with this chapter's content. Keyword: Energy and Energy Transfer

> **UNTAMED SCIENCE**
• Why Is This Inner Tube So Hot?

> **PLANET DIARY**
• Energy and Energy Transfer

> **ART IN MOTION**
• Kinetic and Potential Energy

> **INTERACTIVE ART**
• Types of Energy • Heat Transfer

> **VIRTUAL LAB**
• Exploring Kinetic and Potential Energy

CONTENTS

Lab zone® Enter the Lab zone for hands-on inquiry.

Chapter Lab Investigation:
• Directed Inquiry: Design and Build a Solar Cooker
• Open Inquiry: Design and Build a Solar Cooker

Inquiry Warm-Ups: • What's in a Piece of Coal? • Can You Capture Solar Energy? • Which Bulb Is More Efficient?

Quick Labs: • Observing Oil's Consistency • Fossil Fuels • Producing Electricity • Human Energy Use • Future Energy Use

my science online.com

Go to MyScienceOnline.com to interact with this chapter's content. **Keyword:** Energy Resources

> UNTAMED SCIENCE
• Farming the Wind

> PLANET DIARY
• Energy Resources

> INTERACTIVE ART
• Hydroelectric Power Plant • Nuclear Power Plant

> ART IN MOTION
• Oil: Long to Form, Quick to Use

> REAL-WORLD INQUIRY
• Energy Conservation

 Enter the Lab zone for hands-on inquiry.

△ **Chapter Lab Investigation:**
  • Directed Inquiry: Making Waves
  • Open Inquiry: Making Waves
  • Directed Inquiry: Changing Pitch
  • Open Inquiry: Changing Pitch

△ **Inquiry Warm-Ups:** • What Are Waves?
• What Do Waves Look Like? • How Does a
Ball Bounce? • What Is Sound? • How Does
Amplitude Affect Loudness?

△ **Quick Labs:** • What Causes Mechanical
Waves? • Three Types of Waves • Properties
of Waves • What Affects the Speed of a
Wave? • Wave Interference • Standing Waves
• Understanding Sound • Ear to the Sound
• Listen to This • Pipe Sounds

my science online .com

Go to MyScienceOnline.com to
interact with this chapter's content.
Keyword: Characteristics of Waves

> **UNTAMED SCIENCE**
• Extreme Wave Science!

> **PLANET DIARY**
• Characteristics of Waves

> **INTERACTIVE ART**
• Wave Interference • Properties of Waves

> **ART IN MOTION**
• Wave and Energy Movement • Observing
the Doppler Effect

> **VIRTUAL LAB**
• Bouncing and Bending Light

CONTENTS

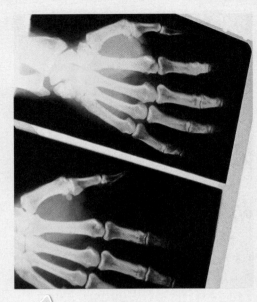

Lab zone® Enter the Lab zone for hands-on inquiry.

Chapter Lab Investigation:
• Directed Inquiry: Changing Colors
• Open Inquiry: Changing Colors

Inquiry Warm-Ups: • How Fast Are
Electromagnetic Waves? • What Is White
Light? • How Do Colors Mix? • Reflection
Wink? • How Can You Make an Image Appear?

Quick Labs: • Electromagnetic Wave
• Waves or Particles? • Wave Differences
• Parts of the Spectrum • Hypotheses
• Observing • Mirror Images • Bent Pencil
• Looking at Images

my science online.com

Go to MyScienceOnline.com to
interact with this chapter's content.
Keyword: Electromagnetic Waves and
Light

> UNTAMED SCIENCE
• The Day the Waves Died

> PLANET DIARY
• Electromagnetic Waves and Light

> INTERACTIVE ART
• Electromagnetic Waves • Modulating
Electromagnetic Waves • Mirrors and Lenses

> ART IN MOTION
• Invisible Information • Refraction,
Reflection, and Rainbows

> VIRTUAL LAB
• Wave or Particle?

CHAPTER 8

Introducing Earth

Lab zone® Enter the Lab zone for hands-on inquiry.

Chapter Lab Investigation:
• Directed Inquiry: Modeling Mantle Convection Currents
• Open Inquiry: Modeling Mantle Convection Currents

Inquiry Warm-Ups: • What Is a System?
• Earth's Interior • Tracing Heat Flow

Quick Labs: • Parts of Earth's System • What Forces Shape Earth? • How Do Scientists Find Out What's Inside Earth? • Build a Model of Earth • How Can Heat Cause Motion in a Liquid?

my science ONLINE .com

Go to MyScienceOnline.com to interact with this chapter's content.
Keyword: Introducing Earth

> **UNTAMED SCIENCE**
• Beyond the Dirt

> **PLANET DIARY**
• Introducing Earth

> **INTERACTIVE ART**
• Earth's System • Heat Transfer

> **ART IN MOTION**
• Convection in Earth's Mantle

> **REAL-WORLD INQUIRY**
• Exploring Earth's Layers

CONTENTS

CHAPTER 9

Minerals and Rocks

Lab zone® Enter the Lab zone for hands-on inquiry.

Chapter Lab Investigation:
• Directed Inquiry: Testing Rock Flooring
• Open Inquiry: Testing Rock Flooring

Inquiry Warm-Ups: • How Does the Rate of Cooling Affect Crystals? • How Do Rocks Compare? • Liquid to Solid • Earth's Coral Reefs • A Sequined Rock • Recycling Rocks

Quick Labs: • Classifying Objects as Minerals • What Is the True Color of a Mineral? • Classify These Rocks • How Do Igneous Rocks Form? • The Rocks Around Us • How Does Pressure Affect Particles of Rock? • What Causes Layers? • How Do Grain Patterns Compare? • Which Rock Came First?

my science ONLINE.com

Go to MyScienceOnline.com to interact with this chapter's content.
Keyword: Minerals and Rocks

> **UNTAMED SCIENCE**
• Climbing Through the Rock Cycle

> **PLANET DIARY**
• Minerals and Rocks

> **INTERACTIVE ART**
• Crystal Systems • Rock Cycle

> **ART IN MOTION**
• Formation of Igneous Rock

> **REAL-WORLD INQUIRY**
• What Would You Build With?

Lab zone ®
**Enter the Lab zone
for hands-on inquiry.**

Chapter Lab Investigation:
• Directed Inquiry: Modeling Sea-Floor Spreading
• Open Inquiry: Modeling Sea-Floor Spreading

Inquiry Warm-Ups: • How Are Earth's Continents Linked Together? • What Is the Effect of a Change in Density? • Plate Interactions

Quick Labs: • Moving the Continents • Mid-Ocean Ridges • Reversing Poles • Mantle Convection Currents

my SCIENCE online .com

Go to MyScienceOnline.com to interact with this chapter's content.
Keyword: Plate Tectonics

> UNTAMED SCIENCE
• Diving Toward Divergence

> PLANET DIARY
• Plate Tectonics

> INTERACTIVE ART
• Continental Drift • Sea-Floor Spreading

> ART IN MOTION
• Changing Earth's Crust

> REAL-WORLD INQUIRY
• Predicting Plate Motion

CONTENTS

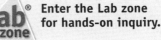
Enter the Lab zone for hands-on inquiry.

Chapter Lab Investigation:
• Directed Inquiry: Finding the Epicenter
• Directed Inquiry: Gelatin Volcanoes

Inquiry Warm-Ups: • Earth's Crust • How Do Seismic Waves Travel? • How Can Seismic Waves Be Detected? • Moving Volcanoes • How Fast Do Liquids Flow? • How Do Volcanoes Change Land?

Quick Labs: • Effects of Stress • Modeling Faults • Modeling Stress • Seismic Waves • Measuring Earthquakes • Seismograph • Earthquake Patterns • Where Are Volcanoes Found? • Volcanic Stages • Volcanic Landforms • Volcanic Activity

my science online.com

Go to MyScienceOnline.com to interact with this chapter's content.
Keyword: Earthquakes and Volcanoes

> UNTAMED SCIENCE
• Why Quakes Shake

> PLANET DIARY
• Earthquakes and Volcanoes

> INTERACTIVE ART
• Seismic Waves • Earthquake Engineering
• Composite Volcano • Volcanoes

> ART IN MOTION
• Stresses and Faults • Volcanic Boundaries

> REAL-WORLD INQUIRY
• Placing a Bay Area Stadium • Volcano

Lab® zone Enter the Lab zone for hands-on inquiry.

Chapter Lab Investigation:
• Directed Inquiry: Investigating Soils and Drainage
• Open Inquiry: Investigating Soils and Drainage

Inquiry Warm-Ups: • How Fast Can It Fizz?
• What Is Soil? • How Can You Keep Soil From Washing Away?

Quick Labs: • Freezing and Thawing
• Rusting Away • It's All on the Surface
• The Contents of Soil • Using It Up • Soil Conservation

my science ONLINE.com

Go to MyScienceOnline.com to interact with this chapter's content.
Keyword: Weathering and Soil

> UNTAMED SCIENCE
• Tafoni, No Bologna

> PLANET DIARY
• Weathering and Soil

> INTERACTIVE ART
• The Forces of Weathering • Soil Layers

> ART IN MOTION
• Mechanical and Chemical Weathering

> REAL-WORLD INQUIRY
• Being Smart About Soil

CONTENTS

Lab zone® Enter the Lab zone for hands-on inquiry.

Chapter Lab Investigation:
• Directed Inquiry: Sand Hills
• Open Inquiry: Sand Hills

Inquiry Warm-Ups: • How Does Gravity Affect Materials on a Slope? • How Does Moving Water Wear Away Rocks? • How Do Glaciers Change the Land? • What Is Sand Made Of? • How Does Moving Air Affect Sediment?

Quick Labs: • Weathering and Erosion • Raindrops Falling • Erosion Cube • Surging Glaciers • Modeling Valleys • Shaping a Coastline • Desert Pavement

my science online.com

Go to MyScienceOnline.com to interact with this chapter's content.
Keyword: Erosion and Deposition

> **PLANET DIARY**
• Carving a Canyon

> **PLANET DIARY**
• Erosion and Deposition

> **ART IN MOTION**
• Effects of Glaciers

> **INTERACTIVE ART**
• Effects of Waves • Mass Movement

> **REAL-WORLD INQUIRY**
• Why Live Where It Floods?

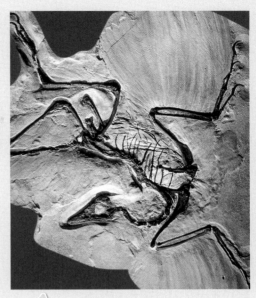

 Enter the Lab zone for hands-on inquiry.

Chapter Lab Investigation:
• Directed Inquiry: Exploring Geologic Time
Through Core Samples
• Open Inquiry: Exploring Geologic Time
Through Core Samples

Inquiry Warm-Ups: • What's in a Rock?
• Which Layer Is the Oldest? • This Is Your Life!
• Dividing History

Quick Labs: • Sweet Fossils • Modeling
Trace Fossils • Modeling the Fossil Record
• How Did It Form? • Going Back in Time
• Graphing the Fossil Record • Modeling an
Asteroid Impact • Cenozoic Timeline

my science online.com

Go to MyScienceOnline.com to interact
with this chapter's content. Keyword:
A Trip Through Geologic Time

> **UNTAMED SCIENCE**
• Riding the Geo-vator

> **PLANET DIARY**
• A Trip Through Geologic Time

> **ART IN MOTION**
• Change Over Geologic Time

> **INTERACTIVE ART**
• Piecing Together the Past • Index Fossils
• Fossil Formation

> **REAL-WORLD INQUIRY**
• How Do You Find the Age of a Rock?

CONTENTS

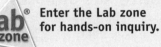 Enter the Lab zone
for hands-on inquiry.

Chapter Lab Investigation:
• Directed Inquiry: Microscope
• Directed Inquiry: A Look Beneath the Skin

Inquiry Warm-Ups: • What Can You See?
• How Large Are Cells? • Detecting Starch
• Yeast Cells • How Is Your Body Organized?
• How Does Your Body Respond?

Quick Labs: • Comparing Cells • Observing
Cells • Gelatin Cell Model • Tissues, Organs,
Systems • What Is a Compound? • What's
That Taste? • Observing Mitosis • Modeling
Mitosis • Observing Cells and Tissues
• Working Together, Acts I and II

my science online.com

Go to MyScienceOnline.com to
interact with this chapter's content.
Keyword: Cells and Human Body
Systems

UNTAMED SCIENCE
• Touring Hooke's Crib!

PLANET DIARY
• Cells and Human Body Systems

INTERACTIVE ART
• Plant and Animal Cells • Specialized Cells
• The Cell Cycle • Body Systems

ART IN MOTION
• The Body's Highway

VIRTUAL LAB
• How Can You Observe Cells?

Untamed Science™

Video Series: Chapter Adventures

Untamed Science created this captivating video series for interactive SCIENCE featuring a unique segment for every chapter of the program.

Featuring videos such as

interactive SCIENCE

This is your book.
You can write in it!

Get Engaged!

At the start of each chapter, you will see two questions: an Engaging Question and the Big Question. Each chapter's Big Question will help you start thinking about the Big Ideas of Science. Look for the Big Q symbol throughout the chapter!

WHAT CAN SHARKS TEACH THESE CAGED SCIENTISTS?

What does it mean to think like a scientist?

Would you ever go diving in a shark cage? If you were a marine biologist, this might be part of your job. To learn more about sharks, marine biologists study them in their natural environment. These Galápagos sharks were observed swimming off of the coast of Hawaii. Marine biologists have learned that a full-grown male Galápagos shark can grow to be 3.7 meters long and eat squid, octopus, and fish, including other sharks.

Infer What information could scientists learn by watching these sharks?

The scientists could estimate how old the sharks are and notice if they are males or females. They might also see how the sharks act around humans.

> **UNTAMED SCIENCE** Watch the **Untamed Science** video to learn more about science.

xxx   What Is Science?

Untamed Science™

Follow the Untamed Science video crew as they travel the globe exploring the Big Ideas of Science.

Interact with your textbook.   **Interact with inquiry.**   **Interact online.**

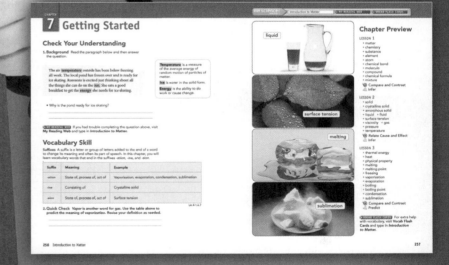

Build Reading, Inquiry, and Vocabulary Skills

In every lesson you will learn new 🔄 Reading and 🔺 Inquiry skills. These skills will help you read and think like a scientist. Vocabulary skills will help you communicate effectively and uncover the meaning of words.

Go Online!

Look for the MyScienceOnline.com technology options. At MyScienceOnline.com you can immerse yourself in amazing virtual environments, get extra practice, and even blog about current events in science.

Master Indiana Standards

Indiana Academic Standards for Science are indicated every step of the way throughout your book.

Explore the Key Concepts.

Each lesson begins with a series of Key Concept questions. The interactivities in each lesson will help you understand these concepts and Unlock the Big Question.

MY PLANET DiARY
for Indiana

At the start of each lesson, My Planet Diary will introduce you to amazing events, significant people, and important discoveries in Indiana or help you to overcome common misconceptions.

Desertification If the soil in a on of moisture and nutrients, the area advance of desertlike conditions in fertile is called **desertification** (dih

One cause of desertification is c is a period when less rain than nor droughts, crops fail. Without plant blows away. Overgrazing of grasslar cutting down trees for firewood ca

Desertification is a serious prob and graze livestock where desertific people may face famine and starvat central Africa. Millions of rural pe cities because they can no longer su

apply it!

Desertification affects many areas around the world.

1 Name Which continent has the most existing desert?

Africa

2 Interpret Maps Where in the United States is the greatest risk of desertification?

The western United Sta

3 Infer Is desertification a threat is existing desert? Explain. Circle an your answer.

No; there are high-risk ar desert, such as along th

4 CHALLENGE If an area is facing d things people could do to possibly li

Sample: People could limi grow plants to provide s

360   Land, Air, and Water Resource

Explain what you know.

Look for the pencil. When you see it, it's time to interact with your book and demonstrate what you have learned.

apply it!

Elaborate further with the Apply It activities. This is your opportunity to take what you've learned and apply it to new situations.

Lab Zone

Look for the Lab zone triangle. This means it's time to do a hands-on inquiry lab. In every lesson, you'll have the opportunity to do many hands-on inquiry activities that will help reinforce your understanding of the lesson topic.

Land Reclamation Fortunately, it is possible to replace land damaged by erosion or mining. The process of restoring an area of land to a more productive state is called **land reclamation.** In addition to restoring land for agriculture, land reclamation can restore habitats for wildlife. Many different types of land reclamation projects are currently underway all over the world. But it is generally more difficult and expensive to restore damaged land and soil than it is to protect those resources in the first place. In some cases, the land may not return to its original state.

FIGURE 4
Land Reclamation
These pictures show land before and after it was mined.

✎ **Communicate** Below the pictures, write a story about what happened to the land.

Sample: Some trees were cut to make room for a mine. When the mining stopped, people replaced the soil and planted grass and trees. In time, the mine became a forest, but it is not the same as the original forest.

rtile area becomes depleted
come a desert. The
as that previously were
uh fih KAY shun).
. For example, a **drought**
lls in an area. During
, the exposed soil easily
y cattle and sheep and
se desertification, too.
People cannot grow crops
has occurred. As a result,
Desertification is severe in
here are moving to the
t themselves on the land.

Key
- Existing desert
- High-risk area
- Moderate-risk area

North America · Europe · Asia · Atlantic Ocean · Pacific Ocean · South America · Africa · Indian Ocean · Australia · Antarctica

in areas where there
on the map to support

moderate-risk areas without existing
ast coast of South America.

ification, what are some
its effects?

vestock overgrazing, limit tree cutting, and
cover even during droughts.

8.NS.8

Assess Your Understanding

1a. Review Subsoil has (less/more) plant and animal matter than topsoil. 8.2.6

b. Explain What can happen to soil if plants are removed?
Soil particles can move, eroding the area.

c. Apply Concepts
that could prev
land reclam
Sample
might
other
farmin

got it? 8.2.6

○ **I get it!** Now I know that soil management is important becau
ways, and poor management causes erosio
depletion, and desertification.

○ **I need extra help with** See TE note.

Go to MY SCIENCE COACH online for help with this subject.

Lab zone Do the Quick Lab Modeling

got it?

Evaluate Your Progress.

After answering the Got It question, think about how you're doing. Did you get it or do you need a little help? Remember, MY SCIENCE COACH is there for you if you need extra help.

Explore the Big Question.

At one point in the chapter, you'll have the opportunity to take all that you've learned to further explore the Big Question.

Pollution and Solutions

What can people do to use resources wisely?

FIGURE 4 ·········
> REAL-WORLD INQUIRY All living things depend on land, air, and water. Conserving these resources for the future is important. Part of resource conservation is identifying and limiting sources of pollution.

✎ **Interpret Photos** On the photograph, write the letter from the key into the circle that best identifies the source of pollution.

Land
Describe at least one thing your community could do to reduce pollution on land.

Pollution Sources

A. Sediments

B. Municipal solid waste

C. Runoff from development

Air
Describe at least one thing your community could do to reduce air pollution.

Water
Describe at least one thing your community could do to reduce water pollution.

Lab zone
Do
Get

▷ Assess Your Under

1a. Define What are sediments?

b. Explain How can bacteria he spill in the ocean?

c. ANSWER What can people do t resources wisely?

d. CHALLENGE Why might a co to recycle the waste they pr would reduce water pollutio

got it? ·········

O **I get it!** Now I know that w can be reduced by

O **I need extra help with**

Go to **my science coac** with this subject.

Answer the Big Question.

Now it's time to show what you know and answer the Big Question.

Review What You've Learned.

**Use the Chapter Study Guide to review the Big Question
and prepare for the quizzes and exams.**

Practice Taking the ISTEP+.

**Apply the Big Question and take a practice test in
the ISTEP+ format.**

INTERACT... WITH YOUR TEXTBOOK...

Go to **MyScienceOnline.com** and immerse yourself in amazing virtual environments.

▷ THE BIG QUESTION

Each online chapter starts with a Big Question. Your mission is to unlock the meaning of this Big Question as each science lesson unfolds.

Unit 4 > Chapter 1 > Lesson 1

| << | The Big Question | Unlock the Big Question | Explore the Big Question | >> |

The Big Question   Check Your Understanding   Vocabulary Skill

Populations and Communities

? The Big Question

Tools

Unit 2 > Chapter 4 > Lesson 1

| Engage & Explore | Explain |

Planet Diary

my planeT DiARY

▷ VOCAB FLASH CARDS

Practice chapter vocabulary with interactive flash cards. Each card has an image, definitions in English and Spanish, and space for your own notes.

Unit 4 > Chapter 1 > Lesson 1

| << | The Big Question | Unlock the Big Question | Explore the Big Question | >> |

The Big Question   Untamed Science   Check Your Understanding   Vocabulary Skill   Vocabulary Flashcards

Vocabulary Flashcards

Tools

Card List   Create-a-Card   10 Cards Left   Test Me

Lesson Cards   My Cards

Birth Rate
Carrying Capacity
Commensalism
Community
Competition
Death Rate
Ecology
Ecosystem
Emigration
Habitat
Host
Immigration
Limiting Factor

Science Vocabulary

▶ Term: **Community**

▶ Definition: **All the different populations that live together in a particular area.**

View Spanish

Add Notes

Card 5 of

Unit 6 > Chapter 1 > Lesson 3

| Engage & Explore | Ex |

Apply It   Directed Virtual Lab

Color in Light

Exit

Reset Lab

Unit 6 > Chapter 1 > Lesson 1

| Engage & Explore | Explain | Elaborate | Evaluate |

Apply It   Do the Math   Art in Motion   Interactive Art   Real World Inquiry

The Nebraska Plains

▶ **Bald Eagle**

Information   Media

Haliaeetus leucocephalus
Bald Eagles are 80-95 cm tall with a wingspan of 180-230 cm. These birds are born with all brown feathers but grow white feathers on their head, neck, and tail.

Layers List   ▲ Show

Next
22 of 22
Back

▷ INTERACTIVE ART

At MyScienceOnline.com, many of the beautiful visuals in your book become interactive so you can extend your learning.

my science online.com | Populations and Communities | > PLANET DIARY | > LAB ZONE | > VIRTUAL LAB

🔄 ➕ 🌐 http://www.myscienceonline.com/

> PLANET DIARY

My Planet Diary online is the place to find more information and activities related to lesson topics.

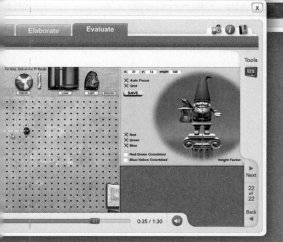

Elaborate | Evaluate

t Everest

Tools

Still Growing! Mount Everest in the Himalayas is the highest mountain on Earth. Climbers who reach the peak stand 8,850 meters above sea level. You might think that mountains never change. But forces inside Earth push Mount Everest at least several millimeters higher each year. Over time, Earth's forces slowly but constantly lift, stretch, bend, and break Earth's crust in dramatic ways!

Planet Diary | Go to Planet Diary to learn more about forces in the Earth's crust.

Next
22 of 22
Back

Find Your Chapter

1 Go to www.myscienceonline.com.

2 Log in with username and password.

3 Click on your program and select your chapter.

Keyword Search

1 Go to www.myscienceonline.com.

2 Log in with username and password.

3 Click on your program and select Search.

4 Enter the keyword (from your book) in the search box.

Other Content Available Online

> UNTAMED SCIENCE Follow these young scientists through their amazing online video blogs as they travel the globe in search of answers to the Essential Questions of Science.

> MY SCIENCE COACH Need extra help? My Science Coach is your personal online study partner. My Science Coach is a chance for you to get more practice on key science concepts. There you can choose from a variety of tools that will help guide you through each science lesson.

> MY READING WEB Need extra reading help on a particular science topic? At My Reading Web you will find a choice of reading selections targeted to your specific reading level.

> VIRTUAL LAB

Get more practice with realistic virtual labs. Manipulate the variables on-screen and test your hypothesis.

? BIG IDEAS OF SCIENCE

Have you ever worked on a jigsaw puzzle? Usually a puzzle has a theme that leads you to group the pieces by what they have in common. But until you put all the pieces together you can't solve the puzzle. Studying science is similar to solving a puzzle. The big ideas of science are like puzzle themes. To understand big ideas, scientists ask questions. The answers to those questions are like pieces of a puzzle. Each chapter in this book asks a big question to help you think about a big idea of science. By answering the big questions, you will get closer to understanding the big idea.

✎ **Before you read each chapter, write about what you know and what more you'd like to know.**

BIGIDEA

Scientists use scientific inquiry to explain the natural world.

Scientists use their senses to investigate the natural world. For example, a scientist could observe these chimpanzees to figure out why they are sticking a stem in the termite mound.

What do you already know about how you study the natural world? ✎ **What more would you like to know?**

_____

_____

Big Questions:

❷ How do scientists investigate the natural world? Chapter 1

❷ How is mathematics important to the world of scientists? Chapter 2

✎ **After reading the chapters, write what you have learned about the Big Idea.**

_____

BIGIDEA

A net force causes an object's motion to change.

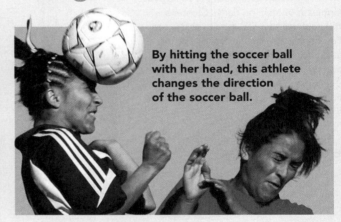

By hitting the soccer ball with her head, this athlete changes the direction of the soccer ball.

What do you already know about how the force of one object can affect the movement of another object? ✎ **What more would you like to know?**

_____

_____

_____

_____

Big Question:

❷ How do objects react to forces? Chapter 3

✎ **After reading the chapter, write what you have learned about the Big Idea.**

_____

Energy can take different forms but is always conserved.

As these skydivers fall, they don't lose any energy—the energy just takes different forms.

What do you already know about what happens to the mass and energy of a candle as it burns?
✏️ **What more would you like to know?**

_____

_____

_____

_____

Big Question:

❓ How is energy conserved in a transformation? Chapter 4

✏️ **After reading the chapter, write what you have learned about the Big Idea.**

_____

_____

_____

Waves transmit energy.

The light and heat that lightning gives off travels in the form of electromagnetic waves.

What do you already know about waves and how they travel from one place to another?
✏️ **What more would you like to know?**

_____

_____

_____

Big Questions:

❓ What are the properties of waves? Chapter 6

❓ How does light interact with matter? Chapter 7

✏️ **After reading the chapters, write what you have learned about the Big Idea.**

_____

_____

_____

_____

Earth's land, water, air, and life form a system.

A severe storm, drought, or wildfire could cause changes in Yellowstone National Park that would affect these bison.

What do you already know about how changes in one part of Earth can affect another part?

✏️ **What would you like to know?**

_____

_____

_____

Big Questions:

❓ What are some of Earth's energy sources? Chapter 5

❓ What is the structure of Earth? Chapter 8

✏️ **After reading the chapters, write what you have learned about the Big Idea.**

_____

_____

Earth is a continually changing planet.

Over millions of years, the Colorado River cut through layers of solid rock to form the Grand Canyon in Arizona.

What do you already know about changes on Earth? ✏️ **What more would you like to know?**

_____

_____

_____

Big Questions:

❓ How do rocks form? Chapter 9

❓ How do moving plates change Earth's crust? Chapter 10

❓ Why do earthquakes and volcanoes occur more in some places than others? Chapter 11

❓ What processes break down rock? Chapter 12

❓ What processes shape the surface of the land? Chapter 13

✏️ **After reading the chapters, write what you have learned about the Big Idea.**

_____

_____

_____

BIGIDEA

Earth is 4.6 billion years old and the rock record contains its history.

This fossil of a turtle is millions of years old.

What do you already know about Earth's history?
✎ **What more would you like to know?**

_____

_____

_____

_____

Big Question:

❓ How do scientists study Earth's past?
Chapter 14

✎ **After reading the chapter, write what you have learned about the Big Idea.**

_____

_____

_____

BIGIDEA

Living things are made of cells.

Nerve cells like this one transmit messages in your body. Other kinds of cells do different jobs.

What do you already know about what a cell does?
✎ **What more would you like to know?**

_____

_____

_____

Big Question:

❓ What are cells made of? Chapter 15

✎ **After reading the chapter, write what you have learned about the Big Idea.**

_____

_____

_____

HOW CAN AN ASTRONAUT STUDY GRAVITY WHILE FLOATING?

How do scientists investigate the natural world?

NASA studies how microgravity, or very little gravity, affects humans, plants, crystals, and liquids. For example, NASA has found that the muscles and bones of astronauts weaken during space missions. Plants grow in different directions, crystals grow larger, and water does not pour as it would on Earth, but falls out in spheres.

⚠ Infer **What other ideas might NASA study in space?**

_____

_____

_____

_____

> UNTAMED SCIENCE Watch the **Untamed Science** video to learn more about science.

Scientific Thinking

Academic Standards for Science

7.NS.1, 7.NS.2, 7.NS.3, 7.NS.4, 7.NS.6, 7.NS.8,
7.NS.9, 7.NS.10, 7.NS.11, 7.DP.2, 7.DP.9

1 Getting Started

Check Your Understanding

1. **Background** Read the paragraph below and then answer the question.

Miki is in the **process** of preparing a stew for dinner at her campsite. After it is cooked, she sets the pot aside to cool. When she returns, the pot is empty. Immediately, she **poses** questions: Who ate the stew? What animals are active in the evening? She soon finds **evidence:** the pot cover, greasy spills, and a stinky smell. The thief is a skunk.

> A **process** is a series of actions or events.
>
> To **pose** is to put forward a question or a problem.
>
> Facts, figures, or signs that help prove a statement are all pieces of **evidence.**

- How does the process of posing questions and looking for evidence help Miki solve the mystery of the missing stew?

_____

_____

> **MY READING WEB** If you had trouble completing the question above, visit **My Reading Web** and type in *Scientific Thinking.*

Vocabulary Skill

Identify Related Word Forms Learn related forms of words to increase your vocabulary. The table below lists forms of words related to vocabulary terms.

Verb	Noun	Adjective
observe, *v.* to gather information using the senses	observation, *n.* facts learned by gathering information using the senses	observable, *adj.* able to be heard, seen, touched, tasted, or smelled
predict, *v.* to state or claim what will happen in the future	prediction, *n.* a statement or claim of what will happen in the future	predictable, *adj.* able to be predicted; behaving in a way that is expected

2. **Quick Check** Complete the sentence with the correct form of the word.

- It is difficult to _____ how much rain will fall.

observing

subjective

data

Number of Chirps per minute

Cricket	15°C	20°C	25°C
1	91	135	180
2	80	124	169
3	89	130	176
4	78	125	158
5	77	121	157

controlled experiment

Chapter Preview

LESSON 1

- science
- observing
- quantitative observation
- qualitative observation
- inferring
- predicting
- classifying
- evaluating
- making models

↺ **Ask Questions**
△ **Predict**

LESSON 2

- skepticism
- ethics
- personal bias
- cultural bias
- experimental bias
- objective
- subjective
- deductive reasoning
- inductive reasoning

↺ **Relate Cause and Effect**
△ **Classify**

LESSON 3

- scientific inquiry
- hypothesis
- variable
- manipulated variable
- responding variable
- controlled experiment
- data
- scientific theory
- scientific law

↺ **Compare and Contrast**
△ **Control Variables**

❯ **VOCAB FLASH CARDS** For extra help with vocabulary, visit **Vocab Flash Cards** and type in *Scientific Thinking.*

Science and the Natural World

🔑 **What Skills Do Scientists Use?**
7.NS.1, 7.NS.2, 7.NS.3, 7.NS.8, 7.NS.11, 7.DP.9

my planeT DiaRY

BIOGRAPHY

The Wild Chimpanzees of Gombe

The following words are from the writings of Jane Goodall, a scientist who studied wild chimpanzees in Africa for many years.

"Once, as I walked through thick forest in a downpour, I suddenly saw a chimp hunched in front of me. Quickly I stopped. Then I heard a sound from above. I looked up and there was a big chimp there, too. When he saw me he gave a loud, clear wailing *wraaaaah*—a spine-chilling call that is used to threaten a dangerous animal. To my right I saw a large black hand shaking a branch and bright eyes glaring threateningly through the foliage. Then came another savage *wraaaah* from behind...I was surrounded." Because Jane stood still, the chimps no longer felt threatened, so they went away.

Answer the question.

What is one advantage and one disadvantage of studying wild animals in their natural environment?

_____

_____

_____

_____

_____

_____

> **PLANET DIARY** Go to **Planet Diary** to learn more about science and the natural world.

Lab zone® Do the Inquiry Warm-Up *Is It Really True?*

Vocabulary
- science • observing • quantitative observation
- qualitative observation • inferring • predicting
- classifying • evaluating • making models

Skills
↻ Reading: Ask Questions
△ Inquiry: Predict

What Skills Do Scientists Use?

Jane Goodall trained herself to become a scientist, or a person who does science. **Science** is a way of learning about the natural world. Science also includes all the knowledge gained by exploring the natural world. 🗝 **Scientists use skills such as observing, inferring, predicting, classifying, evaluating, and making models to study the world.**

Observing **Observing** means using one or more of your senses to gather information. It also means using tools, such as a microscope, to help your senses. By observing chimps like the one in **Figure 1,** Jane Goodall learned what they eat. She also learned what sounds chimps make and even what games they play.

Observations can be either quantitative or qualitative. A **quantitative observation** deals with numbers, or amounts. For example, seeing that you have 11 new e-mails is a quantitative observation. A **qualitative observation** deals with descriptions that cannot be expressed in numbers. Noticing that a bike is blue or that a lemon tastes sour is a qualitative observation.

FIGURE 1 ···
Observing
A chimpanzee uses a rock as a tool to crack open a nut.

✎ **Observe** Write one quantitative observation and one qualitative observation about this chimp.

_____

_____

_____

_____

_____

_____

_____

7.NS.2, 7.NS.3, 7.NS.8

Academic Standards for Science

7.NS.1 Make predictions and develop testable questions based on research and prior knowledge.

7.NS.2 Plan and carry out investigations.

7.NS.3 Collect quantitative data.

7.NS.8 Analyze data.

7.NS.11 Communicate findings using graphs.

7.DP.9 Present evidence using mathematical representations.

↻ **Ask Questions** In the graphic organizer ask a *what, how,* or *why* question based on the text under Observing. As you read, write an answer to your question.

Thinking Like a Scientist

Question

_____

_____

_____

_____

Answer

_____

_____

_____

Inferring One day, Jane watched as a chimp peered into a tree hollow. The chimp picked up a handful of leaves and chewed on them. Then, it took the leaves out of its mouth and pushed them into the hollow. When the chimp pulled the leaves out, Jane saw the gleam of water. The chimp then put the wet leaves back into its mouth. Jane reasoned that there was water in the tree. Jane made three observations. She saw the chimp pick up dry leaves, put them in the hollow, and then pull them out wet. But, Jane was not observing when she reasoned that there was water inside the tree. She was inferring. When you explain or interpret the things you observe, you are **inferring,** or making an inference. Inferring is not guessing. Inferences are based on reasoning from what you already know. They could also be based on assumptions you make about your observations. See what inferences you can make about the chimps in **Figure 2.**

FIGURE 2 ···

Inferring

What can you infer about the chimps and the termite mound?   7.NS.8

✎ **Complete the activities below.**

1. **Observe** In the chart below, write two observations about the chimp on the left.

2. **Infer** Use the observations you wrote to make two related inferences.

Observation	Inference

Predicting Jane's understanding of chimp behavior grew over time. Sometimes, she could predict what a chimp would do next. **Predicting** means making a statement or a claim about what will happen in the future based on past experience or evidence.

By observing, Jane learned that when a chimp was frightened or angry its hairs stood on end. This response was sometimes followed by threatening gestures such as charging, throwing rocks, and shaking trees. Therefore, when Jane saw a chimp with its hair on end, she was able to predict that there was danger.

Predictions and inferences are closely related. While inferences are attempts to explain what is happening or *has* happened, predictions are statements or claims about what *will* happen. If you see a broken egg on the floor by a table, you might infer that the egg had rolled off the table. If, however, you see an egg rolling toward the edge of a table, you can predict that it's about to create a mess.

FIGURE 3
Predicting
Predictions are forecasts of what will happen next.
✎ **Predict Write a prediction about what this angry chimp might do next.**

_____

_____

_____

_____

7.NS.1

do the math!

Like all animals, chimps prefer to eat certain foods when they are available.

1 Graph Use the information in the table to create a bar graph.

2 Label the *x*-axis and the *y*-axis. Then write a title for the graph.

3 Interpret Data Did chimps feed more on seeds or leaves during May?

_____

_____

4 Infer What might chimps eat more of if fruits are not available in June?

_____

_____

_____

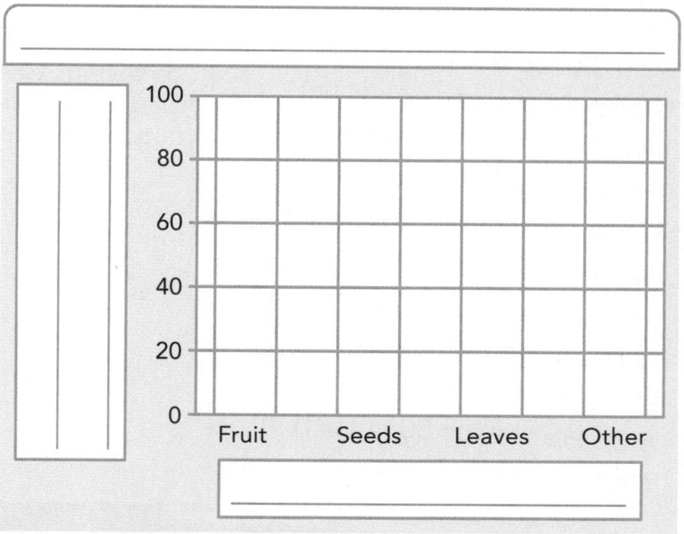

Chimp Diet in May	
Fruits	52%
Seeds	30%
Leaves	12%
Other foods	6%

100
80
60
40
20
0

Fruit   Seeds   Leaves   Other

7.NS.8, 7.DP.9

Classifying

What did chimps do all day? To find out, Jane's research team followed the chimps through the forest. They took detailed field notes about the chimps' behaviors. **Figure 4** shows some notes about Jomeo, an adult male chimp.

Suppose Jane had wanted to know how much time Jomeo spent feeding or resting that morning. She could have found out by classifying Jomeo's actions. **Classifying** is the grouping together of items that are alike in some way. Jane could have grouped together all the information about Jomeo's feeding habits or his resting behavior.

Evaluating

Suppose Jane had found that Jomeo spent most of his time resting. What would this observation have told her about chimp behavior? Before Jane could have reached a conclusion, she would have needed to evaluate her observations. **Evaluating** involves comparing observations and data to reach a conclusion about them. For example, Jane would have needed to compare all of Jomeo's behaviors with those of other chimps to reach a conclusion. She would also need to have evaluated the resulting behavior data of Jomeo and the other chimps.

FIGURE 4 ·····························

> **VIRTUAL LAB** **Classifying**
By classifying the information related to a chimp's resting, climbing, or feeding, a scientist can better understand chimp behavior.

✎ **Classify** Use the chart to classify the details from the field notes.

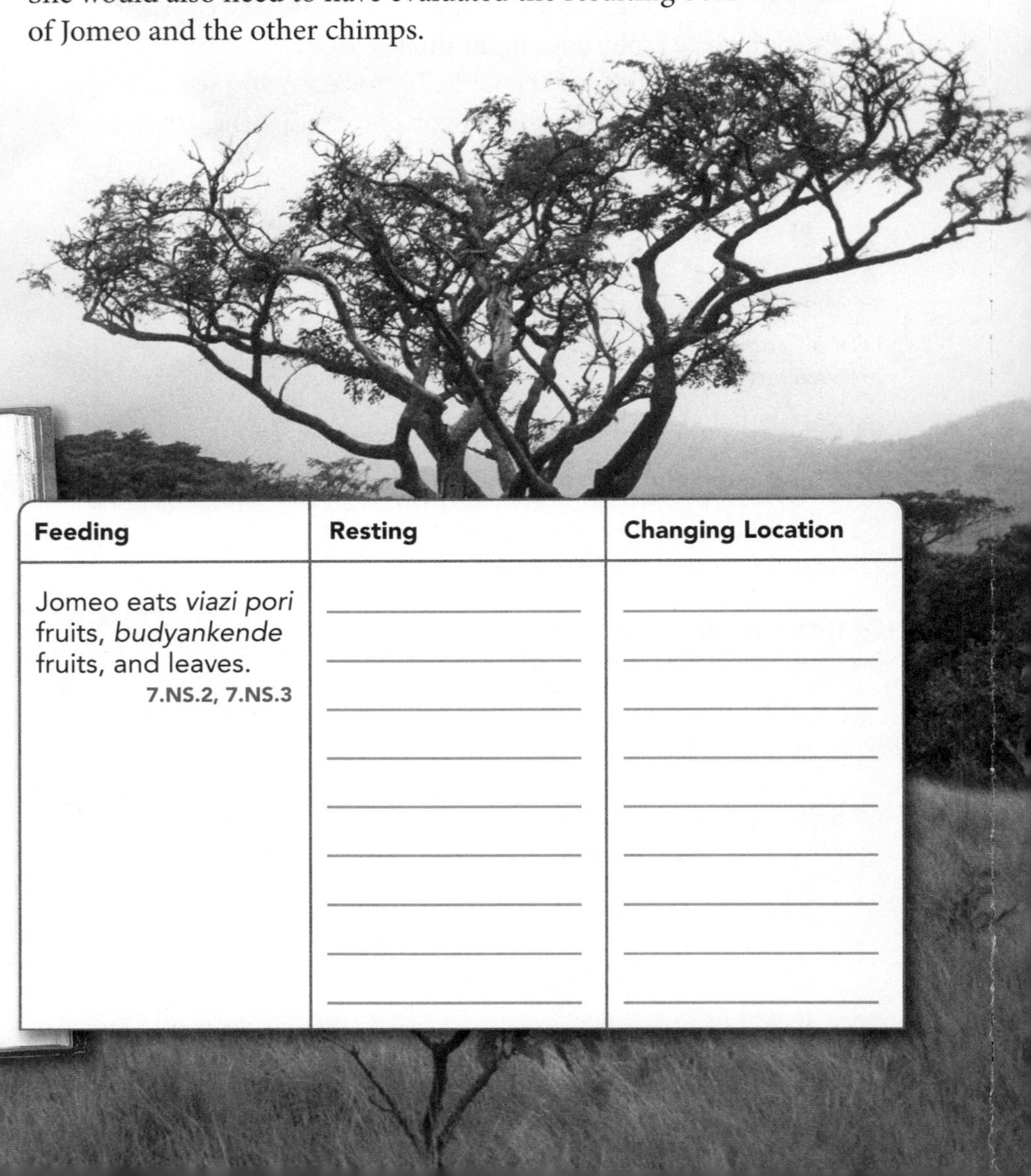

- 6:45 A.M. Jomeo rests in his nest. He lies on his back.
- 6:50 Jomeo leaves his nest, climbs a tree, and feeds on *viazi pori* fruits and leaves.
- 7:16 He wanders along about 175 m from his nest feeding on *budyankende* fruits.
- 8:08 Jomeo stops feeding, rests in a large tree, feeds on *viazi pori* fruits again.
- 8:35 He travels 50 m further, rests by a small lake.

Feeding	Resting	Changing Location
Jomeo eats *viazi pori* fruits, *budyankende* fruits, and leaves. 7.NS.2, 7.NS.3		

Making Models How far do chimps travel? Where do they go? Sometimes, Jane's research team followed a particular chimp for many days at a time. To show the chimp's movements, they might have made a model like the one shown in **Figure 5**. The model shows Jomeo's movements and behaviors during one day. **Making models** involves creating representations of complex objects or processes. Some models can be touched, such as a map. Others are in the form of mathematical equations or computer programs. Models help people study things that can't be observed directly. By using models, Jane and her team shared information that would otherwise be difficult to explain.

FIGURE 5 ···

▶ **INTERACTIVE ART** Making Models

This model shows Jomeo's movements and behaviors during one day. 7.NS.11

✎ **Use the map to answer the questions.**

1. Interpret Maps How far did Jomeo travel during this day?

_____

_____

2. How many times did Jomeo stop to feed?

_____

3. How many times did Jomeo rest?

_____

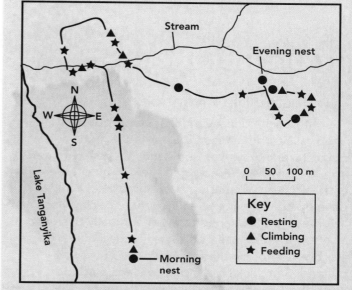

Jomeo's Movements

Stream

Evening nest

N
W · E
S

Lake Tanganyika

0   50   100 m

Morning nest

Key
● Resting
▲ Climbing
★ Feeding

 Do the Quick Lab *Classifying Objects.*

🔑 **Assess Your Understanding**

1a. Compare and Contrast How do observations differ from inferences?

_____

_____

_____

7.NS.1, 7.NS.2, 7.NS.8

b. Classify Do you think this statement is an observation or an inference? *The cat is ill.* Explain your reasoning.

_____

_____

_____

7.NS.1, 7.NS.2, 7.NS.8

got**it?** ···

○ **I get it!** I know that scientists use skills such as _____

_____

○ **I need extra help with** _____

Go to **MY SCIENCE** ⓢ **COACH** *online for help with this subject.*

7.NS.1, 7.NS.2, 7.NS.8

Thinking Like a Scientist

🔑 **What Attitudes Help You Think Scientifically?**
7.NS.1, 7.NS.2

🔑 **What Is Scientific Reasoning?**
7.NS.8, 7.NS.11

MY PLANET DIARY

Incredible Inventions

Most scientific inventions are purposely created and result from curiosity, persistence, and years of hard work. However, some inventions have been accidentally discovered when their inventors were in the process of creating something else. While developing wallpaper cleaner, a type of clay was invented. A coil-shaped toy was originally designed as a spring to be used on ships. Instead of developing a substitute for synthetic rubber, toy putty was created. Self-stick notes, potato chips, and the hook and loop fasteners used on items such as clothing, shoes, and toys are also inventions that were discovered by accident. Like the inventors of these items, your curiosity may help you invent the next "big thing"!

DISCOVERY

Communicate Discuss the following questions with a partner. Write your answers below.

1. Why do you think it is important for scientists to be curious?

_____

_____

2. What might you want to invent? Why?

_____

_____

_____

> **PLANET DIARY** Go to **Planet Diary** to learn more about thinking like a scientist.

Lab zone ® Do the Inquiry Warm-Up *How Keen Are Your Senses?*

Vocabulary

- skepticism • ethics • personal bias • cultural bias
- experimental bias • objective • subjective
- deductive reasoning • inductive reasoning

Skills

- Reading: Relate Cause and Effect
- Inquiry: Classify

What Attitudes Help You Think Scientifically?

Perhaps someone has told you that you have a good attitude. An attitude is a state of mind. Your actions say a lot about your attitude. **Scientists possess certain important attitudes, including curiosity, honesty, creativity, open-mindedness, skepticism, good ethics, and awareness of bias.**

Curiosity One attitude that drives scientists is curiosity. Scientists want to learn more about the topics they study. **Figure 1** shows some things that may spark the interest of scientists.

Honesty Good scientists always report their observations and results truthfully. Honesty is especially important when a scientist's results go against previous ideas or predictions.

Creativity Whatever they study, scientists may experience problems. Sometimes, it takes creativity to find a solution. Creativity means coming up with inventive ways to solve problems or produce new things. Creativity may involve using a variety of sources to answer questions and solve problems.

> **Academic Standards for Science**
>
> **7.NS.1** Make predictions and develop testable questions based on research and prior knowledge.
> **7.NS.2** Plan and carry out investigations as a class, in small groups or independently often over a period of several class lessons.

FIGURE 1 ··················

Curiosity
Curiosity helps scientists learn about the world around them. **7.NS.1**

 Complete these tasks.

1. **Pose Questions** Look at each photo. In each box, write a question you are curious about.

2. **Communicate** With a partner, share and discuss the questions you each wrote.

Open-Mindedness, Skepticism

Awareness of Bias

Curiosity

Scientific Attitudes

Creativity

Honesty

Ethics

FIGURE 2

Attitudes of Scientists
This scientist is carefully conducting an experiment.

✎ **Summarize** After you have read the section What Attitudes Help You Think Scientifically?, write a summary of each scientific attitude in the graphic organizer. **7.NS.2**

Open-Mindedness and Skepticism Scientists need to be open-minded, or capable of accepting new and different ideas. However, open-mindedness should always be balanced by **skepticism,** which is having an attitude of doubt. Skepticism keeps a scientist from accepting ideas that may be untrue.

Ethics Because scientists work with the natural world, they must be careful not to damage it. Scientists need a strong sense of **ethics,** which refers to the rules that enable people to know right from wrong. Scientists must consider all the effects their research may have on people and the environment. They make decisions only after considering the risks and benefits to living things or the environment. For example, scientists test medicine they have developed before the medicine is sold to the public. Scientists inform volunteers of the new medicine's risks before allowing them to take part in the tests. Look at **Figure 2** to review scientific attitudes.

Awareness of Bias What scientists expect to find can influence, or bias, what they observe and how they interpret observations. For example, a scientist might misinterpret the behavior of an animal because of what she already knows about animals.

There are different kinds of bias. **Personal bias** comes from a person's likes and dislikes. For instance, if you like the taste of a cereal, you might think everyone else should, too. **Cultural bias** stems from the culture in which a person grows up. For example, a culture that regards snakes as bad might overlook how well snakes control pests. **Experimental bias** is a mistake in the design of an experiment that makes a particular result more likely. For example, suppose you wanted to determine the boiling point of pure water. If your experiment uses water that has some salt in it, your results would be biased.

✏️ Relate Cause and Effect
In the first paragraph, underline an example of bias. Then circle its effect.

**it!**

Matt likes cheese crackers best and thinks that most other students do too. So he observed what students bought at the vending machine during one lunch. Seven bought crackers, three bought nuts, and none bought raisins. **7.NS.2**

① Circle the evidence of personal bias.

② [CHALLENGE] Describe the experimental bias.

_____

_____

_____

$1.00

$1.25

Salted Peanuts

RAISINS

NET WT. 1 ½ OZ (42.5 g)

$0.75 cheese CRACKERS

NET WT. 1.25 OZ (35 g)

 Do the Quick Lab *Thinking Like a Scientist.*

🔑 Assess Your Understanding

1a. Explain What can bias a scientist's observations?

_____

_____

7.NS.1, 7.NS.2

b. Apply Concepts Debbie discovered a new way to make pizza. What scientific attitude is this an example of?

_____

_____

7.NS.1, 7.NS.2

got it?

○ **I get it!** Now I know that attitudes that help you think scientifically are _____

_____

_____

_____

○ **I need extra help with** _____

Go to **my science ⓢ coach** *online for help with this subject.* **7.NS.1, 7.NS.2**

What Is Scientific Reasoning?

You use reasoning, or a logical way of thinking, when you solve word problems. Scientists use reasoning in their work, too. 🔑 **Scientific reasoning requires a logical way of thinking based on gathering and evaluating evidence.** There are two types of scientific reasoning. Scientific reasoning can be deductive or inductive.

Because scientific reasoning relies on gathering and evaluating evidence, it is objective reasoning. Being **objective** means that you make decisions and draw conclusions based on available evidence. For example, scientists used to think chimps ate only plants. However, Jane Goodall observed chimps eating meat. Based on this evidence, she concluded that chimps ate meat and plants.

In contrast, being **subjective** means that personal feelings have entered into a decision or conclusion. Personal opinions, values, and tastes are subjective because they are based on your feelings about something. For example, if you see a clear stream in the woods, you might take a drink because you think clear water is clean. However, you have not objectively tested the water's quality. The water might contain microorganisms you cannot see and be unsafe to drink.

apply it!

Classify Read the sentences below. Then decide if each example uses objective reasoning or subjective reasoning to reach a conclusion. Place a check mark in the corresponding column.

7.NS.8, 7.NS.11

	Objective	Subjective
Jane Goodall saw a chimp chewing on wet leaves. She reasoned that chimps sometimes used leaves to drink water.		
I like to run. I must be the fastest person in the class.		
Emily is 1.2 m tall. No one else in class is taller than 1 m. So, Emily is the tallest person in class.		
I dislike dogs. Dogs must be the least friendly animals.		

Deductive Reasoning Scientists who study Earth think that the uppermost part of Earth's surface is made up of many sections they call plates. The theory of plate tectonics states that earthquakes should happen mostly where plates meet. There are many earthquakes in California. Therefore, California must be near a place where plates meet. This is an example of deductive reasoning. **Deductive reasoning** is a way to explain things by starting with a general idea and then applying the idea to a specific observation.

You can think about deductive reasoning as being a process. First, you state the general idea. Then you relate the general idea to the specific case you are investigating. Then you reach a conclusion. You can use this process in **Figure 3.** The process for the plate tectonics example is shown here.

- Earthquakes should happen mostly where plates meet.
- California has many earthquakes.
- California must be near a place where plates meet.

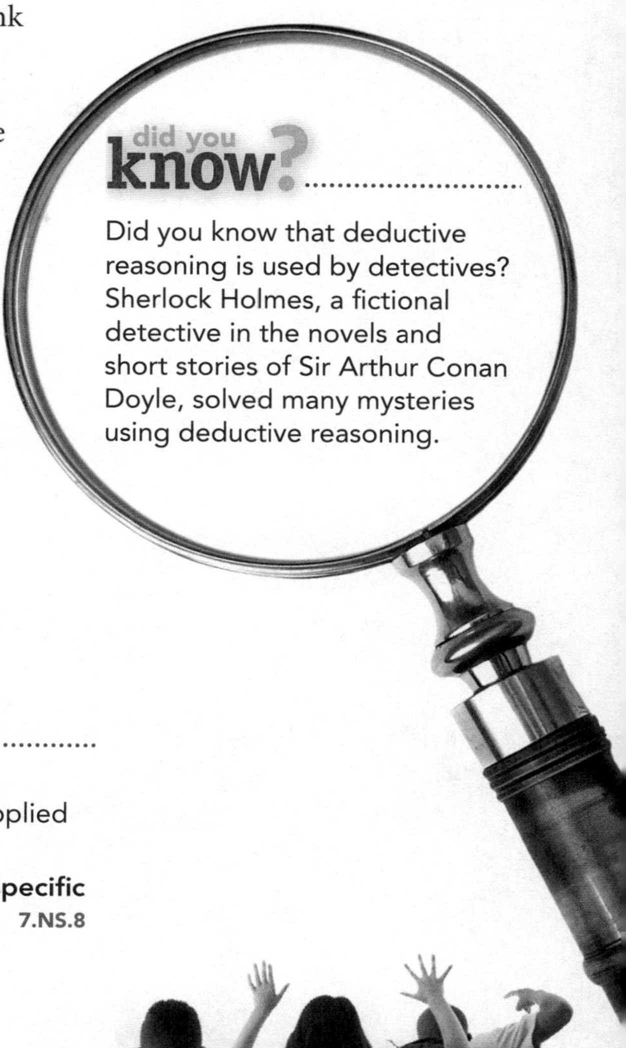

did you know?

Did you know that deductive reasoning is used by detectives? Sherlock Holmes, a fictional detective in the novels and short stories of Sir Arthur Conan Doyle, solved many mysteries using deductive reasoning.

FIGURE 3

Deductive Reasoning

Deductive reasoning occurs when a general idea is applied to a specific example and a conclusion is reached.

Apply Concepts Apply each general idea to a specific example and then draw a conclusion. 7.NS.8

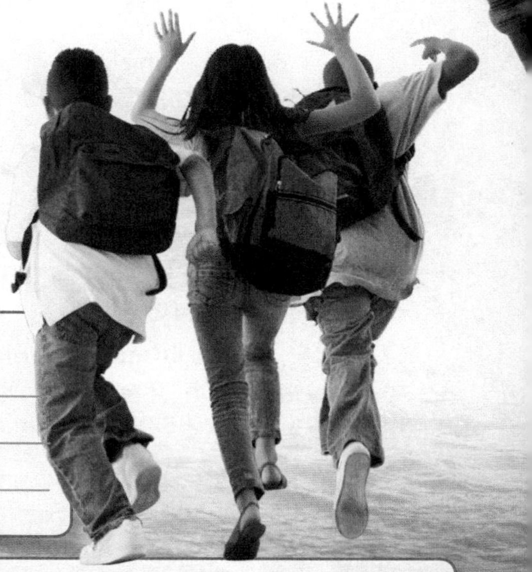

Dinner is always at 6 P.M.

____

Classes end when the bell rings.

____

Triangles have three sides.

____

Inductive Reasoning Scientists also use inductive reasoning, which can be considered the opposite of deductive reasoning. **Inductive reasoning** uses specific observations to make generalizations. For example, suppose you notice that leaf-cutter ants appear to follow other ants along specific paths, as shown in **Figure 4**. The ants follow the paths to sources of food, water, and nest material. Then they return to their nests. These observations about the leaf-cutter ants are specific. From these specific observations you conclude that these ants must communicate to be able to always follow the same path. This conclusion is a generalization about the behavior of leaf-cutter ants based on your observations. Scientists frequently use inductive reasoning. They collect data and then reach a conclusion based on that data.

FIGURE 4 ···

> INTERACTIVE ART **Scientific Reasoning**
Leaf-cutter ants follow a chemical trail to find and harvest leaves.

✎ **Identify** **Look at the statements below. Write *D* next to the statements that use deductive reasoning. Write *I* next to the statements that use inductive reasoning.**

7.NS.8

❶ Turtles have shells. They must use shells for protection. _____

❷ A puddle has frozen. It must be below 0°C outside. _____

❸ Because of gravity, everything that goes up must come down. _____

❹ Many birds fly toward the equator in fall. Birds prefer warm weather. _____

Faulty Reasoning Scientists must be careful not to use faulty reasoning, because it can lead to faulty conclusions. If you draw a conclusion based on too little data, your reasoning might lead you to the wrong general idea. For example, to conclude accurately that all ants communicate with each other, you would have to observe leaf-cutter ants and many other kinds of ants many times. In addition, based on observations of how leaf-cutter ants follow paths, you cannot conclude how they communicated. For example, you cannot say they follow the tiny footprints of the ants ahead of them. Such a conclusion would be a guess not based on observation.

apply it!

Joy drew lines of symmetry on a square. She saw that a rectangle has four straight sides and four right angles, so she drew the same lines of symmetry on a rectangle.

1 Make Models Fold a piece of rectangular notebook paper according to the lines of symmetry Joy drew on the rectangle. Are her lines of symmetry correct? Explain how you know.

_____

_____

7.NS.11

2 Identify Faulty Reasoning Underline Joy's reasoning for drawing the lines of symmetry on the rectangle. What other characteristic should Joy have considered?

_____

_____

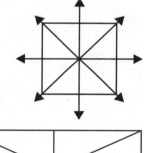

Lab zone® Do the Quick Lab
Using Scientific Thinking.

🔑 Assess Your Understanding

2a. Explain What is a cause of faulty reasoning?

_____

7.NS.8

b. Infer Will scientists who observe the same ants always draw the same conclusion? Why?

_____

_____

7.NS.8

got it?

◯ **I get it!** Now I know that scientific reasoning includes _____

_____

◯ **I need extra help with** _____

Go to MY SCIENCE Ⓢ COACH *online for help with this subject.*   7.NS.8

17

Scientific Inquiry

UNLOCK
THE BIG
?

🔑 **What Is Scientific Inquiry?**
7.NS.1

🔑 **How Do You Design and Conduct an Experiment?**
7.NS.1, 7.NS.2, 7.NS.3, 7.NS.4, 7.NS.6, 7.NS.7, 7.NS.8, 7.NS.9, 7.NS.10, 7.NS.11, 7.DP.2

🔑 **What Are Scientific Theories and Laws?**
7.NS.6, 7.NS.8

my planet diary

The Law of Falling Objects

Misconception: Heavier objects fall faster than lighter ones. This assumption is not true. They actually fall at the same rate, or with the same acceleration. The misconception was introduced by a philosopher named Aristotle and accepted for more than 2,000 years. But in the late 1500s, Galileo Galilei discovered something different—all free-falling objects fall with the same acceleration. To prove this, Galileo performed a number of experiments. Galileo's experiments involved rolling balls with different masses down a ramp called an inclined plane and making careful measurements.

Galileo and one of his acceleration experiments

MISCONCEPTION

Communicate Discuss the following questions with a partner. Write your answers below.

1. Why did Galileo perform experiments to see if all objects fall with the same acceleration?

_____

_____

2. Do you think a feather and a book that are dropped from the same height at the same time will hit the ground at the same time? Explain your answer in terms of Galileo's discovery.

_____

_____

_____

_____

_____

_____

> PLANET DIARY Go to **Planet Diary** to learn more about scientific inquiry.

Lab ®
zone
Do the Inquiry Warm-Up
What's Happening?

Vocabulary

- scientific inquiry
- hypothesis
- variable
- manipulated variable
- responding variable
- controlled experiment
- data
- scientific theory
- scientific law

Skills

- Reading: Compare and Contrast
- Inquiry: Control Variables

What Is Scientific Inquiry?

Chirp, chirp, chirp. It is one of the hottest nights of summer and your bedroom windows are wide open. On most nights, the quiet chirping of crickets gently lulls you to sleep, but not tonight. The noise from the crickets is almost deafening. Why do all the crickets in your neighborhood seem determined to keep you awake tonight? Your thinking and questioning is the start of the **scientific inquiry** process. **Scientific inquiry refers to the diverse ways in which scientists study the natural world and propose explanations based on the evidence they gather.** Some scientists run experiments in labs, but some cannot. For example, geologists use observations of rock layers to draw inferences about how Earth has changed over time.

Posing Questions Scientific inquiry often begins with a question about an observation. Your observation about the frequent chirping may lead you to ask a question: Why are the crickets chirping so much tonight? Questions come from your experiences, observations, and inferences. Curiosity plays a role, too. Because others may have asked similar questions, you should do research to find what information is already known about the topic before you go on with your investigation. Scientists often review the work of others at the start of an investigation. Look at **Figure 1** to pose a scientific question about an observation.

> Academic Standards for Science
>
> **7.NS.1** Make predictions and develop testable questions based on research and prior knowledge.

FIGURE 1 ··
Posing Questions
The photo at the right is of a Roesel's bush cricket from England.

✎ **Pose Questions Make an observation about this cricket. Then pose a question about this observation that you can study.**

_____

_____

_____

7.NS.1

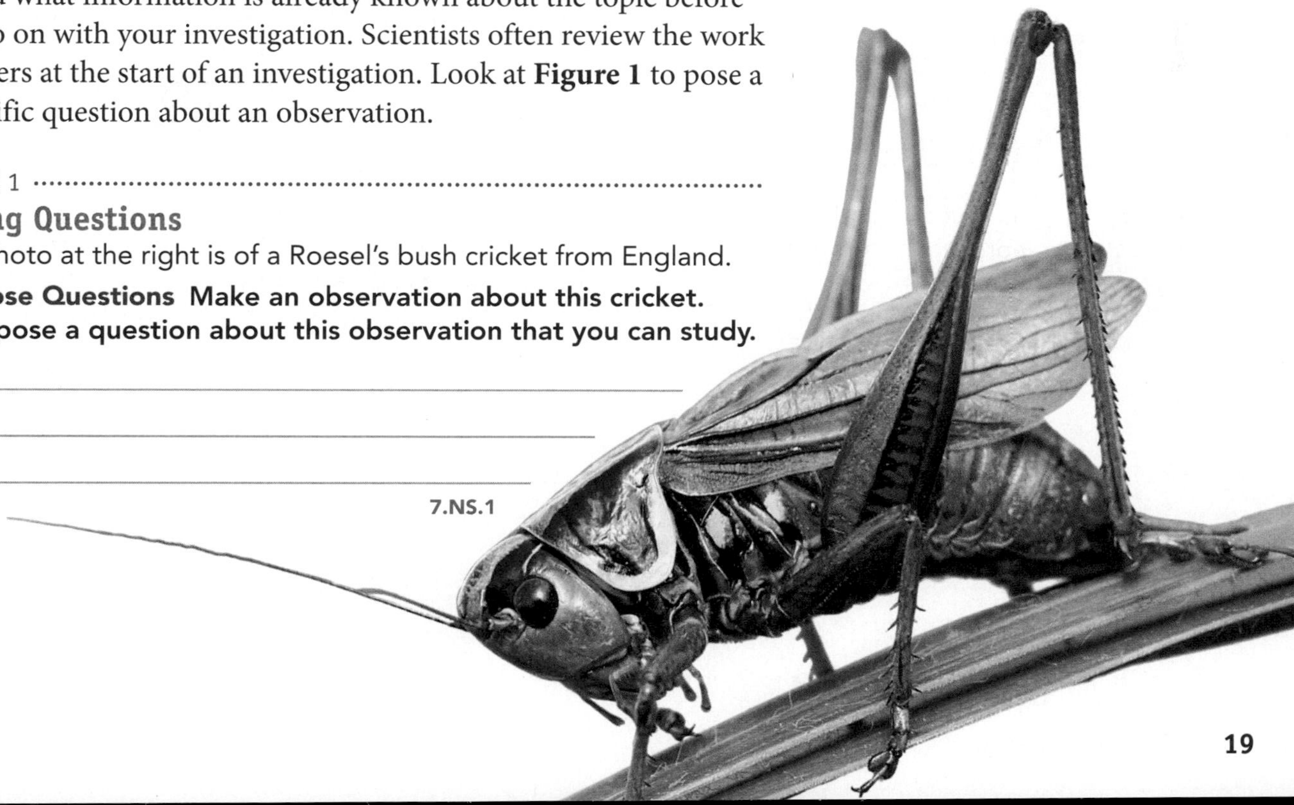

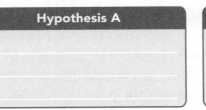

Why has my digital music player stopped working?

Developing a Hypothesis How could you answer your question about cricket chirping? In trying to answer the question, you are developing a hypothesis. A **hypothesis** (plural: *hypotheses*) is a possible answer to a scientific question. You may suspect that the hot temperatures affected the chirping. Your hypothesis would be that cricket chirping increases as a result of warmer air temperatures. Use **Figure 2** to practice developing a hypothesis.

A hypothesis is *not* a fact. In science, a fact is an observation that has been confirmed repeatedly. For example, that a cricket rubs its forelegs together to make the chirping noise is a fact. A hypothesis, on the other hand, is one possible answer to a question. For example, perhaps the crickets only seemed to be chirping more that night because there were fewer other sounds than usual.

In science, a hypothesis must be testable. Researchers must be able to carry out investigations and gather evidence that will either support or disprove the hypothesis. Disproven hypotheses are still useful because they can lead to further investigations.

FIGURE 2 ··

Developing a Hypothesis

✏ **Develop Hypotheses** Write two hypotheses that might answer this student's question.   7.NS.1

Hypothesis A	Hypothesis B

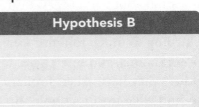 Do the Quick Lab
Scientific Inquiry.

🔑 Assess Your Understanding

1a. Explain Can you test a hypothesis that crickets chirp more when they hide under logs? Explain.

_____

_____

_____

7.NS.1

b. Develop Hypotheses What other hypothesis might explain why crickets chirp more frequently on some nights?

_____

_____

_____

7.NS.1

got it? ···

○ I get it! Now I know that scientific inquiry is _____

_____

○ I need extra help with _____

Go to my science COACH online for help with this subject.   7.NS.1

How Do You Design and Conduct an Experiment?

After developing your hypothesis, you are ready to test it by designing an experiment. 🗝 **An experiment must follow sound scientific principles for its results to be valid.** You know your experiment will involve counting cricket chirps at warm temperatures. But, how will you know how often a cricket would chirp at a low temperature? You cannot know unless you count other cricket chirps at low temperatures for comparison.

Controlling Variables To test your hypothesis, you will observe crickets at different air temperatures. All other **variables,** or factors that can change in an experiment, must be the same. This includes variables such as food and hours of daylight. By keeping these variables the same, you will know that any difference in cricket chirping is due to temperature alone.

The one variable that is purposely changed to test a hypothesis is the **manipulated variable,** or independent variable. The manipulated variable here is air temperature. The factor that may change in response to the manipulated variable is the **responding variable,** or dependent variable. The responding variable here is the number of cricket chirps.

⊙ **Compare and Contrast**
A manipulated variable is (purposely/not purposely) changed. A responding variable is (purposely/not purposely) changed.

apply it!

A student performs an experiment to determine whether 1 g of sugar or 1 g of salt dissolves more quickly in water.

7.NS.1, 7.NS.4

❶ ◣ **Control Variables** Identify the manipulated variable and the responding variable.

_____

_____

7.NS.4

❷ **Identify** What are two other variables in this experiment?

_____

_____

7.NS.4

❸ **Draw Conclusions** Write a hypothesis for this experiment.

_____

_____

7.NS.1

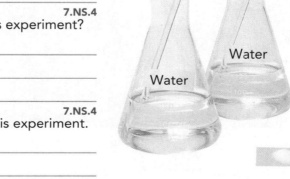

Water

Water

Salt

Sugar

Setting Up a Controlled Experiment

An experiment in which only one variable is manipulated at a time is called a **controlled experiment.** You decide to test the crickets at three different temperatures: 15°C, 20°C, and 25°C, as shown in **Figure 3.** All other variables are kept the same. Otherwise, your experiment would have more than one manipulated variable. Then there would be no way to tell which variable influenced your results.

Experimental Bias

In any experiment there is a risk of introducing bias. For example, if you expect crickets to chirp more at 25°C, you may run experiments at just that temperature. Or, without meaning to, you might bias your results by selecting only the crickets that chirp the most often to test. Having a good sample size, or the number of crickets tested, is also important. Having too few crickets may bias your results because individual differences exist from cricket to cricket.

FIGURE 3 ···

A Controlled Experiment

The manipulated variable in the experiment below is temperature.

✎ **Design Experiments In the boxes, write the number of crickets you would test for this controlled experiment. On the lines below, write three other variables that must be kept the same.**

_____

_____

_____

7.NS.2, 7.NS.4, 7.NS.7, 7.DP.2

Temperature 15°C

Crickets _____

Temperature 20°C

Crickets _____

Temperature 25°C

Crickets _____

Collecting and Interpreting Data You are almost ready to begin your experiment. You decide to test five crickets, one at a time, at each temperature. You also decide to run multiple trials for each cricket. This is because a cricket may behave differently from one trial to the next. Before you begin your experiment, decide what observations you will make and what data you will collect. **Data** are the facts, figures, and other evidence gathered through qualitative and quantitative observations. To organize your data, you may want to make a data table. A data table provides you with an organized way to collect and record your observations. Decide what your table will look like. Then you can start to collect your data.

After your data have been collected, they need to be interpreted. One tool that can help you interpret data is a graph. Graphs can reveal patterns or trends in data. Sometimes, there is more than one interpretation for a set of data. For example, scientists all agree that global temperatures have gone up over the past 100 years. What they do not agree on is the predictions of how much the temperatures are likely to go up over the next 100 years.

do the math!

A data table helps you organize the information you collect in an experiment. Graphing the data may reveal any patterns in your data.

1 Read Graphs Identify the manipulated variable and the responding variable.

_____

_____

_____

_____

2 Read Graphs As the temperature increases from 15°C to 25°C, what happens to the number of chirps per minute?

_____

_____

3 Predict How many chirps per minute would you expect when the temperature is 10°C?

_____

_____

7.NS.1, 7.NS.7, 7.NS.8

Number of Chirps per Minute

Cricket	15°C	20°C	25°C
1	91	135	180
2	80	124	169
3	89	130	176
4	78	125	158
5	77	121	157
Average	83	127	168

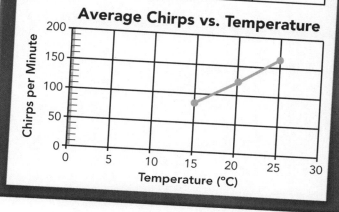

Average Chirps vs. Temperature

(graph: y-axis Chirps per Minute, x-axis Temperature (°C))

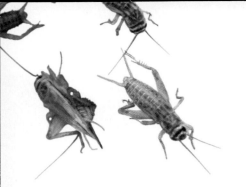

Drawing Conclusions Now you can draw conclusions about your hypothesis. A conclusion is a summary of what you have learned from an experiment. To draw your conclusion, you must examine your data objectively to see if they support or do not support your hypothesis. You also must consider whether you collected enough data.

You may decide that the data support your hypothesis. You conclude that the frequency of cricket chirping increases with temperature. Now, repeat your experiment to see if you get the same results. A conclusion is unreliable if it comes from an experiment with results that cannot be repeated. Many trials are needed before a hypothesis can be accepted as true.

Your data won't always support your hypothesis. When this happens, check your experiment for things that went wrong, or for improvements you can make. Then fix the problem and do the experiment again. If the experiment was done correctly the first time, your hypothesis was probably not correct. Propose a new hypothesis that you can test. Scientific inquiry usually doesn't end once an experiment is done. Often, one experiment leads to another.

Number of Chirps per Minute			
Cricket	15°C	20°C	25°C
1	98	100	120
2	92	95	105
3	101	93	99
4	102	85	97
5	91	89	98
Average	96	92	103

FIGURE 4 ···

▷ VIRTUAL LAB Drawing Conclusions

Sometimes the same experiment can have very different data.   **7.NS.8, 7.NS.9, 7.NS.10**

✐ **Answer the questions below.**

1. **Interpret Tables** Look at the data in the table. Do the data support the hypothesis that crickets chirp more in warmer temperatures? Explain.

_____

_____

_____

2. **Analyze Sources of Error** If the data in this table were yours, what might you do next? Explain.

_____

_____

_____

3. CHALLENGE Can you draw a conclusion from these data? Why or why not?

_____

_____

_____

Communicating Communicating is the sharing of ideas and results with others through writing and speaking. Scientists communicate by giving talks at scientific meetings, exchanging information on the Internet, or publishing articles in scientific journals.

When scientists share the results of their research, they describe their procedures so that others can repeat their experiments. It is important for scientists to wait until an experiment has been repeated many times before accepting a result. Therefore, scientists must keep accurate records of their methods and results. This way, scientists know that the result is accurate. Before the results are published, other scientists review the experiment for sources of error, such as bias, data interpretation, and faulty conclusions.

Sometimes, a scientific inquiry can be part of a huge project in which many scientists are working together around the world. For example, the Human Genome Project involved scientists from 18 different countries. The scientists' goal was to create a map of the information in your cells that makes you who you are. On such a large project, scientists must share their ideas and results regularly. Come up with ideas for communicating the results of your cricket experiment in **Figure 5.**

Vocabulary Identify Related Word Forms *Communication* is the noun form of the verb *communicate*. Write a sentence using the noun *communication*.

The Human Genome Project logo

FIGURE 5 ·······

Communicating Results
Since the Human Genome Project touched upon many areas of science, communication was important.

✎ **Communicate** Get together as a group and write three ways to share the results of your cricket experiment with other students.   7.NS.11

25

EXPLORE THE BIG ?

In a Scientist's Shoes

How do scientists investigate the natural world?

Design an Experiment

QUESTION _____

SCIENTIFIC ATTITUDES INVOLVED _____

_____

HYPOTHESIS _____

VARIABLES

Manipulated Variables _____

Responding Variables _____

Factors to Consider _____

_____

COLLECT DATA

Number of Trials _____

Units of Measure _____

SCIENTIFIC SKILLS USED _____

_____

NEXT STEPS _____

FIGURE 6 ························

> INTERACTIVE ART Think like a scientist to find out if an unfolded, a folded, or a crumpled sheet of paper falls fastest.

✎ **Complete these tasks.**

1. **Design Experiments** Write about your experiment on the notebook.

2. **Communicate** Discuss ways to improve your experiments.
   7.NS.2, 7.NS.3, 7.NS.4, 7.NS.6

Lab zone® Do the Lab Investigation *Keeping Flowers Fresh.*

🔑 Assess Your Understanding

2a. Explain How might using different types of crickets affect the cricket experiment?

_____

_____

_____

_____

7.NS.4, 7.NS.6

b. ANSWER THE BIG ? How do scientists investigate the natural world?

_____

_____

_____

_____

7.NS.2, 7.NS.3, 7.NS.4, 7.NS.6, 7.NS.8, 7.NS.10, 7.NS.11

got it? ························

○ **I get it!** Now I know that an experimental design must _____

_____

○ **I need extra help with** _____

Go to **MY SCIENCE ⓢ COACH** online for help with this subject.   7.NS.2, 7.NS.3, 7.NS.4, 7.NS.6, 7.NS.8, 7.NS.10, 7.NS.11

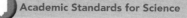

What Are Scientific Theories and Laws?

Academic Standards for Science

7.NS.6 Test predictions with multiple tests.

7.NS.8 Analyze data, using appropriate mathematical manipulation as required, and use it to identify patterns and make inferences based on these patterns.

Sometimes, a large set of related observations can be connected by a single explanation. This explanation can lead to the development of a scientific theory. In everyday life, a theory can be an unsupported guess. Everyday theories are not scientific theories. A **scientific theory** is a well-tested explanation for a wide range of observations and experimental results. For example, according to the atomic theory, all substances are composed of particles called atoms. Atomic theory helps to explain many observations, such as why iron nails rust. Scientists accept a theory only when it can explain the important observations. If the theory cannot explain new observations, then the theory is changed or thrown out. In this way, theories are constantly being developed, revised, or discarded as more information is collected.

A **scientific law** is a statement that describes what scientists expect to happen every time under a particular set of conditions. ☞ **Unlike a theory, a scientific law describes an observed pattern in nature without attempting to explain it.** For example, the law of gravity states that all objects in the universe attract each other. Look at **Figure 7.**

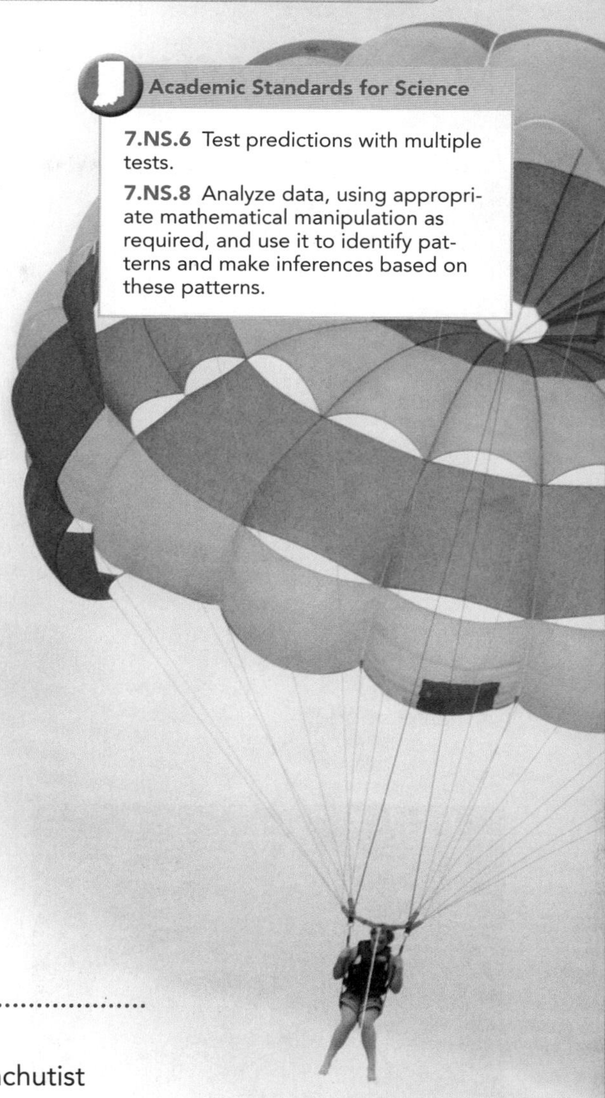

FIGURE 7 ···
A Scientific Law
According to the law of gravity, this parachutist will eventually land on Earth.

✎ **Apply Concepts** Give another example of a scientific law.

_____

_____

_____

 Lab ® Do the Quick Lab
zone *Theories and Laws.*

☞ **Assess Your Understanding**

got it? ···

O **I get it!** Now I know that the difference between a scientific theory and a law is that _____

_____

O **I need extra help with** _____

Go to my science ⓢ **coach** *online for help with this subject.*   7.NS.6, 7.NS.8

27

1 Study Guide

To think like a scientist, you must use _____, _____,

and _____ to observe the world.

LESSON 1 Science and the Natural World
7.NS.1, 7.NS.2, 7.NS.3, 7.NS.8, 7.NS.11, 7.DP.9

Scientists use skills such as observing, inferring, predicting, classifying, evaluating, and making models to study the world.

Vocabulary
- science • observing
- quantitative observation
- qualitative observation • inferring
- predicting • classifying • evaluating
- making models

LESSON 2 Thinking Like a Scientist
7.NS.1, 7.NS.2, 7.NS.8, 7.NS.11

Scientists possess certain important attitudes, including curiosity, honesty, creativity, open-mindedness, skepticism, good ethics, and awareness of bias.

Scientific reasoning requires a logical way of thinking based on gathering and evaluating evidence.

Vocabulary
- skepticism • ethics • personal bias • cultural bias
- experimental bias • objective • subjective
- deductive reasoning • inductive reasoning

LESSON 3 Scientific Inquiry
7.NS.1, 7.NS.2, 7.NS.3, 7.NS.4, 7.NS.6, 7.NS.7, 7.NS.8, 7.NS.9, 7.NS.10, 7.NS.11, 7.DP.2

Scientific inquiry refers to the diverse ways in which scientists study the natural world and propose explanations based on the evidence they gather.

An experiment must follow sound scientific principles for its results to be valid.

Unlike a theory, a scientific law describes an observed pattern in nature without attempting to explain it.

Vocabulary
- scientific inquiry • hypothesis • variable • manipulated variable • responding variable
- controlled experiment • data • scientific theory • scientific law

Review and Assessment

LESSON 1 Science and the Natural World

1. When you explain or interpret an observation, you are

   a. making models.   **b.** classifying.

   c. inferring.   **d.** predicting.

                    7.NS.2

2. When scientists group observations that are alike in some way, they are _____

                    7.NS.2

3. Predict How do scientists use observations to make predictions?

_____

_____

_____

                    7.NS.1

4. Infer Suppose you come home to the scene below. What can you infer happened?

_____

_____

_____

_____

                    7.NS.2

5. Observe What is a quantitative observation you might make in your school cafeteria?

_____

_____

_____

                    7.NS.2

LESSON 2 Thinking Like a Scientist

6. The scientific attitude of having doubt is called

   a. open-mindedness.   **b.** curiosity.

   c. honesty.   **d.** skepticism.

                    7.NS.8

7. When a person allows personal opinions, values, or tastes to influence a conclusion, that person is using _____ reasoning.

                    7.NS.8

8. Compare and Contrast Describe the three types of bias that can influence a science experiment.

_____

_____

_____

_____

_____

_____

_____

                7.NS.1, 7.NS.2

9. Draw Conclusions Why is it important to report experimental results honestly, even when the results might be the opposite of the results you expect to see?

_____

_____

_____

_____

_____

                    7.NS.2

10. **Write About It** A team of scientists is developing a new medicine to improve memory. Write about how the attitudes of curiosity, honesty, creativity, and open-mindedness help the scientists in their work. When might they need to think about ethics? How could bias influence their results?

            7.NS.1, 7.NS.2, 7.NS.8, 7.NS.11

1 Review and Assessment

Scientific Inquiry

11. The facts, figures, and other evidence gathered through observations are called

   a. conclusions.

   b. data.

   c. predictions.

   d. hypotheses.

                               7.NS.3

12. The one variable that is changed to test a hypothesis is

   a. the responding variable.

   b. the other variable.

   c. the manipulated variable.

   d. the dependent variable.

                               7.NS.4

13. A _____ is

a well-tested explanation for a wide range of observations.

                               7.NS.2

14. Communicate What are some ways that scientists communicate with each other?

_____

_____

_____

_____

_____

_____

_____

                            7.NS.10

15. **Write About It** Suppose you want to find out which dog food your dog likes best. Write about the experiment you would design. What variables would you need to control? What kinds of data would you collect? How could you avoid experimental bias?

           7.NS.1, 7.NS.2, 7.NS.3, 7.NS.4,
              7.NS.6, 7.NS.8, 7.NS.10

APPLY THE BIG ? How do scientists investigate the natural world?

16. Central Middle School is having problems with attendance during the winter. Many students get sick and miss school. The principal wants to fix the problem, but she is not sure what to do. One idea is to install hand sanitizer dispensers in the classrooms.

Think about this problem scientifically. What is a possible hypothesis in this situation? What experiment could you design to test it? Mention at least three attitudes or skills that will be important in finding the answer.

_____

_____

_____

_____

_____

_____

_____

_____

_____

_____

_____

_____

7.NS.1, 7.NS.2, 7.NS.3, 7.NS.4, 7.NS.6, 7.NS.8, 7.NS.10

Indiana ISTEP+ Practice

Multiple Choice

Circle the letter of the best answer.

1. Sophia noticed that many birds pick through the seeds in her bird feeder until they get a sunflower seed. What is an inference she could make from this observation?

    A. Birds are attracted to white objects.

    B. Sunflower seeds are crunchy.

    C. Birds do not like seeds.

    D. Birds prefer sunflower seeds.

    .1

2. Which of the following attitudes   good scientists possess?

    A. curiosity about the wor'

    B. certainty that a hypo'   sis is correct

    C. ambition to be far   s and respected

    D. a strong sense c   ltural bias

    7.NS.2

3. Marie   served people at a store. Which is a qua'   ive observation she may have made?

    A   wenty people walked into the store.

    . The store sells clothes.

    C. It was 1:00 P.M.

    D. all of the above

    7.NS.1

4. Tara was collecting data about rainfall by measuring water levels in a bucket in her yard. She saw her dog drinking   om the bucket. This is an example of

    A. cultural bias.

    B. personal bias.

    C. experiment   ias.

    D. data colle   on.

    7.NS.1

Const   ted Response

Wr' your answer to Question 5 on the l   below.

ɔ. What is a scientific theory?

_____

_____

_____

    7.NS.1

Extended Response

Use the graph below and your knowledge of science to help you answer Question 6. Write your answer on a separate sheet of paper.

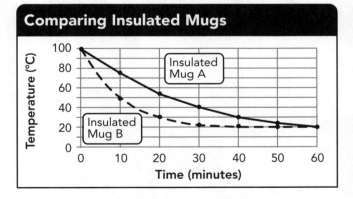

6. This graph compares how well two different brands of insulated mugs retain heat. Describe the variables in the experiment. What conclusion might you draw from the graph?

    7.NS.4, 7.NS.8

When We Think We Know but It Isn't So

Science is a way of thinking and learning about the world. It is not rigid or unchanging. In fact, scientists are constantly learning new things. And sometimes, they make mistakes! That's just what René Blondlot and his co-workers at Nancy University in France did in 1903.

X-rays had just been discovered. Scientists everywhere, including Blondlot, were experimenting with them. In a series of photographs taken in an experiment, Blondlot observed strange lights. He was convinced he had discovered another new form of radiation. He named his discovery the N-ray, in honor of Nancy University where he worked. Dozens of other scientists repeated his experiments expecting to see the lights. Some were convinced that they actually had seen them. But there was one very big problem—N-rays do not exist! Scientists who were skeptical did not see these lights and could not repeat the results of the experiment. It was soon discovered that when they looked for N-rays, Blondlot and his colleagues were just seeing what they expected and hoped to see.

This is a clear case of expectations influencing observations. Because some scientists did not do enough to avoid their bias, they made a big mistake.

Research It Research about Robert W. Wood, the scientist who disproved the existence of N-rays. Write a paragraph summarizing how he came to this conclusion. What questions did he ask?

7.NS.2

◄ René Blondlot was a famous scientist who allowed his ambition to overrule his powers of observation.

READY FOR A CLOSE-UP

Whether they are filming animal behavior in the wild or documenting new medical technologies, science filmmakers never know what's going to happen next. For one film, a filmmaker spent 16 weeks sitting hidden under an animal skin for 14 hours every day, just so he could film bird behavior. To film a lion attack, another film crew put themselves in danger by parking a few meters away from some very hungry lions in the middle of the night.

Making a good science film is about more than getting the perfect shot. Crews working in fragile ecosystems like the Arctic or in deserts take care not to wreck habitats. This means they travel light—sometimes using just one hand-held camera.

Writers and producers also try to avoid bias. If there is more than one theory about a topic, they try to find experts who can discuss each theory, and they present as many facts as possible. The makers of a film about the Jarkov woolly mammoth relied heavily on their scientific advisors to make sure scientific facts weren't sacrificed for a good story.

Patience, an adventurous spirit, and science knowledge are all part of being a great science filmmaker!

Research It Research one species of animal. Write a proposal for a documentary about that animal. Include a list of four or five questions you hope to answer with your film.

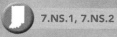

7.NS.1, 7.NS.2

WHY IS THIS SCIENTIST WEIGHING A POLAR BEAR?

How mathematics important to the work of scientists?

> **UNTAMED SCIENCE** Watch the **Untamed Science** video to learn more about how tools help scientists.

Scientists weighed this small female polar bear while she was asleep. They also measured the bear's body and skull. Similar measurements were done on bears throughout the Beaufort Sea of Alaska. The bears live on a frozen portion of the ocean called sea ice. Scientists are also measuring the sea ice to determine how much the ice is shrinking. By taking these measurements, scientists can figure out how the bears are affected by their environment.

Develop Hypotheses Write a hypothesis that could be tested with these scientists' measurements.

_____

_____

_____

Using Mathematics in Science

Academic Standards for Science

7.NS.1, 7.NS.2, 7.NS.3, 7.NS.5, 7.NS.7, 7.NS.8, 7.NS.11

Getting Started

Check Your Understanding

1. Background Read the paragraph below and then answer
the question.

Emi studied hard to prepare for her science lab
investigation. Emi was concerned because her
investigation was **complex.** She had been earning high
marks all year and wanted to maintain this **trend.** Emi
also wanted to use her lab report as a **sample** of her
science work.

> To be **complex** is to have
> many parts.
>
> A **trend** is the general
> direction that something
> tends to move.
>
> A **sample** is a portion of
> something that is used to
> represent the whole thing.

• Why would preparing help Emi maintain her high marks?

_____

_____

▷ MY READING WEB If you had trouble completing the question above,
visit **My Reading Web** and type in *Using Mathematics in Science.*

Vocabulary Skill

Identify Multiple Meanings Some words have more than one meaning.
The table below lists multiple meaning words used in science and in
daily life.

Word	Everyday Meaning	Scientific Meaning
mean	*v.* to indicate; to intend **Example:** They didn't *mean* to hurt her.	*n.* the numerical average **Example:** The *mean* of 11, 7, 5, and 9 is 8.
volume	*n.* the loudness of a sound **Example:** Turn up the *volume* so we can hear the song.	*n.* the amount of space an object or substance takes up **Example:** Record the *volume* of water in the graduated cylinder.

2. Quick Check In the table above, circle the meaning of the word
volume that is used in the following sentence.

• The *volume* of juice in the container is 1.89 liters.

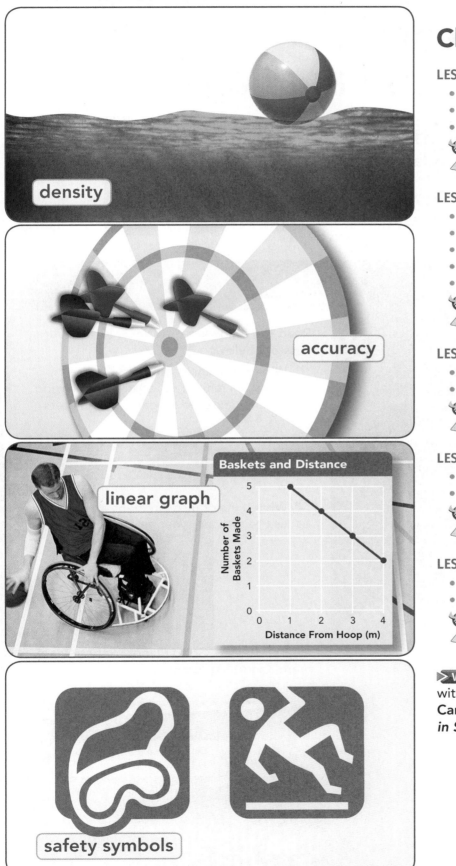

density

accuracy

linear graph

Baskets and Distance

Number of Baskets Made (y-axis: 0–5)
Distance From Hoop (m) (x-axis: 0–4)

safety symbols

Chapter Preview

LESSON 1
- metric system • SI
- mass • weight • volume
- meniscus • density

⟳ **Compare and Contrast**
△ **Measure**

LESSON 2
- estimate • accuracy
- precision • significant figures
- percent error • mean
- median • mode • range
- anomalous data

⟳ **Relate Cause and Effect**
△ **Calculate**

LESSON 3
- graph • linear graph
- nonlinear graph

⟳ **Relate Text and Visuals**
△ **Predict**

LESSON 4
- model • system • input
- process • output • feedback

⟳ **Identify the Main Idea**
△ **Make Models**

LESSON 5
- safety symbol
- field

⟳ **Summarize**
△ **Observe**

> VOCAB FLASH CARDS For extra help with vocabulary, visit **Vocab Flash Cards** and type in *Using Mathematics in Science.*

Measurement—
A Common Language

🔑 **Why Do Scientists Use a
Standard Measurement System?**
7.NS.3, 7.NS.5, 7.NS.8

🔑 **What Are Some SI Units
of Measure?**
7.NS.1, 7.NS.3, 7.NS.5, 7.NS.7, 7.NS.8

my planet Diary

Extreme Measurements

Here are some fascinating animal
measurements.

- The Queen Alexandra's Birdwing butterfly
  has a wingspan of 30 centimeters.

- A newborn giraffe stands 1.8 meters tall.

- When a blue whale exhales, the spray
  from its blowhole can reach up to 9 meters
  into the air.

- A colossal squid's eye measures about
  28 centimeters across.

- With a mass of only 20 grams, the rhinoceros
  beetle can lift 850 times its own mass.

- A hummingbird's egg has a mass
  of about half a gram while
  an ostrich egg has
  a mass of about
  1,500 grams.

Ostrich egg

FUN FACTS

Read the following questions. Write your
answers below.

1. What problems could arise if some
   scientists measured length in inches and
   others measured length in centimeters?

   _____

   _____

   _____

2. What units of measurement would you
   use to measure your height and mass?

   _____

   _____

   _____

   _____

▷ PLANET DIARY ⟩ Go to **Planet Diary** to learn
more about measurement.

Lab ® Do the Inquiry Warm-Up
zone *History of Measurement.*

Hummingbird eggs

Vocabulary
- metric system • SI • mass • weight
- volume • meniscus • density

Skills
- Reading: Compare and Contrast
- Inquiry: Measure

Why Do Scientists Use a Standard Measurement System?

Standard measurement is important. Without it, cooks would use handfuls and pinches instead of cups and tablespoons.

Scientists also use standard measurements. This allows scientists everywhere to repeat experiments. In the 1790s, scientists in France developed the metric system of measurement. The **metric system** is a measurement system based on the number 10. Modern scientists use a version of the metric system called the International System of Units, or **SI** (from the French, *Système International d'Unités*). **Using SI as the standard system of measurement allows scientists to compare data and communicate with each other about their results.** The prefixes used in the SI system are shown in **Figure 1.**

Academic Standards for Science

7.NS.3 Collect quantitative data with appropriate tools and technologies and use appropriate units to label numerical data.

7.NS.5 Use principles of accuracy and precision when making measurement.

7.NS.8 Analyze data and use it to identify patterns and make inferences based on these patterns.

FIGURE 1 ··································
▷ VIRTUAL LAB **SI Prefixes**
SI units are similar to our money units, in which a dime is ten times more than a penny.

✎ **Complete the tasks below.**

1. **Name** In the table at the right, finish filling in the Example column.

2. **Calculate** How many times larger is a *kilo-* than a *deka-*?

_____

_____

7.NS.8

Common SI Prefixes

Prefix	Meaning	Example
kilo- (k)	1,000	_____
hecto- (h)	100	_____
deka- (da)	10	dekameter
no prefix	1	meter
deci- (d)	0.1 (one tenth)	_____
centi- (c)	0.01 (one hundredth)	_____
milli- (m)	0.001 (one thousandth)	_____

 Lab zone Do the Quick Lab *How Many Shoes?*

Assess Your Understanding

got it? ···

○ I get it! Now I know that scientists use a standard measurement system to _____

_____

○ I need extra help with _____

Go to my science COACH *online for help with this subject.*

7.NS.3, 7.NS.5

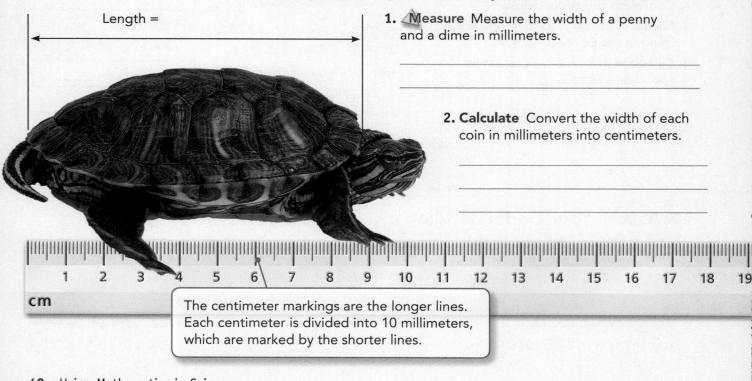
Conversions for Length

1 km	=	1,000 m
1 m	=	100 cm
1 m	=	1,000 mm
1 cm	=	10 mm

What Are Some SI Units of Measure?

Scientists regularly measure attributes such as length, mass, volume, density, temperature, and time. Each attribute is measured in an SI unit.

Length Length is the distance from one point to another. **In SI, the basic unit for measuring length is the meter (m).** Many distances can be measured in meters. For example, you can measure a softball throw or your height in meters. One meter is about the distance from the floor to a doorknob. A tool used to measure length is a metric ruler.

For measuring lengths smaller than a meter, you use the centimeter (cm) and millimeter (mm). For example, the length of this page is about 28 centimeters. For measuring a long distance, such as the distance between cities, you use the unit called a kilometer (km). The table at the left shows you how to convert between different metric length units. Try measuring the turtle's shell in **Figure 2**.

FIGURE 2 ···

Measuring Length

To use a metric ruler, line up one end of an object with the zero mark. Then read the number at the object's other end.

✎ **Use the ruler to measure the length of the turtle's shell and record it above the arrow. Then working in small groups, complete the activity below.** 7.NS.3, 7.NS.5, 7.NS.8

1. **Measure** Measure the width of a penny and a dime in millimeters.

_____

_____

2. **Calculate** Convert the width of each coin in millimeters into centimeters.

_____

_____

_____

Length =

The centimeter markings are the longer lines. Each centimeter is divided into 10 millimeters, which are marked by the shorter lines.

cm 1 2 3 4 5 6 7 8 9 10 11 12 13 14 15 16 17 18 19

Mass A balance, such as the one shown in **Figure 3,** is used to measure mass. **Mass** is a measure of the amount of matter in an object. A balance compares the mass of an object to a known mass. 🔑 **In SI, the basic unit for measuring mass is the kilogram (kg).** The mass of cars, bicycles, and people is measured in kilograms. If you want to measure much smaller masses, you would use grams (g) or milligrams (mg). The table at the right shows how to convert between kilograms, grams, and milligrams.

Unlike mass, **weight** is a measure of the force of gravity acting on an object. A scale is used to measure weight. When you stand on a scale on Earth, gravity pulls you downward. This compresses springs inside the scale. The more you weigh, the more the springs compress. On the moon, the force of gravity is weaker than it is on Earth. So the scale's springs would not compress as much on the moon as on Earth. Unlike weight, your mass on the moon is the same as your mass on Earth.

Conversions for Mass		
1 kg	=	1,000 g
1 g	=	1,000 mg

✏️
⟳ Compare and Contrast
Use the chart to compare and contrast mass and weight.

Alike	Different
_____	_____
_____	_____
_____	_____
_____	_____
_____	_____
_____	_____
_____	_____
_____	_____
_____	_____

FIGURE 3 ·····················

Measuring Mass
A triple-beam balance can be used to measure mass.

✏️ ⚠️Measure **Read the balance to find the mass of the turtle. Record your answer in grams and then in milligrams.**

_____

_____

7.NS.3, 7.NS.5

1 Place an object on the pan.

2 Shift the riders on the beams until they balance the object and the pointer hits 0.

3 Add up the grams shown on all three beams to find the mass.

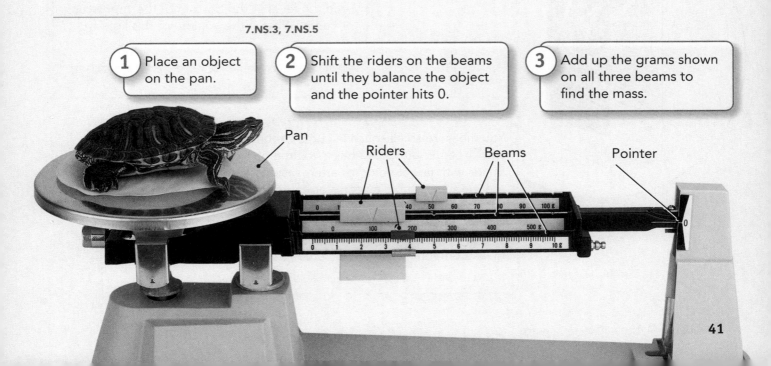

Pan   Riders   Beams   Pointer

41

Conversions for Volume

1 m³	=	1,000,000 cm³
1 cm³	=	1 mL
1 L	=	1,000 mL
1 L	=	1,000 cm³

Volume Instead of measuring your juice, you just look to see how much of the glass you have filled up. **Volume** is the amount of space an object or substance takes up. ⟅⟆ **In SI, the basic unit for measuring volume is the cubic meter (m³).** Other units include the liter (L) and the cubic centimeter (cm³). Cubic meters or centimeters are used to measure the volume of solids. The liter is commonly used for measuring the volume of liquids. The green table shows how to convert between these units.

FIGURE 4 ··

Volume of Liquids, Rectangular Solids, and Irregular Solids

Measuring the volume of liquids and rectangular solids requires different methods.

✎ **Complete the activity on this page. Then follow the steps to measure the volume of an irregular solid on the next page.** 7.NS.3, 7.NS.5

Explain In the boxes, find the volume of the liquid and the cereal box. Below, explain which has a greater volume.

_____

_____

_____

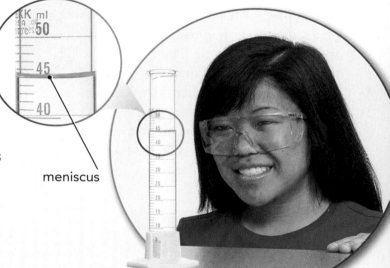

meniscus

Volume of Liquids

You are probably familiar with the liter from seeing 1-liter and 2-liter bottles. You can measure smaller liquid volumes by using milliliters (mL). There are 1,000 milliliters in one liter. To measure the volume of a liquid, read the level at the bottom of the **meniscus,** or curve. What is the volume of this liquid?

_____

25 cm
20 cm
6 cm

Volume of Rectangular Solids

You measure small solids in cubic centimeters (cm³). A cube with 1-centimeter sides has a volume of 1 cubic centimeter. Solids with larger volumes are measured with the cubic meter (m³). A cubic meter is equal to the volume of a cube with 1-meter sides. To calculate a rectangular solid's volume, multiply length times width times height. When you use this formula, you must use the same units for all measurements. What is the cereal box's volume?

_____

Volume of Irregular Solids

Suppose you wanted to measure the volume of a rock. Because of its irregular shape, you cannot measure a rock's length, width, or height. However, you can use the displacement method shown on this page. To use this method, you immerse the object in water and measure how much the water level rises.

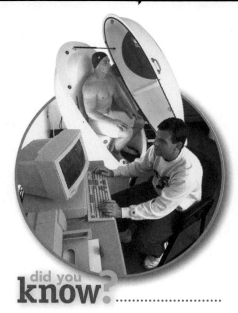

1 Fill a graduated cylinder about two thirds full of water.

What is the volume of water in the graduated cylinder?

_____

2 Place the object into the water. What is the volume of the water plus the object?

_____

3 Find the volume of the object by subtracting the volume of the water alone from the volume of the water plus the object.

What is the volume of the object?

_____

7.NS.3, 7.NS.5

43

Density Look at **Figure 5.** Two objects of the same size can have different masses. This is because different materials have different densities. **Density** is a measure of how much mass is contained in a given volume.

Units of Density Because density is made up of two measurements, mass and volume, an object's density is expressed as a relationship between two units.  **In SI, the basic unit for measuring density is kilograms per cubic meter (kg/m³).** Other units of density are grams per cubic centimeter (g/cm³) and grams per milliliter (g/mL).

FIGURE 5 ··

Comparing Densities

The bowling ball and the beach ball have the same volume but not the same mass.

✎ **Form Operational Definitions** Use this information to decide which object has a greater density. Explain your answer in terms of volume and mass.

_____

_____

_____

do the math!

Calculating Density

The density of an object is the object's mass divided by its volume. To find the density of an object, use the formula below.

$$\text{Density} = \frac{\text{mass}}{\text{volume}}$$

❶ Calculate Find the density of a piece of metal that has a mass of 68 g and a volume of 6 cm³.

_____

❷ Predict Suppose a piece of metal has the same mass as the metal in Question 1 but a greater volume. How would its density compare to the metal in Question 1?

_____

_____

_____

7.NS.1, 7.NS.3, 7.NS.8

Density of Substances The table in **Figure 6** lists the densities of some common substances. The density of a pure substance is the same for all samples of that substance. For example, all samples of pure gold, no matter how large or small, have a density of 19.3 g/cm^3.

Once you know an object's density, you can determine whether the object will float in a given liquid. An object will float if it is less dense than the surrounding liquid. For example, the density of water is 1 g/cm^3. A piece of wood with a density of 0.8 g/cm^3 will float in water. A ring made of pure silver, which has a density of 10.5 g/cm^3, will sink.

FIGURE 6 ···

A Density Experiment

Knowing the density of an object helps you predict how it will float and identify what it is made of.

✎ **Complete the tasks below.**

1. Infer An object has a density of 0.7 g/cm^3. Do you think it floats or sinks in water? Explain.

_____

_____

2. Design Experiments Use what you know about density and measuring tools to describe the steps you might use to determine if a bar of metal is gold. Write your procedure in the notebook.
7.NS.7, 7.NS.8

Densities of Some Common Substances

Substance	Density (g/cm³)
Air	0.001
Ice	0.9
Water	1.0
Aluminum	2.7
Gold	19.3

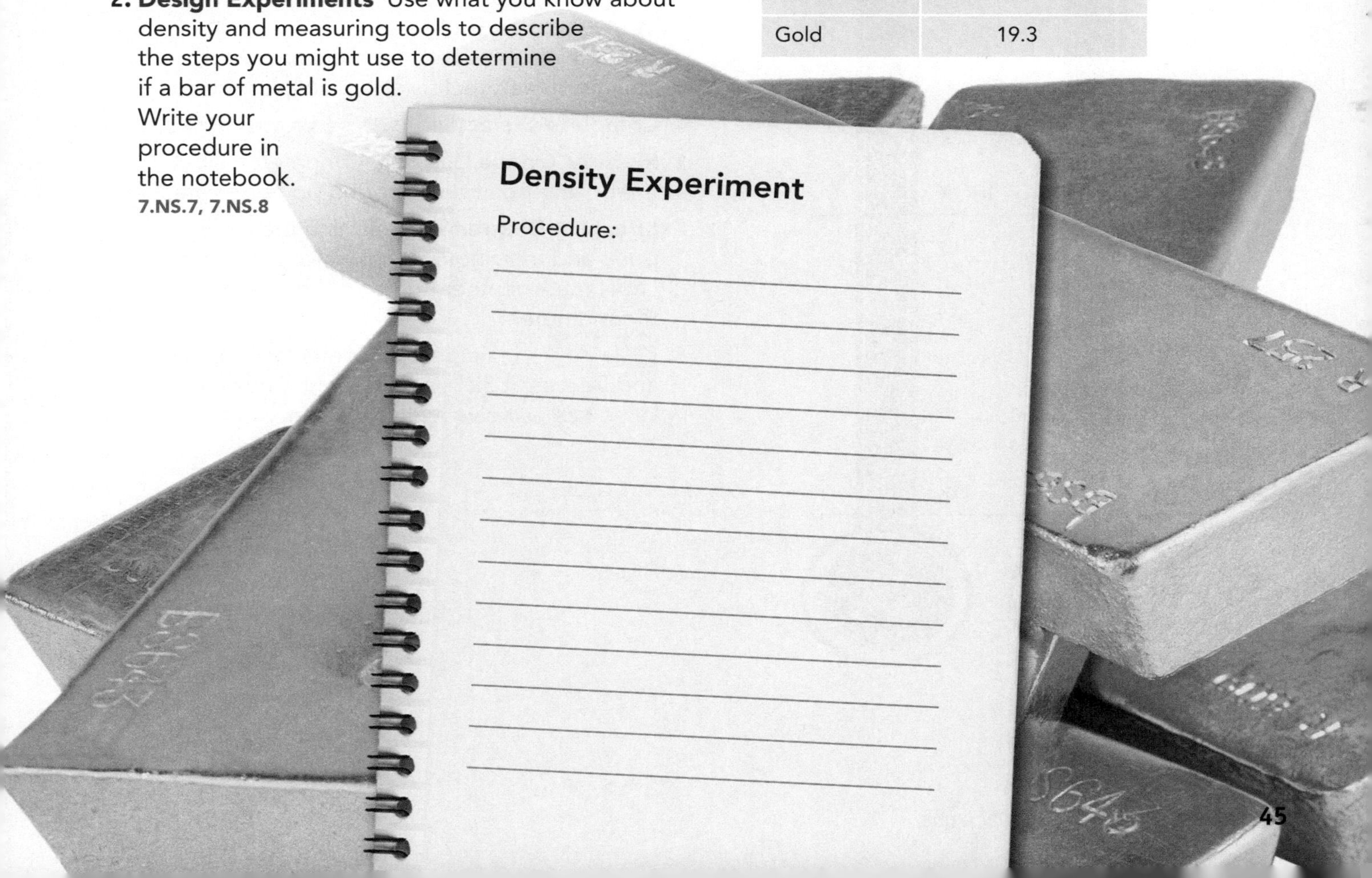

Density Experiment

Procedure:

_____

_____

_____

_____

_____

_____

_____

_____

_____

_____

_____

_____

_____

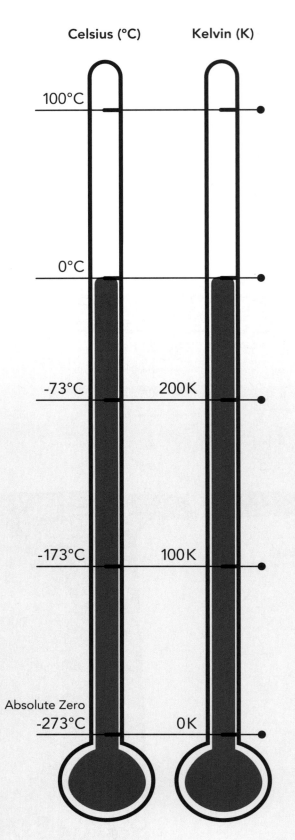

Celsius (°C)   Kelvin (K)

100°C

0°C

-73°C   200 K

-173°C   100 K

Absolute Zero
-273°C   0 K

Temperature Is it cold out this morning? How high will the temperature rise? You probably use temperature measurements often in your everyday life. So do scientists.

Scientists commonly use the Celsius temperature scale to measure temperature. On the Celsius scale, water freezes at 0°C and boils at 100°C. **In addition to the Celsius scale, scientists sometimes use another temperature scale, called the Kelvin scale. In fact, the kelvin (K) is the official SI unit for temperature.** Kelvin is useful in science because there are no negative numbers. Units on the Kelvin scale are the same size as those on the Celsius scale, as shown in **Figure 7.** The table below shows how to convert between Celsius and Kelvin.

A thermometer is used to measure temperature. When you place a liquid thermometer in a substance, the liquid inside the thermometer will increase or decrease in volume. This makes the level rise or fall. Wait until the level stops changing. Then read the number next to the top of the liquid in the thermometer.

FIGURE 7 ···

Temperature Scales
Zero on the Kelvin scale (0 K) is the coldest possible temperature. It is called absolute zero.

✏ **Complete the activities.**   7.NS.3, 7.NS.5, 7.NS.8

1. **Identify** On the Celsius thermometer, label the boiling point and freezing point of water.

2. **Interpret Diagrams** Determine the boiling point and freezing point of water in Kelvins. Label these temperatures on the Kelvin thermometer.

3. CHALLENGE In Fahrenheit, water boils at 212° and freezes at 32°. Are Fahrenheit units the same size as Kelvin units? Explain.

_____

_____

_____

Conversions for Temperature

0°C	=	273 K
100°C	=	373 K

Time You push to run even faster with the finish line in sight. But an opponent is catching up. Just one second can mean the difference between winning and losing. What is a second?

🔑 **The second (s) is the SI unit used to measure time.** Just like all the SI units, the second is divided into smaller units based on the number 10. For example, a millisecond (ms) is one thousandth of a second. You use minutes or hours for longer periods of time. There are 60 seconds in a minute, and 60 minutes in an hour.

Clocks and watches are used to measure time. Some clocks are more accurate than others. Most digital stopwatches measure time accurately to one hundredth of a second, as shown in **Figure 8.** Devices used for timing Olympic events measure time to a thousandth of a second or even closer.

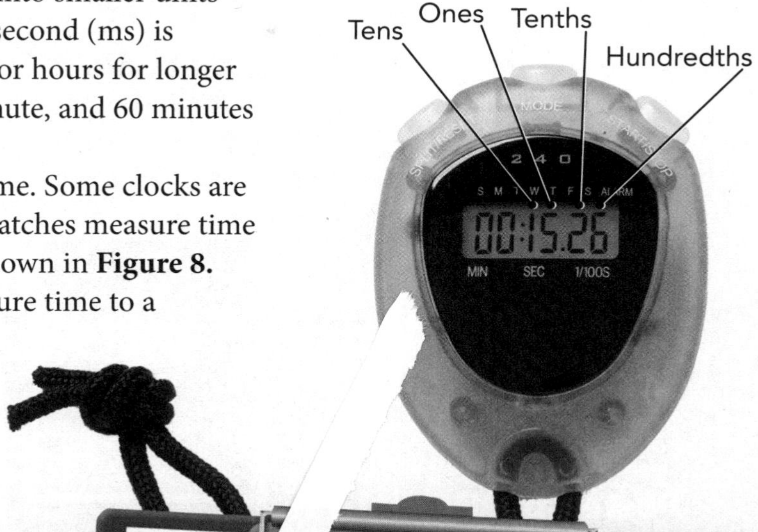

Tens Ones Tenths Hundredths

00:15.26

MIN   SEC   1/100S

FIGURE 8 ···

It's About Time
This stopwatch measured Jessie's best time in a school race.

✏️ **Write Jessie's time in the chart and then complete the activity.**

Interpret Tables In the last column, write the order that the runners finished.

7.NS.8

Runne...	Time	Place
Geo...	00:15.74	
Sa...	00:26.78	
S...	00:20.22	
...ssie		

Lab ® Do the Quick Lab
zone *Measuring Length in Metric.*

🔑 **Assess Your Understanding**

1a. Identify What tool would you use to measure the mass of a baseball?

_____

_____

7.NS.3

b. Sequence What steps would you ta... to determine the density of a base...

_____

_____

_____

_____

got it?

○ **I get it!** Now I know that basic SI units of measurement are _____

_____

_____

_____

○ **I need extra help with** _____

Go to **MY SCIENCE** ⓢ **COACH** online for help with this subject.   7.NS.3

7.NS.3

Mathematics and Science

🔑 **What Math Skills Do Scientists Use?**
7.NS.3, 7.NS.5, 7.NS.8

🔑 **What Math Tools Do Scientists Use?**
7.NS.3, 7.NS.5, 7.NS.8, 7.NS.11

my pLaneT DiaRY for Indiana

BLOG

Posted by: Destini
Location: Monrovia, Indiana

Math is used in our everyday lives whether we realize it or not. Every school morning I wake up at a certain time and get ready for school. In order to allow myself enough time to get completely ready before the bus comes, I add up the minutes it takes for me to shower, get dressed, eat, and take my dog out.

- Shower: 25 minutes
- Get dressed and do my hair: 20 minutes
- Eat: 5 minutes
- Dog out: 2 to 3 minutes

My bus comes at 7:25. So I wake up at 6:30 every morning. I have just enough time to get everything done.

Communicate Discuss the following question with a partner. Write your answer below.

How do you use math in your everyday life?

_____

_____

_____

_____

_____

_____

▷ **PLANET DIARY** Go to **Planet Diary** to learn more about mathematics and science.

Lab zone® Do the Inquiry Warm-Up *How Many Marbles Are There?*

Vocabulary
- estimate
- accuracy
- precision
- significant figures
- percent error
- mean
- median
- mode
- range
- anomalous data

Skills
- ⟳ Reading: Relate Cause and Effect
- △ Inquiry: Calculate

What Math Skills Do Scientists Use?

From measuring to collecting data, scientists use math every day. ⌐ **Math skills that scientists use to collect data include estimation, accuracy and precision, and significant figures.**

Estimation An **estimate** is an approximation of a number based on reasonable assumptions. An estimate is not a guess. It is always based on known information. Scientists often rely on estimates when they cannot obtain exact numbers. Their estimates might be based on indirect measurements, calculations, and models. For example, they may estimate the distance between stars based on indirect measurements because they can't measure the distance directly. Other estimates might be based on a sample.

> **Academic Standards for Science**
>
> **7.NS.3** Collect quantitative data with appropriate tools or technologies and use appropriate units to label numerical data.
>
> **7.NS.5** Use principles of accuracy and precision when making measurement.
>
> **7.NS.8** Analyze data, using appropriate mathematical manipulation as required, and use it to identify patterns and make inferences based on these patterns.

do the math!

Estimation

Estimating from a sample is a quick way to determine the large number of birds in this photo.

1 Interpret Photos How many birds are in the yellow square? This number is your sample.

_____

2 Explain By what number should you multiply the sample to find an estimate for the total number of birds in the total area? Explain your answer.

_____

_____

_____

3 Estimate Calculate your estimate for the total number of birds. Show your work.

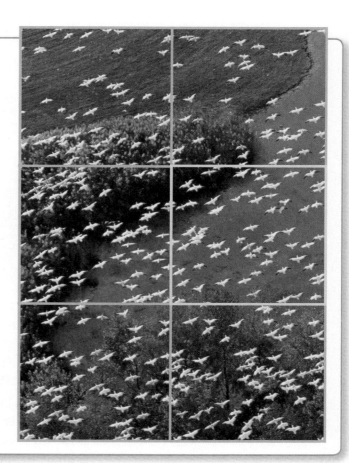

7.NS.3, 7.NS.8

Accuracy and Precision

People often use the words *accuracy* and *precision* to describe the same idea. In science, these words have different meanings. **Accuracy** refers to how close a measurement is to the true or accepted value. **Precision** refers to how close a group of measurements are to each other.

How can you be sure that a measurement is both accurate and precise? First, use a high-quality measurement tool. Second, measure carefully. Finally, repeat the measurement a few times. If your measurement is the same each time, you can assume that it is reliable. A reliable measurement is both accurate and precise. Look at **Figure 1**.

FIGURE 1 ·······················

Accuracy and Precision

In a game of darts, accurate throws land close to the bull's eye. Precise throws land close to one another.

✎ **Apply Concepts** Draw dots on boards C and D to show the situations described.   **7.NS.5**

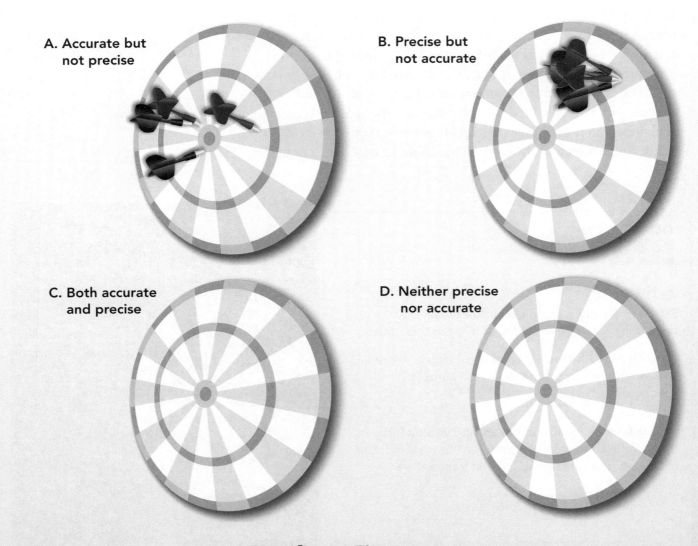

A. Accurate but not precise

B. Precise but not accurate

C. Both accurate and precise

D. Neither precise nor accurate

Significant Figures

Significant figures communicate how precise measurements are. The **significant figures** in a measurement include all digits measured exactly, plus one estimated digit. If the measurement has only one digit, you must assume it is estimated. Use **Figure 2** to learn more about significant figures.

Ruler markings: 0 1 2 3 4 5 6 7 8 9 10 11 12 13 14 15

Adding or Subtracting Measurements

When you add or subtract measurements, your answer can only have as many places after the decimal point as the measurement with the fewest places after the decimal point. For example, suppose you add a tile that is 5.3 centimeters long to a row of tiles that is 21.94 centimeters long. Find the new length of the row.

```
  21.94 cm (2 places after the decimal)
+  5.3  cm (1 place after the decimal)
  27.24 cm → 27.2 cm (1 place after the decimal)
```

If you remove a tile that is 5.3 centimeters long from a row of tiles that is 21.94 centimeters long, what is the new length of the row? How many significant figures are in this measurement?

_____

_____

7.NS.5, 7.NS.8

FIGURE 2 ·····················
Significant Figures

Suppose you are tiling a bathroom. You might estimate that the tile is 5.3 cm long. The measurement 5.3 cm has two significant figures, or sig figs. You are certain of the 5, but you have estimated the 3.

 **Calculate** Read about adding, subtracting, and multiplying measurements. Then complete the activities in the boxes.

Multiplying Measurements

When you multiply measurements, the answer should only have the same number of significant figures as the measurement with the fewest significant figures. For example, suppose you need to find the area of a space that measures 2.25 meters by 3 meters.

```
  2.25 m  (3 sig figs)
×   3 m   (1 sig fig)
  6.75 m² → 7 m² (1 sig fig)
```

Find the area of a space that measures 4.4 meters by 2 meters. How many significant figures are in this measurement?

_____

_____

7.NS.5, 7.NS.8

 Lab zone Do the Quick Lab For Good Measure.

🗝 Assess Your Understanding

1a. Review What math skill do scientists rely on when they cannot obtain exact numbers?

_____

7.NS.3, 7.NS.5

b. Interpret Data Lia measures a wall of her room to be 3.7 meters by 2.45 meters. How many significant figures are in the measurement of its area? Explain.

_____

_____

7.NS.5, 7.NS.8

got it?

○ **get it!** Now I know that the math skills scientists use to collect data include _____

_____

_____

_____

○ I need extra help with _____

Go to **MY SCIENCE** Ⓢ **COACH** online for help with this subject.   7.NS.3, 7.NS.5, 7.NS.8

51

Relate Cause and Effect
Underline the causes of a high percent error.

What Math Tools Do Scientists Use?

Mathematics is just as powerful a tool for analyzing data as it is for collecting it. **Scientists use certain math tools to analyze data. These tools include calculating percent error; finding the mean, median, mode, and range; and checking the reasonableness of data.**

Percent Error Often, scientists must make measurements that already have accepted values. For example, an accepted, or true, value for the density of the metal copper is 8.92 g/cm^3. Suppose you measure the mass and volume of a sample of the metal copper, and calculate a density of 9.37 g/cm^3. You know your calculation is not accurate, but by how much? **Percent error** calculations are a way to determine how accurate an experimental value is. A low percent error means that the result you obtained was accurate. A high percent error means that your result was not accurate. It may not be accurate because you did not measure carefully or something was wrong with your measurement tool.

do the math! Sample Problem

Percent Error

The experimental density of copper is 9.37 g/cm^3. The true value is 8.92 g/cm^3. To calculate the percent error, use the following formula and substitute.

$$\text{Percent error} = \frac{\text{Difference between experimental value and true value}}{\text{true value}} \times 100\%$$

$$\%E = \frac{9.37 \text{ g/cm}^3 - 8.92 \text{ g/cm}^3}{8.92 \text{ g/cm}^3} \times 100\%$$

The percent error in the calculation of the density of copper was 5.04%.

1 Calculate Suppose you measured the density of a silver ring to be 11.2 g/cm^3, but you know that the true value for the density of silver is 10.5 g/cm^3. Find the percent error for the density you measured.

_____

_____

_____

2 CHALLENGE What are two possible sources of error when measuring a sample's mass and volume?

_____

_____

_____

7.NS.3, 7.NS.5, 7.NS.8

Mean, Median, Mode, and Range

Walking along a beach one night, you see a sea turtle laying her eggs in the sand. You start to wonder about sea turtle nests. What is the average number of eggs in a nest? What is the range of eggs in a group of nests? Scientists ask questions like these, too. Their answers come from analyzing data. Use **Figure 3** to analyze sea turtle egg data yourself.

Mean The **mean** is the numerical average of a set of data. To find the mean, add up the numbers in the data set. Then divide the sum by the total number of items you added.

Find the mean for the egg data.

_____

Median The **median** is the middle number in a set of data. To find the median, list all the numbers in order from least to greatest. The median is the middle entry. If a list has an even number of entries, add the two middle numbers together and divide by two to find the median.

Find the median for the egg data.

_____

_____

Mode The **mode** is the number that appears most often in a list of numbers.

Find the mode for the egg data.

_____

Range The **range** of a set of data is the difference between the greatest value and the least value in the set.

Find the range for the egg data.

_____

FIGURE 3 ·····································

Sea Turtle Egg Data

You can use math to analyze the data in the table below about the number of sea turtle eggs in seven nests.

✎ **Calculate** Fill in the boxes with the mean, median, mode, and range of the sea turtle data. 7.NS.3, 7.NS.5, 7.NS.8, 7.NS.11

Nest	Number of Eggs
A	110
B	102
C	94
D	110
E	107
F	110
G	109

Sea Turtles at Nesting Beach

Day	Turtles
Day 1	7
Day 2	7
Day 3	8
Day 4	7
Day 5	2

FIGURE 4 ·····················

Collected Data

On Day 5, only two turtles are at the beach.

✎ **Analyze Experimental Results**
Describe an unknown variable that could have affected the data.

_____

_____

_____

_____

7.NS.8

Reasonable and Anomalous Data

An important part of analyzing any set of data is to ask, "Are these data reasonable? Do they make sense?" For example, suppose a scientist who studies sea turtles measures the ocean water temperature each night for five nights. His data for the first four nights are 26°C, 23°C, 25°C, and 24°C. On the last night, he asks a student to make the measurement. The student records 81 in the data book.

Are the data reasonable? The reading on Day 5 is very different. Some variation in ocean temperature makes sense within a small range. But it doesn't make sense for ocean temperature to rise 57°C in one day, from 24°C to 81°C. The 81°C does not fit with the rest of the data. Data that do not fit with the rest of a data set are **anomalous data.** In this case, the anomalous data are explainable. The student measured °F instead of °C. Sometimes asking whether data are reasonable can uncover sources of error or unknown variables. Investigating the reason for anomalous data can lead to new discoveries.

EXPLORE THE BIG ❓

TURTLE TURF

How is mathematics important to the work of scientists?

THINK LIKE A SCIENTIST

The pale green coloring on the map shows areas where green sea turtles commonly nest in Florida.

FIGURE 5 ·····················

> **INTERACTIVE ART** Scientists use mathematics to help answer the question, "How and why are the number of sea turtle nests in Florida changing?"

✎ **Design Experiments Answer the questions below.**

1 How would you collect accurate and precise turtle nest data?

_____

_____

_____

2 What properties of the nests could you measure?

_____

_____

_____

_____

_____

3 How might a hurricane in Florida cause anamolous nest data?

_____

_____

4 How could you estimate the total number of nests in Florida?

_____

_____

_____

_____

7.NS.3, 7.NS.5, 7.NS.8, 7.NS.11

 Do the Quick Lab
How Close Is It?

🔑 Assess Your Understanding

2a. Describe Why is it important for scientists to calculate percent error?

_____

_____

7.NS.3, 7.NS.5, 7.NS.8, 7.NS.11

b. ANSWER THE BIG **?** How is mathematics important to the work of scientists?

_____

_____

_____

_____

7.NS.3, 7.NS.5, 7.NS.8, 7.NS.11

got it? ·····················

○ **I get it!** Now I know that math tools scientists use to analyze data include _____

_____

_____

_____

○ **I need extra help with** _____

Go to **MY SCIENCE ⓢ COACH** online for help with this subject.   7.NS.3, 7.NS.5, 7.NS.8

3 Graphs in Science

UNLOCK THE BIG **?**

🗝 **What Kinds of Data Do Line Graphs Display?**
7.NS.7, 7.NS.11

🗝 **Why Are Line Graphs Powerful Tools?**
7.NS.1, 7.NS.7, 7.NS.8, 7.NS.11

MY PLANET DIARY

Waste and Recycling Data

The information below shows the amount of waste generated and recovered for recycling per person per day for each year listed.

- **1980:** Generated waste was about 1.68 kg and recovered waste was about 0.16 kg.

- **1990:** Generated waste was about 2.04 kg and recovered waste was about 0.33 kg.

- **2000:** Generated waste was 2.09 kg and recovered waste was about 0.51 kg.

- **2002:** Generated waste was about 2.09 kg and recovered waste was about 0.61 kg.

- **2007:** Generated waste was about 2.09 kg and recovered waste was about 0.70 kg.

SCIENCE STATS

Communicate Discuss the following questions with a partner. Write your answers below.

How do you think society's view on recycling has changed over the years?

_____

_____

_____

_____

_____

▷ **PLANET DIARY** Go to **Planet Diary** to learn more about graphs in science.

Lab zone Do the Inquiry Warm-Up *What's in a Picture?*

Academic Standards for Science

7.NS.7 Keep accurate records in a notebook during investigations.

7.NS.11 Communicate findings using graphs, charts, maps and models through oral and written reports.

What Kinds of Data Do Line Graphs Display?

Could the saying "A watched pot never boils" really be true? Or does it take longer to boil water when there is more water in the pot? You could do an experiment to find out. The table in **Figure 1** shows data from such an experiment. But what do the data mean? Does it take longer to boil a larger volume of water?

Vocabulary
• graph • linear graph • nonlinear graph

Skills
↻ Reading: Relate Text and Visuals
△ Inquiry: Predict

Line Graphs To help see what the data mean, you can use a graph. A **graph** is a "picture" of your data. One kind of graph is a line graph. ☞ **Line graphs display data that show how one variable (the responding variable) changes in response to another variable (the manipulated variable).**

Using Line Graphs Scientists control changes in the manipulated variable. Then they collect data about how the responding variable changes. A line graph is used when a manipulated variable is continuous, which means there are other points between the tested ones. For example, in the water-boiling experiment, many volumes are possible between 500 mL and 2,000 mL.

FIGURE 1 ·····································

▶ INTERACTIVE ART **A Line Graph**
This line graph plots the data from the table below.

✎ **Identify** Identify the manipulated variable and the responding variable in the experiment.

_____

_____

_____

7.NS.7, 7.NS.11

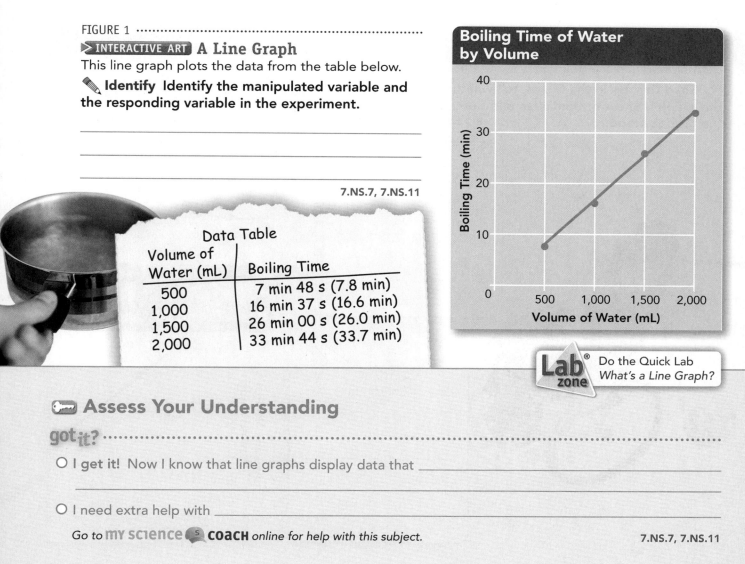

Data Table

Volume of Water (mL)	Boiling Time
500	7 min 48 s (7.8 min)
1,000	16 min 37 s (16.6 min)
1,500	26 min 00 s (26.0 min)
2,000	33 min 44 s (33.7 min)

Boiling Time of Water by Volume

Lab zone® Do the Quick Lab
What's a Line Graph?

☞ Assess Your Understanding

got it? ···

○ I get it! Now I know that line graphs display data that _____

_____

○ I need extra help with _____

Go to MY SCIENCE ⓢ COACH *online for help with this subject.*

7.NS.7, 7.NS.11

⟳ **Relate Text and Visuals**

Underline statements in the text that describe the graphs in Figure 2.

Why Are Line Graphs Powerful Tools?

A line graph in which the data points yield a straight line is a **linear graph.** The kind of graph in which the data points do not fall along a straight line is called a **nonlinear graph.** As shown in **Figure 2,** both kinds of line graphs are useful. 🔑 **Line graphs are powerful tools in science because they allow you to identify trends, make predictions, and recognize anomalous data.**

For example, the graph of experimental data in **Figure 3** on the next page shows that the trend is linear, even though most points do not fall exactly on the line. One point is clearly not part of the trend. It is an anomalous data point. Graphs make it easy to see anomalous data points like this one. When a graph does not have any clear trends, it probably means that the variables are not related.

FIGURE 2 ·······································

Linear Trends

Data plotted in a line graph may show a trend.

✎ **Read Graphs** In the boxes, tell whether the graph is linear or nonlinear, and describe the graph's trend.   7.NS.8, 7.NS.11

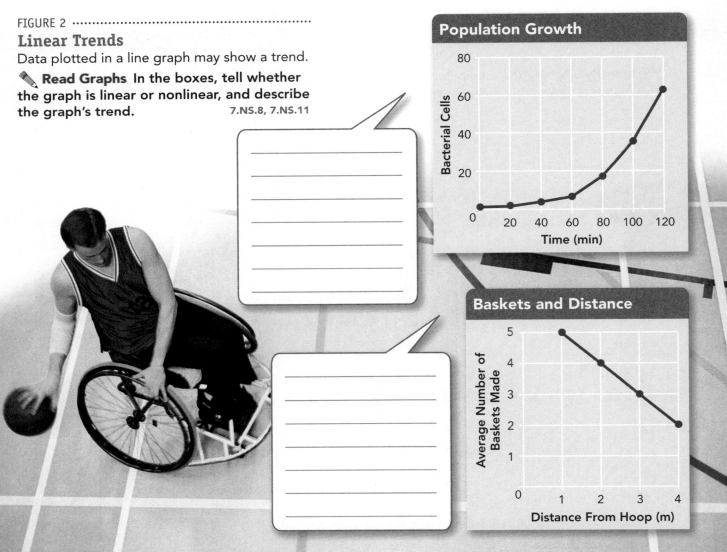

Population Growth

Bacterial Cells (y-axis: 20, 40, 60, 80)

Time (min) (x-axis: 20, 40, 60, 80, 100, 120)

Baskets and Distance

Average Number of Baskets Made (y-axis: 1, 2, 3, 4, 5)

Distance From Hoop (m) (x-axis: 1, 2, 3, 4)

Temperature of Heating Water

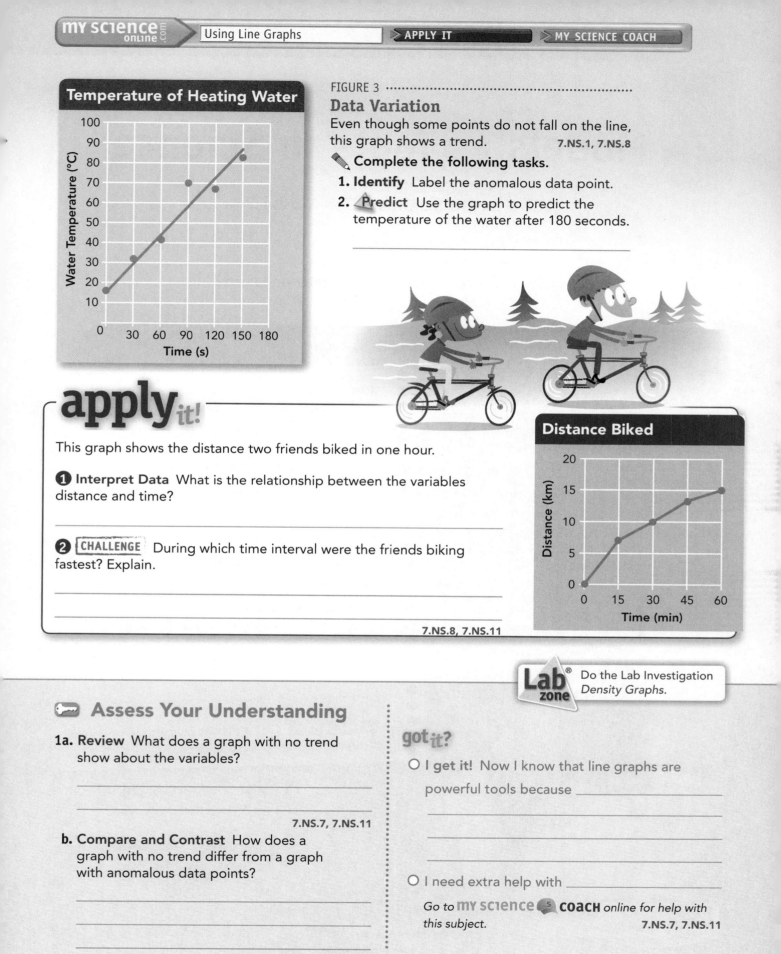

Water Temperature (°C) vs **Time (s)**

FIGURE 3 ···
Data Variation
Even though some points do not fall on the line, this graph shows a trend.   7.NS.1, 7.NS.8

✎ **Complete the following tasks.**

1. **Identify** Label the anomalous data point.
2. **Predict** Use the graph to predict the temperature of the water after 180 seconds.

_____

apply it!

This graph shows the distance two friends biked in one hour.

❶ **Interpret Data** What is the relationship between the variables distance and time?

_____

❷ **CHALLENGE** During which time interval were the friends biking fastest? Explain.

_____
_____

7.NS.8, 7.NS.11

Distance Biked

Distance (km) vs **Time (min)**

Lab zone ® Do the Lab Investigation *Density Graphs.*

🔑 Assess Your Understanding

1a. Review What does a graph with no trend show about the variables?

_____
_____

7.NS.7, 7.NS.11

b. Compare and Contrast How does a graph with no trend differ from a graph with anomalous data points?

_____
_____
_____

7.NS.7, 7.NS.11

got it?

○ **I get it!** Now I know that line graphs are powerful tools because _____

_____
_____
_____

○ **I need extra help with** _____

Go to **my science** ⑤ **coach** online for help with this subject.   7.NS.7, 7.NS.11

Indiana

LESSON

4 Models as Tools in Science

UNLOCK THE BIG ?

🔑 **Why Do Scientists Use Models?**
7.NS.7, 7.NS.11

🔑 **What Is a System?**
7.NS.7, 7.NS.11

🔑 **How Are Models of Systems Used?**
7.NS.7, 7.NS.11

my planet Diary

Flying Through Space

You don't have to be an astronaut to experience what it's like to fly in space. Thanks to technological advances, space flight simulation software programs have been created. These programs range from simple and straightforward to detailed and complicated. Depending on which one you use, you can experience what it might feel like to fly to the moon, command a mission to Mars, and even explore other solar systems. If you've ever wondered what it's like to be an astronaut, now you have the chance to find out!

FUN FACTS

Read the following questions. Write your answers below.

1. Why would a flight simulation software program created today be more realistic than one that was created ten years ago?

_____

_____

_____

_____

2. Would you be able to really fly in space if you knew how to use a space flight simulation software program? Explain.

_____

_____

_____

▷ **PLANET DIARY** Go to **Planet Diary** to learn more about models as tools in science.

Lab zone Do the Inquiry Warm-Up *Scale Models.*

Inside a flight simulator

Vocabulary
- model
- system
- input
- process
- output
- feedback

Skills
- ⟳ Reading: Identify the Main Idea
- △ Inquiry: Make Models

Why Do Scientists Use Models?

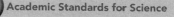

Academic Standards for Science

7.NS.7 Keep accurate records in a notebook during investigations.
7.NS.11 Communicate findings using graphs, charts, maps and models through oral and written reports.

"Who is that model on the cover?" "I still have that model car I built." The word *model* has many meanings. But, as with many words, *model* has a specific meaning in science. In science, a **model** is any representation of an object or process. Pictures, diagrams, computer programs, and mathematical equations are all examples of scientific models.

🔑 **Scientists use models to understand things they cannot observe directly.** For example, scientists use models as reasonable representations of things that are either very large, such as Earth's core, or very small, such as an atom. These kinds of models are physical models—drawings or three-dimensional objects. Other models, such as mathematical equations or word descriptions, are models of processes. Look at the models in **Figure 1**.

FIGURE 1 ·····················

Two Science Models
Models may be three-dimensional objects or equations.

✏️ **Explain** Tell whether each of these models represents an object or a process and why each is useful.

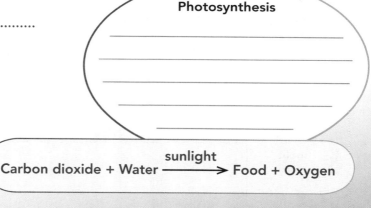

Photosynthesis

_____

_____

_____

_____

Carbon dioxide + Water —sunlight→ Food + Oxygen

Earth's core

_____

_____

_____

_____

_____

Lab zone ® Do the Quick Lab *Making Models.*

🔑 Assess Your Understanding

got it? ·······················

○ **I get it!** Now I know that scientists use models to _____

_____

_____

○ **I need extra help with** _____

Go to my science ⑤ coach *online for help with this subject.* **7.NS.7, 7.NS.11**

What Is a System?

Many things you see and use are systems. For example, a toaster oven, your town's water pipes, and your bicycle are all systems. A **system is a group of parts that work together to perform a function or produce a result.**

Systems have common properties. All systems have input, process, and output. **Input** is the material or energy that goes into a system. **Process** is what happens in a system. **Output** is the material or energy that comes out of a system. In addition, some systems have feedback. **Feedback** is output that changes the system in some way. For example, the heating and cooling system in most homes has feedback. A sensor in the thermostat recognizes when the desired temperature has been reached. The sensor provides feedback that turns the system off temporarily. Look at **Figure 2** to see another example of a system.

✏️ **Identify the Main Idea**
Circle the main idea in the second paragraph. Underline the details.

FIGURE 2 ....

An Everyday System
In a flashlight, many parts work together as a system.

✎ **Apply Concepts** Look at the flashlight and use what you know to fill in the chart.

	Flashlight
Parts of System	
Input	
Process	
Output	7.NS.11

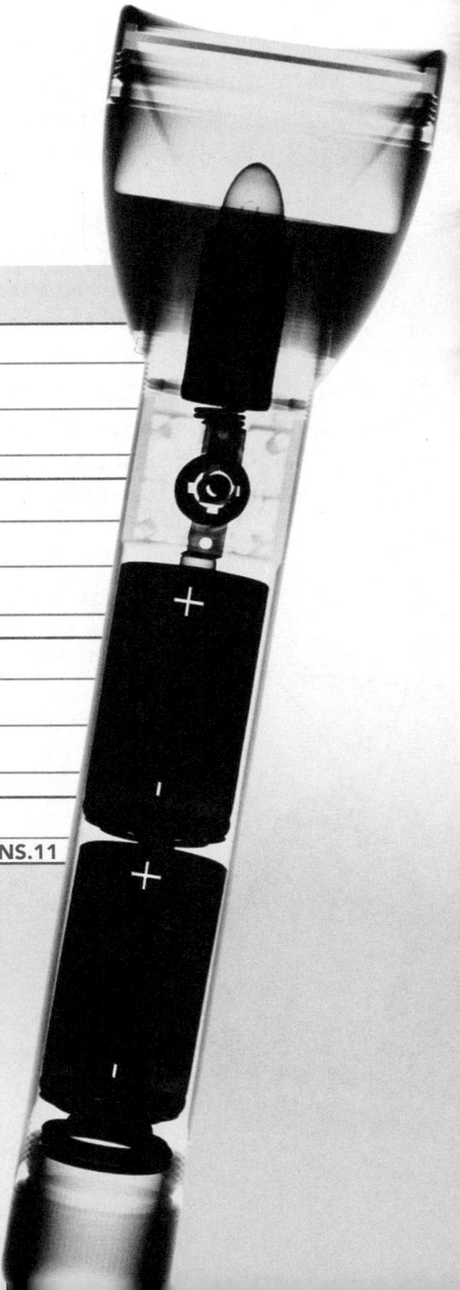

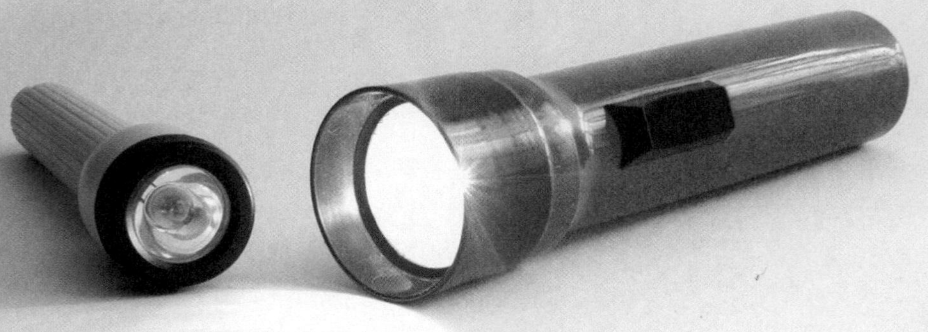

apply it!

Sun, air, land, and water are the parts of a system that produce a sea breeze. During the day, the sun's energy heats both the land and the water. The land and water, in turn, heat the air above them. Air over the land becomes much warmer than the air over water. As the warmer air rises, the cooler air from over the water rushes in to replace it. A sea breeze is the result.

An Afternoon Sea Breeze

1 Warm air rises

2 Cooler air moves to take warm air's place

Warm land   Cool water

1 Identify Identify the input, output, and process of the sea breeze system.

_____

_____

_____

_____

2 CHALLENGE Which parts of this system will change after the sun sets? How will it change?

_____

_____

7.NS.11

Do the Quick Lab *Systems.*

🔑 Assess Your Understanding

1a. List What are the properties of a system?

_____

_____

_____

_____

7.NS.7, 7.NS.11

b. Apply Concepts A student uses a calculator to solve a math problem. Is this an example of a system? Explain your answer.

_____

_____

_____

_____

7.NS.7, 7.NS.11

got it?

○ **I get it!** Now I know that a system is _____

_____

_____

○ **I need extra help with** _____

Go to **my science ⓢ coach** *online for help with this subject.*   7.NS.7, 7.NS.11

How Are Models of Systems Used?

It's easy to identify the materials and energy that make up the inputs and outputs of a system. It's not easy to observe a system's process. 🔑 **Scientists use models to understand how systems work. They also use models to predict changes in a system as a result of feedback or input changes.** However, they keep in mind that predictions based on models are uncertain.

When scientists construct a model of a system, they begin with certain assumptions. These assumptions allow them to make a basic model that accurately reflects the parts of the system and their relationships. A scientist who wants to study how energy moves through living things in an environment might use a model called a food chain. A food chain is a series that shows who eats whom to obtain energy in an environment. The food chain shown in **Figure 3** assumes that largemouth bass only eat flagfish. Largemouth bass actually eat many kinds of animals. However, the model still accurately reflects the relationship between the parts of a system.

Anhinga

Largemouth bass

Flagfish

Algae

FIGURE 3 ·····································

A Basic Model

In this model of a food chain in the Florida Everglades, the algae make food using the sun's energy. Algae are tiny living things that make their own food.

✏️ **Complete the tasks below.**

1. ▲ **Make Models** On the line next to each part of the system, write who eats it.

2. **CHALLENGE** What is the energy source for this system?

_____

7.NS.11

The arrows show the direction in which energy moves. You can "read" an arrow as saying "are eaten by."

Flagfish: _____

Bass: _____

Algae: _____

Modeling a Simple System A food chain is a good model to begin to understand how energy moves through living things in an environment. However, it shows how only a few of those living things are related. So a scientist may build a food web to model a more complete picture of the system. In **Figure 4** you can see a food web with many overlapping food chains. The food web is more detailed than one food chain. But it does not provide information about other factors, such as weather, that affect energy flow in the system.

FIGURE 4 ··

> INTERACTIVE ART **A Model of a Simple System**
This model of an Everglades food web contains overlapping food chains.

✎ **Interpret Diagrams** Study the food web model. On the notebook page write two things you learned from this complex model. 7.NS.7

Alligator

Anhinga

Raccoon

Pig frog

Largemouth bass

Everglades crayfish

Flagfish

Plants, leaves, seeds, and fruits

Algae

Modeling a Complex System Some systems that scientists study are complex. Many parts and many variables interact in these systems. So scientists may use a computer to keep track of all the variables. Because such systems are difficult to model, scientists may model only the specific parts of the system they want to study. Their model may be used to show the processes in the system or to make predictions. For example, the system that involves the melting of sea ice in the Arctic is a complex system. **Figure 5** shows how some parts of that system affect each other.

FIGURE 5

How Arctic Sea Ice Melts
The Arctic sea-ice system can be modeled by a diagram.

✎ **Identify List some of the variables in the Arctic sea-ice system. Then identify the input, process, and output in this model and fill in the boxes.**

_____

_____

7.NS.11

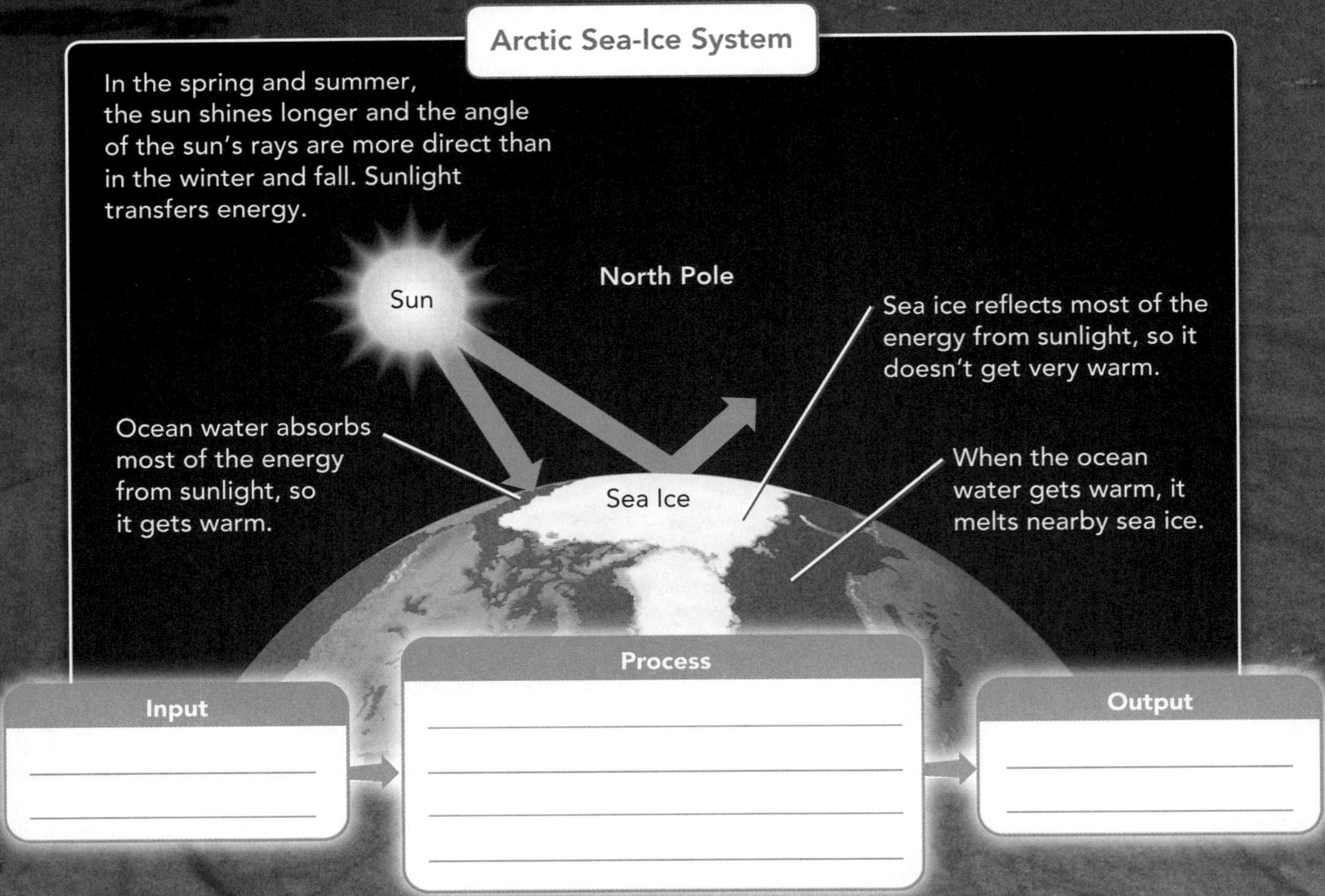

Arctic Sea-Ice System

In the spring and summer, the sun shines longer and the angle of the sun's rays are more direct than in the winter and fall. Sunlight transfers energy.

North Pole

Sun

Sea ice reflects most of the energy from sunlight, so it doesn't get very warm.

Ocean water absorbs most of the energy from sunlight, so it gets warm.

Sea Ice

When the ocean water gets warm, it melts nearby sea ice.

Input	Process	Output

Arctic Sea-Ice System

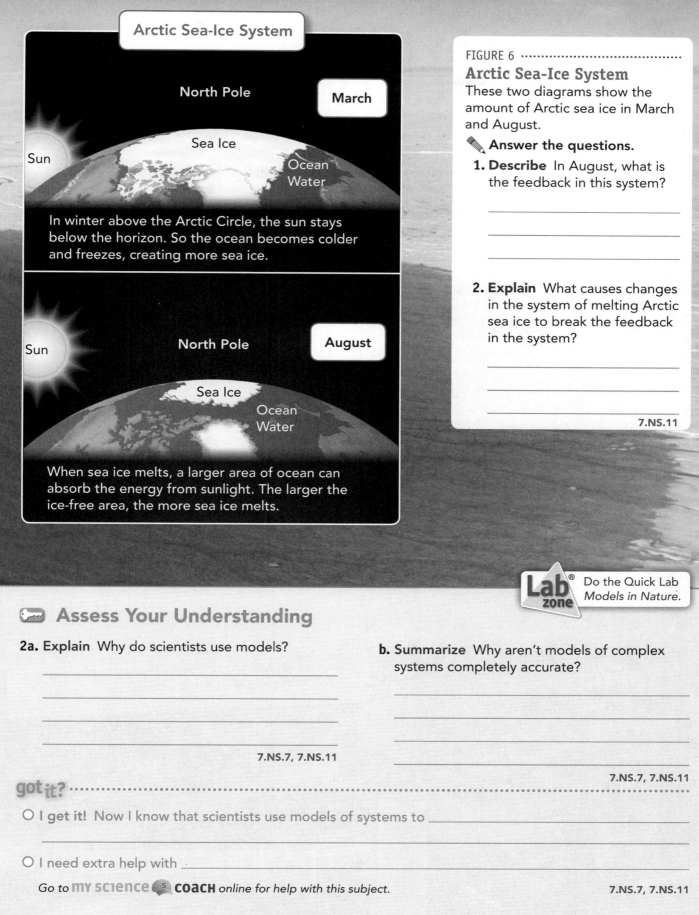

North Pole

March

Sun

Sea Ice

Ocean Water

In winter above the Arctic Circle, the sun stays below the horizon. So the ocean becomes colder and freezes, creating more sea ice.

Sun

North Pole

August

Sea Ice

Ocean Water

When sea ice melts, a larger area of ocean can absorb the energy from sunlight. The larger the ice-free area, the more sea ice melts.

FIGURE 6 ·····························

Arctic Sea-Ice System

These two diagrams show the amount of Arctic sea ice in March and August.

✏ **Answer the questions.**

1. **Describe** In August, what is the feedback in this system?

_____

_____

_____

2. **Explain** What causes changes in the system of melting Arctic sea ice to break the feedback in the system?

_____

_____

_____

7.NS.11

Lab®
zone Do the Quick Lab *Models in Nature.*

🔑 Assess Your Understanding

2a. Explain Why do scientists use models?

_____

_____

_____

_____

7.NS.7, 7.NS.11

b. Summarize Why aren't models of complex systems completely accurate?

_____

_____

_____

_____

7.NS.7, 7.NS.11

got it? ·····························

⚪ **I get it!** Now I know that scientists use models of systems to _____

_____

⚪ **I need extra help with** _____

Go to **my science** ⬤ⁱ **COACH** *online for help with this subject.*

7.NS.7, 7.NS.11

Safety in the Science Laboratory

UNLOCK THE BIG ?

🔑 **Why Prepare for a Laboratory Investigation?**
7.NS.2, 7.NS.11

🔑 **What Should You Do if an Accident Occurs?**
7.NS.2

MY PLANET DIARY

DISASTER

Oil Refinery Explosion

On March 23, 2005, an explosion at an oil refinery in Texas took the lives of 15 people and wounded at least 170 others. Sadly, experts agree that this accident could have been prevented had safety codes not been ignored. Investigators found old, worn equipment and noticed that several repairs had not been made. One positive thing that has come out of this accident is a safety video made by the U.S. Chemical Safety Board. The video is based on the refinery accident and includes safety information about how to prevent such an accident from ever occurring again.

Read the following questions. Write your answers below.

1. How do investigators believe this accident might have been prevented?

_____

_____

_____

2. What kind of information would you include in a safety video based on the accident?

_____

_____

_____

_____

▶ PLANET DIARY Go to **Planet Diary** to learn more about safety in the science laboratory.

Lab zone ® Do the Inquiry Warm-Up *Where Is the Safety Equipment in Your School?*

Vocabulary
- safety symbol
- field

Skills
- Reading: Summarize
- Inquiry: Observe

Why Prepare for a Laboratory Investigation?

After hiking for many hours, you reach the campsite. You rush to set up your tent. The tent is lopsided, but it's up, so you run off with your friends. Later that night, heavy rain falls. Water pours into the tent and soaks you. You look for a flashlight. Then you realize that you forgot to pack one. If you had only prepared better, you would be dry and able to see.

Preparing for a Lab Just like for camping, you must prepare before you begin a laboratory investigation, or lab. **Good preparation helps you stay safe when doing laboratory investigations.** You should prepare for a lab before you do it. Read through any procedures carefully, and make sure you understand all the directions. If anything is unclear, ask your teacher about it before you begin the lab. Investigations may include safety symbols like the ones you see in **Figure 1. Safety symbols** alert you to possible sources of accidents in a laboratory.

Academic Standards for Science

7.NS.2 Plan and carry out investigations as a class, in small groups or independently often over a period of several class lessons.
7.NS.11 Communicate findings using graphs, charts, maps and models.

FIGURE 1 ····················
Safety Symbols
Safety symbols identify how to work carefully and what safety equipment to use.

✎ **Apply Concepts** In the notebook, list symbols that would appear for a lab investigation in which you measure the temperature of water as it heats to boiling.

Safety Symbols

Safety Goggles

Lab Apron

Breakage

Heat-Resistant Gloves

Heating

Poison

Physical Safety

Flames

No Flames

Measuring the Temperature of Water

Lab Safety

_____
_____
_____
_____
_____
_____
_____
_____
_____
_____

FIGURE 2 ··

Safety in the Lab

Recognizing and preventing safety hazards are important skills to practice in the lab.

✎ **Complete the tasks.** 7.NS.11

1. **Make Models** In the empty boxes on each page, draw a safety symbol for wearing closed-toe shoes and one for tying back long hair.

2. CHALLENGE How might the student on this page protect himself from breathing in fumes from the flask or beakers?

_____

_____

_____

_____

Performing a Lab Whenever you do a science lab, your chief concern must be your safety and that of your classmates and your teacher. The most important safety rule is simple: *Always follow your teacher's instructions and the directions exactly.* Never try anything on your own without asking your teacher first.

Figure 2 shows a number of things that you can do to make your lab experience safe and successful. When performing a lab, keep your work area clean and organized. Label all containers so you do not use the wrong chemical accidentally. Also, do not rush through any of the steps. When you need to move around the room, move slowly and carefully so you do not trip or bump into another group's equipment. Finally, always show respect and courtesy to your teacher and classmates.

Wear safety goggles to protect your eyes from chemical splashes, glass breakage, and sharp objects.

Wear an apron to protect yourself and your clothes from chemicals.

Wear heat-resistant gloves when handling hot objects.

Keep your work area clean and uncluttered.

Wear closed-toe shoes when working in the laboratory.

Make sure electric cords are untangled and out of the way.

End-of-Lab Procedures There are important things you need to do at the end of every lab. When you have completed a lab, be sure to clean up your work area. Turn off and unplug any equipment and return it to its proper place. It is very important that you dispose of any waste materials properly. Some wastes should not be thrown in the trash or poured down the drain. Follow your teacher's instructions about proper disposal. Finally, be sure to wash your hands thoroughly after working in the laboratory.

Wear plastic gloves to protect your skin when handling animals, plants, or chemicals.

Tie back long hair to keep it away from flames, chemicals, or equipment.

Handle live animals and plants with care.

Summarize In the boxes provided, summarize the procedures you perform before, during, and after a lab-investigation. **7.NS.2**

Before

During

After

Safety in the Field Some of your science investigations will be done in the **field,** or any area outside a science laboratory. Just as in the laboratory, good preparation helps you stay safe. For example, there can be many safety hazards outdoors. You could encounter severe weather, traffic, wild animals, or poisonous plants. Whenever you set out to work in the field, you should always tell an adult where you will be. Never carry out a field investigation alone. Use common sense to avoid any potentially dangerous situations.

These two students have not taken proper precautions to work in the field.

1 ⚠ **Observe** Identify the clothing that is not appropriate for working in this field environment. **7.NS.2**

_____

_____

2 Draw Conclusions Explain how one piece of clothing a student is wearing might expose the student to hazards in the field.

_____

_____

_____

Lab® **zone** Do the Quick Lab *Be Prepared.*

🔑 **Assess Your Understanding**

1a. List List two things you should do before you begin a lab.

_____

_____

_____

7.NS.2

b. Make Generalizations Why would field investigation take more preparation than a lab investigation?

_____

_____

_____

7.NS.2

got it? ....

○ **I get it!** Now I know that the key to working safely in the lab and in the field is _____

_____

○ **I need extra help with** _____

Go to MY SCIENCE 🔵 ˢ **COACH** *online for help with this subject.* **7.NS.2**

What Should You Do if an Accident Occurs?

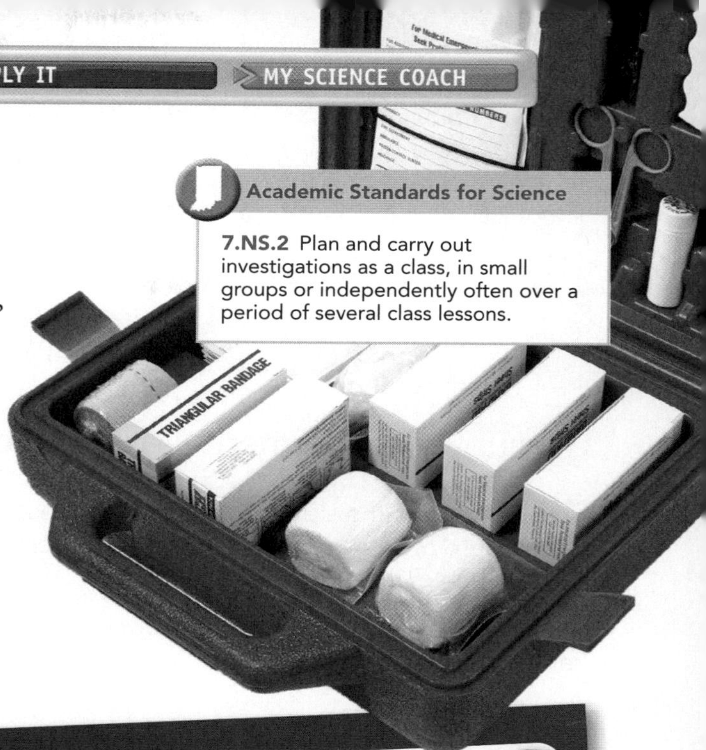

Although you may have prepared carefully, at some point, an accident may occur. Would you know what to do? You should always start by telling an adult.

🔑 **When any accident occurs, no matter how minor, tell your teacher immediately. Then listen to your teacher's directions and carry them out quickly.** Make sure you know the location and the proper use of all the emergency equipment in your laboratory. Knowing safety and first-aid procedures beforehand will prepare you to handle accidents properly. **Figure 3** lists some emergency procedures.

Academic Standards for Science

7.NS.2 Plan and carry out investigations as a class, in small groups or independently often over a period of several class lessons.

FIGURE 3 ·············

In Case of Emergency
These first-aid tips can help you in emergency situations in the lab.

✎ **Read and answer the questions.**

1. **Review** Complete the sentence in the chart to identify the first step in responding to a lab emergency.

2. **Make Judgments** Suppose your teacher is involved in a lab accident. What should you do?   **7.NS.2**

_____

_____

_____

_____

⚠ In Case of an Emergency ⚠

The first thing to do in an emergency is

_____

Injury	What to Do
Burns	Immerse burns in cold water.
Cuts	Cover cuts with a dressing. Apply direct pressure to stop bleeding.
Spills on Skin	Flush the skin with large amounts of water.
Object in Eye	Flush the eye with water. Seek medical help.

Lab zone® Do the Quick Lab *Just in Case.*

🔑 Assess Your Understanding

got**it?** ·············

O **I get it!** Now I know that the first thing I should do in case of an accident is _____

_____

O I need extra help with _____

Go to **my science** ⑤ **coach** online for help with this subject.   **7.NS.2**

REVIEW THE BIG ?

Scientists use mathematics to make _____, and to collect, analyze, and display _____.

LESSON 1 Measurement—A Common Language

7.NS.1, 7.NS.3, 7.NS.5, 7.NS.7, 7.NS.8

🔑 Using SI as the standard system of measurement allows scientists to compare data and communicate with each other about their results.

🔑 In SI, some units of measurement include meter (m), kilogram (kg), cubic meter (m^3), kilograms per cubic meter (kg/m^3), kelvin (K), and second (s).

Vocabulary
• metric system • SI • mass • weight • volume • meniscus • density

---

LESSON 2 Mathematics and Science

7.NS.3, 7.NS.5, 7.NS.8, 7.NS.11

🔑 Math skills that scientists use to collect data include estimation, accuracy and precision, and significant figures.

🔑 Scientists calculate percent error; find the mean, median, mode, and range; and check reasonableness to analyze data.

Vocabulary
• estimate • accuracy • precision
• significant figures • percent error • mean
• median • mode • range • anomalous data

LESSON 3 Graphs in Science

7.NS.1, 7.NS.7, 7.NS.8, 7.NS.11

🔑 Line graphs display data that show how the responding variable changes in response to the manipulated variable.

🔑 Line graphs are powerful tools in science because they allow you to identify trends, make predictions, and recognize anomalous data.

Vocabulary
• graph • linear graph
• nonlinear graph

LESSON 4 Models as Tools in Science

7.NS.7, 7.NS.11

🔑 Models help scientists understand things they cannot observe directly.

🔑 A system is a group of parts that work together to produce a specific function or result.

🔑 Scientists use models to understand how systems work and to predict how systems might change from feedback or input changes.

Vocabulary
• model • system • input • process
• output • feedback

LESSON 5 Safety in the Science Laboratory

7.NS.2, 7.NS.11

🔑 Good preparation helps you stay safe when doing science investigations.

🔑 When any accident occurs, no matter how minor, tell your teacher immediately. Then listen to your teacher's directions and carry them out quickly.

Vocabulary
• safety symbol • field

Review and Assessment

LESSON 1 Measurement— A Common Language

1. The amount of matter an object contains is its

  a. length.   **b.** mass.

  c. weight.   **d.** volume.

                                  7.NS.3

2. The basic SI unit of length is the

_____

                                  7.NS.3

3. Measure 0 K is equal to what temperature in Celsius?

_____

                        7.NS.3, 7.NS.5

4. Compare and Contrast Which of the objects below has a greater volume? Explain.

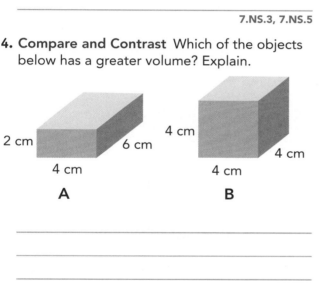

2 cm   6 cm   4 cm

4 cm   4 cm   4 cm

    A   **B**

_____

_____

_____

                                    7.NS.3

5. Calculate A 12.5 g marble displaces 5.0 mL of water. What is its density?

_____

                        7.NS.3, 7.NS.5

6. **Write About It** You are a sports reporter interviewing an Olympic swimmer who lost the silver medal by a few hundredths of a second. Write a one-page interview in which you discuss the meaning of time and the advanced instruments used to measure time.

               7.NS.2, 7.NS.3, 7.NS.5

LESSON 2 Mathematics and Science

7. The significant figures in a measurement

  a. include only the first two digits.

  b. include only the estimated digits.

  c. include only the digits that have been measured exactly.

  d. include all of the digits that have been measured exactly, plus one estimated digit.

                                  7.NS.5

8. _____ refers to how close a measurement is to the true or accepted value.

                                  7.NS.5

9. Apply Concepts What is the median of 7, 31, 86, 6, 20, 85, and 12?

_____

                                    7.NS.8

10. Analyze Sources of Error You rush through your lab activity and obtain a percent error of 50 percent. Why might your percent error be so high?

_____

_____

_____

_____

_____

_____

                              7.NS.5, 7.NS.9

11. math! You measure the mass of a mystery object to be 658 g. The actual mass of the object is 755 g. What is your percent error?

                              7.NS.5, 7.NS.8

2 Review and Assessment

CHAPTER 2

LESSON 3 Graphs in Science

12. A line graph is used when a manipulated variable is

a. responsive. b. linear.

c. continuous. d. anomalous.

7.NS.11

13. A _____ is a graph in which the data points do not fall along a straight line.

7.NS.11

14. Make Generalizations What do line graphs help you see about your data?

_____

_____

_____

_____

7.NS.7, 7.NS.11

LESSON 4 Models as Tools in Science

15. Material or energy that goes into a system is

a. output. b. input.

c. feedback. d. process.

7.NS.11

16. A _____ system has many parts and variables.

7.NS.11

17. **Write About It** The output of the system below is text displayed on the screen. Describe the input and process that produces this output.

YOUR IMAGE HERE

7.NS.11

LESSON 5 Safety in the Science Laboratory

18. The outdoor area in which some of your scientific investigations will be done is called the

a. yard. b. lawn.

c. park. d. field.

7.NS.2

19. Good _____ will help you stay safe when performing scientific investigations.

7.NS.2

20. Make Judgments Why do you think that you should never bring food into a laboratory?

_____

_____

_____

_____

_____

7.NS.2

 APPLY THE BIG **?**

How is mathematics important to the work of scientists?

21. Civil engineers help plan the construction of buildings. Name three ways the engineers use math during the planning process.

_____

_____

_____

_____

_____

_____

_____

_____

_____

_____

7.NS.2

Indiana ISTEP+ Practice

Multiple Choice

Circle the letter of the best answer.
Use the graph to answer Question 1.

1. What is the general trend in the data?

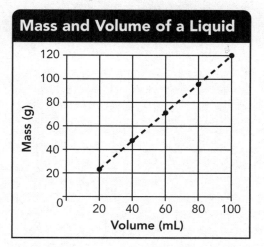

A. linear

B. no trend

C. nonlinear

D. linear at first and then nonlinear

7.NS.8, 7.NS.11

2. A student grows tomatoes for an experiment. Which piece of equipment will be needed to determine the mass of the tomato?

A. graduated cylinder

B. meter stick

C. stopwatch

D. triple-beam balance

7.NS.2, 7.NS.3, 7.NS.5

3. Ranida measured a string and got these measurements: 21.5 cm, 21.3 cm, 21.7 cm, and 21.6 cm. The string actually measures 25.5 cm. Which best describes Ranida's measurements?

A. They were accurate.

B. They were not accurate but they were precise.

C. They were both accurate and precise.

D. They were neither accurate nor precise.

7.NS.3, 7.NS.5, 7.NS.8

4. Ellis measured the mass of five samples of quartz. His results were 39.75 g, 38.91 g, 37.66 g, 39.75 g, and 39.55 g. What was the mean mass of the samples?

A. 39.55 g

B. 39.75 g

C. 39.12 g

D. 38.91 g

7.NS.3, 7.NS.5, 7.NS.8

Constructed Response

Write your answer to Question 5 on the lines below.

5. Tanya measured an object's mass and volume and calculated its density to be 18 g/cm^3. The object's actual density was 15 g/cm^3. How can Tanya find her percent error?

_____

_____

_____

7.NS.5, 7.NS.8

Extended Response

Use the diagram below and your knowledge of science to help you answer Question 6. Write your answer on a separate sheet of paper.

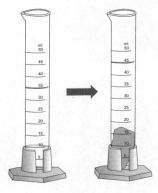

6. Clark decides to measure the volume of a rock he found outside. Based on the diagram above, what method is he using? What is the volume of the rock? Explain your answer.

7.NS.2, 7.NS.3, 7.NS.5, 7.NS.7, 7.NS.8, 7.NS.11

YOU LOST WHAT?!

Differing measurement systems caused the Mars Climate Orbiter to fly off course and vanish. ▼

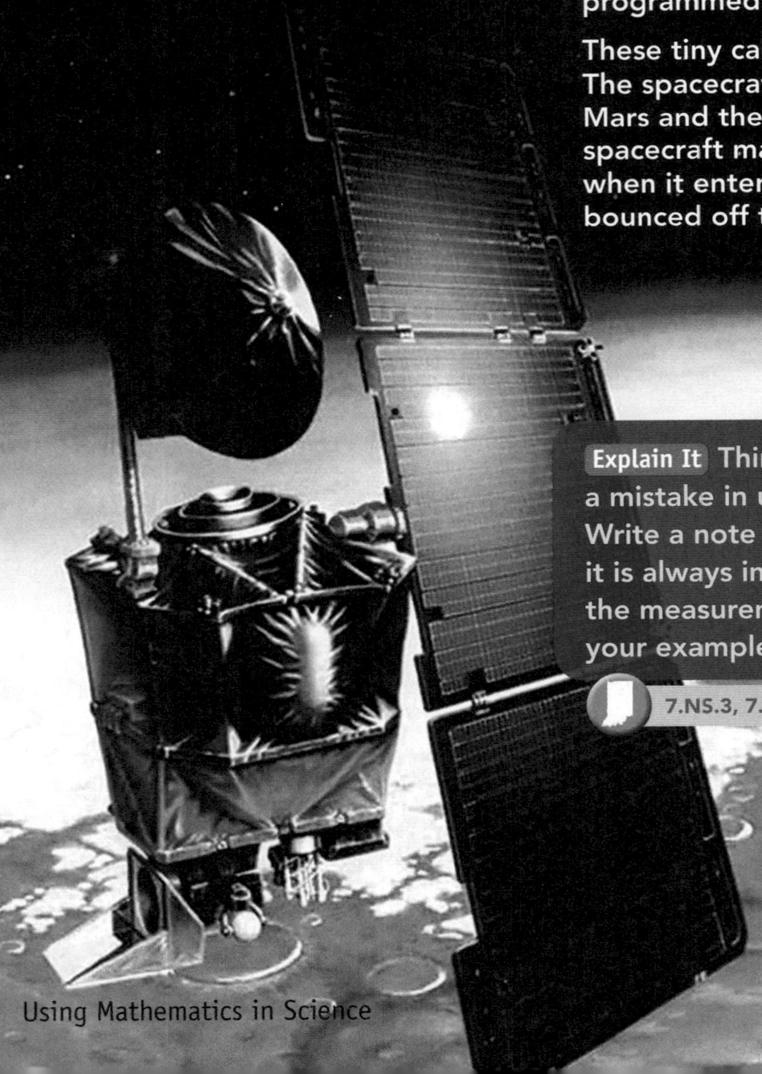

In 1999, the National Aeronautics and Space Administration (NASA) made a 125-million-dollar mistake.

That year, the Mars Climate Orbiter was supposed to orbit Mars for one Martian year (687 Earth days). It was to send back information on the planet's atmosphere, surface, and polar caps. Two different teams worked on the orbiter. A team of engineers designed and built it. A team from NASA worked with the engineers to navigate it.

Both teams overlooked a small, but very important detail. The engineering team measured data using Imperial (English) units, while NASA used the metric system. So NASA's navigators assumed that the unit of measurements used to measure how hard the spacecraft's thrusters fired was Newtons per second. Unfortunately, the engineers had programmed the thrusters in pounds per second!

These tiny calculations added up to a big mistake. The spacecraft traveled too close to the surface of Mars and the signal was lost. The 125-million-dollar spacecraft may have been damaged beyond repair when it entered the Martian atmosphere. If not, it bounced off the atmosphere and was lost in space.

Explain It Think of some other examples where a mistake in units could have disastrous results. Write a note to a friend in which you explain why it is always important to include the units with the measurements you are reporting. Include your examples in the note.

7.NS.3, 7.NS.5

Smallpox
on the loose

These days, most people don't worry about contracting smallpox. The last known victim of smallpox died in 1978 and, even then, smallpox was a rare disease. People thought that smallpox was safely contained in labs and that nobody could get sick with it. Then someone did.

Janet Parker was a medical photographer at the University of Birmingham Medical School in England. Scientists working in a lab below her darkroom were researching the smallpox virus. Unfortunately, the laboratory did not have good safety and containment procedures for the deadly virus. Even now, nobody knows exactly how Janet was exposed to the virus, but one theory is that the virus traveled through the air ducts to the darkroom. She became ill and died in September 1978.

Research It The World Health Organization (WHO) declared smallpox completely gone in 1980. What steps did the WHO take to ensure that no one else would contract the disease? In 2002, the WHO decided not to ask the remaining labs to destroy the smallpox stocks. What value do they think the stocks might have? Write a report that answers these questions and include suggestions on what else could or should be done.

7.NS.2

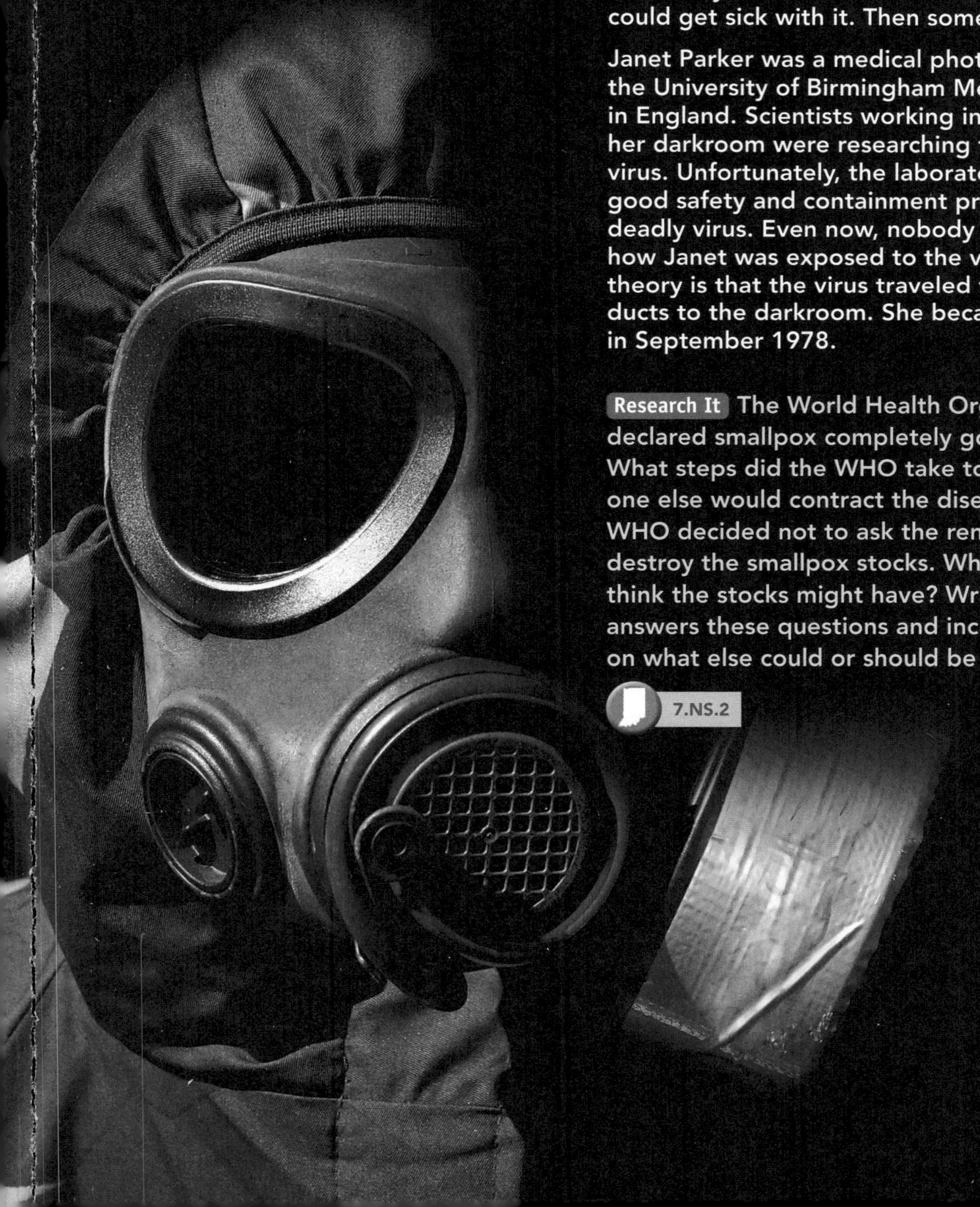

WHY WON'T THIS ACROBAT LAND ON HER HEAD?

How do objects react to forces?

This teen is part of a traveling youth circus that performs in New England. As a circus trouper, she may do stunts such as tumbling and swinging on a trapeze. These stunts often appear to be gravity-defying and dangerous, but the troupers know how to perform in a way that lets them land safely.

Develop Hypotheses **How does this athlete land on her feet?**

_____

_____

_____

_____

_____

_____

> **UNTAMED SCIENCE** Watch the **Untamed Science** video to learn more about forces.

Forces and Motion

Academic Standards for Science

7.1.1, 7.1.5, 7.1.6, 7.1.7, 7.NS.1, 7.NS.1–7.NS.11, 7.DP.1–7.DP.11

3 Getting Started

Check Your Understanding

1. Background Read the paragraph below and then answer the question.

The dashboard of a car displays your speed so that you know how fast you're going. Since this reading doesn't change when you turn, you don't know the car's velocity. If the car did show you your change in velocity, you could calculate the car's acceleration.

> Speed is the distance an object travels per unit of time.
>
> Velocity is speed in a given direction.
>
> Acceleration is the rate at which velocity changes with time.

- What are three ways to accelerate (change velocity)?

_____

_____

> MY READING WEB If you had trouble completing the question above, visit **My Reading Web** and type in **Forces and Motion.**

Vocabulary Skill

Latin Word Origins Many science words in English come from Latin. For example, the word *solar*, which means "of the sun," comes from the Latin *sol*, which means "sun."

Latin Word	Meaning of Latin Word	Example
fortis	strong	force, *n.* a push or pull exerted on an object
iners	inactivity	inertia, *n.* the tendency of an object to resist any change in its motion
centrum	center	centripetal force, *n.* a force that causes an object to move in a circle

2. Quick Check Choose the word that best completes the sentence.

- A _____ always points toward the center of a circle.

force

ZOO

friction

gravity

inertia

Chapter Preview

LESSON 1
- motion
- reference point
- International System of Units
- distance

↻ **Compare and Contrast**
△ **Measure**

LESSON 2
- speed • average speed
- instantaneous speed
- velocity • slope

↻ **Identify Supporting Evidence**
△ **Calculate**

LESSON 3
- acceleration

↻ **Identify the Main Idea**
△ **the Main Idea**
Graph

LESSON 4
- force • newton • net force

↻ **Relate Text and Visuals**
△ **Make Models**

LESSON 5
- friction • sliding friction
- static friction • fluid friction
- rolling friction • gravity
- mass • weight

↻ **Identify Supporting Evidence**
△ **Design Experiments**

LESSON 6
- inertia

↻ **Ask Questions**
△ **Infer**

> VOCAB FLASH CARDS For extra help with vocabulary, visit **Vocab Flash Cards** and type in *Forces and Motion.*

Describing Motion

UNLOCK THE BIG ?

🔑 **When Is an Object in Motion?**

7.1.7, 7.NS.3, 7.NS.5

my planet DiaRY   VOICES FROM HISTORY

Nicolaus Copernicus

Why would anyone think that Earth moves around the sun? After all, on a clear day you can see the sun move across the sky. But Polish astronomer Nicolaus Copernicus realized that an object revolving around you from left to right looks the same as an object standing still while you rotate from right to left. In *On the Revolution of the Heavenly Spheres,* he wrote

Every apparent change in respect of position is due to motion of the object observed, or of the observer, or indeed to an unequal change of both.

This book was published in 1543. It was a summary of more than 30 years of Copernicus's studies on the solar system.

Write your answer to the question below.

For thousands of years, many people thought Earth was the center of the universe. Name one possible reason why they thought this.

_____

_____

_____

_____

_____

_____

▶ PLANET DIARY Go to **Planet Diary** to learn more about motion.

Lab® zone Do the Inquiry Warm-Up *What Is Motion?*

Academic Standards for Science

7.1.7 Demonstrate and describe how an object's speed or direction of motion changes when a force acts upon it and they remain unchanged when the net force acting upon it is zero.

7.NS.3 Collect quantitative data and use appropriate units to label numerical data.

7.NS.5 Use the principles of accuracy and precision when making measurement.

When Is an Object in Motion?

Deciding if an object is in motion isn't as easy as you might think. For example, you are probably sitting in a chair as you read this book. Are you moving? Parts of you are. Your eyes blink and your chest moves up and down. But you would probably say that you are not moving. An object is in **motion** if its position changes relative to another object. Because your position relative to your chair does not change, you could say that you are not in motion.

Vocabulary

- motion • reference point
- International System of Units • distance

Skills

↩ **Reading:** Compare and Contrast

△ **Inquiry:** Measure

Reference Points To decide if you are moving, you use your chair as a reference point. A **reference point** is a place or object used for comparison to determine if something is in motion. 🔑 **An object is in motion if it changes position relative to a reference point.** Objects that are fixed relative to Earth—such as a building, a tree, or a sign—make good reference points.

You may already know what happens if your reference point is moving relative to Earth. Have you ever been in a school bus parked next to another bus? Suddenly, you think that your bus is moving backward. When you look out the window again for a fixed point, you find that your bus isn't moving at all—the other bus is moving forward! Your bus seemed to be moving backward because you had used the other bus as a reference point.

did you know?

Because of Earth's spin, the stars appear to move in circular arcs across the night sky. Only the North Star remains in a fixed position. Historically, sailors have used the North Star to help them navigate.

FIGURE 1 ••••••••••••••••••••••••••••••••••••

▶ **ART IN MOTION** **Reference Point**
The top photo was taken shortly before the bottom photo.

✎ **Answer the following questions.**

1. **Interpret Photos** Did the car that the boy is in move, or did the car in the background move? Explain your answer.

_____

_____

_____

_____

2. **Identify** What objects in this photo make good reference points?

_____

_____

_____

Relative Motion If you use your chair as your reference point as you sit and read, you are not moving. If you choose another object as a reference point, you may be moving.

Suppose you use the sun as a reference point instead of your chair. If you compare your position to the sun, you are moving quite rapidly because you and your chair are on Earth, which revolves around the sun. Earth moves around the sun at a speed of about 30 kilometers every second. So you and everything else on Earth are moving that quickly as well. Going that fast, you could travel from New York City to Los Angeles in about two minutes! Relative to the sun, both you and your chair are in motion. But because you are moving with Earth, you do not seem to be moving.

apply it!

The people in the photo are riding on a spinning carousel.

❶ **Interpret Photos** Are the people moving relative to each other? Are they moving relative to objects on the ground? Explain.

_____

_____

_____

_____

_____

_____

_____

_____

❷ **Explain** How is your choice of reference point important when describing the motion of the people?

_____

_____

_____

_____

_____

_____

_____

_____

Measuring Distance

To describe motion completely, you need to use units of measurement. Scientists use a system of measurement called the **International System of Units** or, in French, *Système International* (SI). **Distance** is the length of the path between two points. The SI unit for length is the meter (m). The distance from the floor to a doorknob is about 1 meter.

Scientists use other units to measure distances much smaller or much larger than a meter. For example, the width of the spider shown in **Figure 2** can be measured in centimeters (cm). The prefix *centi-* means "one hundredth." A centimeter is one hundredth of a meter, so there are 100 centimeters in a meter. For lengths smaller than a centimeter, the millimeter (mm) is used. The prefix *milli-* means "one thousandth," so there are 1,000 millimeters in a meter. Distances much longer than a meter can be measured in kilometers (km). The prefix *kilo-* means "one thousand," so there are 1,000 meters in a kilometer. A straight line between San Francisco and Boston would measure about 4,300 kilometers.

FIGURE 2 ·······························

Measuring Distance

The unit of length that you use to measure distance depends on the size of the distance.

✎ **Answer the following questions.**

1. **Review** Fill in the following common conversions for length.

   1 m = _____ mm

   1 m = _____ cm

   1 km =_____ m

2. ✎ **Measure** What is the distance in centimeters from points A to B on the spider? _____

3. **CHALLENGE** How many of these spiders would fit side by side in the length of 1 meter?

   _____

   _____

   7.NS.3, 7.NS.5

Ⓐ   Ⓑ

Lab ® **zone** Do the Quick Lab *Identifying Motion.*

🗝 Assess Your Understanding

1a. Review A _____
is a place or object used for comparison to
determine if something is in motion.   **7.1.7**

b. Explain Why is it important to know if your reference point is moving?

_____

_____

_____

_____

7.1.7

got it?

○ **I get it!** Now I know that an object is in
motion if _____

_____

_____

_____

○ **I need extra help with** _____

Go to MY SCIENCE ⓢ COACH *online for help with this subject.*   **7.1.7**

Speed and Velocity

UNLOCK
THE BIG
?

🔑 **How Do You Calculate Speed?**
7.1.7, 7.NS.8, 7.DP.9

🔑 **How Do You Describe Velocity?**
7.1.6, 7.1.7, 7.NS.8

🔑 **How Do You Graph Motion?**
7.1.7, 7.NS.1, 7.NS.8, 7.DP.10

my pLaneT DiaRY

BLOG

Posted by: Mallory

Location: Fountain Valley,
California

Once my sister talked me into going to the roller-skating rink with her. I hate skating, but against my better judgment, I agreed to go. I can skate, but I don't go very fast. At the rink, there were these speed skaters, or, as I like to call them, "assassin skaters." The assassin skaters went ridiculously fast. They were probably going approximately 20 miles per hour in the same direction as me. They zipped past me, just barely missing me.

The worst part about going skating was getting stuck behind a group of skaters or a couple. They went so slowly that you had to speed up to get around them.

Communicate Answer the questions. Discuss your answers with a partner.

1. Do all the skaters in the rink move at the same speed? Explain.

_____

_____

_____

2. Describe a sport or activity in which speed is important.

_____

_____

_____

_____

> **PLANET DIARY** Go to **Planet Diary** to learn more about speed and velocity.

Lab ® Do the Inquiry Warm-Up
zone *How Fast and How Far?*

Vocabulary
- speed • average speed
- instantaneous speed
- velocity • slope

Skills
- Reading: Identify Supporting Evidence
- Inquiry: Calculate

How Do You Calculate Speed?

You might describe the motion of an airplane as fast or the motion of a snail as slow. By using these words, you are describing the object's speed. The **speed** of an object is the distance the object moves per unit of time. Speed is a type of rate. A rate tells you the amount of something that occurs or changes in one unit of time.

The Speed Equation 🔑 **To calculate the speed of an object, divide the distance the object travels by the amount of time it takes to travel that distance.** This relationship can be written as an equation.

$$\text{Speed} = \frac{\text{Distance}}{\text{Time}}$$

The speed equation contains a unit of distance divided by a unit of time. If you measure distance in meters and time in seconds, the SI unit for speed is meters per second, or m/s. (The slash is read as "per.") For example, at its cruising altitude, an airplane might travel at a constant speed of 260 m/s. This means that the airplane will travel a distance of 260 meters in 1 second. The speed of a snail is about 1 mm/s. This means that the snail will travel a distance of 1 millimeter in 1 second. The speed of the airplane is much greater than the speed of the snail because the airplane travels much farther than the snail in the same amount of time.

Academic Standards for Science

7.1.7 Demonstrate and describe how an object's speed or direction of motion changes when a force acts upon it and how they remain unchanged when the net force acting upon it is zero.

7.NS.8 Analyze data and use it to identify patterns and make inferences based on these patterns.

7.DP.9 Present evidence using mathematical representations.

Vocabulary High-Use Academic Words Complete the following sentence. The relationship between speed, distance, and time can be written as a(n)

_____

apply it!

The cyclist shown in the diagram is moving at a constant speed of 10 m/s during her ride.

1 **Identify** Draw arrows on the scale to mark how far the cyclist travels after 1, 2, 3, 3.5, and 4 seconds.

2 **CHALLENGE** How long will it take the cyclist to travel 400 meters? **7.NS.8, 7.DP.9**

| 10 | 20 | 30 | 40 |

Distance (m)

FIGURE 1 ·····································

Average Speed

Triathletes A and B are competing in a triathlon. The first two legs of the race are swimming and biking.

✎ **Calculate** Use the data in the boxes below to calculate each triathlete's average speed during the swimming and biking legs of the race. **7.NS.8**

Average Speed When a plane is at its cruising altitude, it can travel at a constant speed for many hours. But the speed of most moving objects is not constant. In a race known as the triathlon, the competitors (or triathletes) first swim, then bike, and finally run. The speeds of the triathletes change throughout the race. They travel slowest when they swim, a little faster when they run, and fastest when they bike.

Although the triathletes do not travel at a constant speed, they do have an average speed throughout the race. To calculate **average speed,** divide the total distance traveled by the total time. For example, suppose a triathlete swims a distance of 3 kilometers in 1 hour. Then the triathlete bikes a distance of 50 kilometers in 3 hours. Finally, the triathlete runs a distance of 12 kilometers in 1 hour. The average speed of the triathlete is the total distance divided by the total time.

$$\text{Total distance} = 3 \text{ km} + 50 \text{ km} + 12 \text{ km} = 65 \text{ km}$$

$$\text{Total time} = 1 \text{ h} + 3 \text{ h} + 1 \text{ h} = 5 \text{ h}$$

$$\text{Average speed} = \frac{65 \text{ km}}{5 \text{ h}} = 13 \text{ km/h}$$

The triathlete's average speed is 13 kilometers per hour.

Leg 1 *Swimming*

Total distance: 3.0 km
Triathlete A's total time: 0.8 h
Triathlete B's total time: 1.0 h

Triathlete A's average speed =

Triathlete B's average speed =

Leg 2 *Biking*

Total distance: 50.0 km
Triathlete A's total time: 3.0 h
Triathlete B's total time: 2.5 h

Triathlete A's average speed =

Triathlete B's average speed =

Instantaneous Speed Suppose Triathlete B passes Triathlete A during the biking leg. At that moment, Triathlete B has a greater instantaneous speed than Triathlete A. **Instantaneous speed** is the speed at which an object is moving at a given instant in time. It is important not to confuse instantaneous speed with average speed. The triathlete with the greatest average speed, not the greatest instantaneous speed, wins the race.

The triathletes run in the third and final leg of the triathlon.

1 △ **Calculate** Use the data from all three legs to solve for each triathlete's average speed.

> **Leg 3** *Running*
> Total distance: 12.0 km
> Triathlete A's total time: 1.2 h
> Triathlete B's total time: 1.0 h

Total distance =	
Triathlete A's total time =	
Triathlete A's average speed =	
Triathlete B's total time =	
Triathlete B's average speed =	

2 Identify Which triathlete finishes first? _____

7.NS.8

Lab zone ® Do the Lab Investigation *Stopping on a Dime.*

🔑 Assess Your Understanding

1a. Identify The (instantaneous/average) speed is the speed of the object at a given instant in time. The (instantaneous/average) speed is the speed of the object over a longer period of time.　　　　7.1.7

b. Apply Concepts The speedometer in a car gives the car's _____ speed.
　　　　7.1.7

got it?

○ **I get it!** Now I know to calculate the speed of an object, I need to _____

_____

○ **I need extra help with** _____

Go to **my science** ⑤ **coach** online for help with this subject.　　　　7.1.7

Academic Standards for Science

7.1.6 Explain that forces have magnitude and direction and those forces can be added to determine the net force acting on an object.

7.1.7 Demonstrate and describe how an object's speed or direction of motion changes when a force acts upon it and how they remain unchanged when the net force acting upon it is zero.

7.NS.8 Analyze data.

Identify Supporting Evidence Underline the reason why velocity is important to air traffic controllers.

How Do You Describe Velocity?

Knowing the speed at which something travels does not tell you everything about its motion. To describe an object's motion, you also need to know its direction. For example, suppose you hear that a thunderstorm is traveling at a speed of 25 km/h. Should you prepare for the storm? That depends on the direction of the storm's motion. Because storms usually travel from west to east in the United States, you probably need not worry if you live west of the storm. You probably should take cover if you live east of the storm.

When you know both the speed and direction of an object's motion, you know the velocity of the object. Speed in a given direction is called **velocity.** You know the velocity of the storm when you know that it is moving 25 km/h eastward.

At times, describing the velocity of moving objects can be very important. For example, air traffic controllers must keep close track of the velocities of the aircraft under their control. These velocities change as airplanes move overhead and on the runways. An error in determining a velocity, either in speed or in direction, could lead to a collision.

Velocity is also important to airplane pilots. For example, the stunt pilots in **Figure 2** make spectacular use of their control over the velocity of their aircraft. Stunt pilots use this control to stay in close formation while flying graceful maneuvers at high speeds.

FIGURE 2 ·······················

Velocity
These stunt pilots are performing at an air show.

Explain Why is velocity and not just speed important to these pilots?

_____

_____

_____

_____

_____

_____

_____

_____

_____

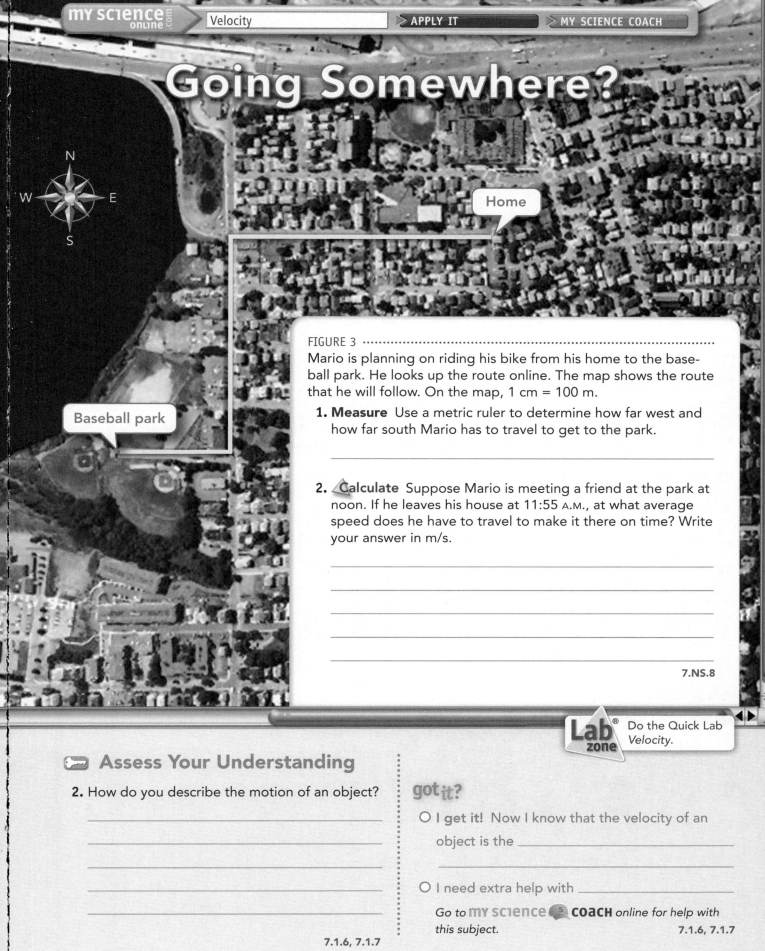

Going Somewhere?

N
W · E
S

Home

Baseball park

FIGURE 3 ···

Mario is planning on riding his bike from his home to the baseball park. He looks up the route online. The map shows the route that he will follow. On the map, 1 cm = 100 m.

1. Measure Use a metric ruler to determine how far west and how far south Mario has to travel to get to the park.

_____

2. Calculate Suppose Mario is meeting a friend at the park at noon. If he leaves his house at 11:55 A.M., at what average speed does he have to travel to make it there on time? Write your answer in m/s.

_____
_____
_____
_____
_____

7.NS.8

Lab zone® Do the Quick Lab *Velocity.*

🔑 Assess Your Understanding

2. How do you describe the motion of an object?

_____
_____
_____
_____

7.1.6, 7.1.7

got it?

○ **I get it!** Now I know that the velocity of an object is the _____

_____

○ **I need extra help with** _____

Go to my science ⑤ coach *online for help with this subject.*   7.1.6, 7.1.7

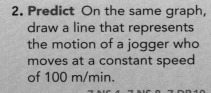
FIGURE 4 ·······························

> INTERACTIVE ART **Constant Speed**

The graph shows the motion of a jogger.

✏ **Use the graph to answer the questions.**

1. Read Graphs What is the jogger's speed?

_____

2. Predict On the same graph, draw a line that represents the motion of a jogger who moves at a constant speed of 100 m/min.

7.NS.1, 7.NS.8, 7.DP.10

How Do You Graph Motion?

The graphs you see in **Figure 4** and **Figure 5** are distance-versus-time motion graphs. 🔑 **You can show the motion of an object on a line graph in which you plot distance versus time.** By tradition, time is shown on the horizontal axis, or *x*-axis. Distance is shown on the vertical axis, or *y*-axis. A point on the line represents the distance an object has traveled during a particular time. The *x* value of the point is time, and the *y* value is distance.

The steepness of a line on a graph is called **slope.** The slope tells you how fast one variable changes in relation to the other variable in the graph. In other words, slope tells you the rate of change. Since speed is the rate that distance changes in relation to time, the slope of a distance-versus-time graph represents speed. The steeper the slope is, the greater the speed. A constant slope represents motion at constant speed.

Calculating Slope You can calculate the slope of a line by dividing the rise by the run. The rise is the vertical difference between any two points on the line. The run is the horizontal difference between the same two points.

$$\text{Slope} = \frac{\text{Rise}}{\text{Run}}$$

In **Figure 4,** using the points shown, the rise is 400 meters and the run is 2 minutes. To find the slope, you divide 400 meters by 2 minutes. The slope is 200 meters per minute.

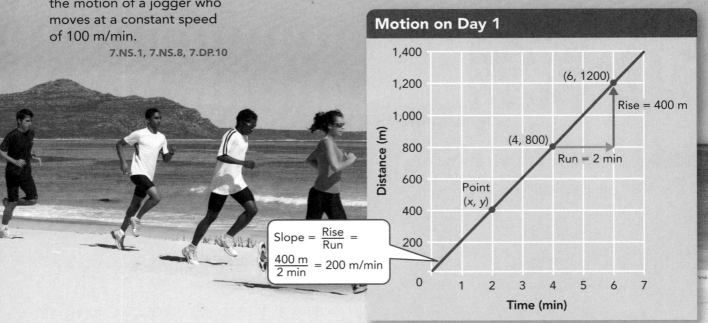

Motion on Day 1

$$\text{Slope} = \frac{\text{Rise}}{\text{Run}} =$$

$$\frac{400 \text{ m}}{2 \text{ min}} = 200 \text{ m/min}$$

Different Slopes Most moving objects do not travel at a constant speed. For example, the graph in **Figure 5** shows a jogger's motion on the second day of training. The line is divided into three segments. The slope of each segment is different. From the steepness of the slopes you can tell that the jogger ran fastest during the third segment. The horizontal line in the second segment shows that the jogger's distance did not change at all. The jogger was resting during the second segment.

FIGURE 5 ·······························
Changing Speed
The graph shows how the speed of a jogger varies during her second day of training.

✏️ **Read Graphs** Find the rise, the run, and the slope for each segment of the graph. Write the answers in the boxes below.

7.NS.8

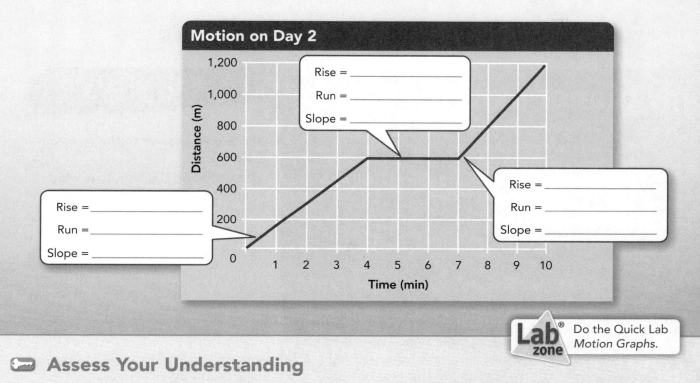

Motion on Day 2

Rise = _____
Run = _____
Slope = _____

Rise = _____
Run = _____
Slope = _____

Rise = _____
Run = _____
Slope = _____

Distance (m): 0, 200, 400, 600, 800, 1,000, 1,200

Time (min): 1 2 3 4 5 6 7 8 9 10

Lab zone   Do the Quick Lab *Motion Graphs.*

🔑 **Assess Your Understanding**

3a. Identify The _____ of a distance-versus-time graph shows you the speed of a moving object.

7.1.7

b. Calculate The rise of a line on a distance-versus-time graph is 900 m and the run is 3 min. What is the slope of the line?

_____

_____

7.1.7, 7.NS.8

c. Apply Concepts Is it possible for a distance-versus-time graph to be a vertical line? Explain.

_____

_____

_____

_____

_____

7.1.7

got it? ·······························

○ **I get it!** Now I know to show the motion of an object on a line graph, you _____

_____

○ **I need extra help with** _____

Go to **my science** ⟩ **COACH** *online for help with this subject.*

7.1.7

Acceleration

🔑 **What Is Acceleration?**
7.1.7, 7.NS.1, 7.NS.8

my planet diary

Jumping Spider

A small spider, less than 2 centimeters long, spots an insect. The spider crouches and crawls forward. Then it lifts its front legs and leaps, landing right on its victim!

Amazingly, a jumping spider can jump 10 to 40 times its body length. To capture prey from that far away, it must accurately estimate its initial velocity. Once the spider jumps, the force of gravity controls its motion, causing it to follow a curved path. Its velocity changes at every point along the path until it lands on its prey.

FUN FACT

Write your answer to the question below.

Think of a sport or activity in which the goal is to hit a target from far away. What are some of the challenges?

_____

_____

_____

_____

_____

> PLANET DIARY Go to **Planet Diary** to learn more about acceleration.

Lab® zone Do the Inquiry Warm-Up *Will You Hurry Up?*

Academic Standards for Science

7.1.7 Demonstrate and describe how an object's speed or direction of motion changes when a force acts upon it and how they remain unchanged when the net force acting upon it is zero.

7.NS.1 Make predictions.

7.NS.8 Analyze data, using appropriate mathematical manipulation as required, and use it to identify patterns and make inferences based on these patterns.

What Is Acceleration?

Suppose you are a passenger in a car stopped at a red light. When the light changes to green, the driver steps on the accelerator. As a result, the car speeds up, or accelerates. In everyday language, acceleration means "the process of speeding up."

Acceleration has a more precise definition in science. Scientists define **acceleration** as the rate at which velocity changes. Recall that velocity describes both the speed and direction of an object. A change in velocity can involve a change in either speed or direction—or both. 🔑 **In science, acceleration refers to increasing speed, decreasing speed, or changing direction.**

Vocabulary
- acceleration

Skills

🎯 Reading: Identify the Main Idea

△ Inquiry: Graph

Changing Speed

Whenever an object's speed changes, the object accelerates. A car that begins to move from a stopped position or speeds up to pass another car is accelerating. People can accelerate too. For example, you accelerate when you coast down a hill on your bike.

Just as objects can speed up, they can also slow down. This change in speed is sometimes called deceleration, or negative acceleration. A car decelerates as it comes to a stop at a red light. A water skier decelerates as the boat slows down.

Changing Direction

Even an object that is traveling at a constant speed can be accelerating. Recall that acceleration can be a change in direction as well as a change in speed. Therefore, a car accelerates as it follows a gentle curve in the road or changes lanes. Runners accelerate as they round the curve in a track. A softball accelerates when it changes direction as it is hit.

Many objects continuously change direction without changing speed. The simplest example of this type of motion is circular motion, or motion along a circular path. For example, the seats on a Ferris wheel accelerate because they move in a circle.

🎯 **Identify the Main Idea**

Underline the main idea in the section called Changing Speed.

FIGURE 1 ·······················

Acceleration

During the game of soccer, a soccer ball can show three types of acceleration— increasing speed, decreasing speed, and changing direction.

✏️ **Interpret Photos** Label the type of acceleration that is occurring in each of the photos.

0.0s   1.0s   2.0s   3.0s

0 m/s   8 m/s   16 m/s   24 m/s

FIGURE 2 ·······························

Acceleration

The airplane is accelerating at a rate of 8 m/s².

✏️ **Predict** Determine the speed of the airplane at 4.0 s and 5.0 s. Write your answers in the boxes next to each airplane.   7.NS.1

Calculating Acceleration Acceleration describes the rate at which velocity changes. If an object is not changing direction, you can describe its acceleration as the rate at which its speed changes. To determine the acceleration of an object moving in a straight line, you calculate the change in speed per unit of time. This is summarized by the following equation.

$$\text{Acceleration} = \frac{\text{Final Speed} - \text{Initial Speed}}{\text{Time}}$$

If speed is measured in meters per second (m/s) and time is measured in seconds, the SI unit of acceleration is meters per second per second, or m/s². Suppose speed is measured in kilometers per hour and time is measured in hours. Then the unit for acceleration is kilometers per hour per hour, or km/h².

To understand acceleration, imagine a small airplane moving down a runway. **Figure 2** shows the airplane's speed after each second of the first three seconds of its acceleration. To calculate the acceleration of the airplane, you must first subtract the initial speed of 0 m/s from its final speed of 24 m/s. Then divide the change in speed by the time, 3 seconds.

$$\text{Acceleration} = \frac{24 \text{ m/s} - 0 \text{ m/s}}{3 \text{ s}}$$

$$\text{Acceleration} = 8 \text{ m/s}^2$$

The airplane accelerates at a rate of 8 m/s². This means that the airplane's speed increases by 8 m/s every second. Notice in **Figure 2** that after each second of travel, the airplane's speed is 8 m/s greater than its speed in the previous second.

FIGURE 3 ·······························

Deceleration

An airplane touches down on the runway with a speed of 70 m/s. It decelerates at a rate of –5 m/s².

✏️ **Predict** Determine the speed of the airplane after each second of its deceleration. Write your answers in the table to the right.

    7.NS.1, 7.NS.8

Time (s)	1	2	3	4
Speed (m/s)				

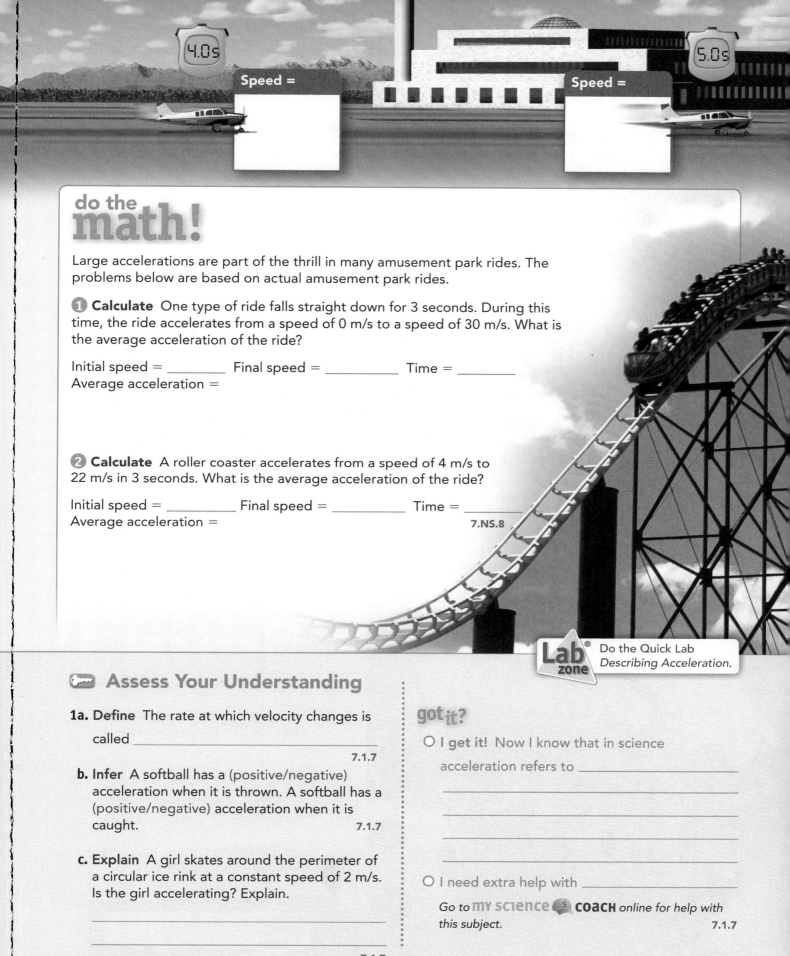

Speed = _____

Speed = _____

4.0s

5.0s

do the math!

Large accelerations are part of the thrill in many amusement park rides. The problems below are based on actual amusement park rides.

1 Calculate One type of ride falls straight down for 3 seconds. During this time, the ride accelerates from a speed of 0 m/s to a speed of 30 m/s. What is the average acceleration of the ride?

Initial speed = _____ Final speed = _____ Time = _____
Average acceleration =

2 Calculate A roller coaster accelerates from a speed of 4 m/s to 22 m/s in 3 seconds. What is the average acceleration of the ride?

Initial speed = _____ Final speed = _____ Time = _____
Average acceleration =

7.NS.8

Lab® zone   Do the Quick Lab
Describing Acceleration.

🔑 Assess Your Understanding

1a. Define The rate at which velocity changes is called _____

7.1.7

b. Infer A softball has a (positive/negative) acceleration when it is thrown. A softball has a (positive/negative) acceleration when it is caught.

7.1.7

c. Explain A girl skates around the perimeter of a circular ice rink at a constant speed of 2 m/s. Is the girl accelerating? Explain.

_____

_____

7.1.7

got it?

○ **I get it!** Now I know that in science acceleration refers to _____

_____

_____

_____

_____

○ **I need extra help with** _____

Go to MY SCIENCE ⓢ COACH *online for help with this subject.*

7.1.7

99

The Nature of Force

UNLOCK THE BIG ?

🗝 **How Are Forces Described?**
7.1.5, 7.1.7, 7.DP.10

🗝 **How Do Forces Affect Motion?**
7.1.6, 7.1.7, 7.NS.8, 7.DP.10

my planet diary

MISCONCEPTIONS

Forced to Change

Misconception: Any object that is set in motion will slow down on its own.

Fact: A force is needed to change an object's state of motion.

A soccer ball sits at rest. You come along and kick it, sending it flying across the field. It eventually slows to a stop. You applied a force to start it moving, and then it stopped all on its own, right?

No! Forces cause *all* changes in motion. Just as you applied a force to the ball to speed it up from rest, the ground applied a force to slow it down to a stop. If the ground didn't apply a force to the ball, it would keep rolling forever without slowing down or stopping.

Answer the questions below.

1. Give an example of a force you apply to slow something down.

_____

_____

2. Where might it be possible to kick a soccer ball and have it never slow down?

_____

_____

_____

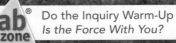 **PLANET DIARY** Go to **Planet Diary** to learn more about forces.

Lab®**zone** Do the Inquiry Warm-Up *Is the Force With You?*

Vocabulary
- force
- net force
- newton

Skills
- Reading: Relate Text and Visuals
- Inquiry: Make Models

How Are Forces Described?

A **force** is a push or a pull. When one object pushes or pulls another object, the first object exerts a force on the second object. Some forces, such as friction, involve direct contact between two objects. Other forces, such as gravity, act between two objects over a distance. You will learn more about these two different types of forces in the next lesson.

🗝 **Like velocity and acceleration, a force is described by its strength and by the direction in which it acts.** The direction and strength of a force can be represented by an arrow. The arrow points in the direction of the force, as shown in **Figure 1.** The length of the arrow tells you the strength of the force—the longer the arrow, the greater the force. The strength of a force is measured in the SI unit called the **newton** (N), after scientist Sir Isaac Newton.

Academic Standards for Science

7.1.5 Describe and investigate how forces between objects can act at a distance, such as magnetic, electrical or gravitational forces, or by means of direct contact between objects.

7.1.7 Demonstrate and describe how an object's speed or direction of motion changes when a force acts upon it and how they remain unchanged when the net force acting upon it is zero.

7.DP.10 Communicate the solution including evidence using drawings.

FIGURE 1 ·······························

Describing Forces

In the photos at the right, two men are celebrating an Olympic victory. Forces cause them to pull each other in for a hug, lean over, and fall into the pool.

✏ **Identify** In the box within each photo, draw an arrow that represents the force acting on the person on the right. The first one is done as an example.

7.DP.10

Do the Quick Lab
What Is Force?

🗝 **Assess Your Understanding**

got it? ···

○ **I get it!** Now I know that forces are described by _____

_____

○ **I need extra help with** _____

Go to my science s **COACH** *online for help with this subject.*

7.1.5, 7.1.7

FIGURE 2 ···

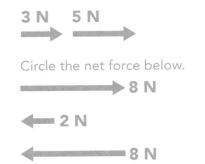

> INTERACTIVE ART Net Force

The change in motion of an object is determined by
the net force acting on the object.

✎ Make Models Calculate and draw an arrow for the
net force for each situation in the boxes below.

7.NS.8, 7.DP.10

16 N

10 N

20 N

10 N

a Net force _____

b Net force _____

Academic Standards for Science

7.1.6 Explain that forces have magnitude and direction and can be added to determine the net force acting on an object.

7.1.7 Demonstrate and describe how an object's speed or direction of motion changes when a force acts upon it and how they remain unchanged when the net force acting upon it is zero.

7.NS.8 Analyze data.

7.DP.10 Communicate the solution using drawings.

✎ ···

↻ **Relate Text and Visuals** Use the information in the text to determine the net force of these two force arrows.

3 N   5 N

Circle the net force below.

→ 8 N

← 2 N

← 8 N

How Do Forces Affect Motion?

Often more than one force acts on an object at the same time. The combination of all the forces on an object is called the **net force.** The net force determines if and how an object will accelerate.

You can find the net force on an object by adding together the strengths of all the individual forces acting on the object. Look at **Figure 2a.** The big dog pushes on the box with a force of 16 N to the right. The small dog pushes on the box with a force of 10 N to the right. The net force on the box is the sum of these forces. The box will accelerate to the right. In this situation, there is a nonzero net force. ⚷ **A nonzero net force causes a change in the object's motion.**

What if the forces on an object aren't acting in the same direction? In **Figure 2b,** the big dog pushes with a force of 20 N. The small dog still pushes with a force of 10 N, but now they're pushing against each other. When forces on an object act in opposite directions, the strength of the net force is found by subtracting the strength of the smaller force from the strength of the larger force. You can still think of this as *adding* the forces together if you think of all forces that act to the right as positive forces and all forces that act to the left as negative forces. The box will accelerate to the right. When forces act in opposite directions, the net force is in the same direction as the larger force.

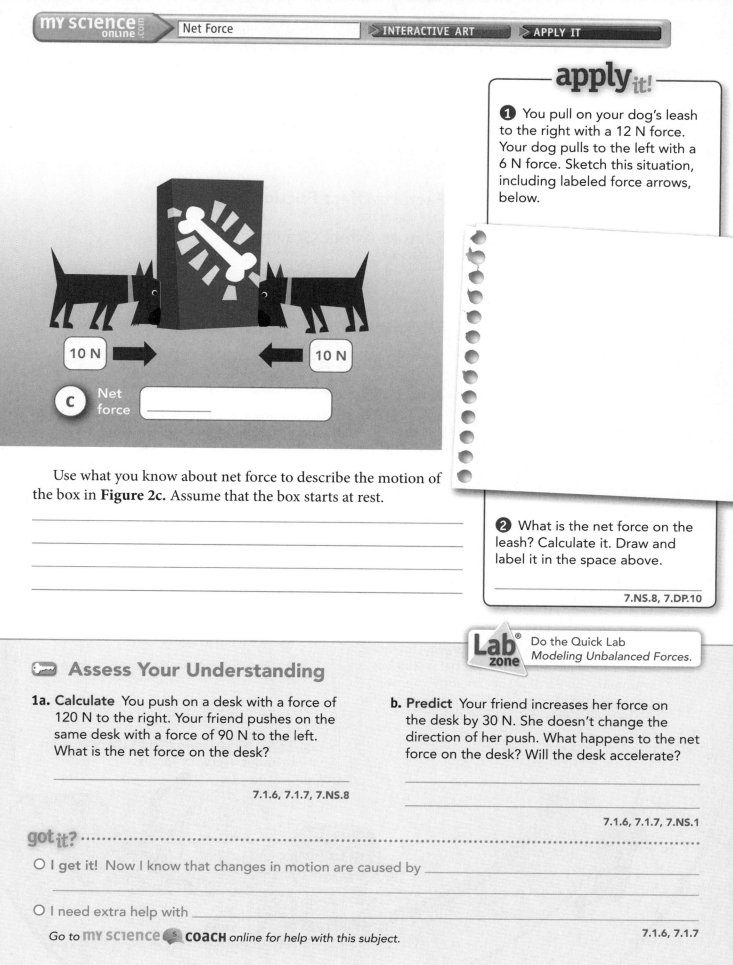

apply it!

❶ You pull on your dog's leash to the right with a 12 N force. Your dog pulls to the left with a 6 N force. Sketch this situation, including labeled force arrows, below.

10 N → ← 10 N

C Net force _____

Use what you know about net force to describe the motion of the box in **Figure 2c.** Assume that the box starts at rest.

_____
_____
_____
_____

❷ What is the net force on the leash? Calculate it. Draw and label it in the space above.

7.NS.8, 7.DP.10

Lab zone Do the Quick Lab
Modeling Unbalanced Forces.

Assess Your Understanding

1a. Calculate You push on a desk with a force of 120 N to the right. Your friend pushes on the same desk with a force of 90 N to the left. What is the net force on the desk?

_____

7.1.6, 7.1.7, 7.NS.8

b. Predict Your friend increases her force on the desk by 30 N. She doesn't change the direction of her push. What happens to the net force on the desk? Will the desk accelerate?

_____
_____

7.1.6, 7.1.7, 7.NS.1

got it?

○ **I get it!** Now I know that changes in motion are caused by _____

○ **I need extra help with** _____

Go to **my science** **COACH** *online for help with this subject.*

7.1.6, 7.1.7

Friction and Gravity

UNLOCK THE BIG ?

🔑 **What Factors Affect Friction?**
7.1.5, 7.NS.2, 7.NS.4, 7.DP.9

🔑 **What Factors Affect Gravity?**
7.1.5, 7.NS.1, 7.NS.8

my PLANET DiARY

CAREERS

Space Athletes

Have you ever seen pictures of astronauts playing golf on the moon or playing catch in a space station? Golf balls and baseballs can float or fly farther in space, where gravitational forces are weaker than they are on Earth. Imagine what professional sports would be like in reduced gravity!

You may not have to imagine much longer. At least one company specializes in airplane flights that simulate a reduced gravity environment. Similar to NASA training flights that astronauts use when preparing to go into space, these flights allow passengers to fly around the cabin. In environments with reduced gravity, athletes can perform jumps and stunts that would be impossible on Earth. As technology improves, permanent stadiums could be built in space for a whole new generation of athletes.

Communicate Discuss these questions with a partner and then answer them below.

1. Sports can be more fun in reduced gravity. What jobs could be harder or less fun to do in space? Why?

_____

_____

_____

2. What kinds of sports do you think could be more fun in space? Why?

_____

_____

_____

▶ PLANET DIARY Go to **Planet Diary** to learn more about everyday forces.

Lab zone® Do the Inquiry Warm-Up *Observing Friction.*

Vocabulary
• friction • sliding friction • static friction
• fluid friction • rolling friction • gravity
• mass • weight

Skills
◉ Reading: Identify Supporting Evidence
◭ Inquiry: Design Experiments

What Factors Affect Friction?

If you slide a book across a table, the surface of the book rubs against the surface of the table. The force that two surfaces exert on each other when they rub against each other is called **friction.** ◌━ **Two factors that affect the force of friction are the types of surfaces involved and how hard the surfaces are pushed together.** The football player in **Figure 1** is pushing on a blocking sled. If his coach wanted to make it harder to move the sled, the coach could change the surface of the sled. Covering the bottom of the sled with rubber would increase friction and make the sled harder to move. In general, smooth surfaces produce less friction than rough surfaces.

What would happen if the football player switched to a much heavier sled? He would find the heavier sled harder to push because it pushes down harder against the ground. Similarly, if you rubbed your hands together forcefully, there would be more friction than if you rubbed your hands together lightly. Friction increases when surfaces push harder against each other.

Friction acts in a direction opposite to the direction of the object's motion. Without friction, a moving object will not stop until it strikes another object.

Academic Standards for Science

7.1.5 Describe and investigate how forces between objects can act at a distance, such as magnetic, electrical or gravitational forces, or by means of direct contact between objects.

7.NS.2 Plan and carry out an investigation.

7.NS.4 Incorporate variables that can be changed, measured or controlled.

7.DP.9 Present evidence using mathematical representations.

Vocabulary Latin Word Origins
Friction comes from the Latin word *fricare*. Based on the definition of friction, what do you think *fricare* means?

○ to burn
○ to rub
○ to melt

FIGURE 1 ···
▶ ART IN MOTION **Friction and Different Surfaces**
The strength of friction depends on the types of surfaces involved. ✎ **Sequence Rank the surfaces above by how hard it would be to push a sled over them, from easiest (1) to hardest (3). (Each surface is flat.) What does this ranking tell you about the amount of friction over these surfaces?**

_____

_____

Sliding Friction

Sliding friction occurs when two solid surfaces slide over each other. Sliding friction is what makes moving objects slow down and stop. Without sliding friction, a penguin that slid down a hill wouldn't stop until he hit a wall!

✎ **Classify** Label five examples of sliding friction and compare with a classmate.

Friction acts opposite the direction of motion.

Direction of motion →

← Friction

Static Friction

Static friction acts between objects that aren't moving. Think about trying to push a couch across the room. If you don't push hard enough, it won't move. The force that's keeping you from moving it is static friction. Once you push hard enough to overcome static friction, the couch starts moving and there is no more static friction. However, there is sliding friction.

✎ **Classify** Label five examples of static friction and compare with a classmate.

Draw an arrow representing the frictional force at work.

Fluid Friction

Fluids, such as water and air, are materials that flow easily. **Fluid friction** occurs when a solid object moves through a fluid. Fluid friction is easier to overcome than sliding friction. This is why sidewalks become slippery when they get wet.

✏️ **Classify Label five examples of fluid friction and compare with a classmate.**

Draw an arrow representing the frictional force at work.

Rolling Friction

When an object rolls across a surface, **rolling friction** occurs. Rolling friction is much easier to overcome than sliding friction for similar materials. That's why it's easy to push a bike along the sidewalk when the wheels can turn, but much harder to push the bike if you're applying the brakes and the tires slide, not roll.

✏️ **Classify Label five examples of rolling friction and compare with a classmate.**

Draw an arrow representing the frictional force at work.

apply it!

Your family is moving and isn't sure how to best overcome friction while moving furniture. You have a spring scale, wood blocks to represent your furniture, and sandpaper, aluminum foil, marbles, and olive oil as possible surfaces to slide your furniture over.

⚠ **Design Experiments Design an experiment that will help you determine which material will reduce friction the most.**

You know that friction occurs between surfaces when they slide against each other. If you measure the applied force required to push something across a surface, you know that your applied force would (increase/decrease) as friction increased.

STEP ① Measure How would you determine your applied force in this experiment?

_____

_____

_____

STEP ② Control Variables What variables would you have to control to keep your results accurate?

_____

_____

_____

STEP ③ Create Data Tables Draw the data table you would use when performing this experiment.

7.NS.2, 7.NS.4, 7.DP.9

🔑 Assess Your Understanding

1a. List Name four types of friction and give an example of each.

_____

_____

_____

_____

_____

7.1.5

b. Classify What types of friction occur between your bike tires and the ground when you ride over cement, ride through a puddle, and apply your brakes?

_____

7.1.5

Lab zone ® Do the Lab Investigation *Sticky Sneakers.*

got it?

○ **I get it!** Now I know that friction is affected by

_____

_____

_____

○ **I need extra help with** _____

_____

Go to **my science** **coach** *online for help with this subject.*

7.1.5

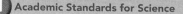

What Factors Affect Gravity?

A skydiver would be surprised if she jumped out of a plane and did not fall. We are so used to objects falling that we may not have thought about why they fall. One person who thought about it was Sir Isaac Newton. He concluded that a force acts to pull objects straight down toward the center of Earth. **Gravity** is a force that pulls objects toward each other.

Universal Gravitation Newton realized that gravity acts everywhere in the universe, not just on Earth. It is the force that makes the skydivers in **Figure 2** fall to the ground. It is the force that keeps the moon orbiting around Earth. It is the force that keeps all the planets in our solar system orbiting around the sun.

What Newton realized is now called the law of universal gravitation. The law of universal gravitation states that the force of gravity acts between all objects in the universe that have mass. This means that any two objects in the universe that have mass attract each other. You are attracted not only to Earth but also to the moon, the other planets in the solar system, and all the objects around you. Earth and the objects around you are attracted to you as well. However, you do not notice the attraction among small objects because these forces are extremely small compared to the force of Earth's attraction.

Academic Standards for Science

7.1.5 Describe and investigate how forces between objects can act at a distance, such as magnetic, electrical or gravitational forces, or by means of direct contact between objects.
7.NS.1 Make predictions.
7.NS.8 Analyze data.

FIGURE 2 ·········

Observing Gravity

Newton published his work on gravity in 1687.

✎ **Observe** What observations might you make today that would lead you to the same conclusions about gravity? Write down your ideas below.

_____

_____

_____

_____

_____

Factors Affecting Gravity

A gravitational force exists between any two objects in the universe. However, you don't see your pencil fly toward the wall the way you see it fall toward Earth. That's because the gravitational force between some objects is stronger than the force between others. You observe only the effects of the strongest gravitational forces. 🗝 **Two factors affect the gravitational attraction between objects: mass and distance.** **Mass** is a measure of the amount of matter in an object. The SI unit of mass is the kilogram.

The more mass an object has, the greater the gravitational force between it and other objects. Earth's gravitational force on near by objects is strong because the mass of Earth is so large. The more massive planets in **Figure 3** interact with a greater gravitational force than the less massive planets. Gravitational force also depends on the distance between the objects' centers. As distance increases, gravitational force decreases. That's why Earth can exert a visible gravitational force on a pencil in your room and not on a pencil on the moon.

✏️ **Identify Supporting Evidence** Underline the factors that determine how strong the gravitational force is between two objects.

FIGURE 3 ·······

Gravitational Attraction

Gravitational attraction depends on two factors: mass and distance. Suppose there was a solar system that looked like this.

✏️ **Interpret Diagrams** Use the diagram below to compare the gravitational force between different planets and their sun. Assume all planets are made of the same material, so bigger planets have more mass. 7.NS.8

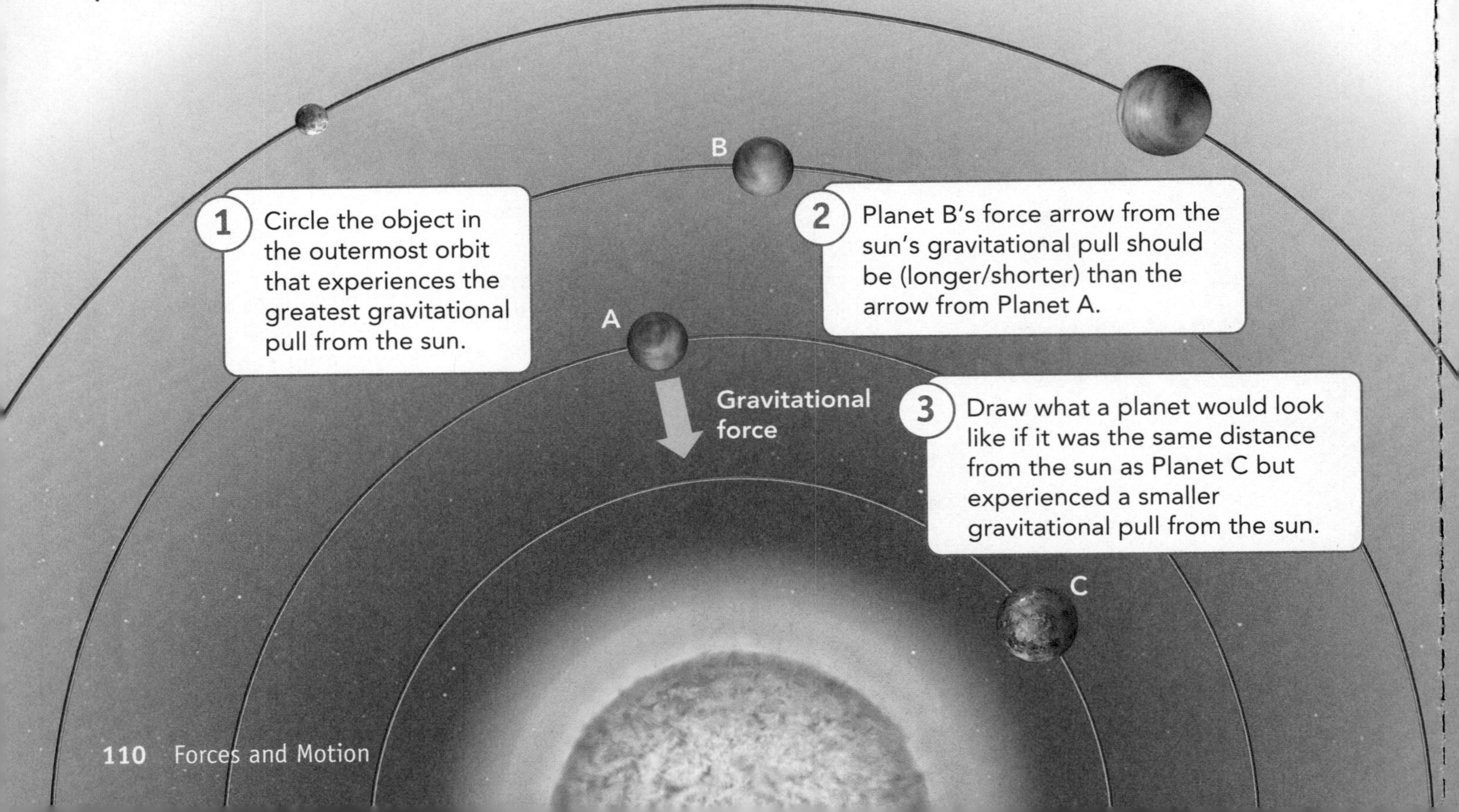

1 Circle the object in the outermost orbit that experiences the greatest gravitational pull from the sun.

2 Planet B's force arrow from the sun's gravitational pull should be (longer/shorter) than the arrow from Planet A.

Gravitational force

3 Draw what a planet would look like if it was the same distance from the sun as Planet C but experienced a smaller gravitational pull from the sun.

Earth
60 N

Moon
____ N

Mars
____ N

Weight and Mass

Weight and Mass Mass is sometimes confused with weight. Mass is a measure of the amount of matter in an object. **Weight** is a measure of the force of gravity on an object. When you stand on a bathroom scale, it displays the gravitational force Earth is exerting on you.

At any given time, your mass is the same on Earth as it would be on any other planet. But weight varies with the strength of the gravitational force. The dog in **Figure 4** has a different weight at different places in the solar system. On the moon, he would weigh about one sixth of what he does on Earth. On Mars, he would weigh just over a third of what he does on Earth.

FIGURE 4 ⋯⋯⋯⋯⋯⋯⋯⋯⋯⋯⋯⋯⋯⋯⋯⋯⋯⋯⋯⋯⋯⋯⋯⋯⋯⋯⋯⋯⋯
Weight and Mass
The Mars Phoenix Lander weighs about 3,400 N on Earth. It weighs about 1,300 N on Mars. ✏ **Predict** The first scale shows the dog's weight on Earth. Predict its weight on the moon and on Mars. Enter those weights in the boxes on the other two scales.
7.NS.1, 7.NS.8

Lab zone® Do the Quick Lab *Calculating.*

Assess Your Understanding

2a. Describe What happens to the gravitational force between two objects when their masses are increased? What happens when the distance between the objects increases?

_____
_____
_____

7.1.5

b. Relate Cause and Effect If the mass of Earth increased, what would happen to your weight? What about your mass?

_____
_____
_____
_____

7.1.5

got it? ⋯⋯⋯

○ **I get it!** Now I know that the factors that affect the gravitational force between objects are _____

_____

○ **I need extra help with** _____

Go to **MY SCIENCE COACH** online for help with this subject.

7.1.5

111

Newton's Laws of Motion

🔑 **What Is Newton's First Law of Motion?**
7.1.7

🔑 **What Is Newton's Second Law of Motion?**
7.1.7, 7.NS.8

🔑 **What Is Newton's Third Law of Motion?**
7.1.7, 7.NS.3, 7.NS.8

MY PLANET DIARY

VOICES FROM HISTORY

Horse Force

"If a horse draws a stone tied to a rope, the horse (if I may so say) will be equally drawn back towards the stone...."

—Sir Isaac Newton

Scientists have used everyday examples to explain their ideas for hundreds of years. The quotation is from Newton's *Mathematical Principles of Natural Philosophy*, which was first published in the 1680s. Newton used this book to set down his laws of motion. These three simple laws describe much of the motion around you, and they continue to be studied today.

Answer the question below.
What current scientific discoveries might be taught in schools hundreds of years from now?

_____
_____
_____
_____
_____

> PLANET DIARY Go to **Planet Diary** to learn more about Newton.

Lab® Do the Inquiry Warm-Up
zone *What Changes Motion?*

What Is Newton's First Law of Motion?

Academic Standards for Science

7.1.7 Demonstrate and describe how an object's speed or direction of motion changes when a force acts upon it and how they remain unchanged when the net force acting upon it is zero.

You would be surprised if a rock started rolling on its own or a raindrop paused in midair. If an object is not moving, it will not start moving until a force acts on it. If an object is moving, it will continue at a constant velocity until a force acts to change its speed or its direction. 🔑 **Newton's first law of motion states that an object at rest will remain at rest unless acted upon by a nonzero net force. An object moving at a constant velocity will continue moving at a constant velocity unless acted upon by a nonzero net force.**

Vocabulary
- inertia

Skills
- Reading: Ask Questions
- Inquiry: Infer

Inertia All objects, moving or not, resist changes in motion. Resistance to change in motion is called inertia (in UR shuh). Newton's first law of motion is also called the law of inertia. Inertia explains many common events, including why you move forward in your seat when the car you are in stops suddenly. You keep moving forward because of inertia. A force, such as the pull of a seat belt, is needed to pull you back. Roller coasters like the one in **Figure 1** have safety bars for the same reason.

Inertia Depends on Mass Some objects have more inertia than others. Suppose you need to move an empty backpack and a full backpack. The greater the mass of an object, the greater its inertia, and the greater the force required to change its motion. The full backpack is harder to move than the empty one because it has more mass and therefore more inertia.

know
The Voyager is a roller coaster in Indiana that holds the world's record for providing the most "air time" of any wooden coaster. This means that your body continues in the direction it's going while the car changes direction rapidly. You become temporarily airborne. Just imagine the feeling of Voyager's 24.2 seconds of air time!

FIGURE 1 ....
Inertia
A roller coaster is hard to stop because it has a lot of inertia. ✏️ ⚠️ **Infer Use Newton's first law of motion to explain why you feel tossed around whenever a roller coaster goes over a hill or through a loop.**

_____

_____

_____

_____

_____

Lab zone Do the Quick Lab
Around and Around.

🔑 Assess Your Understanding

got it?
○ I get it! Now I know that Newton's first law of motion states that _____

_____

○ I need extra help with _____

Go to MY SCIENCE COACH online for help with this subject.

7.1.7

Academic Standards for Science

7.1.7 Demonstrate and describe how an object's speed or direction of motion changes when a force acts upon it and they remain unchanged when the net force acting upon it is zero.

7.NS.8 Analyze data.

What Is Newton's Second Law of Motion?

Which is harder to push, a full shopping cart or an empty one? Who can cause a greater acceleration on a shopping cart, a small child or a grown adult?

Changes in Force and Mass Suppose you increase the force on a cart without changing its mass. The acceleration of the cart will also increase. Your cart will also accelerate faster if something falls out. This reduces the mass of the cart, and you keep pushing just as hard. The acceleration of the sled in **Figure 2** will change depending on the mass of the people on it and the force the sled dogs apply. Newton realized these relationships and found a way to represent them mathematically.

Determining Acceleration 🔑 **Newton's second law of motion states that an object's acceleration depends on its mass and on the net force acting on it.** This relationship can be written as follows.

$$\text{Acceleration} = \frac{\text{Net force}}{\text{Mass}}$$

This formula can be rearranged to show how much force must be applied to an object to get it to accelerate at a certain rate.

$$\text{Net force} = \text{Mass} \times \text{Acceleration}$$

FIGURE 2 ·······························

Newton's Second Law
Suppose that four dogs pull a sled carrying two people.
✏️ **Explain Use words and fill in the pictures to show how you can change the dog/person arrangement to change the sled's acceleration.**

How could you increase the sled's acceleration?

_____

_____

_____

How could you decrease the sled's acceleration?

_____

_____

_____

7.NS.8

Acceleration is measured in meters per second per second (m/s^2). Mass is measured in kilograms (kg). Newton's second law shows that force is measured in kilograms times meters per second per second ($kg \cdot m/s^2$). This unit is also called the newton (N), which is the SI unit of force. One newton is the force required to give a 1-kg mass an acceleration of $1\ m/s^2$.

do the math!

Every year in cities around the world, teams create cars, push them across platforms, and hope they will fly. Unfortunately, the cars always end up accelerating down into the water.

1 **Calculate** If a 100-N net force acts on a 50-kg car, what will the acceleration of the car be?

_____

2 After that same car leaves the platform, gravity causes it to accelerate downward at a rate of $9.8\ m/s^2$. What is the gravitational force on the car?

_____

7.NS.8

 Lab zone® Do the Quick Lab *Newton's Second Law.*

🔑 Assess Your Understanding

1a. Review What equation allows you to calculate the force acting on an object?

_____

7.1.7

b. Calculate What is the net force on a 2-kg skateboard accelerating at a rate of $2\ m/s^2$?

_____

7.1.7, 7.NS.8

c. Predict If the mass of the skateboard doubled but the net force on it remained constant, what would happen to the acceleration of the skateboard?

_____

_____

_____

7.1.7, 7.NS.1

got it? ··

O **I get it!** Now I know that Newton's second law of motion describes the relationship _____

_____

O **I need extra help with** _____

Go to **MY SCIENCE** 🔎 **COACH** *online for help with this subject.*

7.1.7

115

Reaction force Action force

FIGURE 3 ·······························

Action-Reaction Pairs

A swimmer moves because the water pushes her forward when she pushes back on it.

✎ **Interpret Diagrams** Draw arrows to show the action and reaction forces between the gymnast and the balance beam. Draw your own example in the space provided.

Academic Standards for Science

7.1.7 Demonstrate and describe how an object's speed or direction of motion changes when a force acts upon it and they remain unchanged when the net force acting upon it is zero.

7.NS.3 Collect data and use units to label numerical data.

7.NS.8 Analyze data.

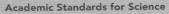

⊙ **Ask Questions** Action and reaction force pairs are all around you, but they aren't always obvious. Write down a question about a situation in which you can't identify what force pairs are at work.

_____

_____

_____

_____

_____

_____

What Is Newton's Third Law of Motion?

If you leaned against a wall and it didn't push back on you, you'd fall through. The force exerted by the wall is equal in strength and opposite in direction to the force you exert on the wall. ⚷ **Newton's third law of motion states that if one object exerts a force on another object, then the second object exerts a force of equal strength in the opposite direction on the first object.** Another way to state Newton's third law is that for every action there is an equal but opposite reaction.

Action-Reaction Pairs Pairs of action and reaction forces are all around you. When you walk, you push backward on the ground with your feet. Think of this as an action force. (It doesn't matter which force is called the "action" force and which is called the "reaction" force.) The ground pushes forward on your feet with an equal and opposite force. This is the reaction force. You can only walk because the ground pushes you forward! In a similar way, the swimmer in **Figure 3** moves forward by exerting an action force on the water with her hands. The water pushes on her hands with an equal reaction force that propels her body forward.

Detecting Motion

If you drop your pen, gravity pulls the pen downward. According to Newton's third law, the pen pulls Earth upward with an equal and opposite reaction force. You see the pen fall. You *don't* see Earth accelerate toward the pen. Remember Newton's second law. If mass increases and force stays the same, acceleration decreases. The same force acts on both Earth and your pen. Since Earth has such a large mass, its acceleration is so small that you don't notice it.

Do Action-Reaction Forces Cancel?

You have learned that two equal forces acting in opposite directions on an object cancel each other out and produce no change in motion. So why don't the action and reaction forces in Newton's third law of motion cancel out as well?

Action and reaction forces do not cancel out because they act on different objects. The swimmer in **Figure 3** exerts a backward action force on the water. The water exerts an equal but opposite forward reaction force on her hands. The action and reaction forces act on different objects—the action force acts on the water and the reaction force acts on her hands.

Unlike the swimmer and the water, the volleyball players in **Figure 4** both exert a force on the *same* object—the volleyball. Each player exerts a force on the ball equal in strength but opposite in direction. The forces on the volleyball are balanced. The ball does not move toward one player or the other.

did you know?

Newton's third law of motion explains why rockets accelerate in space, even though there is no water or air to push off of. Inside rockets, gas is produced. When the rockets push that gas backward out of the rocket, a reaction force occurs that pushes the rocket forward.

FIGURE 4 ·····················
Action-Reaction Forces
All the horizontal forces on the volleyball cancel out.

✎ **Apply Concepts** In the dog illustration above, use Newton's third law of motion to draw and label any missing force arrows for all the objects.

Force on ball

Forces on hands

Force on ball

What Makes a Bug Go *Splat*?

How do objects react to forces?

FIGURE 5 ······························

▷ VIRTUAL LAB Splat! A bug has just flown into the windshield of an oncoming car. The car must have hit the bug much harder than the bug hit the car, right? ✎ **Apply Concepts** Use Newton's laws of motion to make sense of the situation and answer the questions.

A

Buzz!

In order for the bug to fly through the air, a force has to push the bug forward. Identify this force. How does the bug produce it? (*Hint:* Think back to how a swimmer moves through the water.)

_____

_____

_____

_____

_____

The bug was at rest on a tree when it saw the car and decided to fly toward it. If the bug has a mass of 0.05 kg and accelerates at 2 m/s², what's the net force on the bug?

_____

7.NS.3, 7.NS.8

10 - LG - SP

B
Vroom!

The driver hates killing bugs. When she saw one coming toward the windshield, she braked suddenly and hoped it would get out of the way. (Sadly, it did not.) When she hit the brakes, she felt that she was thrown forward. Use one of Newton's laws to explain why.

_____

_____

_____

_____

_____

C
Splat!

The unfortunate bug hits the windshield with a force of 1 N. If you call this the action force, what is the reaction force? Does the car hit the bug any harder than the bug hits the car? Use one of Newton's laws to explain why or why not.

_____

_____

_____

_____

_____

Compare the forces on the bug and the car again. Use another one of Newton's laws to explain why the bug goes *splat* and the car keeps going, without noticeably slowing down.

_____

_____

_____

_____

Lab zone Do the Quick Lab
Interpreting Illustrations.

Assess Your Understanding

2a. Identify A dog pulls on his leash with a 10-N force to the left, but doesn't move. Identify the reaction force.

_____

_____

_____

7.1.7

b. ANSWER THE BIG **?** Using all three of Newton's laws, explain how objects react to forces.

_____

_____

_____

_____

_____

_____

_____

_____

_____

_____

_____

_____

_____

7.1.7

got it?...

○ **I get it!** Now I know that Newton's third law of motion states that _____

_____

_____

_____

_____

○ **I need extra help with** _____

_____

_____

Go to MY SCIENCE ⓢ COACH *online for help with this subject.* 7.1.7

3 Study Guide

REVIEW THE BIG ?

Changes in motion are caused by _____. _____ laws describe these changes in motion.

LESSON 1 Describing Motion
7.1.7, 7.NS.3, 7.NS.5

🔑 An object is in motion if it changes position relative to a reference point.

Vocabulary
• motion
• reference point
• International System of Units
• distance

LESSON 2 Speed and Velocity
7.1.6, 7.1.7, 7.NS.1, 7.NS.8, 7.DP.9, 7.DP.10

🔑 To calculate the speed of an object, divide the distance the object travels by the amount of time it takes to travel the distance.

🔑 When you know both the speed and direction of an object's motion, you know the velocity of the object.

🔑 You can show the motion of an object on a line graph in which you plot distance versus time.

Vocabulary
• speed   • average speed
• instantaneous speed   • velocity   • slope

LESSON 3 Acceleration
7.1.7, 7.NS.1, 7.NS.8

🔑 In science, acceleration refers to increasing speed, decreasing speed, or changing direction.

Vocabulary
• acceleration

LESSON 4 The Nature of Force
7.1.5, 7.1.6, 7.1.7, 7.NS.8, 7.DP.10

🔑 Like velocity and acceleration, a force is described by its strength and by the direction in which it acts.

🔑 A nonzero net force causes a change in the object's motion.

Vocabulary
• force   • newton
• net force

LESSON 5 Friction and Gravity
7.1.5, 7.NS.1, 7.NS.2, 7.NS.4, 7.NS.8, 7.DP.9

🔑 Two factors that affect the force of friction are the types of surfaces involved and how hard the surfaces are pushed together.

🔑 Two factors affect the gravitational attraction between objects: their masses and distance.

Vocabulary
• friction   • sliding friction
• static friction   • fluid friction
• rolling friction   • gravity
• mass   • weight

LESSON 6 Newton's Laws of Motion
7.1.7, 7.NS.3, 7.NS.8

🔑 Objects at rest will remain at rest and objects moving at a constant velocity will continue moving at a constant velocity unless they are acted upon by nonzero net forces.

🔑 The acceleration of an object depends on its mass and on the net force acting on it.

🔑 If one object exerts a force on another object, then the second object exerts a force of equal strength in the opposite direction on the first object.

Vocabulary
• inertia

Review and Assessment

LESSON 1 **Describing Motion**

1. What is the SI unit of distance?

   a. foot   **b.** meter

   c. mile   **d.** kilometer

                                   7.NS.3

2. A change in position with respect to a

reference point is _____

                                   7.1.7

3. Classify Suppose you are in a train. List some objects that make good reference points to determine whether or not the train is moving.

_____

                                   7.1.7

Use the illustration to answer Questions 4 and 5.

4. Compare and Contrast Suppose you are standing on the sidewalk. Describe the direction of your motion relative to the car and the plane.

_____

_____

_____

                                   7.1.7

5. Compare and Contrast Suppose you are riding in the plane. Describe the direction of your motion relative to the person standing on the sidewalk and the car.

_____

_____

_____

_____

                                   7.1.7

LESSON 2 **Speed and Velocity**

6. What quantity can you calculate if you know that a car travels 30 kilometers in 20 minutes?

   a. average speed   **b.** direction

   c. velocity   **d.** instantaneous speed

                                   7.1.7

The graph shows the motion of a remote-control car. Use the graph to answer Questions 7 and 8.

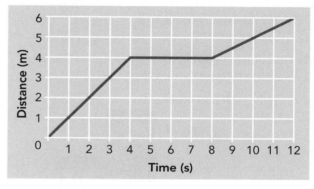

7. Read Graphs During which time period was the car moving the fastest?

_____

                                 7.1.7, 7.NS.8

8. Calculate What was the speed of the car during the first four seconds?

_____

_____

                                 7.1.7, 7.NS.8

LESSON 3 **Acceleration**

9. The rate at which velocity changes is

   a. acceleration.   **b.** direction.

   c. speed.   **d.** velocity.

                                   7.1.7

10. math! A ball is dropped from a window and takes 2 seconds to reach the ground. It starts from rest and reaches a final speed of 20 m/s. What is the ball's acceleration?

_____

_____

_____

                                 7.1.7, 7.NS.8

LESSON 4 **The Nature of Force**

11. When a nonzero net force acts on an object, the force

 a. changes the motion of the object.

 b. must be greater than the reaction force.

 c. does not change the motion of the object.

 d. is equal to the weight of the object.

7.1.5, 7.1.7

12. The SI unit of force is the _____

7.1.7

13. Calculate What is the net force on the box? Be sure to specify direction.

15 N

10 N

7.1.6, 7.NS.8

LESSON 5 **Friction and Gravity**

14. Friction always acts

 a. in the same direction as motion.

 b. opposite the direction of motion.

 c. perpendicular to the direction of motion.

 d. at a 30° angle to the direction of motion.

7.1.5

15. The factors that affect the gravitational force between two objects are _____

_____

7.1.5

16. List What are two ways you can increase the frictional force between two objects?

_____

_____

7.1.5

17. Write About It Design a ride for an amusement park. Describe the ride and explain how friction and gravity will affect the ride's design.

7.1.5, 7.NS.11

LESSON 6 **Newton's Laws of Motion**

18. Newton's second law states that force is equal

 to _____

7.1.7

19. Interpret Diagrams The friction force between the bag and the floor is 4 N. What is the net force acting on the bag? What is the acceleration of the bag?

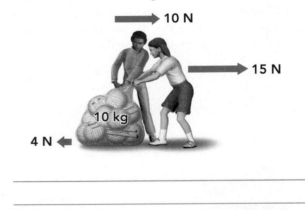

10 N

15 N

10 kg

4 N

_____

_____

_____

7.1.7, 7.NS.3, 7.NS.8

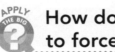 **How do objects react to forces?**

20. Forces are all around you. Describe an example of each of Newton's laws of motion that you experience before you get to school in the morning.

_____

_____

_____

_____

_____

_____

_____

_____

_____

_____

_____

7.1.5, 7.1.7

Indiana ISTEP+ Practice

Multiple Choice

Circle the letter of the best answer.

Force Force

Motion

1. In the balloon diagram above, why don't the two forces cancel each other out?

    A. They are not equal.

    B. They both act on the air.

    C. They both act on the balloon.

    D. They act on different objects.

    7.1.6

2. In a game of tug-of-war, you pull on the rope with a force of 100 N to the right and your friend pulls on the rope with a force of 100 N to the left. What is the net force on the rope?

    A. 200 N to the right

    B. 200 N to the left

    C. 0 N

    D. 100 N to the right

    7.1.6

3. What condition is necessary for an object to make a good reference point?

    A. The object is moving at a constant speed.

    B. The object is accelerating.

    C. The object is fixed relative to the motion you are trying to describe.

    D. The object is large.

    7.1.7

4. Two objects traveling at the same speed have different velocities if they

    A. start at different times.

    B. travel different distances.

    C. have different masses.

    D. move in different directions.

    7.1.6, 7.1.7

Constructed Response

Write your answer to Question 5 on the lines below.

5. Your family is driving to the beach. You travel 200 kilometers in the first two hours. During the next hour, you stop for lunch and only travel 25 kilometers. What was your average speed?

    _____

    _____

    7.1.7, 7.NS.3, 7.NS.8

Extended Response

Use your knowledge of science to help you answer Question 6. Write your answer on a separate sheet of paper.

6. Use all three of Newton's laws of motion to describe what happens when a car starts off at rest, is pushed across a platform, and then accelerates downward.

    7.1.7

Frontiers of Technology

A SAFER Race Track

▲ The SAFER barrier is made up of steel tubes welded together. Behind these tubes are stacks of foam, placed between the barrier and the concrete wall.

Imagine yourself being propelled through space and time at more than 320 km/h (200 mph)—surrounded by 20 other speeding cars. You realize you're headed straight for a concrete wall but there's no time to stop. Indy-car drivers have faced this scenario many times over the past 100 years, sometimes with tragic results.

In 2002, a new type of barrier was introduced at the Indianapolis 500. Instead of a hard concrete wall, a "soft wall" made of steel and polystyrene foam was placed between the track and the concrete. When a car hits the new Steel and Foam Energy Reduction (SAFER) barrier, the steel and foam work together to absorb some of the kinetic energy released by the impact. This protects the driver and gives other drivers additional time and space to avoid the wrecked car.

Design It Design a barrier that absorbs the energy from the impact of a moving object. Brainstorm potential solutions and select your best idea. Then build a prototype and evaluate it with different moving objects. Record data, such as how far the objects bounce back after colliding into the barrier. Graph your data and redesign your solution to improve it. See Appendix A on page 578 for more information about the design process.

7.1.1, 7.1.6, 7.NS.1–7.NS.11, 7.DP.1–7.DP.11

SUPERLUBRICITY

Get a Grip!

There is a substance that doesn't play by the rules of friction. You might be surprised to know it is graphite—the same material found in your pencils, and it has a quality called superlubricity!

When two pieces of graphite slide across each other, if the layers are properly arranged, friction almost disappears. This property makes graphite an excellent dry lubricant. Unlike oils and water- or silicon-based lubricants, graphite won't wet or damage the materials being lubricated.

Scientists are studying graphite because, while they can observe superlubricity, they still can't really describe how it works. Studies are being done to figure out the models of superlubricity, or how it works in different situations.

Test It Find more information about graphite and superlubricity. Design an experiment using lead (which contains graphite) from your pencils to test the friction of graphite sliding across other materials. Keep track of your results and present your findings in a series of graphs and charts.

7.NS.2, 7.NS.3, 7.NS.7, 7.NS.8, 7.NS.11

Colored scanning tunneling micrograph of the surface of graphite. The hexagonal pattern of the graphite surface is related to the way the carbon atoms are arranged. ▼

Graphite is a form of carbon. When it is properly prepared, two layers of graphite can slide across each other with almost no friction. ▶

125

WHAT
MIGHT THESE
COLORS
MEAN?

How is energy conserved in a transformation?

The image at the right is called a thermogram. A special camera measures the electromagnetic radiation of an object and creates a temperature "map." A thermographic camera can be used to find people in a fire, detect when a racehorse might be injured, and spot tumors in humans. By noticing excessive heat in motors, transformers, and pumps, the camera can detect equipment problems before they fail, saving millions of dollars.

Infer Since a thermogram shows temperature, what might the colors you see indicate?

_____

_____

_____

_____

> **UNTAMED SCIENCE** Watch the **Untamed Science** video to learn more about heat.

Energy and Energy Transfer

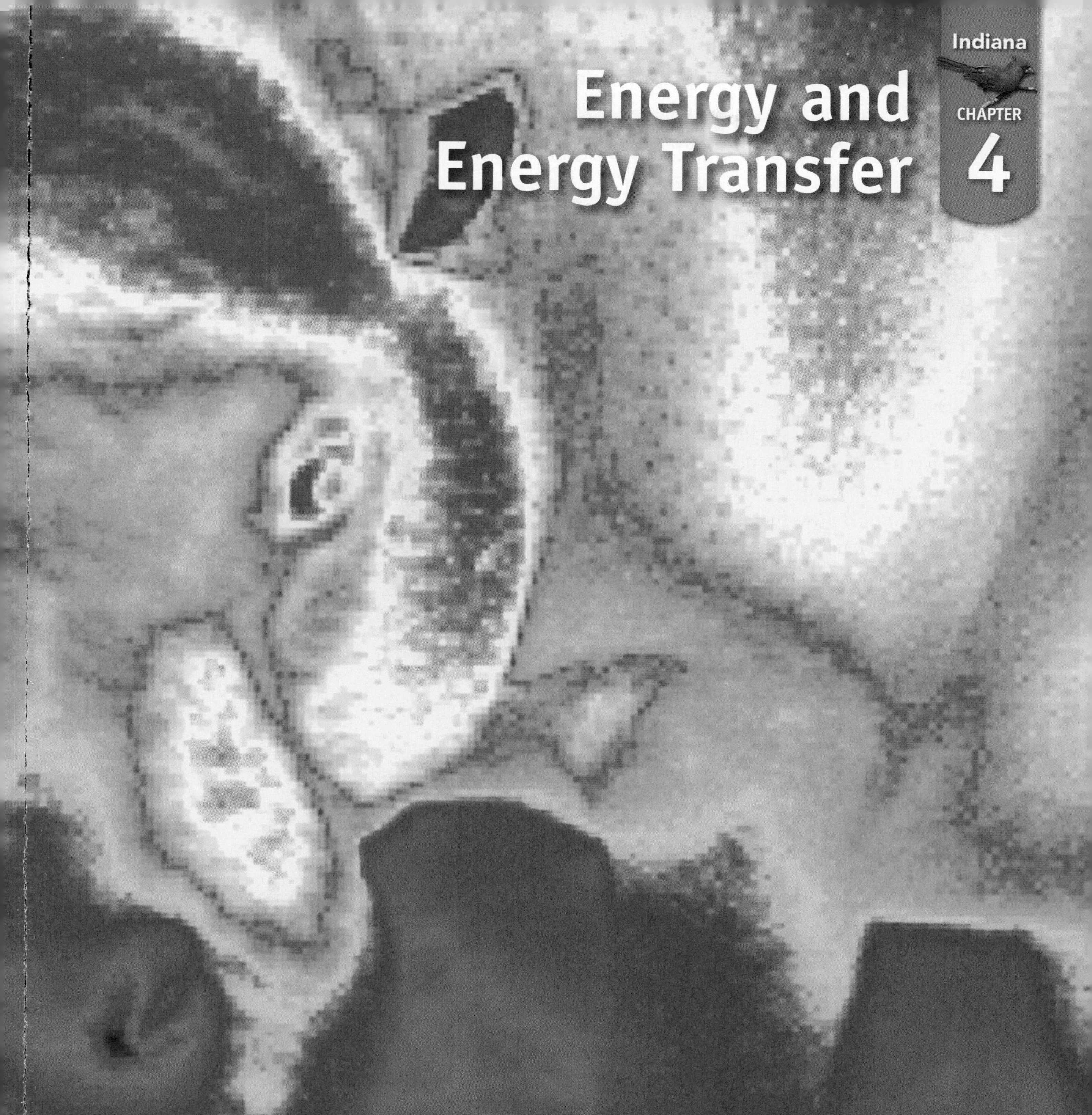

Academic Standards for Science

7.1, 7.1.1, 7.1.2, 7.1.4, 7.4.1, 7.4.2, 7.4.3, 7.4.4, 7.NS.1–7.NS.11, 7.DP.1–7.DP.11

4 Getting Started

Check Your Understanding

1. **Background** Read the paragraph below and then answer the question.

Kiera is swimming in the ocean. Since she is moving, she has **kinetic energy.** Energy is measured in **joules.** Her brother, who swims at the same speed but has more mass, has more kinetic energy. If he slows down, he will have the same amount of kinetic energy as Kiera. While swimming, she notices that it is easier to float in salt water because it has a higher **density** than fresh water.

Kinetic energy is energy an object has due to its motion.

A **joule** is a unit of work equal to one newton-meter.

Density is the ratio of the mass of a substance to its volume.

• What are the two ways you can increase kinetic energy?

_____

> **MY READING WEB** If you had trouble completing the question above, visit **My Reading Web** and type in *Energy and Energy Transfer.*

Vocabulary Skill

Identify Multiple Meanings Some words have several meanings. Words you use every day may have different meanings in science.

Word	Everyday Meaning	Scientific Meaning
friction	*n.* conflict or animosity **Example:** There was a good deal of *friction* between the two friends.	*n.* the force one surface exerts on another when they come into contact **Example:** *Friction* from the pavement can cause your car's tires to squeal.
heat	*v.* to make warm or hot **Example:** The fireplace began to *heat* the room.	*n.* thermal energy moving from a warmer object to a cooler object **Example:** Good insulation can prevent heat loss.

2. **Quick Check** Circle the sentence below that uses the scientific meaning of the word *friction.*
   • Yelling at your brother will only cause more *friction.*
   • The ball slowed to a stop because of *friction.*

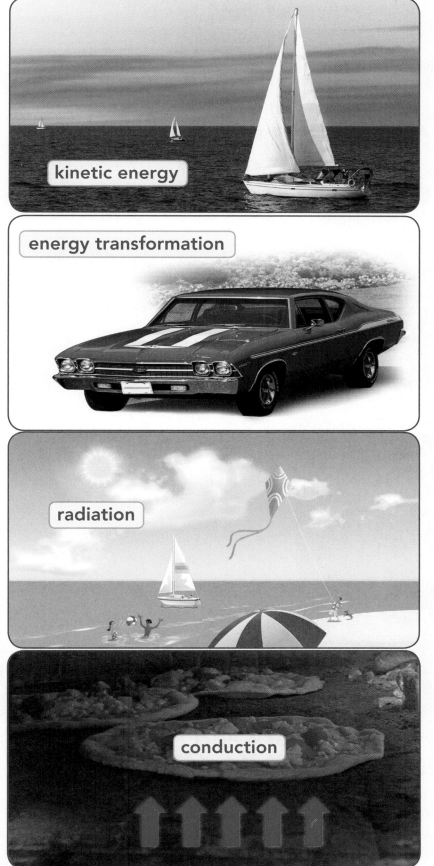

kinetic energy

energy transformation

radiation

conduction

Chapter Preview

LESSON 1
- energy
- power
- kinetic energy
- potential energy
- mechanical energy
- electrical energy
- electromagnetic energy
- nuclear energy
- chemical energy
- thermal energy

  Reading: Interpret Photographs
  Inquiry: Observe

LESSON 2
- energy transformation
- law of conservation of energy
- friction

  Reading: Relate Cause and Effect
  Inquiry: Classify

LESSON 3
- convection
- convection current
- radiation
- conduction

  Compare and Contrast
  Infer

> **VOCAB FLASH CARDS** For extra help with vocabulary, visit **Vocab Flash Cards** and type in *Energy and Energy Transfer.*

The Nature of Energy

UNLOCK
THE BIG
?

🔑 **How Are Work and Energy Related?**
7.1.1, 7.4.1, 7.4.2, 7.4.3, 7.NS.8

🔑 **What Are Some Forms of Energy?**
7.1.1, 7.4.2

MY PLANET DIARY
for Indiana

Blog

Posted by: Shelby

Location: Monrovia, Indiana

I was outside, it was a really sunny day, and I was jumping rope. Jumping rope takes a lot of energy. To get energy you need to eat. Energy is the ability to do work, and when you jump rope you are working to get your feet off the ground long enough to have the rope under you.

After a full day of jumping rope, man was I tired. I walked into the kitchen to get a nice, healthy snack. Then, I could go back outside.

Use your experience to answer the question.

Describe some of the ways you use energy during a typical day in your life.

_____

_____

_____

_____

_____

_____

_____

_____

> PLANET DIARY Go to **Planet Diary** to learn more about energy.

 Do the Inquiry Warm-Up *Pulling at an Angle*

Academic Standards for Science

7.1.1 Explain that when energy is transferred, the total quantity of energy does not change.

7.4.1 Understand that energy is the capacity to do work.

7.4.2 Explain that energy can be used to do work using many processes.

7.4.3 Explain that power is the rate that energy is converted from one form to another.

How Are Work and Energy Related?

Have you ever watched sailboats on a lake? They move across the water without an engine to power them. A sailboat moves because the wind pushes it. Wind is moving air, and because it is moving, wind has energy. **Energy** is the ability to do work or cause change.

Vocabulary
- energy • power • kinetic energy • potential energy
- mechanical energy • electrical energy • electromagnetic energy
- nuclear energy • chemical energy • thermal energy

Skills
- Reading: Interpret Photographs
- Inquiry: Observe

Work Work is done whenever a force exerted on an object makes the object move in the direction of the force. ⬤ **Work is the transfer of energy.** For example, moving air exerts a force on a sailboat, and the sailboat moves. The air does work on the sailboat. When this happens, some of the energy of the wind is transferred to the boat.

The amount of energy the wind has can vary. On some days, the wind blows faster. The wind can then transfer more energy to a sailboat, and the sailboat moves faster. On other days, the wind has less energy and the sailboat will move more slowly.

The moving sailboat has **kinetic energy**, the energy an object has because of its motion. The faster the sailboat moves, the more kinetic energy it has. Energy can also be stored. Stored energy is called **potential energy**. If the wind dies down, the sailboat's engine can be used to move the boat. Potential energy stored in the fuel becomes the kinetic energy of the moving boat.

Power is the rate that work is done. Since work is the transfer of energy, another way to say this is that power is the transfer of energy over time, or the rate that energy is converted from one form to another. Energy is typically measured in joules, so the unit for power is joules per second, or watts.

✎ **Interpret Photographs**
How can you tell that work is being done on the boats?

_____

_____

_____

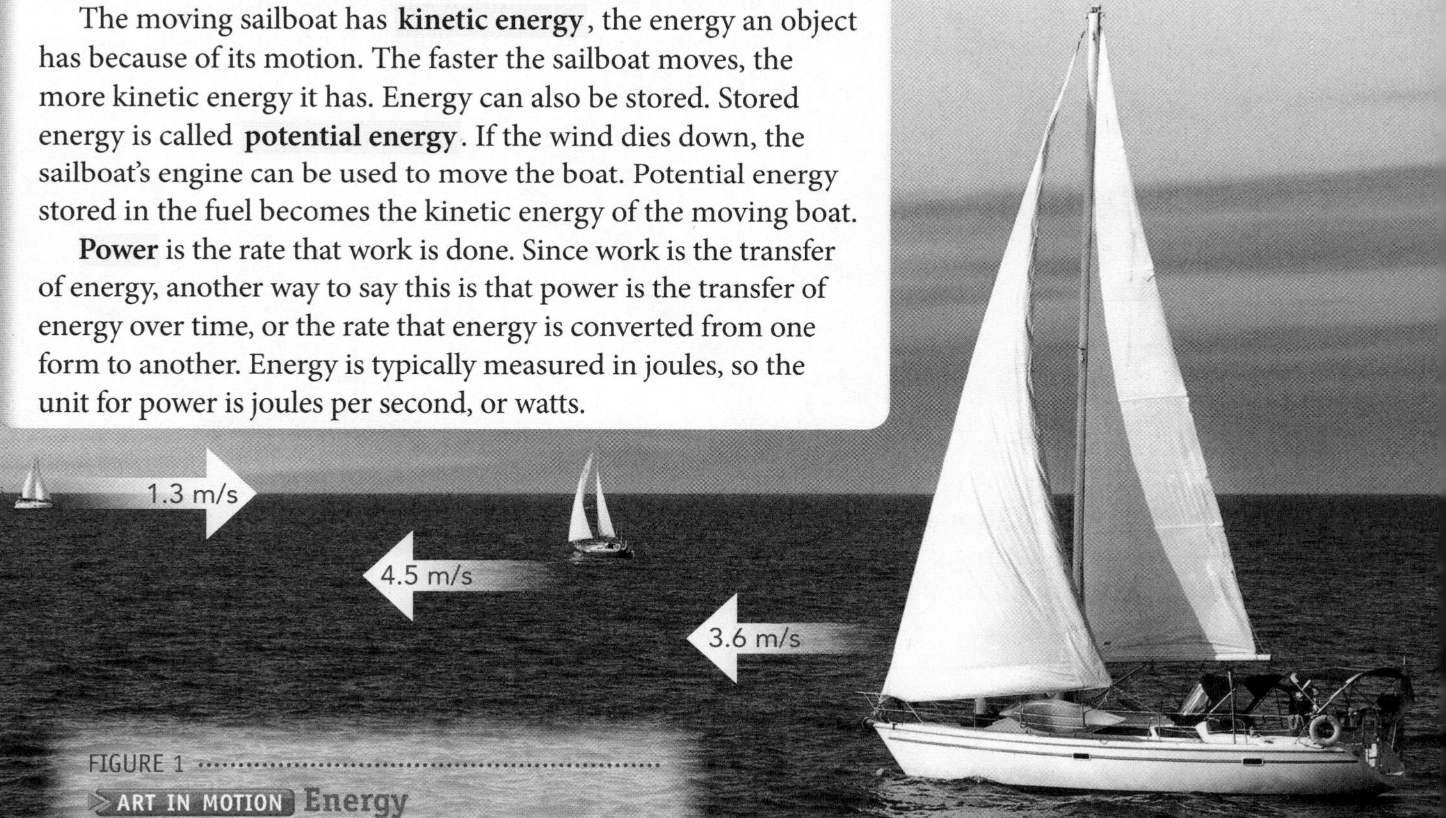

1.3 m/s

4.5 m/s

3.6 m/s

FIGURE 1 ....
▷ ART IN MOTION Energy
The wind pushes on the sails of a sailboat, transferring energy to the boat. Assuming the three boats are the same, draw a circle around the boat with the greatest kinetic energy. Draw a square around the boat with the least kinetic energy.

Mechanical Energy

An object's combined kinetic energy and potential energy is called mechanical energy.

Mechanical energy = Potential energy + Kinetic energy

Mechanical energy is the form of energy associated with an object's motion, position, or shape. For example, the diver shown in **Figure 2** has mechanical energy because he is moving and because of his height above the water. Like all forms of energy, an object with mechanical energy can do work. For example, the diver does work on the diving board when he jumps on it, causing it to bend. Then the diving board does work on the diver as it pushes him upward as it returns to its normal shape. He has both kinetic energy and potential energy.

A bicyclist moving along a flat path has a potential energy of zero relative to the ground. In that case, her mechanical energy equals her kinetic energy. A book sitting on a shelf is not moving, so its kinetic energy is zero. The book's mechanical energy equals its potential energy.

FIGURE 2 ·······

Mechanical Energy

A diver's kinetic and potential energy are constantly changing during a typical springboard dive.

✎ **Apply Concepts** For each point in the dive, complete the text or answer the question.

1 As the diver jumps to start his dive, he has kinetic energy. He also has (gravitational/elastic) potential energy because of his position above the water.

2 As the diver lands on the end of the board, he pushes down on the board, causing it to bend. The board has (gravitational/elastic) potential energy because its shape has changed.

Gravitational Potential Energy The mechanical energy of position, or gravitational potential energy, depends on an object's height relative to a reference point, such as the ground. The higher an object's position, the greater its gravitational potential energy.

Elastic Potential Energy Mechanical energy due to an object's shape is called elastic potential energy. When you push down on a spring, for example, you change its shape. An object that is compressed or stretched out of its normal shape has elastic potential energy. This energy is released when the spring returns to its original shape.

Lab zone® Do the Quick Lab *What Is Work?*

3 Calculate At the highest point in his dive, the diver has potential energy of 1400J and kinetic energy of 350J. What is the diver's mechanical energy?

_____
7.NS.8

4 Right before the diver hits the water, his (kinetic/potential) energy is at its highest.

🔑 **Assess Your Understanding**

1a. Compare and Contrast How are kinetic energy and potential energy different?

_____
_____
_____
7.1.1

b. Review A baseball has potential energy of 11J and kinetic energy of 30J. What is the ball's mechanical energy?

_____
_____
7.1.1

got it? ....

○ **I get it!** Now I know that work is the

_____ and mechanical energy is associated with an object's

_____

○ **I need extra help with** _____

Go to **MY SCIENCE** 🄢 **COACH** *online for help with this subject.* 7.1.1

133

Academic Standards for Science

7.1.1 Explain that when energy is transferred, the total quantity of energy does not change.

7.4.2 Explain that energy can be used to do work in many processes.

What Are Some Forms of Energy?

So far, you have learned that objects have kinetic and potential energy due to their motion, position, or shape. All objects are made up of tiny particles, invisible to the naked eye. Such particles have kinetic energy since they are constantly moving. Together, the particles also have potential energy as a result of their interactions. **Forms of energy associated with particles include electrical energy, nuclear energy, electromagnetic energy, thermal energy, and chemical energy.** All these forms of energy can be used to do work.

Electrical Energy

Electrical energy is the energy of electric charges. Stationary charges have potential energy. Moving charges have both kinetic energy and potential energy. Electrical energy runs computers, televisions, fans, toasters, and other appliances.

Nuclear Energy

Nuclear energy is potential energy stored in an atom's nucleus. Nuclear reactions in the sun produce sunlight. Other nuclear reactions generate electricity in nuclear power plants.

FIGURE 3

INTERACTIVE ART **Forms of Energy**

Classify Circle the different forms of energy and identify the type of energy for each example. Some examples may have more than one type of energy.

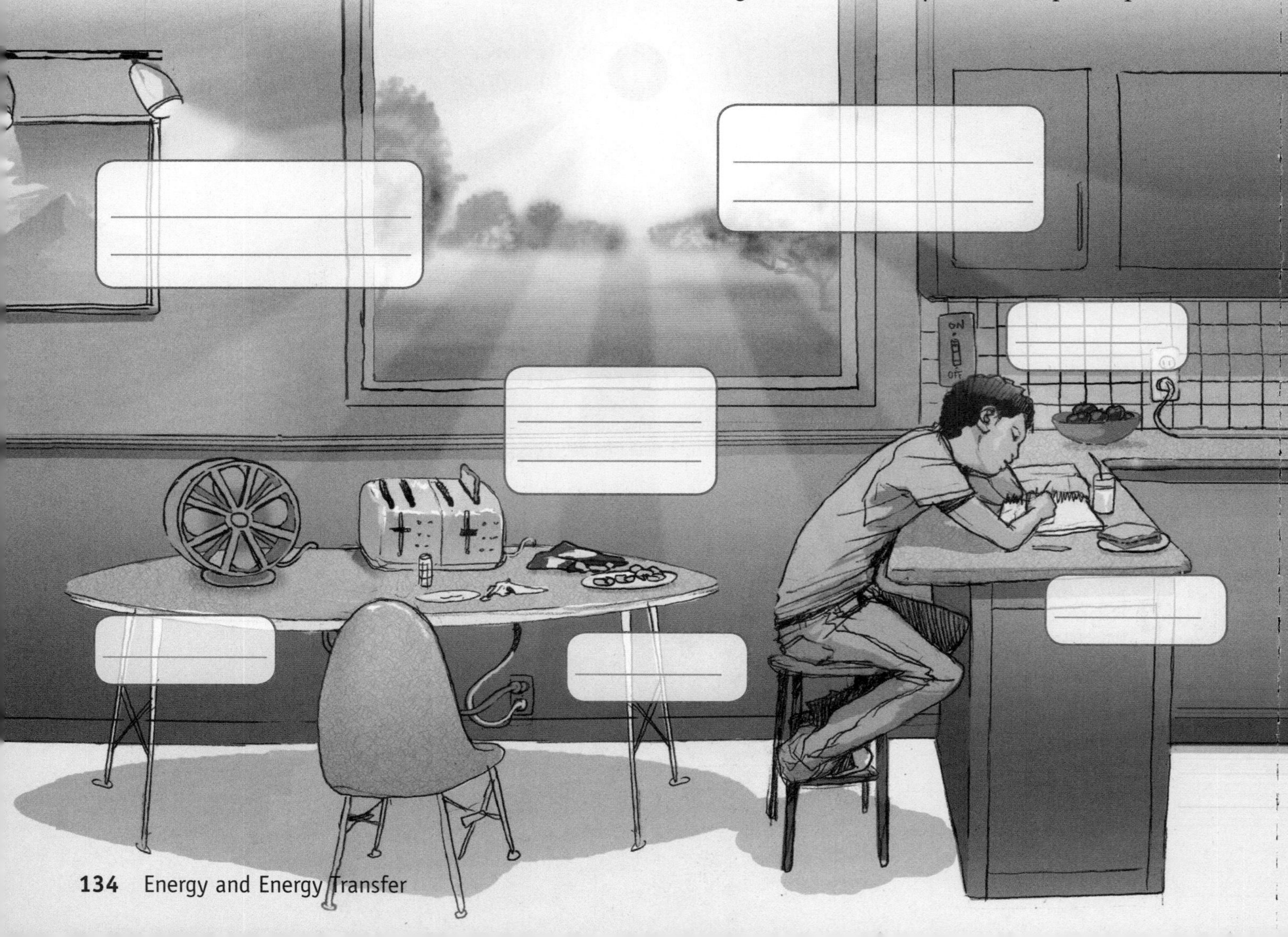

Electromagnetic Energy

Light is an example of **electromagnetic energy**, a form of energy that travels through space in waves. X-rays, radio waves, and microwaves are other examples of electromagnetic energy. The sun and stars give off electromagnetic energy.

Thermal Energy

Thermal energy is the total kinetic and potential energy of the particles within an object. These particles are always moving, so they have kinetic energy. The warmer an object is, the faster its particles move and the more kinetic energy it has. The way the particles are arranged gives them potential energy. So all matter has both kinetic and potential energy, even when at rest.

Chemical Energy

Chemical energy is potential energy stored in chemical bonds. This energy can be released during chemical reactions. When certain chemical bonds are broken, energy is released. The energy you use to move, think, and grow comes from chemical energy in the food you eat.

Lab ® **zone** Do the Quick Lab *Forms of Energy*

🔑 Assess Your Understanding

2a. How do chemical bonds produce energy?

_____

_____

_____

7.1.1

b. What is electromagnetic energy? Give two examples.

_____

_____

7.1.1

got it? ....

○ **I get it!** Now I know that forms of energy include _____

_____

_____

○ **I need extra help with** _____

Go to my science ⓢ coach *online for help with this subject.*

7.1.1

135

Energy Transformation and Conservation

LESSON 2

🔑 **What Happens When is Energy Transferred?**
7.1.1, 7.1.2, 7.4.3, 7.4.4, 7.NS.8

🔑 **How is Energy Conserved When it Is Transformed?**
7.1.1, 7.1.2, 7.4.4, 7.NS.11

UNLOCK THE BIG **?**

my pLaneT DiaRY
for Indiana

DISCOVERY

The Power of Steam

Did you know that before the invention and improvement of the steam engine during the Industrial Revolution, trains were actually pulled by horses?

Steam engines are a type of power system. They are powered by converting the chemical energy found in fuels like coal or wood to the mechanical energy of steam. These machines did everything from pumping water out of underground mines to weaving cloth. They were important in moving raw materials, products, and people thousands of miles from place to place.

At the Indiana Transportation Museum in Noblesville, you'll find a coal-burning steam locomotive named the NKP No. 587. It's one of the last coal-burning steam locomotives to be built and used in the United States.

Communicate Discuss the question with a group of classmates. Write your answer below.

How do you think a steam engine uses fuel to make steam?

_____

_____

_____

_____

_____

_____

> **PLANET DIARY** Go to **Planet Diary** to learn more about energy transformations.

Lab zone Do the Inquiry Warm-Up *Pendulum Swing*

During its 37-year run, NKP No.587 frequently stopped in Indianapolis on its way to Michigan City via Castleton and Noblesville. It was retired in March 1955.

NORFOLK STATE ROAD 587

Vocabulary
- energy transformation
- law of conservation of energy
- friction

Skills
- ⟳ Reading: Relate Cause and Effect
- △ Inquiry: Classify

What Happens When Energy Is Transferred?

A soccer ball sitting on the ground has no kinetic energy. After you kick the ball, it moves across the grass. The moving soccer ball has kinetic energy. Where did the ball get this energy?

Energy Transfers When you swing your foot toward the ball, your foot has kinetic energy. When you make contact with the ball, some of your kinetic energy moves to the ball. The ball gains kinetic energy and your foot loses kinetic energy. Energy is transferred when it moves from one object to another.

If you pour hot tea into a mug, the mug soon becomes warm. Thermal energy moves from the tea to the mug. When you hold the mug in your hands, you feel the warmth when thermal energy moves from the mug to your hands. If you leave the mug of tea sitting on a table for a while, the mug and the tea become cooler. They have less thermal energy. This energy is not lost, however. It is transferred from the tea and the mug to the air around them. **When energy is transferred from one object to another, the total quantity of energy does not change.**

Academic Standards for Science

7.1.1 Explain that when energy is transferred from one system to another, the total quantity of energy does not change.

7.1.2 Describe and give examples of how energy can be transferred from place to place and transformed from one form to another.

7.4.3 Explain that power is the rate that energy is converted from one form to another.

7.4.4 Explain that power systems are used to provide propulsion for engineered products and systems.

FIGURE 1 ···
Energy Transfer
Energy is needed to make things move.

✎ **Relate Cause and Effect**
Draw an arrow on the photograph to show the direction in which energy will be transferred. How will the transfer of energy affect the ball?

7.1.2, 7.NS.8

Lab zone Do the Quick Lab *Energy Transfer*

⟐ Assess Your Understanding

got it? ··

○ I get it! Now I know that when energy is transferred from one object to another, _____

_____

○ I need extra help with _____

Go to **my science** **COACH** *online for help with this subject.*

7.1.1

Academic Standards for Science

7.1.1 Explain that when energy is transferred from one system to another, the total quantity of energy does not change.

7.1.2 Describe and give examples of how energy can be transferred from place to place and transformed from one form to another through radiation, convection and conduction.

7.4.4 Explain that power systems are used to provide propulsion for engineered products and systems.

7.NS.11 Communicate findings using models.

How Is Energy Conserved During a Transformation?

All forms of energy can be transformed into other forms of energy. A change from one form of energy to another is called an **energy transformation**.

Transfers and Transformations An energy transformation is not the same as a transfer of energy. In a transfer of energy, there is no change in form. When a car is moving, mechanical energy is transferred from the car's engine (its power system) to its wheels. The energy does not change form. No transformation takes place. However, energy transformations occur inside the car's engine. Through a series of controlled explosions, the chemical energy in gasoline is transformed into the mechanical energy of moving pistons. This mechanical energy is used to provide propulsion that makes the car move.

Potential energy does not do any work because it cannot be transferred to another object. Potential energy changes only when it is transformed to kinetic energy.

You are a passenger in a car at night. Describe the energy transformations that are taking place to power the car's headlights.

_____

_____

_____

_____

_____

Kinetic and Potential Energy

Kinetic and Potential Energy You may know that one of the most common energy transformations is the transformation between kinetic and potential energy. For instance, when a rock falls off a cliff, potential energy is transformed to kinetic energy.

Figure 2 shows another transformation between kinetic and potential energy. When the toy plane's elastic band is straight (**A**), the propeller does not turn. As a result, the plane does not move. But if you turn the propeller, potential energy is stored in the coiled-up elastic band (**B**). When the propeller is released, the elastic band uncoils quickly. So the propeller turns (**C**). As it turns, the potential energy that was stored in the coils of the elastic band is transformed into the kinetic energy of the propeller. The plane flies.

FIGURE 2 ···

All Wound Up

You can think of the model plane shown below as a system. Energy transformations within the system help the plane to fly.

✎ **Classify** Circle the correct answer in the boxes below.

7.NS.11

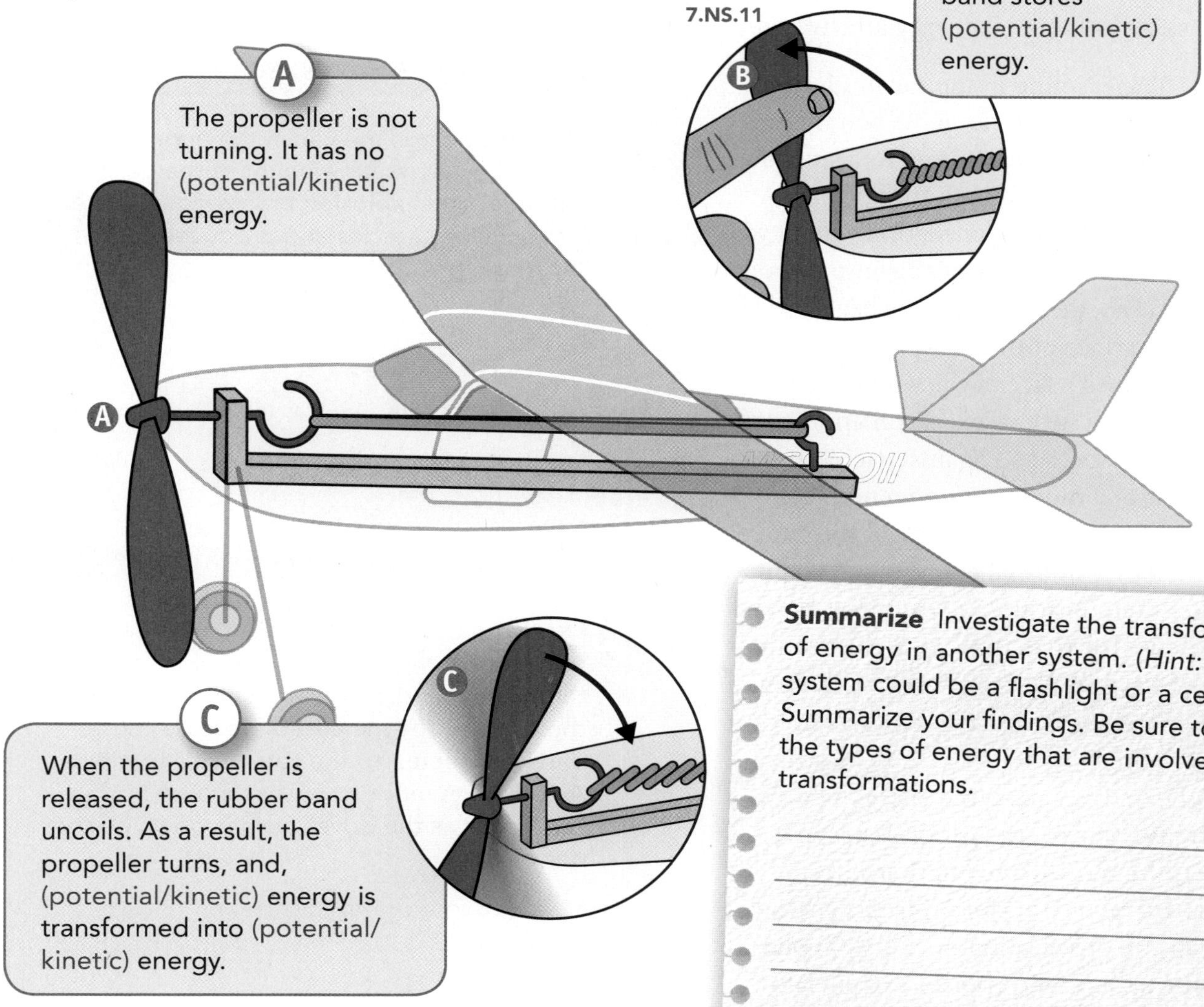

A The propeller is not turning. It has no (potential/kinetic) energy.

B The coiled rubber band stores (potential/kinetic) energy.

C When the propeller is released, the rubber band uncoils. As a result, the propeller turns, and, (potential/kinetic) energy is transformed into (potential/kinetic) energy.

Summarize Investigate the transformation of energy in another system. (*Hint:* Your system could be a flashlight or a cell phone.) Summarize your findings. Be sure to state the types of energy that are involved in your transformations.

_____

_____

_____

_____

_____

Energy Conservation Transformations in energy can make a toy plane fly. Does the plane fly forever? No, the toy plane does not fly forever. But that does not mean that energy is destroyed.

🔑 **In a closed system, as energy is transformed it is neither lost nor created. Rather, energy is conserved.** The scientific principle that energy is neither lost nor created during a transformation is called the **law of conservation of energy.**

Look at **Figure 4.** To show that energy is conserved in a system during a transformation, you would have to add the amounts of all the types of energy in the system before any energy transformation occurred. Then, you would have to add the amounts of each type of energy after all energy transformations were finished. You would find that the total energy before the transformations is the same as the total energy afterwards.

Friction The gasoline in the car in **Figure 3** has energy that makes the car go. When the car uses up the gasoline, the car comes to a stop. So what happened to the gasoline's energy?

To understand what happened, think about what happens when you rub sandpaper against a wooden surface. As you rub, the wood surface heats up. That is because the surface of the sandpaper is rubbing quickly against the surface of the wood. **Friction** is the force that one surface exerts on another surface when two surfaces rub against each other.

When parts of a moving system encounter friction, some of the kinetic energy of the system is transformed into thermal energy. As a result, parts of the system heat up. For example, as the car moves down the road, the car tires encounter friction from the surface of the road. As a result, the kinetic energy of the car decreases as friction heats the car's tires.

Although friction causes the energy of a system to decrease, this energy is not destroyed. As kinetic energy is transformed to thermal energy, the thermal energy is transferred to the surroundings. The law of conservation of energy applies to both transformations and transfers of energy.

✏️ **Summarize** In each step below, describe the energy transformations (if any) that take place in the gasoline. Then fill in the bars on each diagram to the right to show the relative amounts of energy from low to high.

1 The driver pumps the gas from the gas tank into the car.

_____

_____

_____

2 The driver starts the car. In the engine, a spark causes a small amount of the gas to explode. The explosion breaks down the fuel into smaller particles and produces heat in the engine.

_____

_____

_____

_____

3 Explosions continue to produce heat and break down the fuel. As it is broken down, the fuel expands, increasing pressure inside the engine. The increased pressure causes parts connected to the car wheels to move. As the parts move, the wheels turn. So the car moves as the driver pushes down on the gas pedal.

_____

_____

Places!

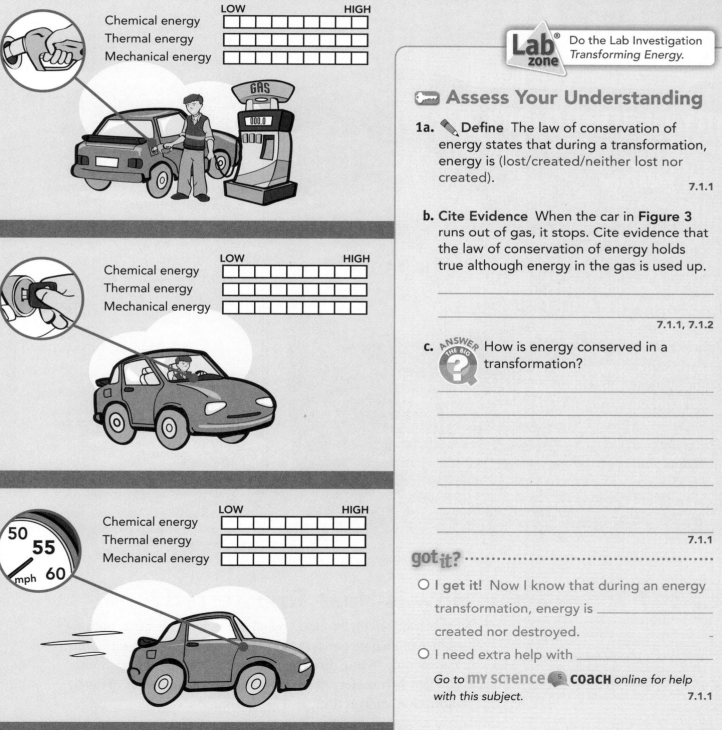

Chemical energy — LOW ☐☐☐☐☐☐☐☐☐☐ HIGH
Thermal energy — ☐☐☐☐☐☐☐☐☐☐
Mechanical energy — ☐☐☐☐☐☐☐☐☐☐

GAS
000.0

Chemical energy — LOW ☐☐☐☐☐☐☐☐☐☐ HIGH
Thermal energy — ☐☐☐☐☐☐☐☐☐☐
Mechanical energy — ☐☐☐☐☐☐☐☐☐☐

Chemical energy — LOW ☐☐☐☐☐☐☐☐☐☐ HIGH
Thermal energy — ☐☐☐☐☐☐☐☐☐☐
Mechanical energy — ☐☐☐☐☐☐☐☐☐☐

50 55 60 mph

How is energy conserved in a transformation?

FIGURE 3 ··

▷ VIRTUAL LAB The energy that is stored in gasoline can be transformed to make cars drive down roads. In the questions below, assume that all of the gasoline is burned in the car's engine.

Lab zone® Do the Lab Investigation *Transforming Energy.*

🔑 Assess Your Understanding

1a. ✎ **Define** The law of conservation of energy states that during a transformation, energy is (lost/created/neither lost nor created).

7.1.1

b. Cite Evidence When the car in **Figure 3** runs out of gas, it stops. Cite evidence that the law of conservation of energy holds true although energy in the gas is used up.

_____

_____

7.1.1, 7.1.2

c. ANSWER THE BIG **?** How is energy conserved in a transformation?

_____

_____

_____

_____

_____

_____

7.1.1

got it? ··

○ **I get it!** Now I know that during an energy

transformation, energy is _____

created nor destroyed.

○ **I need extra help with** _____

Go to **MY SCIENCE ⓢ COACH** *online for help with this subject.* 7.1.1

141

The Transfer of Heat

UNLOCK THE BIG ?

🔑 **How Is Heat Transferred?**

7.1.2, 7.NS.8, 7.NS.11

MY PLANET DIARY

DISASTER

Wild Weather

Hurricanes are intense storms that can cause billions of dollars in damage. These storms form when very warm, moist air rises quickly, creating an area of lower air pressure below. As the air rises, the water vapor in the air condenses, releasing a huge amount of thermal energy. This energy causes swirling winds, which draw in more warm water, feeding the storm. If a hurricane's path takes it over land, the storm can cause massive destruction. However, as the storm moves over land, its energy source—the warm ocean water—is depleted, and the storm eventually fizzles out.

Answer the question below.

Why do hurricanes tend to form in warmer climates?

_____

_____

_____

_____

_____

_____

_____

_____

> PLANET DIARY Go to **Planet Diary** to learn more about hurricanes.

Lab® zone Do the Inquiry Warm-Up *What Does It Mean to Heat Up?*

Academic Standards for Science

7.1.2 Describe and give examples of how energy can be transferred from place to place and transformed from one form to another through radiation, convection and conduction.

7.NS.8 Analyze data.

7.NS.11 Communicate findings using models.

How Is Heat Transferred?

Heat is transferring around you all the time. If it wasn't, nothing would ever change temperature. Heat doesn't transfer randomly. It travels only in one direction and by three different methods. 🔑 **Heat is transferred from warmer areas to cooler areas by conduction, convection, and radiation.**

Vocabulary
- convection
- radiation
- convection current
- conduction

Skills
- Reading: Compare and Contrast
- Inquiry: Infer

Convection

Convection is a type of heat transfer that occurs only in fluids, such as water and air. When air is heated, its particles speed up and move farther apart. This makes the heated air less dense. The heated air rises to float on top of the denser, cooler air. Cooler air flows into its place, heats up, and rises. Previously heated air cools down, sinks, and the cycle repeats. This flow creates a circular motion known as a **convection current.** Convection currents in air cause wind and weather changes.

Radiation

Radiation is the transfer of energy by electromagnetic waves. Radiation is the only form of heat transfer that does not require matter. You can feel the radiation from a fire without touching the flames. The sun's energy travels to Earth through 150 million kilometers of empty space.

Conduction

Conduction transfers heat from one particle of matter to another within an object or between two objects. The fast-moving particles in the floor of the oven collide with the slow-moving particles in the uncooked pizza. This causes the pizza's particles to move faster, making the pizza hotter.

FIGURE 1
Heat Transfer
A wood-fire pizza oven demonstrates three types of heat transfer.

✎ **Apply Concepts** Describe a heat transfer that occurs after the pizza comes out of the oven. What kind of transfer is it?

_____

_____

↻ **Compare and Contrast**
Circle statements on the previous page that describe what the different types of heat transfer have in common. Underline their differences on this page.

143

Where Does Heat Transfer on This Beach?

INTERACTIVE ART Heat transfer goes on all around you all the time, even on the beach. ✎ **Apply Concepts** Fill in the chart below to review the different types of heat transfer. Then, in the illustration, label at least one example of each type of heat transfer. Draw arrows to show how heat is being transferred in each example.

7.NS.11

Type of Heat Transfer	Explanation
Conduction	
Convection	
Radiation	

Lab zone Do the Quick Lab *Visualizing Convection Currents.*

🔑 Assess Your Understanding

1a. Classify What type of heat transfer occurs when eggs cook in a hot pan? Before toasters, people toasted bread by holding it over a fire. What type of heat transfer occurred then? Name the third type of heat transfer and an example of a food cooked by it.

_____

_____

7.1.2

b. Review How does heat flow from one object to another?

_____

_____

_____

_____

_____

7.1.2

got it? ....

○ **I get it!** Now I know that the three methods of heat transfer are _____

_____

○ **I need extra help with** _____

Go to **MY SCIENCE COACH** *online for help with this subject.*

7.1.2

145

The total amount of _____ is the same before and after any transformation.

LESSON 1 **The Nature of Energy**

7.1.1, 7.4.1, 7.4.2, 7.4.3, 7.NS.8

🔑 Work is the transfer of energy.

🔑 Forms of energy include mechanical energy, electrical energy, electromagnetic energy, nuclear energy, chemical energy, and thermal energy.

Vocabulary
- energy • power • kinetic energy • potential energy
- mechanical energy • electrical energy • electromagnetic energy
- nuclear energy • chemical energy • thermal energy

LESSON 2 **Energy Transformation and Conservation**

7.1.1, 7.1.2, 7.4.3, 7.4.4, 7.NS.8, 7.NS.11

🔑 When energy is transferred from one object to another, the total quantity of energy does not change.

🔑 In a closed system, as energy is transformed it is neither lost nor created. Rather, energy is conserved.

Vocabulary
- energy transformation
- law of conservation of energy • friction

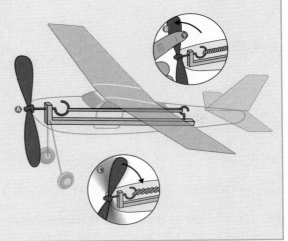

LESSON 3 **The Transfer of Heat**

7.1.2, 7.NS.8, 7.NS.11

🔑 Heat is transferred from warmer areas to cooler areas by conduction, convection, and radiation.

Vocabulary
- convection • convection current
- radiation • conduction

Review and Assessment

LESSON 1 The Nature of Energy

1. Which of these is the energy an object has because of its motion?

  a. kinetic energy.   **b.** nuclear energy.

  c. chemical energy.   **d.** thermal energy.

7.1.1

2. Visible light and x-rays are examples of

_____

7.1.1

3. Gravitational potential energy depends on an

object's _____

_____

7.1.1

4. How is the snowblower in this photo transferring energy?

_____

_____

_____

7.1.1

5. How can electric charges have kinetic energy and potential energy at some times and only potential energy at other times?

_____

_____

_____

_____

_____

7.1.1

LESSON 2 Energy Transformation and Conservation

6. What is the difference between an energy transfer and energy transformation?

_____

_____

_____

_____

_____

7.1.1

7. What is the law of conservation of energy?

_____

_____

_____

_____

_____

7.1.1

8. When light from the sun strikes a solar panel, the panel makes electricity. This is an example of transforming

  a. electromagnetic energy to thermal energy

  b. nuclear energy to chemical energy

  c. electrical energy to mechanical energy

  d. electromagnetic energy to electrical energy

7.1.2

9. Gears and other moving parts of a machine are greased to reduce friction. In terms of energy, explain why this is so important.

_____

_____

_____

_____

_____

_____

_____

_____

7.1.2

147

Review and Assessment

The Transfer of Heat

11. What is the process by which heat transfers from one particle of matter to another when the particles collide?

a. conduction   **b.** convection

c. expansion   **d.** radiation

7.1.2

12. A convection current is _____

_____

_____

7.1.2

13. Classify Identify each example of heat transfer as conduction, convection, or radiation: opening the windows in a hot room; a lizard basking in the sun; putting ice on a sprained ankle.

_____

_____

7.1.2

14. Infer How can heat be transferred across empty space? Explain your answer.

_____

_____

_____

7.1.2

15. Make Judgments Suppose you try to heat your home using a fireplace in one of the rooms. Would a fan be helpful? Explain.

_____

_____

_____

7.1.2

16.  **Write About It** Explain why a school might ask teachers to keep the windows closed and the shades down during a heat wave.

7.1.2, 7.NS.11

 How is energy conserved in a transformation?

17. Coal can be used to power a steam engine. First, coals are burned in a chamber. The heat produced as the coals burn cause water in a second, nearby chamber to boil and change to steam. The steam causes air in the chamber to expand, driving parts of the steam engine that turn the engine's wheels. As the wheels turn, the engine moves down the tracks. Explain how energy is conserved as coal in a steam engine makes the steam engine move.

_____

_____

_____

_____

_____

_____

_____

_____

_____

_____

_____

_____

7.1.1, 7.1.2

Indiana ISTEP+ Practice

Multiple Choice

Circle the letter of the best answer.

1. The table gives the kinetic and potential energy of a 10-kg dog doing various activities.

Activity	Kinetic Energy (J)	Potential Energy (J)
Running	250	0
Playing with a chew toy	10	150
Leaping	200	100
Napping	0	35

During which activity does the dog have the greatest mechanical energy?

A. running
B. playing with a chew toy
C. leaping
D. napping

7.1.1

2. _____ energy does not do any work because it cannot be transferred to another object.

A. potential
B. kinetic
C. mechanical
D. thermal

7.1.2

3. Which of the following statements is true?

A. Convection and conduction are the only two types of heat transfer.
B. Radiation does not require matter to transfer heat.
C. Conduction only occurs in fluids.
D. A hot frying pan cooks eggs through convection.

7.1.2

4. What is gravitational potential energy?

A. mechanical energy due to an object's shape
B. the energy an object has because of its motion
C. energy stored in chemical bonds
D. the mechanical energy of an object's position relative to a reference point

7.1.1

Constructed Response

Write your answer to Question 5 on the lines below.

5. What happens to the kinetic energy of a system as a result of friction?

_____

_____

_____

_____

7.1.1, 7.1.2

Extended Response

Write your answer to Question 6 on a separate sheet of paper.

6. How is energy being transferred in this image?

7.1.1

TECH & DESIGN

Museum of Science

CHARGE IT!

Have you ever noticed how many batteries you use every day? There are batteries in cars, flashlights, cell phones, laptop computers, and even bug zappers! Discarded batteries add up to a lot of waste. Fortunately, rechargeable batteries can help keep the energy flowing and reduce the number of batteries that get thrown out. Can you imagine how many nonrechargeable batteries a cell phone would go through in a month?

Batteries transform chemical energy into electrical energy. To refuel a rechargeable battery, you plug it into a power source—such as an outlet in the wall. The electrical energy reverses the chemical changes, storing the electrical energy as chemical energy. The battery is once again "charged up" and ready to go!

Research It Gasoline-powered cars and hybrid cars have rechargeable batteries. Research how the batteries in gasoline-powered cars and hybrid cars are recharged.

7.NS.2

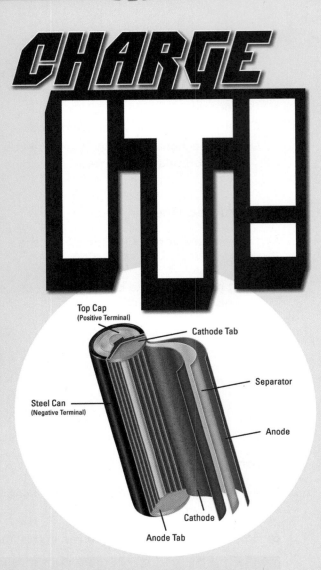

Top Cap
(Positive Terminal)

Cathode Tab

Separator

Steel Can
(Negative Terminal)

Anode

Cathode

Anode Tab

▲ The inside of this rechargeable battery has three long thin layers. A separator separates a positive electrode from a negative electrode. Using the battery causes lithium ions to move from the positive material to the negative one. Applying an electrical charge moves the ions back to the positive electrode.

Museum of Science®

CATCH AND NO RELEASE

A spider's web is more than just a sticky net hanging across an open space. The strong, elastic nature of spider silk ensures that an insect cannot leave once it strikes the web. To make their webs, spiders produce two kinds of silk—dragline silk and capture-spiral silk.

Dragline silk makes up the web's large frame. When an insect crashes into a spider's web, the dragline silk absorbs the force of impact and spreads it out over the entire area of the frame. No matter the mass or speed of the insect, the dragline silk is strong enough to absorb the force.

Capture-spiral silk is the sticky silk at the center of the web. It is more elastic than dragline silk so it stretches and then returns to its shape when an insect strikes it. As it stretches, it transforms the insect's kinetic energy into elastic potential energy. As a result, the insect slows down gradually and doesn't immediately bounce off the web. Once the insect comes to a stop, the stickiness of the capture-spiral thread keeps the prey from leaving.

Spider silk is only one-tenth the diameter of human hair, but it is very strong. In fact, a thread of spider silk can resist more force than a piece of steel of the same size!

Design It Design a spider web using string. First, brainstorm potential designs and document your ideas. Select a design and build a prototype. Then evaluate and test the strength of your design by adding weights until the web breaks. Record the data from your tests and use this information to redesign your prototype. See Appendix A on page 578 for more information about the design process.

7.1.1, 7.1.6, 7.NS.1–7.NS.11, 7.DP.1–7.DP.11

151

HOW CAN WIND KEEP YOUR LIGHTS ON?

What are some of Earth's energy sources?

This man is repairing a wind turbine at a wind farm in Texas. Most wind turbines are at least 30 meters off the ground where the winds are fast. Wind speed and blade length help determine the best way to capture the wind and turn it into power. **Develop Hypotheses** Why **do you think people are working to increase the amount of power we get from wind?**

_____

_____

_____

_____

_____

_____

▶ **UNTAMED SCIENCE** Watch the **Untamed Science** video to learn more about energy resources.

Energy Resources

Academic Standards for Science

7.1.3, 7.4.1, 7.4.2, 7.4.3, 7.NS.1–7.NS.11, 7.DP.1–7.DP.11

5 Getting Started

Check Your Understanding

1. Background Read the paragraph below and then answer the question.

Aisha loves visiting her grandmother at work. Her grandmother says that the building she works in was designed to help conserve **natural resources.** Most of the building's electricity comes from **renewable resources,** such as sunlight and wind, instead of from **nonrenewable resources,** such as oil or coal.

A **natural resource** is any material that occurs naturally in the environment and is used by people.

A **renewable resource** is either always available or is naturally replaced in a short time.

A **nonrenewable resource** is a resource that is not replaced within a useful time frame.

• What is one example of a natural resource?

_____

_____

▶ **MY READING WEB** If you had trouble completing the question above, visit **My Reading Web** and type in *Energy Resources.*

Vocabulary Skill

High-Use Academic Words High-use academic words are words that are used frequently in classrooms. Look for the words below as you read this chapter.

Word	Definition	Example
scarce	*adj.* rare; in limited supply	Tickets for the concert are becoming *scarce* because of the demand.
emit	*v.* to give off	When the oven is on, it *emits* heat, making the whole apartment warmer.

2. Quick Check Choose the word from the table above that best completes each sentence.

• Motor vehicles _____ chemicals that contribute to air pollution.

• As people continue to use oil faster than it can be replaced, it will become _____.

fossil fuel

solar energy

biomass fuel

energy conservation

Chapter Preview

LESSON 1
- fuel
- fossil fuel
- hydrocarbon
- petroleum
- refinery
- petrochemical

◉ **Summarize**
△ **Communicate**

LESSON 2
- solar energy
- hydroelectric power
- biomass fuel
- gasohol
- geothermal energy
- nuclear fission
- reactor vessel
- fuel rod
- control rod

◉ **Relate Cause and Effect**
△ **Infer**

LESSON 3
- efficiency
- insulation
- energy conservation

◉ **Identify the Main Idea**
△ **Observe**

▷ **VOCAB FLASH CARDS** For extra help with vocabulary, visit **Vocab Flash Cards** and type in **Energy Resources.**

Fossil Fuels

UNLOCK
THE BIG
?

🔑 **What Are the Three Major Fossil Fuels?**
7.1.3, 7.4.2, 7.4.4, 7.NS.8

🔑 **Why Are Fossil Fuels Nonrenewable Resources?**
7.1.3, 7.4.4, 7.NS.8

MY PLANET DiARY
for Indiana

TECHNOLOGY

Scratching the Surface

Mining coal is a tough job! Coal deposits are limited and usually located under deep layers of dirt and soil. When coal was first mined in Indiana in the 1830s, the only way to get to it was by digging dangerous underground tunnels. However, as technology developed, larger and more powerful land-moving machines allowed miners to remove or "strip" away the top layer of ground, exposing the coal. But even today, machinery has limitations. Indiana's miners are required to work deeper and deeper underground to reach what's left of coal deposits.

Communicate Discuss the question with a partner. Write your answer below.

Read the text and look at the chart. What is a possible explanation for the decrease in surface mining and increase in underground mining in recent years?

_____

_____

_____

_____

▷ PLANET DIARY Go to **Planet Diary** to learn more about fossil fuels.

Lab zone® Do the Inquiry Warm-Up *What's in a Piece of Coal?*

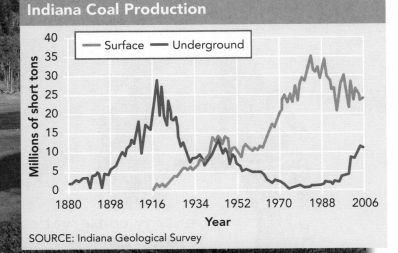

Indiana Coal Production

— Surface — Underground

Millions of short tons

40
35
30
25
20
15
10
5
0

1880 1898 1916 1934 1952 1970 1988 2006
Year

SOURCE: Indiana Geological Survey

Vocabulary
- fuel • fossil fuel • hydrocarbon
- petroleum • refinery
- petrochemical

Skills
- ↻ Reading: Summarize
- △ Inquiry: Communicate

What Are the Three Major Fossil Fuels?

Whether you travel in a car or a bus, walk, or ride your bike, you use some form of energy. The source of that energy is fuel. A **fuel** is a substance that provides energy, such as heat, light, motion, or electricity. This energy is the result of a chemical change.

Most of the energy used today comes from organisms that lived hundreds of millions of years ago. As these plants, animals, and other organisms died, their remains piled up. Layers of sand, rock, and mud buried the remains. Over time, heat and the pressure of the layers changed the remains into other substances. **Fossil fuels** are the energy-rich substances formed from the remains. ⊏⊐ **The three major fossil fuels are coal, oil, and natural gas.**

Fossil fuels are made of hydrocarbons. **Hydrocarbons** are chemical compounds that contain carbon and hydrogen atoms. When the fossil fuels are burned, the atoms react. They combine with oxygen to form new molecules. These reactions release energy in the forms of heat and light.

Burning fossil fuels provides more energy per kilogram than burning other fuels. One kilogram of coal, for example, can provide twice as much energy as one kilogram of wood. Oil and natural gas can provide three times as much energy as an equal mass of wood.

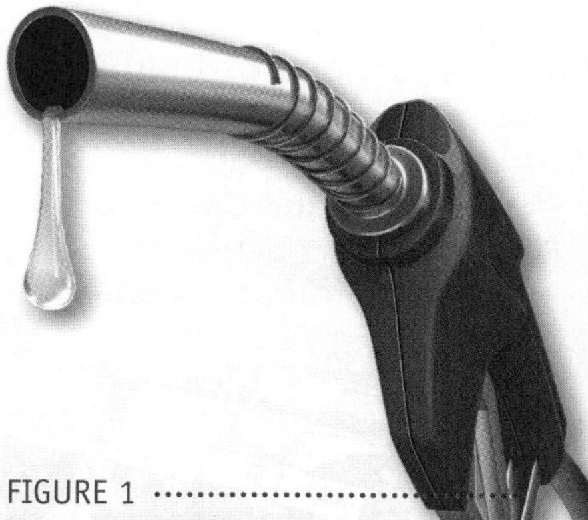

Academic Standards for Science

7.1.3 Recognize and explain how different ways of obtaining, transforming, and distributing energy have different environmental consequences.

7.4.2 Explain that energy can be used to do work using many processes.

7.4.4 Explain that power systems are used to provide propulsion for engineered products and systems.

7.NS.8 Analyze data.

FIGURE 1 ·····················

Fossil Fuels in Everyday Life
Fossil fuels have many common uses.

✎ **Identify** Fill in the chart with ways that you or other people use the three fossil fuels in daily life.

Fossil Fuel	Common Uses	Uses in Your Life
Coal	• Used to generate half of all U.S. electricity • Used to make products like fertilizer and medicine • When heated, used to make steel	
Oil	• As gasoline and diesel fuels, used to power vehicles • Used to heat homes • Used to make plastics and other petroleum products	
Natural gas	• Used to generate electricity • Used to cook food • Used to heat homes	

Coal People have burned coal to produce heat for thousands of years. For much of that time, wood was more convenient and cheaper than coal for most people. But during the 1800s, the huge energy needs of growing industries made it worthwhile to find, mine, and transport coal. Today, coal makes up about 22 percent of the fuel used in the United States. Most of that coal fuels electrical power plants.

Before coal can be used to produce energy, it has to be removed from the ground. Miners use machines to chop the coal into chunks and lift it to the surface. Coal mining can be a dangerous job. Thousands of miners have been killed or injured in mining accidents. Many more suffer from lung diseases. Fortunately, modern safety procedures and better equipment have made coal mining safer, although it is still very dangerous.

Coal is the most plentiful fossil fuel in the United States. It is fairly easy to transport and provides a lot of energy when burned. But coal also has some disadvantages. Coal mining can increase erosion. Runoff from coal mines can cause water pollution. Burning most types of coal results in more air pollution than using other fossil fuels. See **Figure 2**.

Figure 3 shows how plant remains build up over time and form coal.

FIGURE 2 ·····

Pros and Cons of Coal Use
Coal mining, shown above, is a dangerous job.

✎ **Compare and Contrast**
Fill in the chart below using information from the text.

Pros and Cons of Coal Use	
Pros	**Cons**

FIGURE 3 ··

Coal Formation
Coal formation takes millions of years.

Decomposing Plant Matter
When swamp plants die, their
decomposing remains build up.

Peat
Over time, plant remains pile up and
form peat. Peat can be burned as fuel.

Coal
Under increasing pressure from sediments,
peat is compacted. Eventually, peat becomes
coal. Coal is a more efficient fuel than peat.

✎

Summarize Explain the process
of coal formation in your own words.

_____

_____

_____

FIGURE 4 ·······················

> ART IN MOTION Oil Formation

Oil is formed in a process similar to coal.

🖎 **Interpret Diagrams** Use what you know to fill in the steps of oil formation in the diagrams below.

300–400 million years ago

_____

_____

_____

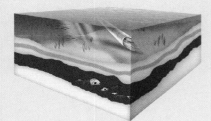

50–100 million years ago

_____

_____

_____

Today

_____

_____

_____

_____

Oil Oil is a thick, black, liquid fossil fuel. It formed from the remains of small animals, algae, and other organisms that lived in oceans and shallow inland seas hundreds of millions of years ago. **Petroleum** is another name for oil. Petroleum comes from the Latin words *petra* (rock) and *oleum* (oil). Petroleum accounts for more than one third of the energy produced in the world. Fuel for most cars, airplanes, trains, and ships comes from petroleum. Many homes are heated by oil as well.

Most oil deposits are located underground in tiny holes in sandstone or limestone. **Figure 4** shows how oil is formed. The oil fills the holes somewhat like the way water fills the holes of a sponge. Because oil deposits are usually located deep below the surface, finding oil is difficult. Scientists can use sound waves to test an area for oil. Even using this technique, scientists may not always locate wells that will produce a usable amount of oil.

FIGURE 5 ·······················

Oil Pipeline

Workers build an oil pipeline in Russia.

7.NS.8

When oil is first pumped out of the ground, it is called crude oil. To be made into useful products, crude oil must undergo a process called refining. A factory in which crude oil is heated and separated into fuels and other products is called a **refinery.** Many of the products that you use every day are made from crude oil. **Petrochemicals** are compounds that are made from oil. Petrochemicals are used to make plastics, paints, medicines, and cosmetics.

apply it!

Over 2,500 species of plants and animals live in Lake Baikal, in Russia. Eighty percent of these species live nowhere else on Earth. One of those species is the Baikal seal—one of only three freshwater seal species on Earth. The seal and other species were threatened when oil companies planned to build the world's longest oil pipeline within 800 meters of the lake's shore. The pipe-line would bring oil from Russia's interior to China and ports along the Pacific Ocean. Citizens were concerned that oil leaks and spills would damage the lake. They worked together to convince the oil companies to move the pipeline 40 kilometers to the north. The design of the new pipeline protects the lake and also delivers oil to places that need it.

Communicate An oil pipeline is proposed in your area near a body of water you think is important. Using Lake Baikal as an example, write a letter to the editor of your local paper explaining what you think should be done about the pipeline and why. Give your letter a headline.

_____
_____
_____
_____
_____
_____
_____
_____
_____
_____
_____
_____
_____
_____
_____
_____

Natural Gas Natural gas is a mixture of methane and other gases. Natural gas forms from some of the same organisms as oil. Because it is less dense than oil, natural gas often rises above an oil deposit, forming a pocket of gas in the rock.

Pipelines transport natural gas from its source to the places where it is used. If all the gas pipelines in the United States were connected, they would reach to the moon and back—three times! Natural gas can also be compressed into a liquid and stored in tanks as fuel for trucks and buses.

Natural gas has several benefits. It produces large amounts of energy, but has lower levels of many air pollutants compared to coal or oil. It is also easy to transport once pipelines are built. One cost of natural gas is that it is highly flammable. A gas leak can cause explosions and fires. If you use natural gas in your home, you probably are familiar with the "gas" smell alerting you when there is unburned gas in the air. You may be surprised to learn that natural gas actually has no odor. What causes the strong smell? Gas companies add a chemical with a distinct smell to the gas so that people can detect a gas leak.

FIGURE 6 ·····························
Natural Gas
A gas-top burner uses natural gas to cook food.
✎ **Analyze Costs and Benefits** Fill in the boxes with some costs and benefits of natural gas.

Costs of Natural Gas	Benefits of Natural Gas
_____	_____
_____	_____
_____	_____
_____	_____
_____	_____
_____	_____

Lab ® Do the Quick Lab *Observing Oil's Consistency.*
zone

🗝 Assess Your Understanding

1a. Define What are petrochemicals?

_____
_____
_____

7.1.3

b. Make Judgments Should the federal government decide where to build oil or natural gas pipelines? Explain.

_____
_____
_____

7.1.3

got‍it? ·······························

○ **I get it!** Now I know that the three major fossil fuels are_____

○ **I need extra help with** _____

Go to **MY SCIENCE COACH** online for help with this subject.

7.1.3, 7.4.2

Why Are Fossil Fuels Nonrenewable Resources?

The many advantages of using fossil fuels as an energy source have made them essential to modern life. 🔑 **Since fossil fuels take hundreds of millions of years to form, they are considered nonrenewable resources.** Earth's known oil reserves, or the amount of oil that can currently be used, took 500 million years to form. Fossil fuels will run out if they are used faster than they are formed.

Many nations that consume large amounts of fossil fuels have very small reserves or supplies. They have to buy oil, natural gas, and coal from nations with large supplies to make up the difference. The United States, for example, uses about one quarter of all the oil produced in the world. But only two percent of the world's oil supply is located in this country. The uneven distribution of fossil fuel reserves has often been a cause of political problems in the world.

Academic Standards for Science

7.1.3 Recognize and explain how different ways of obtaining, transforming, and distributing energy have different environmental consequences.

7.NS.8 Analyze data, using appropriate mathematical manipulation as required, and use it to identify patterns and make inferences based on these patterns.

do the math!

Use the graph to answer the questions below.

1 Read Graphs Which energy source generates the most electricity in the United States? _____

2 Calculate What percentage of the fuels in the graph are fossil fuels? _____

3 CHALLENGE How might this graph look in 50 years? Give reasons to support your answer. _____

_____

_____

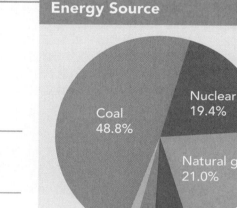

Recent Electricity Production in the United States by Energy Source

Coal 48.8%

Nuclear 19.4%

Natural gas 21.0%

Petroleum 1.6%

Other 3.2%

Hydroelectric 6.0%

7.NS.8

Lab zone®   Do the Quick Lab *Fossil Fuels.*

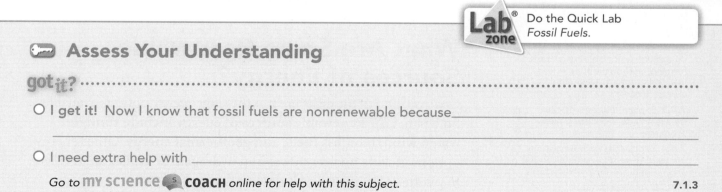

🔑 **Assess Your Understanding**

got it? ....

○ **I get it!** Now I know that fossil fuels are nonrenewable because_____

_____

○ **I need extra help with** _____

Go to **my SCIENCE** ○ **COACH** *online for help with this subject.*   7.1.3

Renewable Sources of Energy

UNLOCK THE BIG ?

🔑 **What Are Some Renewable Sources of Energy?**
7.1.3, 7.4.2, 7.4.4, 7.NS.8

🔑 **How Does a Nuclear Power Plant Produce Electricity?**
7.1.3, 7.4.2, 7.4.4

my pLaneT DiaRY

An Unlikely Decision

T. Boone Pickens's family taught him the value of hard work during the Great Depression of the 1930s. At 11, he delivered newspapers. By 26, he founded his own oil and gas company and became rich. In 2007, T. Boone Pickens surprised everyone by announcing plans to build the world's largest wind farm. He insisted the country must replace oil with wind and solar power. Even though he still promotes oil, he was one of the first oil businessmen to admit a change was needed. "I've been an oil man all my life," Pickens said, "but this is one emergency we can't drill our way out of."

BIOGRAPHY

Communicate Discuss these questions with a group of classmates. Write your answers below.

1. Why do you think Pickens's decision was so surprising?

_____

_____

2. Do you think more focus should be put on finding sources of energy other than oil? Why or why not?

_____

_____

> PLANET DIARY Go to **Planet Diary** to learn more about renewable energy.

Lab zone Do the Inquiry Warm-Up
Can You Capture Solar Energy?

Academic Standards for Science

7.1.3 Recognize and explain how different ways of obtaining, transforming, and distributing energy have different environmental consequences.

7.4.2 Explain that energy can be used to do work using many processes.

7.4.4 Explain that power systems are used to provide propulsion for engineered products and systems.

7.NS.8 Analyze data.

What Are Some Renewable Sources of Energy?

Coal, oil, and natural gas are not the only energy options available on Earth. 🔑 **Renewable sources of energy include sunlight, water, wind, biomass fuels, and geothermal energy.** Other energy options include nuclear power and hydrogen. Scientists are trying to put these energy sources to work.

Vocabulary

- solar energy
- hydroelectric power
- biomass fuel
- gasohol
- geothermal energy
- nuclear fission
- reactor vessel
- fuel rod
- control rod

Skills

- Reading: Relate Cause and Effect
- Inquiry: Infer

Solar Energy

The warmth you feel on a sunny day is **solar energy,** or energy from the sun. The sun constantly gives off energy in the forms of light and heat. Solar energy is the source, directly or indirectly, of most other renewable energy resources. In one hour, Earth receives enough solar energy to meet the energy needs of the world for an entire year. Solar energy does not cause pollution. It will not run out for billions of years.

So why hasn't solar energy replaced energy from fossil fuels? One reason is that solar energy is only available when the sun is shining. Another problem is that the energy Earth receives from the sun is very spread out. To obtain a useful amount of power, it is necessary to collect solar energy from a large area.

Solar Power Plants One way to capture the sun's energy involves using giant mirrors. In a solar power plant, rows of mirrors focus the sun's rays to heat a tank of water. The water boils. This creates steam. The steam can then be used to generate electricity.

Solar Cells Solar energy can be converted directly into electricity in a solar cell. When light hits the cell, an electric current is produced. Solar cells power some calculators, lights, and other small devices.

Relate Cause and Effect
Underline one way solar energy is collected and circle the way it is used.

did you know?

Photovoltaic cells, or solar cells, are named for the Greek word for light, *photo,* and electricity pioneer Alessandro Volta.

FIGURE 1 ········

Everyday Solar Power

Many objects, including calculators, street lights, and even backpacks that charge electronic devices, can be powered by the sun.

✎ **Describe** What object in your everyday life would you like to run on solar power? Would you want the sun to be its only power source? Why?

_____

_____

_____

_____

_____

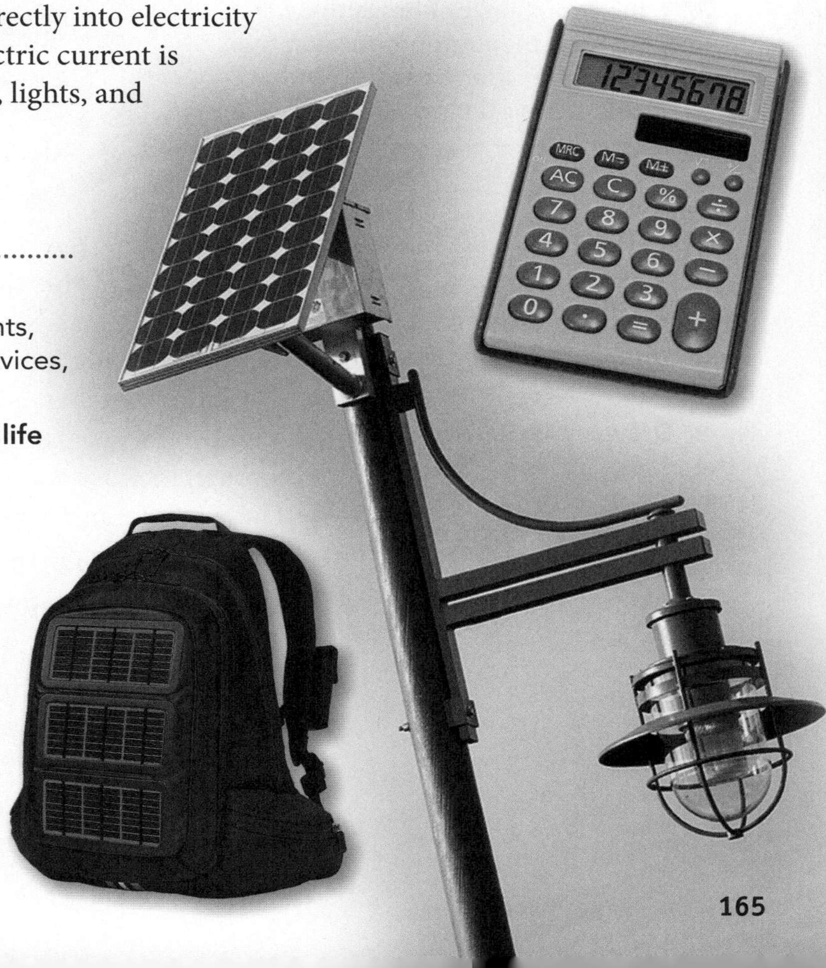

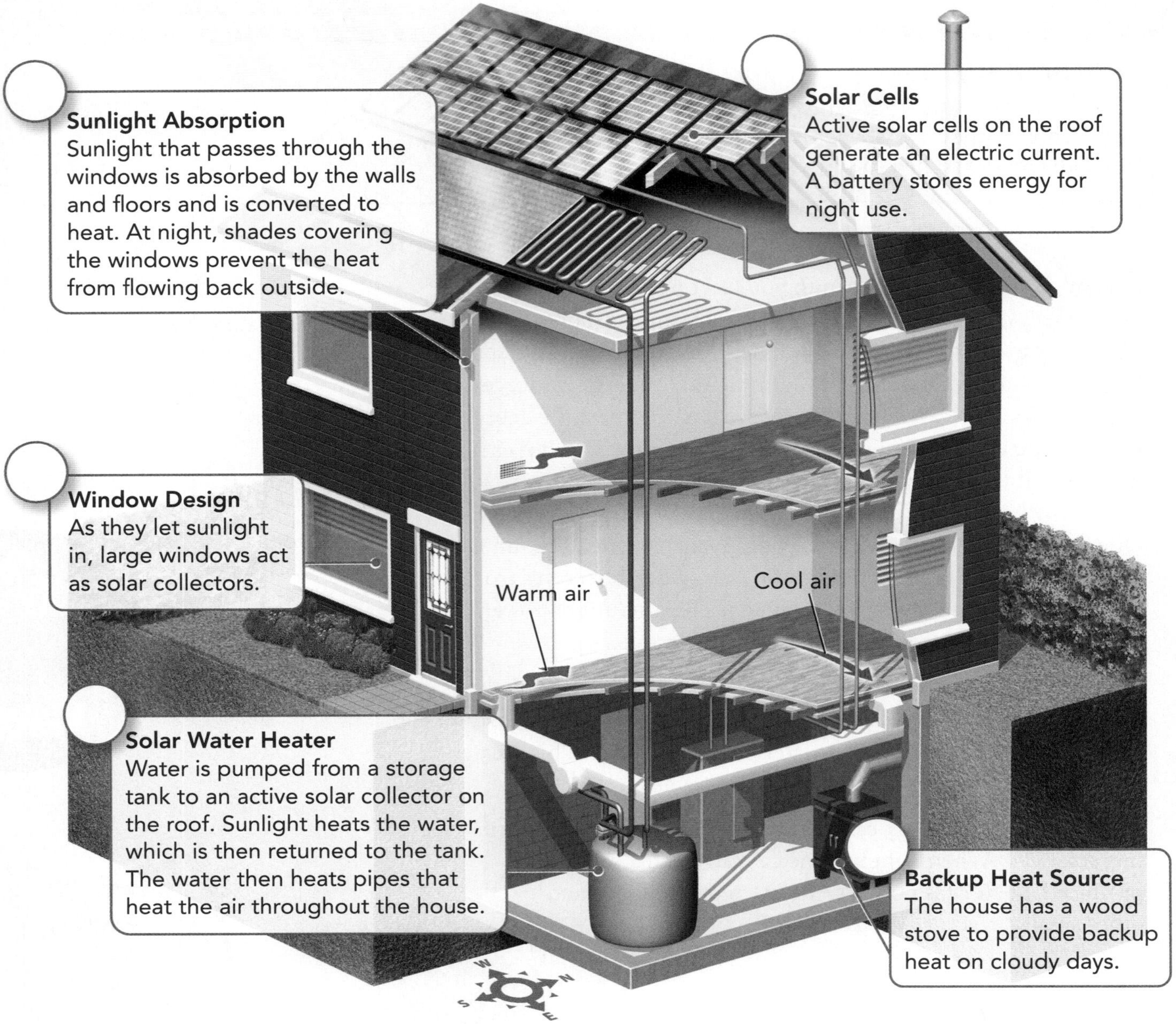

Sunlight Absorption
Sunlight that passes through the windows is absorbed by the walls and floors and is converted to heat. At night, shades covering the windows prevent the heat from flowing back outside.

Solar Cells
Active solar cells on the roof generate an electric current. A battery stores energy for night use.

Window Design
As they let sunlight in, large windows act as solar collectors.

Warm air

Cool air

Solar Water Heater
Water is pumped from a storage tank to an active solar collector on the roof. Sunlight heats the water, which is then returned to the tank. The water then heats pipes that heat the air throughout the house.

Backup Heat Source
The house has a wood stove to provide backup heat on cloudy days.

FIGURE 2 ·······································

Solar-Powered House
This house takes advantage of active and passive solar heating.

⚠**Infer** Draw a checkmark in the blank circles on the passive sources of solar energy. Draw a star in the blank circles on the active sources.

Passive Solar Heating Solar energy can be used to heat buildings with passive solar systems. A passive solar system converts sunlight into heat, or thermal energy. The heat is then distributed without using pumps or fans. Passive solar heating is what occurs in a parked car on a sunny day. Solar energy passes through the car's windows and heats the seats and other car parts. These parts transfer heat to the air, warming the inside of the car. The same principle can be used to heat a home.

Active Solar Heating An active solar system captures the sun's energy, and then uses pumps and fans to distribute the heat. First, light strikes the dark metal surface of a solar collector. There, it is converted to thermal energy. Water is pumped through pipes in the solar collector to absorb the thermal energy. The heated water then flows to a storage tank. Finally, pumps and fans distribute the heat throughout the building. Refer to **Figure 2.**

Hydroelectric Power
Solar energy is the indirect source of water power. In the water cycle, energy from the sun heats water on Earth's surface. The heat turns the water into water vapor. The vapor condenses and falls back to Earth as rain, sleet, hail, or snow. As the water flows over land, it provides another source of energy.

Hydroelectric power is electricity produced by flowing water. A dam across a river blocks the flow of water, creating a body of water called a reservoir. When a dam's gates are opened, water flows through tunnels at the bottom of the dam. As the water moves through the tunnels, it turns turbines (like a fan's blades). The turbines are connected to a generator. Once a dam is built, generating electricity is inexpensive. But dams can prevent some fish species from breeding. They can also damage aquatic habitats.

Capturing the Wind
Like water power, wind energy is also an indirect form of solar energy. The sun heats Earth's surface unevenly. As a result, different areas of the atmosphere have different temperatures and air pressures. The differences in pressure cause winds to form as air moves from one area to another.

Wind can be used to turn a turbine and generate electricity. Wind farms consist of many wind turbines. Together, the wind turbines generate large amounts of power. Wind is the fastest-growing energy source in the world. Wind energy does not cause pollution. In places where fuels are difficult to transport, wind energy is the major source of power if it is available.

Nuclear Power
Like water and wind power, nuclear power does not produce air pollution since no fuel is burned. Instead, the energy released from the splitting of atoms is used to create steam that turns turbines. This process can be dangerous and even cause explosions if too much energy is released. Wastes generated by nuclear plants can be dangerous if disposed of improperly.

FIGURE 3 ·······················
Hydroelectric and Wind Power
Hydroelectric and wind power do not rely on fossil fuels.
✎ **Compare and Contrast**
List similarities and differences between water and wind power in the Venn diagram.

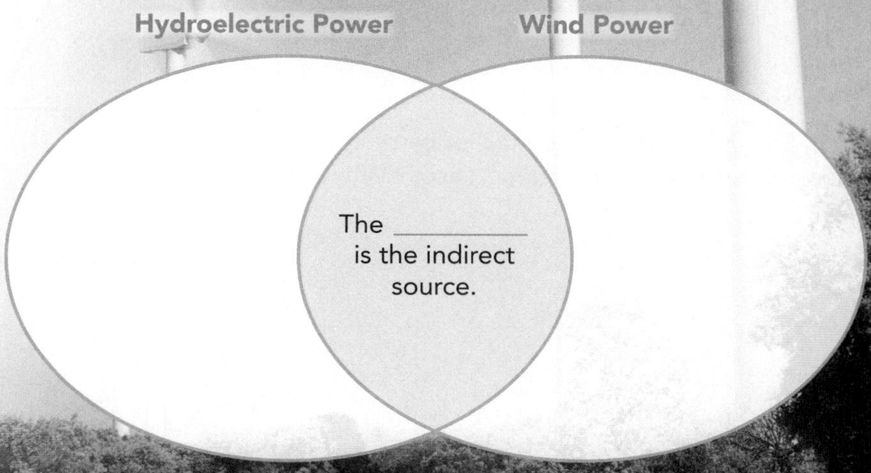

Hydroelectric Power

Wind Power

The _____ is the indirect source.

167

Biomass Fuels

Wood was probably the first fuel ever used for heat and light. Wood belongs to a group of fuels called **biomass fuels.** Biomass fuels are made from living things. Other biomass fuels include leaves, food wastes, and even manure. As fossil fuel supplies shrink, people are taking a closer look at biomass fuels. For example, when oil prices rose in the early 1970s, Hawaiian farmers began burning sugar cane wastes to generate electricity.

In addition to being burned as fuel, biomass materials can be converted into other fuels. For example, corn, sugar cane, and other crops can be used to make alcohol. Adding alcohol to gasoline forms **gasohol.** Gasohol can be used as fuel for cars. Bacteria can produce methane gas by decomposing biomass materials in landfills. That methane can be used to heat buildings. And some crops, such as soybeans, can produce oil. The oil can be used as fuel, which is called biodiesel fuel.

Biomass fuels are renewable resources. But it takes time for new trees to replace those that have been cut down. And it is expensive to produce alcohol and methane in large quantities. As a result, biomass fuels are not widely used today in the United States. But as fossil fuels become scarcer, biomass fuels may provide another source for meeting energy needs.

FIGURE 4 ·····················

Corn Power
Biomass fuels come from living things, such as corn. It takes about 11.84 kilograms of corn to make one gallon of fuel!

apply it!

What can happen when a food crop is used for fuel? The relationship is plotted with two curves on the graph.

❶ **Interpret Graphs** According to the graph, as demand for corn increases, what happens to the supply?

_____

❷ **CHALLENGE** How would the price of corn change as demand for fuel increases? Why?

_____
_____
_____
_____

7.NS.8

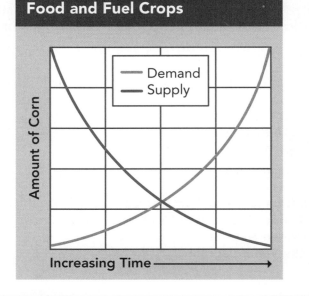

Supply and Demand for Food and Fuel Crops

- Demand
- Supply

Amount of Corn

Increasing Time ⟶

Tapping Earth's Energy

Below Earth's surface are pockets of very hot liquid rock called magma. In some places, magma is very close to the surface. The intense heat from Earth's interior that warms the magma is called **geothermal energy.**

In certain regions, such as Iceland and New Zealand, magma heats underground water to the boiling point. In these places, the hot water and steam can be valuable sources of energy. For example, in Reykjavík, Iceland, 90 percent of the homes are heated by water warmed underground in this way. Geothermal energy can also be used to generate electricity, as shown in **Figure 5.**

Geothermal energy does have disadvantages. There are only a few places where Earth's crust is thin enough for magma to come close to the surface. Elsewhere, very deep wells would be needed to tap this energy. Drilling deep wells is very expensive. Even so, geothermal energy is likely to become a good method for meeting energy needs for some locations in the future.

FIGURE 5 ·······················

Geothermal Power in Iceland

Geothermal power plants like the one shown here use heat from Earth's interior to generate electricity.

✎ **Infer** On the diagram below, draw Earth's crust and show where magma might be located in relation to Iceland's surface.

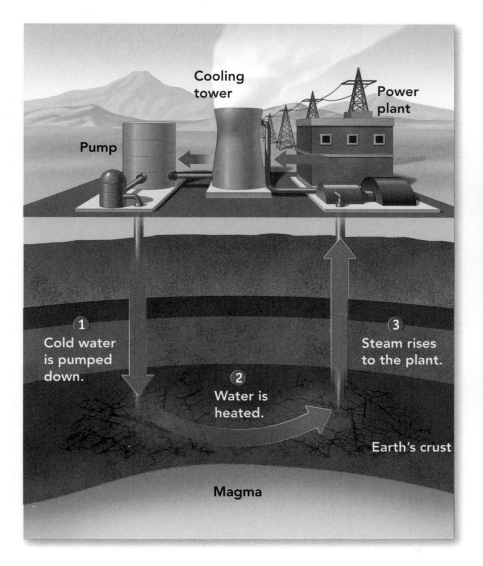

The Energy Around Us

EXPLORE THE BIG ?

What are some of Earth's energy sources?

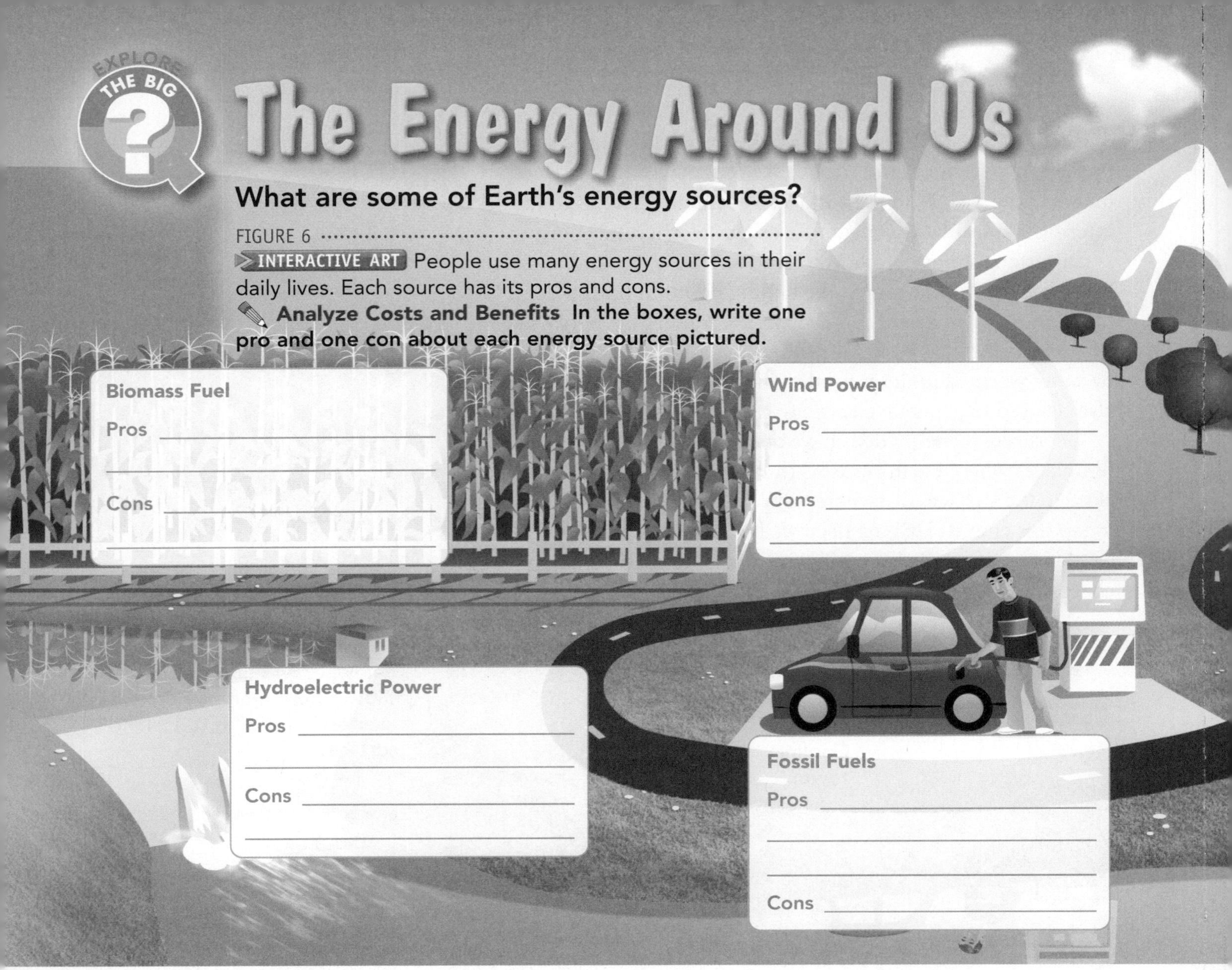

FIGURE 6 ....

> **INTERACTIVE ART** People use many energy sources in their daily lives. Each source has its pros and cons.

✏ **Analyze Costs and Benefits** In the boxes, write one pro and one con about each energy source pictured.

Biomass Fuel

Pros _____

_____

Cons _____

_____

Wind Power

Pros _____

_____

Cons _____

_____

Hydroelectric Power

Pros _____

_____

Cons _____

_____

Fossil Fuels

Pros _____

_____

Cons _____

_____

✏

Vocabulary High-Use Academic Words The word *emit* means "to give off." What do vehicles that run on hydrogen fuel cells emit?

_____

_____

_____

_____

Electric Cars and Hydrogen Fuel Cells

You may have heard about or even seen battery-powered electric cars. But what about cars that use hydrogen fuel cells? Both technologies, battery-powered electric cars and hydrogen fuel cells, have been developed to use renewable energy. See **Figure 6.**

Electric cars run entirely on batteries, and you plug them into an outlet to recharge them. The electricity used can be generated by power plants that use hydroelectric or solar energy. Some electric cars have adaptors that let you recharge them in minutes.

Some cars can run on hydrogen. They have tanks called hydrogen fuel cells that hold hydrogen instead of gasoline. Many power plants can use excess energy to break water molecules apart to make hydrogen. This hydrogen can then be pumped into cars. Cars that run on hydrogen fuel cells emit water vapor, not exhaust.

Geothermal Energy

Pros _____

_____

Cons _____

_____

Solar Power

Pros _____

_____

Cons _____

_____

Hydrogen

Hydrogen Power

Pros _____

_____

Cons _____

_____

Nuclear Power

Pros _____

_____

Cons _____

_____

Lab zone® Do the Lab Investigation *Design and Build a Solar Cooker.*

🔑 Assess Your Understanding

1a. Review What forms of energy are provided by the sun?_____

7.1.3

b. Explain Are biomass fuels renewable? Why?_____

_____

7.1.3

c. ANSWER THE BIG ❓ What are some of Earth's energy sources?

_____

_____

_____

_____

_____

7.1.3, 7.4.2

got it? ....

○ **I get it!** Now I know that alternative energy sources include_____

_____

○ **I need extra help with** _____

Go to **MY SCIENCE** Ⓢ **COACH** *online for help with this subject.*

7.1.3, 7.4.2

How Does a Nuclear Power Plant Produce Electricity?

Nuclear power plants generate much of the world's electricity. They generate about 20 percent of the electricity in the United States and more than 70 percent in France. Controlled nuclear fission reactions take place inside nuclear power plants. **Nuclear fission** is the splitting of an atom's nucleus into two nuclei. The splitting releases a lot of energy. **In a nuclear power plant, the heat released from fission reactions is used to turn water into steam. The steam then turns the blades of a turbine to generate electricity.** Look at the diagram of a nuclear power plant in **Figure 7**. In addition to the generator, it has two main parts: the reactor vessel and the heat exchanger.

Reactor Vessel The **reactor vessel** is the part of the nuclear reactor in which nuclear fission occurs. The reactor contains rods of radioactive uranium called **fuel rods.** When several fuel rods are placed close together, a series of fission reactions occurs.

If the reactor vessel gets too hot, control rods are used to slow down the chain reactions. **Control rods,** made of the elements cadmium, boron or hafnium, are inserted near the fuel rods. The elements absorb particles released during fission and slow the speed of the chain reactions. The control rods can then be removed to speed up the chain reactions again.

FIGURE 7 ....

> **INTERACTIVE ART** **Nuclear Power Plants**
Nuclear power plants are designed to turn the energy from nuclear fission reactions into electricity.

✎ **Interpret Diagrams** Where does nuclear fission occur in the plant?

_____

_____

7.4.2

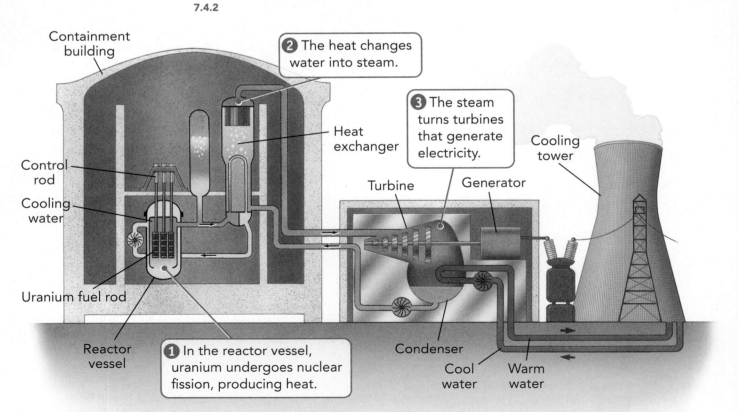

Containment building

2 The heat changes water into steam.

3 The steam turns turbines that generate electricity.

Heat exchanger

Cooling tower

Control rod

Cooling water

Turbine   Generator

Uranium fuel rod

Reactor vessel

1 In the reactor vessel, uranium undergoes nuclear fission, producing heat.

Condenser

Cool water   Warm water

Heat Exchanger Heat is removed from the reactor vessel by water or another fluid that is pumped through the reactor. This fluid passes through a heat exchanger. There, the fluid boils water to produce steam. The steam runs the electrical generator. The steam is condensed again and pumped back to the heat exchanger.

The Risks of Nuclear Power At first, people thought that nuclear fission would provide an almost unlimited source of clean, safe energy. But accidents at nuclear power plants have led to safety concerns. In 1986, the reactor vessel in a nuclear power plant in Chernobyl, Ukraine, overheated. The fuel rods generated so much heat that they started to melt. This condition is called a meltdown. The excess heat caused a series of explosions, which injured or killed dozens of people immediately. In addition, radioactive materials escaped into the environment and killed many more people.

Plant operators can avoid accidents at nuclear facilities through careful planning and by improving safety features. A more difficult problem is the disposal of radioactive wastes. Radioactive wastes remain dangerous for many thousands of years. Scientists must find ways to store these wastes safely for very long periods of time.

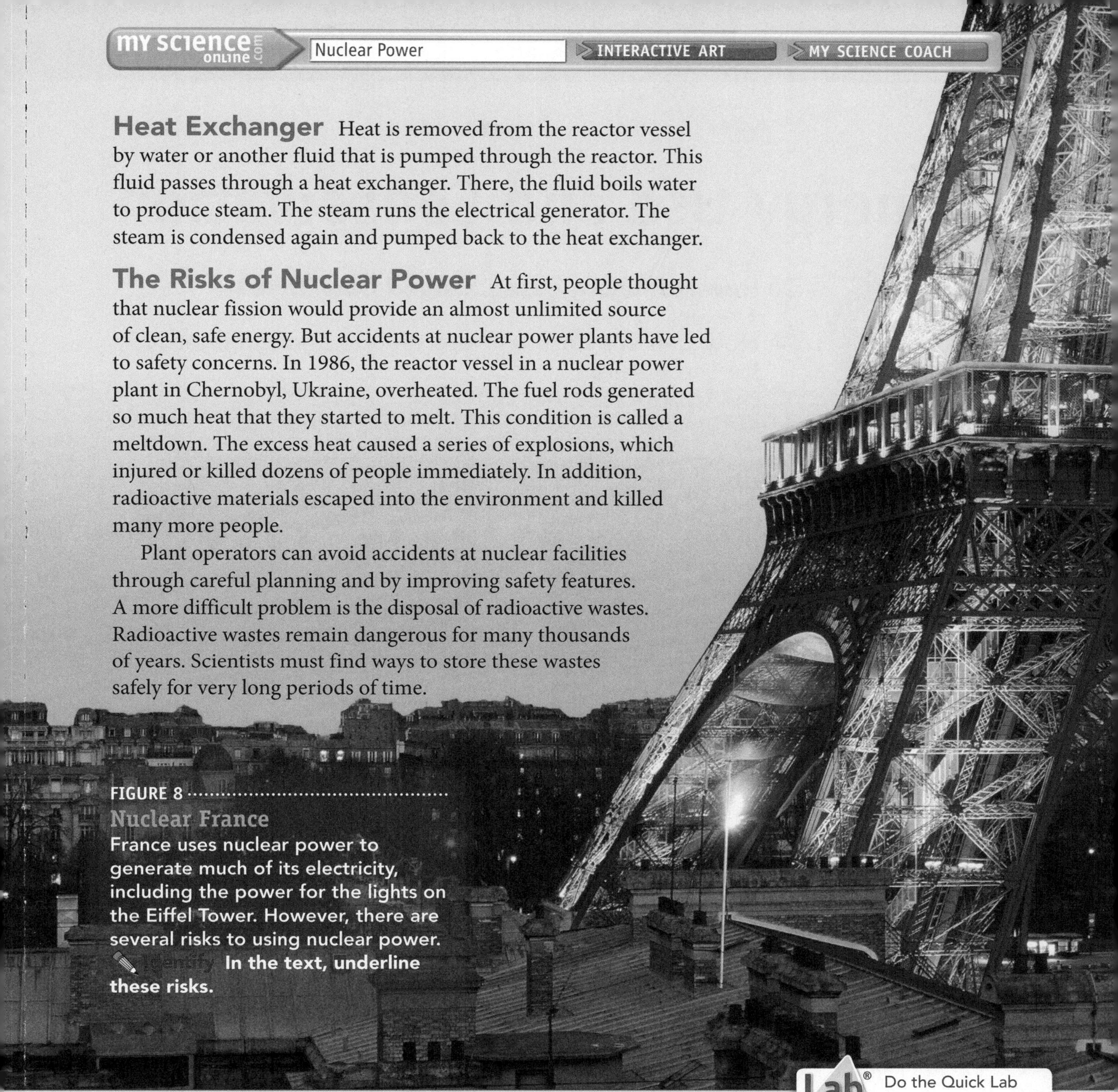

FIGURE 8 ....

Nuclear France
France uses nuclear power to generate much of its electricity, including the power for the lights on the Eiffel Tower. However, there are several risks to using nuclear power.
✎ Identify In the text, underline these risks.

 Lab zone
Do the Quick Lab
Producing Electricity.

🔑 **Assess Your Understanding**

got it? ....

○ I get it! Now I know that nuclear power plants produce energy by _____

_____

○ I need extra help with _____

Go to **my science** ⓢ **coach** *online for help with this subject.*   7.1.3, 7.4.2

Energy Use and Conservation

UNLOCK THE BIG ?

🔑 How Has Energy Use Changed Over Time?
7.1.3, 7.4.4

🔑 How Can We Ensure There Will Be Enough Energy for the Future?
7.1.3, 7.4.1, 7.4.3, 7.4.4, 7.NS.2, 7.NS.11

my PLANET DiARY

TECHNOLOGY

House of Straw

What was that first little pig thinking? Was he just lazy—building a house of straw as quickly as he could without much thought? Or was he helping the environment? It turns out that straw is one of the best materials for keeping warm air inside in cold weather and keeping hot air outside in hot weather. Builders place stacks of straw along the exterior walls of a building and then seal the straw with mud. Bales of straw are natural and cheap, since straw is left over after grain is harvested. It's no wonder that more and more people are using straw to insulate their homes!

Communicate Write your answers below.

1. How does using straw for insulation save energy?

_____

_____

_____

2. Why is using straw for insulation good for the environment?

_____

_____

_____

▶ PLANET DIARY Go to Planet Diary to learn more about energy use and conservation.

Lab zone® Do the Inquiry Warm-Up Which Bulb Is More Efficient?

Vocabulary
- efficiency • insulation
- energy conservation

Skills
- ↻ Reading: Identify the Main Idea
- △ Inquiry: Observe

How Has Energy Use Changed Over Time?

Energy, beyond using your own muscle power, is essential to the way most people live. The methods people use to obtain energy have changed, especially in the last 200 years. ⊂⊐ **For most of human history, people burned wood for energy. Only recently have fossil fuels become the main energy source.**

Eventually, people harnessed the power of other renewable resources. Ships used tall sails to capture wind energy. Flowing water turned wheels connected to stones that ground grain into flour.

Wood, wind, and water were also the main sources of energy in the United States until the nineteenth century. Coal gained in popularity as a fuel during the westward expansion of the railroads. Coal remained the dominant fuel until 1951, when it was replaced by oil and natural gas.

Today, scientists are continually looking for new and better fuels to meet the world's energy needs. As fossil fuel supplies continue to decrease, the interest in renewable energy sources has increased. With more focus on protecting the environment, scientists are working to meet our energy needs while reducing and eliminating many sources of pollution.

Academic Standards for Science

7.1.3 Recognize and explain how different ways of obtaining, transforming, and distributing energy have different environmental consequences.

7.4.4 Explain that power systems are used to provide propulsion for engineered products and systems.

↻ **Identify the Main Idea**
Energy use has changed over time. On the timeline, label and shade the periods in which coal and oil were the dominant fuel sources in the United States.

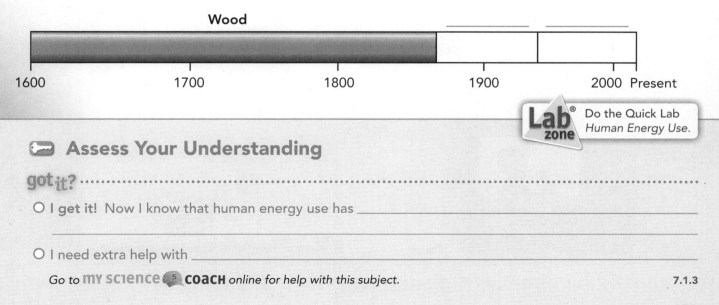

Wood				
1600	1700	1800	1900	2000 Present

Lab zone® Do the Quick Lab *Human Energy Use.*

⊂⊐ Assess Your Understanding

got it? ....

○ **I get it!** Now I know that human energy use has _____

_____

○ **I need extra help with** _____

Go to **my science** ⑤ **coach** *online for help with this subject.*

7.1.3

Academic Standards for Science

7.1.3 Explain how different ways of obtaining, transforming, and distributing energy have environmental consequences.

7.4.1 Understand that energy is the capacity to do work.

7.4.3 Explain that power is the rate that energy is converted from one form to another.

7.4.4 Explain that power systems are used to provide propulsion.

7.NS.2 Carry out investigations.

7.NS.11 Communicate findings.

FIGURE 1 ·······························

> REAL-WORLD INQUIRY **Wasting Energy**

Many things, such as lights and appliances, use energy. If people do not use these things properly, energy can be wasted.

⚠Observe **Circle everything in this scene that is wasting energy.**

How Can We Ensure There Will Be Enough Energy for the Future?

What would happen if the world ran out of fossil fuels today? The heating and cooling systems in most buildings would stop functioning. Forests would disappear as people began to burn wood for heating and cooking. Cars, buses, and trains would be stranded wherever they ran out of fuel. About 70 percent of the world's electric power would disappear. Since televisions, computers, and telephones depend on electricity, communication would be greatly reduced. Lights and most home appliances would no longer work.

Although fossil fuels won't run out immediately, they also won't last forever. Most people think that it makes sense to use fuels more wisely now to avoid fuel shortages in the future. 🔑 **One way to preserve our current energy resources is to increase the efficiency of our energy use. Another way is to conserve energy whenever possible.** Refer to **Figure 1.**

Energy Efficiency One way to make energy resources last longer is to use fuels more efficiently. **Efficiency** is the percentage of energy that is actually used to perform work. The rest of the energy is "lost" to the surroundings, usually as heat. People have developed many ways to increase energy efficiency.

Heating and Cooling One method of increasing the efficiency of heating and cooling systems is insulation. **Insulation** is a layer of material that traps air. This helps block the transfer of heat between the air inside and outside a building. You have probably seen insulation made of fiberglass. It looks like pink cotton candy. A layer of fiberglass 15 centimeters thick insulates a room as well as a brick wall 2 meters thick!

Trapped air can act as insulation in windows too. Many windows consist of two panes of glass with space in between them. The air between the panes of glass acts as insulation.

Lighting Much of the electricity used for home lighting is wasted. For example, less than 10 percent of the electricity that an incandescent light bulb uses is converted into light. The rest is given off as heat. In contrast, compact fluorescent bulbs use about one fourth as much energy to provide the same amount of light.

FIGURE 2 ···
Solutions to Wasting Energy
There are many ways to save energy in a home.
✎ **Explain** Pick at least three of the things you circled in the scene and explain what people could do to stop wasting energy.

Ways to Conserve Energy

177

Transportation Engineers have improved the energy efficiency of cars by designing better engines and batteries. For instance, many new cars use high-efficiency hybrid engines that go twice as far on a tank of fuel than other cars. Buses in some cities are now entirely electric, running on high-power rechargeable batteries. New kinds of batteries allow some electric cars to drive hundreds of kilometers before recharging.

Another way to save energy is to reduce the number of cars on the road. In many communities, public transit systems provide an alternative to driving. Other cities encourage carpooling and bicycling. Many cities now set aside lanes for cars containing two or more people.

apply it!

1 You have been put in charge of designing an ad campaign for your area to get more people to use public transportation. Design a poster that will get people's attention and inform them about their choices. On your poster, list at least three reasons why people should use public transportation. Give your poster a title.

2 Describe Where would you want to display your poster? Why?

_____

_____

3 CHALLENGE How else could you increase awareness about public transportation?

_____

_____

_____

7.NS.2, 7.NS.11

Energy Conservation Another approach to making energy resources last longer is conservation. **Energy conservation** means reducing energy use.

You can reduce your personal energy use by changing your behavior in some simple ways. For example, if you walk to the store instead of getting a ride, you are conserving the gasoline it would take to drive to the store.

While these suggestions seem like small things, multiplied by millions of people they add up to a lot of energy saved for the future.

FIGURE 3 ···

Energy Conservation in Your Everyday Life
Even students like you can conserve energy.
✎ **Communicate With a partner, think of ways you can conserve energy in your daily life. Write your answers in the notebook.**

Lab® zone Do the Quick Lab *Future Energy Use.*

🔑 **Assess Your Understanding**

1a. Define What does it mean to say that something is "energy efficient"?

_____

_____

_____

_____
7.1.3

b. Solve Problems What are some strategies a city could use to increase energy conservation?

_____

_____

_____

_____
7.1.3

got it? ··

○ **I get it!** Now I know that ensuring that the future has enough energy requires _____

_____

○ **I need extra help with** _____

Go to MY SCIENCE ⓢ COACH *online for help with this subject.*
7.1.3

Study Guide

Earth has many energy sources, including _____ such as coal; the sun, which can be used for _____; and flowing water, which can be used for hydroelectric power.

LESSON 1 Fossil Fuels

7.1.3, 7.4.2, 7.NS.8

🔑 The three major fossil fuels are coal, oil, and natural gas.

🔑 Since fossil fuels take hundreds of millions of years to form, they are considered nonrenewable resources.

Vocabulary
- fuel • fossil fuel
- hydrocarbon
- petroleum • refinery
- petrochemical

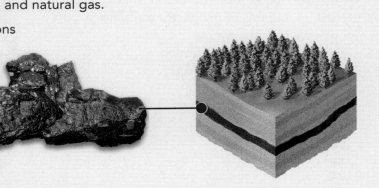

LESSON 2 Renewable Sources of Energy

7.1.3, 7.4.2, 7.4.4, 7.NS.8

🔑 Renewable sources of energy include sunlight, water, wind, biomass fuels, and geothermal energy.

🔑 In a nuclear power plant, the heat released from fission reactions is used to change water into steam. The steam then turns the blades of a turbine to generate electricity.

Vocabulary
- solar energy • hydroelectric power • biomass fuel • gasohol
- geothermal energy • nuclear fission
- reactor vessel • fuel rod • control rod

LESSON 3 Energy Use and Conservation

7.1.3, 7.4.1, 7.4.3, 7.4.4, 7.NS.2, 7.NS.11

🔑 For most of human history, the main fuel source was wood. Only recently have fossil fuels become the main energy source.

🔑 One way to preserve our current energy resources is to increase the efficiency of our energy use. Another way is to conserve energy whenever possible.

Vocabulary
- efficiency • insulation • energy conservation

Review and Assessment

LESSON 1 Fossil Fuels

1. What is one similarity among oil, coal, and natural gas?

  a. They are all petrochemicals.

  b. They all must be processed in a refinery.

  c. They are all gases at room temperature.

  d. They are all formed from the remains of dead organisms.

                        7.1.3

2. Fossil fuels take hundreds of millions of years to form, and therefore are considered _____ energy sources.

                        7.1.3

3. Compare and Contrast Describe one main use for each fuel: coal, oil, and natural gas.

_____

_____

_____

_____

_____

_____

                    7.1.3, 7.4.2

4. Sequence How does coal form?

_____

_____

_____

_____

_____

_____

                    7.1.3

5. Write About It Imagine a day without fossil fuels. Describe your day, from when you wake up until when you eat lunch. Identify each time you would have used energy from fossil fuels.

                    7.1.3, 7.4.2

LESSON 2 Renewable Sources of Energy

6. Which of the following is not a biomass fuel?

  a. gasohol   **b.** methane from landfills

  c. hydrogen   **d.** sugar cane wastes

                    7.1.3

7. Running water can be used as an energy source to produce _____ power.

                    7.1.3

8. Apply Concepts Fill in the boxes with two benefits and two costs of hydrogen power.

Benefits	Costs
_____	_____
_____	_____
_____	_____
_____	_____
_____	_____

                    7.1.3

9. Interpret Photos Explain how a nuclear power plant, like the one pictured below, produces energy.

_____

_____

_____

_____

_____

_____

                    7.1.3

181

LESSON 3 Energy Use and Conservation

10. What is efficiency?

a. the percentage of energy that is lost to the environment as heat

b. the percentage of energy that is used to perform work

c. the percentage of energy that is conserved when work is done

d. the percentage of energy that is wasted when electronics are left on

7.1.3, 7.4.1, 7.4.3

11. _____

involves using less energy, helping energy

resources last longer.

7.1.3

12. Draw Conclusions How is energy use today different from energy use 200 years ago?

_____

_____

_____

_____

_____

_____

_____

_____

7.1.3

13. Solve Problems Describe three actions a person can take to conserve energy.

_____

_____

_____

_____

_____

_____

_____

_____

7.1.3

 APPLY THE BIG **What are some of Earth's energy sources?**

14. Earth's energy sources include both renewable and nonrenewable resources. Name at least three sources of energy that could be used in a classroom like the one below. Then describe the ideal energy source for generating most of your school's electricity and explain why you chose this source.

_____

_____

_____

_____

_____

_____

_____

_____

_____

_____

_____

_____

7.1.3, 7.4.2

Indiana ISTEP+ Practice

Multiple Choice

Circle the letter of the best answer.

1. Which statement is best supported by the table below?

2007 Global Oil Production and Use

Country	Oil production global rank	Oil use global rank
United States	3	1
Russia	1	6
China	5	3
Brazil	15	8

   A. Brazil produces more oil than China.
   B. Russia produces the most oil.
   C. China consumes the most oil.
   D. The United States consumes and produces the most oil in the world.

   7.1.3, 7.NS.8

2. Which of the following is not a fossil fuel?
   A. oil
   B. coal
   C. natural gas
   D. wood

   7.1.3

3. The interior of a car heats up on a sunny day because of
   A. solar cells.
   B. active solar heating.
   C. passive solar heating.
   D. direct solar heating.

   7.1.3

4. How does a nuclear power plant produce energy?
   A. with solar panels
   B. through nuclear fission reactions
   C. with geothermal heat
   D. through nuclear meltdown reactions

   7.1.3

Constructed Response

Write your answer to Question 5 on the lines below.

5. How does increasing the efficiency of energy use help preserve energy resources?

   _____

   _____

   _____

   7.1.3

Extended Response

Use the diagram below and your knowledge of science to help you answer Question 6. Write your answer on a separate sheet of paper.

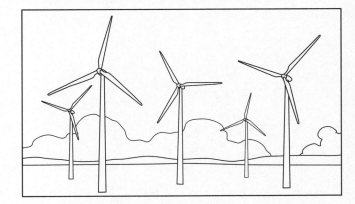

6. Describe how energy is produced in the diagram above. Then, describe one advantage and one disadvantage of this source.

   7.1.3, 7.4.2

Think Like a Scientist

How Low Is Low-Impact?

This electric car is charged by attaching an electric cord to an outlet. However, the source of the electricity may be a fossil fuel-based power plant.

Hybrid engines, windmills, low-impact this, alternative-energy that—everywhere you look, people are trying to find ways to create energy by using renewable resources. Sometimes, a technology seems to conserve energy, but in reality it has hidden costs. For example, electric cars do not release air pollutants during use, but the method that is used to generate the electricity for the car may cause pollution. Is the electricity really "clean"?

Evaluating the costs and benefits of different technologies is an important scientific skill. Use the following questions to sharpen your decision-making skills.

What is the source? What materials are used to create or power the technology? How are they obtained?

What are the products? What is produced when the technology is created or used? How do these products affect the environment? How are these products stored, recycled, or disposed of?

How does it affect our lives? Does using a technology encourage people to use more energy? If it does, do the benefits of the technology outweigh the environmental costs?

Every technology has costs and benefits. However, it is important to be able to evaluate new technologies to find out if the benefits outweigh the costs!

Write About It In a group, discuss the questions listed above. Can you think of ways to add to them or to change them? Then, create an Environmental Decision-Making Guide and use it to evaluate two of the energy technologies described in this chapter.

7.1.3, 7.1.4, 7.NS.8, 7.NS.11

Life on an Oil Rig

This professional's office is on a huge steel platform that is half the area of a football field, surrounded by water. With much of Earth's oil located under the ocean floor, petroleum engineers must go where the oil is. Many of them work on offshore oil rigs—large drilling platforms that extract oil from under the ocean floor.

Conditions far out in the the ocean can be harsh or dangerous. Large equipment, fires, and even hurricanes threaten workers' safety. However, far out in the ocean, workers on oil rigs can see sharks, manta rays, and other marine life.

Petroleum engineers study geology, physics, and chemistry to understand the properties of rock formations that contain oil. They use high-tech remote sensing equipment to find oil and computer modeling software to figure out how to get the oil out of the ocean's floor.

Write About It Find out more about life on an offshore oil rig. Then, write a diary or blog entry that describes a week in the life of an offshore petroleum engineer.

7.1.3, 7.NS.11

OFFSHORE PETROLEUM ENGINEER

▲ The Petronius platform is located in the Gulf of Mexico.

Hydrokinetic Energy

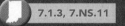

Whirlpool! Maelstrom! Vortex! Do these words make you think of a rushing spiral of water, sucking fish and boats into its center? Not all vortexes sink ships. Fish and whales cause little vortexes when they swim. As the animals move, they create turbulence in the water. Turbulent water moves away from the animal and gives it a little push.

An engineer named Michael Bernitsas has developed a device that uses this effect to generate electricity. As currents push water around a cylindrical device, a vortex forms. As the vortex moves away from the device, the cylinder moves up and down. The device then converts that mechanical energy into electrical energy. Bernitsas has even improved the device by adding mechanical "fish tails" to the generators! Bernitsas is still testing his system, but he hopes that it can someday be used to help meet society's needs for a renewable source of energy.

Design It Find out more about how fish swim. Then, design a model fish that moves efficiently in the water. Brainstorm potential designs and document your ideas. Choose one design and build a prototype. Test and evaluate your prototype in the water. Redesign to improve your solution. See Appendix A on page 578 for more information about the design process.

7.NS.1–7.NS.11, 7.DP.1–7.P.11

HOW WOULD YOU DESCRIBE WAVES?

What are the properties of waves?

Imagine a sunny day on a calm sea. It seems as if you can see to the edge of the world. Suddenly, the clouds roll in, and the waves begin to get larger and faster. Soon, you can barely see past the next wave. One after another, they batter the sailboat, making it pitch and roll like a wild roller coaster. **Draw Conclusions** What are some features of waves?

_____

_____

_____

_____

_____

_____

> **UNTAMED SCIENCE** Watch the **Untamed Science** video to learn more about waves.

Waves and Sound

Academic Standards for Science

7.1.4, 7.NS.1, 7.NS.3, 7.NS.8, 7.NS.11, 7.DP.2, 7.DP.9, 7.DP.10

6 Getting Started

Check Your Understanding

1. **Background** Read the paragraph below and then answer the question.

At a public pond, Lionel skips stones and tosses rocks into the water, sending waves in all directions. Nearby, Ali floats a wooden boat. Both boys observe the properties of the waves. The rocks make higher waves than the stones. They watch the interaction of the waves and the boat. The boat bounces violently as the higher waves travel under it.

Something **floats** if it moves or rests on the surface of a liquid without sinking.

The **properties** of something are its characteristic qualities or features.

Interaction is the combined action or effect that things have on each other.

• What example in the paragraph suggests that the properties of waves might affect a floating object?

_____

_____

_____

▷ MY READING WEB If you had trouble completing the question above, visit **My Reading Web** and type in *Waves and Sound.*

Vocabulary Skill

Identify Multiple Meanings Some words have more than one meaning. Consider the everyday and scientific meanings of the words below.

Word	Everyday Meaning	Scientific Meaning
reflection	*n.* serious thought or consideration	*n.* the bouncing back of a wave from a surface
frequency	*n.* the rate at which something occurs	*n.* the number of waves that pass a point in a certain time

2. **Quick Check** Circle in the chart the meaning of *reflection* as it is used in the following sentence: An echo is the *reflection* of a sound wave.

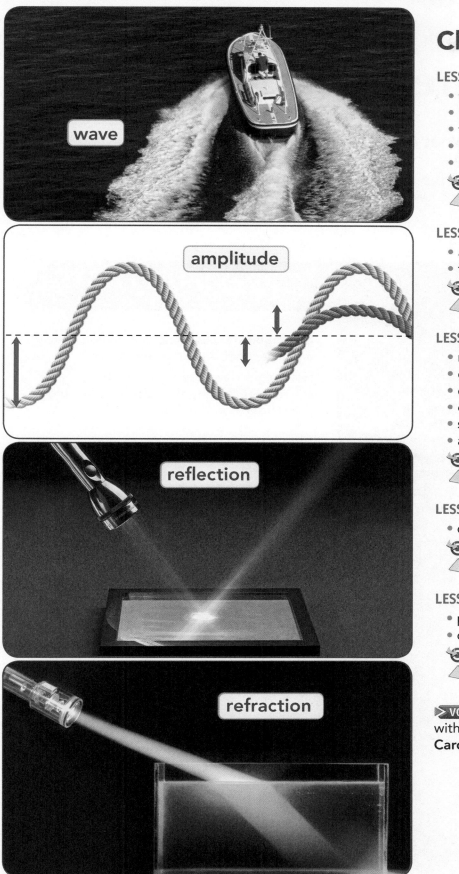

wave

amplitude

reflection

refraction

Chapter Preview

LESSON 1
- wave • energy • medium
- mechanical wave • vibration
- transverse wave • crest • trough
- longitudinal wave • compression
- rarefaction

⟳ **Summarize**
△ **Predict**

LESSON 2
- amplitude • wavelength
- frequency • hertz

⟳ **Identify the Main Idea**
△ **Calculate**

LESSON 3
- reflection • refraction
- diffraction • interference
- constructive interference
- destructive interference
- standing wave • node
- antinode • resonance

⟳ **Relate Cause and Effect**
△ **Observe**

LESSON 4
- density

⟳ **Identify the Main Idea**
△ **Graph**

LESSON 5
- pitch • loudness • intensity
- decibel • Doppler effect

⟳ **Compare and Contrast**
△ **Make Models**

> **VOCAB FLASH CARDS** For extra help with vocabulary, visit **Vocab Flash Cards** and type in **Waves and Sound**.

189

What Are Waves?

UNLOCK THE BIG

?

🔑 **What Forms Mechanical Waves?**
7.1.4

🔑 **What Are the Types of Mechanical Waves?**
7.1.4, 7.NS.1, 7.DP.10

MY PLANET DIARY

FUN FACTS

The Power of Waves

Where does the energy that powers your school come from? It may be from oil, gas, or coal. You also may have heard of using the sun or wind as energy sources. But did you know that ocean waves could be used as an energy source, too? Mechanical systems placed in the ocean or along the shore transform the energy from waves into electricity. Unlike oil, gas, or coal, the energy from ocean waves will not run out. Although wave energy technology is still very new, many scientists are optimistic about its possible use around the world.

Communicate Discuss this question with a partner. Write your answer below.

How might wave energy impact the environment? Consider both intended and unintended consequences.

_____

_____

_____

_____

_____

_____

_____

▶ PLANET DIARY Go to **Planet Diary** to learn more about waves.

Lab zone® Do the Inquiry Warm-Up *What Are Waves?*

Vocabulary

- wave • energy • medium • mechanical wave
- vibration • transverse wave • crest • trough
- longitudinal wave • compression • rarefaction

Skills

○ Reading: Summarize

△ Inquiry: Predict

What Forms Mechanical Waves?

You have probably seen and felt water waves while swimming. But did you know that many kinds of waves affect you daily? Sound and light are very different from water waves, but they are waves, too.

Characteristics of Waves What is a wave? A **wave** is a disturbance involving the transfer of energy from place to place. In science, **energy** is defined as the ability to do work. For example, the energy of a water wave can lift an object on the water's surface as the wave passes under it. But after the wave passes, the water is calm again.

Most waves need something to travel through. For example, sound waves can travel through air, water, and even solid materials. Water waves travel along the surface of the water. A wave can even travel along an object, such as a rope. The material through which a wave travels is called a **medium.** Gases (such as air), liquids (such as water), and solids (such as ropes) can all act as mediums. Waves that require a medium to travel are called **mechanical waves.**

> **Academic Standards for Science**
>
> **7.1.4** Recognize and provide evidence how light, sound and other waves have energy and how they interact with different materials.

○ **Summarize** On the notebook paper, summarize the text on this page in your own words.

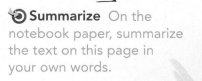

CHALLENGE The news media, such as newspapers and television stations, carry current events worldwide. Explain how the way news travels is similar to the way a wave travels.

_____

_____

_____

_____

_____

Waves and Energy
Energy is needed to make a wave. **Mechanical waves form when a source of energy causes a medium to vibrate.** A **vibration** is a repeated back-and-forth or up-and-down motion. Moving objects have energy, which they can transfer to a medium to produce waves. For example, as you see in **Figure 1,** a motorboat's propeller can transfer energy to calm water. As a result, the particles that make up the water start to vibrate. The vibrations move through the water, resulting in a wave.

FIGURE 1 ···
Forming a Mechanical Wave
A source of energy in a medium can cause a mechanical wave to form.

✎ **Explain** Draw an arrow from each box to the correct part of the photo. Then tell your reason for each choice in the boxes.

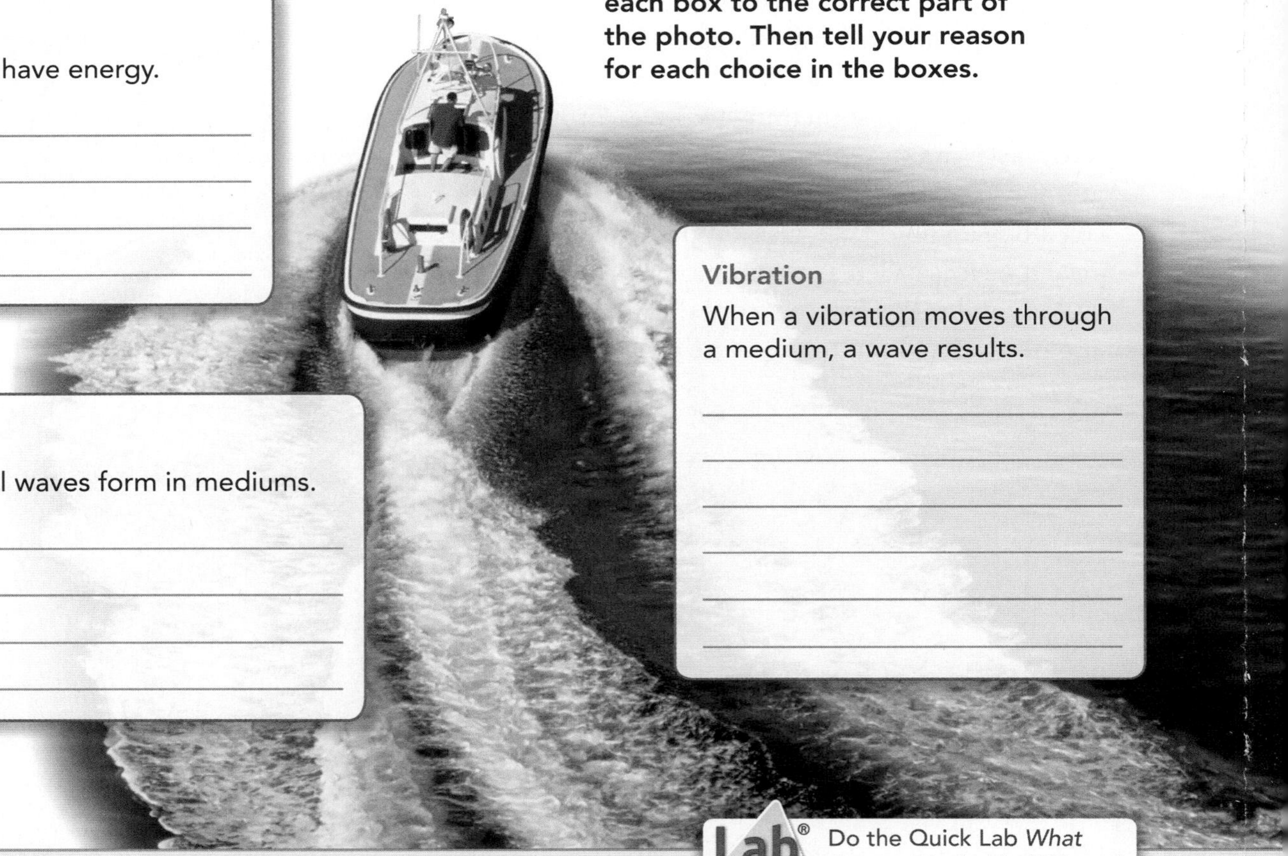

Energy Source
Moving objects have energy.

_____

_____

_____

Medium
Mechanical waves form in mediums.

_____

_____

_____

Vibration
When a vibration moves through a medium, a wave results.

_____

_____

_____

_____

Lab zone® Do the Quick Lab *What Causes Mechanical Waves?*

⚷ Assess Your Understanding

got it? ···

○ I get it! Now I know that a mechanical wave forms when _____

_____

○ I need extra help with _____

Go to MY SCIENCE ⚷ COACH *online for help with this subject.*

7.1.4

What Are the Types of Mechanical Waves?

Waves move through mediums in different ways. 🔑 **The three types of mechanical waves are transverse waves, longitudinal waves, and surface waves.** These waves are classified by how they move through mediums.

Transverse Waves When you make a wave on a rope, the wave moves from one end of the rope to the other. However, the rope itself moves up and down or from side to side, at right angles to the direction in which the wave travels. A wave that vibrates the medium at right angles, or perpendicular, to the direction in which the wave travels is called a **transverse wave.**

Making a transverse wave on a rope forms high and low points along the rope. A high point on a transverse wave is called a **crest**, and a low point is called a **trough** (trawf). In **Figure 2,** you can see that the red ribbon on the rope is first at a crest and then at a trough. As the wave moves through the rope, the ribbon moves up and down between crests and troughs. The dashed line shows the rope's position before it was moved. It is called the rest position.

Academic Standards for Science

7.1.4 Recognize and provide evidence how light, sound and other waves have energy and how they interact with different materials.

7.NS.1 Make predictions and develop testable questions.

7.DP.10 Communicate the solution using drawings.

Vocabulary Identify Multiple Meanings The word *trough* has more than one meaning. Write two sentences that use the word, one showing its everyday meaning and one showing its scientific meaning.

_____

_____

_____

_____

_____

FIGURE 2 ....

Motion in a Transverse Wave

When you shake out a bedsheet or move a rope up and down, you create a transverse wave.

✎ **Complete the tasks.**

1. **Identify** Label the crest, trough, and rest position.

2. **Relate Text and Visuals** Draw a vertical line through the purple arrows and a horizontal line through the blue arrow until it touches the vertical line. What angle did you draw?

_____

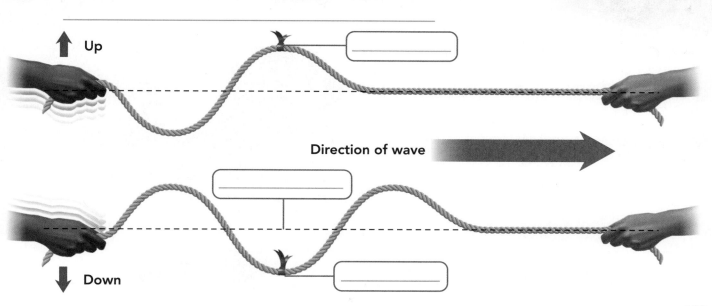

Up

Direction of wave

Down

193

FIGURE 3 ··

Motion in a Longitudinal Wave

Fixed points on a transverse wave vibrate up and down. Fixed points on a longitudinal wave, such as the one marked by the red ribbon, vibrate back and forth.

✏️ **Interpret Diagrams** Label the areas of compression and rarefaction in the diagram.

Longitudinal Waves If you push and pull one end of a spring toy, you can produce a longitudinal wave like the one shown in **Figure 3**. Notice that the coils in the spring move back and forth in the same direction, or parallel, to the wave's motion. A **longitudinal wave** (lawn juh TOO duh nul) vibrates the medium in the same direction in which the wave travels. Also, notice how the spacing between the coils varies. Some coils are close together, while others are farther apart. An area where the coils are close together is called a **compression** (kum PRESH un). An area where the coils are spread out is called a **rarefaction** (rair uh FAK shun).

As compressions and rarefactions travel along the spring toy, each coil moves forward and then back. The energy travels from one end of the spring to the other, in the form of a wave. After the wave passes, each coil returns to its starting position.

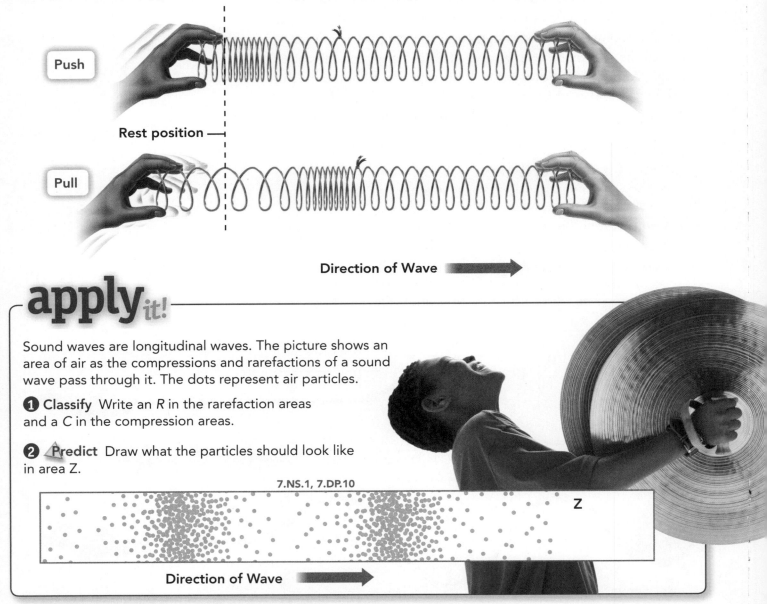

Push

Rest position —

Pull

Direction of Wave ➡️

apply it!

Sound waves are longitudinal waves. The picture shows an area of air as the compressions and rarefactions of a sound wave pass through it. The dots represent air particles.

❶ **Classify** Write an *R* in the rarefaction areas and a *C* in the compression areas.

❷ **Predict** Draw what the particles should look like in area Z.

7.NS.1, 7.DP.10

Z

Direction of Wave ➡️

Surface Waves

Surface Waves Surface waves are combinations of transverse and longitudinal waves. This type of wave travels along a surface that separates two mediums. Ocean waves are the most familiar surface wave. An ocean wave travels at the surface between water and air. When a wave passes through water, the water (and anything on it) vibrates up and down, like a transverse wave on a rope. The water also moves back and forth slightly in the direction that the wave is traveling, like the coils of a spring. But unlike the coils of a spring, water does not compress. The up-and-down and back-and-forth movements combine to make each particle of water move in a circle, as you see in **Figure 4**.

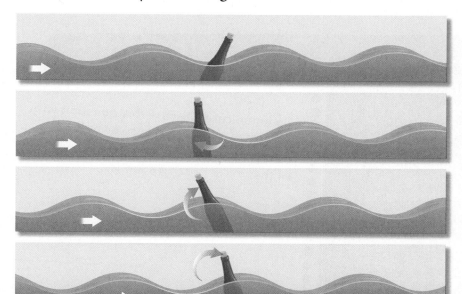

FIGURE 4 ·······························

> **ART IN MOTION** **Waves Transfer Energy**

A wave moves the bottle in a circular motion. After the wave passes, the bottle returns to where it started.

✎ **Predict In the empty box, draw what the next picture should look like.**

7.NS.1, 7.DP.10

 Do the Quick Lab *Three Types of Waves.*

🔑 Assess Your Understanding

1a. Review Compared to the direction it travels, at what angle does a transverse wave vibrate a medium?

_____

_____

7.1.4

b. Compare and Contrast How are transverse and longitudinal waves alike and different?

_____

_____

7.1.4

got it?

○ **I get it!** Now I know that the three types of mechanical waves are _____

_____

_____

_____

○ **I need extra help with** _____

Go to **MY SCIENCE COACH** *online for help with this subject.*

7.1.4

Properties of Waves

🔑 **What Are the Amplitude, Wavelength, Frequency, and Speed of a Wave?**
7.1.4, 7.NS.3, 7.NS.8

🔑 **How Are Frequency, Wavelength, and Speed Related?**
7.1.4, 7.NS.1, 7.NS.8

my PLANET DiaRY

DISCOVERY

The Sound of Romance

Bzzzzzzzzz! Bzzzzzzzzz! What's that noise? It's the sound of a mosquito buzzing in your ear. This distinct buzzing sound comes from sound waves formed as a mosquito beats its wings. Researchers recently discovered that the buzzing sound of female mosquitoes attracts male mosquitoes. When a male mosquito meets a female, he quickly adjusts his own buzz to match the frequency of the sound waves created by the female. Researchers think that this matched buzzing frequency aids in mosquito mating.

Communicate Discuss this question with a partner. Write your answer below.

What are two other animals you know of that make buzzing sounds?

_____

_____

_____

_____

_____

_____

▶ **PLANET DIARY** Go to **Planet Diary** to learn more about wave properties.

Lab zone® Do the Inquiry Warm-Up *What Do Waves Look Like?*

Vocabulary
- amplitude
- wavelength
- frequency
- hertz

Skills
- Reading: Identify the Main Idea
- Inquiry: Calculate

What Are the Amplitude, Wavelength, Frequency, and Speed of a Wave?

Waves may vary greatly. For example, waves can be long or short. They can carry a little energy or a lot of energy. They can be transverse or longitudinal. However, all waves have common properties—amplitude, wavelength, frequency, and speed. **Amplitude describes how far the medium in a wave moves. Wavelength describes a wave's length, and frequency describes how often it occurs. Speed describes how quickly a wave moves.**

Amplitude The height of a wave's crest depends on its amplitude. **Amplitude** is the maximum distance the medium vibrates from the rest position. For a water wave, this distance is how far the water particles move above or below the surface level of calm water. High waves have more energy than low waves. The more energy a wave has, the greater its amplitude.

A transverse wave is shown in **Figure 1.** Its amplitude is the maximum distance the medium moves up or down from its rest position. The amplitude of a longitudinal wave is a measure of how compressed or rarefied the medium becomes. When the compressions are dense, it means the wave's amplitude is large.

FIGURE 1 ···

Amplitude

The amplitude of a transverse wave is the maximum distance the medium vibrates from the rest position.

✎ **Label the parts of the wave. Then answer the question.**

Measure What is the amplitude of the wave in centimeters?

7.NS.3

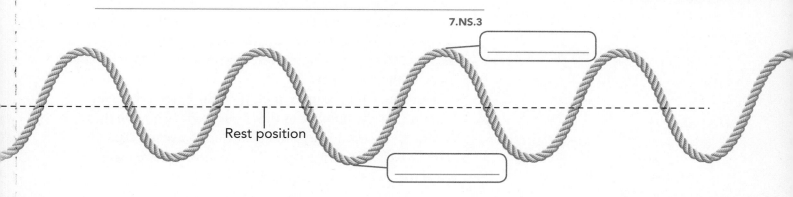

Rest position

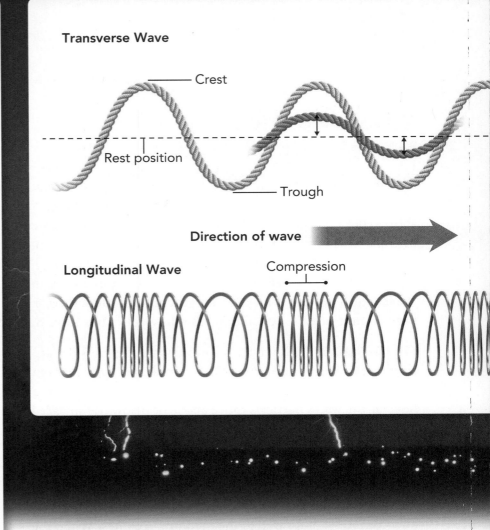

Transverse Wave

Crest

Rest position

Trough

Direction of wave

Longitudinal Wave

Compression

FIGURE 2 ···

Properties of Waves

All waves have amplitude, wavelength, frequency, and speed.

✎ **Read the text on these pages before filling in the boxes and answering these questions.** 7.NS.8

1. **Name** Which transverse wave has the shortest wavelength?

_____

_____

2. **Apply Concepts** If a transverse wave travels 10 meters in 5 seconds, what is its speed?

_____

3. **Draw Conclusions** How does a shorter wavelength affect the frequency of a wave?

_____

_____

_____

_____

_____

_____

_____

_____

··············· ✎ ···············

🌀 **Identify the Main Idea** Read the text. Underline the main idea in each of the three sections.

Wavelength A wave travels a certain distance before it starts to repeat. The distance between two corresponding parts of a wave is its **wavelength.** You can find the wavelength of a transverse wave by measuring the distance from crest to crest as shown in **Figure 2.** For a longitudinal wave, the wavelength is the distance between compressions.

Frequency The **frequency** of a wave is the number of waves that pass a given point in a certain amount of time. For example, if you make waves on a rope so that one wave passes by a point every second, the frequency is 1 wave per second. Move your hand up and down more quickly and you increase the frequency.

Frequency is measured in units called **hertz** (Hz), and is defined as the number of waves per second. A wave that occurs every second has a frequency of 1 wave per second (1/s) or 1 Hz. If two waves pass every second the frequency is 2 waves per second (2/s) or 2 Hz.

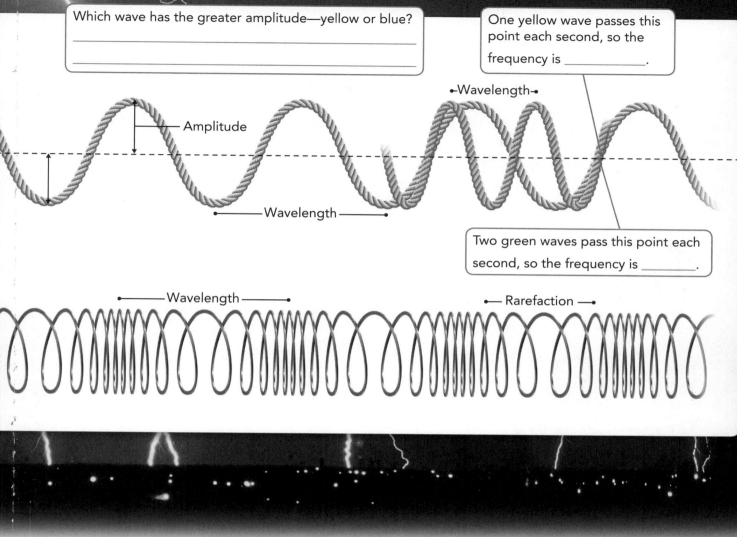

Which wave has the greater amplitude—yellow or blue?
_____
_____

Amplitude

One yellow wave passes this point each second, so the frequency is _____.

←Wavelength→

Two green waves pass this point each second, so the frequency is _____.

Wavelength

Wavelength

Wavelength

Rarefaction

Speed Different waves travel at different speeds. Think about watching a distant thunderstorm on a hot summer day. The thunder occurs the instant the lightning flashes, but the light and sound reach you seconds apart. This happens because light waves travel much faster than sound waves. In fact, light waves travel about a million times faster than sound waves!

The speed of a wave is how far the wave travels in a given amount of time. You can determine a wave's speed by dividing the distance it travels by the time it takes to travel that distance. Sound, for example, travels about 990 meters in 3 seconds in air when the temperature is 0°C. Therefore, its speed is 330 m/s in these conditions. As long as the temperature of the medium (air) doesn't change, the speed of sound will stay the same.

Lab zone® Do the Quick Lab *Properties of Waves.*

🔑 **Assess Your Understanding**

got it? ....

○ **I get it!** Now I know that for any wave, amplitude describes _____
_____,
wavelength describes _____,
frequency describes _____
_____,
and speed describes _____
_____

○ **I need extra help with** _____

Go to MY SCIENCE 🔊 COACH *online for help with this subject.*

7.1.4

How Are Frequency, Wavelength, and Speed Related?

You just learned that you can calculate the speed of a wave by dividing the distance it travels by the time it takes to travel that distance. But you can also calculate the speed of a wave if you know its wavelength and frequency. **The speed, wavelength, and frequency of a wave are related by a mathematical formula.**

$$\text{Speed} = \text{Wavelength} \times \text{Frequency}$$

If you know two quantities in the formula, you can calculate the third quantity. For example, if you know a wave's speed and wavelength, you can calculate its frequency. If you know the speed and frequency, you can calculate the wavelength.

$$\text{Frequency} = \frac{\text{Speed}}{\text{Wavelength}}$$

$$\text{Wavelength} = \frac{\text{Speed}}{\text{Frequency}}$$

The speed of a wave remains constant if the medium, temperature, and pressure do not change. For example, all sound waves travel at the same speed in air at a given temperature and pressure. Even if a sound wave's frequency changes, its speed stays the same. So, if the frequency of a sound wave increases, its wavelength must decrease to maintain a constant speed.

do the math!

The table shows measurements of some properties of a sound wave in water and in air.

1 Calculate Using what you know about the relationship between wavelength, frequency, and speed, fill in the table.

2 CHALLENGE What can this table tell you about the speed of a wave?

Medium	Wavelength	Frequency	Speed
Water	_____	200 Hz	1500 m/s
Water	3.75 m	400 Hz	_____
Air (20°C)	10 m	_____	343 m/s
Air (20°C)	_____	17.15 Hz	343 m/s

_____

_____

_____

7.NS.8

THE BIG ❓

Ride the waves

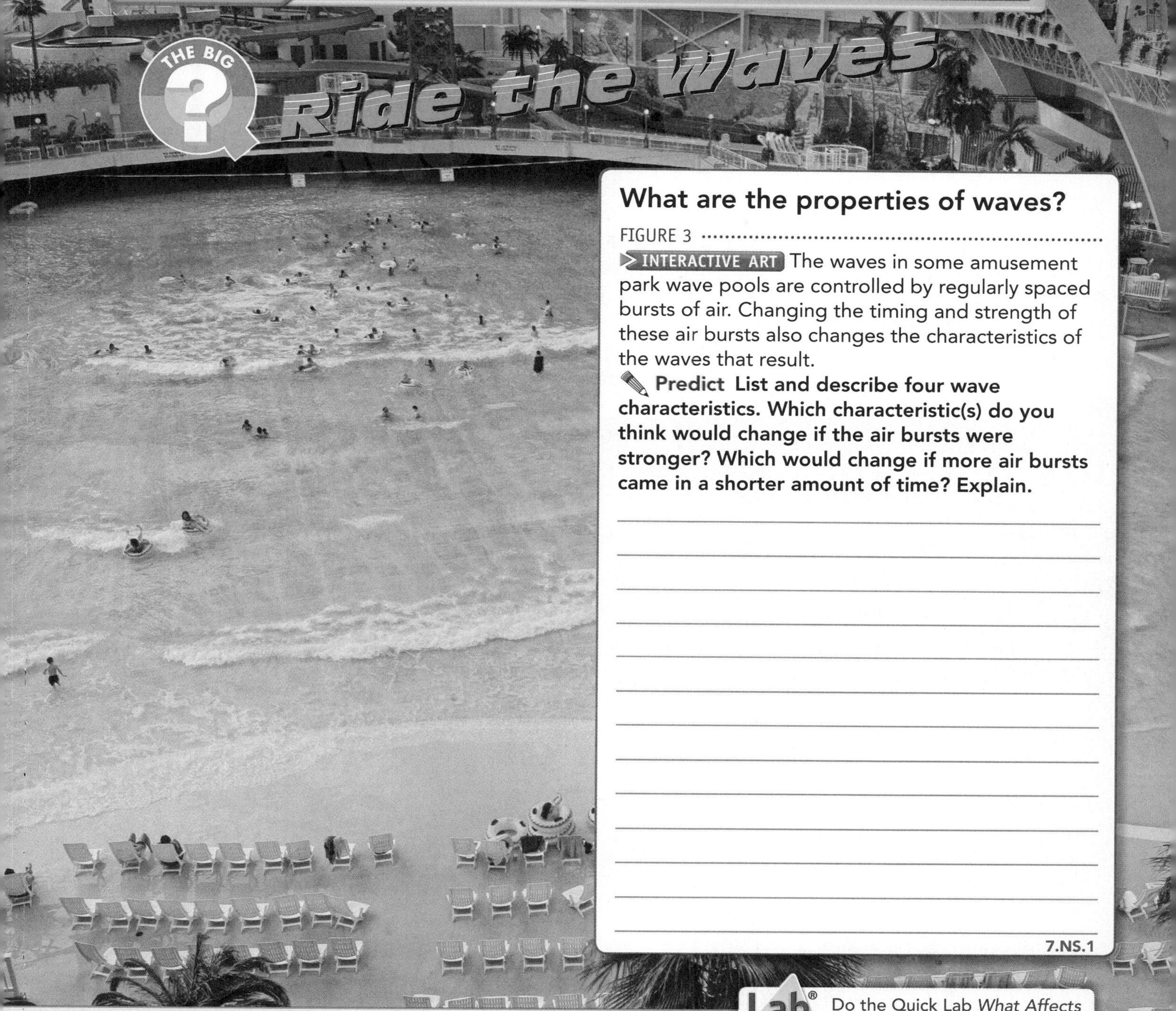

What are the properties of waves?

FIGURE 3 ·······································

▸ INTERACTIVE ART The waves in some amusement park wave pools are controlled by regularly spaced bursts of air. Changing the timing and strength of these air bursts also changes the characteristics of the waves that result.

✎ **Predict** List and describe four wave characteristics. Which characteristic(s) do you think would change if the air bursts were stronger? Which would change if more air bursts came in a shorter amount of time? Explain.

_____

_____

_____

_____

_____

_____

_____

_____

_____

_____

_____

_____

7.NS.1

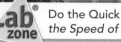

Do the Quick Lab *What Affects the Speed of a Wave?*

🔑 Assess Your Understanding

1a. ANSWER THE BIG ❓ What are the properties of waves?

_____

7.1.4

b. Calculate A wave's frequency is 2 Hz and its wavelength is 4 m. What is the wave's speed?

_____

7.1.4, 7.NS.8

got it?

○ **I get it!** Now I know that wavelength, frequency, and speed are related by the formula _____

_____

○ **I need extra help with** _____

Go to my science ▪ coach *online for help with this subject.*

7.1.4

Interactions of Waves

UNLOCK THE BIG ?

🔑 **What Changes the Direction of a Wave?**
7.1.4, 7.NS.1, 7.NS.8

🔑 **What Are the Two Types of Wave Interference?**
7.1.4, 7.NS.8

🔑 **How Do Standing Waves Form?**
7.1.4, 7.NS.8, 7.DP.2, 7.DP.10

my planet diary

DISASTER

The Fall of Galloping Gertie

"My breath was coming in gasps; my knees were raw and bleeding, my hands bruised and swollen.... Safely back at the toll plaza, I saw the bridge in its final collapse and saw my car plunge into the Narrows."

This dramatic piece of writing is a witness's real-life account of the collapse of the Tacoma Narrows Bridge in Tacoma, Washington, on November 7, 1940.

Prior to its collapse, the suspension bridge was known for its swaying and rolling in the wind. This motion happened so regularly that the bridge was nicknamed "Galloping Gertie." Only four months after its construction, the bridge collapsed into the waters of Puget Sound during a windstorm. Although a disaster, Galloping Gertie's collapse became a valuable teaching tool for engineers.

Lab® Do the Inquiry Warm-Up
zone *How Does a Ball Bounce?*

Communicate Discuss the following questions with a partner. Write your answers below.

1. Why is "Galloping Gertie" an appropriate nickname for the bridge?

_____

_____

2. If you were an engineer studying this bridge collapse, what is one thing you would research?

_____

_____

▷ **PLANET DIARY** Go to **Planet Diary** to learn more about waves interacting.

Vocabulary

- reflection • refraction • diffraction • interference
- constructive interference • destructive interference
- standing wave • node • antinode • resonance

Skills

↻ Reading: Relate Cause and Effect

△ Inquiry: Observe

What Changes the Direction of a Wave?

If you toss a ball against a wall, the ball bounces back in a new direction. Like a ball, waves can also change direction. ⊂▭⊃ **Waves change direction by reflection, refraction, and diffraction.**

Reflection When a wave hits a surface, any part of the wave that cannot pass through the surface bounces back. This interaction with a surface is called **reflection.** Reflection happens often in your everyday life. When you looked in your mirror this morning you used reflected light to see yourself. The echo you hear when you shout in an empty gym is also a reflection.

In **Figure 1** you can see how light waves are reflected. All reflected waves obey the law of reflection.

> **Academic Standards for Science**
>
> **7.1.4** Recognize and provide evidence how light, sound and other waves have energy and how they interact with different materials.
>
> **7.NS.1** Make predictions.
>
> **7.NS.8** Analyze data, using appropriate mathematical manipulation as required, and use it to identify patterns and make inferences based on these patterns.

FIGURE 1 ·····················

The Law of Reflection

The law of reflection states that the angle of incidence equals the angle of reflection.

✎ **Explain** Read the sequence of steps, matching each step to its letter in the photo. If the angle of incidence is 45°, explain what the angle of reflection would be.

_____

_____

_____

_____

_____

_____

7.NS.8

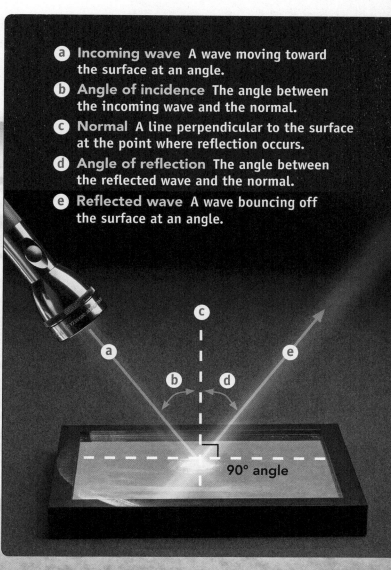

a **Incoming wave** A wave moving toward the surface at an angle.

b **Angle of incidence** The angle between the incoming wave and the normal.

c **Normal** A line perpendicular to the surface at the point where reflection occurs.

d **Angle of reflection** The angle between the reflected wave and the normal.

e **Reflected wave** A wave bouncing off the surface at an angle.

90° angle

Refraction Have you ever ridden a skateboard and gone off the sidewalk onto grass? If so, you know it's hard to keep moving in a straight line. The front wheel on the side moving onto the grass slows down. The front wheel still on the sidewalk continues to move fast. The difference in the speeds of the two front wheels causes the skateboard to change direction.

Like a skateboard that changes direction, changes in speed can cause waves to change direction. Look at **Figure 2.** When a wave enters a new medium at an angle, one side of the wave changes speed before the other side. This causes the wave to bend. Bending occurs because different parts of the wave travel at different speeds. **Refraction** is the bending of waves due to a change in speed.

Waves do not always bend when entering a new medium. No bending occurs if a wave enters a new medium at a right angle. Bending does not occur if the speed of the wave in the new medium is the same as the speed of the wave in the old medium.

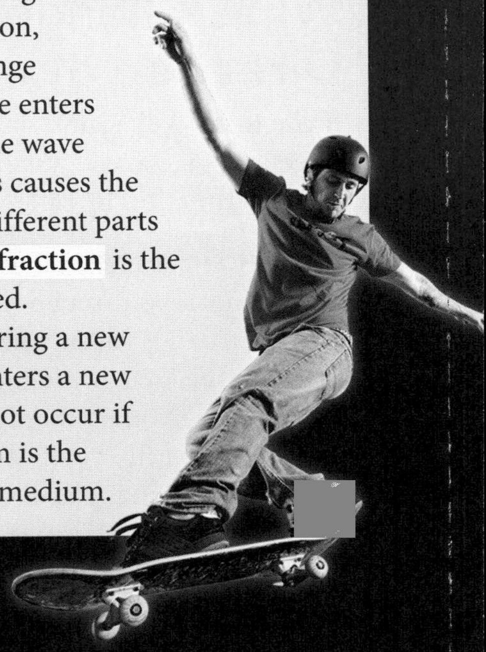

↻ Relate Cause and Effect
In the second paragraph, circle the cause of refraction and underline the effect of refraction.

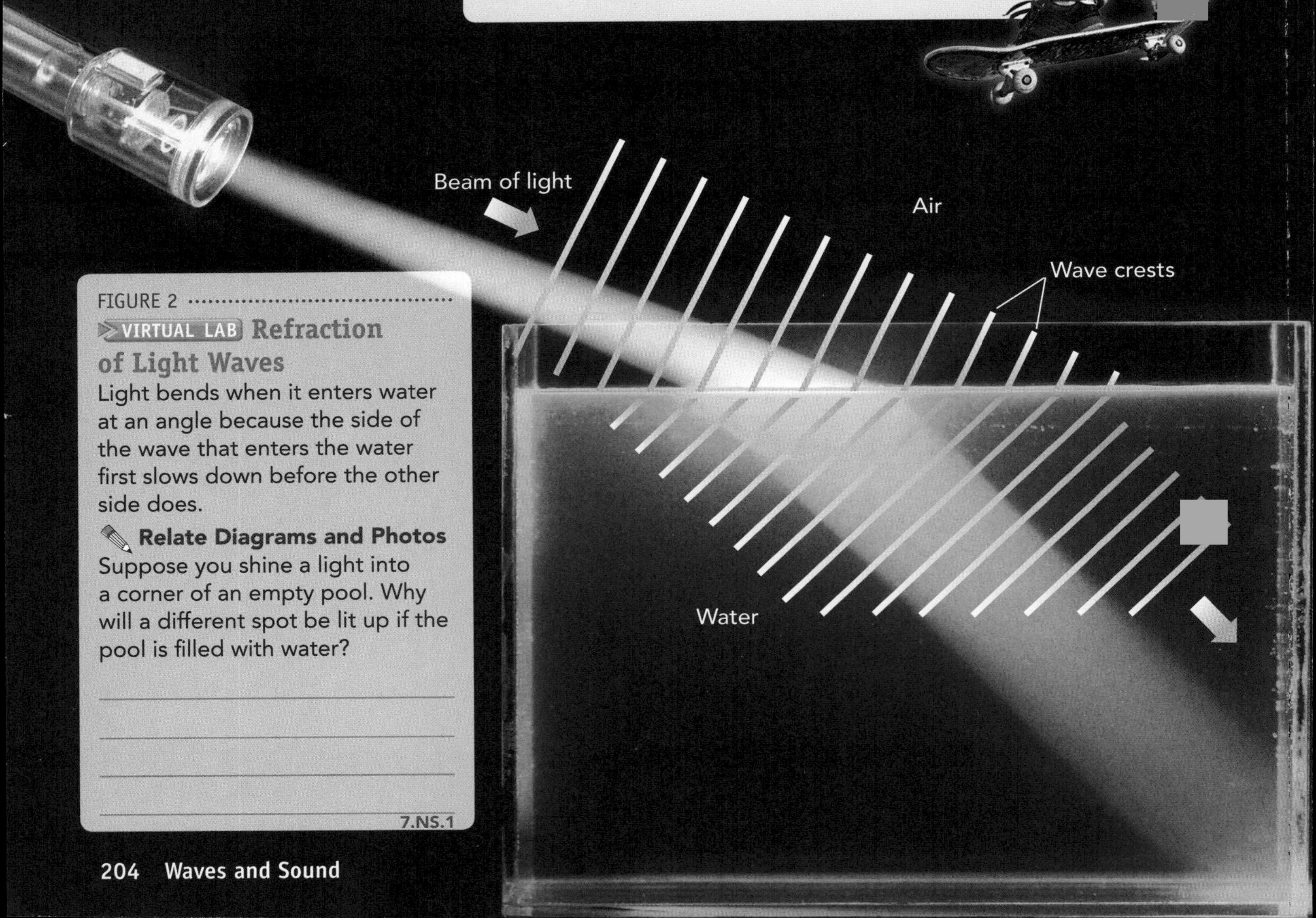

Beam of light

Air

Wave crests

FIGURE 2 ·······················
▶ VIRTUAL LAB **Refraction of Light Waves**
Light bends when it enters water at an angle because the side of the wave that enters the water first slows down before the other side does.

✏ **Relate Diagrams and Photos**
Suppose you shine a light into a corner of an empty pool. Why will a different spot be lit up if the pool is filled with water?

_____

_____

_____

_____

7.NS.1

Water

Diffraction Waves sometimes bend around barriers or pass through openings. When a wave moves around a barrier or through an opening in a barrier, it bends and spreads out. These wave interactions are called **diffraction.** Two examples of diffraction are shown in **Figure 3**.

FIGURE 3 ·······························
The Diffraction of Water Waves
Water waves diffract when they encounter canals or shorelines.

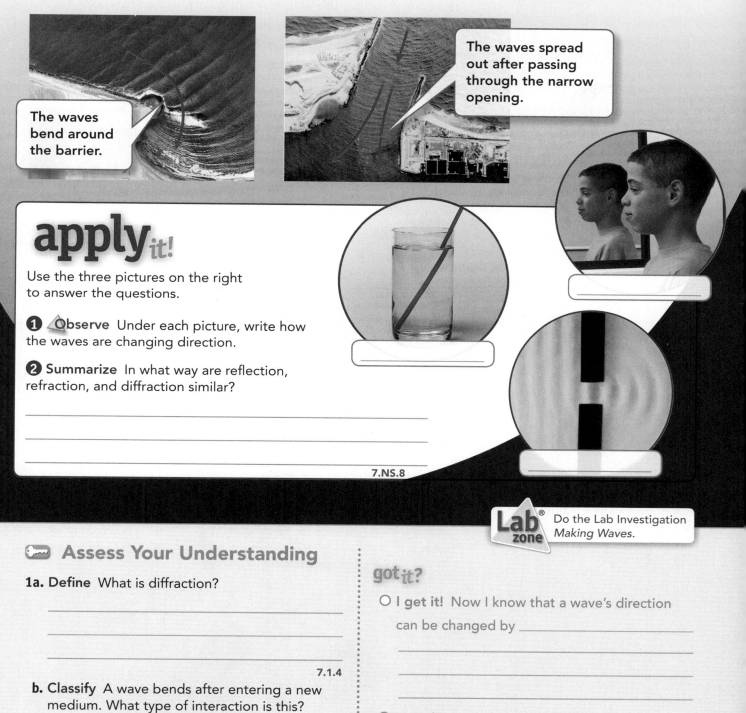

The waves bend around the barrier.

The waves spread out after passing through the narrow opening.

apply it!

Use the three pictures on the right to answer the questions.

❶ ⚠ **Observe** Under each picture, write how the waves are changing direction.

❷ **Summarize** In what way are reflection, refraction, and diffraction similar?

_____

_____

_____

7.NS.8

Lab zone Do the Lab Investigation *Making Waves.*

🔑 Assess Your Understanding

1a. Define What is diffraction?

_____

_____

7.1.4

b. Classify A wave bends after entering a new medium. What type of interaction is this?

_____

_____

7.1.4

got it?

○ **I get it!** Now I know that a wave's direction can be changed by _____

_____

_____

○ **I need extra help with** _____

Go to **MY SCIENCE** 🅢 **COACH** *online for help with this subject.*

7.1.4

What Are the Two Types of Wave Interference?

Have you ever seen soccer balls collide? The balls bounce off each other because they cannot be in the same place at the same time. Surprisingly, this is not true of waves. Unlike two balls, two waves can overlap when they meet. **Interference** is the interaction between waves that meet. **There are two types of interference: constructive and destructive.**

Constructive Interference Interference in which waves combine to form a wave with a larger amplitude than any individual wave's amplitude is called **constructive interference.** You can think of constructive interference as waves "helping each other," or adding their energies. For example, in **Figure 4,** when the crests of two waves overlap, they make a higher crest. If two troughs overlap, they make a deeper trough. In both cases, the amplitude of the combined crests or troughs increases.

did you know?

Interference is responsible for the iridescent colors seen in oil films, soap bubbles, and the feathers of some birds, like the common grackle. The structure of the bird's feathers creates the interference. The bright colors are only seen at specific angles of reflection.

FIGURE 4 ·······················

Constructive Interference

✎ **Infer** Explain what the black dotted line represents. Then tell what happens to the direction of each wave when the waves meet.

_____

_____

_____

_____

_____

7.NS.8

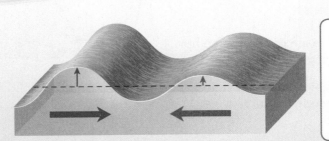

❶ Two waves approach each other. The wave on the left has a greater amplitude.

❷ The crest's new amplitude is the sum of the amplitudes of the original crests.

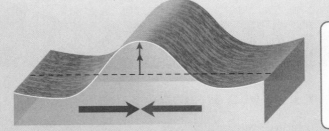

❸ The waves continue on as if they had not met.

Destructive Interference Interference in which two waves combine to form a wave with a smaller amplitude than either original wave had is called **destructive interference.** Destructive interference can occur when the crest of one wave overlaps the trough of another wave. If the crest has a larger amplitude than the trough of the other wave, the crest "wins" and part of it remains. If the original trough had a larger amplitude than the crest of the other wave, the result is a trough. If a crest and trough have equal amplitudes, they will completely cancel as shown in **Figure 5.** Destructive interference is used in noise-canceling headphones to block out distracting noises in a listener's surroundings.

FIGURE 5 ·······················

> INTERACTIVE ART **Destructive Interference**

✎ Observe **Look at the pictures below. In the boxes, describe the steps of destructive interference.**

① _____

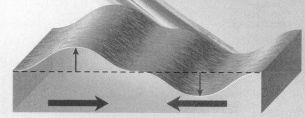

② _____

③ _____

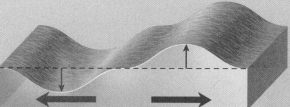

 Do the Quick Lab *Wave Interference.*

🔑 **Assess Your Understanding**

got it? ···

○ **I get it!** Now I know that the two types of wave interference are _____

_____

○ I need extra help with _____

Go to **my science** 💬 **coach** *online for help with this subject.*

7.1.4

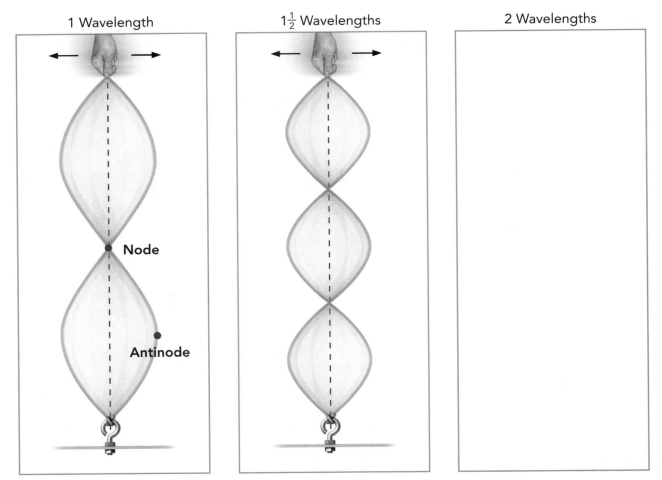

Academic Standards for Science

7.1.4 Recognize and provide evidence how light, sound and other waves have energy and how they interact with different materials.

7.NS.8 Analyze data and use it to make inferences and identify patterns.

7.DP.2 Brainstorm potential solutions.

7.DP.10 Communicate the solution using drawings.

FIGURE 6 ··

Standing Waves

As the frequency of the standing wave increases, more nodes and antinodes are created.

✎ **Complete the tasks.**

1. **Identify** In the second box, label the nodes and antinodes.

2. **CHALLENGE** In the third box, draw the next standing wave in the series, and label its nodes and antinodes.

7.NS.8, 7.DP.10

How Do Standing Waves Form?

If you tie a rope to a doorknob and shake the free end, waves will travel down the rope, reflect at the end, and come back. The reflected waves will meet the incoming waves and interference occurs. 🔑 **If the incoming wave and reflected wave have just the right frequency, they combine to form a wave that appears to stand still. This wave is called a standing wave.** A **standing wave** is a wave that appears to stand in one place, even though it is two waves interfering as they pass through each other.

Nodes and Antinodes In a standing wave, destructive interference produces points with zero amplitude, called **nodes,** as shown in **Figure 6.** The nodes are always evenly spaced along the wave. At points in the standing wave where constructive interference occurs, the amplitude is greater than zero. Points of maximum amplitude on a standing wave are called **antinodes.** The antinodes always occur halfway between two nodes.

1 Wavelength $1\frac{1}{2}$ Wavelengths   2 Wavelengths

Node

Antinode

Resonance Have you ever pushed a child on a swing? At first the swing is difficult to push. But once it is going, you need only a gentle push to keep it going. This is because the swing has a natural frequency. Even small pushes that are in rhythm with the swing's natural frequency produce large increases in the swing's amplitude.

Most objects have at least one natural frequency of vibration. Standing waves occur in an object when it vibrates at a natural frequency. If a nearby object vibrates at the same frequency, it can cause resonance. **Resonance** is an increase in the amplitude of a vibration that occurs when external vibrations match an object's natural frequency.

The Tacoma Narrows Bridge, or "Galloping Gertie," may have collapsed because of resonance. Storm winds are said to have resonated with the natural frequency of the bridge. This caused the amplitude of the bridge's sway to increase until the bridge collapsed. You can see the result of the collapse in **Figure 7.**

FIGURE 7 ·······································
The Power of Resonance
Winds blew as fast as 67 km/h during the storm in which the Tacoma Narrows Bridge collapsed.

✎ **Redesign What might engineers do differently when designing a new bridge for this location?**

_____

_____

_____

7.DP.2

Lab zone ® Do the Quick Lab
Standing Waves.

🔑 **Assess Your Understanding**

2a. Describe What causes resonance to occur?

_____

_____

_____

7.1.4

b. ⟳ **Relate Cause and Effect** What causes nodes to form in a standing wave?

_____

_____

_____

7.1.4

got it?

○ **I get it!** Now I know that standing waves form

when _____

_____

_____

_____

○ **I need extra help with** _____

Go to **MY SCIENCE** ⓢ **COACH** *online for help with this subject.*

7.1.4

The Nature of Sound

UNLOCK THE BIG ?

🔑 **What Is Sound?**
7.1.4

🔑 **What Factors Affect the Speed of Sound?**
7.1.4, 7.NS.1, 7.NS.8, 7.DP.9

my PLANET DiARY

FUN FACTS

Thunder and Lightning

It's a hot, sticky summer day, and the sky is filled with dark clouds. Suddenly, a flash of light zigzags through the air! A few seconds later, you hear the loud crack of thunder.

The lightning you see causes the thunder you hear. The reason you see lightning before you hear thunder is because light travels much faster than sound. You can use this fact to figure out how close the storm is. After you see a flash of lightning, count off the seconds until you hear the thunder. Divide the number of seconds by five. The result gives the approximate distance (in miles) to the storm.

Write your answer to the question below.
You notice that the time between seeing the lightning and hearing the thunder is increasing. What does this mean?

_____

_____

_____

_____

_____

▶ **PLANET DIARY** Go to **Planet Diary** to learn more about the nature of sound.

Lab zone Do the Inquiry Warm-Up *What Is Sound?*

Academic Standards for Science

7.1.4 Recognize and provide evidence how light, sound and other waves have energy and how they interact with different materials.

What Is Sound?

Here is a riddle: If a tree falls in a forest and no one hears it, does the tree make a sound? To a scientist, a falling tree makes a sound whether someone hears it or not. When a tree falls, the energy with which it strikes the ground causes a disturbance. Particles in the ground and the air begin to vibrate, or move back and forth. The vibrations create a sound wave as the energy travels through two mediums—air and the ground. 🔑 **Sound is a disturbance that travels through a medium as a longitudinal wave.**

Vocabulary
- density

Skills
↻ Reading: Identify the Main Idea
△ Inquiry: Graph

Making Sound Waves
A sound wave begins with a vibration. Look at the drum shown in **Figure 1.** When the side of the drum (called the drumhead) is struck, it vibrates rapidly in and out. These vibrations disturb nearby air particles. Each time the drumhead moves outward, it pushes air particles together, creating a *compression*. When the drumhead moves inward, the air particles bounce back and spread out, creating a *rarefaction*. These compressions and rarefactions travel through the air as longitudinal waves.

How Sound Waves Travel
Like other mechanical waves, sound waves carry energy through a medium without moving the particles of the medium along. Each particle of the medium vibrates as the disturbance passes. When the disturbance reaches your ears, you hear the sound.

A common medium for sound is air. But sound can travel through solids and liquids, too. For example, when you knock on a solid wooden door, the particles in the wood vibrate. The vibrations make sound waves that travel through the door. When the waves reach the other side of the door, they make sound waves in the air.

Vocabulary Identify Multiple Meanings Review the multiple meanings of the words in the Getting Started section and answer the question. What is the material through which sound waves travel?

_____

FIGURE 1 ·······························
Sound Waves
As the drumheads vibrate, they create sound waves that travel through the air.

✎ **Interpret Diagrams** Label each box as a compression or a rarefaction. Explain how you knew what to label them.

_____
_____
_____
_____

Wavelength

FIGURE 2 ·····················

Diffraction

Diffraction occurs when sound waves pass through an opening such as a doorway.

✏️ **Identify** Which diagram—A, B, or C—correctly shows what happens to sound waves when they pass through the doorway? Explain your answer.

_____

_____

_____

_____

_____

_____

_____

_____

Diffraction of Sound Waves

Have you ever wondered why when you are sitting in a classroom you can hear your friends talking in the hallway before they walk through the doorway? You hear them because sound waves do not always travel in straight lines. Sound waves can diffract, or bend, around the edges of an opening, such as a doorway.

Sound waves can also diffract around obstacles or corners. This is why you can hear someone who is talking in the hallway before the person walks around the corner. The sound waves bend around the corner. Then they spread out so you can hear them even though you cannot see who is talking. Remember this the next time you want to tell a secret!

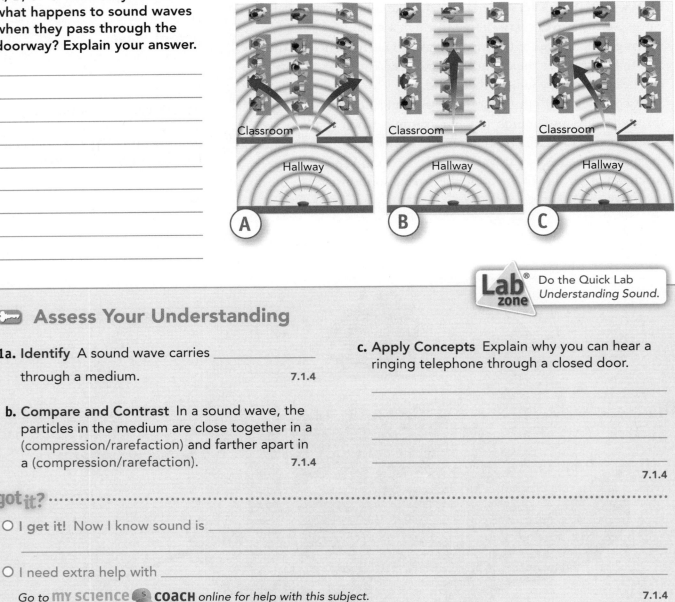

A   B   C

Lab ® Do the Quick Lab
zone *Understanding Sound.*

🔑 Assess Your Understanding

1a. Identify A sound wave carries _____ through a medium.   7.1.4

b. Compare and Contrast In a sound wave, the particles in the medium are close together in a (compression/rarefaction) and farther apart in a (compression/rarefaction).   7.1.4

c. Apply Concepts Explain why you can hear a ringing telephone through a closed door.

_____

_____

_____

_____
7.1.4

got**it?** ··

○ **I get it!** Now I know sound is _____

_____

○ **I need extra help with** _____

Go to **MY SCIENCE COACH** online for help with this subject.   7.1.4

What Factors Affect the Speed of Sound?

Suppose you were in a stadium watching the baseball player in **Figure 3.** You might see the bat hit the ball before you hear the hit. It is possible to see an action before you hear it because sound travels much more slowly than light. At room temperature, about 20°C, sound travels through air at 342 m/s. This is nearly 900,000 times slower than the speed of light! But the speed of sound is not always 342 m/s. Sound waves travel at different speeds in different media. 🗝 **The speed of sound depends on the temperature, stiffness, and density of the medium the sound travels through.**

Temperature In a given liquid or gas, sound travels more slowly at lower temperatures than at higher temperatures. Why? At lower temperatures, the particles of a medium move more slowly than at higher temperatures. It is more difficult for the particles to move, and they return to their original positions more slowly.

Academic Standards for Science

7.1.4 Recognize and provide evidence how light, sound and other waves have energy and how they interact with different materials.

7.NS.1 Make predictions.

7.NS.8 Analyze data, using appropriate mathematical manipulation as required, and use it to identify patterns and make inferences based on these patterns.

7.DP.9 Present evidence using mathematical representations.

FIGURE 3 ......

Speed of Sound in Air

How fast the sound of the bat hitting the ball travels depends on the air temperature. The data in the table show how the speed of sound in air changes with temperature.

✏️ **Use the data to answer the questions.**

7.NS.1, 7.NS.8, 7.DP.9

Air Temperature (°C)	Speed (m/s)
−20	318
−10	324
0	330
10	336
20	342

1. **Graph** Create a line graph. Plot temperature on the horizontal axis and speed on the vertical axis. Give the graph a title.

2. **Predict** What might the speed of sound be at 30°C? _____

213

Stiffness Years ago, Native Americans put their ears to the ground to find out if herds of bison or other animals were nearby. By listening for sounds in the ground they could hear the herds sooner than if they listened for sounds in the air. What is it about the state of the medium—solid, liquid, or gas—that determines the speed of sound?

The speed of sound depends on the stiffness of the medium. Sound travels more quickly in stiff media because when the particles of the medium are compressed, they quickly spread out again. For example, steel is stiffer than wood. If you knocked on both a wooden and steel door of the same thickness, the steel door would transmit the sound more easily. Sound also travels better over long distances in stiff media because sound waves lose energy more slowly than in less stiff media.

Solids are stiffer than liquids or gases. The particles in a solid are close together, so they bounce back and forth quickly as the compressions and rarefactions of the sound waves pass by. Most liquids are not as stiff as solids. So sound does not travel as fast in liquids as it does in solids. Gases are not very stiff. Sound generally travels the slowest in gases.

did you know?

An astronaut riding a vehicle on the surface of the moon would not hear the sound of the engine. Sound can travel only if there is a medium. There are no air molecules to compress or expand on the moon, so there is no sound.

do the math! Analyzing Data

The table shows the speed of sound in different media. Use the data to answer the following questions.

1 Interpret Tables In general, does sound travel faster in solids, liquids, or gases?

_____

2 Infer Which substance is stiffer—air or water?

_____

3 Infer What is the stiffest substance in the table?

_____

4 Apply Concepts Suppose you put your ear to a steel fence. You tell your friend to yell and tap the fence at the same time from far away. Which do you think that you will hear first, the yell or the tap? Why?

_____

_____

_____

_____

5 CHALLENGE How many times faster does sound travel in a diamond than in air?

_____

_____

Speed of Sound	
Medium	Speed (m/s)
Gases (20°C)	
Air	342
Helium	977
Liquids (20°C)	
Mercury	1,450
Fresh water	1,482
Solids	
Lead	1,200
Plastic	1,800
Hardwood	4,000
Steel	5,200
Diamond	12,000

7.NS.8

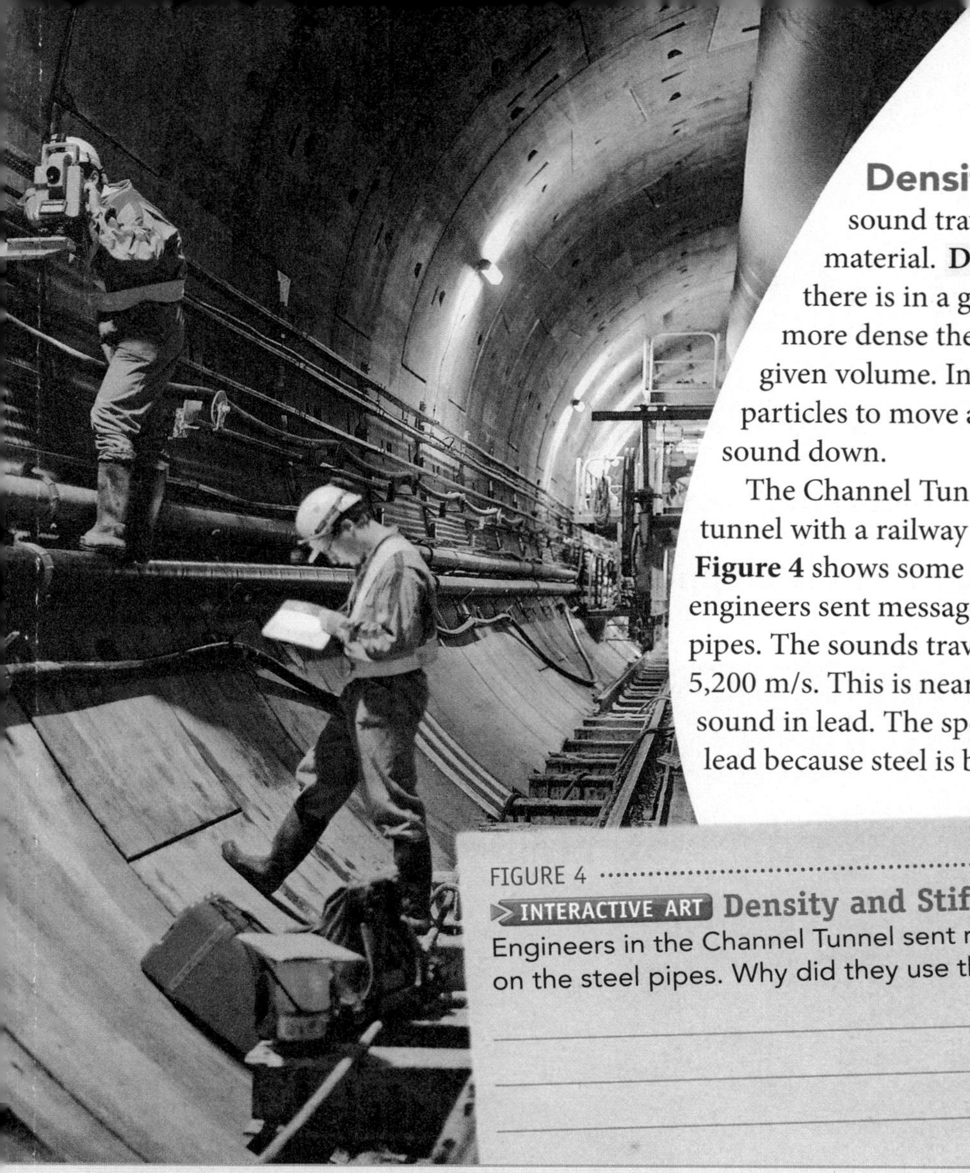

Density In materials of the same stiffness, sound travels more slowly in the denser material. **Density** is how much matter or mass there is in a given amount of space or volume. The more dense the material, the more mass it has in a given volume. In denser materials, it is harder for the particles to move as sound waves pass by. This slows sound down.

The Channel Tunnel is a 50-kilometer-long undersea tunnel with a railway connecting England and France. **Figure 4** shows some engineers working in the tunnel. The engineers sent messages to each other by tapping on the steel pipes. The sounds traveled through the pipes at a speed of 5,200 m/s. This is nearly four times faster than the speed of sound in lead. The speed of sound in steel is greater than in lead because steel is both less dense and stiffer than lead.

FIGURE 4 ······································

> INTERACTIVE ART **Density and Stiffness**
Engineers in the Channel Tunnel sent messages to each other by tapping on the steel pipes. Why did they use the steel pipes to communicate?

_____

_____

_____

Lab zone ® Do the Quick Lab
Ear to the Sound.

🔑 **Assess Your Understanding**

2a. Explain Why does sound usually travel faster in solids than in liquids or gases?

_____

_____

_____

7.1.4

b. Apply Concepts The sounds from a marching band travel (faster/slower) when the air temperature is 30°C than when the air temperature is 20°C.   7.1.4, 7.NS.8

c. Develop Hypotheses Steel is denser than plastic, yet sound travels faster in steel than in plastic. Develop a hypothesis to explain why.

_____

_____

_____

_____

_____

_____

_____

7.1.4, 7.NS.1

got it? ···

◯ **I get it!** Now I know the speed of sound depends on _____

_____

◯ **I need extra help with** _____

Go to MY SCIENCE ⓢ COACH *online for help with this subject.*   7.1.4

Properties of Sound

UNLOCK THE BIG ?

🔑 **What Affects Pitch?**
7.1.4, 7.NS.11, 7.DP.10

🔑 **What Affects Loudness?**
7.1.4, 7.NS.8

🔑 **What Causes the Doppler Effect?**
7.1.4

MY PLANET DIARY

Silent Call

To get a dog's attention, a dog trainer blows into a small whistle. But you don't hear a thing. Dogs can hear frequencies well above the human range of hearing. Frequency is measured in hertz (Hz), or the number of sound waves a vibrating object gives off per second. A higher frequency means that the sound has a higher pitch. The table compares the range of frequencies that humans and various animals can hear.

Use the data in the table to answer the following question.

Which animal can hear the widest range of frequencies?

_____

_____

_____

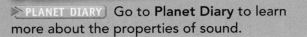 **PLANET DIARY** Go to **Planet Diary** to learn more about the properties of sound.

SCIENCE STATS

Animal	Range of Hearing (in Hertz)
Human	20–20,000
Dog	67–45,000
Mouse	1,000–91,000
Cat	45–64,000
Bullfrog	100–2,500
Elephant	16–12,000

 **Lab zone**® Do the Inquiry Warm-Up *How Does Amplitude Affect Loudness?*

What Affects Pitch?

Pitch is an important property of sound that you may already know about. Have you ever described someone's voice as "high-pitched" or "low-pitched"? The **pitch** of a sound is a description of how high or low the sound seems to a person. 🔑 **The pitch of a sound you hear depends on the frequency of the sound wave.** Sound waves with a high frequency have a high pitch. Sound waves with a low frequency have a low pitch.

Vocabulary
- pitch • loudness • intensity • decibel
- Doppler effect

Skills
↺ Reading: Compare and Contrast

△ Inquiry: Make Models

The frequency of a sound wave depends on how fast the source of the sound is vibrating. For example, when you speak or sing, air from your lungs rushes past your vocal cords, making them vibrate. This produces sound waves. To sing specific pitches, or notes, you use muscles in your throat to stretch or relax your vocal cords. When your vocal cords stretch, they vibrate more quickly as the air rushes by them. This creates higher-frequency sound waves that have higher pitches. When your vocal cords relax, lower-frequency sound waves with lower pitches are produced.

Frequency is measured in hertz (Hz). For example, a frequency of 50 Hz means 50 vibrations per second. A trained soprano voice can produce frequencies higher than 1,000 Hz. A bass singer can produce frequencies lower than 80 Hz. Young people can normally hear sounds with frequencies between 20 Hz and 20,000 Hz.

FIGURE 1 ....

Pitch
The female soprano singer sings high notes and the male bass singer sings low notes.   7.NS.11, 7.DP.10

△ **Make Models** In the bubble above the bass singer, draw lines to represent the frequency of the sound wave for a low note. Then explain your drawing.

_____

_____

_____

_____

Lab zone Do the Lab Investigation *Changing Pitch.*

🔒 Assess Your Understanding

got it? ....

○ **I get it!** Now I know the pitch of a sound that you hear depends on_____

_____

○ **I need extra help with** _____

Go to **my science** ⑤ **coach** *online for help with this subject.*   7.1.4

217

Academic Standards for Science

7.1.4 Recognize and provide evidence how light, sound and other waves have energy and how they interact with different materials.

7.NS.8 Analyze data, using appropriate mathematical manipulation as required, and use it to identify patterns and make inferences based on these patterns.

What Affects Loudness?

Loudness is another important property of sound. You probably already know about loudness. For example, the closer you are to a sound, the louder it is. Also, a whisper in your ear can be just as loud as a shout from a block away. **Loudness** describes your awareness of the energy of a sound. **The loudness of a sound depends on the energy and intensity of the sound wave.**

Energy If you hit a drum lightly, you hear a sound. If you hit the drum harder, you hear a louder sound. Why? When you hit a drum harder, you transfer more energy to it. This causes the amplitude, or the distance the drumhead moves from its rest position, to increase. A sound source vibrating with a large amplitude produces a sound wave with a large amplitude. Recall that the greater the amplitude of a wave, the more energy it has. So the more energy a sound wave has, the louder it sounds.

Intensity If you were to move closer to the stage shown in **Figure 2,** the voices of the performers would sound louder. Why? Close to the sound source, a sound wave covers a small area. As a wave travels away from the source, it covers more area. The total energy of the wave, however, stays the same. Therefore, the closer a sound wave is to its source, the more energy it has in a given area. The amount of energy a sound wave carries per second through a unit area is its **intensity.** A sound wave of greater intensity sounds louder.

FIGURE 2

Intensity

Sound waves spread out as they travel away from the source.

Interpret Diagrams Rank the intensity of a sound wave at the three locations. A ranking of 1 is the greatest. Write your answers in the boxes. Explain your answers.

____

____

____

____

____

____

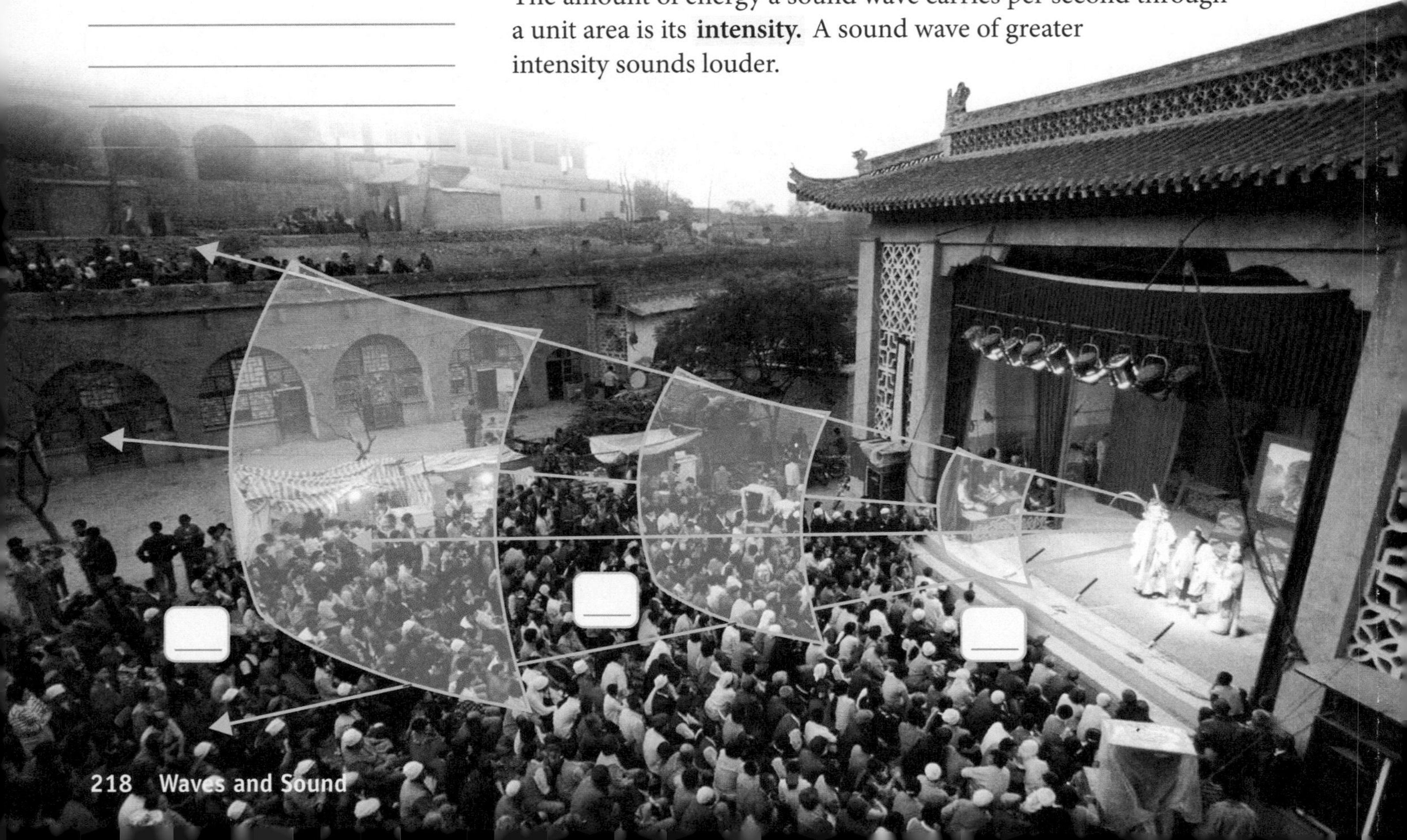

Measuring Loudness

Measuring Loudness The loudness of different sounds is compared using a unit called the **decibel** (dB). The table in the Apply It below compares the loudness of some familiar sounds. The loudness of a sound you can barely hear is about 0 dB. A 10-dB increase in loudness represents a tenfold increase in the intensity of the sound. For example, a 10-dB sound is ten times more intense than a 0-dB sound. A 20-dB sound is 100 times more intense than a 0-dB sound and ten times more intense than a 10-dB sound. Sounds louder than 100 dB can cause damage to your ears, especially if you listen to those sounds for long periods of time. For this reason, airport workers, like the one shown to the right, wear hearing protection.

Use the table to answer the questions.

① Which sounds louder, a rock concert or a jet plane at takeoff?_____

② Which sounds could be dangerous to your ears?

_____

_____

③ Calculate How much more intense is a 20-dB whisper than the threshold of human hearing?

_____

④ **CHALLENGE** How much more intense is a 90-dB hair dryer than 60-dB street traffic?

_____

Measuring Loudness	
Sound	Loudness (dB)
Threshold of human hearing	0
Whisper	15–20
Normal conversation	40–50
Busy street traffic	60–70
Hairdryer	80–90
Rock concert	110–120
Headphones at peak volume	120
Jet plane at takeoff	120–160

7.NS.8

 Lab zone Do the Quick Lab *Listen to This.*

🔑 Assess Your Understanding

1a. Review The amount of energy a sound wave carries per second through a unit area is its

_____

7.1.4

b. Describe The intensity of a sound wave (increases/decreases) with distance. 7.1.4

c. Calculate An 80-dB sound is _____ times more intense than a 60-dB sound.

7.1.4, 7.NS.8

got it?

○ **I get it!** Now I know that the loudness of a sound depends on _____

_____

_____

○ **I need extra help with** _____

Go to **my science** **coach** *online for help with this subject.* 7.1.4

Academic Standards for Science

7.1.4 Recognize and provide evidence how light, sound and other waves have energy and how they interact with different materials.

What Causes the Doppler Effect?

Have you ever listened to the siren of a firetruck on its way to a fire? If so, then you probably noticed that as the truck goes by, the pitch of the siren drops. But the pitch of the siren stays constant for the firefighters in the truck. The siren's pitch changes only if it is moving toward or away from a listener.

The change in frequency of a wave as its source moves in relation to an observer is called the **Doppler effect.** If the waves are sound waves, the change in frequency is heard as a change in pitch. The Doppler effect is named after the Austrian scientist Christian Doppler (1803–1853). 🔧 **The Doppler effect occurs because the motion of the source causes the waves to either get closer together or spread out.**

Figure 3 shows how sound waves from a moving source behave. Each time the siren sends out a new wave, the firetruck moves ahead in the same direction as the waves in front of the truck. This causes the waves to get closer together. Because the waves are closer together, they have a shorter wavelength and a higher frequency as they reach observers in front of the truck. As the truck moves away, it travels in the opposite direction of the sound waves behind it. This causes the waves to spread out. Because they spread out, the waves have a longer wavelength and a lower frequency as they reach the observers behind the truck.

✏️ **Compare and Contrast**
The waves in front of a moving sound source have a (shorter/longer) wavelength. The waves behind a moving sound source have a (shorter/longer) wavelength.

FIGURE 3 ·······························

▶ ART IN MOTION **The Doppler Effect**
As the firetruck speeds by, observers hear a change in the pitch of the siren. ✏️ **Identify Circle the answer that describes the pitch that the observers hear.**

People behind the firetruck hear a (lower/higher) pitch than the firefighters in the truck hear.

People standing in front of the firetruck hear a (lower/higher) pitch than the firefighters in the truck hear.

FIRE DEPARTMENT

FIGURE 4 ···

Headphones turn an electrical signal into sound waves.

1 An electrical signal travels up a wire.

2 The electrical signal causes a magnet to vibrate.

3 The magnet is attached to a thin cone of material. The vibrating cone sends sound waves through the air.

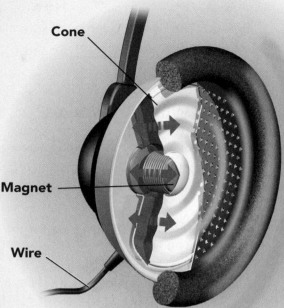

Cone

Magnet

Wire

⟳ **Compare and Contrast** Compare how a drum and headphones produce sounds of higher pitch and greater loudness.

_____

_____

_____

_____

_____

_____

_____

 Lab zone® Do the Quick Lab *Pipe Sounds.*

🔑 Assess Your Understanding

2. What determines the pitch and loudness of sound?

_____

_____

_____

_____

7.1.4

got it?

○ **I get it!** Now I know that the Doppler effect occurs because _____

_____

_____

○ **I need extra help with** _____

Go to **my science** ⑤ **coach** *online for help with this subject.*

7.1.4

 6 Study Guide

The basic properties of waves are _____, _____,
_____ **, and** _____ **.**

LESSON 1 What Are Waves?

7.1.4, 7.NS.1, 7.DP.10

🔑 Mechanical waves form when a source of energy causes a medium to vibrate.

🔑 The three types of mechanical waves are transverse waves, longitudinal waves, and surface waves.

Vocabulary
- wave • energy • medium • mechanical wave • vibration • transverse wave • crest
- trough • longitudinal wave • compression • rarefaction

LESSON 2 Properties of Waves

7.1.4, 7.NS.1, 7.NS.3, 7.NS.8

🔑 Amplitude describes how far the medium in a wave moves. Wavelength describes a wave's length, and frequency describes how often it occurs. Speed describes how quickly a wave moves.

🔑 The speed, wavelength, and frequency of a wave are related by a mathematical formula: Speed = Wavelength × Frequency.

Vocabulary
- amplitude • wavelength • frequency • hertz

LESSON 3 Interactions of Waves

7.1.4, 7.NS.1, 7.NS.8, 7.DP.2, 7.DP.10

🔑 Waves change direction by reflection, refraction, and diffraction.

🔑 There are two types of interference: constructive and destructive.

🔑 If the incoming wave and reflected wave have just the right frequency, they combine to form a standing wave.

Vocabulary
- reflection • refraction • diffraction • interference
- constructive interference • destructive interference
- standing wave • node • antinode • resonance

LESSON 4 The Nature of Sound

7.1.4, 7.NS.1, 7.NS.8, 7.DP.9

🔑 Sound is a disturbance that travels through a medium as a longitudinal wave.

🔑 The speed of sound depends on the temperature, stiffness, and density of the medium the sound travels through.

Vocabulary
- density

LESSON 5 Properties of Sound

7.1.4, 7.NS.8, 7.NS.11, 7.DP.10

🔑 The pitch of a sound you hear depends on the frequency of the sound wave.

🔑 The loudness of a sound depends on the energy and intensity of the sound wave.

🔑 The Doppler effect occurs because the motion of the source causes the waves to either get closer together or spread out.

Vocabulary
- pitch • loudness • intensity • decibel
- Doppler effect

Review and Assessment

LESSON 1 What Are Waves?

1. A wave transfers

   a. energy.   **b.** particles

   c. water.   **d.** air.

                        7.1.4

2. _____ form when a source of energy causes a medium to vibrate.

                        7.1.4

3. Relate Cause and Effect Suppose ripples move from one side of a lake to the other. Does the water move across the lake? Explain.

_____

_____

_____

_____

                        7.1.4

LESSON 2 Properties of Waves

4. The distance between two crests is a wave's

   a. amplitude.   **b.** wavelength.

   c. frequency.   **d.** speed.

                        7.1.4

5. The _____ of a wave is the number of waves that pass a given point in a certain amount of time.

                        7.1.4

6. Calculate Find the frequency of the wave.

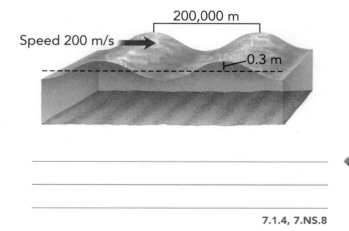

200,000 m

Speed 200 m/s

0.3 m

_____

_____

_____

                7.1.4, 7.NS.8

LESSON 3 Interactions of Waves

7. The bending of a wave due to a change in speed is called

   a. interference.   **b.** reflection.

   c. diffraction.   **d.** refraction.

                        7.1.4

8. _____ occurs when external vibrations match an object's natural frequency.

                        7.1.4

9. Predict Two waves are traveling toward each other. The crests from the waves meet. Describe what happens.

_____

_____

_____

_____

_____

                  7.1.4, 7.NS.1

10. Draw Conclusions If you push a shopping cart and one wheel hits a rough patch of concrete, it is difficult to steer the cart in a straight line. Explain how this is similar to refraction of a wave as it enters a new medium.

_____

_____

_____

_____

_____

_____

_____

                        7.1.4

11. Write About It Wave interaction occurs often in the environment. Describe three different ways that you could observe waves changing direction in an indoor swimming pool. Mention as many types of waves as possible.

                        7.1.4

LESSON 4 The Nature of Sound

12. What term describes how much matter or mass there is in a given volume?

   a. stiffness   **b.** density

   c. temperature   **d.** diffraction

                                   7.1.4

13. If you increase the temperature of a liquid or gas, a sound wave will travel _____

                                   7.1.4

14. Summarize What three properties of a medium affect the speed of sound?

_____

_____

                                   7.1.4

15. Make Models In the circles below, draw the air particles in a compression and rarefaction of the same sound wave.

                          7.1.4, 7.DP.10

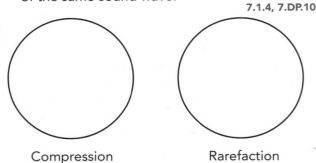

    Compression   Rarefaction

16. Relate Cause and Effect Why is a vibration of an object necessary for a sound wave to form?

_____

_____

_____

                                   7.1.4

17. Infer Thunder and lightning happen at the same time. Explain why you see the lightning before you hear the thunder.

_____

_____

_____

                                   7.1.4

LESSON 5 Properties of Sound

18. What property of sound describes your awareness of the energy of a sound?

   a. loudness   **b.** intensity

   c. pitch   **d.** elasticity

                                   7.1.4

19. As a sound wave travels, its intensity decreases because _____

_____

                                   7.1.4

20. Relate Cause and Effect As a car drives past a person standing on a sidewalk, the driver keeps a hand on the horn. How does the pitch of the horn differ for the driver and the person standing on the sidewalk?

_____

_____

_____

_____

_____

                                   7.1.4

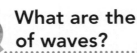

What are the properties of waves?

21. During a storm, a TV reporter says, "The ocean waves are 3 meters high. They are about 45 meters apart and are hitting the shore every 15 seconds." Think about the four basic properties of waves and describe these ocean waves using the correct science words. (*Hint:* You will need to do some calculations first.)

_____

_____

_____

_____

_____

                                7.1.4, 7.NS.8

Indiana ISTEP+ Practice

Multiple Choice

Circle the letter of the best answer.

1. Two waves approach each other as shown in the diagram below. What will be the amplitude of the wave produced when the crests from each wave meet?

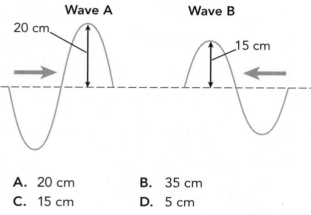

Wave A   **Wave B**

20 cm

15 cm

A. 20 cm	**B.** 35 cm
C. 15 cm	**D.** 5 cm

7.1.4, 7.NS.8

2. Fishing boats use sonar to locate schools of fish. What characteristic of sound is most important for this application of sonar?

   A. Sound waves reflect off some surfaces.

   B. Sound waves diffract around corners.

   C. Sound waves interfere when they overlap.

   D. Sound waves spread out from a source.

7.1.4

3. The speed of a wave in a spring is 3 m/s. If the wavelength is 0.1 m, what is the frequency?

A. 30 Hz	**B.** 0.3 Hz
C. 30 m/s	**D.** 0.3 m/s

7.1.4, 7.NS.8

4. Which of the following is true about standing waves?

   A. Constructive interference produces points with zero amplitude.

   B. The nodes are unevenly spaced along the wave.

   C. The amplitude of antinodes is greater than nodes.

   D. Nodes are points of maximum energy on the wave.

7.1.4

Constructed Response

Write your answer to Question 5 on the lines below.

5. Why does sound intensity decrease as the distance from the source increases?

   _____

   _____

   _____

7.1.4

Extended Response

Use the diagram and your knowledge of science to help you answer Question 6. Write your answer on a separate sheet of paper.

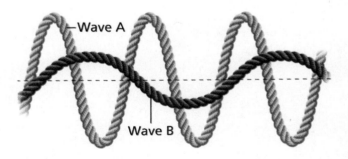

Wave A

Wave B

6. The waves shown above travel at the same speed. Which wave has the higher frequency? Which has the longer wavelength? Which has the greater amplitude?

7.1.4, 7.NS.11

Wall of water

For as long as humans have sailed on the oceans, ships have disappeared without explanation. People chalked these losses up to bad luck and bad weather. A mysterious phenomenon, proven in 2004 to exist, may finally explain why some large ships are never seen again.

Waves in water usually behave like the other waves around them. Most waves in an area are about the same height and move at the same rate. Ocean waves are rarely more than 15 meters in height and usually form rolling hills of water. But freak monster waves can top 30 meters in height, forming huge walls of water!

Some monster waves form where two currents meet and their waves combine. The weather may be responsible for other monster waves. If an ordinary large wave travels at the same speed and in the same direction as the wind for more than 12 hours, the extra push from the wind can cause the wave to reach monster heights. Some monster waves seem to grow out of normal ocean wave patterns. Physicists theorize that these unstable waves absorb energy from the surrounding waves and grow to vast heights.

Most ships are not designed to withstand 30-meter-high waves, so it's no wonder that little has been found but wreckage. Fortunately, scientists are working on ways to protect ships and sailors in the face of these enormous destructive waves.

Model It Research how so-called monster waves focus and amplify the effects of surrounding waves. Use computer technology to create a diagram or to model the effects. Explain your diagram or model to a classmate.

7.1.4, 7.NS.2, 7.NS.11

An Operatic Superpower

Can someone really break a glass by singing a high note? It may seem like a superpower, but the human voice does have the power to shatter a crystal wine glass! This feat is commonly credited to opera singers because they have very powerful and well-trained voices.

Many wine glasses are made of a type of glass called crystal. The molecules in a crystal glass are arranged in a repeating pattern that forms a repeating internal structure. If you tap a crystal object, you can hear a clear tone. That tone is the natural resonant frequency of vibration for that crystal. When the crystal is exposed to a sound at that frequency, the molecules of the crystal vibrate. When the glass vibrates too much, the shape of the glass distorts, which causes the glass to crack. The cracks expand very rapidly, and the crystal shatters.

A trained singer can reproduce the natural frequency of a crystal glass. If the singer can sing the tone of the crystal's natural frequency loudly enough, the singing can shatter the glass!

Design It Resonant frequencies can also be used to make music. Glass harps use wine glasses filled with varying amounts of water to create different notes. The player runs a moistened finger around the rim of each glass. The size of the glass and the amount of water determine which note sounds. Research to learn more about how glass harps work. Then design an experiment to test the amount of water needed to create different pitches. Create a one-page procedure for your experiment.

7.1.4, 7.NS.2, 7.NS.11

WHY CAN YOU SEE A CITY IN THIS SCULPTURE?

How does light interact with matter?

Cloud Gate, a 110-ton sculpture in Chicago, Illinois, is made of highly polished stainless steel. The buildings that you see in the sculpture are a reflection of the city of Chicago.

Predict **If you were standing directly in front of this sculpture, what would you see? Explain your answer.**

_____

_____

_____

_____

_____

_____

> UNTAMED SCIENCE Watch the **Untamed Science** video to learn more about light.

Electromagnetic Waves and Light

Academic Standards for Science

7.1.4, 7.NS.1, 7.NS.2, 7.NS.8, 7.NS.11

7 Getting Started

Check Your Understanding

1. Background Read the paragraph below and then answer the question.

> Jamal wakes up early to write a term paper. As the sun rises, it **transmits** sunlight through the window. The light **reflects** off of his computer screen, making it difficult for him to read the words he types. He pulls down the window shade knowing it will **absorb** some of the light.

> To **transmit** is to pass something from one place to another.
>
> To **reflect** is to throw something back.
>
> To **absorb** is to take something in or soak it up.

• Why does the window create a problem for Jamal?

_____

_____

▶ **MY READING WEB** If you had trouble completing the question above, visit **My Reading Web** and type in *Electromagnetic Waves and Light.*

Vocabulary Skill

Use Prefixes A prefix is a word part that is added at the beginning of a root or base word to change its meaning. Knowing the meaning of prefixes will help you figure out new words.

Prefix	Meaning	Example
micro-	small, tiny	microscope
tele-	distant, operating at a distance	telescope
con-	together with, jointly	concave mirror, convex mirror
trans-	through	translucent

2. Quick Check Choose the word from the table that best completes the sentence.

You need a _____ to view the planets in any detail.

pigment

plane mirror

mirage

convex lens

Chapter Preview

LESSON 1
- electromagnetic wave
- electromagnetic radiation
- polarized light
- photoelectric effect • photon

⟳ **Identify the Main Idea**
△ **Calculate**

LESSON 2
- electromagnetic spectrum
- radio waves • microwaves
- radar • infrared rays
- thermogram • visible light
- ultraviolet rays • X-rays
- gamma rays

⟳ **Summarize**
△ **Communicate**

LESSON 3
- transparent • translucent
- opaque • primary color
- secondary color
- complementary color • pigment

⟳ **Identify the Main Idea**
△ **Predict**

LESSON 4
- ray • regular reflection • image
- diffuse reflection • plane mirror
- virtual image • concave mirror
- optical axis • focal point
- real image • convex mirror

⟳ **Compare and Contrast**
△ **Classify**

LESSON 5
- index of refraction • mirage
- lens • concave lens
- convex lens

⟳ **Ask Questions**
△ **Interpret Data**

▷ **VOCAB FLASH CARDS** For extra help with vocabulary, visit **Vocab Flash Cards** and type in *Electromagnetic Waves and Light.*

The Nature of Electromagnetic Waves

UNLOCK THE BIG ?

🔑 **What Makes Up an Electromagnetic Wave?**
7.1.4, 7.NS.8

🔑 **What Models Explain How Electromagnetic Waves Behave?**
7.1.4, 7.NS.1

MY PLANET DIARY

Posted by:
Jordan

Location:
Hopkinton, Massachusetts

Life is truly a lot easier with a cell phone. I could contact anybody I would possibly need to, such as my parents or emergency care, if there were an emergency. If I were without a cell phone, who knows what could happen? I like having a cell phone to talk to friends, my parents, and my family. Also, it's easier to have my own phone to use when I want to make a call. Like most people I know, I use my cell phone every day. I can always contact people I need to with a cell phone and it's great to have.

BLOG

Read the following questions. Write your answers below.

1. In what situation might Jordan need to use a cell phone? Who would he call?

_____

_____

_____

2. For what reason would you use a cell phone most?

_____

_____

> PLANET DIARY Go to **Planet Diary** to learn more about electromagnetic waves.

Lab zone Do the Inquiry Warm-Up *How Fast Are Electromagnetic Waves?*

Academic Standards for Science

7.1.4 Recognize and provide evidence how light, sound and other waves have energy and how they interact with different materials.

7.NS.8 Analyze data, using appropriate mathematical manipulation as required, and use it to identify patterns and make inferences based on these patterns.

What Makes Up an Electromagnetic Wave?

As you sit at your desk and read this book, you are surrounded by waves you cannot see or hear. There are radio waves, microwaves, infrared rays, visible light, ultraviolet rays, and tiny amounts of X-rays and gamma rays. These waves are all electromagnetic waves.

Vocabulary
- electromagnetic wave • electromagnetic radiation
- polarized light • photoelectric effect • photon

Skills
- Reading: Identify the Main Idea
- Inquiry: Calculate

Characteristics of Electromagnetic Waves

An **electromagnetic wave** is a transverse wave that involves the transfer of electric and magnetic energy. **An electromagnetic wave is made up of vibrating electric and magnetic fields that move through space or some medium at the speed of light.**

An electromagnetic wave can begin with the movement of charged particles, all of which have electric fields around them. As the particles change speed or direction, a vibrating electric field is created, which in turn produces a vibrating magnetic field. The vibrating magnetic field creates a vibrating electric field. The electric and magnetic fields produce each other repeatedly. The result is an electromagnetic wave, shown in **Figure 1.** Note that the two fields vibrate at right angles to one another.

Energy The energy that electromagnetic waves transfer through matter or space is called **electromagnetic radiation.** Electromagnetic waves do not require a medium such as air, so they can transfer energy through a vacuum, or empty space.

FIGURE 1 ·····························
Electromagnetic Wave
An electromagnetic wave travels through space at the speed of light—about 300,000 kilometers per second.

✏️ **Calculate** How long will it take sunlight to travel the 150 million kilometers to Earth? Use a calculator to solve the problem.

_____

_____

_____

7.NS.8

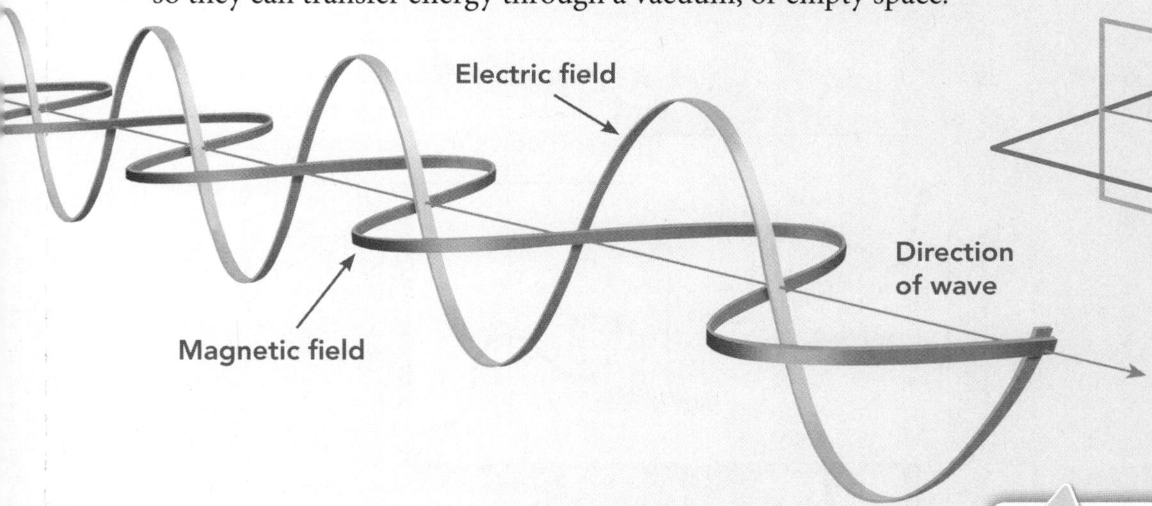

Electric field

Magnetic field

Direction of wave

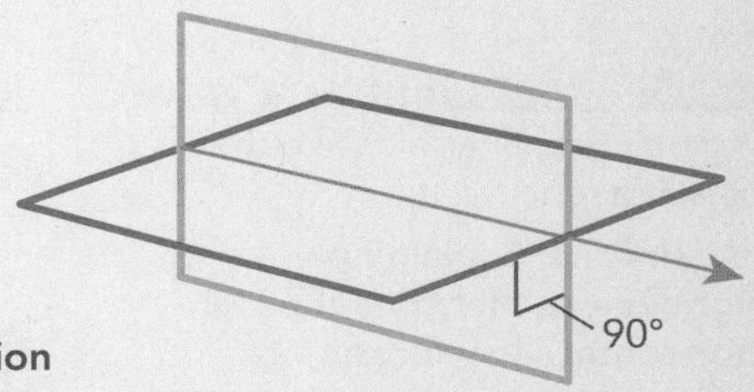

90°

Fields are at right angles to each other.

Lab® zone Do the Quick Lab *What Is an Electromagnetic Wave Made Of?*

Assess Your Understanding

got it? ·······························

○ **I get it!** Now I know that electromagnetic waves are made of _____

_____

○ **I need extra help with** _____

Go to MY SCIENCE COACH online for help with this subject.

7.1.4

Identify the Main Idea
Circle the main idea in the first paragraph. Underline the details.

What Models Explain How Electromagnetic Waves Behave?

Two different models are needed to explain the behavior of electromagnetic waves. A wave model best explains many of the behaviors, but a particle model best explains others. Light is an electromagnetic wave. It has many properties of waves but can also act as though it is a stream of particles.

Wave Model of Light When light passes through a polarizing filter, it has the properties of a wave. An ordinary beam of light consists of waves that vibrate in all directions. A polarizing filter acts as though it has tiny slits aligned in only one direction. The slits can be horizontal or vertical. When light enters a polarizing filter, only some waves can pass through it. The light that passes through is called **polarized light.**

To help you understand the wave model, think of light waves like transverse waves on a rope. They vibrate in all directions. If you shake a rope through a fence with vertical slits, only waves that vibrate up and down will pass through, as shown in **Figure 2.** The other waves are blocked. A polarizing filter acts like the slits in a fence. It allows only waves that vibrate in one direction to pass through it.

FIGURE 2 ·······················

> **VIRTUAL LAB** **Light as a Wave**
A polarizing filter acts like the slits in a fence.

✏ **Predict** Explain how light waves that pass through horizontal slits vibrate.

_____

_____

_____

_____

7.NS.1

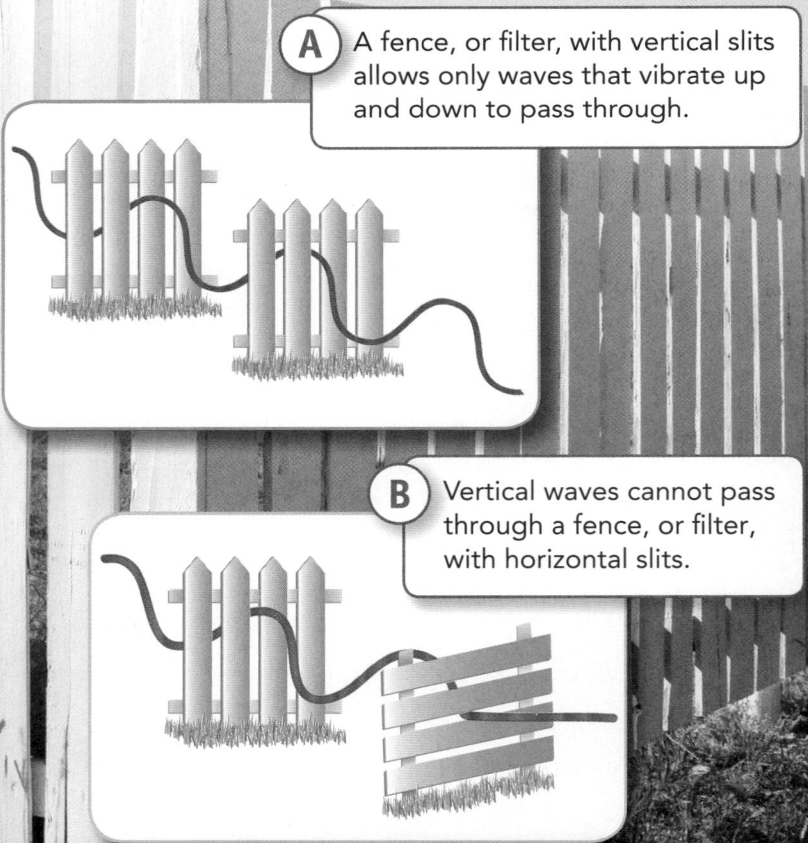

A A fence, or filter, with vertical slits allows only waves that vibrate up and down to pass through.

B Vertical waves cannot pass through a fence, or filter, with horizontal slits.

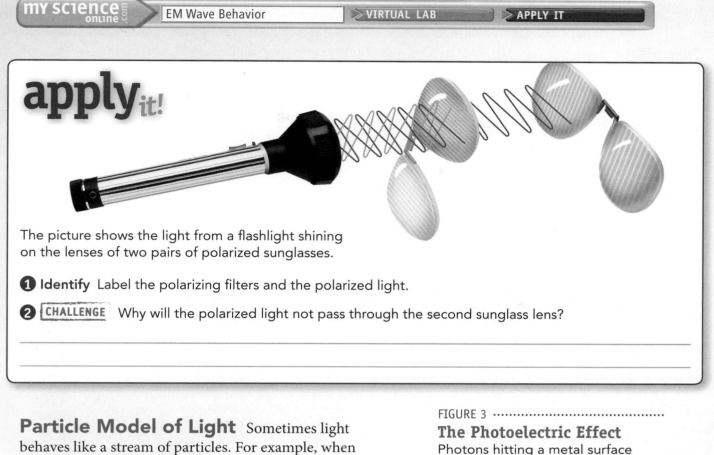

apply it!

The picture shows the light from a flashlight shining on the lenses of two pairs of polarized sunglasses.

1 **Identify** Label the polarizing filters and the polarized light.

2 CHALLENGE Why will the polarized light not pass through the second sunglass lens?

_____

_____

Particle Model of Light
Sometimes light behaves like a stream of particles. For example, when a beam of high frequency light shines on some metals, it causes tiny particles to move. These particles are called electrons. Sometimes light can even cause an electron to move so much that it is knocked out of the metal, as shown in **Figure 3.** This is called the **photoelectric effect.** This effect can be explained by thinking of light as a stream of tiny packets, or particles, of energy. Each packet of light energy is called a **photon.** For the effect to occur, each photon must contain enough energy to knock an electron free from the metal.

FIGURE 3 ···

The Photoelectric Effect
Photons hitting a metal surface knock out electrons.

Dim blue light or ultraviolet rays

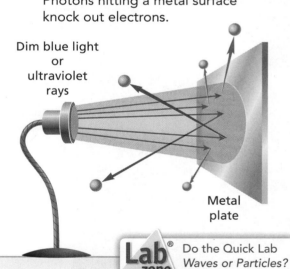

Metal plate

Lab zone® Do the Quick Lab *Waves or Particles?*

🔑 Assess Your Understanding

1a. Define A _____ is a tiny packet of energy.   7.1.4

b. Describe What does a polarizing filter do?

_____

_____

_____

7.1.4

got it?

○ **I get it!** Now I know that the models that explain how electromagnetic waves behave are _____

_____

○ **I need extra help with** _____

Go to **my science** 🅢 **coach** *online for help with this subject.*   7.1.4

Waves of the Electromagnetic Spectrum

🔑 **How Do Electromagnetic Waves Compare?**
7.1.4

🔑 **What Makes Up the Electromagnetic Spectrum?**
7.1.4, 7.NS.8

my pLaneT DiaRY

DISCOVERY

Hey, Where Did It Go?

What would you do if you had an invisibility cloak? This idea might not be as far-fetched as it sounds. Scientists have actually been working on creating a way to make objects invisible! Researchers have created a device that can change the direction of microwaves, so that they flow around a test object. This rerouting causes the object to look invisible at microwave frequencies. Unfortunately, people cannot see microwaves, which means the object isn't invisible to us. But, who knows, maybe one day you'll be able to put on one of these "cloaks" and move around completely unseen!

Answer the question below.

If a device like this is developed for visible light, how do you think a scientist who studies animals in nature might use it?

_____

_____

_____

_____

_____

> PLANET DIARY Go to **Planet Diary** to learn more about the electromagnetic spectrum.

Do the Inquiry Warm-Up
What Is White Light?

Vocabulary

- electromagnetic spectrum • radio waves • microwaves
- radar • infrared rays • thermogram • visible light
- ultraviolet rays • X-rays • gamma rays

Skills

- **Reading:** Summarize
- **Inquiry:** Communicate

How Do Electromagnetic Waves Compare?

Can you imagine trying to take a photo with a radio or heating your food with X-rays? Light, radio waves, and X-rays are all electromagnetic waves. But each has properties that make it more useful for some purposes than others. **All electromagnetic waves travel at the same speed in a vacuum, but they have different wavelengths and different frequencies.** A vacuum is a space that contains no air or other gas.

Visible light is the only range of wavelengths your eyes can see. Your radio detects radio waves, which have much longer wavelengths than visible light. X-rays, on the other hand, have much shorter wavelengths than visible light.

For waves in any medium, as the wavelength decreases, the frequency increases. Waves with the longest wavelengths have the lowest frequencies. Waves with the shortest wavelengths have the highest frequencies. The higher the frequency of a wave, the higher its energy.

Academic Standards for Science

7.1.4 Recognize and provide evidence how light, sound and other waves have energy and how they interact with different materials.

FIGURE 1 ······

Comparing Electromagnetic Waves

Different types of electromagnetic waves have different wavelengths.

✎ **Complete these tasks.**

1. **Label** Write the names *visible light*, *radio waves*, and *X-rays* in the correct boxes on the diagram.

2. **Draw Conclusions** Which wave has the highest energy? Explain.

_____
_____
_____
_____
_____

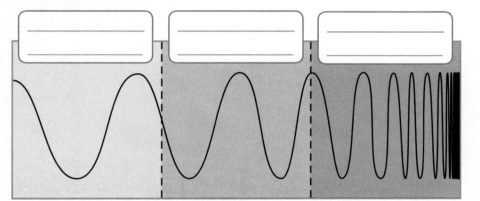

 Do the Quick Lab *Differences Between Waves.*

🔑 Assess Your Understanding

got it? ······

○ **I get it!** Now I know that electromagnetic waves have different _____
_____ but the same _____

○ **I need extra help with** _____

Go to **my science** s **coach** *online for help with this subject.*

7.1.4

Academic Standards for Science

7.1.4 Recognize and provide evidence how light, sound and other waves have energy and how they interact with different materials.

7.NS.8 Analyze data and use it to identify patterns.

What Makes Up the Electromagnetic Spectrum?

There are many different types of electromagnetic waves. The complete range of electromagnetic waves placed in order of increasing frequency is called the **electromagnetic spectrum.** 🔑 **The electromagnetic spectrum is made up of radio waves, microwaves, infrared rays, visible light, ultraviolet rays, X-rays, and gamma rays.** The full spectrum is shown in **Figure 2.**

Radio Waves Electromagnetic waves with the longest wavelengths and the lowest frequencies are **radio waves.** Radio waves are used in broadcasting to carry signals for radio programs. A broadcast station sends out radio waves at certain frequencies. Your radio picks up the radio waves and converts them into an electrical signal. The electrical signal is then converted into sound.

FIGURE 2 ....

The Electromagnetic Spectrum

The electromagnetic spectrum can be broken up into different categories.

✎ **Interpret Diagrams** Use the word bank to fill in the boxes in the diagram. Do microwaves or ultraviolet waves have longer wavelengths? Which have higher frequencies? **7.NS.8**

_____

_____

_____

Word Bank

Shortest wavelength	Longest wavelength
Highest frequency	Lowest frequency

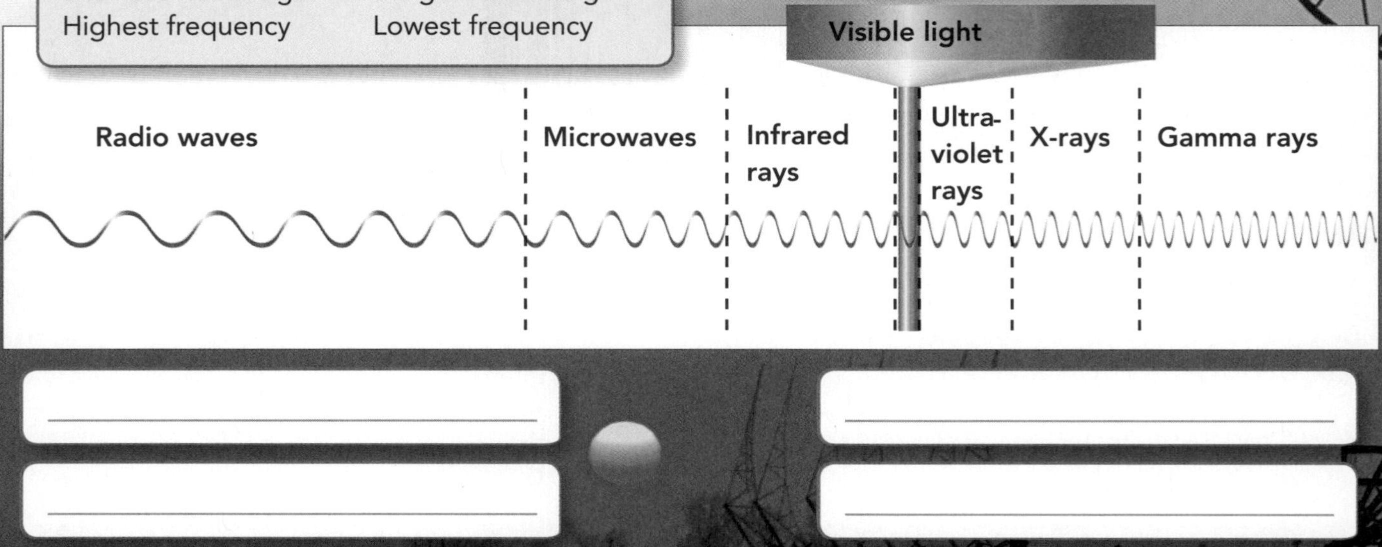

Visible light

Radio waves | Microwaves | Infrared rays | Ultra-violet rays | X-rays | Gamma rays

Microwaves **Microwaves** have shorter wavelengths and higher frequencies than radio waves do. When you think about microwaves, you probably think of microwave ovens that cook and heat food. But microwaves have many other uses, including cellular phone communication and radar.

Radar stands for **ra**dio **d**etection **and r**anging. **Radar** is a system that uses reflected microwaves to detect objects and measure their distance and speed. To measure distance, a radar device sends out microwaves that reflect off an object. The time it takes for the reflected waves to return is used to calculate the object's distance. To measure speed, a radar device uses the Doppler effect. For example, suppose a police radar gun sends out microwaves that reflect off a car. Because the car is moving, the frequency of the reflected waves is different from the frequency of the original waves. The difference in frequency is used to calculate the car's speed.

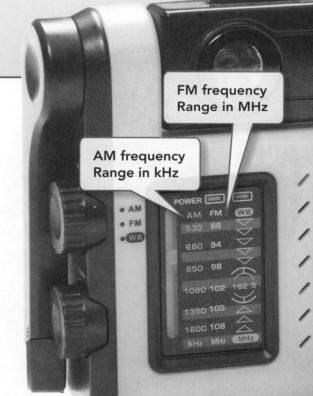

FM frequency Range in MHz

AM frequency Range in kHz

apply it!

Radio stations are broadcast in two different frequency ranges. The ranges are the kilohertz range (kHz) for AM stations and the megahertz range (MHz) for FM stations. The prefix *kilo-* means "thousand"; *mega-* means "million."

1 **Interpret Data** What is the frequency range of the AM band on the radio? Of the FM band?

_____

_____

2 **Interpret Photos** Approximately what frequencies are being tuned in on each band?

_____

_____

3 CHALLENGE The units kHz and MHz stand for kilohertz and megahertz, respectively. If 1 MHz = 1000 kHz, which waves (AM or FM) have longer wavelengths? Explain.

_____

_____

_____

7.NS.8

239

Infrared Rays

Infrared Rays If you turn on an electric stove's burner, you can feel it warm up before the heating element starts to glow. The invisible heat you feel is infrared radiation, or infrared rays. **Infrared rays** are electromagnetic waves with wavelengths shorter than those of microwaves. They have higher frequencies and therefore more energy than microwaves. Because you can feel the energy of infrared rays as heat, these rays are often called heat rays. Heat lamps have bulbs that give off mainly infrared rays. They are used to keep things warm, such as food in a cafeteria or young animals in an incubator.

Most objects give off some infrared rays. Warmer objects give off infrared rays with more energy and higher frequencies than cooler objects. An infrared camera uses infrared rays instead of visible light to take pictures called thermograms. A **thermogram** is an image that shows regions of different temperatures in different colors, as shown in **Figure 3**.

FIGURE 3 ···

The Uses of Infrared Rays

Infrared rays are used in devices such as heat lamps and TV remote controls.

Complete these tasks.

1. **Interpret Diagrams** List the labeled areas on the thermogram from hottest to coolest.

_____

7.NS.8

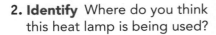

Heat lamp

2. **Identify** Where do you think this heat lamp is being used?

_____

_____

_____

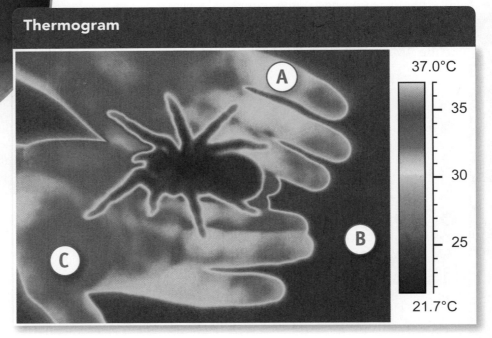

Thermogram

A

B

C

37.0°C

35

30

25

21.7°C

Visible light waves with the longest wavelengths appear red in color.

The shortest wavelengths of visible light appear violet in color.

Sequence What are the colors of the visible spectrum in order, starting with red?

_____

_____

_____

_____

Interpret Photos Which color has the highest frequency?

_____

_____

FIGURE 4 ··

The Visible Spectrum
Refraction of white light from the sun by raindrops separates the light into the colors of the visible spectrum.

✏ **Answer the questions in the boxes to the left and below.**

△ **Communicate** Talk with a partner. Describe other times when you have seen the visible spectrum.

_____

_____

_____

_____

_____

_____

_____

_____

Visible Light
Electromagnetic waves that you can see are called **visible light.** They make up only a small part of the electromagnetic spectrum. Visible light waves have shorter wavelengths and higher frequencies than infrared rays.

Visible light that appears white is actually a mixture of many colors. Recall that light waves bend, or refract, when they enter a new medium. So, when white light passes through rain drops, a rainbow can result, like the one in **Figure 4**.

Ultraviolet Rays
Electromagnetic waves with wavelengths just shorter than those of visible light are called **ultraviolet rays.** Ultraviolet rays have higher frequencies than visible light, so they carry more energy. The energy of ultraviolet rays can damage or kill living cells. For example, too much exposure to ultraviolet rays can burn your skin and over time may cause skin cancer. However, small doses of ultraviolet rays are useful. They cause skin cells to produce vitamin D, which is needed for healthy bones and teeth.

did you know?
The Environmental Protection Agency of the United States tracks ultraviolet light levels in Texas and throughout the country. The agency's UV index rates ultraviolet exposure on a scale of 1 to 11+. High ratings result in UV exposure warnings. These warnings let people know how long they can be out in the sun safely without sunblock.

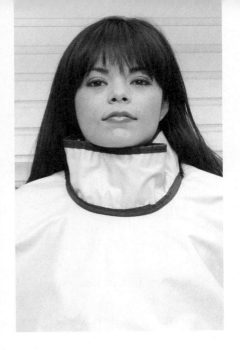

FIGURE 5 ·····································

Lead Apron

X-rays are often used to look at bones and teeth.

✎ **Explain** Why does a dentist cover you with a lead apron to take X-rays of your teeth?

_____

_____

_____

_____

X-rays Electromagnetic waves with wavelengths just shorter than those of ultraviolet rays are **X-rays.** Their frequencies are just a little higher than ultraviolet rays. Because of their high frequencies, X-rays carry more energy than ultraviolet rays and can penetrate most matter. Dense matter, such as bone or lead, absorbs X-rays so they do not pass through. Therefore, X-rays are used to make images of bones and teeth. However, too much exposure to X-rays can cause cancer. See **Figure 5.**

X-rays can also be used in industry and engineering. Engineers can use an X-ray image of a steel or concrete structure to find cracks. Dark areas on the X-ray film show the cracks.

Gamma Rays Electromagnetic waves with the shortest wavelengths and highest frequencies are **gamma rays.** Since they have the greatest amount of energy, gamma rays are the most penetrating of electromagnetic waves. Because of their penetrating ability, these rays are used to examine the body's internal structures. A patient can be injected with a fluid that emits gamma rays. Then, a gamma-ray detector can form an image of the inside of the body.

Some radioactive substances and certain nuclear reactions produce gamma rays. Some objects in space emit bursts of gamma rays. However, these rays are blocked by Earth's atmosphere. Astronomers think that explosions of distant stars produce these gamma rays.

✎ **Summarize** In your own words, write a summary of the section about gamma rays.

_____

_____

_____

_____

_____

_____

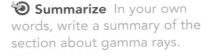

X-rays

FIGURE 6 ·····································
> INTERACTIVE ART The electromagnetic spectrum includes many kinds of waves.

✎ **Complete the activities.**

1. **Identify** Label each kind of wave on the electromagnetic spectrum.

2. **Classify** Circle the name of the highest energy waves.

3. **Apply Concepts** On the notebook page, describe the uses of two kinds of waves.

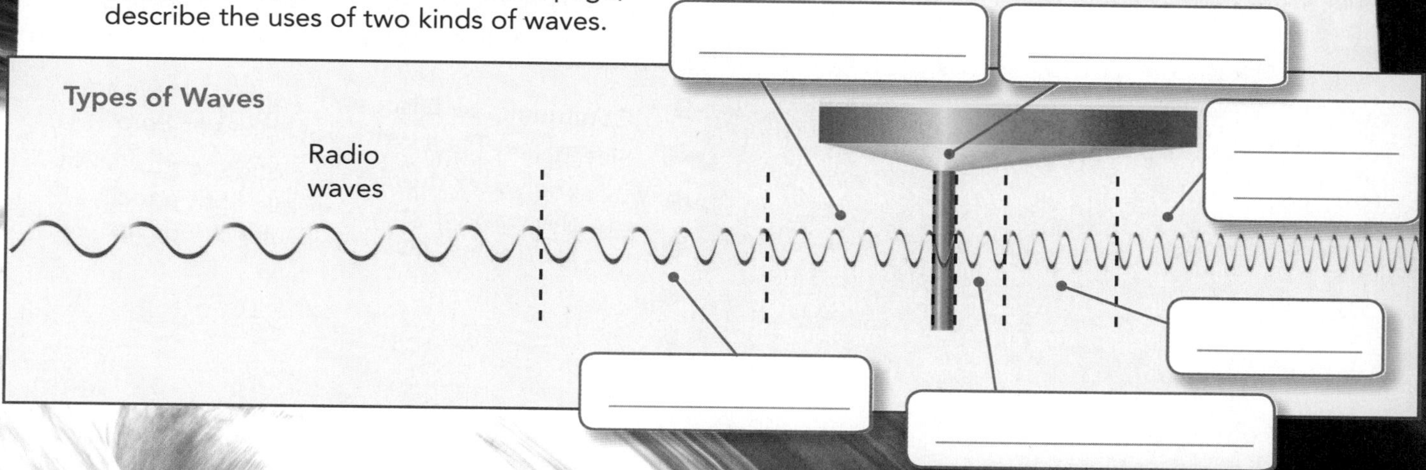

Types of Waves

Radio waves

Do the Quick Lab *Parts of the Electromagnetic Spectrum.*

🔑 Assess Your Understanding

1a. Explain How do ultraviolet rays help your bones and teeth?

_____

_____

_____

_____

7.1.4

b. Classify What kinds of waves make up the electromagnetic spectrum?

_____

_____

_____

_____

_____

7.1.4

got it? ···

○ **I get it!** Now I know the electromagnetic spectrum is made up of _____

_____

○ **I need extra help with** _____

Go to **MY SCIENCE** 🅢 **COACH** online for help with this subject.

7.1.4

Light and Color

UNLOCK THE BIG

🔑 **What Determines Color?**
7.1.4, 7.NS.1

🔑 **How Do Colors Combine?**
7.1.4

my pLaneT DiaRY

FUN FACTS

Why Is the Sky Blue?

Why does the sky look blue on a clear, sunny day? The answer has to do with the nature of light.

The sun gives off white light. White light is made up of many colors. The different colors of light have different wavelengths. Red light has a longer wavelength than blue light. As the sun's light passes through our atmosphere, gas molecules in the air scatter the sunlight. The blue wavelengths get scattered the most, so the sky appears blue!

Communicate Discuss this question with a classmate. Then write your answer below.

The water droplets in clouds scatter all of the wavelengths of visible light equally. How does this explain why clouds are white?

_____

_____

_____

_____

> PLANET DIARY Go to **Planet Diary** to learn more about color.

Lab zone ® Do the Inquiry Warm-Up *How Do Colors Mix?*

Academic Standards for Science

7.1.4 Recognize and provide evidence how light, sound and other waves have energy and how they interact with different materials.

7.NS.1 Make predictions.

What Determines Color?

Why is the grass green or a daffodil yellow? To understand why objects have different colors, you need to know how light can interact with an object. When light strikes an object, the light can be reflected, transmitted, or absorbed. Think about a pair of sunglasses. If you hold the sunglasses in your hand, you can see light that reflects off the lenses. If you put the sunglasses on, you see light that is transmitted through the lenses. The lenses also absorb some light. That is why objects appear darker when seen through the lenses.

Vocabulary

• transparent • translucent • opaque • primary color
• secondary color • complementary color • pigment

Skills

Reading: Identify the Main Idea
Inquiry: Predict

Classifying Materials Lenses, like all objects, are made of different materials. Most materials can be classified as transparent, translucent, or opaque based on what happens to light that strikes the material.

A material that transmits most of the light that strikes it is called **transparent.** Light passes through a transparent material without being scattered. This allows you to see clearly what is on the other side. Water, air, and clear glass are all transparent materials. In **Figure 1,** the window shown in the photo is partially fogged up by condensation. The center of the window, where the condensation has been wiped away, is transparent. The fogged-up part of the window is translucent. A **translucent** (trans LOO sunt) material scatters the light that passes through it. You can usually see something behind a translucent object, but the details are blurred. Wax paper and frosted glass are translucent materials.

A material that reflects or absorbs all of the light that strikes it is called **opaque** (oh PAYK). You cannot see through opaque materials because light cannot pass through them. In **Figure 1,** the wood and snow shown in the photo are opaque. Metals and tightly woven fabric are other examples of opaque materials.

Identify the Main Idea
Underline the main idea under the red heading Classifying Materials.

FIGURE 1 ·······

Types of Materials
The windows contain transparent, translucent, and opaque sections. ✎ Relate Diagrams and Photos **Suppose the ball was placed behind the three-sectional window below. Draw what you would see inside the dashed circle.**

7.NS.1

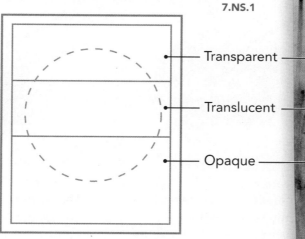

— Transparent —

— Translucent —

— Opaque —

Vocabulary Prefixes How does knowing the meaning of the prefix *trans-* help you remember what happens to light that strikes a translucent object?

_____

_____

_____

_____

Opaque Objects

The color of an opaque object depends on the wavelengths of light that the object reflects. Every opaque object absorbs some wavelengths of light and reflects others. 🔑 **The color of an opaque object is the color of the light it reflects.** For example, look at the apple shown at the top of **Figure 2.** The apple appears red because it reflects red wavelengths of light. The apple absorbs the other colors of light. The leaf looks green because it reflects green light and absorbs the other colors.

Objects can appear to change color if you view them in a different color of light. In red light, the apple appears red because there is red light for it to reflect. But the leaf appears black because there is no green light to reflect. In green light, the leaf looks green but the apple looks black. And in blue light, both the apple and the leaf look black.

Transparent and Translucent Objects

Materials that are transparent or translucent allow only certain colors of light to pass through them. They reflect or absorb the other colors. 🔑 **The color of a transparent or translucent object is the color of the light it transmits.** For example, when white light shines through transparent blue glass, the glass appears blue because it transmits blue light.

White light

FIGURE 2 ···

▶VIRTUAL LAB **Color of an Opaque Object**
The color an apple appears to be depends on the color of the light that strikes it. ✎ **Infer Circle the correct answers in the text below each apple.**

Red light

Green light

Blue light

The apple appears red because it (absorbs/reflects) red light. The leaves look black because they (absorb/reflect) red light.

The apple appears black because it (absorbs/reflects) green light. The leaves look green because they (absorb/reflect) green light.

The apple appears black because it (absorbs/reflects) blue light. The leaves look black because they (absorb/reflect) blue light.

Transparent or translucent materials are used to make color filters. For example, a red color filter is red because it allows only red light to pass through it. When you look at an object through a color filter, the color of the object may appear different than when you see the object in white light.

The lenses in sunglasses are often color filters. For example, lenses tinted yellow are yellow filters. When you put on those sunglasses, some objects appear to change color. The color you see depends on the color of the filter and on the color of the object as it appears in white light.

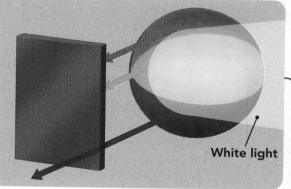

White light

Predict Imagine looking at the beach ball at the right through a red, green, or blue filter. Predict how each section of the beach ball would appear. In the diagrams below, label each section of the beach ball with its corresponding color.

Red filter	Green filter	Blue filter

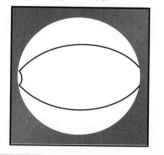 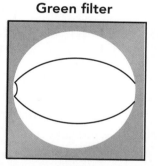 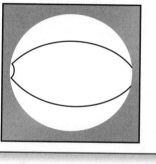

7.NS.1

Lab zone® Do the Quick Lab *Developing Hypotheses.*

Assess Your Understanding

1a. Identify A(n) _____ object reflects or absorbs all the light that strikes it.　　7.1.4

b. Apply Concepts A person wearing a blue shirt is standing in sunlight. What color(s) of light does the shirt reflect? What color(s) of light does the shirt absorb?

_____

_____
　　　　　　　　　　　　　　　　　7.1.4

c. Predict Suppose you are wearing green-tinted glasses. What color would a blue shirt appear through these glasses? _____
　　　　　　　　　　　　7.1.4, 7.NS.1

got it?

○ I get it! Now I know that the color of an opaque object is _____

_____

and the color of a transparent or translucent object is _____

_____

○ I need extra help with _____

_____

Go to MY SCIENCE ⓢ COACH *online for help with this subject.*
　　　　　　　　　　　　　　　　7.1.4

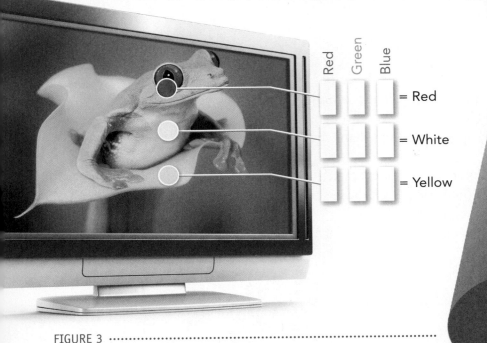

FIGURE 3 ···

Primary Colors of Light

The primary colors of light are red, green, and blue. A television produces many colors using only the primary colors of light. ✎ **Identify Check off the primary color(s) that will produce the color in each circled part of the TV screen.**

Academic Standards for Science

7.1.4 Recognize and provide evidence how light, sound and other waves have energy and how they interact with different materials.

Mixing light

List at least three examples of mixing light.

_____

_____

_____

_____

_____

_____

How Do Colors Combine?

Color is used in painting, photography, theater lighting, and printing. People who work with color must learn how to produce a wide range of colors using just a few basic colors. Three colors that can combine to make any other color are called **primary colors.** Two primary colors combine in equal amounts to produce a **secondary color.**

Mixing Light The primary colors of light are red, green, and blue. 🔑 **When the three primary colors of light are combined in equal amounts, they produce white light.** If they are combined in different amounts, the primary colors can produce other colors. For example, red and green combine to form yellow light. Yellow is a secondary color of light because two primary colors produce it. The secondary colors of light are yellow (red + green), cyan (green + blue), and magenta (red + blue). **Figure 3** shows the primary and secondary colors of light.

A primary and a secondary color can combine to make white light. Any two colors that combine to form white light are called **complementary colors.** Yellow and blue are complementary colors, as are cyan and red, and magenta and green.

A television produces many colors using only the primary colors of light. The picture on a TV screen is made up of little bars of red, green, and blue light. By varying the brightness of each colored bar, the television can produce thousands of different colors.

Mixing Pigment

How does an artist produce the many shades of colors you see in a painting? Inks, paints, and dyes contain **pigments,** or colored substances that are used to color other materials. Pigments absorb some colors and reflect others. The color you see is the result of the colors that a particular pigment reflects.

Mixing colors of pigments is different from mixing colors of light. As pigments are added together, fewer colors of light are reflected and more are absorbed. The more pigments that are combined, the darker the mixture looks.

Cyan, yellow, and magenta are the primary colors of pigments. 🔑 **When the three primary colors of pigments are combined in equal amounts, they produce black.** By combining pigments in varying amounts, you can produce many other colors. If you combine two primary colors of pigments, you get a secondary color, as shown in **Figure 4.** The secondary colors of pigments are red, green, and blue.

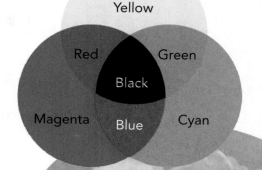

FIGURE 4 ···

Primary Colors of Pigment

Oil painters use a tray called a *palette* to hold and mix pigments. ✏️ **Identify Write the names of the primary colors that combine to produce the secondary color at the end of each statement.**

_____ + _____ = red

_____ + _____ = green

_____ + _____ = blue

 Lab zone Do the Lab Investigation *Changing Colors.*

🔑 Assess Your Understanding

2a. Identify What are the primary colors of light? What are the primary colors of pigment?

_____

_____

_____

_____

7.1.4

b. Compare and Contrast The result of mixing the primary colors of light in equal amounts is the color _____. The result of mixing the primary colors of pigment in equal amounts is the color _____.

7.1.4

got it? ···

○ **I get it!** Now I know that to produce white light you combine _____

_____

○ **I need extra help with** _____

Go to **my science** 💬 **coach** online for help with this subject.

7.1.4

Reflection and Mirrors

What Are the Kinds of Reflection?
7.1.4

What Types of Images Do Mirrors Produce?
7.1.4, 7.NS.8

MY PLANET DiARY

DISCOVERY

Periscope

In a submarine hidden beneath the ocean's surface, a captain peered into a long tube to see possible threats in the sea and air above. This sight tube, called a periscope, was designed by the Frenchman Marie Davey in 1854. Davey's periscope contained two mirrors, one placed at each end of a vertical tube. The mirrors were set parallel to each other and at 45 degrees to the vertical. The reflective surfaces faced each other. When light from an object on the surface reflected downward, an image appeared to the eye. People in submerged submarines could see what was above them!

Write your answer to the question below.

Imagine you are in a submerged submarine looking through a periscope. What are some things you might see?

_____

_____

_____

_____

_____

_____

▷ PLANET DIARY Go to **Planet Diary** to learn more about mirrors.

Lab zone® Do the Inquiry Warm-Up
How Does Your Reflection Wink?

Academic Standards for Science

7.1.4 Recognize and provide evidence how light, sound and other waves have energy and how they interact with different materials.

What Are the Kinds of Reflection?

Why do you see a reflection of yourself in a mirror but not on a page of your textbook? To answer this question, you need to understand how a surface reflects light. To show how light reflects, you can represent light waves as straight lines called **rays.** You may recall that light obeys the law of reflection—the angle of reflection equals the angle of incidence. ⌾ **The two ways in which a surface can reflect light are regular reflection and diffuse reflection.**

Vocabulary
- ray • regular reflection • image • diffuse reflection
- plane mirror • virtual image • concave mirror
- optical axis • focal point • real image • convex mirror

Skills
- Reading: Compare and Contrast
- Inquiry: Classify

Regular reflection occurs when parallel rays of light hit a smooth surface. All of the light rays reflect at the same angle because of the smooth surface. So you see a clear image. An **image** is a copy of the object formed by reflected or refracted rays of light. Shiny surfaces such as metal, glass, and calm water produce regular reflection.

Diffuse reflection occurs when parallel rays of light hit an uneven surface. Each light ray obeys the law of reflection but hits the surface at a different angle because the surface is uneven. Therefore, each ray reflects at a different angle. You either don't see an image or the image is not clear. Most objects reflect light diffusely. This is because most surfaces are not smooth. Even surfaces that appear to be smooth, such as a piece of paper, have small bumps that reflect light at different angles.

FIGURE 1 ·······························

Diffuse and Regular Reflection
✎ **Identify** Label the kind of reflection that occurs on each surface.

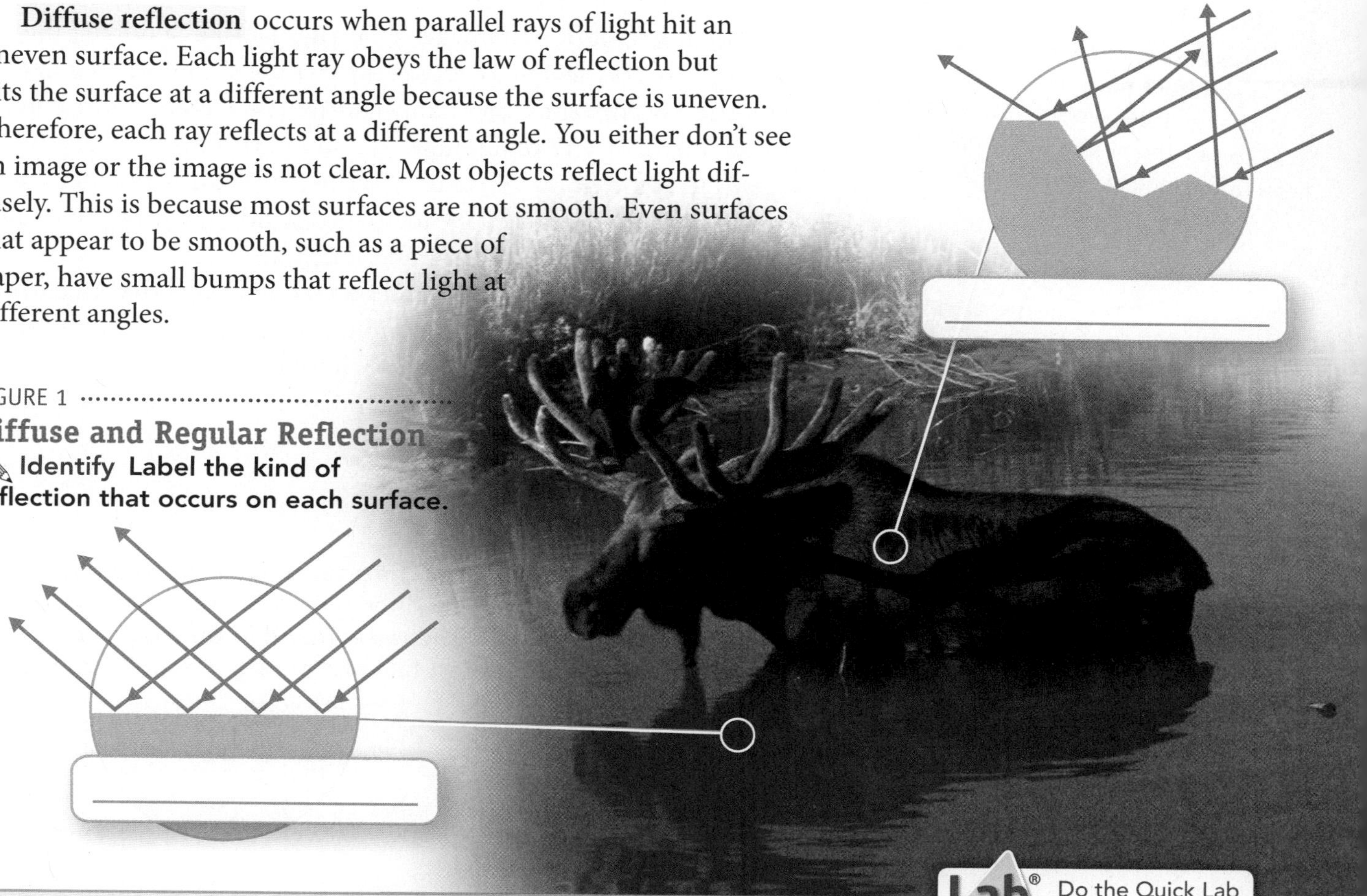

Lab ® zone Do the Quick Lab *Observing.*

🔑 Assess Your Understanding

got it? ··

○ **I get it!** Now I know the two kinds of reflection are_____

_____

○ **I need extra help with** _____

Go to **MY SCIENCE** ⓢ **COACH** *online for help with this subject.*

7.1.4

Academic Standards for Science

7.1.4 Recognize and provide evidence how light, sound and other waves have energy and how they interact with different materials.

7.NS.8 Analyze data, using appropriate mathematical manipulation as required, and use it to identify patterns and make inferences based on these patterns.

What Types of Images Do Mirrors Produce?

Have you ever looked at yourself in the curved mirrors of a fun house? If so, you know that your image looks different than it does in a flat mirror. Your image may look tall and skinny at one point and short and wide at another point. To understand why your image changes, you need to learn about the types of mirrors.

Plane Mirror Did you look into a mirror this morning to brush your teeth? If you did, you probably used a plane mirror. A **plane mirror** is a flat sheet of glass that has a smooth, silver-colored coating on one side. Often this coating is on the back of the glass to protect it from damage. When light strikes a mirror, the coating reflects the light. Because the coating is smooth, regular reflection occurs and a clear image forms. The image you see in a plane mirror is a **virtual image**—an image that forms where light seems to come from. "Virtual" describes something that does not really exist. Your image appears to be behind the mirror, but you can't reach behind the mirror and touch it.

🔑 **A plane mirror produces a virtual image that is upright and the same size as the object.** But the image is not quite the same as the object. The left and right of the image are reversed. For example, when you look in a mirror, your right hand appears to be a left hand in the image.

Plane Mirror

Pretend your friend has never seen her image in a plane mirror. How would you describe to her the similarities and differences between her image and the real her?

_____

_____

_____

_____

_____

_____

_____

_____

FIGURE 2 ·······································

Image in a Plane Mirror

A plane mirror forms a virtual image. The reflected light rays appear to come from behind the mirror, where the image forms.

✏️ Interpret Photos Is the raised hand in the image an image of the dancer's left hand or her right hand? Explain.

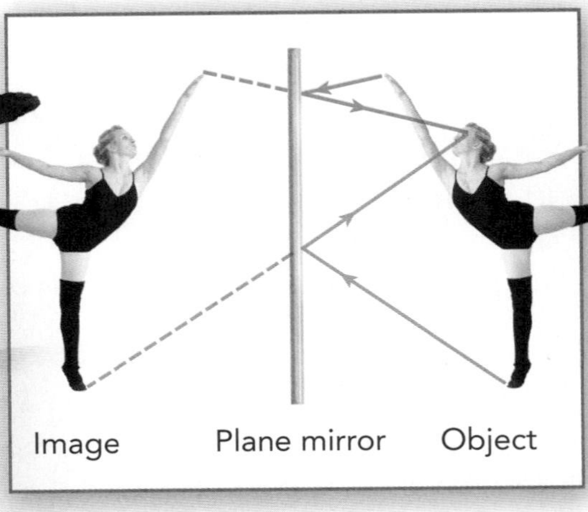

_____

_____

Image   Plane mirror   Object

Concave Mirrors A mirror with a surface that curves inward like the inside of a bowl is a **concave mirror. Figure 3** shows how a concave mirror can reflect parallel rays of light so that they meet at a point. Notice that the rays of light shown are parallel to the optical axis. The **optical axis** is an imaginary line that divides a mirror in half, much like the equator that divides Earth into northern and southern halves. The point at which rays parallel to the optical axis reflect and meet is called the **focal point.**

The type of image that is formed by a concave mirror depends on the location of the object. 🔑 **Concave mirrors can produce real or virtual images.** A **real image** forms when light rays actually meet. If the object is farther away from the mirror than the focal point, the reflected rays form a real image. Unlike a virtual image, a real image can be projected on a surface such as a piece of paper. Real images are upside down. A real image may be smaller, larger, or the same size as the object.

If an object is between the mirror and the focal point, the reflected rays form a virtual image. Virtual images formed by a concave mirror are always larger than the object. Concave mirrors produce the magnified images you see in a makeup mirror.

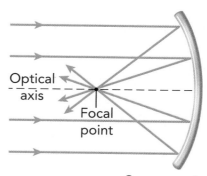

Concave mirror

FIGURE 3 ·············

Concave Mirror

A concave mirror reflects rays of light parallel to the optical axis back through the focal point. The figures below show how a concave mirror can produce both real and virtual images.

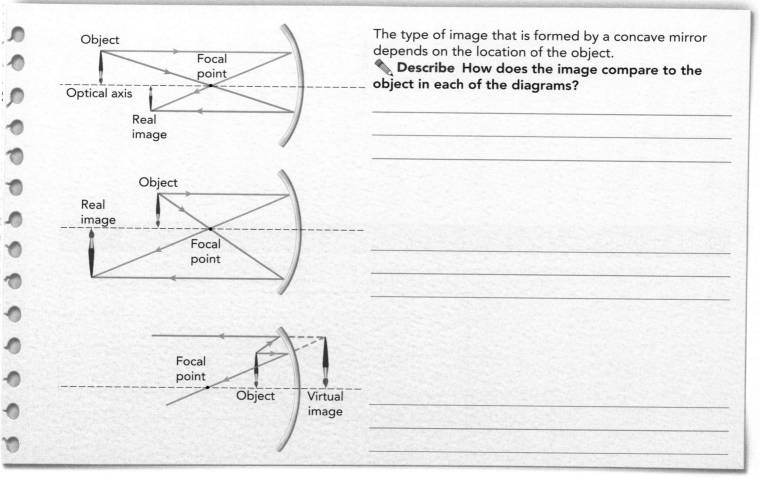

The type of image that is formed by a concave mirror depends on the location of the object.

✎ **Describe** How does the image compare to the object in each of the diagrams?

_____

_____

_____

_____

_____

_____

_____

_____

.... ✏ ....

⟲ **Compare and Contrast**

Compare and contrast the shape
of a convex mirror and a concave
mirror.

_____

_____

_____

_____

Convex Mirrors A mirror with a surface that curves out-ward is called a **convex mirror. Figure 4a** shows how convex mirrors reflect parallel rays of light. The reflected rays spread out but appear to come from a focal point behind the mirror. The focal point of a convex mirror is the point from which the rays appear to come. 🔑 **A convex mirror produces a virtual image that is always smaller than the object.**

Perhaps you have seen this warning on a car mirror: "Objects in mirror are closer than they appear." Convex mirrors are used in cars as passenger-side mirrors. The advantage of a convex mirror is that it allows you to see a larger area than you can with a plane mirror. The disadvantage is that the image is reduced in size. As a result, the image appears to be farther away than it actually is. The driver must understand this and adjust for it.

FIGURE 4 ···

▷ INTERACTIVE ART **Convex Mirror**

a. Light rays parallel to the optical axis reflect as if they came from the focal point behind a convex mirror.

b. ✏ CHALLENGE **Extend the two reflected rays behind the mirror to where they intersect. This is the top of the virtual image. Draw the image.**   7.NS.8

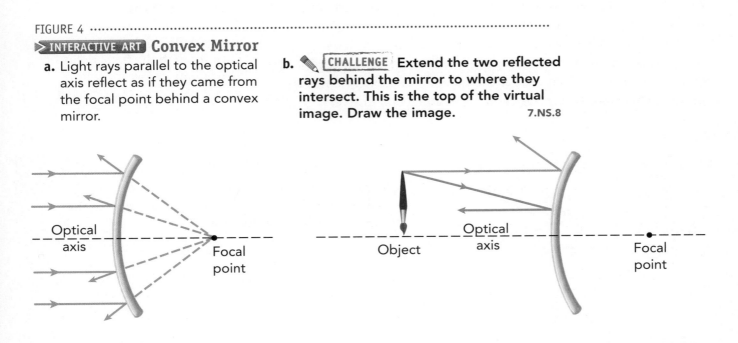

Complete the table to review the different types of images formed by mirrors.

Mirror	Location of Object	Is the image real or virtual?	Is the image upright or upside down?	What is the size of the image compared to the object?
Plane	Anywhere	_____	_____	_____
Concave	Farther than the focal point	_____	_____	_____
	Closer than the focal point	_____	_____	_____
Convex	Anywhere	_____	_____	_____

7.NS.8

apply it!

Each of the photos shows an application of a curved mirror. A bus driver uses the mirror in the top photo to check for traffic. A boy uses the mirror in the bottom photo to put in contact lenses.

1 ⚠ **Classify** Which type of curved mirror is in the top photo?_____

2 ⚠ **Classify** Which type of curved mirror is in the bottom photo?_____

3 Explain Why is the mirror in the top photo more useful than a plane mirror for checking traffic?

_____

_____

_____

4 Explain Why is the mirror in the bottom photo more useful than a plane mirror for putting in contact lenses?

_____

_____

_____

Lab zone Do the Quick Lab *Mirror Images.*

🔑 Assess Your Understanding

1a. Define A(n) _____ is a copy of an object formed by reflected or refracted rays of light.
7.1.4

b. ⚠ **Classify** A _____ mirror can form real and virtual images. _____ and _____ mirrors form only virtual images.
7.1.4

c. Apply Concepts Which type of mirror would you use if you wanted to project an image on a screen? Why?

_____

_____

_____
7.1.4

got it? ···

○ **I get it!** Now I know that the two types of images produced by mirrors are real _____

_____

○ I need extra help with _____

Go to **MY SCIENCE COACH** *online for help with this subject.*
7.1.4

255

Indiana

LESSON
5 Refraction and Lenses

UNLOCK THE BIG ?

🗝 **What Causes Light Rays to Bend?**
7.1.4, 7.NS.1, 7.NS.8

🗝 **What Determines the Type of Image Formed by a Lens?**
7.1.4, 7.NS.8

MY PLANET DIARY

BIOGRAPHY

Isaac Newton

Sir Isaac Newton (1642–1727) may be best known as the man who came up with the theory of gravity. But Newton, who was born in England, made numerous other important contributions to both math and science, including defining the laws of motion and co-founding the field of calculus. In the 1660s, Newton investigated the laws of light and color. In his famous book *Opticks*, he describes how he passed sunlight through a prism to prove that white light consists of many colors. Newton was knighted in 1705 and was the first scientist to be buried at Westminster Abbey.

Communicate Write your answers to the questions below. Then discuss your answers with a partner.

1. How did Newton prove that sunlight consists of many colors?

_____

_____

2. Describe a discovery that you made through experimentation.

_____

_____

_____

_____

_____

> **PLANET DIARY** Go to **Planet Diary** to learn more about lenses.

Lab zone® Do the Inquiry Warm-Up *How Can You Make an Image Appear?*

Vocabulary
- index of refraction • mirage • lens
- concave lens • convex lens

Skills
- Reading: Ask Questions
- Inquiry: Interpret Data

What Causes Light Rays to Bend?

A fish tank can play tricks on your eyes. If you look through the side of a fish tank, a fish seems closer than if you look at it from the top. If you look through the corner of the tank, you may see the same fish twice. Look at **Figure 1.** You see one image of the fish through the front of the tank and another through the side. The two images appear in different places! How can this happen?

Refraction can cause you to see something that may not actually be there. As you look at a fish in a tank, the light coming from the fish to your eye bends as it passes through three different mediums. The mediums are water, the glass of the tank, and air. As the light passes from one medium to the next, it is refracted. **When light rays enter a new medium at an angle, the change in speed causes the rays to bend.**

Academic Standards for Science

7.1.4 Recognize and provide evidence how light, sound and other waves have energy and how they interact with different materials.

7.NS.1 Make predictions.

7.NS.8 Analyze data and use it to identify patterns.

FIGURE 1 ·····················

Optical Illusion in a Fish Tank

There is only one fish in this tank, but refraction makes it look as though there are two.

Communicate Discuss with a classmate some other examples of how the appearance of objects in water is different than in the air. Describe these examples below.

_____

_____

_____

_____

_____

_____

_____

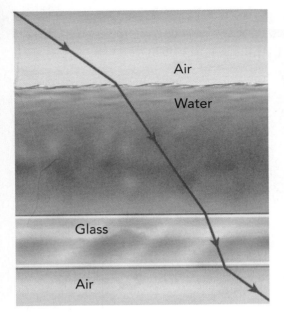

FIGURE 2

Refraction of Light
The light ray bends as it passes through different mediums.
✏️ **Interpret Diagrams** In which medium does light travel the fastest?

Refraction in Different Mediums

Some mediums cause light to bend more than others. **Figure 2** shows how the path of a light ray changes as it passes from one medium to another. When light passes from air into water, the light slows down. Light slows down again and bends even more when it passes from water into glass. When light passes from glass back into air, the light speeds up. Notice that the ray that leaves the glass is traveling in the same direction as it was before it entered the water. Light travels fastest in air, a little slower in water, and slower still in glass.

Glass causes light to bend more than either air or water does. Another way to say this is that glass has a higher index of refraction than either air or water. The **index of refraction** of a medium is a measure of how much a light ray bends when it enters that medium. The higher the index of refraction of a medium, the more it bends light. The index of refraction of water is 1.33. The index of refraction of glass is about 1.5. So light is bent more by glass than by water.

do the math! Analyzing Data

Bending Light

The table shows the index of refraction of some common mediums. **Use the data to answer the following questions.**

1 🔺**Interpret Data** Which medium causes the greatest change in the direction of a light ray that enters at an angle?

_____

2 🔺**Interpret Data** According to the table, which tend to bend light more, solids or liquids?

_____

3 **Predict** Would you expect light to bend if it entered corn oil at an angle after it traveled through glycerol? Explain.

_____
_____

Index of Refraction	
Medium	Index of Refraction
Air (gas)	1.00
Water (liquid)	1.33
Ethyl alcohol (liquid)	1.36
Quartz (solid)	1.46
Corn oil (liquid)	1.47
Glycerol (liquid)	1.47
Glass, crown (solid)	1.52
Sodium chloride (solid)	1.54
Zircon (solid)	1.92
Diamond (solid)	2.42

7.NS.1, 7.NS.8

Prisms and Rainbows Recall that when white light enters a prism, each wavelength is refracted by a different amount. The longer the wavelength, the less the wave is bent by a prism. Red, with the longest wavelength, is refracted the least. Violet, with the shortest wavelength, is refracted the most. This difference in refraction causes white light to spread out into the colors of the spectrum—red, orange, yellow, green, blue, and violet.

The same process occurs in water droplets suspended in the air. When white light from the sun shines through the droplets, a rainbow may appear. The water droplets act like tiny prisms, refracting and reflecting the light and separating the colors.

EXPLORE THE BIG ?

Water + Light = A rainbow

How does light interact with matter?
FIGURE 3 ·······

> ART IN MOTION

A rainbow forms when light is reflected and refracted by water droplets suspended in the air. The diagram shows the path of a light ray that strikes a water droplet. ✏ **Interpret Diagrams Use the diagram to answer the questions.**

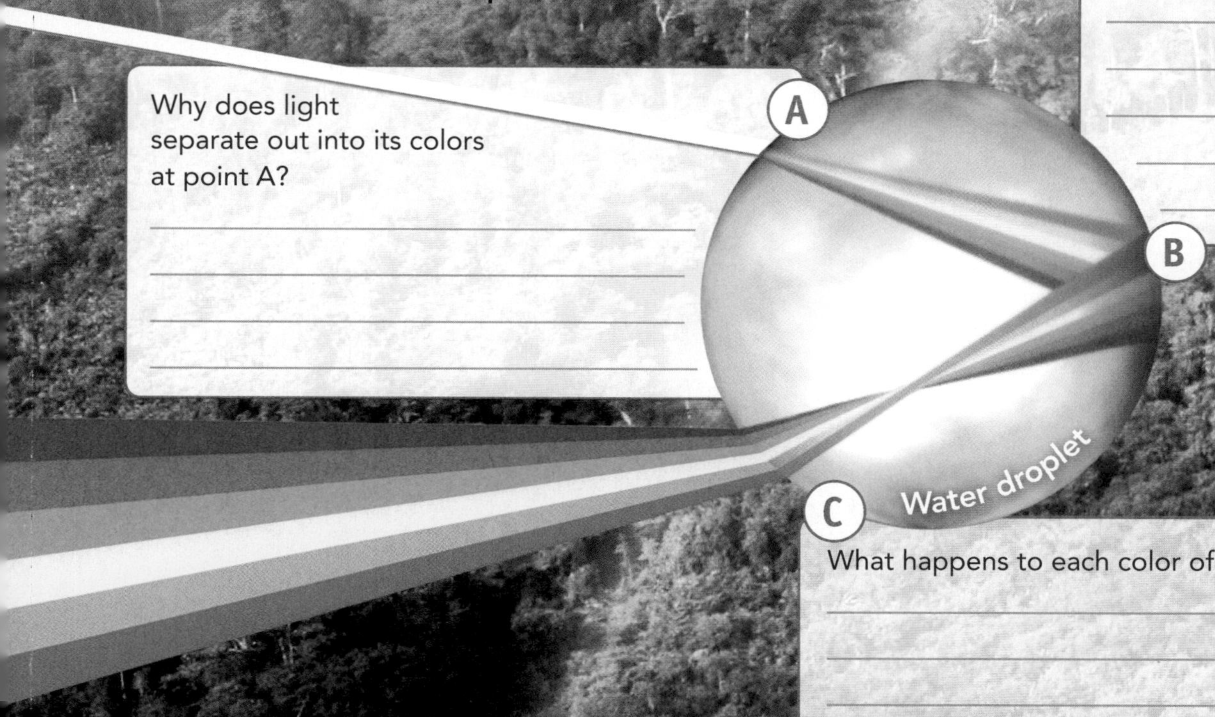

Why does light separate out into its colors at point A?

_____

_____

_____

What happens to each color of light at point B?

_____

_____

_____

_____

A

B

C Water droplet

What happens to each color of light at point C?

_____

_____

_____

259

Ask Questions Before reading about mirages, ask a *What* or *How* question. As you read, write the answer to your question below.

_____

_____

_____

FIGURE 4 ······························

Mirage
The puddles and reflections on the road are mirages.

Mirages You're traveling in a car on a hot day, and you notice that the road ahead looks wet. Yet when you get there, the road is dry. Did the puddles dry up? No, the puddles were never there! You saw a **mirage** (mih RAHJ)—an image of a distant object caused by refraction of light. The puddles on the road are light rays from the sky that are refracted to your eyes.

Figure 4 shows a mirage. Notice that there appears to be a reflection of the vehicle in the road. The air just above the road is hotter than the air higher up. Light travels faster in hot air. So light rays from the vehicle that travel toward the road are bent upward by the hot air. Your brain assumes that these rays traveled in a straight line. So the rays look as if they have reflected off a smooth surface. What you see is a mirage.

Lab zone® Do the Quick Lab *Bent Pencil*.

Assess Your Understanding

1a. Identify A material's _____ is a measure of how much a ray of light bends when it enters that material from air.   7.1.4

b. Predict If a glass prism were in a medium with the same index of refraction, would it separate white light into different colors? Explain.

_____

_____

_____
                                      7.1.4

c. ANSWER THE BIG ? How does light interact with matter?

_____

_____

_____

_____

_____

_____
                                      7.1.4

got it? ···

O **I get it!** Now I know that the reason light rays bend when they enter a new medium at an angle is because _____

O **I need extra help with** _____

Go to MY SCIENCE ⓢ COACH *online for help with this subject.*   7.1.4

What Determines the Type of Image Formed by a Lens?

Any time you look through binoculars, a camera, or eyeglasses, you are using lenses to bend light. A **lens** is a curved piece of glass or other transparent material that refracts light. A lens forms an image by refracting light rays that pass through it. Like mirrors, lenses can have different shapes. 🔑 **The type of image formed by a lens depends on the shape of the lens and the position of the object.**

Concave Lenses A **concave lens** is thinner in the center than at the edges. When light rays traveling parallel to the optical axis pass through a concave lens, they bend away from the optical axis and never meet. A concave lens can produce only virtual images because parallel light rays passing through the lens never meet.

Look at the book to the right. Notice that the words seen through the lens appear smaller than the words outside of the lens. The words seen through the lens are virtual images. A concave lens always produces a virtual image that is upright and smaller than the object. **Figure 5a** shows how a concave lens forms an image. The image is located where the light rays appear to come from.

Academic Standards for Science

7.1.4 Recognize and provide evidence how light, sound and other waves have energy and how they interact with different materials.

7.NS.8 Analyze data, using appropriate mathematical manipulations as required, and use it to identify patterns and make inferences based on these patterns.

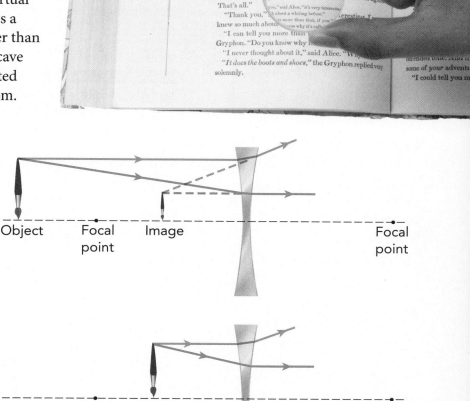

FIGURE 5 ·············

Concave Lens

a. A concave lens produces a virtual image that is upright and smaller than the object.

b. ✎ Apply Concepts Locate this object's image. Extend the two light rays straight back to the same side of the lens as the object. The point where they intersect is the location of the image. Draw the image.

261

Convex Lenses

A **convex lens** is thicker in the center than at the edges. As light rays parallel to the optical axis pass through a convex lens, they are bent toward the center of the lens. The rays meet at the focal point of the lens and continue to travel beyond. The more curved the lens, the more it refracts light. A convex lens acts like a concave mirror, because it focuses rays of light.

An object's position relative to the focal point determines whether a convex lens forms a real or virtual image. Look at **Figure 6.** Notice that the words seen through the lens are larger than the words outside of the lens. The words seen through the lens are virtual images. When an object is between the lens and the focal point, the refracted rays form a virtual image. The image forms on the same side of the lens as the object and is larger than the object. If the object is outside of the focal point, the refracted rays form a real image on the other side of the lens. The real image can be smaller, larger, or the same size as the object. The diagrams in **Figure 7** show how a convex lens forms real and virtual images.

FIGURE 6 ·····························

Convex Lens

When an object is inside the focal point, the image seen through a convex lens is larger than the object. ✎ **Identify** Name a device that uses this type of lens.

_____

_____

Lenses

List some devices that use lenses.

_____

_____

_____

_____

_____

_____

FIGURE 7 ···

▷ **INTERACTIVE ART** **How a Convex Lens Works**

The type of image formed by a convex lens depends on the object's position. ✎ **Classify** Label which image is virtual and which image is real.

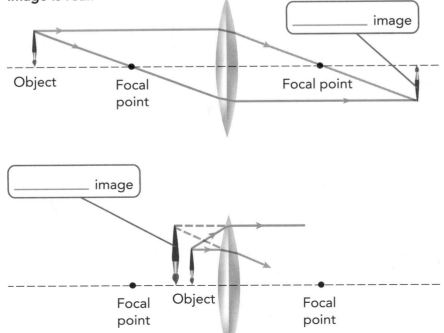

_____ image

Object   Focal point   Focal point

_____ image

Focal point   Object   Focal point

apply it!

① Interpret Photos These photos show parallel rays of light passing through a convex lens and a concave lens. Why do you suppose a convex lens is called a converging lens and a concave lens is called a diverging lens?

_____

_____

_____

Convex lens

Concave lens

② Review Complete the Lenses and Mirrors table. Use the table to answer Question 3.

③ Summarize A convex lens acts like a _____ mirror. A concave lens acts like a _____ mirror.

④ CHALLENGE Suppose a convex lens and a concave mirror are underwater. Compared to the way they work in air, which one do you expect will be more affected by the water? Why?

_____

_____

_____

_____

Lenses and Mirrors

Type of Mirror or Lens	Real, Virtual, or Both Types of Images	Upright, Inverted, or Both Types of Images
Concave Mirror	Both	_____
Convex Mirror	_____	Upright
Concave Lens	_____	_____
Convex Lens	_____	_____

7.NS.8

Lab zone Do the Quick Lab
Looking at Images.

🔑 Assess Your Understanding

2a. Define A _____ is a curved piece of glass or other transparent material that refracts light.   7.1.4

b. Compare and Contrast Describe the shapes of a concave lens and a convex lens.

_____

_____

_____
                                               7.1.4

c. Make Generalizations Use **Figure 7** to explain how you can you tell whether a convex lens will produce a real or virtual image.

_____

_____

_____

_____

_____
                                               7.1.4

got it? ···

○ **I get it!** Now I know that the type of image formed by a lens depends on _____

_____

○ **I need extra help with** _____

Go to MY SCIENCE ⓢ COACH *online for help with this subject.*   7.1.4

7 Study Guide

When light interacts with matter, it can be _____ , _____ , or _____ .

LESSON 1 The Nature of Electromagnetic Waves

7.1.4, 7.NS.1, 7.NS.8

🔑 An electromagnetic wave is made up of vibrating electric and magnetic fields that move through space or some medium at the speed of light.

🔑 Two different models are needed to explain the behavior of electromagnetic waves. A wave model best explains many of the behaviors, but a particle model best explains others.

Vocabulary
- electromagnetic wave • electromagnetic radiation
- polarized light • photoelectric effect • photon

LESSON 2 Waves of the Electromagnetic Spectrum

7.1.4, 7.NS.8

🔑 All electromagnetic waves travel at the same speed in a vacuum, but they have different wavelengths and different frequencies.

🔑 The electromagnetic spectrum is made up of radio waves, microwaves, infrared rays, visible light, ultraviolet rays, X-rays, and gamma rays.

Vocabulary
- electromagnetic spectrum • radio waves
- microwaves • radar • infrared rays • thermogram
- visible light • ultraviolet rays • X-rays • gamma rays

LESSON 3 Light and Color

7.1.4, 7.NS.1, 7.DP.10

🔑 The color of an opaque object is the color of the light it reflects. The color of a transparent or translucent object is the color of the light it transmits.

🔑 When the three primary colors of light are combined in equal amounts, they produce white light. When the three primary colors of pigment are combined in equal amounts, they produce black.

Vocabulary
- transparent • translucent • opaque • primary color
- secondary color • complementary color • pigment

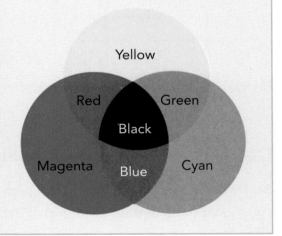

LESSON 4 Reflection and Mirrors

7.1.4, 7.NS.8

🔑 The two ways in which a surface can reflect light are regular reflection and diffuse reflection.

🔑 The three common types of mirrors are plane, concave, and convex.

Vocabulary
- ray • regular reflection • image
- diffuse reflection • plane mirror
- virtual image • concave mirror
- optical axis • focal point
- real image • convex mirror

LESSON 5 Refraction and Lenses

7.1.4, 7.NS.1, 7.NS.8, 7.DP.10

🔑 When light rays enter a new medium at an angle, the change in speed causes them to bend.

🔑 The type of image formed by a lens depends on the shape of the lens and the position of the object.

Vocabulary
- index of refraction • mirage • lens
- concave lens • convex lens

Review and Assessment

LESSON 1 The Nature of Electromagnetic Waves

1. An electromagnetic wave consists of

  a. AM and FM waves.

  b. electrons and protons.

  c. electric and magnetic fields.

  d. particles of a medium.   7.1.4

2. The _____ model of light describes the behavior of light when it acts as a stream of photons.   7.1.4

3. Compare and Contrast Explain how polarized light is different from non-polarized light.

_____

_____

_____

_____

_____

   7.1.4

4. Observe How do you know that electromagnetic waves can travel through a vacuum?

_____

_____

_____

_____

   7.1.4

5. 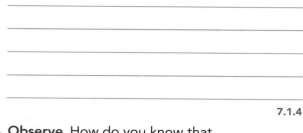 **Write About It** Suppose you go shopping for sunglasses with a friend. He likes a pair of sunglasses labeled *polarized lenses*. Using what you learned in this lesson, explain to him how polarizing sunglasses work.

   7.1.4

LESSON 2 Waves of the Electromagnetic Spectrum

6. The electromagnetic waves with the longest wavelengths and lowest frequencies are

  a. radio waves.   **b.** infrared rays.

  c. X-rays.   **d.** gamma rays.   7.1.4

7. _____ is the only type of electromagnetic wave that you can see. 7.1.4

Use the graph below to answer Questions 8 and 9.

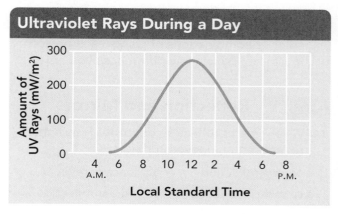

Ultraviolet Rays During a Day

8. Interpret Graphs What is the amount of ultraviolet rays at 8 P.M.?

_____

   7.1.4, 7.NS.8

9. Infer What is the cause of the peak in the graph line at 12 P.M.?

_____

_____

   7.1.4, 7.NS.8

10. Classify Night vision goggles allow you to see warm objects in a dark environment. Which type of electromagnetic wave do they detect?

_____

_____

   7.1.4

Review and Assessment

Light and Color

11. A type of material that reflects or absorbs all of the light that strikes it is called

   a. translucent.   **b.** transparent.

   c. reflective.   **d.** opaque.

                              7.1.4

12. Colors that combine to make any other color are called _____

                              7.1.4

13. **Write About It** Helena works in the lighting crew for a theater. She needs to create a red spotlight on the stage. Kimi is a painter. He wants to create red paint for the background in a new painting. Use the terms *primary color* and *complementary color* to explain what color or combinations of colors each person must use. Explain any differences you note.

                              7.1.4

Reflection and Mirrors

14. What type of reflection describes how light reflects off an uneven surface?

   a. real reflection   **b.** concave reflection

   c. diffuse reflection   **d.** regular reflection

                              7.1.4

15. Light rays obey the law of reflection, which states that _____

                              7.1.4

16. **Apply Concepts** Can a plane mirror produce a real image? Explain.

                              7.1.4

Refraction and Lenses

17. A curved piece of glass or other transparent material that is used to refract light is called a

   a. prism.   **b.** lens.

   c. mirage.   **d.** mirror.   7.1.4

18. A _____ lens can produce only virtual images because parallel light rays passing through the lens never meet.   7.1.4

19. **math!** Quartz has an index of refraction of 1.46. Diamond has an index of refraction of 2.42. In which material does a light ray entering from air slow down more? Explain.

                            7.1.4, 7.NS.8

 How does light interact with matter?

20. Explain why the beam of light changes direction when it enters the water.

Indiana ISTEP+ Practice

Multiple Choice

Circle the letter of the best answer.

1. What would you add to the picture below so that light does not hit the final screen?

   A. another light bulb
   B. a filter with horizontal slits
   C. a filter with vertical slits
   D. none of the above

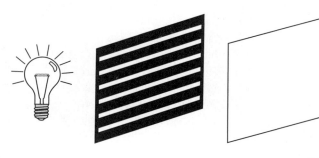

7.1.4

2. A convex lens can produce a real or a virtual image. Which type of mirror is most similar to a convex lens?

   A. concave mirror
   B. convex mirror
   C. plane mirror
   D. none of the above

7.1.4

3. You view an American flag through sunglasses that are tinted green. What colors do you see?

   A. green and blue
   B. red and black
   C. blue and red
   D. black and green

7.1.4

4. Which of the following groups of electromagnetic waves is listed correctly in order of increasing energy?

   A. X-rays, visible light, radio waves
   B. radio waves, visible light, X-rays
   C. infrared rays, visible light, radio waves
   D. visible light, gamma rays, X-rays

7.1.4

Constructed Response

Write your answer to Question 5 on the lines below.

5. The index of refraction for water is 1.33 and for glass it is 1.5. What happens to the speed of light when light travels from glass into water?

   _____

   _____

   _____

   _____

   _____

7.1.4

Extended Response

Use the diagram below and your knowledge of science to help you answer Question 6. Write your answer on a separate sheet of paper.

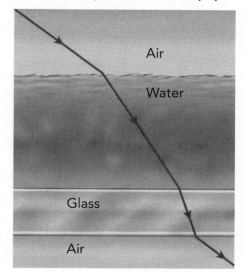

6. Explain why the path of the light ray changes as it travels through the different mediums.

7.1.4

Frontiers of Technology

Seeing Double

Lens

Light from star

Viewing mirror reflects light to eyepiece.

Concave mirror reflects light.

▲ Isaac Newton built the first model for a reflecting telescope in 1688.

Binoculars are really a set of two telescopes—one for each eye—that magnify distant objects. When scientists want to look at something even farther away, they can now turn to the world's largest pair of binoculars: the Large Binocular Telescope (LBT) on Mount Graham in Arizona.

The 120-million-dollar LBT is the world's most powerful optical telescope. It provides scientists with pictures and data of a huge area of space. The LBT has two massive mirrors that work together. Each mirror has a diameter of 8.4 meters! The mirrors gather light and allow scientists to look deeper into the universe than ever before. In fact, the LBT provides the same resolution as a 22.8-meter telescope—that's about as big as two school buses! It also has a larger field for collecting images than any single telescope, allowing scientists to see more.

Design It Research how mirrors work in a reflecting telescope. Make a model or draw a diagram of how a reflecting telescope works. Show how the angles of reflection would work with the mirrors placed at two different angles. Which angles will work best? Present your model or drawing to your class.

7.1.4, 7.NS.2, 7.NS.11

The world's largest binoculars peer into space. ▶

Hiding in Plain Sight

The South African dwarf chameleon has mastered the art of the quick change! This lizard can change the color of its skin in response to light, temperature, and other environmental factors.

Each of the four layers of the dwarf chameleon's skin plays a role in its brilliant appearance. The top layer is clear, so light passes right through it. The second layer has cells that contain a yellow pigment. The third layer doesn't have a specific color—it has cells that scatter light. The way these cells scatter light is similar to the way Earth's atmosphere scatters light, reflecting blue light especially well. The bottom layer of a dwarf chameleon's skin contains a pigment called melanin, which absorbs red light. Hormones control how the melanin is arranged in this layer. The melanin moves in response to light, temperature, and other environmental factors. As the melanin moves, the color of the chameleon's skin changes.

The chameleon's color results from the combination of the reflected light from the underlying layers of skin. When mostly blue light reflected from the third layer combines with light from the yellow layer, the chameleon is bright green.

The third layer of the dwarf chameleon's skin reflects blue light, which combines with the yellow in the second layer to make the chameleon appear bright green. ▼

Model It Use a piece of clear plastic wrap, yellow plastic wrap, a small prism, and white or blue paper to model the top three layers of the chameleon's skin. Does changing the angle of the prism change the color you see through the layers of "skin"? Draw a diagram of your model, and describe how changing the color of the bottom layer and the angle of the prism change the colors you see.

7.1.4, 7.NS.2, 7.NS.11

HOW DEEP INTO EARTH CAN THIS CLIMBER GO?

What is the structure of Earth?

Descending into a canyon, this climber will get nearer to the center of Earth. But how close will he get? As climbers move down through narrow, dark passages of rock and dirt, they sometimes have to dig their way through. Some spelunkers, or cave explorers, have even descended into caves over 2,000 meters deep—the length of nearly 22 football fields!

> **UNTAMED SCIENCE** Watch the **Untamed Science** video to learn more about Earth's structure.

Predict If this climber could go all the way down to Earth's center, what materials other than dirt and solid rock might he find along the way? Explain your answer.

_____

_____

_____

_____

Introducing Earth

Academic Standards for Science

7.1.2, 7.2, 7.2.1, 7.2.2, 7.2.4, 7.2.7, 7.NS.1, 7.NS.8, 7.NS.11

8 Getting Started

Check Your Understanding

1. Background Read the paragraph below and then answer the question.

On a field trip, Paula sees that beach cliffs near the sea have worn away. "Where do the cliffs go?" she asks. Her teacher says, "The cliffs are exposed to natural **forces** all year. The harsh weather breaks the cliffs into pieces. **Gravity** causes the pieces to fall to the sea. Waves then shape the pieces into small **particles,** which wash away."

> A **force** is a natural power that acts on an object.
>
> **Gravity** is the force that makes objects fall toward Earth's center.
>
> A **particle** is a very small fragment of a much larger object.

• What forces change the beach cliffs each year?

_____

_____

▷ MY READING WEB If you had trouble answering the question above, visit **My Reading Web** and type in **Introducing Earth.**

Vocabulary Skill

Identify Related Word Forms You can increase your vocabulary by learning related word forms. If you know that the noun *energy* means "the ability to do work," you can figure out the meaning of the adjective *energetic*.

Verb	Noun	Adjective
destroy to reduce to pieces	destruction the process of reducing to pieces	destructive tending to cause damage or to reduce to pieces
radiate to release energy	radiation energy released in the form of rays or waves	radiant released as waves or rays

2. Quick Check Review the words related to *destroy*. Then circle the correct form of the word *destroy* in the following sentence.

• The (destruction/destructive) winds of a hurricane can be very dangerous.

system

hydrosphere

basalt

convection current

Chapter Preview

LESSON 1
- system
- energy
- atmosphere
- geosphere
- hydrosphere
- biosphere
- constructive force
- destructive force

⟳ **Ask Questions**
△ **Draw Conclusions**

LESSON 2
- seismic wave
- pressure
- crust
- basalt
- granite
- mantle
- lithosphere
- asthenosphere
- outer core
- inner core

⟳ **Identify Supporting Evidence**
△ **Interpret Data**

LESSON 3
- radiation
- convection
- conduction
- density
- convection current

⟳ **Relate Cause and Effect**
△ **Communicate**

▸ **VOCAB FLASH CARDS** For extra help with vocabulary, visit **Vocab Flash Cards** and type in *Introducing Earth.*

The Earth System

UNLOCK THE BIG ?

🔑 **What Are the Main Parts of the Earth System?**
7.2, 7.2.1, 7.NS.1

🔑 **How Do Constructive and Destructive Forces Change Earth?**
7.2.7, 7.NS.8

MY PLANET DIARY

BLOG

Posted by: Nicole

Location: Medfield, Massachusetts

This past summer my family and I went to the Grand Canyon. The Grand Canyon was carved by the Colorado River. It was so cool, looking down from the edge and seeing a small line that is the river and the rock layers in all different colors. I was amazed that mules could carry you down into the canyon.

Read the text and answer the questions.

1. How did the Colorado River change the landscape that existed before the Grand Canyon formed?

_____

_____

2. What else would you like to learn about the Colorado River?

_____

_____

_____

_____

▶ PLANET DIARY Go to **Planet Diary** to learn more about how natural forces change Earth's features.

 Lab zone® Do the Inquiry Warm-Up *What Is a System?*

Academic Standards for Science

7.2 Core Standard Describe how earth processes have shaped the topography of the earth.

7.2.1 Describe how the earth is a layered structure composed of lithospheric plates, a mantle and a dense core.

7.NS.1 Make predictions and develop testable questions based on research and prior knowledge.

What Are the Main Parts of the Earth System?

The Grand Canyon is made up of different parts. Rock forms the canyon walls. Water flows through the canyon in the form of a river, which carves away the rock. Animals such as deer drink the river's water. And air fills the canyon, allowing the animals to breath. All these parts work together. So the environment of the Grand Canyon can be thought of as a system. A **system** is a group of parts that work together as a whole. **Figure 1** shows how air, water, rock, and life work together in another part of Earth.

Vocabulary

- system • energy • atmosphere • geosphere
- hydrosphere • biosphere • constructive force
- destructive force

Skills

↻ Reading: Ask Questions

△ Inquiry: Draw Conclusions

Earth as a System The Earth system involves a constant flow of matter through different parts. For example, you may know that in the *water cycle,* water evaporates from the ocean, rises into the atmosphere, and then falls from the sky as rain. The rainwater then flows into and over Earth, and then back into the ocean.

You might be surprised to learn that rock, too, cycles through the Earth system. For example, new rock can form from molten material inside Earth called *magma.* This material can rise to the surface and harden on land to form new rock. The new rock can then erode into small pieces. The pieces can be washed into the ocean, where they may sink to the bottom as small particles, or *sediment.* If enough of the small particles collect, the weight of the sediment can crush all the particles together. The particles can then be cemented together to form new rock. The flow of rock through the Earth system is called the *rock cycle.*

The constant flow, or cycling, of matter through the Earth system is driven by energy. **Energy** is the ability to do work. The energy that drives the Earth system has two main sources: heat from the sun and heat flowing out of Earth as it cools.

FIGURE 1 ·····················
All Systems Go!
The many parts of the Earth system all work together.

✎ **Develop Hypotheses** Look at the photograph. Choose one part of the Earth system—rock, water, air, or life—and describe how the other parts might be affected if the first part were removed.

_____
_____
_____
_____
_____
_____
_____
_____
_____
_____
_____
_____
_____

7.NS.1

Parts of the Earth System

Earth contains air, water, land, and life. Each of these parts forms its own part, or "sphere." 🔑 **The Earth system has four main spheres: the atmosphere, the hydrosphere, the geosphere, and the biosphere. As a major source of energy for Earth processes, the sun can be considered part of the Earth system as well.** Each part of the Earth system can be studied separately. But the four parts are interconnected, as shown in **Figure 2.**

One of the most important parts of the Earth system is—you! Humans greatly affect the air, water, land, and life of Earth. For instance, the amount of paved land, including roads and parking lots, in the United States is now larger than the state of Georgia.

FIGURE 2 ·······························

▶ INTERACTIVE ART **The Earth System**

Earth's four spheres can affect one another.

✎ **Interpret Photos** Read the descriptions of Earth's four spheres. On the lines in each box, write the spheres that are interacting with each other in the small photograph next to the box.

Atmosphere

Earth's outermost layer is a mixture of gases—mostly nitrogen and oxygen. It also contains dust particles, cloud droplets, and the rain and snow that form from water vapor. It contains Earth's weather, and is the foundation for the different climates around the world. Earth's **atmosphere** (AT muh sfeer) is the relatively thin envelope of gases that forms Earth's outermost layer.

_____

_____

Geosphere

Nearly all of Earth's mass is found in Earth's solid rocks and metals, in addition to other materials. Earth's **geosphere** (GEE uh sfeer) has three main parts: a metal core, a solid middle layer, and a rocky outer layer.

_____

_____

Hydrosphere

About three quarters of Earth is covered by a relatively thin layer of water. Earth's water can take the form of oceans, glaciers, rivers, lakes, groundwater, and water vapor. Of the surface water, most is the salt water of the ocean. Only a tiny part of the hydrosphere is fresh water that is drinkable by humans. The **hydrosphere** (HY druh sfeer) contains all of Earth's water.

_____

_____

Feedback Within a System For years, the ice in glaciers at Glacier National Park in Montana has been melting. The melting is caused by rising temperatures. As the volume of ice in the glaciers has decreased, the land around the glaciers has become warmer. The warmer land melts the glaciers even faster.

Melting of the glaciers in Glacier National Park is an example of a process called *feedback*. When feedback occurs, a system returns—or feeds back—to itself data about a change in the system. In Glacier National Park, the ground around the melting glaciers feeds back warmer temperatures to the glaciers. Feedback can increase the effects of a change, as in the case of warming glaciers, or slow the effects down. Feedback demonstrates how changes in one part of the Earth system might affect the other parts. For example, the feedback of melting glaciers affects the geosphere (the ground), hydrosphere (glaciers), and atmosphere (climate).

Ask Questions Write a question about feedback. Then read the text and answer your question.

_____

_____

_____

_____

_____

_____

Biosphere

Life exists at the tops of mountains, deep underground, at the bottom of the ocean, and high up in the atmosphere. In fact, life exists in all kinds of conditions. But life as we know it cannot exist without water. The parts of Earth that contain living organisms make up the **biosphere** (BI uh sfeer).

_____

_____

_____

Lab zone® Do the Quick Lab *Parts of Earth's System.*

Assess Your Understanding

1a. Review The Earth system consists of the sun and four main _____
7.2

b. Classify The sphere that contains humans is the _____
7.2

c. Evaluate the Impact on Society Give one example of how humans affect the hydrosphere. Then explain how this change impacts society.

_____

_____

_____
7.2

got it?

○ **I get it!** Now I know that the main parts of the Earth system are _____

_____

_____

_____

○ **I need extra help with** _____

_____

Go to MY SCIENCE ⓢ COACH *online for help with this subject.*
7.2

Academic Standards for Science

7.2.7 Use geological features such as karst topography and glaciation to explain how large-scale physical processes have shaped the land.

7.NS.8 Analyze data, using appropriate mathematical manipulation as required.

FIGURE 3 ·······················

From Sea to Mountain
Constructive forces raised the Himalaya Mountains.

✎ **Answer the questions.**

1. **Explain** Why are ammonite fossils found in the Himalayas?

_____

_____

_____

_____

_____

_____

_____

_____

2. **Calculate** Many peaks in the Himalayas are 7,300 meters or more above sea level. About how high above India's capital, New Delhi, are these peaks?

_____

7.NS.8

How Do Constructive and Destructive Forces Change Earth?

Suppose you left a movie camera running in one spot for the next 100 million years and then you watched the movie in fast motion. You would see lands forming and mountains rising up—but you would also see them eroding back down again. 🔑 **Lands are constantly being created and destroyed by competing forces.**

Constructive Forces The Himalayas are Earth's highest mountains. But rock in the Himalayas contains *fossils*, or remains, of ocean animals such as ammonites. How could creatures that once lived at the bottom of the sea be found at the top of the world?

The Himalayas are the result of the collision of two sections of Earth's *lithosphere*, or Earth's top layer of stiff, solid rock. This layer is broken into huge pieces, or *plates*, that move slowly over Earth. The slow movement of Earth's plates is called *plate tectonics*.

The Himalayas are the result of the collision of the plate that carries India with the plate that carries China. Over millions of years, as these plates collided, their edges were squeezed slowly upward. This process lifted up the ocean floor and formed the Himalayas, shown in **Figure 3.**

Forces that construct, or build up, mountains are called **constructive forces.** 🔑 **Constructive forces shape the land's surface by building up mountains and other landmasses.** Volcanoes build up Earth's surface by spewing lava that hardens into rock. Earthquakes build landmasses by lifting up mountains and rock.

Ammonite

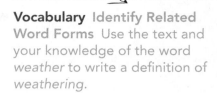
Destructive Forces While the Himalayas are being built up, they are also being torn down. Ice, rain, wind, and changing temperatures tear the rock apart. This process is called *weathering*. After the rock is torn apart, gravity pulls it downward. Eventually, rivers and streams carry away most of the eroded material.

Because forces such as ice, rain, wind, and changing temperatures wear down, or destroy, landmasses, they are called **destructive forces.** 🔑 **Destructive forces destroy and wear away landmasses through processes like erosion and weathering.** *Erosion* is the wearing down and carrying away of land by natural forces such as water, ice, or wind.

Vocabulary Identify Related Word Forms Use the text and your knowledge of the word *weather* to write a definition of *weathering*.

_____

_____

_____

_____

_____

Since 1983, lava from Kilauea has covered more than 100 square kilometers of land in Hawaii. Here, lava flows into the Pacific Ocean. When it reaches the water, it cools quickly. The cooled lava hardens to form new rock.

❶ ◢ **Draw Conclusions** The forces that cause lava to erupt are (constructive/destructive) forces.

❷ [CHALLENGE] Other than the weather, what force wears down the new rock formed by the magma from Kilauea?

_____

_____

 Do the Quick Lab *What Forces Shape Earth?*

🔑 **Assess Your Understanding**

2a. Review Forces that erode mountains are called (constructive/destructive) forces.   **7.2.7**

b. List List the destructive forces that act on mountains to erode them.

_____

_____

                                    7.2.7

c. Relate Cause and Effect How do destructive forces change Earth?

_____

_____

_____

_____

                                    7.2.7

got it? ....

○ **I get it!** Now I know that constructive and destructive forces change Earth by _____

○ **I need extra help with** _____

  Go to MY SCIENCE ⒮ COACH *online for help with this subject.*   **7.2.7**

Earth's Interior

🗝 **How Do Geologists Learn About Earth's Interior?**
7.2.1

🗝 **What Are the Features of Earth's Crust, Mantle, and Core?**
7.2.1, 7.2.2, 7.NS.8, 7.NS.11

my planeT DiaRY

Inside Earth

Deep inside Earth, our planet is constantly changing. Dr. Samuel B. Mukasa, a geochemist at the University of Michigan, studies some of these changes. He examines rocks in Antarctica that have been brought up to Earth's surface by magma. When he examines these rocks, he looks for elements that occur only in very small amounts. These elements can offer telltale signs of processes occurring near the boundary between Earth's crust and its mantle—or even at deeper levels. By studying rocks at Earth's surface, Dr. Mukasa is helping us understand Earth's interior.

CAREERS

Read the text and then answer the question.

How is Dr. Mukasa able to study Earth's interior without actually seeing it?

_____

_____

_____

_____

_____

> PLANET DIARY Go to **Planet Diary** to learn more about Earth's interior.

Lab zone Do the Inquiry Warm-Up *Earth's Interior.*

Academic Standards for Science

7.2.1 Describe how the earth is a layered structure composed of lithospheric plates, a mantle and a dense core.

How Do Geologists Learn About Earth's Interior?

Processes that affect Earth's surface are often a result of what's going on inside Earth. But what's inside Earth? This question is very difficult to answer, because geologists are unable to see deep inside Earth. But geologists have found other methods to study the interior of Earth. 🗝 **Geologists have used two main types of evidence to learn about Earth's interior: direct evidence from rock samples and indirect evidence from seismic waves.**

Vocabulary

- seismic wave • pressure • crust • basalt
- granite • mantle • lithosphere • asthenosphere
- outer core • inner core

Skills

- ➲ Reading: Identify Supporting Evidence
- ⚠ Inquiry: Interpret Data

Evidence From Rock Samples Geologists have drilled holes as deep as 12.3 kilometers into Earth. The drills bring up samples of rock. These rocks give geologists clues about Earth's structure and conditions deep inside Earth, where the rocks formed. In addition, volcanoes sometimes blast rock to the surface from depths of more than 100 kilometers. These rocks provide more information about Earth's interior. Also, in laboratories, geologists have re-created conditions inside Earth to see how rock behaves. For instance, they focus laser beams on pieces of rock while squeezing the rock with great force.

Evidence From Seismic Waves To study Earth's interior, geologists use an indirect method. When earthquakes occur, they produce **seismic waves** (SYZ mik). Geologists record the seismic waves and study how they travel through Earth. The speed of seismic waves and the paths they take give geologists clues about the structure of the planet. That is, the paths of seismic waves reveal areas inside Earth where the makeup or form of material changes. To better understand how seismic waves can reveal Earth's interior, look at how the paths of ocean waves "reveal" the island shown in **Figure 1.**

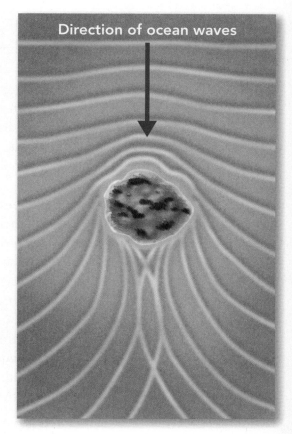
Direction of ocean waves

FIGURE 1 ································

Waves

Paths of ocean waves change when the waves reach an island.

✎ **Infer** Geologists have found that the paths of seismic waves change when the waves reach specific depths inside Earth. What can you infer about Earth's structure from this observation?

_____

_____

_____

_____

 Do the Quick Lab *How Do Scientists Find Out What's Inside Earth?*

☞ Assess Your Understanding

got it? ···

○ **I get it!** Now I know that to learn about Earth's interior, geologists use two main types of evidence: _____

_____

○ I need extra help with _____

Go to my science ⓢ coach *online for help with this subject.*

Academic Standards for Science

7.2.1 Describe how the earth is a layered structure composed of lithospheric plates, a mantle and a dense core.

7.2.2 Recognize that the earth possesses a magnetic field that is detectable at the surface within a compass.

7.NS.8 Analyze data, using appropriate mathematical manipulation as required.

7.NS.11 Communicate findings using graphs, charts, and models.

FIGURE 2 ·······························

Pressure and Depth

The deeper that this swimmer goes, the greater the pressure from the surrounding water.

✎ **Compare and Contrast** How is the water in the swimming pool similar to Earth's interior? How is it different? (*Hint:* Consider both temperature and pressure in your answer.)

_____

_____

_____

_____

_____

_____

_____

_____

_____

_____

What Are the Features of Earth's Crust, Mantle, and Core?

Today, scientists know that Earth's interior is made up of three main layers. Each of Earth's layers covers the layers beneath it, much like the layers of an onion. 🔑 **The three main layers of Earth are the crust, the mantle, and the core. These layers vary greatly in size, composition, temperature, and pressure.**

Although each layer of Earth has its own characteristics, some properties apply throughout all of Earth. For example, the deeper inside Earth, the greater the mass of the rock that is pressing down from above. **Pressure** results from a force pressing on an area. Because of the weight of the rock above, pressure inside Earth increases with depth. 🔑 **The deeper down inside Earth, the greater the pressure.** Look at **Figure 2**. Pressure inside Earth increases much like pressure in the swimming pool increases.

The mass of rock that presses down from above affects the temperature inside Earth. 🔑 **The temperature inside Earth increases as depth increases.** Just beneath Earth's surface, the surrounding rock is cool. But at about 20 meters down, the rock starts to get warmer. For every 40 meters of depth from that point, the temperature typically rises 1 Celsius degree. The rapid rise in temperature continues for several tens of kilometers. Eventually, the temperature increases more slowly, but steadily. The high temperatures inside Earth are the result of the great pressures squeezing rock and the release of energy from radioactive substances. Some heat is also left over from the formation of Earth 4.6 billion years ago.

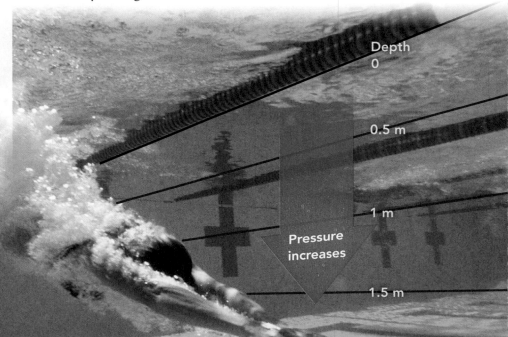

Depth
0

0.5 m

1 m

Pressure
increases

1.5 m

2 m

The Crust In the summer, you might climb a mountain or hike down into a shaded valley. During each of these activities, you are interacting with Earth's **crust,** the layer of rock that forms Earth's outer skin. 🔑 **The crust is a layer of solid rock that includes both dry land and the ocean floor.** The main elements in the crust are oxygen and silicon, as shown in **Figure 3.**

The crust is much thinner than the layer that lies beneath it. In most places, the crust is between 5 and 40 kilometers thick. It is thickest under high mountains—where it can be as thick as 80 kilometers—and thinnest beneath the ocean.

The crust that lies beneath the ocean is called oceanic crust. The composition of oceanic crust is nearly constant. Its overall composition is much like basalt, with small amounts of ocean sediment on top. **Basalt** (buh SAWLT) is a dark, fine-grained rock.

Continental crust, the crust that forms the continents, contains many types of rocks. So, unlike oceanic crust, its composition varies greatly. But overall the composition of continental crust is much like granite. **Granite** is a rock that usually is a light color and has coarse grains. Both granite and basalt have more oxygen and silicon than they have any other element.

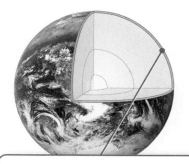

Read the text on this page and then fill in the missing information below.

Layer: _____

Thickness: _____

FIGURE 3 ·······································

Earth's Crust

The crust is Earth's outer layer of solid rock.

The Earth's Crust

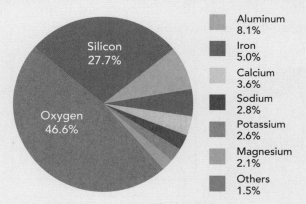

- Silicon 27.7%
- Oxygen 46.6%
- Aluminum 8.1%
- Iron 5.0%
- Calcium 3.6%
- Sodium 2.8%
- Potassium 2.6%
- Magnesium 2.1%
- Others 1.5%

Note: Percentages given are by weight.

The circle graph above shows the composition of Earth's crust.

✏️ **Use the graph and the text on this page to complete the activities below.**

1. **Read Graphs** In total, how much of Earth's crust is made up of oxygen and silicon?

   _____

   7.NS.8

2. **Summarize** Fill in the missing information in the two charts at the right.

Oceanic crust

Oceanic crust

Typical rock: _____

Relative grain size: _____

Color: _____

Continental crust

Typical rock: _____

Relative grain size: _____

Color: _____

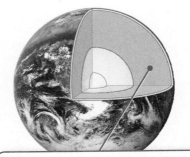

The Mantle
About 40 kilometers beneath dry land, the rock in Earth's interior changes. Rock here contains more magnesium and iron than rock above it. The rock below the boundary is the solid material of the **mantle,** a layer of hot rock. 🔑 **The mantle is made of rock that is very hot, but solid. Scientists divide the mantle into layers based on the physical characteristics of those layers. Overall, the mantle is nearly 3,000 kilometers thick.**

The Lithosphere
The uppermost part of the mantle is brittle rock, like the rock of the crust. Both the crust and the uppermost part of the mantle are strong, hard, and rigid. So geologists often group the crust and uppermost mantle into a single layer called the **lithosphere** (LITH uh sfeer). As shown in **Figure 4,** Earth's lithosphere averages about 100 kilometers thick.

The Asthenosphere
Below the lithosphere, the material is hotter and under increasing pressure. As a result, the part of the mantle just beneath the lithosphere is less rigid than the rock above. Over thousands of years this part of the mantle can bend like a metal spoon. But it's still solid. If you kicked it, you would stub your toe. This soft layer is called the **asthenosphere** (as THEN uh sfeer).

The Mesosphere
Beneath the asthenosphere, the mantle is hot but more rigid. The stiffness of the *mesosphere* is the result of increasingly high pressure. This layer includes a region called the transition zone, which lies just beneath the asthenosphere. It also includes the lower mantle, which extends down to Earth's core.

Read the text on this page and then fill in the missing information below.

Layer: _____

Thickness: _____

_____

FIGURE 4 ····························

Mantle Piece

Earth's mantle is nearly 3,000 kilometers thick. The rigid lithosphere rests on the softer material of the asthenosphere.

✎ **Describe** Fill in the information in the boxes next to the diagram of the upper mantle.

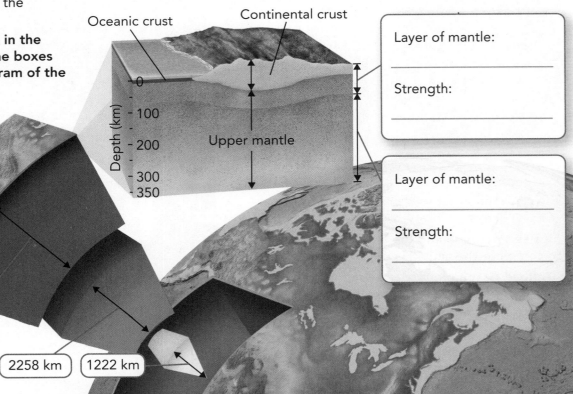

Oceanic crust

Continental crust

Depth (km)

0

100

200

300

350

Upper mantle

Layer of mantle: _____

Strength: _____

Layer of mantle: _____

Strength: _____

2811–2886 km   2258 km   1222 km

The Core Below the mantle lies Earth's core.  **The core is made mostly of the metals iron and nickel. It consists of two parts—a liquid outer core and a solid inner core.** The outer core is 2,258 kilometers thick. The inner core is a solid ball. Its radius is 1,222 kilometers. The total radius of the core is 3,480 kilometers. Earth's core occupies the center of the planet.

Outer Core and Inner Core The **outer core** is a layer of molten metal surrounding the inner core. Despite enormous pressure, the outer core is liquid. The **inner core** is a dense ball of solid metal. In the inner core, extreme pressure squeezes the atoms of iron and nickel so much that they cannot spread out to become liquid.

Currently, most evidence suggests that both parts of the core are made of iron and nickel. But scientists have found data suggesting that the core also contains oxygen, sulfur, and silicon.

> **Read the text on this page and then fill in the missing information below.**
>
> Layer: _____
>
> Radius: _____

FIGURE 5 ···
The Core of It
Earth's core consists of two separate layers.

✎ **Review** Put each term below in its proper place in the Venn diagram.

solid metal	molten metal
iron	nickel
dense ball	liquid layer

Outer Core   Both   Inner Core

do the math! Analyzing Data

Temperature Inside Earth
The graph shows how temperatures change between Earth's surface and the core.

❶ **Read Graphs** Between what depths does Earth's temperature increase the slowest?

_____

❷ **CHALLENGE** Why does the graph show a temperature of 16°C at 0 meters of depth?

_____

_____

❸ ⚠ **Interpret Data** How does temperature change with depth in Earth's interior?

_____

_____

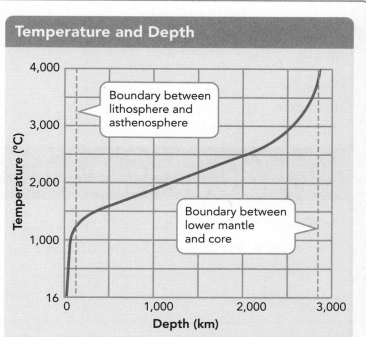

Temperature and Depth

Boundary between lithosphere and asthenosphere

Boundary between lower mantle and core

7.NS.8

285

Identify Supporting Evidence How can iron filings provide evidence that a bar magnet has a magnetic field?

_____

_____

_____

_____

_____

The Core and Earth's Magnetic Field Scientists think that movements in the liquid outer core create Earth's magnetic field. Because Earth has a magnetic field, the planet acts like a giant bar magnet. Earth's magnetic field affects the whole planet.

To understand how a magnetic field affects an object, look at the bar magnet shown in **Figure 6.** If you place the magnet on a piece of paper and sprinkle iron filings on the paper, the iron filings line up with the bar's magnetic field. If you could surround Earth with iron filings, they would form a similar pattern.

When you use a compass, the compass needle aligns with the lines of force in Earth's magnetic field. These lines meet at Earth's magnetic poles. So the needle points to Earth's _magnetic_ north pole, which is not the same location as Earth's _geographic_ North Pole.

EXPLORE THE BIG ? Earth's Interior

What is the structure of Earth?

FIGURE 7 ··

▶ **REAL-WORLD INQUIRY** Earth is divided into distinct layers. Each layer has its own characteristics.

1. Summarize Draw each of Earth's layers. Include both the outer core and the inner core. Label each layer. Then, complete the chart below.

	Thickness/Radius	Composition	Solid/Liquid
Crust:			
Mantle:			
Outer core:			
Inner core:			
TOTAL:	6,371 km		

2. Compare and Contrast Pick any two points inside Earth and label them A and B. Compare and contrast Earth at those two points.

My Point A is in the _____

My Point B is in the_____

_____

_____

_____

7.NS.8, 7.NS.11

FIGURE 6 ·····························

Earth's Magnetic Field
Earth's magnetic field has a north and south pole, like the magnetic field at each end of a magnet.

✎ **Name** Which pole will a compass needle in North America point to? (Underline the correct label for the pole on the globe.)

7.2.2

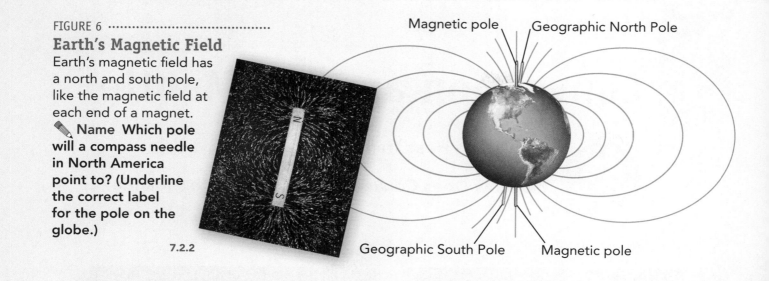

Magnetic pole   Geographic North Pole

Geographic South Pole   Magnetic pole

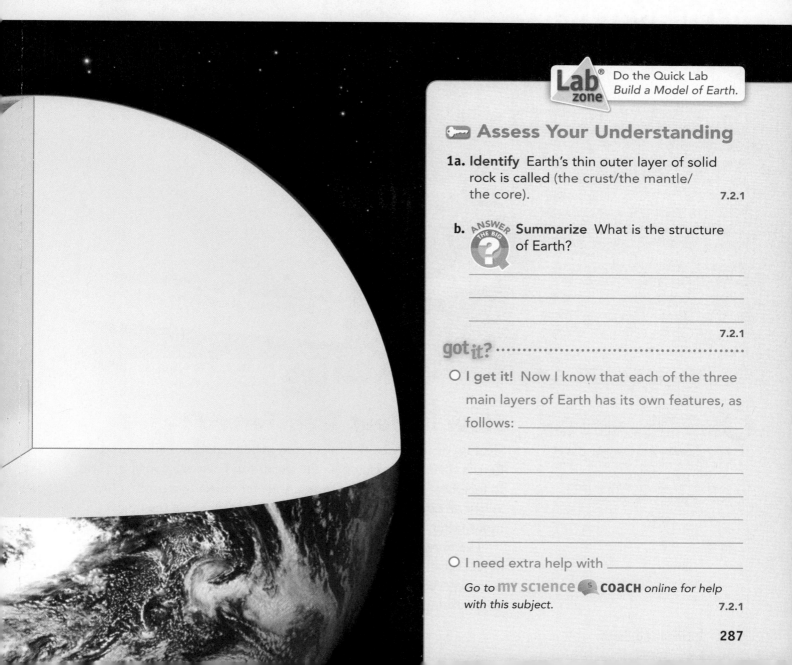

Lab zone® Do the Quick Lab
Build a Model of Earth.

🔑 Assess Your Understanding

1a. Identify Earth's thin outer layer of solid rock is called (the crust/the mantle/ the core).   7.2.1

b. ANSWER THE BIG **?** **Summarize** What is the structure of Earth?

_____

_____

_____

7.2.1

got it? ·····································

○ **I get it!** Now I know that each of the three main layers of Earth has its own features, as follows: _____

_____

_____

_____

_____

○ **I need extra help with** _____

Go to **MY SCIENCE** ◯ᔆ **COACH** *online for help with this subject.*   7.2.1

Convection and the Mantle

UNLOCK THE BIG ?

🔑 **How Is Heat Transferred?**
7.1.2

🔑 **How Does Convection Occur in Earth's Mantle?**
7.1.2, 7.2.4

my planet diary

Lighting Up the Subject

Misconception: Rock cannot flow.

Did you know that the solid rock in Earth's mantle can flow like a fluid? To learn how, look at this image of a lava lamp. Heat from a bulb causes solid globs of wax at the bottom of the lamp to expand. As they expand, the globs become less dense. The globs then rise through the more dense fluid that surrounds them.

In Earth's mantle, great heat and pressure create regions of rock that are less dense than the rock around them. Over millions of years, the less dense rock slowly rises—like the solid globs in the lava lamp!

MISCONCEPTION

✏️ **Compare and Contrast** Think about your own observations of liquids that flow. Then answer the question below.

How is flowing rock different from flowing water?

_____

_____

_____

_____

> PLANET DIARY Go to **Planet Diary** to learn more about Earth's mantle.

Lab zone Do the Inquiry Warm-Up Tracing Heat Flow.

🔵 **Academic Standards for Science**

7.1.2 Describe and give examples of how energy can be transferred from place to place and transformed from one form to another through radiation, convection and conduction.

How Is Heat Transferred?

Heat is constantly being transferred inside Earth and all around Earth's surface. For example, the warm sun heats the cooler ground. In fact, heat always moves from a warmer object to a cooler object. When an object is heated, the particles that make up the object move faster. The faster-moving particles have more energy.

The movement of energy from a warmer object to a cooler object is called heat transfer. 🔑 **There are three types of heat transfer: radiation, convection, and conduction.** Look at **Figure 1** to see examples of heat transfer.

Vocabulary
- radiation • convection
- conduction • density
- convection current

Skills
↺ Reading: Relate Cause and Effect

△ Inquiry: Communicate

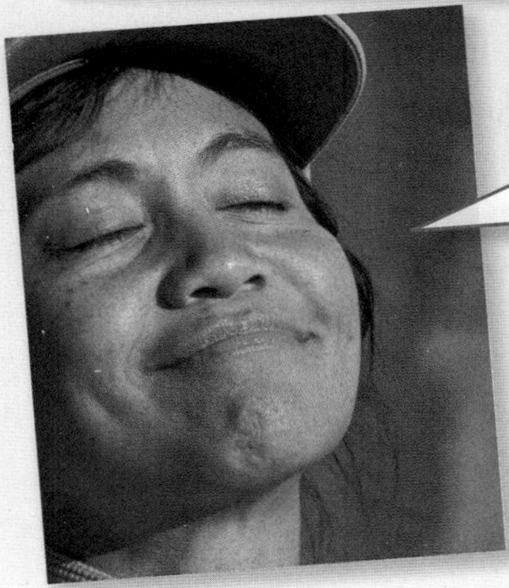

Radiation

The sun constantly transfers light and heat through the air, warming your skin. The transfer of energy that is carried in rays like light is called **radiation**.

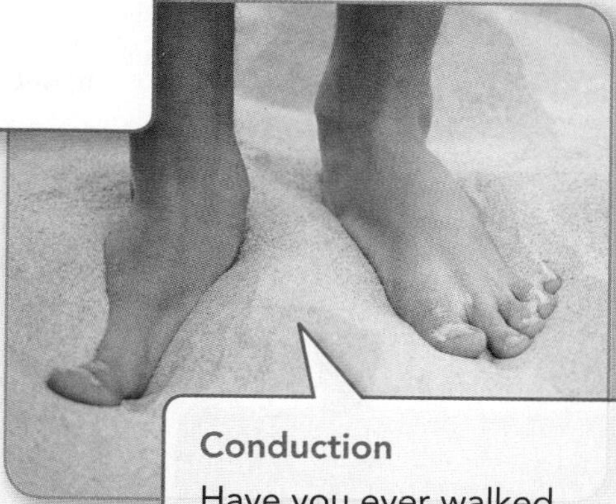

Conduction

Have you ever walked barefoot over hot sand? Your feet can feel as if they are burning! That is because the sand transfers its heat to your skin. Heat transfer between materials that are touching is called **conduction**.

Convection

Seagulls often soar on warm air currents. The currents are created as warm air rises from the ground. The warm air heats cooler air above it. Heat transfer by the movement of a fluid is called **convection**.

FIGURE 1 ·····················

〉 **INTERACTIVE ART** **Heat Transfer**
In each type of heat transfer, heat moves from a warmer object to a colder object.

△ **Communicate** Work with a classmate to think of other examples of conduction, convection, and radiation. (*Hint:* Think of different ways to cook food.) Write your answers in the spaces provided.

Radiation

_____

_____

Conduction

_____

_____

Convection

_____

_____

 Do the Quick Lab *How Can Heat Cause Motion in a Liquid?*

🔑 Assess Your Understanding

got_it? ··

○ **I get it!** Now I know that the three types of heat transfer are _____

○ **I need extra help with** _____

Go to **my science** ⓢ **COACH** *online for help with this subject.*

Academic Standards for Science

7.1.2 Describe and give examples of how energy can be transferred from place to place and transformed from one form to another through radiation, convection and conduction.

7.2.4 Explain how convection currents in the mantle cause lithospheric plates to move.

How Does Convection Occur in Earth's Mantle?

Recall that Earth's mantle and core are extremely hot. How is heat transferred within Earth?

Convection Currents When you heat soup on a stove, convection occurs in the soup. That is, the soup at the bottom of the pot gets hot and expands. As the soup expands, its density decreases. **Density** is a measure of how much mass there is in a given volume of a substance. For example, most rock is more dense than water because a given volume of rock has more mass than the same volume of water.

The warm, less dense soup above the heat source moves upward and floats over the cooler, denser soup, as shown in **Figure 2**. Near the surface, the warm soup cools, becoming denser. Gravity then pulls the colder soup back down to the bottom of the pot. Here, it is reheated and rises again.

✎ **Relate Cause and Effect**
What three processes or forces combine to set convection currents in motion?

_____

_____

_____

_____

_____

FIGURE 2 ·······················
Convection Currents
In a pot of soup, convection currents flow as the hotter, less dense soup rises and the cooler, more dense soup sinks.

A constant flow begins. Cooler, denser soup sinks to the bottom of the pot. At the same time, warmer, less dense soup rises. The flow that transfers heat within a fluid is called a **convection current.** 🗝 **Heating and cooling of a fluid, changes in the fluid's density, and the force of gravity combine to set convection currents in motion.** Without heat, convection currents eventually stop.

apply it!

Hot springs are common in Yellowstone National Park. Here, melted snow and rainwater seep to a depth of 3,000 meters, where a shallow magma chamber heats the rock of Earth's crust. The rock heats the water to over 200°C and keeps it under very high pressure.

❶ **Compare and Contrast** The heated water is (more/less) dense than the melted snow and rainwater.

❷ **CHALLENGE** What might cause convection currents in a hot spring?

_____

_____

Convection Currents in Earth Inside Earth, heat from the core and the mantle act like the stove that heats the pot of soup. That is, large amounts of heat are transferred by convection currents within the core and mantle. ⊙ **Heat from the core and the mantle itself causes convection currents in the mantle.** To see how these currents work in the core and mantle, look at **Figure 3.**

How is it possible for mantle rock to flow? Over millions of years, the great heat and pressure in the mantle have caused solid mantle rock to warm and flow very slowly. Many geologists think plumes of mantle rock rise slowly from the bottom of the mantle toward the top. The hot rock eventually cools and sinks back through the mantle. Over and over, the cycle of rising and sinking takes place. Convection currents like these have been moving inside Earth for more than four billion years!

There are also convection currents in the outer core. These convection currents cause Earth's magnetic field.

did you know?

Convection currents may form on planets other than Earth. For example, scientists believe that the Great Red Spot on Jupiter may be the result of storms that have convection currents.

FIGURE 3 ·····················

ART IN MOTION Mantle Convection

✏️ **Interpret Diagrams** Place the following labels in the boxes for Points A and B:

hotter	less dense	sinks
colder	more dense	rises

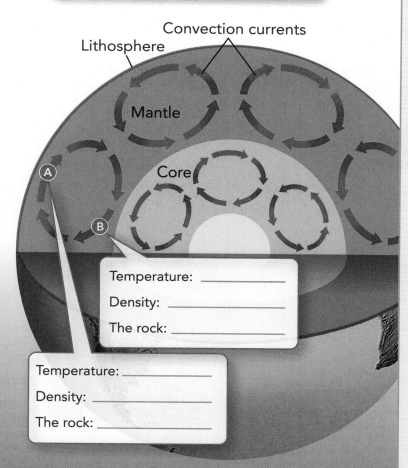

Convection currents
Lithosphere
Mantle
Core

Ⓐ
Ⓑ

Temperature: _____
Density: _____
The rock: _____

Temperature: _____
Density: _____
The rock: _____

Lab zone ® Do the Lab Investigation *Modeling Mantle Convection Currents.*

⊙ **Assess Your Understanding**

1a. Explain A convection current transfers (heat / air) within a fluid. 7.1.2

b. Infer In which part of Earth's core do convection currents occur? _____
7.2.4

c. Predict What would happen to the convection currents in the mantle if Earth's interior eventually cooled down? Why?

_____
_____
_____
_____
_____

7.1.2, 7.2.4, 7.NS.1

got it? ·····························

○ **I get it!** Now I know that convection currents in the mantle are caused by_____
_____
_____

○ **I need extra help with** _____

Go to **my science** ⑤ **COACH** online for help with this subject. 7.1.2, 7.2.4

REVIEW THE BIG ?

Earth consists of three main layers. The _____ is the outermost layer. The _____ is made up of rock that is hot but solid. The _____ occupies Earth's center.

LESSON 1 The Earth System

7.2, 7.2.1, 7.2.7, 7.NS.1, 7.NS.8

🔑 The Earth system has four main spheres: the atmosphere, the hydrosphere, the geosphere, and the biosphere. As a major source of energy for Earth processes, the sun can be considered part of the Earth system as well.

🔑 Lands are constantly being created and destroyed by competing forces. Constructive forces shape the land's surface by building up mountains and other landmasses. Destructive forces destroy and wear away landmasses through processes like erosion and weathering.

Vocabulary
• system   • energy   • atmosphere   • geosphere   • hydrosphere
• biosphere   • constructive force   • destructive force

LESSON 2 Earth's Interior

7.2.1, 7.2.2, 7.NS.8, 7.NS.11

🔑 Geologists have used two main types of evidence to learn about Earth's interior: direct evidence from rock samples and indirect evidence from seismic waves.

🔑 The deeper down inside Earth, the greater the pressure. The temperature inside Earth increases as depth increases.

🔑 The three main layers of Earth are the crust, the mantle, and the core. The crust is a layer of solid rock that includes dry land and ocean floor. The mantle is about 3,000 km thick and is made of very hot, solid rock. The core is mostly iron and nickel. It consists of a liquid outer core and a solid inner core.

Vocabulary
• seismic wave   • pressure   • crust   • basalt   • granite   • mantle
• lithosphere   • asthenosphere   • outer core   • inner core

LESSON 3 Convection and the Mantle

7.1.2, 7.2.4

🔑 There are three types of heat transfer: radiation, convection, and conduction.

🔑 Heating and cooling of a fluid, changes in the fluid's density, and the force of gravity combine to set convection currents in motion.

🔑 Heat from the core and the mantle itself causes convection currents in the mantle.

Vocabulary
• radiation   • convection   • conduction   • density   • convection current

Review and Assessment

LESSON 1 The Earth System

1. Which is part of Earth's hydrosphere?

   a. liquid outer core   **b.** solid inner core

   c. granite   **d.** ocean water

                               7.2

2. Earth's system has two sources of energy,
which are _____

_____

_____

                               7.1.2

3. Infer Explain how the hydrosphere and
biosphere interact in this swamp.

_____

_____

_____

                               7.2

4. Classify Are the forces that cause lava to
erupt from a volcano and flow over Earth's
surface constructive or destructive forces?
Explain.

_____

_____

_____

_____

                               7.2.6

5. **Write About It** If the amount of paved land in
the United States continues to increase, how
might the biosphere be affected?

                              7.NS.1

LESSON 2 Earth's Interior

6. What is the relatively soft layer of the upper
mantle called?

   a. continental crust   **b.** lithosphere

   c. asthenosphere   **d.** inner core

                               7.2.1

7. To learn about Earth's structure, geologists use
seismic waves, which are _____

_____

_____

                               7.2.1

8. Relate Cause and Effect What do scientists
think produces Earth's magnetic field?

_____

_____

_____

_____

                           7.2.1, 7.2.2

9. Sequence Name each layer of Earth, starting
from Earth's center. Include both layers of the
core and all layers of the mantle.

_____

_____

_____

_____

                               7.2.1

10. Summarize What is the relationship between
temperature and depth inside Earth? Is this
relationship the same for pressure?

_____

_____

_____

_____

                               7.2.1

11. **Write About It** Compare and contrast oceanic
crust with continental crust. In your answer, be
sure to consider the composition and thickness
of both types of crust.

                               7.2.1

8 Review and Assessment

Convection and the Mantle

12. What is the transfer of heat by direct contact of particles of matter called?

  a. conduction   **b.** radiation

  c. convection   **d.** pressure

                             7.1.2

13. Compared to air and water, most rock has a high density, which means it has _____

_____

_____

14. Identify Name the two layers below Earth's surface in which convection takes place.

_____
                                  7.2.4

15. Explain What conditions allow rock in the mantle to flow?

_____

_____

_____
                                  7.2.4

16. Develop Hypotheses Suppose a certain part of the mantle is cooler than the parts surrounding it. What might happen to the cooler rock? In your answer, discuss the role of gravity.

_____

_____

_____

_____
                              7.2.4, 7.NS.1

What is the structure of Earth?

17. Suppose you could travel to the center of Earth. You must design a special vehicle for your journey. What equipment should your vehicle include so that it could travel through each layer of Earth shown below? Also, what conditions should your vehicle be able to withstand? Consider temperature, pressure, and the hardness of each layer of Earth.

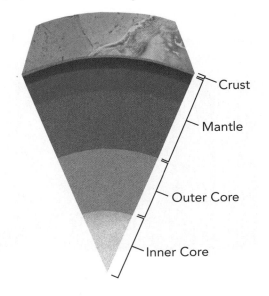

Crust

Mantle

Outer Core

Inner Core

_____

_____

_____

_____

_____

_____

_____

_____

_____

_____

_____

_____
                              7.2.1

Indiana ISTEP+ Practice

Multiple Choice

Circle the letter of the best answer.

1. The illustration below shows a pot of boiling water.

   What process is heating the water?

   A. radiation   **B.** conduction

   C. convection   **D.** destruction

   7.1.2

2. Which part of Earth's system is made up of plants and animals?

   A. biosphere   **B.** hydrosphere

   C. atmosphere   **D.** geosphere

   7.2

3. Which part of Earth's interior is made mostly of nickel and iron and has liquid and solid parts?

   A. lithosphere   **B.** crust

   C. asthenosphere   **D.** core

   7.2.1

4. What is one result of convection currents in Earth's outer core?

   A. erosion
   B. Earth's magnetic field
   C. melted glaciers
   D. Earth's force of gravity

   7.2.4

Constructed Response

Write your answer to Question 5 on the lines below.

5. How do pressure and temperature change inside Earth as depth increases?

   _____

   _____

   _____

   7.2.1

Extended Response

Use the illustration below and your knowledge of science to help you answer Question 6. Write your answer on a separate piece of paper.

6. Describe how Earth's spheres are interacting in the scene pictured below. Also describe any notable constructive and destructive forces.

7.2.7

A Slice of Earth

If you could dig a hole that went straight through to the other side of the world, on your way down you'd see all of the layers underneath Earth's surface.

Of course, digging that kind of hole would be impossible. But if we want to see a slice of Earth, and all its layers, we have another tool. Seismic tomography lets us see Earth's layers as 3-D images. A computer uses data on the size and speed of seismic waves to make these images.

The sudden release of stored energy under Earth's crust sends seismic waves in all directions and causes an earthquake. The waves travel out from the center of the earthquake. Density, pressure, and temperature affect how quickly these seismic waves move through the layers of rock underground. Waves can also bend or bounce back where they meet a boundary between layers.

Scientists are able to record the speed and size of the seismic waves from thousands of earthquakes. Combining this data allows scientists to use computers to create models of Earth's interior.

Design It Design a small structure that can withstand the force of an earthquake. Brainstorm potential solutions and document your designs. Choose your best idea and build a prototype. Test and evaluate the prototype by simulating the effects of an earthquake. Record how well the structure withstands the earthquake simulation. Use this data to redesign your structure. See Appendix A on page 578 for more information about the design process.

7.NS.1–7.NS.11, 7.DP.1–7.DP.11

This seismic tomography image shows a cross-section of Earth's crust and mantle. The colors show materials of different densities that are rising or sinking as part of convection currents in the mantle. The blue line on the map shows that this "slice" of Earth extends from the Pacific Ocean eastward to western Africa. ▶

Setting Sights on Spectacular Sites

You may have seen them near a road, tunnel, or bridge building site, looking through a leveling instrument—a device that looks like a camera on a tripod. Land surveyors collect detailed data about land, such as shape, contour, and elevation, in order to map out what the finished project will look like. They use a variety of mapping instruments from simple measuring tapes to complex satellite photography.

Write About It Research the skills and training that land surveyors need. Write a job posting communicating the skills and training an employer might look for in a land surveyor.

 7.NS.2, 7.NS.11

Where Are We?

Centuries ago, people invented navigational instruments for determining compass direction, latitude, and longitude. Mapmakers created the first scientific maps using a magnetic compass nearly 900 years ago. Later inventions, such as accurate clocks called chronometers, helped mapmakers determine longitude accurately. Today, many people use the latest navigational technology, like Global Positioning System (GPS) technology, in their cars! Since the early days of travel and transportation, navigational tools have shaped science and history.

Research It Create a timeline showing a history of navigational devices and how they changed people's ability to travel. Choose one device and write a paragraph explaining how that device works and how it affected navigation and travel.

 7.NS.2, 7.NS.11

HOW DID THIS ROCK GET HERE?

How do rocks form?

The famous naturalist John Muir first climbed to the summit of Cathedral Peak in 1869. Located in the Sierra Nevada Range in California, it is 3,308 meters in elevation. Cathedral Peak is mostly composed of granite, a mixture of quartz, feldspar, and other minerals such as hornblende and mica. Looking down from this tall, narrow peak, you would probably feel like you were on top of the world!

Develop Hypotheses **How might this towering piece of rock have gotten here?**

_____

_____

_____

_____

_____

> **UNTAMED SCIENCE** Watch the **Untamed Science** video to learn more about minerals and rocks.

Minerals and Rocks

Academic Standards for Science

7.1.3, 7.2.5, 7.NS.1, 7.NS.2, 7.NS.8, 7.NS.11

Check Your Understanding

1. **Background** Read the paragraph below and then answer the question.

Judy filled a glass jar with water. She put a lid on the jar and put the jar in the freezer. Overnight, the water, which was a **liquid,** froze into ice, which is a **solid.** But Judy had forgotten that ice occupies a larger **volume** than the same mass of water. So when the water froze, it expanded and cracked the jar.

A **liquid** is a substance that flows and whose shape, but not volume, can be changed.

A **solid** is a substance that resists changing shape.

Volume is the amount of space that matter occupies.

• What variable changed to turn the liquid water into solid ice?

_____

_____

> **MY READING WEB** If you had trouble completing the question above, visit **My Reading Web** and type in *Minerals and Rocks.*

Vocabulary Skill

Latin Word Origins Many science words in English come from Latin. For example, *granite* comes from the Latin *granum,* meaning "grain." Granite is a rock that has large, visible grains.

Latin Word	Meaning of Latin Word	Example
erosus	eaten away	erosion, *n.* a process by which a mountain is broken into pieces
folium	leaf	foliated, *adj.* with thin, flat layers
caementum	stones and chips from a quarry	cementation, *n.* process in which bits of rock are glued together

2. **Quick Check** Choose the word from the table that best completes the sentence.
   • Rocks that have their grains arranged in flat layers are said to be

_____

crystal

texture

clastic rock

rock cycle

Chapter Preview

LESSON 1
- mineral • inorganic • crystal
- streak • luster
- Mohs hardness scale • cleavage
- fracture • geode • crystallization
- solution • vein

🔁 Relate Text and Visuals
🔺 Form Operational Definitions

LESSON 2
- rock-forming mineral • granite
- basalt • grain • texture
- igneous rock • sedimentary rock
- metamorphic rock

🔁 Identify the Main Idea
🔺 Observe

LESSON 3
- extrusive rock
- intrusive rock

🔁 Relate Cause and Effect
🔺 Interpret Data

LESSON 4
- sediment • weathering • erosion
- deposition • compaction
- cementation • clastic rock
- organic rock • chemical rock

🔁 Identify the Main Idea
🔺 Infer

LESSON 5
- foliated

🔁 Relate Cause and Effect
🔺 Observe

LESSON 6
- rock cycle

🔁 Sequence
🔺 Classify

▷ **VOCAB FLASH CARDS** For extra help with vocabulary, visit **Vocab Flash Cards** and type in *Minerals and Rocks.*

Properties of Minerals

UNLOCK
THE BIG

?

🔑 **What Is a Mineral?**
7.2.5

🔑 **How Are Minerals Identified?**
7.2.5, 7.NS.8

🔑 **How Do Minerals Form?**
7.2.5, 7.NS.8

MY PLANET DIARY for Indiana

FUN FACTS

Glowing with Charm

Indiana is brimming with pride over its calcite! Calcite is a mineral found in many caves in Indiana and it used in construction as well as products like toothpaste. But even a mineral needs good lighting to look its best. When calcite is exposed to ultraviolet (UV) light, it can glow red, pink, green, or blue. The color it glows depends on the amount of other substances in the calcite sample.

Communicate Discuss the question with a partner. Write your answer below.

How might you use a UV light to identify substances in a calcite sample?

_____

_____

_____

_____

_____

> PLANET DIARY Go to **Planet Diary** to learn more about minerals.

Lab zone Do the Inquiry Warm-Up *How Does the Rate of Cooling Affect Crystals?*

Academic Standards for Science

7.2.5 Describe the origin and physical properties of igneous, metamorphic and sedimentary rocks and how they are related through the rock cycle.

What Is a Mineral?

Look at the two substances in **Figure 1.** On the left is a hard chunk of coal. On the right are beautiful quartz crystals. Both are solid materials that form beneath Earth's surface. But which is a mineral?

Defining Minerals How are minerals defined? 🔑 **A mineral is a naturally occurring solid that can form by inorganic processes and that has a crystal structure and a definite chemical composition.** For a substance to be a **mineral,** it must have all five of these characteristics. So, is either quartz or coal a mineral?

Vocabulary

- mineral • inorganic • crystal • streak • luster
- Mohs hardness scale • cleavage • fracture
- geode • crystallization • solution • vein

Skills

↻ **Reading:** Relate Text and Visuals

△ **Inquiry:** Form Operational Definitions

Naturally Occurring

All minerals are substances that are formed by natural processes. Quartz forms naturally as molten material called magma cools and hardens beneath Earth's surface. Coal forms naturally from the remains of plants that are squeezed tightly together.

Solid

A mineral is always a solid, with a definite volume and shape. The particles that make up a solid are packed together very tightly, so they cannot move like the particles that make up a liquid. Coal and quartz are solids.

Crystal Structure

The particles of a mineral line up in a pattern that repeats over and over again. The repeating pattern of a mineral's particles forms a solid called a **crystal.** A crystal has flat sides, called faces, that meet at sharp edges and corners. The quartz in **Figure 1** has a crystal structure. In contrast, most coal lacks a crystal structure.

Forms by Inorganic Processes

All minerals must be able to form by **inorganic** processes. That is, every mineral must be able to form from materials that were not a part of living things. Quartz can form naturally as magma cools. Coal comes only from living things—the remains of plants that lived millions of years ago. But some minerals that can form from inorganic processes may also be produced by living things.

Definite Chemical Composition

A mineral has a definite chemical composition. This means that a mineral always contains certain elements in definite proportions. An element is a substance composed of a single kind of atom.

Quartz always contains one atom of silicon for every two atoms of oxygen. The elements in coal can vary over a wide range.

Quartz

Coal

FIGURE 1 ·······························

Are They or Aren't They?

To be classified as a mineral, a substance must satisfy five requirements.

✏ **Classify** Complete the checklist. Are quartz and coal minerals or only naturally occurring substances?

_____

_____

_____

Mineral Characteristics	Quartz	Coal
Naturally occurring	✔	✔
Can form by inorganic processes		
Solid		
Crystal structure		
Definite chemical composition		

Minerals, Compounds, and Elements

Almost all minerals are compounds. In a compound, two or more elements are combined so that the elements no longer have distinct properties. For example, the mineral cinnabar is composed of the elements sulfur and mercury. Sulfur is bright yellow. Mercury is a silvery liquid at room temperature. But cinnabar has solid, shiny, red crystals.

Different minerals have a different combination of elements. For example, a crystal of quartz has one atom of silicon for every two atoms of oxygen. This ratio is constant for all varieties of quartz. Each mineral in the garnet group of minerals has three atoms of silicon for every twelve atoms of oxygen. But garnets also contain other elements, in set ratios. **Figure 2** shows one variety of garnet.

Some elements occur in nature in a pure form, and not as part of a compound. Elements such as copper, silver, and gold are also minerals. Almost all pure, solid elements are metals.

FIGURE 2 ⋯⋯⋯⋯⋯⋯⋯⋯

Elements and Compounds in Minerals

Quartz and the garnet minerals contain the elements silicon and oxygen. At room temperature, pure silicon is a hard, dark gray solid. Oxygen is a colorless gas.

✏️ **Describe** Choose either quartz or garnet. Then, choose silicon or oxygen. When your element is part of a mineral, how is it different from its pure form?

_____

_____

_____

_____

_____

_____

_____

Rose quartz   Almandine garnet

Lab zone® Do the Quick Lab *Classifying Objects as Minerals.*

🔑 Assess Your Understanding

1a. Summarize All minerals must be able to form from (organic/inorganic) processes.

7.2.5

b. Explain What, specifically, makes a process inorganic?

_____

_____

7.2.5

c. Classify Amber is a material used in jewelry. It forms only by the process of pine tree resin hardening into stone. Is amber a mineral? Explain.

_____

_____

_____

7.2.5

got it? ⋯⋯⋯

○ **I get it!** Now I know that to be classified as a mineral, a substance must be _____

_____

○ **I need extra help with** _____

Go to **MY SCIENCE ⓢ COACH** *online for help with this subject.*

7.2.5

How Are Minerals Identified?

Geologists have identified more than 4,000 minerals. But telling these minerals apart can often be a challenge. 🔑 **Each mineral has characteristic properties that can be used to identify it.**

Academic Standards for Science

7.2.5 Describe the origin and physical properties of igneous, metamorphic and sedimentary rocks and how they are related through the rock cycle.

7.NS.8 Analyze data, using appropriate mathematical manipulation as required.

Color

Both minerals shown here are the color gold. But only one is the mineral gold. In fact, only a few minerals have their own characteristic color.

FIGURE 3 ·····

Is All That Glitters Really Gold?
Both minerals shown here are gold in color.

✎ **Identify** Circle the mineral that you think is gold. (Answer at bottom of page.)

Streak

The **streak** of a mineral is the color of its powder. Although the color of a mineral can vary, its streak does not. However, the streak color and the mineral color are often different. For example, pyrite has a gold color but its streak is greenish black.

Galena   Hematite   Malachite

FIGURE 4 ·····

Scratching the Surface
The color of any particular mineral's streak does not vary.

✎ **Infer** Which is more useful when identifying a mineral: the mineral's color or the mineral's streak?

_____

Luster

Luster is the term used to describe how light is reflected from a mineral's surface. For example, minerals such as galena that contain metals often have a metallic luster. Quartz has a glassy luster. Other terms used to describe luster include earthy, silky, waxy, and pearly.

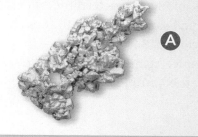

FIGURE 5 ·····

Upon Reflection
Geologists use many terms to describe the luster of minerals.

✎ **Describe** Choose any item in your classroom that reflects light. In one word, describe its luster.

Item: _____

Luster: _____

Metallic
Galena

Silky
Malachite

Waxy, greasy, or pearly

Talc

A. Gold B. Pyrite

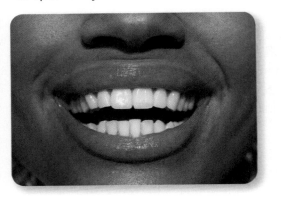

Hardness When you want to identify a mineral, one of the most useful clues to use is the mineral's hardness. In 1812, Austrian Friedrich Mohs, a mineral expert, invented a scale to help identify minerals by how hard they are. The **Mohs hardness scale** is used to rank the hardness of minerals. The scale assigns a mineral's hardness a ranking from 1 to 10, as shown in **Figure 6.**

Hardness can be determined by a scratch test. A mineral can scratch any mineral softer than itself, but can be scratched by any mineral that is harder. For example, suppose you found a deposit of azurite. Azurite is not on the Mohs scale, but you would like to determine its hardness. So you take a small sample and try to scratch it with talc, gypsum, and calcite. But none of these minerals scratch your sample. Apatite, rated 5 on the scale, does scratch it. Therefore, the hardness of azurite is probably about 4.

FIGURE 6

Mohs Hardness Scale

Geologists determine a mineral's hardness by comparing it to the hardness of the minerals on the Mohs scale.

✎ **Explain** Read the description of each mineral at the right. Place each mineral's name in its proper location in the scale.

Topaz It can scratch quartz but not corundum.

Gypsum A fingernail can easily scratch it.

Apatite A steel knife can scratch it.

Diamond Extremely hard, it can scratch all known common minerals.

Quartz It can scratch feldspar but not topaz.

1 Talc The softest mineral, talc flakes when scratched by a fingernail.

2 _____

3 Calcite A fingernail cannot scratch it, but a copper penny can.

4 Fluorite A steel knife can easily scratch it.

5 _____

Increasing hardness

Calculating Density

For many minerals, different samples of a mineral all have the same density. So geologists can use density to help identify mineral samples. To do so, they use the following formula.

$$\text{Density} = \frac{\text{Mass}}{\text{Volume}}$$

You find a sample of the mineral magnetite. The sample has a mass of 151.0 g and a volume of 29.0 cm³. What is the density of magnetite?

_____

_____

_____

7.NS.8

Density Each mineral has a characteristic density. Recall that density is the mass in a given space, or mass per unit volume. No matter how large or small the mineral sample is, the density of that mineral always remains the same. For example, the density of quartz is 2.6 g/cm³. The density of diamond is 3.5 g/cm³.

To measure density, geologists use a balance to first determine the precise mass of a mineral sample. Then they place the mineral in water to determine how much water the sample displaces. The volume of the displaced water equals the volume of the sample. The mineral's density can then be calculated using the formula below.

$$\text{Density} = \frac{\text{Mass}}{\text{Volume}}$$

You can compare the density of two mineral samples of about the same size. Just pick them up and heft them, or feel their weight, in your hands. The sample that feels heavier is probably also denser.

6 **Feldspar**
It can't be scratched by a steel knife but can scratch window glass.

7 _____

8 _____

9 **Corundum**
It can scratch topaz.

10 _____

FIGURE 7 ·····························

Halite

Quartz

Crystal Structure

Each mineral has its own crystal structure.

✎ **Answer the questions.**

1. **List** What two features do geologists use to classify crystals?

_____

_____

_____

_____

2. CHALLENGE Does a quartz crystal have more or fewer faces than a halite crystal?

_____

Crystal Structure The atoms that make up a mineral line up in a regular pattern. This pattern repeats over and over. The repeating pattern of a mineral's atoms forms a mineral's crystal structure. All the crystals of a mineral have the same crystal structure. Scientists can use crystal structure to identify very small mineral samples. For example, scientists can bounce a powerful beam of particles off very small crystals. Because the atoms that make up minerals line up in regular patterns, these beams produce distinct patterns of light.

As shown in **Figure 7,** different minerals have crystals that are shaped differently. Halite crystals are cubic. That is, they are shaped like a cube. You can break a large piece of halite into smaller pieces. But the smaller pieces still contain crystals that are perfect cubes.

Geologists classify crystals by the number of faces, or sides, on the crystal. They also measure the angles at which the faces meet.

What Do You Know?

✎ **Interpret Photographs** The photograph shows crystals of the mineral stibnite. Read the text about how minerals are identified. Then identify which of stibnite's characteristic properties you can infer from the photograph. Which properties would you need to test before being able to identify the mineral?

_____

_____

_____

_____

_____

_____

_____

_____

Cleavage and Fracture

You may be familiar with how the mineral mica can split apart to form flat sheets. A mineral that splits easily along flat surfaces has the property called **cleavage**.

Whether a mineral has cleavage depends on how the atoms in its crystals are arranged. The way atoms are arranged in mica allows it to split easily in one direction. **Figure 8** shows cleavage in mica.

Most minerals do not split apart evenly. Instead, they have a characteristic type of fracture. **Fracture** describes how a mineral looks when it breaks apart in an irregular way. For example, when quartz breaks, it produces curved, shell-like surfaces.

Special Properties

Some minerals can be identified by special physical properties. Calcite bends light to produce double images, as shown in **Figure 9**. Other minerals conduct electricity, glow when placed under ultraviolet light, or are magnetic.

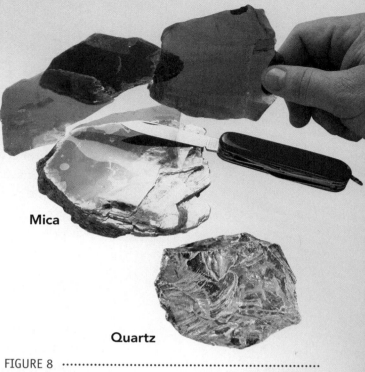

Mica

Quartz

FIGURE 8 ·····························
Fracture and Cleavage
How a mineral breaks apart can help to identify it.

Form Operational Definitions Observe the examples of cleavage and fracture above. Based on your observations, write a definition of cleavage in your own words.

_____

_____

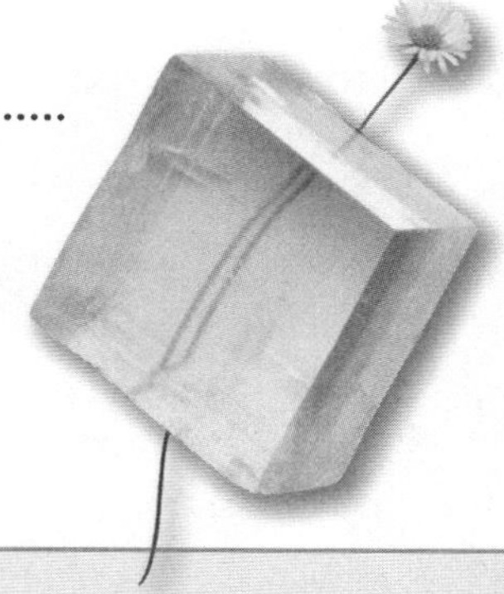

FIGURE 9 ·····························
Special Properties
Calcite bends light to produce a double image.

 Lab zone® Do the Quick Lab *Identifying Minerals.*

🔑 Assess Your Understanding

2a. Summarize Geologists identify minerals by examining their _____

_____

_____

7.2.5

b. Design Experiments Lodestone is magnetic. How might you identify whether a mineral sample might be lodestone?

_____

_____

_____

7.2.5

got it? ··

○ **I get it!** Now I know that the characteristic properties used to identify minerals are _____

_____

○ **I need extra help with** _____

Go to MY SCIENCE ⓢ COACH *online for help with this subject.*

7.2.5

7.2.5 Describe the origin and physical properties of igneous, metamorphic and sedimentary rocks and how they are related through the rock cycle.

7.NS.8 Analyze data.

How Do Minerals Form?

On a rock-collecting field trip, you find an egg-shaped rock about the size of a football. Later, at a geologic laboratory, you split the rock open. The rock is hollow! Its inside surface sparkles with large amethyst crystals. Amethyst is a type of quartz.

You have found a geode, as shown in **Figure 10**. A **geode** (JEE ohd) is a rounded, hollow rock that is often lined with mineral crystals. Geologists believe that crystals probably form inside a geode when water containing dissolved minerals seeps into a crack or hollow in a rock. Slowly, crystallization occurs, lining the inside with large crystals that are often perfectly formed. **Crystallization** is the process by which atoms are arranged to form a material that has a crystal structure. ☞ **In general, minerals can form in three ways. Some minerals form from organic processes. Other minerals can crystallize from materials dissolved in solutions. Finally, many minerals crystallize as magma and lava cool.**

Organic Minerals All minerals can form by inorganic processes. ☞ **However, some minerals can also form by organic processes.** For instance, ocean animals such as clams and corals produce shells and skeletons made out of the mineral calcite.

FIGURE 10

Geodes

Water seeping into a crack in a rock can result in the formation of a geode.

✎ **Sequence** Complete the graphic organizer to show how a geode forms in four steps.

Geode
A crack or hollow forms in a rock.

↓

_____
_____
_____
_____

↓

_____
_____
_____

↓

The geode is complete.

Minerals From Solutions

Sometimes the elements and compounds that form minerals can be dissolved in water to form solutions. A **solution** is a mixture in which one substance is dissolved in another. ⟸ **When elements and compounds that are dissolved in water leave a solution, crystallization occurs.** Minerals can form in this way in bodies of water on Earth's surface. But the huge selenite crystals shown in **Figure 11** formed from a solution of hot water that cooled underground.

Minerals Formed by Evaporation

Some minerals form when solutions evaporate. For example, when the water in salt water evaporates, it leaves behind salt crystals.

In a similar way, deposits of the mineral halite formed over millions of years when ancient seas slowly evaporated. Such halite deposits are found in the American Southwest and along the Gulf Coast. Gypsum and calcite can also form by evaporation. Sometimes, gypsum forms in the shape of a rose.

A gypsum "rose"

Minerals From Hot Water Solutions

Deep underground, magma can heat water to a high temperature. The hot water can dissolve the elements and compounds that form minerals. When the hot water solution begins to cool, the elements and compounds leave the solution and crystallize as minerals. For example, quartz can crystallize from out of a hot water solution. Pure silver is also often deposited from a hot water solution. Gold, too, can be deposited in this way.

Pure metals that crystallize from hot water solutions underground often form veins. A **vein** is a narrow channel or slab of a mineral that is different from the surrounding rock.

Silver

FIGURE 11
Selenite
These huge selenite crystals in a cave in Mexico formed from the crystallization of minerals in a solution.

311

Minerals From Magma and Lava

Many minerals form from magma and lava. **Minerals form as hot magma cools inside the crust, or as lava hardens on the surface. When these liquids cool to a solid state, they form crystals.** The size of the crystals depends on several factors. The rate at which the magma cools, the amount of gas the magma contains, and the chemical composition of the magma all affect crystal size.

Magma and lava are often rich in oxygen and silicon. Minerals that contain these elements are called *silicates*. Together, silicates make up a majority of Earth's crust.

Minerals From Magma

Magma that remains deep below the surface cools slowly over thousands of years. Slow cooling leads to the formation of large crystals. Quartz, feldspar, tourmaline, and mica are common silicate minerals that form from magma.

Tourmaline

Minerals From Lava

If magma erupts to the surface and becomes lava, the lava will cool quickly. There will be no time for large crystals to form. Instead, small crystals form. Leucite and olivine are silicate minerals that can form in lava.

Olivine

FIGURE 12

Where Minerals Form

Minerals can form by crystallization of magma and lava or by crystallization of materials dissolved in water.

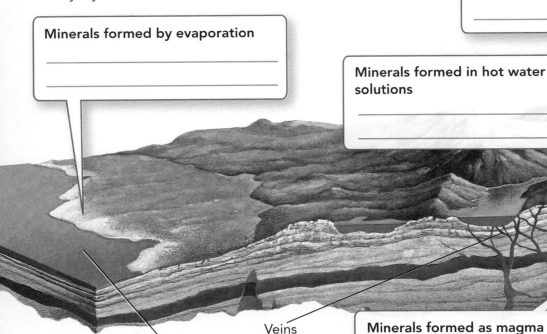

Minerals formed by evaporation
_____
_____

Minerals formed as lava cools
_____

Minerals formed in hot water solutions
_____
_____

Veins

Water containing dissolved minerals

Minerals formed as magma cools
_____
_____

Cooling magma

Relate Text and Visuals
Review the text on this page and on the previous page. Underline the name of each mineral the first time it is mentioned. Then place each mineral in its correct place in **Figure 12**.

Where Mineral Resources Are Found

Earth's crust is made up mostly of the common rock-forming minerals combined in various types of rock. Less common minerals are not found evenly throughout the crust. Instead, several processes can concentrate these minerals, or bring them together, in deposits. An *ore* is a deposit of valuable minerals contained in rocks. Iron ores may contain the iron-bearing minerals pyrite, magnetite, and hematite. Lead ores may contain galena. These ores are mined and the iron or lead is separated from the rock. Graphite and sulfur are sometimes also mined. **Figure 13** shows some major mining areas.

FIGURE 13 ·

Ores

✏ **Interpret Maps** Copper, aluminum, zinc, iron, and nickel can be used in making refrigerators. Which of these metals might the United States need to import for its refrigerators?

_____

_____

7.NS.8

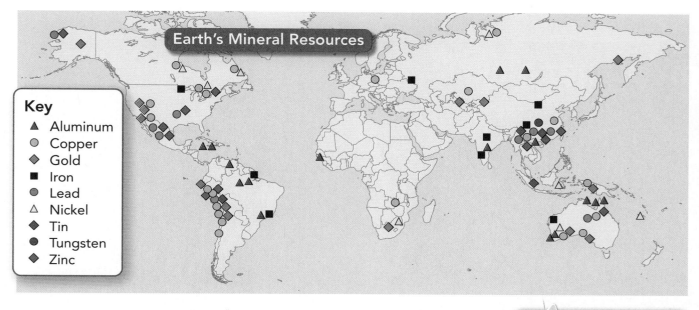

Earth's Mineral Resources

Key
- ▲ Aluminum
- ○ Copper
- ◆ Gold
- ■ Iron
- ● Lead
- △ Nickel
- ◆ Tin
- ● Tungsten
- ◆ Zinc

Lab® **zone** Do the Quick Lab *Crystal Hands.*

🦴 Assess Your Understanding

3a. Review Magma below Earth's surface cools (slowly/quickly).

7.2.5

b. Predict Slow cooling of magma leads to what size mineral crystals?

_____

_____

7.2.5

c. Develop Hypotheses A certain rock has large crystals of feldspar, mica, and quartz. Explain how and where the rock might have formed.

_____

_____

_____

7.2.5

got it? ·

○ **I get it!** Now I know that the three general ways minerals form are when _____

_____

_____

○ **I need extra help with** _____

Go to **MY SCIENCE** 🔊 **COACH** *online for help with this subject.*

7.2.5

313

Classifying Rocks

UNLOCK
THE BIG
? How Do Geologists Classify Rocks?
7.2.5

my planeT DiaRY

FIELD TRIP

The Lonely Giant

In the midst of Wyoming stands a lonely giant: Mount Moran. Its peak stands more than 3,800 meters above sea level. If you climb Mount Moran, you'll crawl across slabs of rock. These slabs formed deep beneath Earth's surface. Here, great temperatures and pressures changed one type of rock into the rock of the slabs. As you continue to climb, a thick, vertical strip of darker stone suddenly appears. This rock is volcanic rock. Finally, when you reach the top, you find a 15-meter cap of sandstone. This rock formed when many tiny particles were squeezed tightly together over millions of years. So Mount Moran contains rocks that formed in three different ways.

Read the text and then answer the questions.

1. In your own words, describe one way in which rocks formed on Mount Moran.

_____

_____

2. If you were climbing Mount Moran, how might you be able to tell one rock from another?

_____

_____

> PLANET DIARY Go to **Planet Diary** to learn more about the three main groups of rocks.

Lab zone® Do the Inquiry Warm-Up *How Do Rocks Compare?*

Vocabulary
- rock-forming mineral • granite • basalt • grain
- texture • igneous rock • sedimentary rock
- metamorphic rock

Skills
↩ Reading: Identify the Main Idea
△ Inquiry: Observe

How Do Geologists Classify Rocks?

If you were a geologist, how would you examine a rock for the first time? You might look at the outside surfaces. But you would also probably use a hammer to break open a small sample of the rock and look at the inside. ⚷ **To study a rock sample, geologists observe the rock's mineral composition, color, and texture.**

Mineral Composition and Color Rocks are made of mixtures of minerals and other materials. Some rocks contain only a single mineral. Other rocks contain several minerals. The granite in **Figure 1,** for example, is made up of quartz, feldspar, mica, and hornblende. About 20 minerals make up most of the rocks of Earth's crust. These minerals are known as **rock-forming minerals.** The minerals that make up granite are rock-forming minerals.

A rock's color provides clues to the rock's mineral composition. For example, **granite** is generally a light-colored rock that has high silica content. That is, it is rich in the elements silicon and oxygen. **Basalt** is a dark-colored rock that has a lower silica content than granite has. But unlike granite, basalt has mineral crystals that are too small to be seen with the naked eye. As with minerals, color alone does not provide enough information to identify a rock.

Academic Standards for Science

7.2.5 Describe the origin and physical properties of igneous, metamorphic and sedimentary rocks and how they are related through the rock cycle.

FIGURE 1 ·······························

Granite
Granite is generally made up of only a few common minerals.

△**Observe** How would you describe the overall color of this rock? What minerals cause the color (or colors) you chose?

_____

_____

_____

_____

_____

_____

Feldspar

Hornblende

Quartz

Mica

Granite

Texture Most rocks are made up of particles of minerals or other rocks, which geologists call **grains.** Grains give the rock its texture. **Texture** is the look and feel of a rock's surface. To describe the texture of a rock, geologists use terms that are based on the size, shape, and pattern of the grains.

Grain Size

Rocks with grains that are large and easy to see are said to be coarse grained. Fine-grained rocks have grains that are so small they can be seen only with a microscope.

Fine grain — Slate

Coarse grain — Diorite

No visible grain — Flint

Grain Shape

In some rocks, grain shape results from the shape of the mineral crystals that form the rock. Other rocks have a grain shape that results from rounded or jagged bits of several rocks.

Rounded grain — Conglomerate

Jagged grain — Breccia

Grain Pattern

In banded rocks, grains can lie in a pattern of flat layers or can form swirls or colored bands. Nonbanded rocks have grains that do not lie in any visible pattern.

Nonbanded — Quartzite

Banded — Gneiss

apply it!

This photograph shows part of a coarse-grained rock. Read the text on this page and then answer the questions.

❶ **Observe** Is this rock banded or nonbanded? _____

❷ **Infer** Based on this rock's appearance, what type of rock might it be? _____

❸ **CHALLENGE** Gneiss forms when very high pressure and temperature are applied to existing rock. How might these conditions explain the wavy pattern in this rock?

_____
_____
_____
_____

Origin Using the characteristics of color, texture, and mineral composition, geologists can classify a rock according to its origin. A rock's origin is the way that the rock formed. 🔑 **Geologists have classified rocks into three major groups: igneous rock, sedimentary rock, and metamorphic rock.**

Each of these groups of rocks forms in a different way, as shown in **Figure 2. Igneous rock** (IG nee us) forms from the cooling of magma or lava. The magma hardens underground to form rock. The lava erupts, cools, and hardens to form rock on Earth's surface.

Most **sedimentary rock** (sed uh MEN tur ee) forms when small particles of rocks or the remains of plants and animals are pressed and cemented together. Sedimentary rock forms in layers that are buried below the surface. **Metamorphic rock** (met uh MAWR fik) forms when a rock is changed by heat or pressure, or by chemical reactions. Most metamorphic rock forms deep underground.

🔄 **Identify the Main Idea**
Read the text on this page. Underline how each of the three major groups of rocks forms.

FIGURE 2 ·····················
Rock Origins
Rocks are classified by the way they formed.

✏️ **Interpret Diagrams** Using the sentences you underlined, label each diagram with the rock origin it represents.

 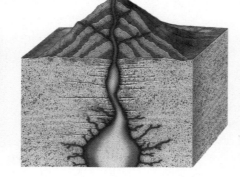 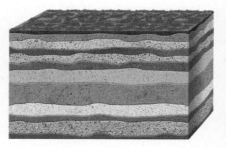

Do the Quick Lab
Classify These Rocks.

🔑 **Assess Your Understanding**

1a. Review Geologists classify rocks according to their _____

7.2.5

b. Explain How do igneous rocks form?

_____

_____

7.2.5

c. Classify Pumice is a type of rock that forms from molten material that erupts violently from a volcano. To what group of rock does pumice belong?

_____

_____

7.2.5

got it? ··

○ **I get it!** Now I know that geologists classify rocks into three major groups called _____

_____

○ **I need extra help with** _____

Go to MY SCIENCE ⓢ COACH *online for help with this subject.*

7.2.5

Igneous Rocks

🔑 **How Do Geologists Classify Igneous Rocks?**
7.2.5, 7.NS.8

🔑 **How Are Igneous Rocks Used?**
7.2.5

MY PLANET DIARY

Arctic Diamonds

If you were looking for diamonds, where would you start? Maybe in a helicopter flying over the Arctic Circle?

In the 1980s, a pair of geologists used a helicopter to search for diamonds in Canada. The pair knew that diamonds form more than 100 kilometers under Earth's surface. They also knew that after diamonds form, powerful eruptions of magma can thrust the diamonds to the surface through volcanic pipes. As the magma cools and hardens, the diamonds are trapped inside volcanic rock.

The geologists found a source for diamonds after searching for several years. Now, diamond mines in Canada produce one of the world's most valuable crops of diamonds!

DISCOVERY

Discuss this question with a group of classmates. Write your answer below.

If you wanted to try to find diamonds, what type of rock might you look for? Why?

_____

_____

_____

▷ PLANET DIARY Go to **Planet Diary** to learn more about volcanic rocks.

Lab zone Do the Inquiry Warm-Up *Liquid to Solid.*

Academic Standards for Science

7.2.5 Describe the origin and physical properties of igneous, metamorphic and sedimentary rocks and how they are related through the rock cycle.
7.NS.8 Analyze data.

How Do Geologists Classify Igneous Rocks?

Look at **Figure 1.** All the rocks shown in the figure are igneous rocks. But do all these rocks look the same? No, because even though all igneous rocks form from magma or lava, igneous rocks can look vastly different from each other. 🔑 **Igneous rocks are classified by their origin, texture, and mineral composition.**

Vocabulary
- extrusive rock
- intrusive rock

Skills
- Reading: Relate Cause and Effect
- Inquiry: Interpret Data

Origin Igneous rock may form on or beneath Earth's surface. **Extrusive rock** is igneous rock formed from lava that erupted onto Earth's surface. Basalt is the most common extrusive rock.

Igneous rock that formed when magma hardened beneath the surface of Earth is called **intrusive rock.** The most abundant type of intrusive rock in continental crust is granite. Granite forms tens of kilometers below Earth's surface and over hundreds of thousands of years or longer.

Texture Different igneous rocks may have similar mineral compositions and yet have very different textures. The texture of an igneous rock depends on the size and shape of its mineral crystals. The only exceptions to this rule are the different types of volcanic glass—igneous rock that lacks a crystal structure.

Rapidly cooling lava forms fine-grained igneous rocks with small crystals or no crystals at all. Slowly cooling magma forms coarse-grained rocks, such as granite, with large crystals. So, intrusive and extrusive rocks usually have different textures. For example, intrusive rocks have larger grains than extrusive rocks. Extrusive rocks have a fine-grained or glassy texture. **Figure 1** shows the textures of different igneous rocks.

Vocabulary Latin Word Origins *Ignis* means "fire" in Latin. What is "fiery" about igneous rocks?

_____

_____

_____

_____

_____

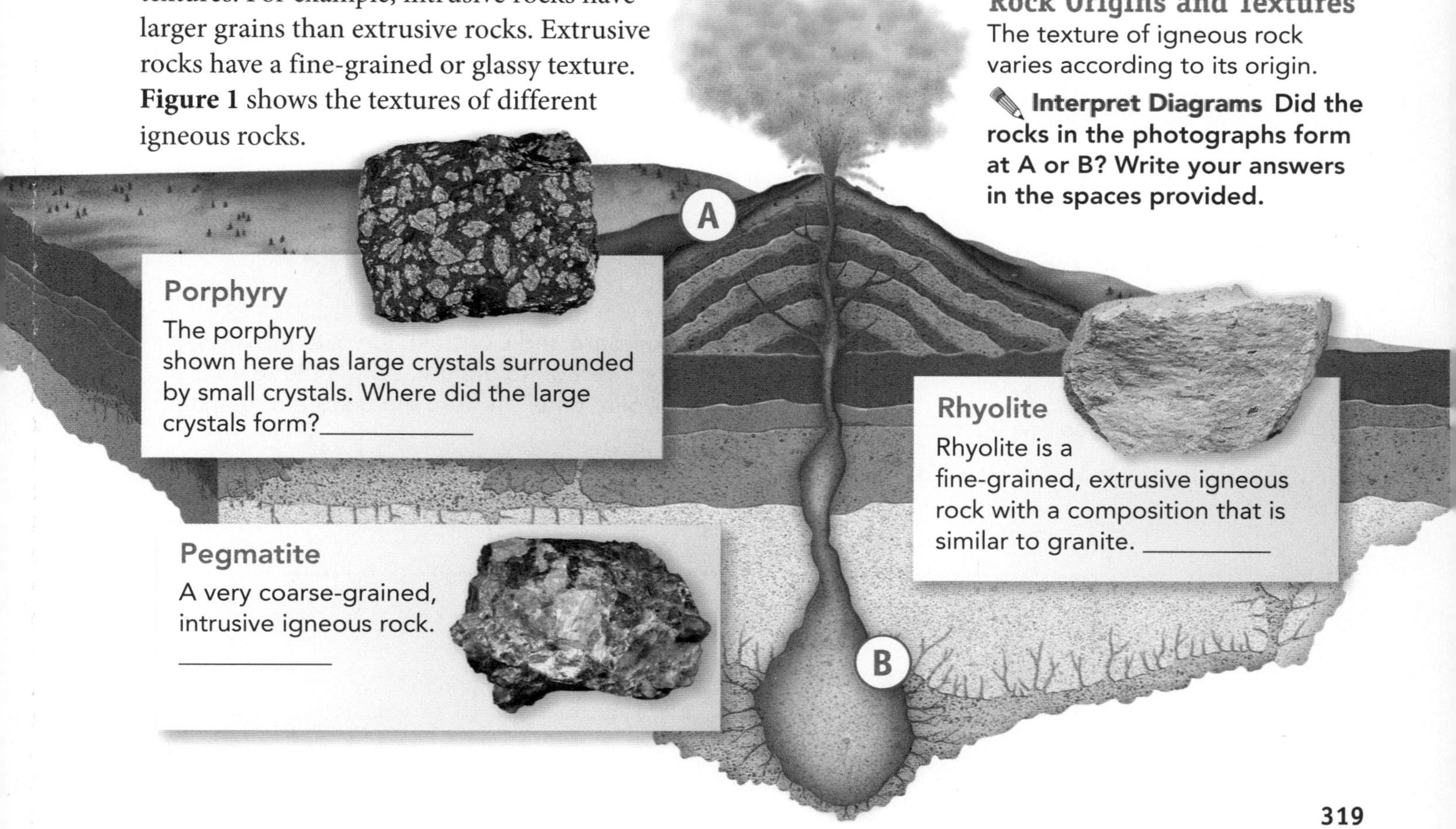

FIGURE 1 ·······························

> ART IN MOTION **Igneous Rock Origins and Textures** The texture of igneous rock varies according to its origin.

✎ **Interpret Diagrams** Did the rocks in the photographs form at A or B? Write your answers in the spaces provided.

Porphyry
The porphyry shown here has large crystals surrounded by small crystals. Where did the large crystals form?_____

Rhyolite
Rhyolite is a fine-grained, extrusive igneous rock with a composition that is similar to granite. _____

Pegmatite
A very coarse-grained, intrusive igneous rock.

_____

A

B

319

apply it!

Diorite is a coarse-grained intrusive igneous rock. It is a mixture of feldspar and dark-colored minerals such as hornblende and mica. The proportion of feldspar and dark minerals in diorite can vary.

1 ⚠ **Interpret Data** What mineral is most abundant in the sample of diorite illustrated by the graph?

_____

2 CHALLENGE How would the color of the diorite change if it contained less hornblende and more feldspar? Explain.

_____

_____

_____

_____

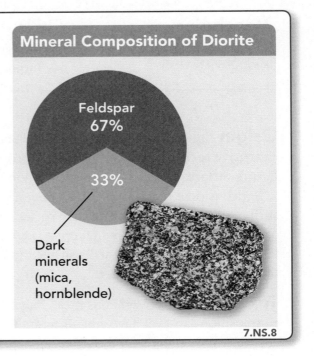

Mineral Composition of Diorite

Feldspar 67%

33%

Dark minerals (mica, hornblende)

7.NS.8

Mineral Composition

Recall that the silica content of magma and lava can vary. Lava that is low in silica usually forms dark-colored rocks such as basalt. Basalt contains feldspar as well as certain dark-colored minerals, but does not contain quartz.

Magma that is high in silica usually forms light-colored rocks, such as granite. Granite's mineral composition determines its color, which can be light gray, red, or pink. Granite that is rich in reddish feldspar is a speckled pink. But granite rich in hornblende and dark mica is light gray with dark specks. Quartz crystals in granite add light gray or smoky specks.

✎ **Relate Cause and Effect**
What determines the color of granite?

◯ Its mineral composition

◯ Its density

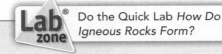
Lab zone Do the Quick Lab *How Do Igneous Rocks Form?*

🔑 Assess Your Understanding

1a. Identify Rhyolite is an (intrusive/extrusive) igneous rock.

7.2.5

b. Summarize How does rhyolite form?

_____

_____

7.2.5

c. Compare and Contrast Rhyolite has a similar composition to granite. Why is the texture of rhyolite different from the texture of granite?

_____

_____

_____

got it? ···

◯ **I get it!** Now I know that igneous rocks are classified according to their _____

_____

◯ **I need extra help with** _____

Go to MY SCIENCE COACH online for help with this subject.

7.2.5

How Are Igneous Rocks Used?

Academic Standards for Science

7.2.5 Describe the origin and physical properties of igneous, metamorphic and sedimentary rocks and how they are related through the rock cycle.

Many igneous rocks are hard, dense, and durable. 🔑 **People throughout history have used igneous rock for tools and building materials.**

Granite has a long history of use as a building material. More than 3,500 years ago, the ancient Egyptians used granite to build statues. About 600 years ago, the Incas of Peru built fortresses out of great blocks of granite and other igneous rock. You can see part of one of their fortresses in **Figure 2.** In the United States during the 1800s and early 1900s, granite was widely used to build bridges and public buildings. Today, thin, polished sheets of granite are used in curbstones and floors. Another igneous rock, basalt, can be used for cobblestones. It can also be crushed and used as a material in landscaping and in roads.

Igneous rocks such as pumice and obsidian also have important uses. The rough surface of pumice forms when gas bubbles are trapped in fast-cooling lava, leaving spaces in the rock. The rough surface makes pumice a good abrasive for cleaning and polishing. Ancient Native Americans used obsidian to make sharp tools for cutting and scraping. Obsidian cools very quickly, without forming crystals. So it has a smooth, shiny texture like glass. Perlite, formed by the rapid cooling of magma or lava, is often mixed with soil and used for starting vegetable seeds.

▲ Ollantaytambo

FIGURE 2 ·····················

Building Blocks

Igneous rock has long been used as a building material, such as for this Incan fortress in Peru.

✏️ **Work With Design Constraints** A fortress must be strong enough to withstand violent attacks. Why might the Incas have chosen igneous rock to build their fortress near Ollantaytambo in Peru?

_____

_____

_____

_____

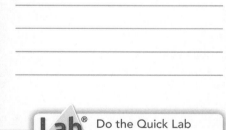 Do the Quick Lab
The Rocks Around Us.

🔑 **Assess Your Understanding**

got it? ···························

○ **I get it!** Now I know that throughout history, people have used igneous rocks for

_____

○ **I need extra help with** _____

Go to my science  coach *online for help with this subject.*   7.2.5

321

Sedimentary Rocks

UNLOCK THE BIG ?

🔑 **How Do Sedimentary Rocks Form?**
7.2.5

🔑 **What Are the Three Major Types of Sedimentary Rocks?**
7.2.5, 7.NS.1

🔑 **How Are Sedimentary Rocks Used?**
7.2.5

MY PLANET DIARY

The Cutting Edge

If you had to carve tools out of stone, would you know which rocks to use? Dr. Beverly Chiarulli, an archaeologist at Indiana University of Pennsylvania, studies stone tools that were used by people in Pennsylvania 10,000 years ago. Dr. Chiarulli has found that these people crafted spearheads out of the sedimentary rocks called chert and jasper. Chert is hard and has a very fine texture. It is brittle, but does not fracture along thin, even planes. So, chert can be shaped somewhat easily by flaking off chips, producing the sharp edges needed for spearheads.

CAREERS

Read the text and then answer the question.

What properties of chert allow it to be carved into sharp spearheads?

_____

_____

_____

_____

▶ PLANET DIARY Go to **Planet Diary** to learn more about sedimentary rocks.

Lab zone Do the Inquiry Warm-Up *Acid Test for Rocks.*

Academic Standards for Science

7.2.5 Describe the origin and physical properties of igneous, metamorphic and sedimentary rocks and how they are related through the rock cycle.

How Do Sedimentary Rocks Form?

The banks of a cool stream may be made up of tiny sand grains, mud, and pebbles. Shells, leaves, and even bones may also be mixed in. All of these particles are examples of sediment. **Sediment** is small, solid pieces of material that come from rocks or living things.

Sedimentary rocks form when sediment is deposited by water and wind, as shown in **Figure 1**. 🔑 **Most sedimentary rocks are formed through a sequence of processes: weathering, erosion, deposition, compaction, and cementation.**

Vocabulary
- sediment • weathering • erosion • deposition
- compaction • cementation • clastic rock
- organic rock • chemical rock

Skills
↪ **Reading: Identify the Main Idea**

△ **Inquiry: Infer**

Deposition
Water can carry sediment to a lake or ocean. Here, the material is deposited in layers as it sinks to the bottom. **Deposition** is the process by which sediment settles out of the water or wind carrying it.

Weathering and Erosion
Rock on Earth's surface is constantly broken up by **weathering**—the effects of freezing and thawing, plant roots, acid, and other forces on rock. After the rock is broken up, the fragments are carried away as a result of **erosion**—the process by which running water, wind, or ice carry away bits of broken-up rock.

Compaction
Thick layers of sediment build up gradually over millions of years. The weight of new layers can squeeze older sediments tightly together. The process that presses sediments together is **compaction.**

Cementation
While compaction is taking place, some minerals in the rock slowly dissolve in the water. **Cementation** is the process in which dissolved minerals crystallize and glue particles of sediment together.

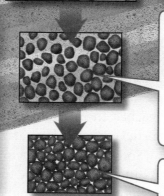

FIGURE 1 ·····················

How Sedimentary Rock Forms
Sedimentary rocks form through a series of processes over millions of years.

✎ **Sequence** Put the terms listed in the word bank in the proper sequence to show how mountains can change into sedimentary rock.

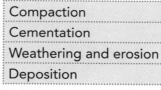

| Compaction |
| Cementation |
| Weathering and erosion |
| Deposition |

☐ ⟶ ☐ ⟶ ☐ ⟶ ☐

Lab zone Do the Quick Lab *How Does Pressure Affect Particles of Rock?*

⚷ Assess Your Understanding

got it? ···

○ **I get it!** Now I know that most sedimentary rocks are formed through the processes of _____

_____

○ **I need extra help with** _____

Go to **my science** ⑤ **COACH** *online for help with this subject.*

Academic Standards for Science

7.2.5 Describe the origin and physical properties of igneous, metamorphic and sedimentary rocks and how they are related through the rock cycle.

7.NS.1 Make predictions based on research or prior knowledge.

Identify the Main Idea

Clastic rocks are grouped by the size of the _____ _____ they contain.

FIGURE 2 ·····················

Clastic Rocks

Clastic rocks are sedimentary rocks that form from particles of other rocks.

✎ **Identify** Match the clastic rocks to the four photographs below them. Write your answer in the spaces provided.

What Are the Three Major Types of Sedimentary Rocks?

Geologists classify sedimentary rocks according to the type of sediments that make up the rock. ⚷ **The three major groups of sedimentary rocks are clastic rocks, organic rocks, and chemical rocks.** Different processes form each of these types of rocks.

Clastic Rocks Most sedimentary rocks are made up of broken pieces of other rocks. A **clastic rock** is a sedimentary rock formed when rock fragments are squeezed together. The fragments can range in size from clay particles that are too small to be seen without a microscope to large, heavy boulders. Clastic rocks are grouped by the size of the rock fragments, or particles, of which they are made. Some common clastic rocks, shown in **Figure 2,** are shale, sandstone, conglomerate, and breccia (BRECH ee uh).

Shale forms from tiny particles of clay. Water deposits the clay particles in thin, flat layers. Sandstone forms from the sand on beaches, the ocean floor, riverbeds, and sand dunes. Most sand particles consist of quartz.

Some clastic sedimentary rocks contain rock fragments that are of different sizes. If the fragments have rounded edges, they form conglomerate. Fragments with sharp edges form breccia.

Shale
Fossils are often found in shale, which tends to split into flat pieces.
_____

Sandstone
Many small holes between sand grains allow sandstone to absorb water.
_____

Conglomerate
Rock fragments with rounded edges make up conglomerate.
_____

Breccia
Rock fragments with sharp edges form breccia.
_____

1 2 3 4

Organic Rocks You may be familiar with the rocks called coal and limestone, shown in **Figure 3.** Both are sedimentary rocks. But instead of forming from particles of other rocks, they form from the remains of material that was once living. **Organic rock** forms where the remains of plants and animals are deposited in layers. The term "organic" refers to substances that once were part of living things or were made by living things.

Coal forms from the remains of swamp plants buried in water. As layer upon layer of plant remains build up, the weight of the layers squeezes the decaying plants together. Over millions of years, they slowly change into coal.

Limestone forms in the ocean, where many living things, such as coral, clams, and oysters, have hard shells or skeletons made of calcite. When these ocean animals die, their shells pile up on the ocean floor. Over millions of years, compaction and cementation can change the thick sediment into limestone.

did you know?

Many of Indiana's official state buildings and monuments are built from limestone quarried in southern Indiana. In 1971, the General Assembly officially designated limestone as the state stone.

FIGURE 3 ·······

Organic Rocks

Organic rocks such as limestone and coal are sedimentary rocks that form from the remains of living things.

✎ **Sequence** Complete the graphic organizers to show how coal and limestone form.

Coal
Remains of swamp plants are buried in water.

↓

_____

↓

_____

↓

Over millions of years, coal forms.

Limestone
Ocean animals with hard shells or skeletons die.

↓

_____

↓

_____

↓

Sediment is slowly changed to limestone.

325

**it!**

These rock "towers" in Mono Lake, California, are made of tufa, a form of limestone. Tufa forms from water solutions that contain dissolved materials. The towers formed under water. They became exposed when the water level in the lake dropped as a result of water needs for the city of Los Angeles. Read the text about the major types of sedimentary rocks. Then answer the questions.

1 Classify Tufa is a (clastic/organic/chemical) sedimentary rock.

2 Infer What mineral was dissolved in the waters of Mono Lake and later crystallized to form the rock towers?

_____

7.NS.1

3 [CHALLENGE] When acid comes into contact with calcite, the acid bubbles. How can geologists use acid to confirm that the rock towers are made of limestone?

_____

_____

_____

_____

Chemical Rocks Limestone can also form when calcite that is dissolved in lakes, seas, or underground water comes out of a solution and forms crystals. This kind of limestone is considered a chemical rock. **Chemical rock** forms when minerals dissolved in a water solution crystallize. Chemical rocks can also form from mineral deposits that are left when seas or lakes evaporate. For example, rock salt is made of the mineral halite, which forms by evaporation.

® Do the Quick Lab
What Causes Layers?

🔑 Assess Your Understanding

1a. Review Shale forms from tiny particles of (clay/sand/mica).

7.2.5

b. Describe How is clay deposited to form shale?

_____

_____

_____

7.2.5

c. Infer You come across a thick deposit of shale that forms a layer in the ground. What can you infer about the area's past environment?

_____

_____

_____

_____

7.2.5

got it? •

○ **I get it!** Now I know that the three major types of sedimentary rocks are _____

_____

○ **I need extra help with** _____

Go to MY SCIENCE 🔊 COACH *online for help with this subject.*

7.2.5

How Are Sedimentary Rocks Used?

🔑 **People have used sedimentary rocks throughout history for many different purposes, including for tools and building materials.** Chert was used to make spearheads by people who lived in Pennsylvania more than 10,000 years ago. Other people also made arrowheads out of flint for thousands of years. Flint is a hard rock, yet it can be shaped to a point. It forms when small particles of silica settle out of water.

Sedimentary rocks such as sandstone and limestone have been used as building materials for thousands of years. Both types of stone are soft enough to be cut easily into blocks or slabs. The White House in Washington, D.C., is built of sandstone. Today, builders use sandstone and limestone on the outside walls of buildings, such as the building shown in **Figure 4**. Limestone also has industrial uses. For example, it is used in making cement and steel.

Carnegie Library
(Jeffersonville,
Indiana) ▼

Academic Standards for Science

7.2.5 Describe the origin and physical properties of igneous, metamorphic and sedimentary rocks and how they are related through the rock cycle.

FIGURE 4 ·····························

> REAL-WORLD INQUIRY

Building With Limestone

Limestone is a popular building material. However, acid rain reacts with the calcite in limestone, damaging buildings made from it.

✏ **Evaluate the Design** Do the benefits of constructing limestone buildings outweigh the damage acid rain causes to these buildings? Explain.

_____

_____

Lab zone® Do the Lab Investigation
Testing Rock Flooring.

🔑 Assess Your Understanding

got it? ···

O **I get it!** Now I know that throughout history, people have used sedimentary rocks for _____

_____

O **I need extra help with** _____

Go to MY SCIENCE COACH *online for help with this subject.*

7.2.5

Metamorphic Rocks

UNLOCK THE BIG ?

🔑 **What Are Metamorphic Rocks?**

7.2.5, 7.NS.1

MY PLANET DIARY

MISCONCEPTION

Rock Dough

Misconception:
Rocks do not change form.

Did you know that heat can change a rock's form without melting it? To understand how, think of what happens when you bake cookies. You might mix flour, eggs, sugar, and baking powder in a bowl. When you bake the raw dough in a hot oven, the dough changes into cookies.

Heat can change rock, too. If hot magma or lava come near rock, the heat can "bake" the rock. The ingredients in the rock—the minerals—might not melt. But the heat can still change the rock into a new form!

Read the text and then answer the question below.

Does rock have to melt in order to change form? Explain.

_____

_____

_____

_____

_____

_____

> **PLANET DIARY** Go to **Planet Diary** to learn more about how rocks can change form.

Lab zone Do the Inquiry Warm-Up *A Sequined Rock.*

Academic Standards for Science

7.2.5 Describe the origin and physical properties of igneous, metamorphic and sedimentary rocks and how they are related through the rock cycle.

7.NS.1 Make predictions based on research or prior knowledge.

What Are Metamorphic Rocks?

You may be surprised to learn that heat can change rock like a hot oven changes raw cookie dough. But deep inside Earth, both heat and pressure are much greater than at Earth's surface. When great heat and pressure are applied to rock, the rock can change both its shape and its composition. 🔑 **Any rock that forms from another rock as a result of changes in heat or pressure (or both heat and pressure) is a metamorphic rock.**

Vocabulary
- foliated

Skills
- Reading: Relate Cause and Effect
- Inquiry: Observe

How Metamorphic Rocks Form Metamorphic rock can form out of igneous, sedimentary, or other metamorphic rock. Many metamorphic rocks are found in mountains or near large masses of igneous rock. Why are metamorphic rocks commonly found in these locations? The answer lies inside Earth.

The heat that can change a rock into metamorphic rock can come from pockets of magma. For instance, pockets of magma can rise through the crust. The high temperatures of these pockets can change rock into metamorphic rock. Collisions between Earth's plates can also push rock down toward the heat of the mantle.

Very high pressure can also change rock into metamorphic rock. For instance, plate collisions cause great pressure to be applied to rocks while mountains are being formed. The pressure can deform, or change the physical shape of, the rock, as shown in **Figure 1**. Also, the deeper that a rock is buried in the crust, the greater the pressure on that rock. Under very high temperature or pressure (or both), the minerals in a rock can be changed into other minerals. At the same time, the appearance, texture, and crystal structure of the minerals in the rock change. The rock eventually becomes a metamorphic rock.

FIGURE 1 ·······································
Metamorphic Rock
The rock in the photograph was once sedimentary rock. Now, it is metamorphic rock.

✎ **Develop Hypotheses** What changed the rock? Make sure your answer explains the rock's current appearance.

_____

_____

_____

_____

_____

7.NS.1

Deformed metamorphic rock in eastern Connecticut ▲

329

Relate Cause and Effect
Read the text on this page.
Underline each sentence that
describes how one type of
rock changes into another
type of rock.

How Metamorphic Rocks Are Classified

While metamorphic rocks are forming, intense heat changes the size and shape of the grains, or mineral crystals, in the rock. Extreme pressure squeezes rock so that the mineral grains may line up in flat, parallel layers. **Geologists classify metamorphic rocks according to the arrangement of the grains making up the rocks.**

Foliated Rocks Metamorphic rocks that have their grains arranged in either parallel layers or bands are said to be foliated. **Foliated** describes the thin, flat layering found in most metamorphic rocks. For instance, the crystals in granite can be flattened to create the foliated texture of gneiss. Slate is also a common foliated rock. Heat and pressure change the sedimentary rock shale into slate. Slate is basically a denser, more compact version of shale. But as shale changes into slate, the mineral composition of the shale can change.

Nonfoliated Rocks Some metamorphic rocks are nonfoliated. The mineral grains in these rocks are arranged randomly. Marble and quartzite are metamorphic rocks that have a nonfoliated texture. Quartzite forms out of quartz sandstone. The weakly cemented quartz particles in the sandstone recrystallize to form quartzite, which is extremely hard. Quartzite looks smoother than sandstone, as shown in **Figure 2.** Finally, marble usually forms when limestone is subjected to heat and pressure deep beneath the surface.

FIGURE 2

Presto!

Great heat and pressure can change one type of rock into another.

Classify Label each rock *sedimentary,* *igneous,* or *metamorphic.* Indicate whether the metamorphic rocks are foliated. Then shade the correct arrowhead to show which rock can form from the other rock.

Granite

Gneiss

Heat and pressure

Quartzite

Sandstone

Heat and pressure

How Metamorphic Rocks Are Used Marble and slate are two of the most useful metamorphic rocks. Marble has an even grain, so it can be cut into thin slabs or carved into many shapes. And marble is easy to polish. So architects and sculptors use marble for many statues and buildings, such as the Tower of Pisa. Like marble, slate comes in many colors, including gray, red, and purple. Because it is foliated, slate splits easily into flat pieces. These pieces can be used for roofing, outdoor walkways, and as trim for stone buildings. **The metamorphic rocks marble and slate are important materials for building and sculpture.**

Tower of Pisa ▶

Although marble, quartzite, and slate are all metamorphic rocks, they are used in different ways.

1 △ **Observe** Look around your school or neighborhood. What examples of metamorphic rock can you find? How is each metamorphic rock used? Write your answers in the notebook at the right.

2 [CHALLENGE] Why are chess pieces sometimes made of marble?

_____

_____

_____

Lab zone Do the Quick Lab *How Do Grain Patterns Compare?*

Assess Your Understanding

1a. Define What is a metamorphic rock?

_____

_____

_____

_____

_____

7.2.5

b. Identify Faulty Reasoning Suppose great heat completely melts a certain deposit of rock, which then hardens into new rock. You might think that the new rock is metamorphic. But it isn't. Why not?

_____

_____

_____

7.2.5

got it? ·

○ I get it! Now I know that certain metamorphic rocks are used for _____

○ I need extra help with _____

Go to MY SCIENCE ⓢ COACH *online for help with this subject.*

7.2.5

The Rock Cycle

UNLOCK THE BIG ?

🔑 **What Is the Rock Cycle?**
7.2.5

MY PLANET DIARY

Rolling Along

The Himalaya Mountains are eroding at a rate of about 2.5 millimeters per year. That's about one tenth as fast as your fingernails grow! But the Himalayas were formed millions of years ago. So imagine the total mass of rock that has fallen down the mountain and that has then been swept out to sea. Over millions of years, the piled weight of eroded particles will squeeze the bits together on the sea floor. New rock will form. Then, ancient bits of the Himalayas will be recycled inside new rock.

Read the text and then answer the question.

How could small pieces of the Himalayas form new rock?

_____

_____

▶ PLANET DIARY Go to **Planet Diary** to learn more about the rock cycle.

FUN FACT

Lab zone Do the Inquiry Warm-Up *Recycling Rocks.*

Ⓘ **Academic Standards for Science**

7.2.5 Describe the origin and physical properties of igneous, metamorphic and sedimentary rocks and how they are related through the rock cycle.

What Is the Rock Cycle?

Natural forces act on the Himalayas. In fact, rock in Earth's crust is always changing. 🔑 **Forces deep inside Earth and at the surface produce a slow cycle that builds, destroys, and changes the rocks in the crust.** The **rock cycle** is a series of processes that occur on Earth's surface and in the crust and mantle that slowly change rocks from one kind to another. For example, weathering can break down granite into sediment that later forms sandstone.

Vocabulary
* rock cycle

Skills
↻ Reading: Sequence
△ Inquiry: Classify

One Pathway Through the Rock Cycle

There are many pathways by which rocks move through the rock cycle. For example, Stone Mountain, near Atlanta, Georgia, is made of granite. The granite in Stone Mountain, shown in **Figure 1,** formed millions of years ago below Earth's surface as magma cooled.

After the granite had formed, the forces of mountain building slowly pushed the granite upward. Then, over millions of years, weathering and erosion began to wear away the granite. Today, particles of granite constantly break off the mountain and become sand. Streams carry the sand to the ocean. What might happen next?

Over millions of years, layers of sand might pile up on the ocean floor. Slowly, the sand would be compacted by its own weight. Or perhaps calcite that is dissolved in the ocean water would cement the particles together. Over time, the quartz that once formed the granite of Stone Mountain could become sandstone, which is a sedimentary rock.

Sediment could keep piling up on the sandstone. Eventually, pressure would compact the rock's particles until no spaces were left between them. Silica, the main ingredient in quartz, would replace the calcite cement. The rock's texture would change from gritty to smooth. After millions of years, the standstone would have changed into the metamorphic rock quartzite.

↻ **Sequence** Number the materials that move through the rock cycle at Stone Mountain in the sequence given in the text:

_____ Sand

_____ Granite

_____ Quartzite

FIGURE 1 ·······················

Stone Mountain

The granite in Stone Mountain is moving through the rock cycle.

✎ **Answer the questions.**

1. △ **Classify** As shown in the photograph, trees can grow on the mountain. Their roots might break up the granite. What step of the rock cycle do the trees play a role in?

_____

2. **CHALLENGE** Does the rock cycle stop after the quartzite has formed? Explain.

_____

_____

_____

_____

_____

_____

The Rock Cycle

How do rocks form?

FIGURE 2 ···

✏️ ▷ INTERACTIVE ART **Be a Rock Star!**
Through melting, weathering and erosion, and heat and pressure, the rock cycle constantly changes rocks from one type into another type.

Interpret Diagrams Study the diagram. Then fill in each blank arrow with the correct term: *melting, weathering and erosion*, or *heat and pressure*. (*Hint*: To fit your answers, abbreviate "weathering and erosion" as "w & e.")

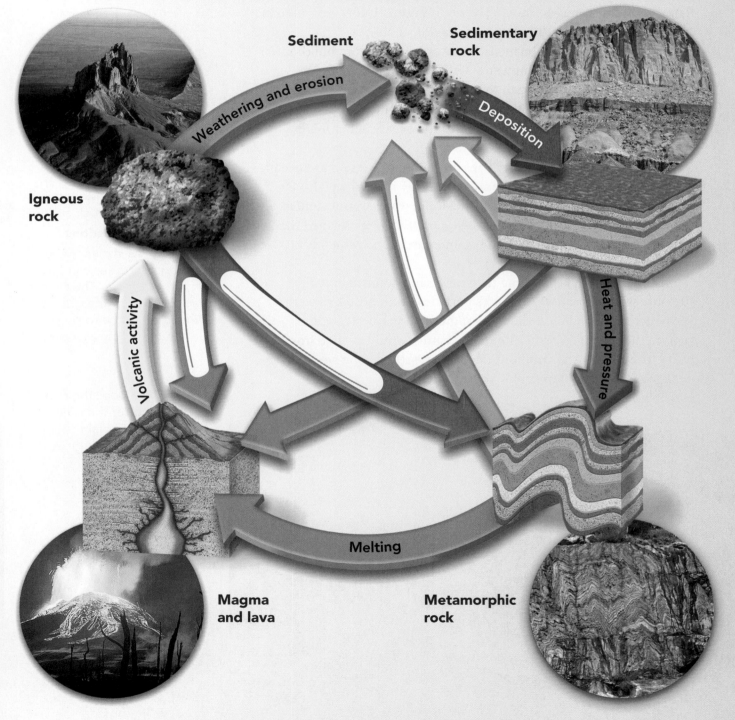

Sediment

Sedimentary rock

Weathering and erosion

Deposition

Igneous rock

Volcanic activity

Heat and pressure

Melting

Magma and lava

Metamorphic rock

The Rock Cycle and Plate Tectonics
The changes of the rock cycle are closely related to plate tectonics. Recall that Earth's lithosphere is made up of huge plates. These plates move slowly over Earth's surface as the result of convection currents in Earth's mantle. As the plates move, they carry the continents and ocean floors with them. Plate movements help drive the rock cycle by helping to form magma, the source of igneous rocks.

Where oceanic plates move apart, magma formed from melted mantle rock moves upward and fills the gap with new igneous rock. Where an oceanic plate is subducted beneath a continental plate, magma forms and rises. The result is a volcano made of igneous rock. A collision of continental plates may push rocks so deep that they melt to form magma, leading to the formation of igneous rock.

Sedimentary rock can also result from plate movement. For example, the collision of continental plates can be strong enough to push up a mountain range. Then, weathering and erosion begin. The mountains are worn away. This process leads to the formation of sedimentary rock.

Finally, a collision between continental plates can push rocks down deep beneath the surface. Here, heat and pressure could change the rocks to metamorphic rock.

Conservation of Material in the Rock Cycle
Constructive and destructive forces build up and destroy Earth's landmasses. But as the rock in Earth's crust moves through the rock cycle, material is not lost or gained. For example, a mountain can erode to form sediment, all of which can eventually form new rock.

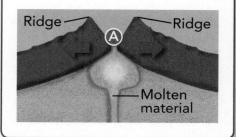

Do the Quick Lab
Which Rock Came First?

🔑 Assess Your Understanding

1a. Name The rock cycle builds, destroys, and changes the rock in Earth's (crust/core).

7.2.5

b. ANSWER THE BIG **?** **Describe** How do rocks form?

_____

_____

_____

_____

_____

_____

_____

7.2.5

got it? ···

○ **I get it!** Now I know that the rock cycle is _____

_____

_____

○ **I need extra help with** _____

Go to MY SCIENCE ⓢ COACH online for help with this subject.

7.2.5

REVIEW THE BIG ❓

In the rock cycle, rocks form through three main processes: _____,

_____, and _____.

LESSON 1 Properties of Minerals

7.2.5, 7.NS.8

🔑 A mineral is a natural solid that can form by inorganic processes and that has a crystal structure and a definite chemical composition.

🔑 Each mineral has characteristic properties.

🔑 Minerals form from cooling of magma and lava, from solutions, or from organic processes.

Vocabulary
• mineral • inorganic • crystal • streak • luster
• Mohs hardness scale • cleavage • fracture
• geode • crystallization • solution • vein

LESSON 2 Classifying Rocks

7.2.5

🔑 To study a rock sample, geologists observe the rock's mineral composition, color, and texture.

🔑 Geologists have classified rocks into three major groups: igneous rock, sedimentary rock, and metamorphic rock.

Vocabulary
• rock-forming mineral • granite • basalt
• grain • texture • igneous rock
• sedimentary rock • metamorphic rock

LESSON 3 Igneous Rocks

7.2.5, 7.NS.8

🔑 Igneous rocks are classified by their origin, texture, and mineral composition.

🔑 People throughout history have used igneous rock for tools and building materials.

Vocabulary
• extrusive rock
• intrusive rock

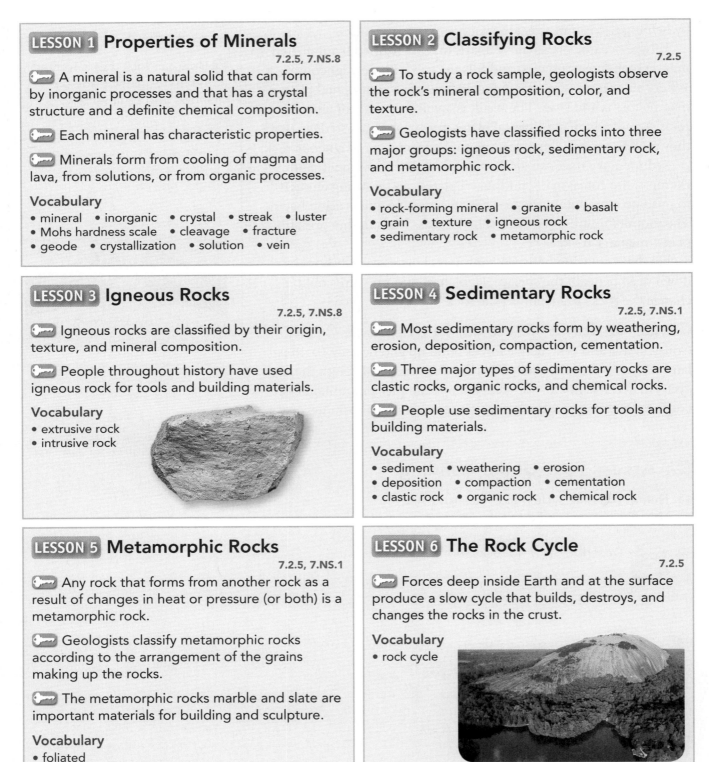

LESSON 4 Sedimentary Rocks

7.2.5, 7.NS.1

🔑 Most sedimentary rocks form by weathering, erosion, deposition, compaction, cementation.

🔑 Three major types of sedimentary rocks are clastic rocks, organic rocks, and chemical rocks.

🔑 People use sedimentary rocks for tools and building materials.

Vocabulary
• sediment • weathering • erosion
• deposition • compaction • cementation
• clastic rock • organic rock • chemical rock

LESSON 5 Metamorphic Rocks

7.2.5, 7.NS.1

🔑 Any rock that forms from another rock as a result of changes in heat or pressure (or both) is a metamorphic rock.

🔑 Geologists classify metamorphic rocks according to the arrangement of the grains making up the rocks.

🔑 The metamorphic rocks marble and slate are important materials for building and sculpture.

Vocabulary
• foliated

LESSON 6 The Rock Cycle

7.2.5

🔑 Forces deep inside Earth and at the surface produce a slow cycle that builds, destroys, and changes the rocks in the crust.

Vocabulary
• rock cycle

Review and Assessment

LESSON 1 Properties of Minerals

1. Streak is the color of a mineral's

a. luster.   b. cleavage.

c. powder.   d. fracture.

7.2.5

2. During crystallization, _____ are arranged to form a material with a crystal structure.

7.2.5

3. Compare and Contrast Fill in the table to compare the characteristics of a mineral and a material that is not a mineral.

	Hematite	Brick
Natural	✔	✘
Can form by inorganic processes		
Solid		
Crystal structure		
Definite chemical composition		

7.2.5, 7.NS.11

LESSON 2 Classifying Rocks

4. A rock that forms from many small fragments of other rocks is a(n)

a. igneous rock.   b. sedimentary rock.

c. metamorphic rock.   d. extrusive rock.

7.2.5

5. The 20 or so minerals that make up most of the rocks of Earth's crust are known as

_____

7.2.5

Use the photograph to answer Question 6.

6. Interpret Photographs Describe the texture of this rock.

_____

_____

7.2.5

LESSON 3 Igneous Rocks

7. What kind of igneous rock usually contains large crystals?

a. organic   b. clastic

c. intrusive   d. extrusive

7.2.5

8. An igneous rock's color is primarily determined by its _____

7.2.5

9. Relate Cause and Effect What conditions lead to the formation of large crystals in an igneous rock?

_____

_____

7.2.5

10. ✏ **Write About It** Describe the texture of granite. Also describe granite's mineral composition and explain granite's origin.

7.2.5

LESSON 4 Sedimentary Rocks

11. You find a deposit of organic limestone. In what type of setting did it probably form?

a. the ocean   b. a volcano

c. a swamp   d. sand dunes

7.2.5

12. Shale is a clastic rock, meaning that it forms when _____ are squeezed or cemented together (or both).

7.2.5

13. Name A certain rock contains large, jagged pieces of other rocks, cemented by fine particles. What type of rock is this? Explain.

_____

_____

7.2.5

14. ✏ **Write About It** You find a rock with fossils in it. Is this rock more likely to be a sedimentary rock than an igneous rock? Explain.

7.2.5

LESSON 5 Metamorphic Rocks

15. A metamorphic rock in which the grains line up in layers is called a

    a. chemical rock.   **b.** clastic rock.

    c. nonorganic rock.   **d.** foliated rock.

                                      7.2.5

16. Two types of foliated rock are

_____

                                      7.2.5

17. Infer Why do you think slate might be denser than shale?

_____

_____

                                      7.2.5

18. Develop Hypotheses Why do the crystals in gneiss line up in bands?

_____

_____

_____

                              7.2.5, 7.NS.1

LESSON 6 The Rock Cycle

19. The process by which metamorphic rock changes to igneous rock begins with

    a. melting.   **b.** erosion.

    c. deposition.   **d.** crystallization.

                                      7.2.5

20. _____ can turn igneous rock into sediment.

                                      7.2.5

21. **Write About It** Use the diagram to describe two ways metamorphic rock can change into sedimentary rock.

                                      7.2.5

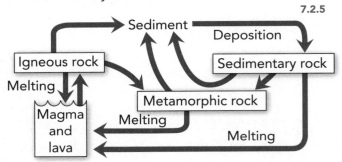

How do rocks form?

22. While hiking through a mountain range, you use a chisel and hammer to remove the three rock samples shown below. Classify the rocks you found as either igneous, sedimentary, or metamorphic. Then, describe the textures of each rock. Also describe the processes that formed each rock.

_____

_____

_____

_____

_____

_____

_____

_____

_____

_____

_____

_____

_____

_____

_____

_____

_____

_____

                                      7.2.5

Indiana ISTEP+ Practice

Multiple Choice

Circle the letter of the best answer.

1. The diagrams below show four different mineral samples.

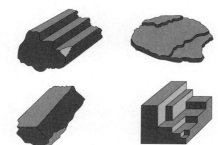

Which mineral property is best shown by the samples?

A. crystal structure

B. cleavage

C. hardness

D. color

7.2.5

2. You find a rock in which the grains are arranged in wavy, parallel bands of white and black crystals. What kind of rock have you probably found?

A. igneous   **B.** sedimentary

C. metamorphic   **D.** extrusive

7.2.5

3. Which statement best describes how an extrusive igneous rock forms?

A. Magma cools quickly on Earth's surface.

B. Magma cools slowly to form granite.

C. Magma cools quickly below Earth's surface.

D. Magma cools slowly beneath Earth's surface.

7.2.5

4. Which process causes many sedimentary rocks to have visible layers?

A. eruption   **B.** intrusion

C. crystallization   **D.** deposition

7.2.5

Constructed Response

Write your answer to Question 5 on the lines below.

5. If heat and pressure inside Earth cause the texture and crystal structure of a rock to change, what new class of rock is formed?

_____

_____

_____

7.2.5

Extended Response

Use the diagram below and your knowledge of science to help you answer Question 6. Write your answer on a separate piece of paper.

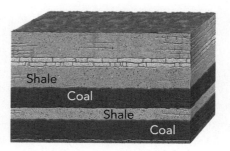

6. Describe the environment that probably existed millions of years ago where these rocks formed. Explain your reasoning.

7.2.5

Science and Society

STRUGGLING TO SURVIVE

An old problem has resurfaced in Arizona and New Mexico. The Navajo homeland in this region rests on one of the richest uranium reserves in the United States. Uranium mining in this area first began in the 1950s and stopped in the 1970s. When the mining companies left, many of them did not remove radioactive waste or seal the mine tunnels. This has greatly affected the health of the Navajo people who live and work near the old mines.

Years later, mining companies have come back to the Navajo homeland and the area around it. This time, they want to use solution mining, which uses water to flush out the uranium ore. This method is less dangerous than underground mining, but it can still contaminate the groundwater. And because the area is mostly desert, mining could use up scarce water.

Uranium is used for fuel in nuclear reactors that generate electricity. These reactors do not add carbon to the atmosphere, so some people think we should use them, instead of coal-fired power plants, to meet our electricity needs. The Navajo who live in an area with both coal and uranium must try to make decisions that will be good for their community both in the present and in the future.

Research It Working in a group, research (a) the uses of uranium, (b) the environmental impact of uranium mining, (c) the effect mining has had on the Navajo people's health, and (d) the effect mining has had on Navajo communities, environment, and people. As a group, write a paper weighing the costs and benefits of using solution mining to extract uranium ore.

7.1.3, 7.NS.2, 7.NS.11

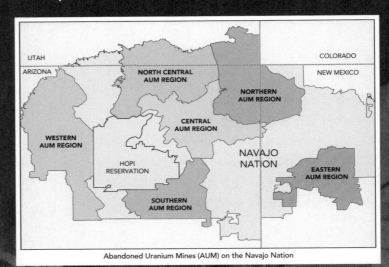

Abandoned Uranium Mines (AUM) on the Navajo Nation

Waiter, There's a MINERAL in My Soup!

While minerals form part of Earth's crust, they do not simply stay there until somebody picks them up. The minerals that make up Earth's crust are made up of elements that living things need, such as calcium. Over time, the minerals containing elements dissolve in water. Elements become part of our food because vegetables absorb them from the soil. When we eat the vegetables, we also take in the elements.

Calcium is one of the most important elements for your body because it helps build strong bones and teeth. It can be found in dairy products like milk, yogurt, and cheese, as well as broccoli and canned salmon.

Iron helps transport oxygen from your lungs to the rest of your body, and helps form red blood cells. Beef, tuna, eggs, and whole wheat bread are great sources of iron.

Potassium helps your muscles and nervous system work properly. Bananas, tomatoes, oranges, potatoes with skins, and peanuts are rich in potassium.

Zinc helps your immune system stay strong. A healthy immune system helps you fight off illnesses and infections. Zinc can be found in pork, lamb, beans, and lentils.

Design It Plan one day's worth of meals (breakfast, lunch, dinner). Include as many foods rich in essential elements as possible in your plan.

7.2.5, 7.NS.2

IS THIS CRACK IN EARTH GROWING?

THE BIG ?

How do moving plates change Earth's crust?

You may think that Earth's crust is one huge, solid piece. In fact, Earth's surface is broken into several pieces—like a cracked eggshell. One of the cracks runs through the middle of this lake in Iceland.

Infer Why do you think this crack in Earth's crust might get wider?

_____

_____

_____

_____

_____

_____

_____

> **UNTAMED SCIENCE** Watch the **Untamed Science** video to learn more about Earth's crust.

Plate Tectonics

Academic Standards for Science

7.2.4, 7.NS.1, 7.NS.2, 7.NS.8, 7.NS.11, 7.DP.1–7.DP.11

10 Getting Started

Check Your Understanding

1. **Background** Read the paragraph below and then answer the question.

> Maria took a train from Oregon to Georgia. The train rode across the entire **continent** of North America. It rode up and down the Rocky Mountains, which form a **boundary** between America's east and west. The conductor said, "These mountains are part of Earth's **crust**."

A **continent** is a large landmass.

A **boundary** is the point or line where one region ends and another begins.

The **crust** is the outer layer of Earth.

- What is the crust?

_____

_____

> **MY READING WEB** If you had trouble answering the question above, visit **My Reading Web** and type in *Plate Tectonics*.

Vocabulary Skill

Use Prefixes A prefix is a word part that is added at the beginning of a root or base word to change its meaning. Knowing the meaning of prefixes will help you figure out new words.

Prefix	Meaning	Example
mid-	at or near the middle	mid-ocean ridge, *n.* a chain of mountains that runs along the middle of the ocean floor
sub-	below, beneath, under	subduction, *n.* a process by which part of Earth's crust sinks downward

2. **Quick Check** Choose the word from the table that best completes the sentence below.
   - Oceanic crust is pushed beneath continental crust during

   _____.

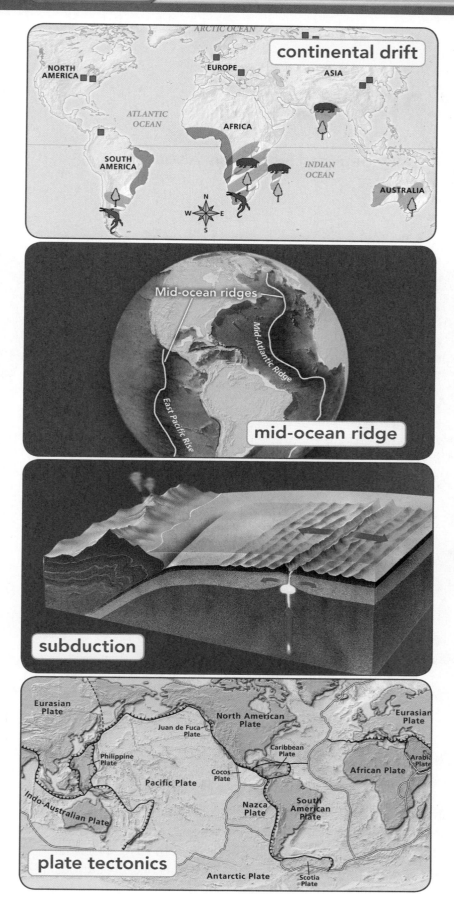

continental drift

mid-ocean ridge

subduction

plate tectonics

Chapter Preview

LESSON 1
- continental drift
- Pangaea
- fossil

↻ Ask Questions

△ Infer

LESSON 2
- mid-ocean ridge
- sea-floor spreading
- deep-ocean trench
- subduction

↻ Relate Text and Visuals

△ Develop Hypotheses

LESSON 3
- plate
- divergent boundary
- convergent boundary
- transform boundary
- plate tectonics
- fault
- rift valley

↻ Relate Cause and Effect

△ Calculate

▷ VOCAB FLASH CARDS For extra help with vocabulary, visit **Vocab Flash Cards** and type in *Plate Tectonics.*

345

UNLOCK
THE BIG
?

🔑 **What Was Wegener's Hypothesis About the Continents?**
7.2.4, 7.NS.8

mY PLaneT DiaRY

A Puzzled Look

Scientists have long noticed that Earth's continents look as though they could fit together like pieces of a jigsaw puzzle. This was an idea that Alfred Wegener suggested in 1910. "Doesn't the east coast of South America fit exactly against the west coast of Africa, as if they had once been joined?" he asked. "This is an idea I'll have to pursue."

VOICES FROM HISTORY

Communicate Discuss Wegener's idea with a partner. Then answer the questions.

1. Why did Wegener think that the continents might once have been joined?

_____

_____

_____

2. If you were Wegener, what other evidence would you look for to show that the continents had once been joined?

_____

_____

> PLANET DIARY Go to **Planet Diary** to learn more about the continents.

Lab® zone Do the Inquiry Warm-Up *How Are Earth's Continents Linked Together?*

🏛 **Academic Standards for Science**

7.2.4 Explain how convection currents in the mantle cause lithospheric plates to move causing fast changes like earthquakes and volcanic eruptions, and slow changes like creation of mountains and formation of new ocean floor.
7.NS.8 Analyze data.

What Was Wegener's Hypothesis About the Continents?

Have you ever looked at a world map and noticed how the coastlines of Africa and South America seem to match up? For many years, scientists made this same observation! In 1910, a German scientist named Alfred Wegener (VAY guh nur) became curious about why some continents look as though they could fit together.

Vocabulary
- continental drift
- Pangaea
- fossil

Skills
- Reading: Ask Questions
- Inquiry: Infer

According to Wegener, the continents of Earth had moved. **Wegener's hypothesis was that all the continents were once joined together in a single landmass and have since drifted apart.** Wegener's idea that the continents slowly moved over Earth's surface became known as **continental drift.**

According to Wegener, the continents were joined together in a supercontinent, or single landmass, about 300 million years ago. Wegener called the supercontinent **Pangaea** (pan JEE uh).

Over tens of millions of years, Pangaea began to break apart. The pieces of Pangaea slowly moved to their present locations, shown in **Figure 1.** These pieces became the continents as formed today. In 1915, Wegener published his evidence for continental drift in a book called *The Origin of Continents and Oceans.*

Evidence From Land Features Land features on the continents provided Wegener with evidence for his hypothesis. On the next page, **Figure 2** shows some of this evidence. For example, Wegener pieced together maps of Africa and South America. He noticed that mountain ranges on the continents line up. He noticed that coal fields in Europe and North America also match up.

Pangaea means "all lands" in Greek. Why is this a suitable name for a supercontinent?

_____

_____

_____

_____

_____

FIGURE 1 ·····················

Piecing It All Together

The coastlines of some continents seem to fit together like a jigsaw puzzle.

✎ **Use the map to answer the questions.**

1. **Interpret Maps** Draw an arrow to match the numbered coast with the lettered coast that seems to fit with it.

   ❶   ⓐ
   ❷   ⓑ
   ❸   ⓒ
   ❹   ⓓ

2. △ **Infer** How would a continent's climate change if it drifted closer to the equator?

_____

_____

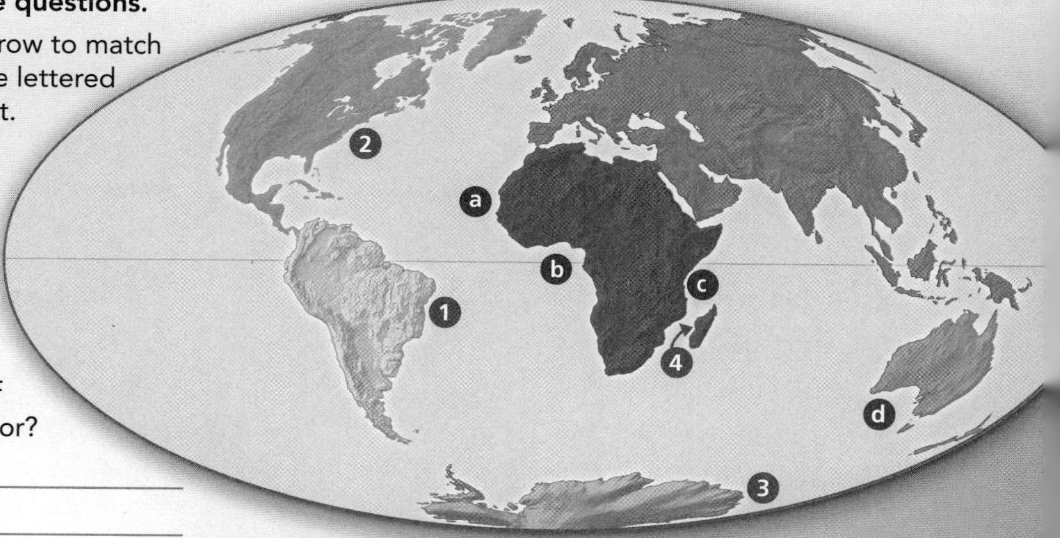

7.NS.8

FIGURE 2 ·······················

> **INTERACTIVE ART** **Pangaea and Continental Drift**

Many types of evidence suggest that Earth's landmasses were once joined together.

Infer On the top map of Pangaea, draw where each piece of evidence on the bottom map would have been found. Use a different symbol or color for each piece of evidence, and provide a key. Then label the continents.

7.NS.8

Evidence From Fossils

Wegener also used fossils to support his hypothesis for continental drift. A **fossil** is any trace of an ancient organism that has been preserved in rock. For example, *Glossopteris* (glaw SAHP tuh ris) was a fernlike plant that lived 250 million years ago. *Glossopteris* fossils have been found in Africa, South America, Australia, India, and Antarctica, as shown in **Figure 2**. The occurrence of *Glossopteris* on landmasses that are now separated by oceans indicates that Pangaea once existed.

Other examples include fossils of the freshwater reptiles *Mesosaurus* and *Lystrosaurus*. These fossils have also been found in places now separated by oceans. Neither reptile could have swum great distances across salt water. Wegener inferred that these reptiles lived on a single landmass that had since split apart.

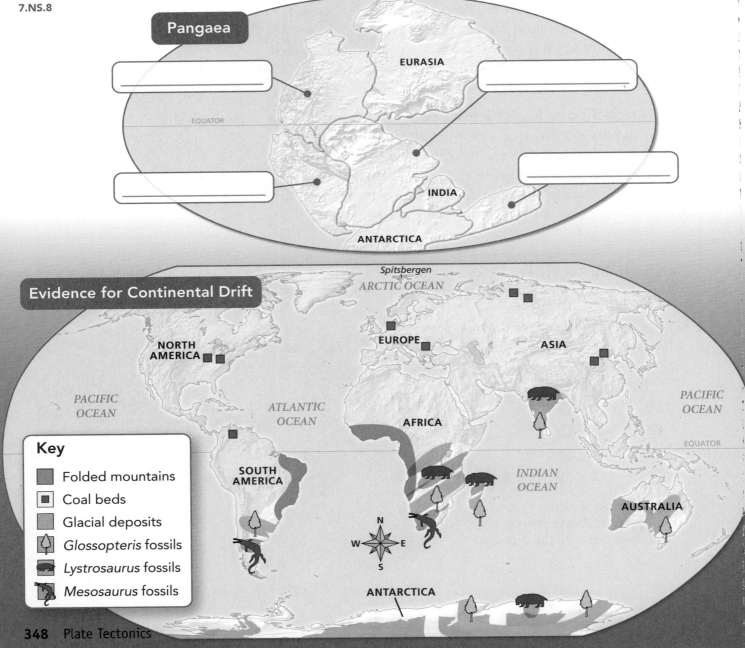

Pangaea

EURASIA

EQUATOR

INDIA

ANTARCTICA

Evidence for Continental Drift

Spitsbergen
ARCTIC OCEAN

NORTH AMERICA

EUROPE

ASIA

PACIFIC OCEAN

ATLANTIC OCEAN

AFRICA

PACIFIC OCEAN

EQUATOR

Key

Folded mountains

Coal beds

Glacial deposits

Glossopteris fossils

Lystrosaurus fossils

Mesosaurus fossils

SOUTH AMERICA

INDIAN OCEAN

AUSTRALIA

N
W   E
S

ANTARCTICA

Evidence From Climate
Wegener used evidence of climate change to support his hypothesis. As a continent moves toward the equator, its climate gets warmer. As a continent moves toward the poles, its climate gets colder. In either case, the continent carries along with it the fossils and rocks that formed at all of its previous locations.

For example, fossils of tropical plants are found on Spitsbergen, an island in the Arctic Ocean. When these plants lived about 300 million years ago, the island must have had a warm, mild climate. Wegener said the climate changed because the island moved.

Wegener's Hypothesis Rejected
Wegener attempted to explain how continental drift took place. He suggested that the continents plowed across the ocean floors. But Wegener could not provide a satisfactory explanation for the force that pushes or pulls the continents. Because Wegener could not identify the cause of continental drift, most geologists of his time rejected his idea.

✏️
Ask Questions Write a question relating to climate and Wegener's hypothesis. Read the text and answer your question.

_____
_____
_____
_____
_____
_____
_____

Deep scratches have been found in rocks in South Africa. Such scratches are caused only by glaciers that move across continents. But the climate of South Africa is too mild today for glaciers to form.

1 **Infer** South Africa was once (colder/warmer) than it is today.

2 **CHALLENGE** What can you infer about South Africa's former location?

_____
_____

Do the Quick Lab
Moving the Continents.

🔑 Assess Your Understanding

1a. Review Based on evidence from land features, fossils, and climate, Wegener concluded that continents (sink/rise/move).

7.2.4

b. Predict Wegener said that because continents move, they can collide with each other. How could colliding continents explain the formation of mountains?

_____
_____
_____

7.2.4

got it?

○ **I get it!** Now I know Wegener's hypothesis about the continents stated that _____
_____
_____
_____

○ I need extra help with _____

Go to MY SCIENCE COACH online for help with this subject.

7.2.4

Sea-Floor Spreading

UNLOCK THE BIG Q

🔑 **What Are Mid-Ocean Ridges?**
7.2.4, 7.NS.8

🔑 **What Is Sea-Floor Spreading?**
7.2.4, 7.NS.11

🔑 **What Happens at Deep-Ocean Trenches?**
7.2.4, 7.NS.1

my PLANeT DiaRY

DISCOVERY

Marie Tharp

Have you ever tried to draw something you can't see? By 1952, geologists Marie Tharp and Bruce Heezen had set to work mapping the ocean floor. Tharp drew details of the ocean floor based on data taken from ships. The data showed how the height of the ocean floor varied. Tharp's maps, which were first published in 1957, helped to confirm the hypothesis of continental drift.

Think about what structures might lie beneath Earth's oceans. Then answer the question.

Do you think the ocean has valleys and mountains? Explain.

_____

_____

_____

_____

> PLANET DIARY Go to **Planet Diary** to learn more about the ocean floor.

 Do the Inquiry Warm-Up *What Is the Effect of a Change in Density?*

Academic Standards for Science

7.2.4 Explain how convection currents in the mantle cause lithospheric plates to move causing fast changes like earthquakes and volcanic eruptions, and slow changes like creation of mountains and formation of new ocean floor.

7.NS.8 Analyze data.

What Are Mid-Ocean Ridges?

When scientists such as Marie Tharp drew maps showing features of the ocean floor, they made a surprising discovery. In certain places, the floor of the ocean appeared to be stitched together like the seams of a baseball! The seams curved along the ocean floors for great distances, as shown in **Figure 1.**

Scientists found that the seams formed mountain ranges that ran along the middle of some ocean floors. Scientists called these mountain ranges **mid-ocean ridges.** 🔑 **Mid-ocean ridges form long chains of mountains that rise up from the ocean floor.**

Vocabulary
- mid-ocean ridge
- deep-ocean trench
- sea-floor spreading
- subduction

Skills
↻ Reading: Relate Text and Visuals
△ Inquiry: Develop Hypotheses

In the mid-1900s, scientists mapped mid-ocean ridges using *sonar*. Sonar is a device that uses sound waves to measure the distance to an object. Scientists found that mid-ocean ridges extend into all of Earth's oceans. Most mid-ocean ridges lie under thousands of meters of water. Scientists also discovered that a steep-sided valley splits the tops of some mid-ocean ridges. The ridges form the longest mountain ranges on Earth. They are longer than the Rockies in North America and longer than the Andes in South America.

FIGURE 1 ·······························
Ocean Floors
7.NS.8

Mid-ocean ridges rise from the sea floor like stitches on the seams of a baseball.

✎ **Interpret Diagrams** Look at the diagram below. Then use the scale to answer each question. Be sure to measure from the *front* of the diagram.

1. How far below sea level is the peak of the ridge?

_____

2. How high does the ridge rise from the sea floor?

_____

3. CHALLENGE How deep below the peak is the valley marking the center of the ridge?

_____

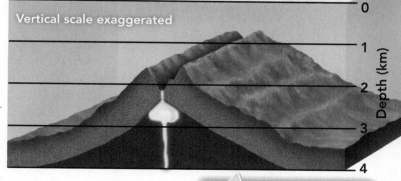

Vertical scale exaggerated

Depth (km)
0
1
2
3
4

Do the Quick Lab
Mid-Ocean Ridges.

🔑 Assess Your Understanding

got**it?** ···

○ **I get it!** Now I know that mid-ocean ridges form _____

_____

○ **I need extra help with** _____

Go to **my science** **coach** *online for help with this subject.*

7.2.4

What Is Sea-Floor Spreading?

By the 1960s, geologists had learned more about mid-ocean ridges. They found that mid-ocean ridges continually add new material to the ocean floor. They called this process **sea-floor spreading.**

Sea-floor spreading begins at a mid-ocean ridge, which forms along a crack in the oceanic crust. Along the ridge, new molten material from inside Earth rises, erupts, cools, and hardens to form a solid strip of rock. **Sea-floor spreading adds more crust to the ocean floor. At the same time, older strips of rock move outward from either side of the ridge.**

Figure 2 shows evidence that geologists have found for sea-floor spreading.

Pillow lava on the ocean floor

Evidence From Ocean Material

In the central valley of mid-ocean ridges, scientists have found rocks shaped like pillows. Such rocks form only when molten material hardens quickly after erupting under water.

Ridge

Magnetic striping on both sides of the Juan de Fuca ridge

Evidence From Magnetic Stripes

Rock on the ocean floor forms from molten material. As the material erupts, cools, and hardens, magnetic minerals inside the rock line up in the direction of Earth's magnetic poles. These minerals form unseen magnetic "stripes" on the ocean floor. But the magnetic poles occasionally reverse themselves. So each stripe defines a period when molten material erupted and hardened while Earth's magnetic poles did not change.

Scientists found that the pattern of magnetic stripes on one side of a mid-ocean ridge is usually a mirror image of the pattern on the other side of the ridge. The matching patterns show that the crust on the two sides of the ridge spread from the ridge at the same time and at the same rate.

Evidence From Drilling Samples

Scientists drilled into the ocean floor to obtain rock samples. They found that the farther away from a ridge a rock sample was taken, the older the rock was. The youngest rocks were always found at the center of the ridges. Recall that at the ridge center, molten material erupts and cools to form new crust. The rocks' age showed that sea-floor spreading had taken place.

Ocean floor samples taken in 2006

FIGURE 2 ·······················

> INTERACTIVE ART **Sea-Floor Spreading**

Some mid-ocean ridges have a valley that runs along their center. Evidence shows that molten material erupts through this valley. The material then hardens to form the rock of the ocean floor.

✎ **Color the right half of the diagram to show magnetic striping. How does your drawing show evidence of sea-floor spreading?**

_____

_____

_____

> **Relate Text and Visuals**
How does the diagram show that new crust forms from molten material?

_____

_____

_____

_____

_____

_____

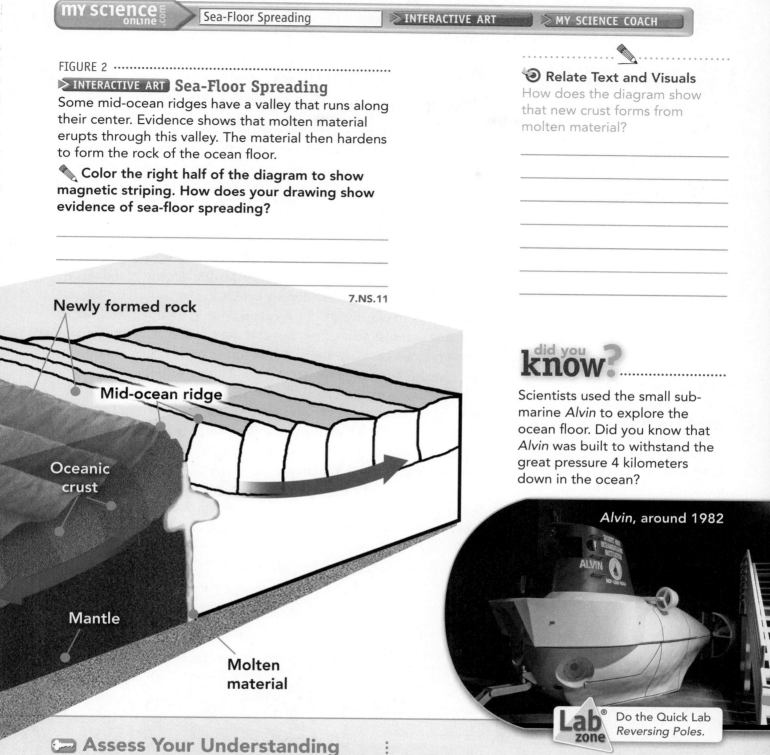

7.NS.11

Newly formed rock

Mid-ocean ridge

Oceanic crust

Mantle

Molten material

did you know?·····················

Scientists used the small submarine *Alvin* to explore the ocean floor. Did you know that *Alvin* was built to withstand the great pressure 4 kilometers down in the ocean?

Alvin, around 1982

Lab zone Do the Quick Lab *Reversing Poles.*

🔑 **Assess Your Understanding**

1a. Review In sea-floor spreading, new crust is added at a (mid-ocean ridge/magnetic stripe).

7.2.4

b. Apply Concepts Suppose Earth's magnetic polarity changed many times over a short period. What pattern of striping at a mid-ocean ridge would you expect to find?

_____

_____

7.2.4

got it?

O **I get it!** Now I know that sea-floor spreading is the process in which _____

_____

O **I need extra help with** _____

Go to my science ⑤ coach *online for help with this subject.*

7.2.4

What Happens at Deep-Ocean Trenches?

Does the ocean floor keep getting wider without stopping? No, eventually the ocean floor plunges into deep underwater canyons. These canyons are called **deep-ocean trenches.** At a deep-ocean trench, the oceanic crust bends downward. 🔑 **In a process taking tens of millions of years, part of the ocean floor sinks back into the mantle at deep-ocean trenches.**

The Process of Subduction When a washcloth is placed in water, the water soaks into it. So, the density of the washcloth increases. The higher density causes the washcloth to sink.

Changes in density affect the ocean floor in a similar way. Recall that new oceanic crust is hot. But as it moves away from the mid-ocean ridge, it cools. As it cools, it becomes more dense. Eventually, as it moves, the cool, dense crust might collide with the edge of a continent. Gravity then pulls the older, denser oceanic crust down beneath the trench and back into the mantle, as shown in **Figure 3.**

The process by which the ocean floor sinks beneath a deep-ocean trench and back into the mantle again is called **subduction** (sub DUC shun). As subduction occurs, crust closer to a mid-ocean ridge moves away from the ridge and toward a deep-ocean trench. Sea-floor spreading and subduction often work together. They move the ocean floor as if it were on a giant conveyor belt.

FIGURE 3 ·······

Subduction

Oceanic crust created along a mid-ocean ridge is destroyed at a deep-ocean trench. During the process of subduction, oceanic crust sinks down beneath the trench into the mantle.

✏️ **Summarize Label the mantle, the mid-ocean ridge, and the deep-ocean trench. For locations A and B, circle the correct choice for each statement.**

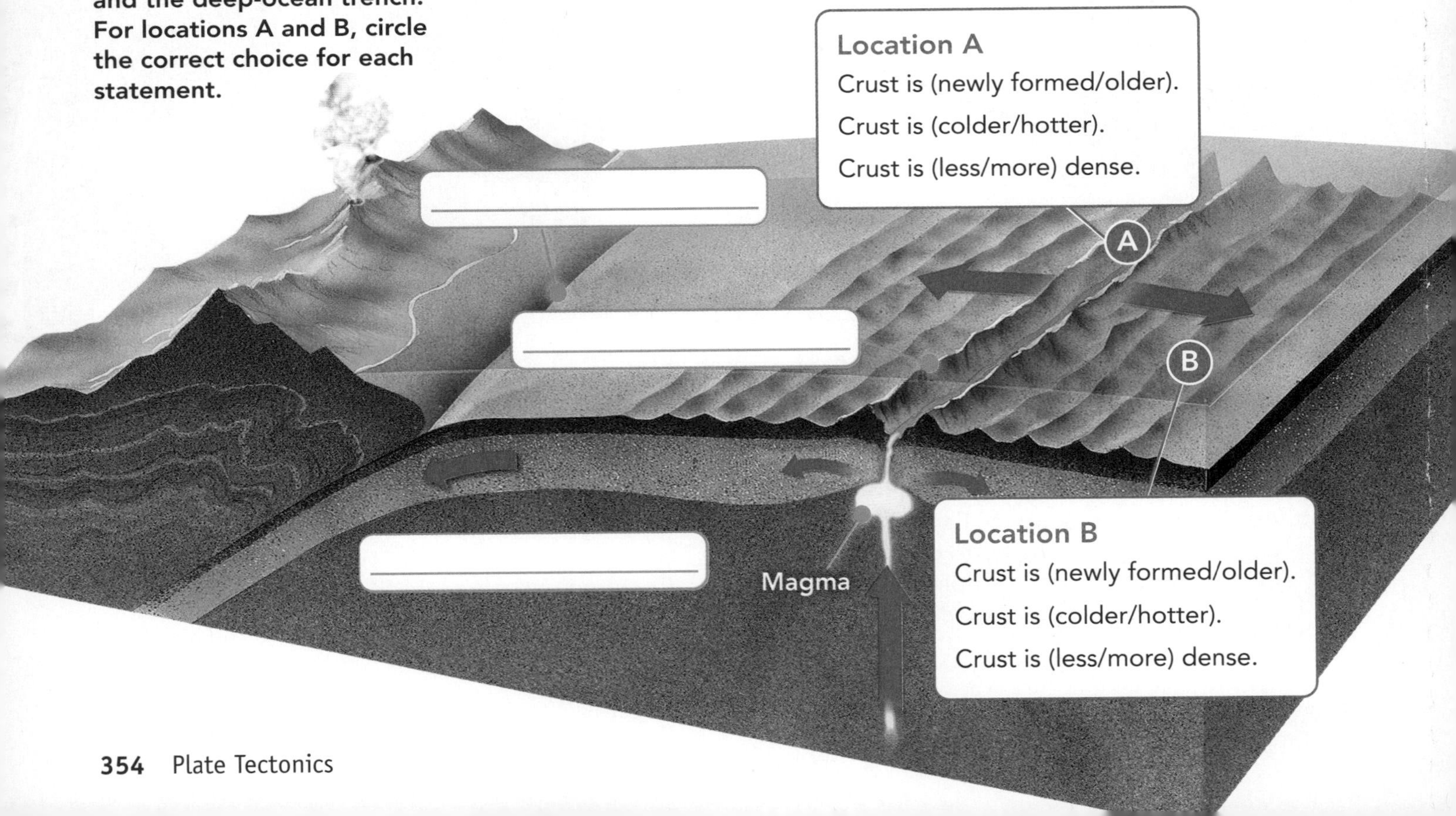

Location A
Crust is (newly formed/older).
Crust is (colder/hotter).
Crust is (less/more) dense.

Magma

Location B
Crust is (newly formed/older).
Crust is (colder/hotter).
Crust is (less/more) dense.

apply it!

The deepest part of the ocean is along the Mariana Trench. This trench is one of several trenches (shown in yellow) in the Pacific Ocean. After reading the main text in this lesson, answer the questions below.

1 Infer At the Pacific Ocean's deep-ocean trenches, oceanic crust is (spread/subducted).

2 Develop Hypotheses The Pacific Ocean is shrinking. Explain this fact in terms of subduction at deep-ocean trenches and spreading at mid-ocean ridges.

_____

_____

_____

_____

_____

_____

_____

7.NS.1

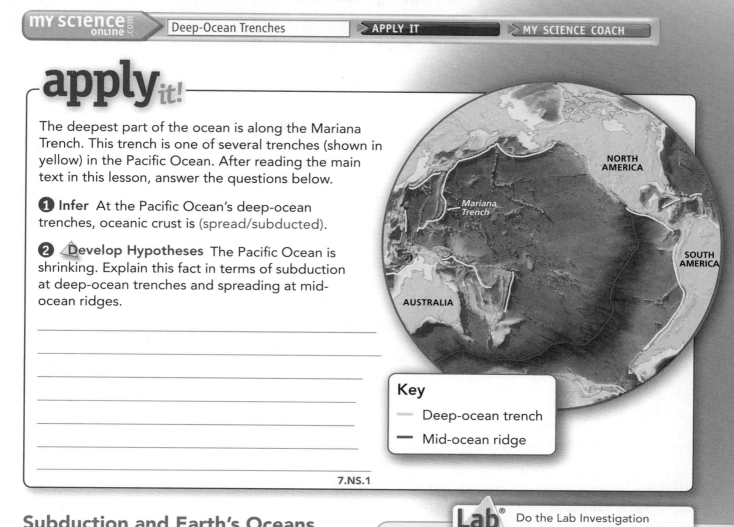

Key

--- Deep-ocean trench

— Mid-ocean ridge

Subduction and Earth's Oceans

The processes of subduction and sea-floor spreading can change the size and shape of the oceans. Because of these processes, the ocean floor is renewed about every 200 million years. That is the time it takes for new rock to form at the mid-ocean ridge, move across the ocean, and sink into a trench.

The sizes of Earth's oceans are determined by how fast new crust is being created at mid-ocean ridges and how fast old crust is being swallowed up at deep-ocean trenches. An ocean surrounded by many trenches may shrink. An ocean with few trenches will probably grow larger.

For example, the Atlantic Ocean is expanding. This ocean has only a few short trenches. As a result, the spreading ocean floor has almost nowhere to go. Along the continental margins, the oceanic crust of the Atlantic Ocean floor is attached to the continental crust of the continents around the ocean. So as the Atlantic's ocean floor spreads, the continents along its edges also move. Over time, the whole ocean gets wider.

Lab zone | Do the Lab Investigation
Modeling Sea-Floor Spreading.

🔑 Assess Your Understanding

2a. Review Subduction takes place at (mid-ocean ridges/deep-ocean trenches).

7.2.4

b. Relate Cause and Effect Why does subduction occur?

_____

_____

_____

_____

7.2.4

got it? •

○ **I get it!** Now I know that at deep-ocean trenches _____

_____

○ **I need extra help with** _____

Go to **my science** ⓢ **coach** online for help with this subject.

7.2.4

355

Indiana

LESSON 3

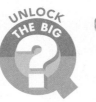

The Theory of Plate Tectonics

UNLOCK THE BIG Q

What Is the Theory of Plate Tectonics?
7.2.4, 7.NS.8

my planet Diary

Slip-Sliding Away

In 30 million years, this airplane might take one hour longer to fly from New York to London than it takes today. That's because these two cities are moving slowly apart as they ride on pieces of Earth's crust.

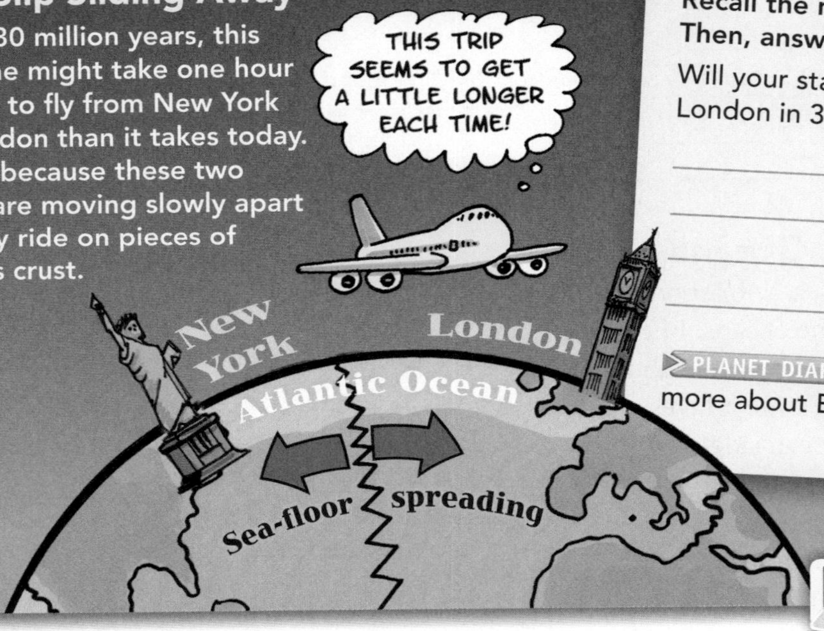

THIS TRIP SEEMS TO GET A LITTLE LONGER EACH TIME!
New York
London
Atlantic Ocean
Sea-floor spreading

FUN FACT

Recall the name of your state capital. Then, answer the question below.

Will your state capital be farther from London in 30 million years? Explain.

____

____

____

____

PLANET DIARY Go to **Planet Diary** to learn more about Earth's crust.

Lab zone® Do the Inquiry Warm-Up *Plate Interactions.*

Academic Standards for Science

7.2.4 Explain how convection currents in the mantle cause lithospheric plates to move causing fast changes like earthquakes and volcanic eruptions, and slow changes like creation of mountains and formation of new ocean floor.

7.NS.8 Analyze data, using appropriate mathematical manipulation as required.

What Is the Theory of Plate Tectonics?

Have you ever dropped a hard-boiled egg? The eggshell cracks into uneven pieces. Earth's lithosphere, its solid outer shell, is like that eggshell. It is broken into pieces separated by cracks. These pieces are called **plates.** Earth's major tectonic plates are shown in **Figure 1.**

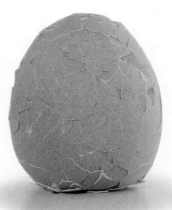

Vocabulary

- plate • divergent boundary • convergent boundary
- transform boundary • plate tectonics • fault
- rift valley

Skills

↻ Reading: Relate Cause and Effect

△ Inquiry: Calculate

Earth's plates meet at boundaries. Along each boundary, plates move in one of three ways. Plates move apart, or diverge, from each other at a **divergent boundary** (dy VUR junt). Plates come together, or converge, at a **convergent boundary** (kun VUR junt). Plates slip past each other along a **transform boundary.**

In the mid-1960s, geologists combined what they knew about sea-floor spreading, Earth's plates, and plate motions into a single theory called **plate tectonics.** 🔑 **The theory of plate tectonics states that Earth's plates are in slow, constant motion, driven by convection currents in the mantle.** Plate tectonics explains the formation, movement, and subduction of Earth's plates.

Mantle Convection and Plate Motions
What force is great enough to move the continents? Earth's plates move because they are the top part of the large convection currents in Earth's mantle. During subduction, gravity pulls denser plate edges downward, into the mantle. The rest of the plate also moves. The motion of the plates is like the motion of liquid in a pot of soup heating on a stove.

FIGURE 1 ·······························
▸ REAL-WORLD INQUIRY

Earth's Plates
Plate boundaries divide the lithosphere into large plates.

✎ **Interpret Maps** Draw arrows at all the boundaries of the Pacific plate, showing the directions in which plates move. (*Hint:* First, study the map key.)

7.NS.8

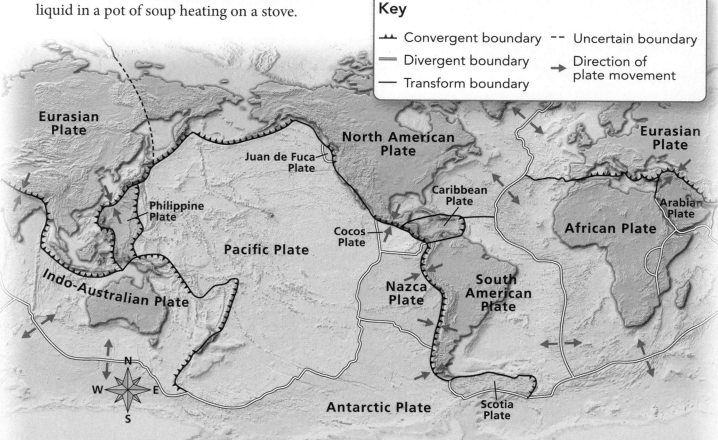

Key

⩚ Convergent boundary   -- Uncertain boundary

= Divergent boundary   → Direction of plate movement

— Transform boundary

Eurasian Plate

Juan de Fuca Plate

North American Plate

Philippine Plate

Caribbean Plate

Cocos Plate

Pacific Plate

Indo-Australian Plate

Nazca Plate

South American Plate

African Plate

Arabian Plate

Eurasian Plate

Antarctic Plate

Scotia Plate

N W E S

357

Relate Cause and Effect

What has caused the location of Earth's continents to change over time?

_____

Plate Motions Over Time Scientists use satellites to measure plate motion precisely. The plates move very slowly— from about 1 to 12 centimeters per year. The North American and Eurasian plates move apart at a rate of 2.5 centimeters per year. That's about as fast as your fingernails grow. Because the plates have been moving for tens to hundreds of millions of years, they have moved great distances.

Over time, the movement of Earth's plates has greatly changed the location of the continents and the size and shape of the oceans. As plates move, they change Earth's surface, producing earthquakes, volcanoes, mountain ranges, and deep-ocean trenches. Geologists have evidence that, before Pangaea existed, other supercontinents formed and split apart over the last billion years. Pangaea itself formed when Earth's landmasses moved together about 350 to 250 million years ago. Then, about 200 million years ago, Pangaea began to break apart, as shown in **Figure 2**.

FIGURE 2 ···

> INTERACTIVE ART **Plate Motion**

Since the breakup of Pangaea, the continents have taken about 200 million years to move to their present location.

✎ **Use the maps to answer the questions.**

1. **Interpret Maps** List three examples of continents that have drifted apart from each other.

_____

_____

_____

_____

_____

2. [CHALLENGE] Which two landmasses that were not connected to each other in Pangaea have collided on Earth today?

_____

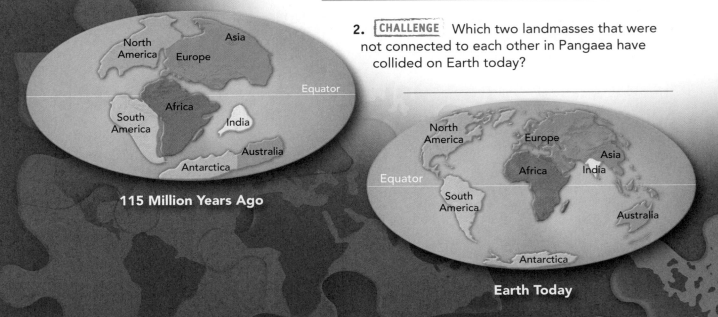

200 Million Years Ago

Pangaea — Equator

115 Million Years Ago

North America — Asia — Europe — Africa — South America — India — Australia — Antarctica — Equator

Earth Today

North America — Europe — Asia — Africa — India — South America — Australia — Antarctica — Equator

Plate Boundaries

Recall that the edges of Earth's plates meet at plate boundaries. **Faults**—breaks in Earth's crust where rocks have slipped past each other—form along these boundaries. Convection currents in Earth's mantle cause the plates to move. As the plates move, they collide, pull apart, or grind past each other. These movements produce great changes in Earth's surface and on the ocean floor. These changes include the formation of volcanoes, mountain ranges, and deep-ocean trenches.

Divergent Boundaries

Can a crack in Earth's crust be so wide that people can walk through it? In Iceland it can! There, two plates move slowly away from each other. **Figure 3** shows part of the crack that has formed as these two plates have moved apart over time.

Recall that plates move away from each other at a divergent boundary. Most divergent boundaries occur along the mid-ocean ridges, where new crust is added during sea-floor spreading. But in a few places, the mid-ocean ridge rises above sea level. Volcanic activity of the mid-Atlantic ridge is also seen in Iceland.

Where pieces of Earth's crust diverge on land, a deep valley called a **rift valley** forms. Several rift valleys make up the East African rift system. There, the crust is slowly pulling apart over a wide area.

Vocabulary Prefixes Read the text about the three types of plate boundaries. Circle the correct meaning of each prefix given here.

Di- = (away/together/along)

Con- = (away/together/along)

Trans- = (away/together/along)

FIGURE 3 ··

Breaking Up Is Hard to Do

Two plates separate to form a great crack in Iceland, marking a divergent boundary.

✎ **Interpret Diagrams** Draw arrows on the diagram to show how plates move at a divergent boundary. Then describe how the plates move.

_____

_____

_____

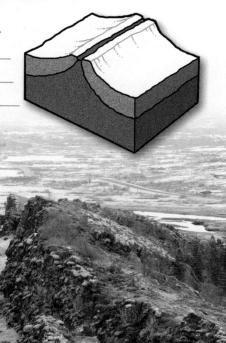

do the math!

Plates move at very slow rates. These rates are from about 1 to 12 cm per year. To calculate rates of motion, geologists use the following formula.

$$\text{Rate} = \frac{\text{Distance}}{\text{Time}}$$

△ **Calculate** The Pacific plate is sliding past the North American plate. In 10 million years, the plate will move 500 km. What is the Pacific plate's rate of motion? Express your answer in centimeters per year.

7.NS.8

FIGURE 4 ·······················

The Andes

The Andes Mountains formed at a convergent boundary.

✎ **Interpret Diagrams** Draw arrows on the diagram to show how plates move when they converge. Then describe how the plates move.

_____

_____

_____

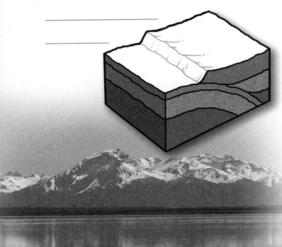

Convergent Boundaries The Andes Mountains run for 8,900 kilometers along the west coast of South America. Here, two plates collide. Recall that a boundary where two plates come together, or collide, is called a convergent boundary.

What happens when two plates collide? The density of the plates determines which one comes out on top. Oceanic crust becomes cooler and denser as it spreads away from the mid-ocean ridge. Where two plates carrying oceanic crust meet at a trench, the plate that is more dense sinks under the less dense plate.

A plate carrying oceanic crust can also collide with a plate carrying continental crust. Oceanic crust is more dense than continental crust. The more dense oceanic crust can push up the less dense continental crust. This process has formed the Andes, as shown in **Figure 4.** Meanwhile, the more dense oceanic crust also sinks as subduction occurs. Water eventually leaves the sinking crust and rises into the wedge of the mantle above it. This water lowers the melting point of the mantle in the wedge. As a result, the mantle partially melts and rises up as magma to form volcanoes.

Two plates carrying continental crust can also collide. Then, neither piece of crust is dense enough to sink far into the mantle. Instead, the collision squeezes the crust into high mountain ranges.

EXPLORE THE BIG Q?

Earth's Changing Crust

How do moving plates change Earth's crust?

FIGURE 6 ···························

▶ **ART IN MOTION** As plates move, they produce mountains, volcanoes, and valleys as well as mid-ocean ridges and deep-ocean trenches.

✎ **Identify** Fill in the blanks with the correct terms from the list on the next page. (*Hint:* Some points use more than one term.)

Molten material

Molten material

Transform Boundaries Recall that a transform boundary is a place where two plates slip past each other, moving in opposite directions. Beneath the surface of a transform boundary, the sides of the plates are rocky and jagged. So, the two plates can grab hold of each other and "lock" in place. Forces inside the crust can later cause the two plates to unlock. Earthquakes often occur when the plates suddenly slip along the boundary that they form. However, crust is neither created nor destroyed at transform boundaries. The San Andreas fault, shown in **Figure 5,** is one example of a transform boundary.

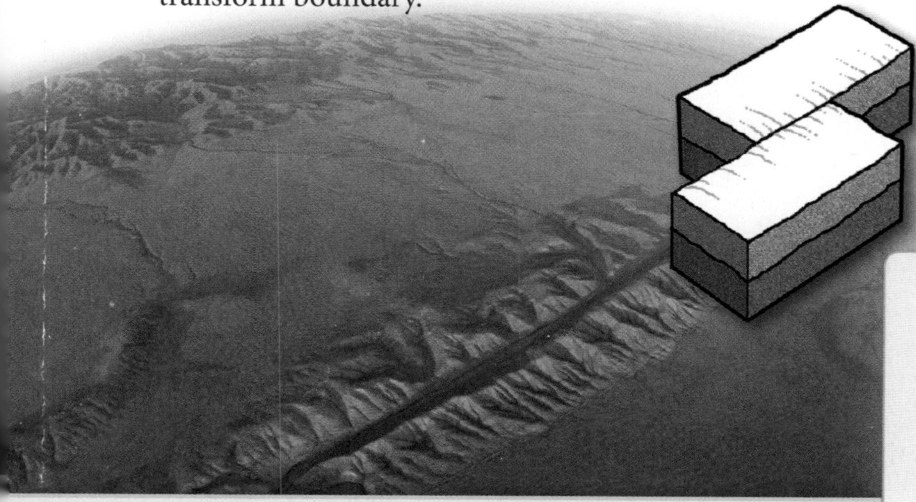

FIGURE 5 ·······························

Fault Line
The San Andreas fault in California marks a transform boundary.

✎ **Interpret Diagrams** Draw arrows on the diagram to show how plates move at a transform boundary. Then describe how the plates move.

_____

_____

_____

Rift valley	Mountains	Convection
Volcanoes	Subduction	Oceanic crust
Sea-floor spreading	Mid-ocean ridge	Convergent boundary
Transform boundary	Continental crust	Deep-ocean trench
Divergent boundary		

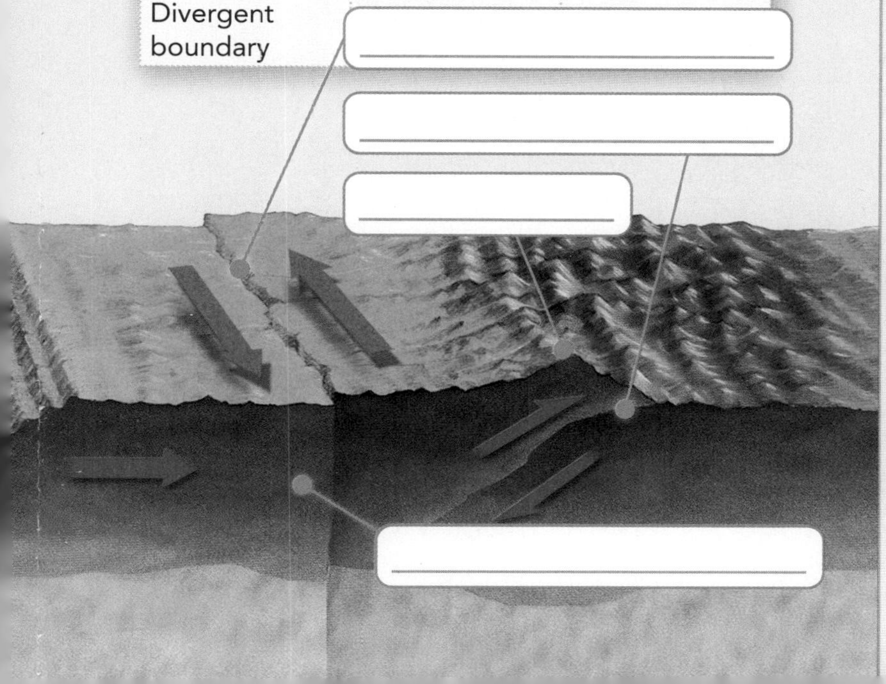

Lab ® **zone** Do the Quick Lab *Mantle Convection Currents.*

🔑 **Assess Your Understanding**

1a. Review Moving plates form convergent, divergent, or _____ boundaries.

7.2.4

b. ANSWER THE BIG ❓ **Summarize** How do moving plates change Earth's crust?

_____

_____

_____

_____

_____

_____

_____

_____

_____

7.2.4

got it? ·······························

○ **I get it!** Now I know that the three types of plate boundaries are _____

_____

○ **I need extra help with** _____

Go to MY SCIENCE ⓢ COACH *online for help with this subject.*

7.2.4

361

CHAPTER

10 Study Guide

New crust forms at _____. Crust is subducted and destroyed at _____. Mountains form where plates _____.

LESSON 1 Drifting Continents

7.2.4, 7.NS.8

🔑 Wegener's hypothesis was that all the continents were once joined together in a single landmass and have since drifted apart.

Vocabulary
- continental drift
- Pangaea
- fossil

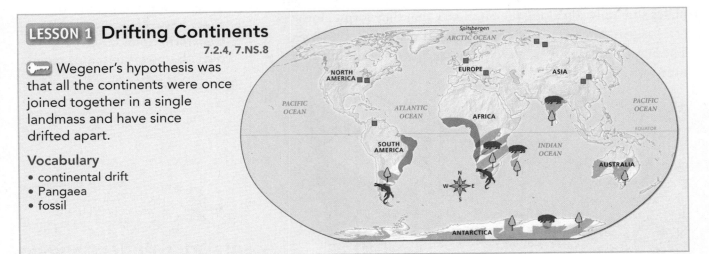

LESSON 2 Sea-Floor Spreading

7.2.4, 7.NS.1, 7.NS.8, 7.NS.11

🔑 Mid-ocean ridges form long chains of mountains that rise up from the ocean floor.

🔑 Sea-floor spreading adds more crust to the ocean floor. At the same time, older strips of rock move outward from either side of the ridge.

🔑 In a process taking tens of millions of years, part of the ocean floor sinks back into the mantle at deep-ocean trenches.

Vocabulary
- mid-ocean ridge
- sea-floor spreading
- deep-ocean trench
- subduction

LESSON 3 The Theory of Plate Tectonics

7.2.4, 7.NS.8

🔑 The theory of plate tectonics states that Earth's plates are in slow, constant motion, driven by convection currents in the mantle.

Vocabulary
- plate
- divergent boundary
- convergent boundary
- transform boundary
- plate tectonics
- fault
- rift valley

Review and Assessment

LESSON 1 Drifting Continents

1. What did Wegener think happens during continental drift?

a. Continents move. **b.** Continents freeze.

c. The mantle warms. **d.** Convection stops.

7.2.4

2. Wegener thought that all the continents were once joined together in a supercontinent that he called _____.

7.2.4

3. Draw The drawing shows North America and Africa. Circle the parts of the coastlines of the two continents that were joined in Pangaea.

7.2.4

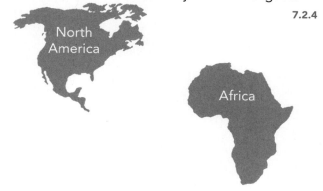

North America

Africa

4. Make Judgments Wegener proposed that mountains form when continents collide, crumpling up their edges. Was Wegener's idea about how mountains form consistent with his hypothesis of continental drift? Explain.

_____

_____

_____

_____

7.2.4

5. Write About It Michelle is a scientist working in Antarctica. She learns that fossils of *Glossopteris* have been found on Antarctica. Her colleague Joe, working in India, has also found *Glossopteris* fossils. Write a letter from Michelle to her colleague explaining how these fossils could be found in both places. Define *continental drift* in your answer and discuss how it explains the fossil findings.

7.2.4

LESSON 2 Sea-Floor Spreading

6. In which areas does subduction of the ocean floor take place?

a. rift valleys **b.** the lower mantle

c. mid-ocean ridges **d.** deep-ocean trenches

7.2.4

7. A mid-ocean ridge is a _____

_____

that rises up from the ocean floor.

7.2.4

8. Compare and Contrast Look at the diagram. Label the area where new crust forms.

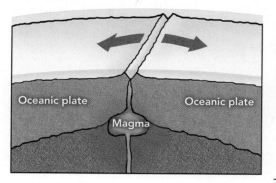

Oceanic plate   Oceanic plate

Magma

7.2.4

9. Apply Concepts Why are the oldest parts of the ocean floor no older than about 200 million years?

_____

_____

_____

7.2.4

10. Sequence Place the following steps of sea-floor spreading in their correct sequence.

A. The molten material cools and hardens, forming a strip of rock along the ocean floor.

B. The strip of rock moves away from the ridge.

C. Molten material from inside Earth rises to the ocean floor at a mid-ocean ridge.

_____

7.2.4

11. Write About It How is pillow lava evidence of sea-floor spreading?

7.2.4

363

12. At which boundary do two plates pull apart?

    a. convergent   **b.** transform

    c. divergent   **d.** mantle-crust

                  7.2.4

13. When a divergent boundary occurs on land, it forms a _____.

                   7.2.4

Use the diagram to answer Questions 14–15.

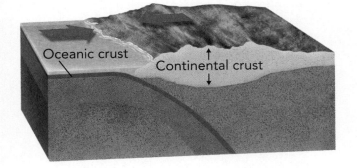

Oceanic crust   Continental crust

14. Classify What type of plate boundary is shown in the diagram?

    _____

                   7.2.4

15. Predict What type of landforms will result from the plate movement shown in the diagram?

    _____

                   7.2.4

16. Compare and Contrast How does the density of oceanic crust differ from that of continental crust? Why is this difference important?

    _____

    _____

    _____

                   7.2.4

17. math! It takes 100,000 years for a plate to move about 2 kilometers. What is the rate of motion in centimeters per year?

                7.2.4, 7.NS.8

How do moving plates change Earth's crust?

18. Summarize Suppose Earth's landmasses someday all move together again. Describe the changes that would occur in Earth's oceans and Earth's landmasses. Use the map and the theory of plate tectonics to explain your ideas.

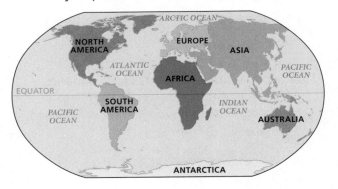

    _____

    _____

    _____

    _____

    _____

    _____

    _____

    _____

    _____

    _____

    _____

    _____

    _____

    _____

    _____

    _____

                   7.2.4, 7.NS.1

Indiana ISTEP+ Practice

Multiple Choice

Circle the letter of the best answer.

1. The diagram shows a process in Earth's crust.

Which statement best describes the process in the diagram?

A. Converging plates form mountains.

B. Converging plates form volcanoes.

C. Diverging plates form mountains.

D. Diverging plates form a rift valley.

7.2.4

2. What is one piece of evidence that caused Wegener to think that continents moved?

A. He found an old map of the world that showed movement.

B. He found similar fossils on different continents that are separated by oceans.

C. He proved his hypothesis with an experiment that measured movement.

D. He observed the continents moving with his own eyes.

7.2.4

3. Which of the following is evidence for sea-floor spreading?

A. matching patterns of magnetic stripes found in the crust of the ocean floor

B. new rock found farther from mid-ocean ridges than older rock

C. pieces of different crust found on different continents

D. changes in climate on the continent of Africa

7.2.4

4. What force causes the movement of Earth's plates?

A. convection currents

B. pressure

C. sound waves

D. cooling

7.2.4

Constructed Response

Write your answer to Question 5 on the lines below.

5. What happens to new oceanic crust at a mid-ocean ridge?

_____

_____

_____

7.2.4

Extended Response

Use the map below and your knowledge of science to help you answer Question 6. Write your answer on a separate piece of paper.

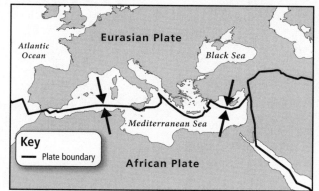

6. The African plate is moving toward the Eurasian plate at a rate of a few centimeters per year. How will this area change in 100 million years? In your answer, consider how the continents will change and how the Mediterranean Sea will change.

7.2.4

365

ALVIN:2.0

AN EXTREME MAKEOVER

For years, *Alvin*, the world's oldest research submarine, has worked hard. *Alvin* carries scientists deep into the ocean. The research submarine has made over 4,400 dives—some as deep as 4,500 meters beneath the water's surface. With the help of *Alvin*, scientists have discovered everything from tube worms to the wreck of the *Titanic*. But *Alvin* allows scientists to see only the top 63 percent of the ocean. The rest of the ocean lies even deeper than 4,500 meters, where *Alvin* can't go.

Enter *Alvin* 2.0—*Alvin's* replacement. It is bigger and faster, with more windows and improved sensors. It can go down to 6,500 meters and carry heavier samples. *Alvin* 2.0 allows scientists to see most of the ocean.

With better and deeper access to the ocean, scientists are excited about all of the new and weird discoveries they'll make with *Alvin* 2.0.

▼ Presenting . . .
the new *Alvin!*

Design It Research more about *Alvin* 2.0's capabilities. Think about a new feature that you would like to add to *Alvin* 2.0. What needs would your feature meet? Brainstorm potential designs and document your work with labeled drawings. Select your best idea and explain what materials you could use to create a prototype. Tell how you would test, evaluate, and redesign your prototype to better meet the needs you identified. See Appendix A on page 578 for more information about the design process.

🔵 7.NS.1, 7.NS.2, 7.NS.11, 7.DP.1–7.DP.11

Museum of Science

An Ocean Is Born

In one of the hottest, driest places in the world, Earth's crust is cracking.

In the Afar region of Ethiopia, Earth's tectonic plates are moving apart. Here, Earth's crust is so thin that magma has been able to break through the surface. As the plates drifted farther apart, the crust sank to form a valley that is 59 kilometers long!

Today volcanoes, earthquakes, and hydrothermal fields tell us how thin the crust is, and how the plates are pulling apart. Eventually, this valley could sink deep enough to allow salt water from the nearby Red Sea to move in and form an ocean. This ocean could split Africa apart. Although it could take millions of years for an actual ocean to form, scientists are excited to witness the steps that will lead to its birth.

Research It Research a major change in Earth's surface caused by plate movement. Try to find at least two different accounts of the event. Create a timeline or a storyboard showing when and how the change occurred.

7.2.3, 7.NS.2, 7.NS.11

▲ Tectonic plates are pulling apart in this dry, hot area in the Afar region of Ethiopia.

▲ Lava seeps out of a crack in the lava lake on top of Erfa Ale, the highest mountain in the Afar region. Scientists must wear protective clothing in this extremely hot, dangerous environment.

WHAT COULD CAUSE THIS BUILDING TO TOPPLE?

THE BIG ?

Why do earthquakes and volcanoes occur more often in some places than in others?

Earthquakes can strike without a moment's notice. The ground can buckle and buildings can topple, as happened to this building in Taiwan in 1999. These disasters may seem like random events. But the structure of Earth suggests a different conclusion. ▷Predict **Do you think geologists can predict where and when an earthquake will occur? Explain.**

_____

_____

_____

_____

_____

_____

▷ **UNTAMED SCIENCE** Watch the **Untamed Science** video to learn more about earthquakes.

Earthquakes and Volcanoes

Academic Standards for Science

7.2.4, 7.NS.1, 7.NS.5, 7.NS.8, 7.NS.11

11 Getting Started

Check Your Understanding

1. **Background** Read the paragraph below and then answer the question.

Mr. Carenni said, "For today's activity, let's make a model of Earth's crust. We can think of the **crust** as a thin film of ice resting on top of a much thicker layer of hard, packed snow. Now let's suppose that the ice breaks into pieces. On Earth, these pieces are called **plates.** The edges of the plates are called **boundaries.** "

The **crust** is Earth's rocky, outer layer.

A **plate** is one of the large pieces that Earth's crust is broken into.

Boundaries are lines along which something ends.

- Suppose two pieces of ice are pushed slowly together. What might happen to the edges of the pieces?

_____

_____

> **MY READING WEB** If you had trouble answering the question above, visit **My Reading Web** and type in *Earthquakes and Volcanoes.*

Vocabulary Skill

High-Use Academic Words High-use words are words that are used frequently in academic reading, writing, and discussions. These words are different from key terms because they appear in many subject areas.

Word	Definition	Example
surface	*n.* the exterior or outermost layer of an object	The *surface* of Earth is very rocky.
stage	*n.* a point in a process	Middle age is one *stage* of life.
hazard	*n.* a possible danger	Forest fires can be a *hazard* for people living near the woods.

2. **Quick Check** Choose the word from the table that best completes the sentence.

- When a volcano erupts, the lava can be a _____ for cities and towns nearby.

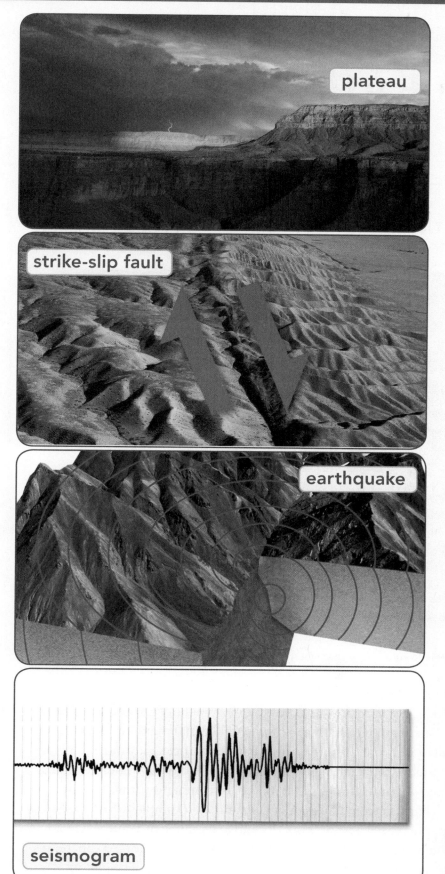

plateau

strike-slip fault

earthquake

seismogram

Chapter Preview

LESSON 1
- stress • tension • compression
- shearing • normal fault • reverse fault • strike-slip fault • plateau

↻ Relate Cause and Effect
△ Make Models

LESSON 2
- earthquake • focus • epicenter
- P wave • S wave • surface wave
- seismograph • Modified Mercalli scale • magnitude • Richter scale
- moment magnitude scale

↻ Sequence
△ Infer

LESSON 3
- seismogram

↻ Identify the Main Idea
△ Predict

LESSON 4
- volcano • magma • lava • Ring of Fire • island arc • hot spot

↻ Relate Text and Visuals
△ Develop Hypotheses

LESSON 5
- magma chamber • pipe • vent
- lava flow • crater • silica
- pyroclastic flow • dormant
- extinct

↻ Outline
△ Communicate

LESSON 6
- caldera • cinder cone
- composite volcano • shield volcano • volcanic neck • dike
- sill • batholith

↻ Relate Cause and Effect
△ Predict

> VOCAB FLASH CARDS For extra help with vocabulary, visit **Vocab Flash Cards** and type in *Earthquakes and Volcanoes.*

371

Forces in Earth's Crust

UNLOCK THE BIG ?

🔑 **How Does Stress Change Earth's Crust?**
7.2.4

🔑 **How Do Faults Form?**
7.2.4

🔑 **How Does Plate Movement Create New Landforms?**
7.2.4, 7.NS.1, 7.NS.11, 7.DP.10

MY PLANET DiARY

Still Growing!

Mount Everest in the Himalayas is the highest mountain on Earth. Climbers who reach the peak stand 8,850 meters above sea level. You might think that mountains never change. But forces inside Earth push Mount Everest at least several millimeters higher each year. Over time, Earth's forces slowly but constantly lift, stretch, bend, and break Earth's crust in dramatic ways!

MISCONCEPTION

✏️ **Communicate** Discuss the following question with a classmate. Write your answer below.

How long do you think it took Mount Everest to form? Hundreds of years? Thousands? Millions? Explain.

_____

_____

_____

_____

▶ **PLANET DIARY** Go to **Planet Diary** to learn more about forces in Earth's crust.

Lab zone Do the Inquiry Warm-Up *How Does Stress Affect Earth's Crust?*

🏛 **Academic Standards for Science**

7.2.4 Explain how convection currents in the mantle cause lithospheric plates to move causing fast changes like earthquakes and volcanic eruptions and slow changes like creation of mountains and formation of new ocean floor.

How Does Stress Change Earth's Crust?

Rocks are hard and stiff. But the movement of Earth's plates can create strong forces that slowly bend or fold many rocks like a caramel candy bar. Like the candy bar, some rocks may only bend and stretch when a strong force is first applied to them. But beyond a certain limit, all rocks in Earth's brittle upper crust will break.

Forces created by plate movement are examples of stress. **Stress** is a force that acts on rock to change its shape or volume. Geologists often express stress as force per unit area. Because stress increases as force increases, stress adds energy to the rock. The energy is stored in the rock until the rock changes shape or breaks.

Vocabulary
- stress • tension • compression • shearing
- normal fault • reverse fault • strike-slip fault • plateau

Skills
- ⟳ Reading: Relate Cause and Effect
- △ Inquiry: Make Models

Three kinds of stress can occur in the crust—tension, compression, and shearing. 🔑 **Tension, compression, and shearing work over millions of years to change the shape and volume of rock.** Most changes in the crust occur only very slowly, so that you cannot directly observe the crust bending, stretching, or breaking. **Figure 1** shows the three types of stress.

Tension Rock in the crust can be stretched so that it becomes thinner in the middle. This process can make rock seem to act like a piece of warm bubble gum. The stress force that pulls on the crust and thins rock in the middle is called **tension.** Tension occurs where two plates pull apart.

Compression One plate pushing against another plate can squeeze rock like a giant trash compactor. The stress force that squeezes rock until it folds or breaks is called **compression.** Compression occurs where two plates come together.

Shearing Stress that pushes a mass of rock in two opposite directions is called **shearing.** Shearing can cause rock to break and slip apart or to change its shape. Shearing occurs where two plates slip past each other.

FIGURE 1 ···

▷ ART IN MOTION **Stress in Earth's Crust**
Stress can push, pull, or squeeze rock in Earth's crust.
✎ **Apply Concepts Look at the pair of arrows in the second diagram. These arrows show how tension affects rock. Draw a pair of arrows on the third diagram to show how compression affects rock. Then, draw a pair of arrows on the bottom diagram to show how shearing acts on rock.**

Before stress

Tension

Compression

Shearing

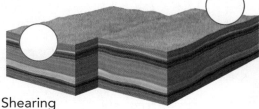

Lab® zone Do the Quick Lab
Effects of Stress.

🔑 Assess Your Understanding

got it? ··

○ **I get it!** Now I know that stress changes Earth's crust by changing the _____

○ I need extra help with _____

Go to my science ⁵ coach *online for help with this subject.*

Academic Standards for Science

7.2.4 Explain how convection currents in the mantle cause lithospheric plates to move causing fast changes like earthquakes and volcanic eruptions and slow changes like creation of mountains and formation of new ocean floor.

How Do Faults Form?

Recall that a fault is a break in the rock of the crust where rock surfaces slip past each other. Most faults occur along plate boundaries, where the forces of plate motion push or pull the crust so much that the crust breaks. 🔑 **When enough stress builds up in rock, the rock breaks, creating a fault.** There are three main types of faults: normal faults, reverse faults, and strike-slip faults.

Normal Faults The Rio Grande River flows through a wide valley in New Mexico. Here, tension has pulled apart two pieces of Earth's crust, forming the valley. Where rock is pulled apart by tension in Earth's crust, normal faults form. In a **normal fault,** the fault cuts through rock at an angle, so one block of rock sits over the fault, while the other block lies under the fault. The block of rock that sits over the fault is called the *hanging wall.* The rock that lies under the fault is called the *footwall.* The diagram of the normal fault in **Figure 2** shows how the hanging wall sits over the footwall. When movement occurs along a normal fault, the hanging wall slips downward. Normal faults occur where two plates diverge, or pull apart.

FIGURE 2 ···

> ART IN MOTION **Faults**

The three main types of faults are defined by the direction in which rock moves along the fault. ✏️ **Observe In the descriptions below the first two diagrams, fill in the blanks to indicate how rock moves. In both of these diagrams, label the hanging wall and footwall.**

Key

➡️ Movement along the fault

➡️ Force deforming the crust

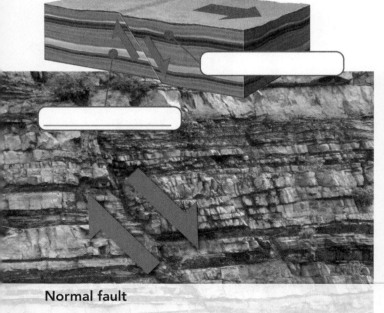

Normal fault

In a normal fault, the hanging wall _____ _____ relative to the footwall.

Reverse fault

In a reverse fault, the hanging wall moves _____ relative to the footwall.

Reverse Faults

The northern Rocky Mountains rise high above the western United States and Canada. These mountains were gradually lifted up over time by movement along reverse faults. A **reverse fault** has the same structure as a normal fault, but the blocks move in the reverse direction. That is, the hanging wall moves up and the footwall moves down. **Figure 2** shows a reverse fault. Reverse faults form where compression pushes the rock of the crust together.

Strike-Slip Faults

The hilly plains in southern California are split by the San Andreas fault, shown in **Figure 2.** Here, shearing has produced a strike-slip fault. In a **strike-slip fault,** the rocks on either side of the fault slip past each other sideways, with little up or down motion. A strike-slip fault that forms the boundary between two plates is called a transform boundary. The San Andreas fault is an example of a transform boundary.

Lab zone | Do the Quick Lab Modeling Faults.

apply it!

The low angle of a thrust fault allows rock in the hanging wall to be pushed great distances. For example, over millions of years, rock along the Lewis thrust fault in Glacier National Park has moved 80 kilometers.

1 **Identify** Based on the arrows showing fault movements in the diagram, a thrust fault is a type of (normal fault/reverse fault).

2 **CHALLENGE** Why might the type of rock in the hanging wall of the Lewis thrust fault be different from the type of rock in the footwall?

_____

_____

_____

_____

Strike-slip fault

Rocks on either side of a strike-slip fault move past each other.

🔑 Assess Your Understanding

1a. Review When enough stress builds up in brittle rock, the rock breaks, causing a

_____ to form. 7.2.4

b. Infer A geologist sees a fault along which blocks of rock in the footwall have moved higher relative to blocks of rock in the hanging wall. What type of fault is this? 7.2.4

_____

got it? ···

○ **I get it!** Now I know that faults form when

_____

○ **I need extra help with** _____

_____

Go to **my science COACH** online for help with this subject. 7.2.4

375

7.2.4 Explain how convection currents in the mantle cause lithospheric plates to move causing fast changes like earthquakes and volcanic eruptions and slow changes like creation of mountains and formation of new ocean floor.

7.NS.1 Make predictions.

7.NS.11 Communicate findings using models.

7.DP.10 Communicate the solution using drawings.

Vocabulary Identify Multiple Meanings Underline the sentence that uses the scientific meaning of *fold*.

- The rock looked as crushed as my shirts if I don't fold them.
- Rock that bends without breaking may form a fold.

FIGURE 3

Folded Rock

Folds in rock shorten and thicken the Earth's crust. Over time, this process can form mountains. **Make Models Hold down the right edge of this page. Then, push the left edge toward the center of the book. Is this activity a good model for showing how folded rock forms? Explain.**

_____

_____

_____

_____

_____

_____

_____

_____

7.NS.11

How Does Plate Movement Create New Landforms?

Most changes in the crust occur so slowly that they cannot be observed directly. But what if you could speed up time so that a billion years passed by in minutes? Then, you could watch the movement of Earth's plates fold, stretch, and uplift the crust over wide areas. 🔑 **Over millions of years, the forces of plate movement can change a flat plain into features such as anticlines and synclines, folded mountains, fault-block mountains, and plateaus.**

Folding Earth's Crust Have you ever skidded on a rug that wrinkled up as your feet pushed it across the floor? Sometimes plate movements can cause Earth's crust to fold much like the rug. Then, rocks stressed by compression may bend without breaking.

How Folds Form Folds are bends in rock that form when compression shortens and thickens Earth's crust. A fold can be a few centimeters across or hundreds of kilometers wide. **Figure 3** shows folds in rock that were exposed when a road was cut through a hillside in California.

Place your fingers here and push the left edge of the page.

How Anticlines and Synclines Form Geologists use the terms *anticline* and *syncline* to describe upward and downward folds in rock. A fold in rock that bends upward into an arch is an anticline (AN tih klyn), as shown in **Figure 4.** A fold in rock that bends downward to form a V shape is a syncline (SIN klyn). Anticlines and synclines are found in many places where compression forces have folded the crust. The central Appalachian Mountains in Pennsylvania are folded mountains made up of anticlines and synclines.

How Folded Mountains Form The collision of two plates can cause compression and folding of the crust over a wide area. Folding produced some of the world's largest mountain ranges. The Himalayas in Asia and the Alps in Europe formed when pieces of the crust folded during the collision of two plates. These mountains formed over millions of years.

FIGURE 4 ···

Anticlines and Synclines
Compression can cause folds in the crust. Two types of folding are anticlines, which arch up, and synclines, which dip down.
Relate Cause and Effect Draw arrows to show the direction in which forces act to compress the crust. (*Hint*: Review the information on compression in this lesson.) Then label the anticline and the syncline.

When two normal faults cause valleys to drop down on either side of a block of rock, what type of landform results?

_____

_____

Stretching Earth's Crust

If you traveled by car from Salt Lake City to Los Angeles, you would cross the Great Basin. This region contains many mountains separated by broad valleys, or basins. The mountains form from tension in Earth's crust that causes faulting. Such mountains are called fault-block mountains.

How do fault-block mountains form? Where two plates move away from each other, tension forces create many normal faults. Suppose two normal faults cause valleys to drop down on either side of a block of rock. This process is shown in the diagram that accompanies the photograph in **Figure 5.** As the hanging wall of each normal fault slips downward, the block in between now stands above the surrounding valleys, forming a fault-block mountain.

FIGURE 5 ·······································

Tension and Normal Faults

As tension forces pull the crust apart, two normal faults can form a fault-block mountain range, as you can see in the diagram below. The mountain range in the photograph is in the Great Basin. Valleys can also form as a result of two normal faults.

Predict Label the hanging wall and the two footwalls in diagram A. In diagram B, draw the new position of the hanging wall after movement occurs. Describe what happens.

_____

_____

_____

_____

7.NS.1

A Before movement occurs along the faults.

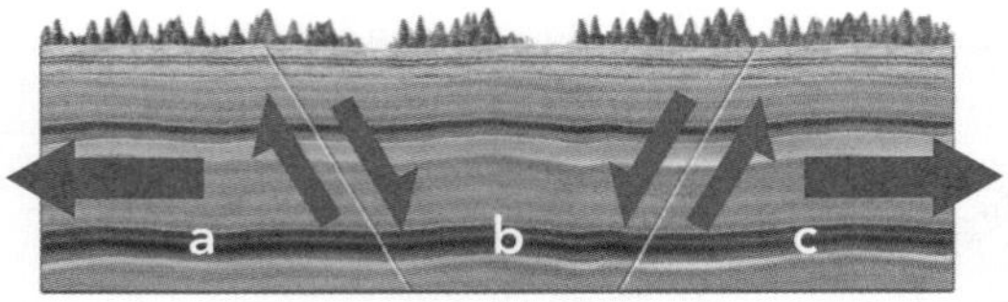

a._____

b._____

c._____

B Draw the outcome after movement occurs along the faults.

Fault-block mountains

Key

 Movement along the fault

 Force deforming the crust

Uplifting Earth's Crust The forces that raise mountains can also uplift, or raise, plateaus. A **plateau** is a large area of flat land elevated high above sea level. Some plateaus form when forces in Earth's crust push up a large, flat block of rock. Like a fancy sandwich, a plateau consists of many different flat layers, and is wider than it is tall. Forces deforming the crust uplifted the Colorado Plateau in the "Four Corners" region of Arizona, Utah, Colorado, and New Mexico. **Figure 6** shows one part of that plateau in northern Arizona.

FIGURE 6 ·········
The Kaibab Plateau
The Kaibab Plateau forms the North Rim of the Grand Canyon. The plateau is the flat-topped landform in the right half of the photograph.

Look at the sequence of drawings below. In your own words, describe what happens in the last two diagrams.

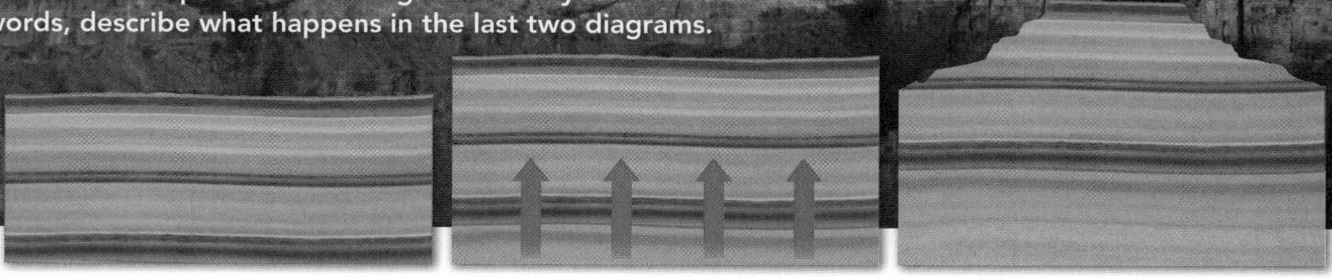

A flat, layered block of rock lies somewhere in Earth's crust.

_____
_____
_____
_____

_____
_____
_____
_____

Lab zone® Do the Quick Lab
Modeling Stress.

🔑 Assess Your Understanding

2a. Review Normal faults often occur when two plates (come together/pull apart).   **7.2.4**

b. Interpret Diagrams Look at the diagram that accompanies the photograph in **Figure 5.** Does the block of rock in the middle move up as a result of movement along the normal faults? Explain.

_____
_____
_____
_____
_____
_____

7.2.4

got it? ··

○ **I get it!** Now I know that plate movements create new features by _____

_____
_____
_____
_____

○ **I need extra help with** _____

_____

Go to **MY SCIENCE COACH** *online for help with this subject.*   **7.2.4**

Earthquakes and Seismic Waves

UNLOCK THE BIG

🔑 **What Are Seismic Waves?**
7.2.4, 7.NS.8, 7.NS.11

🔑 **How Are Earthquakes Measured?**
7.2.4, 7.NS.8

🔑 **How Is an Epicenter Located?**
7.2.4, 7.NS.8

my planeT DiaRY

DISASTER

Witness to Disaster

On May 12, 2008, a major earthquake struck China. American reporter Melissa Block was conducting a live radio interview in that country at the moment the earthquake struck.

"What's going on?" Block asked. She remained on the air and continued: "The whole building is shaking. The whole building is SHAKING."

Block watched as the ground moved like waves beneath her feet. The top of the church across the street started to fall down. For minutes, the ground continued to vibrate under Block's feet. The earthquake that day killed about 87,000 people.

—NPR.com

✎ **Communicate** Discuss these questions with a group of classmates. Write your answers below.

1. What does Melissa Block's experience tell you about the way the ground can move during an earthquake?

_____

_____

2. How do you think you would react during an earthquake or other disaster?

_____

_____

_____

▷ PLANET DIARY Go to **Planet Diary** to learn more about earthquakes.

Lab zone ® Do the Inquiry Warm-Up *How Do Seismic Waves Travel Through Earth?*

Vocabulary

- earthquake   • focus   • epicenter   • P wave
- S wave   • surface wave   • seismograph
- Modified Mercalli scale   • magnitude   • Richter scale
- moment magnitude scale

Skills

⟳ Reading: Sequence

△ Inquiry: Infer

What Are Seismic Waves?

Earth is never still. Every day, worldwide, several thousand earthquakes are detected. An **earthquake** is the shaking and trembling that results from movement of rock beneath Earth's surface. Most earthquakes are too small to notice. But a large earthquake can crack open the ground, shift mountains, and cause great damage.

Cause of Earthquakes   The forces of plate movement cause earthquakes. Plate movements produce stress in Earth's crust, adding energy to rock and forming faults. Stress increases along a fault until the rock slips or breaks, causing an earthquake. In seconds, the earthquake releases an enormous amount of stored energy. Some of the energy released during an earthquake travels in the form of seismic waves. 🔑 **Seismic waves are vibrations that are similar to sound waves. They travel through Earth carrying energy released by an earthquake.** The speed and path of the waves in part depend on the material through which the waves travel.

Academic Standards for Science

7.2.4 Explain how convection currents in the mantle cause lithospheric plates to move causing fast changes like earthquakes and volcanic eruptions and slow changes like creation of mountains and formation of new ocean floor.

7.NS.8 Analyze data and use it to make inferences.

7.NS.11 Communicate findings using maps and models through written reports.

Earthquake   Path of seismic waves

A

B

C

apply it!

Earthquakes start below the surface of Earth. But an earthquake's seismic waves do not carry energy only upward, toward Earth's surface. They also carry energy downward, through Earth's interior.

1 Look at the drawing showing Earth's interior. At which point(s) can seismic waves be detected?

○ A only
○ A and B
○ A, B, and C

2 △ **Infer** At which point do you think the seismic waves will have the most energy? Why?

_____

_____

_____

7.NS.8

Sequence Number the following in the order in which seismic waves would be felt:

__ At an earthquake's epicenter

__ At a distance of 500 km from the earthquake's focus

__ At the earthquake's focus

Types of Seismic Waves

Like a pebble thrown into a pond, the seismic waves of an earthquake race out in every direction from the earthquake's focus. The **focus** (FOH kus) is the area beneath Earth's surface where rock that was under stress begins to break or move. This action triggers the earthquake. The point on the surface directly above the focus is called the **epicenter** (EP uh sen tur).

Most earthquakes start in the lithosphere, within about 100 kilometers beneath Earth's surface. Seismic waves carry energy from the earthquake's focus. This energy travels through Earth's interior and across Earth's surface. That happened in 2002, when a powerful earthquake ruptured the Denali fault in Alaska, shown in **Figure 1.**

There are three main categories of seismic waves. These waves are P waves, S waves, and surface waves. But an earthquake sends out only P and S waves from its focus. Surface waves can develop wherever P and S waves reach the surface.

FIGURE 1

INTERACTIVE ART **Seismic Waves**

The diagram shows how seismic waves traveled during an earthquake along the Denali fault.

Explain **Match the two points in the diagram to the two terms below them. Then, write a short, science-based news article that describes how, why, and where the earthquake took place. Include a headline.**

earthBLOG

ENTRY 1

Write your headline here.

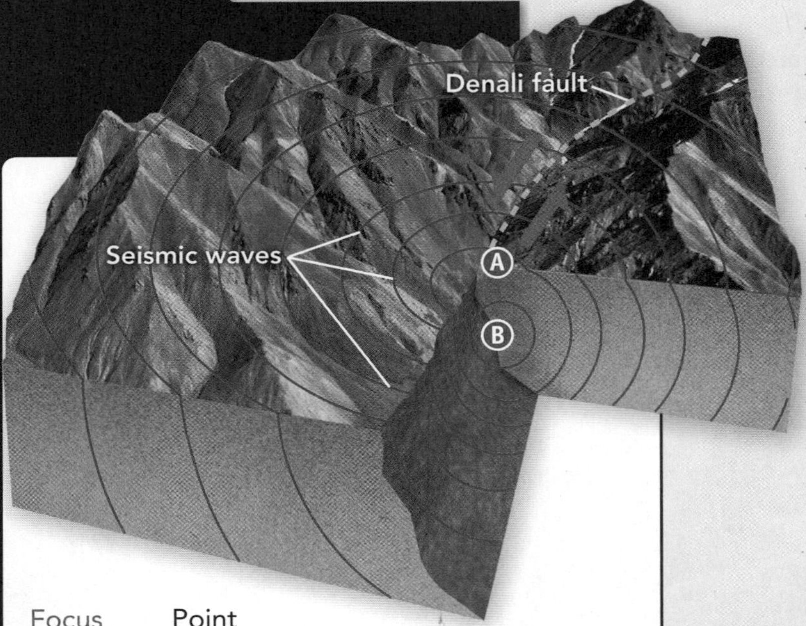

Denali fault

Seismic waves

Ⓐ

Ⓑ

Focus   Point _____

Epicenter Point _____

7.NS.11

P Waves The first waves to arrive are primary waves, or P waves. **P waves** are seismic waves that compress and expand the ground like an accordion. Like the other types of seismic waves, P waves can damage buildings. Look at **Figure 2A** to see how P waves move.

S Waves After P waves come secondary waves, or S waves. **S waves** are seismic waves that can vibrate from side to side (as shown in **Figure 2B**) or up and down. Their vibrations are at an angle of 90° to the direction that they travel. When S waves reach the surface, they shake structures violently. While P waves travel through both solids and liquids, S waves cannot move through liquids.

Surface Waves When P waves and S waves reach the surface, some of them become surface waves. **Surface waves** move more slowly than P and S waves, but they can produce severe ground movements. These waves produce movement that is similar to waves in water, where the water's particles move in a pattern that is almost circular. Surface waves can make the ground roll like ocean waves (**Figure 2C**) or shake buildings from side to side.

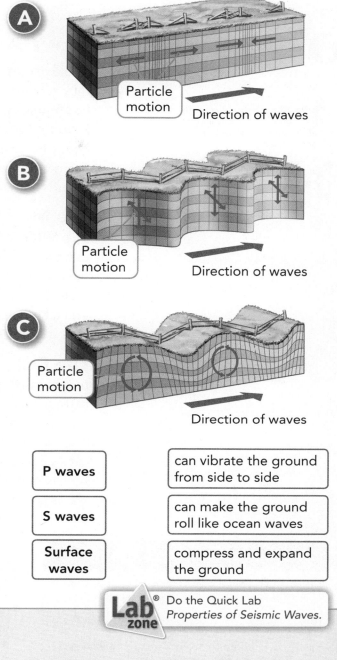

FIGURE 2 ·······························

P, S, and Surface Waves
Earthquakes release stored energy as seismic waves.
✎ **Describe Draw a line from each type of seismic wave to the movement it causes.**

P waves		can vibrate the ground from side to side
S waves		can make the ground roll like ocean waves
Surface waves		compress and expand the ground

Lab zone® Do the Quick Lab
Properties of Seismic Waves.

🔑 **Assess Your Understanding**

1a. Review The energy released by an earthquake moves out from the earthquake's

_____ in the form of seismic waves.

7.2.4

b. Predict Small earthquakes occur along a certain fault several times a year. Why might geologists worry if no earthquakes occur for 25 years?

_____

_____

_____

7.2.4, 7.NS.1

got it? ··

○ **I get it!** Now I know that seismic waves are_____

_____

○ **I need extra help with** _____

Go to **my science** ⓢ **coach** *online for help with this subject.*

7.2.4

How Are Earthquakes Measured?

Geologists monitor earthquakes by measuring the seismic waves they produce. This is done in two ways. 🔧 **The amount of earthquake damage or shaking that is felt is rated using the Modified Mercalli scale. The magnitude, or size, of an earthquake is measured on a seismograph using the Richter scale or moment magnitude scale.** A **seismograph** is an instrument that records and measures an earthquake's seismic waves.

The Modified Mercalli Scale

The **Modified Mercalli scale** rates the amount of shaking from an earthquake. The shaking is rated by people's observations, without the use of any instruments. This scale is useful in regions where there aren't many instruments to measure an earthquake's strength. The table in **Figure 3** describes the 12 steps of the Mercalli scale. To rank examples of damage, look at the photographs in **Figure 3**.

The Richter Scale

An earthquake's **magnitude** is a single number that geologists assign to an earthquake based on the earthquake's size. There are many magnitude scales. These scales are based on the earliest magnitude scale, called the **Richter scale.** Magnitude scales like the Richter scale rate the magnitude of small earthquakes based on the size of the earthquake's waves as recorded by seismographs. The magnitudes take into account that seismic waves get smaller the farther a seismograph is from an earthquake.

Rank	Description
I–III	People notice vibrations like those from a passing truck. Unstable objects disturbed.
IV–VI	Some windows break. Plaster may fall.
VII–IX	Moderate to heavy damage. Buildings jolted off foundations.
X–XII	Great destruction. Cracks appear in ground. Waves seen on surface.

FIGURE 3 ·····························

▶ INTERACTIVE ART **Modified Mercalli Scale**
The Modified Mercalli scale uses Roman numerals to rate the damage and shaking at any given location, usually close to the earthquake. ✏️ **Classify Assign a Modified Mercalli rating to each photograph.**

The Moment Magnitude Scale

Geologists use the **moment magnitude scale** to rate the total energy an earthquake releases. News reports may mention the Richter scale, but the number quoted is almost always an earthquake's moment magnitude. To assign a magnitude to an earthquake, geologists use data from seismographs and other sources. The data allow geologists to estimate how much energy the earthquake releases. **Figure 4** gives the magnitudes of some recent, strong earthquakes.

Comparing Magnitudes

An earthquake's moment magnitude tells geologists how much energy was released by an earthquake. Each one-point increase in magnitude represents the release of roughly 32 times more energy. For example, a magnitude 6 earthquake releases 32 times as much energy as a magnitude 5 earthquake.

An earthquake's effects increase with magnitude. Earthquakes with a magnitude below 5 are small and cause little damage. Those with a magnitude above 6 can cause great damage. The most powerful earthquakes, with a magnitude of 8 or above, are rare. In the 1900's, only three earthquakes had a magnitude of 9 or above. More recently, the 2004 Sumatra earthquake had a magnitude of 9.2.

FIGURE 4 ⋯⋯⋯⋯⋯⋯⋯⋯⋯⋯⋯⋯⋯
Earthquake Magnitude

The table gives the moment magnitudes of some recent earthquakes.

Magnitude	Location	Date
9.2	Sumatra (Indian Ocean)	December 2004
7.9	China	May 2008
7.6	Turkey	August 1999
6.6	Japan	October 2004
5.4	California	July 2008

[CHALLENGE] Approximately how many times stronger was the earthquake in Turkey than the earthquake in Japan?

_____

did you **know?** ⋯⋯⋯⋯⋯⋯⋯⋯

Earthquakes are not exactly uncommon in the Hoosier State. This map shows the locations of earthquakes in and around Indiana from 1800 through 1995.

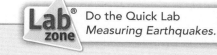

Lab ® Do the Quick Lab
zone *Measuring Earthquakes.*

🔑 Assess Your Understanding

2a. Identify The _____ scale rates earthquakes based on the amount of energy that is released.

7.2.3

b. Infer Suppose the moment magnitude of an earthquake is first thought to be 6, but is later found to be 8. Would you expect the earthquake damage to be more or less serious? Why?

_____

_____

_____

7.2.3

got it? ⋯⋯⋯⋯⋯⋯⋯⋯⋯⋯⋯⋯⋯

○ **I get it!** Now I know that to measure earthquakes, geologists use seismic waves to determine _____

_____

_____

○ **I need extra help with** _____

_____

Go to **my science** ⓢ **coach** *online for help with this subject.*

7.2.3

385

7.2.4 Explain how convection currents in the mantle cause lithospheric plates to move causing fast changes like earthquakes and volcanic eruptions and slow changes like creation of mountains and formation of new ocean floor.

7.NS.8 Analyze data, using appropriate mathematical manipulation as required, and use it to identify patterns and make inferences based on these patterns.

How Is an Epicenter Located?

When an earthquake occurs, geologists try to pinpoint the earthquake's epicenter. Why? Locating the epicenter helps geologists identify areas where earthquakes may occur in the future. 🔑 **Geologists use seismic waves to locate an earthquake's epicenter.** To do this, they use data from thousands of seismograph stations set up all over the world. However, you can use a simpler method to find an earthquake's epicenter.

Recall that seismic waves travel at different speeds. P waves arrive at a seismograph first. Then S waves follow close behind. Look at the graph, P and S Waves, below. Suppose you know when P waves arrived at a seismograph after an earthquake, and when S waves arrived. You can read the graph to find the distance from the seismograph to the epicenter. Notice that the farther away an earthquake is from a given point, the greater the time between the arrival of the P waves and the S waves.

Suppose you know the distance of three seismograph stations from an epicenter. You can then draw three circles to locate the epicenter. Look at **Figure 5**. The center of each circle is a particular seismograph's location. The radius of each circle is the distance from that seismograph to the epicenter. The point where the three circles intersect is the location of the epicenter.

do the math!

Seismic Wave Speeds

Seismographs at five observation stations recorded the arrival times of the P and S waves produced by an earthquake. These data were used to draw the graph.

1 **Read Graphs** What variable is shown on the x-axis of the graph? What variable is shown on the y-axis?

_____

2 **Estimate** How long did it take the S waves to travel 2,000 km?

_____

3 **Estimate** How long did it take the P waves to travel 2,000 km?

_____

4 **Calculate** What is the difference in the arrival times of the P waves and the S waves at 2,000 km? At 4,000 km?

_____

_____

P and S Waves

7.NS.8

FIGURE 5 ·············

Determining an Earthquake's Epicenter

The map shows how to find the epicenter of an earthquake using data from three seismographic stations. ✏ **Interpret Maps** Suppose a fourth seismographic station is located in San Diego. What was the approximate difference in arrival times of P and S waves here?

_____

7.NS.8

Hint: Use the map scale to determine how far San Diego is from the epicenter. Then, use the graph on the previous page to find your answer.

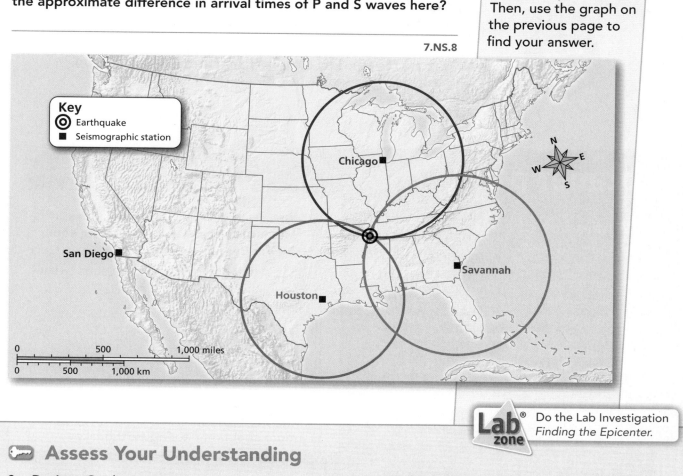

Do the Lab Investigation
Finding the Epicenter.

🔑 Assess Your Understanding

3a. Review Geologists use _____ to locate an earthquake's epicenter.

7.2.4

b. Identify What can geologists measure to tell how far an earthquake's epicenter is from a particular seismograph?

_____

_____

7.2.4

c. Apply Concepts Suppose an earthquake occurs somewhere in California. Could a seismograph on Hawaii be used to help locate the epicenter of the earthquake? Why or why not?

_____

_____

_____

_____

7.2.4

got it? ·············

○ **I get it!** Now I know that geologists can locate an earthquake's epicenter by using_____

_____

○ I need extra help with _____

Go to **MY SCIENCE COACH** *online for help with this subject.*

7.2.4

Monitoring Earthquakes

UNLOCK THE BIG ?

🔑 **How Do Seismographs Work?**
7.2.4, 7.NS.8

🔑 **What Patterns Do Seismographic Data Reveal?**
7.2.4, 7.NS.1, 7.NS.8, 7.NS.10

MY PLANET DiARY

Whole Lot of Shaking Going On

Is the ground moving under your school? A project that will monitor shaking underneath the entire nation might help you find out!

In 2004, scientists in the USArray project placed 400 seismographs across the western United States. Every month, 18 seismographs are picked up and moved east, "leapfrogging" the other seismographs. The map below shows one arrangement of the array. The seismic data that are obtained will help scientists learn more about our active Earth!

FUN FACT

✏️ **Communicate** Discuss this question with a group of classmates. Write your answer below.

When the array arrives in your state, what information might it provide?

_____

_____

_____

_____

▶ PLANET DIARY Go to **Planet Diary** to learn more about monitoring earthquakes.

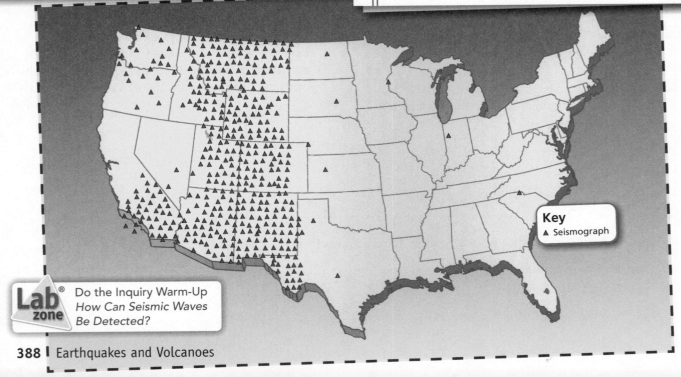

Key
▲ Seismograph

Lab zone Do the Inquiry Warm-Up *How Can Seismic Waves Be Detected?*

Vocabulary
- seismogram

Skills
- ⟳ Reading: Identify the Main Idea
- △ Inquiry: Predict

How Do Seismographs Work?

Today, seismographs are complex electronic devices. Some laptop computers and car air bags contain similar devices that detect shaking. But a simple seismograph, like the one in **Figure 1,** can consist of a heavy weight attached to a frame by a spring or wire. A pen connected to the weight rests its point on a drum that can rotate. As the drum rotates, the pen in effect draws a straight line on paper wrapped tightly around the drum. 🔑 **Seismic waves cause a simple seismograph's drum to vibrate, which in turn causes the pen to record the drum's vibrations.** The suspended weight with the pen attached moves very little. This allows the pen to stay in place and record the drum's vibrations.

Measuring Seismic Waves When you write a sentence, the paper stays in one place while your hand moves the pen. But in a seismograph, it's the pen that remains stationary while the paper moves. Why is this? All seismographs make use of a basic principle of physics: Whether it is moving or at rest, every object resists any change to its motion. A seismograph's heavy weight resists motion during an earthquake. But the rest of the seismograph is anchored to the ground and vibrates when seismic waves arrive.

Academic Standards for Science

7.2.4 Explain how convection currents in the mantle cause lithospheric plates to move causing fast changes like earthquakes and volcanic eruptions and slow changes like creation of mountains and formation of new ocean floor.

7.NS.8 Analyze data, and use it to identify patterns and make inferences.

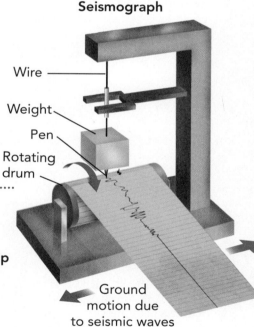

Seismograph

- Wire
- Weight
- Pen
- Rotating drum
- Ground motion due to seismic waves

FIGURE 1 ······

Recording Seismic Waves
In a simple seismograph, a pen attached to a suspended weight records an earthquake's seismic waves.

✎ **Make Models** To mimic the action of a seismograph, hold the tip of a pencil on the right edge of the seismograph paper below. Have a classmate pull the right edge of the book away from your pencil while the classmate also "vibrates" the book side to side.

FIGURE 2 ··································

Seismograms

When an earthquake's seismic waves reach a simple seismograph, the seismograph's drum vibrates. The vibrations are recorded by the seismograph's pen, producing a seismogram, as shown on the top diagram.

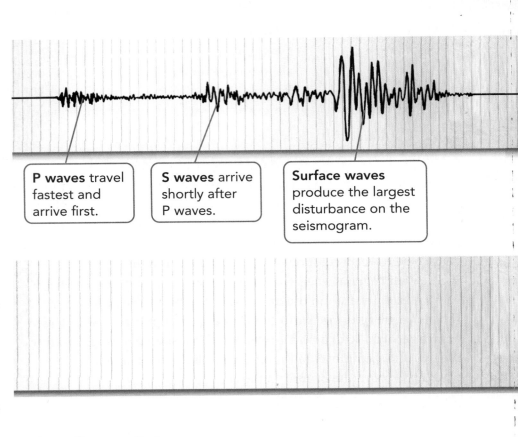

P waves travel fastest and arrive first.

S waves arrive shortly after P waves.

Surface waves produce the largest disturbance on the seismogram.

CHALLENGE An aftershock is a smaller earthquake that occurs after a larger earthquake. Draw the seismogram that might be produced by a seismograph during an earthquake and its aftershock. Label the earthquake and the aftershock.

7.NS.8

Reading a Seismogram You have probably seen the zigzagging lines used to represent an earthquake. The pattern of lines, called a **seismogram,** is the record of an earthquake's seismic waves produced by a seismograph. Study the seismogram in **Figure 2.** Notice when the P waves, S waves, and surface waves arrive. The height of the lines drawn by the seismograph is greater for a more severe earthquake or an earthquake closer to the seismograph.

 Do the Quick Lab
Design a Seismograph.

🔑 Assess Your Understanding

1a. Review The height of the lines on a seismogram is (greater/less) for a stronger earthquake.   7.2.4

b. Interpret Diagrams What do the relatively straight, flat portions of the seismogram at the top of **Figure 2** represent?

_____

_____

_____

_____

7.2.4

got it?

○ **I get it!** Now I know that a simple seismograph works when _____

_____

_____

_____

○ I need extra help with _____

Go to MY SCIENCE ⓢ COACH *online for help with this subject.*   7.2.4

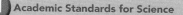

What Patterns Do Seismographic Data Reveal?

Geologists use seismographs to monitor earthquakes. Other devices that geologists use detect slight motions along faults. Yet even with data from many different devices, geologists cannot yet predict when and where an earthquake might strike. **But from past seismographic data, geologists have created maps of where earthquakes occur around the world. The maps show that earthquakes often occur along plate boundaries.** Recall that where plates meet, plate movement stores energy in rock that makes up the crust. This energy is eventually released in an earthquake.

Earthquake Risk in North America Earthquake risk largely depends on how close a given location is to a plate boundary. In the United States, two plates meet along the Pacific coast in California, Washington state, and Alaska, causing many faults. Frequent earthquakes occur in California, where the Pacific plate and the North American plate meet along the San Andreas fault. In Washington, earthquakes result from the subduction of the Juan de Fuca plate beneath the North American plate. Recall that during subduction, one plate is forced down under another plate.

Academic Standards for Science

7.2.4 Explain how convection currents in the mantle cause lithospheric plates to move causing fast changes like earthquakes and volcanic eruptions and slow changes like creation of mountains and formation of new ocean floor.

7.NS.1 Make predictions based on prior knowledge.

7.NS.8 Analyze data, and use it to identify patterns and make inferences.

Identify the Main Idea
Underline the sentence in the second paragraph that describes the main factor in determining earthquake risk for a given location.

apply it!

The map shows areas where serious earthquakes are likely to occur, based on the location of past earthquakes across the United States.

1 Interpret Maps The map indicates that serious earthquakes are most likely to occur (on the east coast/in the midsection/on the west coast) of the United States.

2 Predict Based on the evidence shown in the map, predict where you think plate boundaries lie. Explain your reasoning.

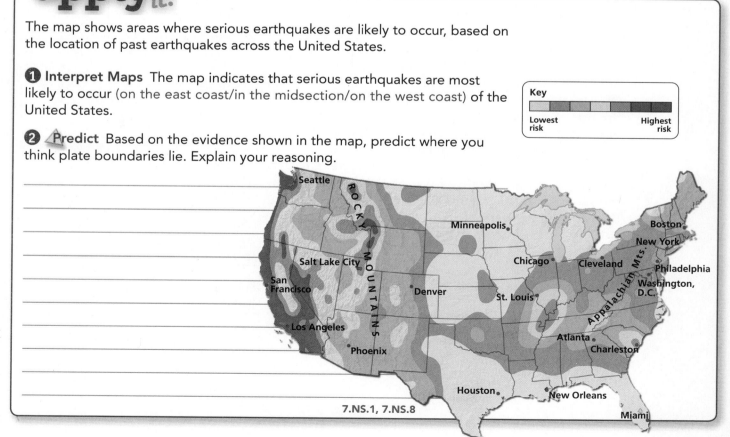

Key

Lowest risk — Highest risk

7.NS.1, 7.NS.8

391

Earthquake Risk Around the World Many of the world's earthquakes occur in a vast area of geologic activity called the Ring of Fire. In this area, plate boundaries form a ring around the Pacific Ocean. Volcanoes as well as earthquakes are common along these boundaries. The Ring of Fire includes the west coast of Central America and the west coast of South America. Strong earthquakes have occurred in countries along these coasts, where plates converge. Across the Pacific Ocean, the Pacific Plate collides with several other plates. Here, Japan, Indonesia, New Zealand, and New Guinea are seismically very active.

India, China, and Pakistan also have been struck by large earthquakes. In this area of the world, the Indo-Australian Plate collides with the Eurasian Plate. Earthquakes are also common where the Eurasian Plate meets the Arabian and African plates.

EXPLORE
THE BIG
?

Earthquakes, Volcanoes, and Plate Tectonics

Why do earthquakes and volcanoes occur more often in some places than in others?

FIGURE 3 ···

▶ **REAL-WORLD INQUIRY** Earthquakes Around the World

Earthquakes are closely linked to plate tectonics. The map shows where past earthquakes have occurred in relation to plate boundaries.

✎ **Make Judgments** Draw an outline tracing the plate boundaries that make up the Ring of Fire. Then, look at North America. Draw a star where buildings should be built to withstand earthquakes. Put an X where there is less need to design buildings to withstand strong shaking. Do the same for another continent (not Antarctica). Explain your answers.

_____

_____

_____

_____

_____

_____

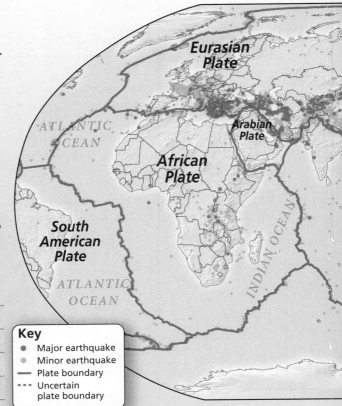

Key
- ● Major earthquake
- ● Minor earthquake
- — Plate boundary
- --- Uncertain plate boundary

7.NS.8

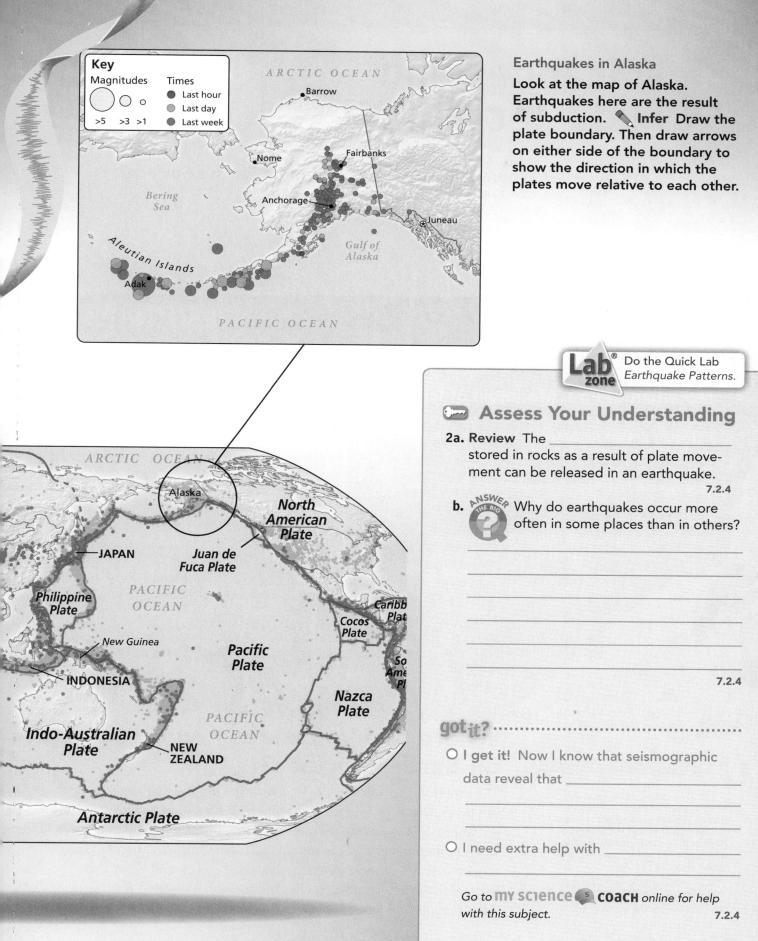

Key

Magnitudes

>5 >3 >1

Times

- Last hour
- Last day
- Last week

ARCTIC OCEAN

Barrow

Nome

Fairbanks

Anchorage

Juneau

Bering Sea

Gulf of Alaska

Aleutian Islands

Adak

PACIFIC OCEAN

ARCTIC OCEAN

Alaska

North American Plate

JAPAN

Juan de Fuca Plate

Philippine Plate

PACIFIC OCEAN

New Guinea

Caribb Plat

Cocos Plate

INDONESIA

Pacific Plate

So Ame Pl

Nazca Plate

PACIFIC OCEAN

Indo-Australian Plate

NEW ZEALAND

Antarctic Plate

Earthquakes in Alaska

Look at the map of Alaska. Earthquakes here are the result of subduction. ✎ **Infer** Draw the plate boundary. Then draw arrows on either side of the boundary to show the direction in which the plates move relative to each other.

Lab zone Do the Quick Lab *Earthquake Patterns.*

🔑 Assess Your Understanding

2a. Review The _____ stored in rocks as a result of plate movement can be released in an earthquake.

7.2.4

b. ANSWER THE BIG ❓ Why do earthquakes occur more often in some places than in others?

_____

_____

_____

_____

_____

_____

7.2.4

got it? ....

○ **I get it!** Now I know that seismographic data reveal that _____

_____

_____

○ **I need extra help with** _____

_____

Go to **MY SCIENCE** Ⓢ **COACH** online for help with this subject.

7.2.4

393

Volcanoes and Plate Tectonics

LESSON 4

UNLOCK THE BIG ?

🔑 **Where Are Volcanoes Found on Earth's Surface?**

7.2.4, 7.NS.1, 7.NS.8

my planet diary

Mountain of Fire, Mountain of Ice

Climbers who struggle up the snow-packed slopes of Mount Erebus on Antarctica may be in for an unpleasant surprise. Balls of scorching molten rock three meters across might come hurtling out of the air and land just steps from climbers' feet! Why? Because Mount Erebus is one of Earth's southernmost volcanoes.

Scientists believe that Mount Erebus lies over an area where material from Earth's mantle rises and then melts. The melted material reaches the surface at Mount Erebus.

FIELD TRIP

Read the text and then answer the question.

How did Mount Erebus form?

_____

_____

_____

_____

_____

_____

▷ PLANET DIARY Go to **Planet Diary** to learn more about volcanoes.

Lab zone® Do the Inquiry Warm-Up *Moving Volcanoes.*

🇮🇳 **Academic Standards for Science**

7.2.4 Explain how convection currents in the mantle cause lithospheric plates to move causing fast changes like earthquakes and volcanic eruptions and slow changes like creation of mountains and formation of new ocean floor.

7.NS.1 Make predictions based on research and prior knowledge.

7.NS.8 Analyze data.

Where Are Volcanoes Found on Earth's Surface?

The eruption of a volcano can be awe-inspiring. Molten material can be spewed high into the atmosphere. Villages can be buried in volcanic ash. A **volcano** is a mountain that forms in Earth's crust when molten material, or magma, reaches the surface. **Magma** is a molten mixture of rock-forming substances, gases, and water from the mantle. When magma reaches the surface, it is called **lava.** After magma and lava cool, they form solid rock.

Vocabulary
- volcano
- magma
- lava
- Ring of Fire
- island arc
- hot spot

Skills
↪ **Reading:** Relate Text and Visuals
△ **Inquiry:** Develop Hypotheses

Volcanoes and Plate Boundaries Are volcanoes found randomly across Earth? No, in general, volcanoes form a regular pattern on Earth. To understand why, look at the map in **Figure 1.** Notice how volcanoes occur in many great, long belts. 🗝 **Volcanic belts form along the boundaries of Earth's plates.**

Volcanoes can occur where two plates pull apart, or diverge. Here, plate movements cause the crust to fracture. The fractures in the crust allow magma to reach the surface. Volcanoes can also occur where two plates push together, or converge. As the plates push together, one plate can sink beneath the other plate. Water that is brought down with the sinking plate eventually helps to form magma, which rises to the surface.

The **Ring of Fire,** shown in **Figure 1,** is one major belt of volcanoes. It includes the many volcanoes that rim the Pacific Ocean. The Ring of Fire includes the volcanoes along the coasts of North and South America and those in Japan and the Philippines.

↪ **Relate Text and Visuals**
Volcanoes often form belts along plate boundaries. How does **Figure 1** illustrate that this statement holds true for North America?

_____

_____

_____

_____

_____

_____

FIGURE 1 ···

The Ring of Fire
The Ring of Fire is a belt of volcanoes that circles the Pacific Ocean. As with most of Earth's volcanoes, these volcanoes form along boundaries of tectonic plates.

△ **Develop Hypotheses** Circle a volcano on the map that does not fall along a plate boundary. Why did this volcano form here? Write your answer below. Revise your answer after finishing the lesson.

Original Hypothesis: _____

_____

_____

_____

Revised Hypothesis: _____

_____

_____

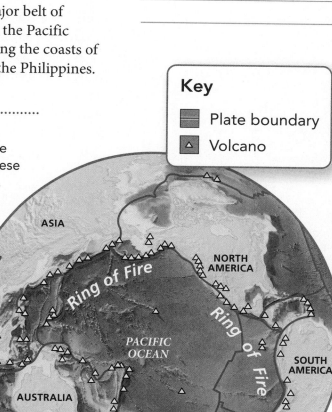

Key
▬ Plate boundary
△ Volcano

ASIA
NORTH AMERICA
Ring of Fire
PACIFIC OCEAN
Ring of Fire
SOUTH AMERICA
AUSTRALIA
△ Mt. Erebus
ANTARCTICA

7.NS.1

FIGURE 2 ....

▶ ART IN MOTION

Volcanoes and Converging Boundaries

Volcanoes often form where two plates collide.

✎ **Compare and Contrast** Shade the arrows to show the direction of plate movement. Then compare and contrast the ways volcanoes form at A and B.

_____

_____

_____

_____

_____

_____

_____

_____

_____

_____

_____

Diverging Boundaries Volcanoes form along the mid-ocean ridges, where two plates move apart. Mid-ocean ridges form long, underwater mountain ranges that sometimes have a rift valley down their center. Along the rift valley, lava pours out of cracks in the ocean floor. This process gradually builds new mountains. Volcanoes also form along diverging plate boundaries on land. For example, large volcanoes are found along the Great Rift Valley in East Africa.

Converging Boundaries Many volcanoes form near converging plate boundaries, where two oceanic plates collide. Through subduction, the older, denser plate sinks into the mantle and creates a deep-ocean trench. Water in the sinking plate eventually leaves the crust and rises into the wedge of the mantle above it. As a result, the melting point of the mantle in the wedge is lowered. So, the mantle partially melts. The magma that forms as a result rises up. This magma can break through the ocean floor, creating volcanoes.

The resulting volcanoes sometimes create a string of islands called an **island arc.** Look at **Figure 2.** The curve of an island arc echoes the curve of its deep-ocean trench. Major island arcs include Japan, New Zealand, the Aleutians, and the Caribbean islands.

Volcanoes also occur where an oceanic plate is subducted beneath a continental plate. Collisions of this type produced the volcanoes of the Andes Mountains in South America. In the United States, plate collisions also produced the volcanoes of the Pacific Northwest, including Mount St. Helens and Mount Rainier.

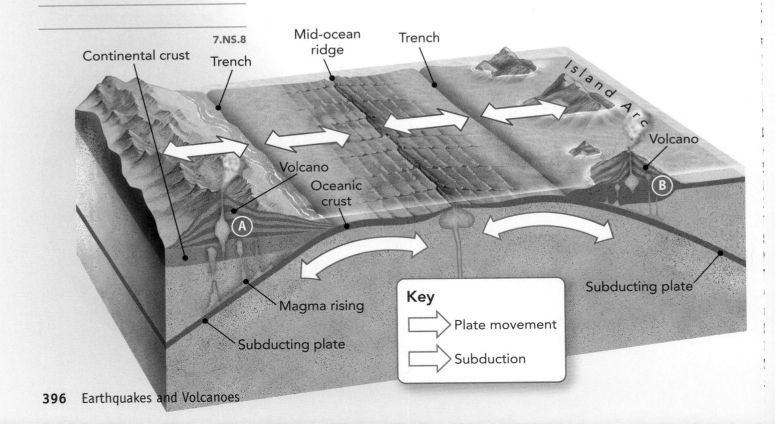

7.NS.8

Continental crust · Trench · Mid-ocean ridge · Trench · Island Arc · Volcano · Volcano · Oceanic crust · B · A · Magma rising · Subducting plate

Key
⇨ Plate movement
⇨ Subduction

Hot Spots Not all volcanoes form along plate boundaries. Some volcanoes are the result of "hot spots" in Earth's mantle. A **hot spot** is an area where material from deep within Earth's mantle rises through the crust and melts to form magma. 🔑 **A volcano forms above a hot spot when magma erupts through the crust and reaches the surface.** Hot spots stay in one place for many millions of years while the plate moves over them. Some hot spot volcanoes lie close to plate boundaries. Others lie in the middle of plates. Yellowstone National Park in Wyoming marks a huge hot spot under the North American plate.

apply it!

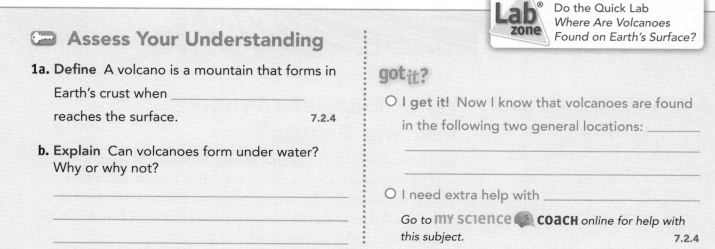

The Hawaiian Islands have formed one by one as the Pacific plate drifts slowly over a hot spot. This process has taken millions of years.

❶ The hot spot is currently forming volcanic mountains on the island of (Oahu/Maui/Hawaii).

❷ Do you think Maui will erupt again? Why or why not?

_____

_____

❸ **CHALLENGE** Which island is older—Kauai or Maui? Why?

_____

_____

_____

_____

7.NS.1

🔑 Assess Your Understanding

1a. Define A volcano is a mountain that forms in Earth's crust when _____ reaches the surface.   7.2.4

b. Explain Can volcanoes form under water? Why or why not?

_____

_____

_____

7.2.4

Lab zone® Do the Quick Lab *Where Are Volcanoes Found on Earth's Surface?*

got it?

○ **I get it!** Now I know that volcanoes are found in the following two general locations: _____

_____

_____

○ **I need extra help with** _____

Go to MY SCIENCE Ⓢ COACH *online for help with this subject.*   7.2.4

LESSON

5 Volcanic Eruptions

UNLOCK THE BIG ?

🔑 **What Happens When a Volcano Erupts?**
7.2.4, 7.NS.8

🔑 **What Are the Stages of Volcanic Activity?**
7.2.4, 7.NS.1, 7.NS.8

MY PLANET DIARY

FUN FACTS

Hotheaded!

Can lava look like hair from the top of your head? It often does in Hawaii! Here, hikers may come across thin strands of hardened material that shimmer like gold in the sunlight. These thin strands are Pele's hair (PAY layz). Pele is the Hawaiian goddess of volcanoes and fire. Her "hair" is actually volcanic glass! It forms when tiny drops of molten lava fly into the air. The wind stretches these drops into threads that are as thin as hair. The glass strands then settle in crevices in the ground, forming clumps.

Read the text. Then answer the question.
How does Pele's hair form?

_____

_____

_____

_____

_____

> PLANET DIARY Go to **Planet Diary** to learn more about lava.

Lab zone® Do the Inquiry Warm-Up
How Fast Do Liquids Flow?

Academic Standards for Science

7.2.4 Explain how convection currents in the mantle cause lithospheric plates to move causing fast changes like earthquakes and volcanic eruptions and slow changes like creation of mountains and formation of new ocean floor.

7.NS.8 Analyze data.

What Happens When a Volcano Erupts?

Lava begins as magma. Magma usually forms in the somewhat soft layer of hot, solid rock that lies in the upper mantle, just below a layer of harder rock. The magma is less dense than the material that is around it. So it rises into any cracks in the rock above. If this magma reaches the surface, a volcano can form.

Vocabulary
- magma chamber • pipe • vent • lava flow • crater
- silica • pyroclastic flow • dormant • extinct

Skills
Reading: Outline

Inquiry: Communicate

Inside a Volcano A volcano is more than a large, cone-shaped mountain. Inside a volcano is a system of passageways through which magma moves, as shown in **Figure 1.**

- **Magma chamber** All volcanoes have a pocket of magma beneath the surface. Beneath a volcano, magma collects in a **magma chamber.** During an eruption, the magma forces its way through one or more cracks in Earth's crust.
- **Pipe** Magma moves upward through a **pipe,** a long tube that extends from Earth's crust up through the top of the volcano, connecting the magma chamber to Earth's surface.
- **Vent** Molten rock and gas leave the volcano through an opening called a **vent.** Some volcanoes have a single central vent at the top. But volcanoes often have vents on the sides also.
- **Lava flow** A **lava flow** is the spread of lava as it pours out of a vent.
- **Crater** A **crater** is a bowl-shaped area that may form at the top of a volcano around the central vent.

Vocabulary High-Use Academic Words A system is a group of parts that function as a whole. Describe why a volcano might be considered a system.

_____

_____

_____

_____

_____

FIGURE 1 ·······························

Inside a Volcano
A volcano is made up of many different parts.

Identify Place each word in its proper place in the diagram.

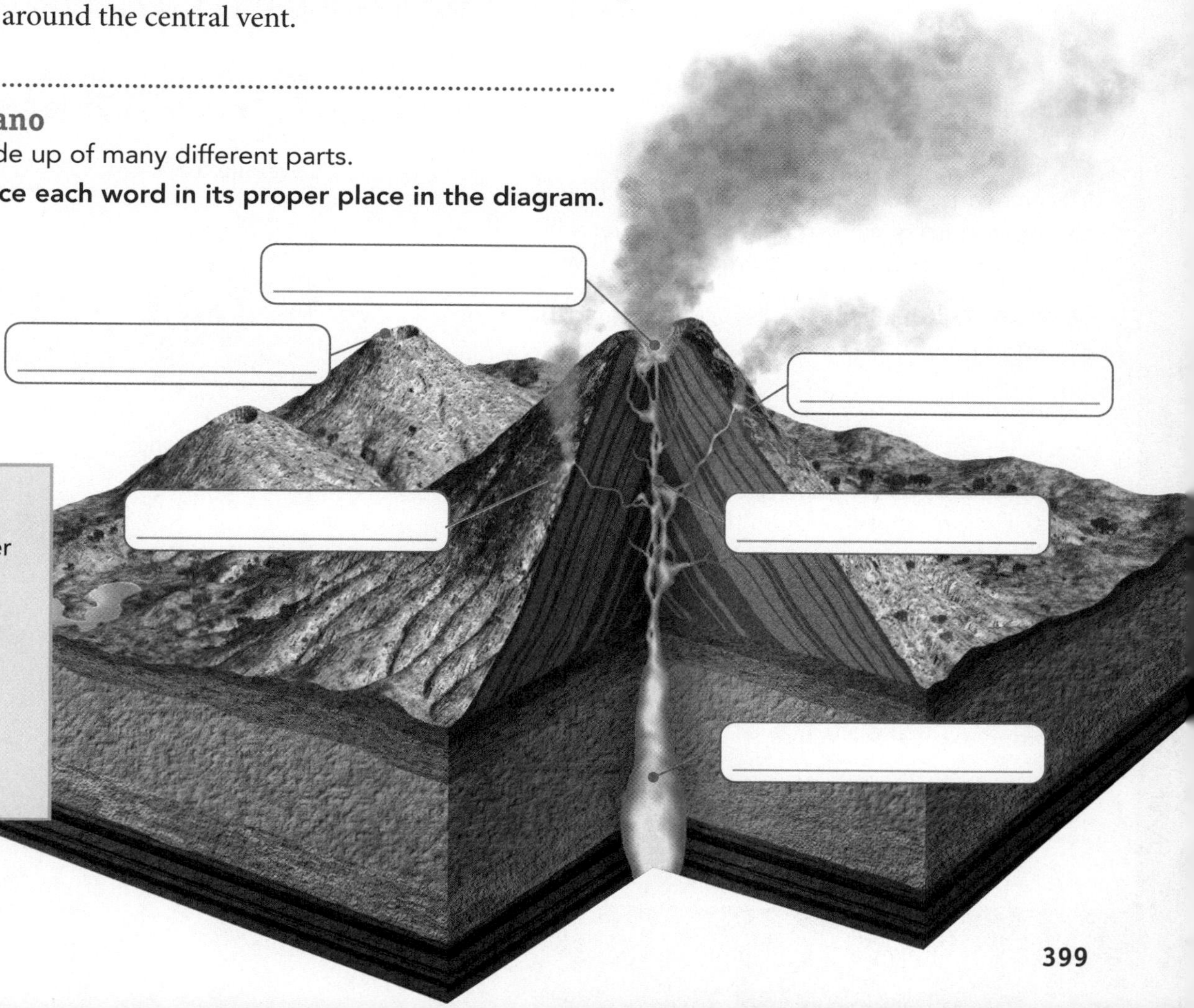

Word Bank

Magma chamber

Pipe

Central vent

Side vent

Lava flow

Crater

399

A Volcanic Eruption

Perhaps you know that dissolved carbon dioxide gas is trapped in every can of soda. But did you know that dissolved gases are trapped in magma? These dissolved gases are under great pressure. During an eruption, as magma rises toward the surface, the pressure of the surrounding rock on the magma decreases. The dissolved gases begin to expand, forming bubbles. These bubbles are much like the bubbles in the soda can. As pressure falls within the magma, the size of the gas bubbles increases greatly. These expanding gases exert great force. **When a volcano erupts, the force of the expanding gases pushes magma from the magma chamber through the pipe until it flows or explodes out of the vent.** Once magma escapes from the volcano and becomes lava, the remaining gases bubble out.

Two Types of Volcanic Eruptions

Some volcanic eruptions occur gradually, over days, months, or even years. Others are great explosions. **Geologists classify volcanic eruptions as quiet or explosive.** Whether an eruption is quiet or explosive depends in part on the magma's silica content and whether the magma is thin and runny or thick and sticky. **Silica** is a material found in magma that forms from the elements oxygen and silicon. Temperature also helps determine how fluid, or runny, magma is.

did you know?

Stromboli volcano lies on an island off the coast of Italy. The volcano has been erupting almost constantly for at least 2,400 years! Expanding gases dissolved in magma cause the eruption to be nearly constant.

do the math!

Magma Composition

Magma varies in composition. It is classified according to the amount of silica it contains. The less silica that the magma contains, the more easily it flows.

1 Read Graphs What materials make up both types of magma?

_____

2 Read Graphs Which type of magma has more silica? How much silica does this magma contain?

_____

_____

3 [CHALLENGE] Which of these magmas do you think might erupt in a dramatic explosion? Why?

_____

_____

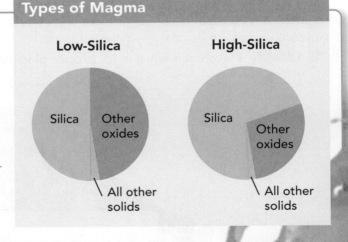

Types of Magma

Low-Silica

Silica | Other oxides

All other solids

High-Silica

Silica | Other oxides

All other solids

7.NS.8

Quiet Eruptions A volcano erupts quietly if its magma is hot or low in silica. Hot, low-silica magma is thin and runny and flows easily. The gases in the magma bubble out gently. Low-silica lava oozes quietly from the vent and can flow for many kilometers.

Quiet eruptions can produce different types of lava, as shown in **Figure 2.** The different types of lava harden into different types of rock. Pahoehoe (pah HOH ee hoh ee) forms from fast-moving, hot lava that is thin and runny. The surface of pahoehoe looks like a solid mass of ropelike coils. Aa (AH ah) forms from lava that is cooler and thicker. The lava that aa forms from is also slower-moving. Aa has a rough surface consisting of jagged lava chunks.

Mostly quiet eruptions formed the Hawaiian Islands. On the island of Hawaii, lava pours from the crater near the top of Kilauea. Lava also flows out of long cracks on the volcano's sides. In general, the temperature of magma and lava can range from about 750°C to 1175°C—hot enough to melt copper! Quiet eruptions have built up the island of Hawaii over hundreds of thousands of years.

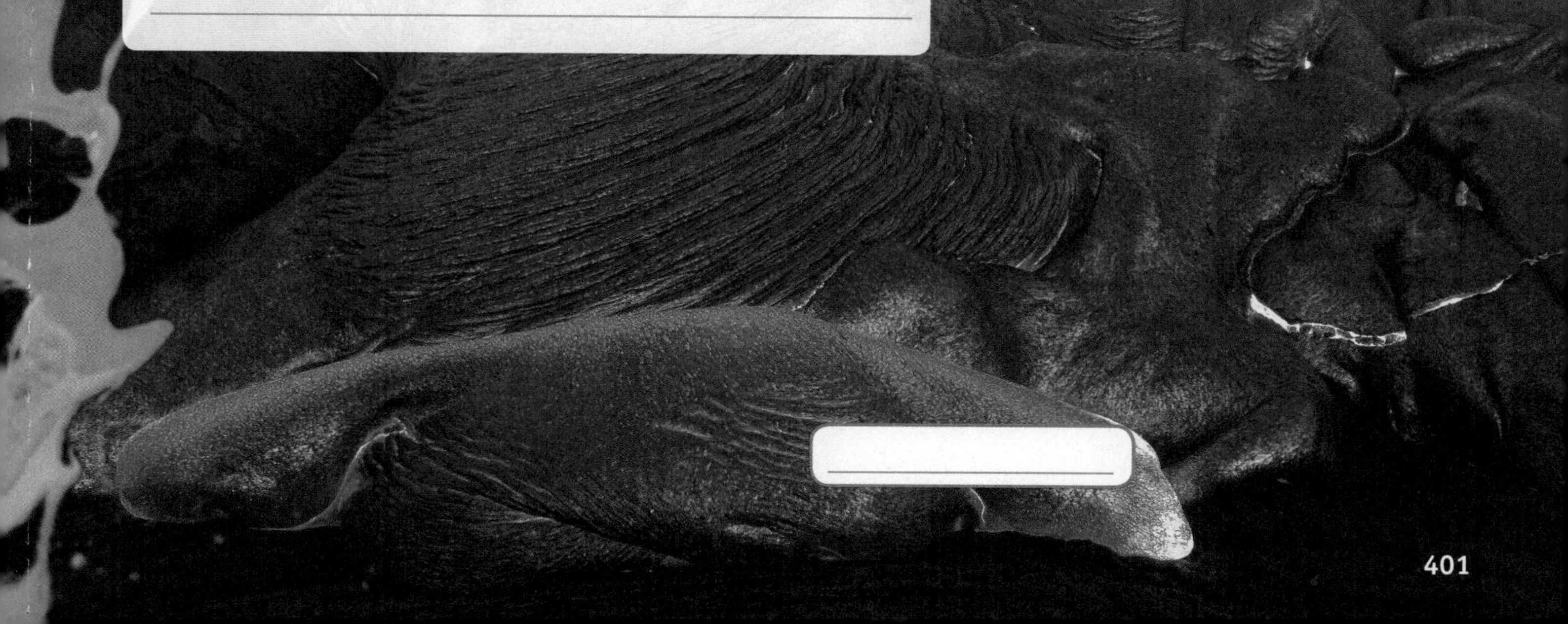

FIGURE 2 ···
Lava From Quiet Eruptions
Quiet eruptions can produce two different types of lava.

✎ **Interpret Photographs** Which lava is hardening to form aa? Which is hardening to form pahoehoe? Write your answers in the spaces provided. Then, in your own words, describe the texture of each type of rock.

_____

_____

_____

_____

_____

_____

Outline Review the text on this page and on the previous page. Then complete the following outline.

Types of Volcanic Eruptions

1. Quiet eruption

   a. Kilauea

   b. _____

2. Explosive eruption

   a. _____

   b. High-silica magma

Explosive Eruptions A volcano erupts explosively if its magma is high in silica. High-silica magma is thick and sticky. This type of magma can build up in the volcano's pipe, plugging it like a cork in a bottle. Dissolved gases, including water vapor, cannot escape from the thick magma. The trapped gases build up pressure until they explode. The erupting gases and steam push the magma out of the volcano with incredible force. That's what happened during the eruption of Mount St. Helens in Washington State. This eruption is shown in **Figure 3.**

An explosive eruption throws lava powerfully into the air where it breaks into fragments that quickly cool and harden into pieces of different sizes. The smallest pieces are volcanic ash. Volcanic ash is made up of fine, rocky particles as small as a speck of dust. Pebble-sized particles are called cinders. Larger pieces, called bombs, may range from the size of a golf ball to the size of a car.

FIGURE 3 ·······························

What a Blast!

The explosive eruption of Mount St. Helens in 1980 blew off the top of the mountain.

Explain Read the text in this section. In your own words, explain how dissolved gases caused Mount St. Helens to erupt explosively.

_____

_____

_____

_____

_____

_____

_____

_____

Before 1980 eruption

During 1980 eruption

After 1980 eruption

Volcano Hazards Both quiet eruptions and explosive eruptions can cause damage far from a crater's rim. For example, during a quiet eruption, lava flows from vents, setting fire to, and often burying, everything in its path. A quiet eruption can cover large areas with a thick layer of lava.

During an explosive eruption, a volcano can belch out a mixture of dangerous materials such as hot rock and ash. This mixture of materials can form a fast-moving cloud that rushes down the sides of the volcano. A **pyroclastic flow** (py roh KLAS tik) is the mixture of hot gases, ash, cinders, and bombs that flow down the sides of a volcano when it erupts explosively. Landslides of mud, melted snow, and rock can also form from an explosive eruption. **Figure 4** shows one result of an explosive eruption.

FIGURE 4 ··

Volcano Hazards
In 1991, Mount Pinatubo in the Philippines erupted explosively.

Communicate What hazards did Mount Pinatubo present to towns near the volcano? Consider the effects of lava, ash, and gases. Work in a small group. List your answers here.

_____

_____

_____

_____

_____

_____

_____

_____

Do the Lab
Investigation
Gelatin Volcanoes.

🔑 Assess Your Understanding

1a. Review Two types of volcanic eruptions are

_____

7.2.4

b. Infer Some volcanoes have great glaciers on their slopes. Why might these glaciers be a hazard if a volcano erupts?

_____

_____

_____

_____

7.2.4

got it?

○ **I get it!** Now I know that when a volcano erupts, the force of the expanding gases

_____

_____

○ **I need extra help with** _____

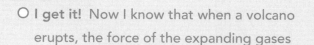

Go to MY SCIENCE ⓢ COACH *online for help with this subject.*

7.2.4

Academic Standards for Science

7.2.4 Explain how convection currents in the mantle cause lithospheric plates to move causing fast changes like earthquakes and volcanic eruptions and slow changes like creation of mountains and formation of new ocean floor.

7.NS.1 Make predictions and develop testable questions based on research and prior knowledge.

7.NS.8 Analyze data, and use it to identify patterns and make inferences.

What Are the Stages of Volcanic Activity?

The activity of a volcano may last from less than a decade to more than 10 million years. But most long-lived volcanoes do not erupt continuously. You can see the pattern of activity by looking at the eruptions of volcanoes in the Cascade Range, shown in **Figure 5.** Mount Jefferson has not erupted in at least 15,000 years. Will it ever erupt again? 🔑 **Geologists often use the terms active, dormant, or extinct to describe a volcano's stage of activity.**

An active, or live, volcano is one that is erupting or has shown signs that it may erupt in the near future. A **dormant,** or sleeping, volcano is a volcano that scientists expect to awaken in the future and become active. An **extinct,** or dead, volcano is a volcano that is unlikely to ever erupt again. For example, hot-spot volcanoes may become extinct after they drift away from the hot spot.

Changes in activity in and around a volcano may give warning shortly before a volcano erupts. Geologists use special instruments to detect these changes. For example, tiltmeters can detect slight surface changes in elevation and tilt caused by magma moving underground. Geologists can also monitor gases escaping from the volcano. They monitor the many small earthquakes that occur around a volcano before an eruption. The upward movement of magma triggers these earthquakes. Also, rising temperatures in underground water may signal that magma is nearing the surface.

FIGURE 5 ···

Cascade Volcanoes

The Cascade volcanoes have formed as the Juan de Fuca plate sinks beneath the North American plate.

✏️ **Develop Hypotheses** Answer the questions.

1. Circle the three volcanoes that appear to be the most active.

2. Why might geologists still consider Mount Jefferson to be an active volcano?

_____

_____

7.NS.8

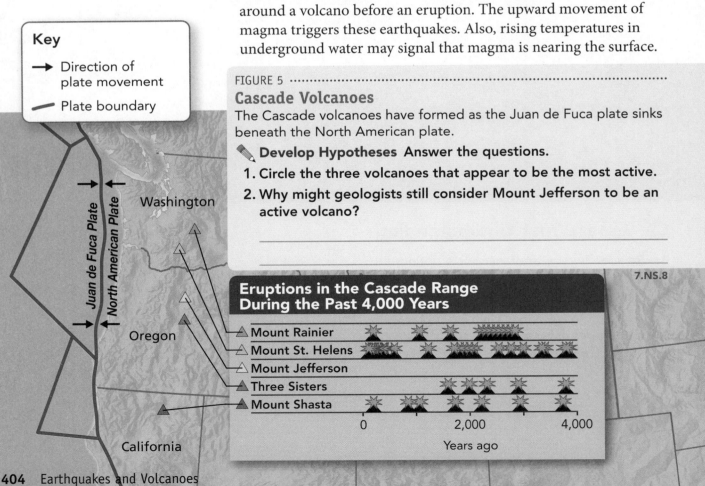

Key

→ Direction of plate movement

— Plate boundary

Juan de Fuca Plate

North American Plate

Washington

Oregon

California

Eruptions in the Cascade Range During the Past 4,000 Years

Mount Rainier
Mount St. Helens
Mount Jefferson
Three Sisters
Mount Shasta

0   2,000   4,000

Years ago

MT. RAINIER

How does a volcano erupt?

FIGURE 6 ···

>> REAL-WORLD INQUIRY Mount Rainier

Mount Rainier is part of the Cascade volcanoes. All past eruptions of Mount Rainier have included ash and lava.

Magma at Mount Rainier

60% Silica

40% Other material

North American plate

Seattle

Mount Rainier

Juan de Fuca plate

✎ **Predict** How might Mount Rainier erupt in the future? Use the information given here. Include the role of plate tectonics in your answer. Also discuss Mount Rainier's history and its current stage of activity. (*Hint:* Look at Figure 5.)

_____

_____

_____

_____

_____

_____

_____

_____

_____

_____

_____

_____

7.NS.1

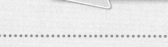

Lab® zone Do the Quick Lab *Volcanic Stages.*

🔑 Assess Your Understanding

2a. Identify A volcano that is currently erupting is called an (active/dormant/extinct) volcano.

7.2.4

b. How does a volcano erupt?

_____

_____

_____

_____

_____

7.2.4

got it? ·····································

○ I get it! Now I know that the three stages in

the life cycle of a volcano are _____

_____

_____

○ I need extra help with _____

_____

Go to MY SCIENCE ⓢ COACH online for help with this subject.

7.2.4

Volcanic Landforms

UNLOCK
THE BIG
?

🗝 **What Landforms Do Lava and Ash Create?**
7.2.4, 7.NS.1, 7.NS.8

🗝 **What Landforms Does Magma Create?**
7.2.4, 7.NS.5, 7.NS.8

my PLANET DiARY

BLOG

Posted by: Jackson

Location: West Hills, California

I was subjected to the sight of an active, dangerous volcano. We were on Hawaii, in a small aircraft over the Big Island.

The volcano was quite large—maybe a few miles in diameter. Out of the top of this volcano, there was an immense pillar of smoke, being blown out to sea by the Hawaiian winds. Judging by the patterns of the hardened lava on the slopes of the volcano, it was a shield volcano. The whole area was literally oozing with volcanic activity. Quite a few large depressions had formed where presumably there had been a magma pocket that collapsed in on itself.

Answer the questions below.

1. What landforms were created by the volcano that Jackson saw?

_____
_____
_____

2. If you had a chance to visit Hawaii, would you prefer to see a volcano from an airplane or from the ground? Explain.

_____
_____
_____
_____

> PLANET DIARY Go to **Planet Diary** to learn more about volcanic landforms.

Lab zone® Do the Inquiry Warm-Up *How Do Volcanoes Change Land?*

Vocabulary

- caldera • cinder cone • composite volcano
- shield volcano • volcanic neck • dike • sill
- batholith

Skills

↪ Reading: Relate Cause and Effect

△ Inquiry: Predict

What Landforms Do Lava and Ash Create?

Lava has built up much of the islands of Hawaii. In fact, for much of Earth's history, volcanic activity on and beneath Earth's surface has built up Earth's land areas and formed much of the ocean crust. **Volcanic eruptions create landforms made of lava, ash, and other materials. These landforms include shield volcanoes, cinder cone volcanoes, composite volcanoes, and lava plateaus. Other landforms include calderas, which are the huge holes left by the collapse of volcanoes.** A caldera is shown in **Figure 1**.

Academic Standards for Science

7.2.4 Explain how convection currents in the mantle cause lithospheric plates to move causing fast changes like earthquakes and volcanic eruptions and slow changes like creation of mountains and formation of new ocean floor.

7.NS.1 Make predictions and develop testable questions based on research and prior knowledge.

7.NS.8 Analyze data.

FIGURE 1 ·····························
How a Caldera Forms
Crater Lake in Oregon fills an almost circular caldera.

✏ **Interpret Diagrams** In your own words, describe what is happening in the sequence of diagrams below.

7.NS.8

Calderas

Large eruptions can empty the main vent and magma chamber beneath a volcano. With nothing to support it, the mountain top may collapse inward. A **caldera** (kal DAIR uh) is the hole left when a volcano collapses. A lake can form, filling the hole. If the volcano erupts again, a steep-walled cone may form in the middle.

407

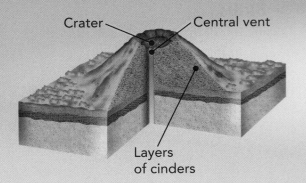

Crater — Central vent

Layers
of cinders

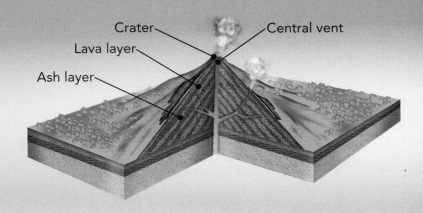

Crater — Central vent
Lava layer
Ash layer

Cinder Cone Volcanoes

If a volcano's magma has high silica content, it will be thick and sticky. So the volcano can erupt explosively, producing ash, cinders, and bombs. These materials can build up around the vent in a steep, cone-shaped hill or small mountain that is called a **cinder cone.** For example, Paricutín in Mexico erupted in 1943 in a farmer's cornfield. The volcano built up a cinder cone that was about 400 meters high.

Composite Volcanoes

Sometimes, the silica content of magma can vary. So eruptions of lava flows alternate with explosive eruptions of ash, cinder, and bombs. The result is a composite volcano. **Composite volcanoes** are tall, cone-shaped mountains in which layers of lava alternate with layers of ash. Mount Fuji in Japan and Mount St. Helens in Washington State are composite volcanoes. Composite volcanoes can be more than 4,800 meters tall.

FIGURE 2 ···

Volcanic Mountains

Lava from volcanoes cools and hardens to form lava plateaus and three types of mountains.

✎ **Read the text at the top of these two pages. Then answer the questions.**

1. **Classify** Identify the type of volcanic landform shown in each of the two photographs at the right.

2. CHALLENGE Use the graphic organizer to compare and contrast two types of volcanoes.

	Volcano Type: _____	Volcano Type: _____
Typical size		
Shape		
How the volcano forms		

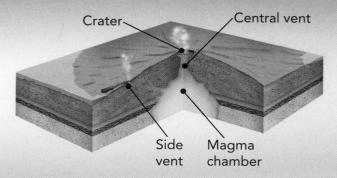

Crater — Central vent

Side vent — Magma chamber

Fissures — New lava layer

Lava layers

Shield Volcanoes

At some spots on Earth's surface, thin layers of lava pour out of a vent and harden on top of previous layers. Such lava flows slowly build a wide, gently sloping mountain called a **shield volcano.** Hot spot volcanoes that form on the ocean floor are usually shield volcanoes. For example, in Hawaii, Mauna Loa rises 9,000 meters from the ocean floor!

Lava Plateaus

Lava can flow out of several long cracks in an area. The thin, runny lava floods the area and travels far before cooling and solidifying. After millions of years, repeated floods of lava can form high, level plateaus. These plateaus are called lava plateaus. The Columbia Plateau is a lava plateau that covers parts of Washington State, Oregon, and Idaho.

apply it!

The Hawaiian Islands are very fertile, or able to support plant growth. In fact, many areas near volcanoes have rich, fertile soil. The rich soil forms after hard lava and ash break down. The ash releases substances that plants need to grow.

❶  **Predict** What type of industry might you expect to find on land near volcanoes?

_____

7.NS.1

❷ **Analyze Costs and Benefits** Lava flows could force people to flee their homes on the island of Hawaii. But in 2006, sales from crops on the island totaled over $153 million. Are the risks worth the rewards? Explain.

_____

_____

_____

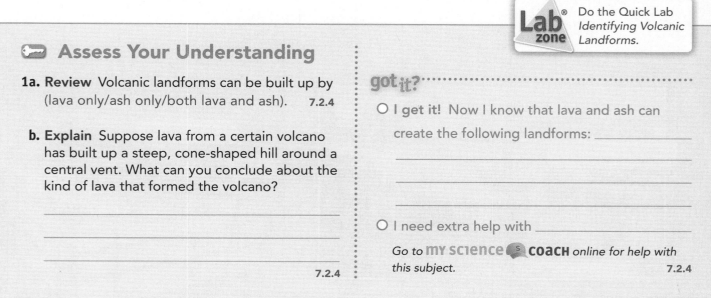

Lab zone ® Do the Quick Lab *Identifying Volcanic Landforms.*

🔑 Assess Your Understanding

1a. Review Volcanic landforms can be built up by (lava only/ash only/both lava and ash). **7.2.4**

b. Explain Suppose lava from a certain volcano has built up a steep, cone-shaped hill around a central vent. What can you conclude about the kind of lava that formed the volcano?

_____

_____

_____

7.2.4

got it?

○ **I get it!** Now I know that lava and ash can create the following landforms: _____

_____

_____

○ **I need extra help with** _____

Go to MY SCIENCE ⑤ COACH *online for help with this subject.* 7.2.4

Academic Standards for Science

7.2.4 Explain how convection currents in the mantle cause lithospheric plates to move causing fast changes like earthquakes and volcanic eruptions and slow changes like creation of mountains and formation of new ocean floor.

7.NS.5 Use principals of accuracy when making measurements.

7.NS.8 Analyze data, using appropriate mathematical manipulation as required, and use it to identify patterns and make inferences base on these patterns.

Relate Cause and Effect

What type of landform can be created when magma hardens in a volcano's pipe?

○ Sill

○ Dike

○ Volcanic neck

What Landforms Does Magma Create?

Sometimes magma cools and hardens into rock before reaching the surface. Over time, forces such as flowing water, ice, or wind may strip away the layers above the hardened magma and expose it. **Features formed by magma include volcanic necks, dikes, and sills, as well as dome mountains and batholiths.**

Volcanic Necks Look at **Figure 3.** The landform that looks like a giant tooth stuck in the ground is Shiprock in New Mexico. Shiprock formed when magma hardened in an ancient volcano's pipe. Later, the softer rock around the pipe wore away, exposing the harder rock inside. A **volcanic neck** forms when magma hardens in a volcano's pipe and the surrounding rock later wears away.

Dikes and Sills Magma that forces itself across rock layers hardens into a **dike.** Magma that squeezes between horizontal rock layers hardens to form a **sill.**

FIGURE 3 ·····

Volcanic Necks, Dikes, and Sills

A dike extends outward from Shiprock, a volcanic neck in New Mexico.

Identify Label the formations. How can you tell which is which?

Volcanic neck

Dike

Sill

CANADA
British Columbia batholith
Idaho batholith
PACIFIC OCEAN
UNITED STATES
Sierra Nevada batholith
Baja batholith

Key
Batholith
0   200 mi
0   200 km

Dome Mountains
Bodies of hardened magma can create dome mountains. A dome mountain forms when uplift pushes a large body of hardened magma toward the surface. The hardened magma forces the layers of rock to bend upward into a dome shape. Eventually, the rock above the dome mountain wears away, leaving it exposed. This process formed the Black Hills in South Dakota.

Batholiths
How large can landforms created by magma be? Look at the map in **Figure 4.** A **batholith** (BATH uh lith) is a mass of rock formed when a large body of magma cools inside the crust. Batholiths form the core of many mountain ranges. Over millions of years, the overlying rock wears away, allowing the batholith to move upward. Flowing water and grinding ice slowly carve the batholith into mountains.

FIGURE 4 ···
Batholiths
Batholiths are common in the western United States. The mountains shown here are part of the Sierra Nevada batholith.

✎ **Measure** About how long is the Sierra Nevada batholith? (*Hint:* Use the map and map key.)

_____

7.NS.5, 7.NS.8

Lab zone®
Do the Quick Lab
How Can Volcanic Activity Change Earth's Surface?

🔑 Assess Your Understanding

2a. Review Dikes and sills are two examples of landforms created when (magma/lava) forces its way through cracks in the upper crust.

7.2.4

b. Identify What feature forms when magma cuts across rock layers?

_____

7.2.4

c. Infer Which is older—a dike or the rock layers the dike cuts across? Explain.

_____

_____

_____

_____

7.2.4

got it? ···

○ **I get it!** Now I know that magma creates landforms such as _____

_____

○ **I need extra help with** _____

Go to **my science** ⓢ **coach** *online for help with this subject.*

7.2.4

11 Study Guide

Earthquakes often occur along _____ , where _____

_____ stores energy in rock that makes up the crust.

LESSON 1 Forces in Earth's Crust
7.2.4, 7.NS.1, 7.NS.11

🔑 Tension, compression, and shearing work over millions of years to change the shape and volume of rock.

🔑 When enough stress builds up in rock, the rock breaks, creating a fault.

🔑 Plate movement can change a flat plain into features such as folds, folded mountains, fault-block mountains, and plateaus.

Vocabulary
- stress • tension • compression • shearing
- normal fault • reverse fault • strike-slip fault
- plateau

LESSON 3 Monitoring Earthquakes
7.2.4, 7.NS.1, 7.NS.8

🔑 Seismic waves cause a simple seismograph's drum to vibrate, which in turn causes the pen to record the drum's vibrations.

🔑 From past seismographic data, geologists have created maps of where earthquakes occur around the world. The maps show that earthquakes often occur along plate boundaries.

Vocabulary
- seismogram

LESSON 5 Volcanic Eruptions
7.2.4, 7.NS.1, 7.NS.8

🔑 When a volcano erupts, the force of the expanding gases pushes magma from the magma chamber through the pipe until it flows or explodes out of the vent.

🔑 Geologists classify volcanic eruptions as quiet or explosive.

🔑 Geologists often use the terms active, dormant, or extinct to describe a volcano's stage of activity.

Vocabulary
- magma chamber • pipe • vent • lava flow
- crater • silica • pyroclastic flow • dormant
- extinct

LESSON 2 Earthquakes and Seismic Waves
7.2.4, 7.NS.8, 7.NS.11

🔑 Seismic waves carry energy produced by an earthquake.

🔑 The amount of earthquake damage or shaking that is felt is rated using the Modified Mercalli scale. An earthquake's magnitude, or size, is measured using the Richter scale or moment magnitude scale.

🔑 Geologists use seismic waves to locate an earthquake's epicenter.

Vocabulary
- earthquake • focus • epicenter • P wave
- S wave • surface wave • seismograph
- Modified Mercalli scale • magnitude
- Richter scale • moment magnitude scale

LESSON 4 Volcanoes and Plate Tectonics
7.2.4, 7.NS.1, 7.NS.8

🔑 Volcanic belts form along the boundaries of Earth's plates.

🔑 A volcano forms above a hot spot when magma erupts through the crust and reaches the surface.

Vocabulary
- volcano • magma • lava • Ring of Fire
- island arc • hot spot

LESSON 6 Volcanic Landforms
7.2.4, 7.NS.1, 7.NS.5, 7.NS.8

🔑 Volcanic eruptions create landforms made of lava, ash, and other materials. These landforms include shield volcanoes, cinder cone volcanoes, composite volcanoes, calderas, and lava plateaus.

🔑 Features formed by magma include volcanic necks, dikes, sills, mountains, and batholiths.

Vocabulary
- caldera • cinder cone • composite volcano
- shield volcano • volcanic neck • dike • sill
- batholith

Review and Assessment

LESSON 1 Forces in Earth's Crust

1. Which force squeezes Earth's crust to make the crust shorter and thicker?

a. tension   **b.** normal

c. shearing   **d.** compression

7.2.4

2. Rocks on either side of a _____ fault slip past each other with little up and down motion.

7.2.4

3. List Give two examples of mountain ranges in the world that have been caused by folding.

_____

_____

_____

7.2.4

LESSON 2 Earthquakes and Seismic Waves

4. Which of these scales rates earthquake damage at a particular location?

a. focus   **b.** Modified Mercalli

c. Richter   **d.** moment magnitude

7.2.4

5. Interpret Diagrams Label the diagram to show the directions an S wave travels and vibrates.

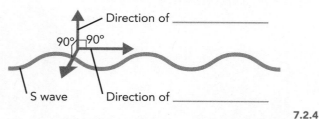

Direction of _____

90°   90°

S wave   Direction of _____

7.2.4

6. math! Seismograph A records P waves at 6:05 P.M. and S waves at 6:10 P.M. Seismograph B records P waves at 6:10 P.M. and S waves at 6:25 P.M. What is the difference in the arrival times at each device? Which device is closer to the earthquake's epicenter?

_____

_____

_____

7.2.4, 7.NS.8

LESSON 3 Monitoring Earthquakes

7. In which type of location is earthquake risk the greatest?

a. at plate centers   **b.** on big plates

c. at plate boundaries   **d.** on small plates

7.2.4

8. **Write About It** There is a high risk of earthquakes along the San Andreas fault in California. What is happening in Earth's crust along the fault to cause this high earthquake risk? Use the theory of plate tectonics in your answer.

7.2.4

LESSON 4 Volcanoes and Plate Tectonics

9. At what point does magma become lava?

a. below a vent   **b.** inside a pipe

c. at Earth's surface   **d.** in Earth's mantle

7.2.4

10. Magma reaches the surface by erupting through a volcano, which is a _____

_____

_____

11. Interpret Diagrams Look at the diagram below. Draw an arrow to indicate the direction of plate movement.

Oceanic plate

Hot spot

7.2.4

LESSON 5 Volcanic Eruptions

12. What type of rock forms from thin and runny, fast-moving lava?

a. pyroclastic   **b.** silica

c. aa   **d.** pahoehoe

7.2.4

13. As magma rises to the surface during an eruption, pressure on the magma decreases, allowing gas bubbles to _____

7.2.4

14. Define What is an extinct volcano?

_____

_____

7.2.4

15. Predict How might a volcano be hazardous for plants and animals that live nearby?

_____

_____

_____

7.2.4, 7.NS.1

LESSON 6 Volcanic Landforms

16. What type of volcanic mountain is composed of layers of lava that alternate with layers of ash?

a. cinder cone   **b.** composite volcano

c. shield volcano   **d.** caldera

7.2.4

17. Sometimes magma creates batholiths, which

are _____

_____

_____

7.2.4

18. Write About It Compare and contrast dikes and sills.

7.2.4, 7.NS.11

APPLY THE BIG ? Why do earthquakes and volcanoes occur more often in some places than in others?

19. An architect is hired to design a skyscraper in the Indonesian city of Jakarta, which is near the Ring of Fire. The architect must follow special building codes that the city has written. What might those codes be for and why are they important in Jakarta?

_____

_____

_____

_____

_____

_____

_____

7.2.4

Indiana ISTEP+ Practice

Multiple Choice

Circle the letter of the best answer.

1. The diagram below shows a mass of rock affected by stress.

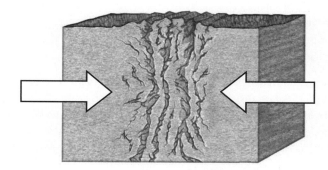

What type of stress process is shown in this diagram?

A. pulling apart   B. tension

C. compression   D. shearing

7.2.4

2. Which of the following landforms is formed by magma?

A. caldera

B. dome mountain

C. cinder cone volcano

D. composite volcano

7.2.4

3. Which scale would a geologist use to estimate the total energy released by an earthquake?

A. Modified Mercalli scale

B. Richter scale

C. epicenter scale

D. moment magnitude scale

7.2.4

4. What do we call a volcano that has not erupted in a long time but that scientists believe may erupt sometime in the future?

A. dormant   B. active

C. extinct   D. island arc

7.2.4

Constructed Response

Write your answer to Question 5 on the lines below.

5. What is the first step in the formation of a hot-spot volcano?

_____

_____

7.2.4

Extended Response

Use the diagram below and your knowledge of science to help you answer Question 6. Write your answer on a separate piece of paper.

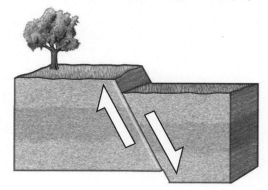

6. Explain the process that forms a normal fault and leads to an earthquake along the fault. Describe the fault, the type of stress that produces it, and events that occur before and during the earthquake.

7.2.4

Congratulations, It's an Island!

On November 15, 1963, a fiery eruption shot out from the icy sea, off the south coast of Iceland, spewing gigantic clouds of ash.

A new island, Surtsey, formed. A volcanic eruption began 130 meters under the sea and forced volcanic ash to the surface. Eventually, the layers of lava and ash formed a volcanic cone that rose above sea level—the birth of Surtsey.

Eruptions continued for nearly four years as steady flows of lava moved outward and cooled in the sea. By the end, Surtsey had an area of 2.7 square kilometers.

It takes a long time for a new island to cool down! At the very base of the island, water flows through layers of loose rocks. When it makes contact with the extremely hot magma chamber deep under the sea, the water evaporates. Steam travels through the layers of porous rock at the base of the island, heating the island up.

To protect Surtsey's environment, the government of Iceland allows only a handful of scientists to visit the delicate new environment. Surtsey is a natural laboratory that gives scientists valuable information on how plant and animal populations begin on a volcanic island.

Research It The arrival of living things on Surtsey is an example of primary succession. Research the organisms that live on Surtsey, or in another area of newly formed lava rock. Make a storyboard showing primary succession on Surtsey or on the area you have researched.

7.NS.2, 7.NS.11

▲ Island of Surtsey today. People are not allowed to live on the island, but scientists who have permission to research there have built a research station.

Volcanologists have a seriously hot job. They investigate how, where, and when volcanoes all over the world erupt. You might find a volcanologist studying on the slopes of Mount St. Helens in Washington State, or investigating the crater of Krakatoa in Indonesia. They also try to predict eruptions.

Volcanologists have to take safety very seriously—after all, they work around actively erupting volcanoes! They have to watch out for volcanic gases and landslides. Volcanology is not all about adventures in the field, though. Volcanologists study Earth sciences, math, and physics in order to understand what they observe in the field. They also spend time writing about what they learn, so that other people can learn from their research.

Research It Research the history of a volcano that has been studied by volcanologists. Based on your research, describe how the volcano has erupted and try to predict if and when it might erupt again.

7.2.3, 7.NS.1, 7.NS2, 7.NS.11

A Dangerous Job

AN EXPLOSIVE SECRET

Scientists once believed that explosive volcanic eruptions could not happen deep under water. Instead, they thought, lava seeped slowly from undersea volcanoes.

But in 2008, scientists found jagged pieces of glassy volcanic rock around undersea volcanoes in the Arctic Ocean. Seeping lava does not cause jagged glassy rocks. Explosive eruptions do.

The Gakkel Ridge is a long crack in the floor of the Arctic Ocean. The two sides of the crack are spreading apart slowly. As a result, gas builds up in pockets of magma beneath the ridge. Eventually the pressure of this gas causes explosive volcanic eruptions. The eruptions release lava, heat, gases, and trace metals into the ocean water. The jagged rocks that scientists found came from these explosions.

Ice cap covering North Pole

▲ The Gakkel Ridge (in red) is located under the Arctic Ocean.

Research It Research volcanic activity along another mid-ocean ridge, such as the Juan de Fuca Ridge. Prepare a graphic organizer comparing the timing, intensity, and volcanic activities along the two mid-ocean ridges.

7.2.3, 7.NS.2, 7.NS.11

WHY DOES THIS ROCK LOOK LIKE A SPONGE?

What processes break down rock?

What could make a rock so full of holes? These rock formations, called *tafoni*, are found along the coast of California at Salt Point State Park. Develop Hypotheses **Explain what you think caused the holes in these rock formations.**

_____

_____

_____

_____

_____

_____

_____

▶ **UNTAMED SCIENCE** Watch the **Untamed Science** video to learn more about the forces that break down rock.

Weathering and Soil

Academic Standards for Science

7.2.6, 7.2.7, 7.NS.1, 7.NS.2, 7.NS.8, 7.DP.9, 7.DP.10

12 Getting Started

Check Your Understanding

1. **Background** Read the paragraph below and then answer the question.

The **minerals** that make up a rock determine some of the rock's properties. The properties of a rock can change in two ways: **physical changes** and **chemical changes.** Physical changes change the shape or size of a rock, but not its composition. Chemical changes can change minerals into other substances, changing the composition of the rock.

> **Minerals** are naturally occurring, inorganic solids that have specific crystal structures and specific chemical compositions.
>
> A **physical change** is any change that does not alter the chemical composition of a substance.
>
> A **chemical change** produces one or more new substances.

• How can you tell if a physical change has occurred in a rock?

_____

_____

> **MY READING WEB** If you had trouble answering the question above, visit **My Reading Web** and type in *Weathering and Soil.*

Vocabulary Skill

Suffixes A suffix is a letter or group of letters added to the end of a word to change its meaning and often its part of speech. The suffix *-ation* added to a verb can form a noun that means "process of" or "action of." For example, the suffix *-ation* added to *observe* forms the noun *observation*.

Suffix	Meaning	Part of Speech	Examples
-ation, -sion	Process of, action of	Noun	Abrasion, oxidation, conservation
-ing	Showing continuous action	Noun or adjective	Weathering, plowing

2. **Quick Check** Circle the correct words to complete the sentence.
• People who (conserve/conservation) energy are contributing to energy (conserve/conservation).

mechanical weathering

soil

decomposer

contour plowing

Chapter Preview

LESSON 1
- uniformitarianism
- erosion
- weathering
- mechanical weathering
- chemical weathering
- abrasion
- frost wedging
- oxidation
- permeable

🔁 **Relate Cause and Effect**
△ **Control Variables**

LESSON 2
- soil
- bedrock
- humus
- fertility
- loam
- pH scale
- soil horizon
- topsoil
- subsoil
- decomposer

🔁 **Ask Questions**
△ **Form Operational Definitions**

LESSON 3
- natural resource
- soil conservation
- crop rotation
- contour plowing
- conservation plowing

🔁 **Summarize**
△ **Observe**

▷ **VOCAB FLASH CARDS** For extra help with vocabulary, visit **Vocab Flash Cards** and type in *Weathering and Soil.*

Rocks and Weathering

UNLOCK THE BIG ?

🔑 **What Breaks Down Rocks?**
7.2.7, 7.NS.1

🔑 **What Causes Weathering?**
7.2.7, 7.NS.8

🔑 **How Fast Does Weathering Occur?**
7.2.7, 7.NS.8, 7.DP.9

my planeT DiARY

DISCOVERY

Wearing Away Mars

Does this scene look like a desert? It is—but not on Earth! These rocks are found on Mars. Blowing sand wears away some rocks on the surface. Fog containing acid dissolves and breaks down other rocks. Over time, the rocks break down into small particles, covering the planet with reddish sand.

🖉 **Communicate** After you read about the rocks on Mars, answer these questions with a partner.

1. What are two processes that break down rocks on Mars?

_____

_____

2. Give an example of rocks you have seen that were changed by natural processes.

_____

_____

_____

Lab zone Do the Inquiry Warm-Up *How Fast Can It Fizz?*

▶ PLANET DIARY Go to **Planet Diary** to learn more about rocks and weathering.

Academic Standards for Science

7.2.7 Use geological features such as karst topography and glaciation to explain how large-scale physical processes have shaped the land.

7.NS.1 Make predictions based on research or prior knowledge.

What Breaks Down Rocks?

Even the hardest rocks wear down over time—on Earth or on Mars. Natural processes break down rocks and carry the pieces away.

How do scientists know what processes shaped Earth in the past? Geologists make inferences based on the principle of **uniformitarianism** (yoon uh fawrm uh TAYR ee un iz um). This principle states that the geologic processes that operate today also operated in the past. Scientists can infer that ancient landforms and features formed through the same processes they observe today.

Vocabulary
- uniformitarianism • erosion • weathering
- mechanical weathering • chemical weathering
- abrasion • frost wedging • oxidation • permeable

Skills
- Reading: Relate Cause and Effect
- Inquiry: Control Variables

Erosion
Erosion (ee ROH zhun) is the process of wearing down and carrying away rocks. Erosion includes the breaking of rocks into smaller pieces. It also involves the removal of rock particles by wind, water, ice, or gravity.

Weathering
Weathering is the process that breaks down rock and other substances. Heat, cold, water, ice, and gases all contribute to weathering. The forces that wear down mountains like those in **Figure 1** also cause bicycles to rust, paint to peel, and sidewalks to crack. **Erosion works continuously to weather and carry away rocks at Earth's surface.**

FIGURE 1 ···
Effects of Weathering
The Sierra Nevada (below) are much younger than the Appalachians (right). ✎ **Predict How might the Sierras change in the future? Explain your answer.**

_____

_____

_____

7.NS.1

Lab zone® Do the Quick Lab
Freezing and Thawing.

Assess Your Understanding

got it?···

O I get it! Now I know that erosion and weathering_____

_____

O I need extra help with _____

Go to **my science** 🔊 **coach** *online for help with this subject.*

7.2.7

What Causes Weathering?

If you hit a rock with a hammer, the rock may break into pieces. Some forces of weathering break rock into pieces, as a hammer does. The type of weathering in which rock is physically broken into smaller pieces is called **mechanical weathering.** A second type of weathering, called chemical weathering, also breaks down rock. **Chemical weathering** is the process that breaks down rock through chemical changes.

Mechanical Weathering If you have seen rocks that are cracked or split in layers, then you have seen rocks that have undergone mechanical weathering. Mechanical weathering usually works slowly. But over very long periods of time, it does more than wear down rocks. Mechanical weathering, as part of erosion, eventually wears away whole mountains.

FIGURE 2 ·······················

> **INTERACTIVE ART** **Forces of Mechanical Weathering**

✎ **Classify** Match each description to an example shown in the photos on the next page.

[CHALLENGE] How might more than one agent of mechanical weathering operate in the same place?

_____

_____

_____

_____

_____

1 **Animal Actions**

Animals that burrow in the ground—including moles, gophers, prairie dogs, and some insects—loosen and break apart rocks in the soil.

2 **Freezing and Thawing**

When water freezes in a crack in a rock, it expands and makes the crack bigger. The process of frost wedging also widens cracks in sidewalks and causes potholes in streets.

3 **Plant Growth**

Plant roots enter cracks in rocks. As roots grow, they force the cracks apart. Over time, the roots of even small plants can pry apart cracked rocks.

4 **Release of Pressure**

As erosion removes material from the surface of a mass of rock, pressure on the rock is reduced. This release of pressure causes the outside of the rock to crack and flake off like the layers of an onion.

5 **Abrasion**

Sand and other rock particles that are carried by wind, water, or ice can wear away exposed rock surfaces like sandpaper on wood.

Agents of Mechanical Weathering 🔑 The

natural agents of mechanical weathering include freezing and thawing, release of pressure, plant growth, actions of animals, and abrasion. **Abrasion** (uh BRAY zhun) refers to the wearing away of rock by rock particles carried by water, ice, wind, or gravity. Human activities, such as mining and farming, can also cause weathering.

In cool climates, the most important agent of mechanical weathering is the freezing and thawing of water. Water seeps into cracks in rocks and freezes there, expanding as it freezes. The ice then forces the rock apart. Wedges of ice in rocks widen and deepen cracks. This process is called **frost wedging.** When the ice melts, water seeps deeper into the cracks. With repeated freezing and thawing, the cracks slowly expand until pieces of rock break off.

Chemical Weathering

Chemical weathering can produce new minerals as it breaks down rock. For example, granite is made up of several minerals, including feldspars. As a result of chemical weathering, the feldspar minerals eventually change to clay.

Chemical and mechanical weathering often work together. Chemical weathering creates holes or soft spots in rock, so the rock breaks apart more easily. As rocks break into pieces, more surface area is exposed to chemical weathering, as shown in **Figure 3**.

Agents of Chemical Weathering

The agents of chemical weathering include water, oxygen, carbon dioxide, living organisms, and acid rain.

Water Water weathers some rock by dissolving it. Water also carries other substances that dissolve or break down rock, including oxygen, carbon dioxide, and other chemicals.

FIGURE 3

Weathering and Surface Area

Weathering breaks rock into smaller pieces. While the pieces are usually irregularly shaped, you can model the process with cubes. The diagram shows what would happen if a rock cube broke into smaller cubes.

✎ **Calculate By how much does the surface area increase? How would the rate of weathering change?**

_____

_____

_____

7.NS.8

FIGURE 4 ·······························

> ART IN MOTION   Chemical Weathering

Acid rain chemically weathered the statue of the lion.

✏ **Infer** Which agent of chemical weathering most likely formed this limestone cavern?

_____

_____

_____

Lab zone ® Do the Quick Lab *Rusting Away.*

🔑 **Assess Your Understanding**

1a. Define (Mechanical/chemical) weathering physically breaks rock into smaller pieces.

7.2.7

b. Classify Circle the examples of chemical weathering. Underline the examples of mechanical weathering. Freezing and thawing, oxidation, water dissolving chemicals, abrasion, acid rain

7.2.7

c. Predict Many ancient monuments are made of marble. Some are located in highly polluted cities. How might the pollution affect the monuments?

_____

_____

_____

7.2.7, 7.NS.1

got it? ·····································

○ **I get it!** Now I know that weathering is

caused by_____

_____

○ **I need extra help with** _____

Go to MY SCIENCE ⒮ COACH *online for help with this subject.*

7.2.7

Oxygen The oxygen gas in air is an important cause of chemical weathering. Iron combines with oxygen in the presence of water in a process called **oxidation.** The product of iron oxidation is rust. Rust makes rock soft and crumbly and gives it a red or brown color.

Carbon Dioxide Another gas found in air, carbon dioxide, also causes chemical weathering when it dissolves in water. The result is a weak acid called carbonic acid. Carbonic acid easily weathers some kinds of rocks, such as marble and limestone.

Living Organisms As a plant's roots grow, they produce weak acids that slowly dissolve rock around the roots. Lichens—plantlike organisms that grow on rocks—also produce weak acids.

Acid Rain Rainwater is naturally slightly acidic. Burning coal, oil, and gas for energy can pollute the air with sulfur, carbon, and nitrogen compounds. These compounds react with water vapor in clouds, making acids that are stronger than normal rainwater. These acids mix with raindrops and fall as acid rain. Acid rain causes very rapid chemical weathering of rock.

427

How Fast Does Weathering Occur?

Visitors to New England's historic cemeteries may notice a surprising fact. Slate tombstones carved in the 1700s are less weathered and easier to read than marble gravestones from the 1800s. Why is this so? Some kinds of rocks weather more rapidly than others. **The most important factors that determine the rate at which weathering occurs are the type of rock and the climate.**

Type of Rock The minerals that make up the rock determine how fast it weathers. Rocks that are made of minerals that do not dissolve easily will weather slowly. Rocks weather faster if they are made of minerals that do dissolve easily.

Some rocks weather more easily because they are permeable. **Permeable** (PUR mee uh bul) means that a material is full of tiny, connected air spaces that allow water to seep through it. The spaces increase the surface area of the rock. As water seeps through the spaces in the rock, it carries chemicals that dissolve the rock. The water also removes material broken down by weathering.

do the math!

Which Weathered Faster?

The data table shows how much stone was lost due to weathering for two identical pieces of limestone from different locations.

1 Graph Use the data to make a double-line graph. Be sure to label the axes and provide a key and a title.

2 Draw Conclusions (Stone A/Stone B) weathered at a faster rate.

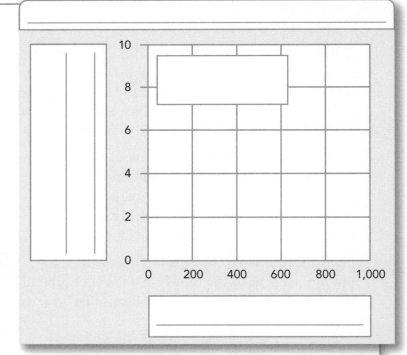

3 Infer What can you infer caused the difference in the rates of weathering?

_____

_____

Weathering Rates of Limestone		
Time (years)	Thickness of Stone Lost (mm)	
	Stone A	Stone B
200	1.75	0.80
400	3.50	1.60
600	5.25	2.40
800	7.00	3.20
1,000	8.75	4.00

7.NS.8, 7.DP.9

Climate

Climate refers to the average weather conditions in an area. Both chemical and mechanical weathering occur faster in wet climates. Rainfall provides the water needed for chemical changes as well as for freezing and thawing.

Chemical reactions occur faster at higher temperatures. That is why chemical weathering occurs more quickly where the climate is both hot and wet. Human activities, such as those that produce acid rain, also increase the rate of weathering.

> **⊙ Relate Cause and Effect**
> Underline the reason that chemical weathering occurs faster in hot climates.

apply it!

Tombstones 1 and 2 are both around 200 years old and are in the same cemetery.

❶ (Stone 1/Stone 2) has weathered more.

❷ What might explain the difference?

_____

_____

_____

❸ **Control Variables** How do you know that the type of rock is the only difference between the tombstones?

_____

_____

Stone 1

Stone 2

 Do the Quick Lab
It's All on the Surface.

🔑 Assess Your Understanding

2a. ⊙ Relate Cause and Effect Why does permeable rock weather more quickly than less permeable rock?

_____

_____

_____

7.2.7

b. Infer Why are tombstones in a cemetery useful for comparing rates of weathering?

_____

_____

_____

7.2.7

got it?

○ **I get it!** Now I know that the rate of weathering depends on_____

_____

○ **I need extra help with** _____

Go to **MY SCIENCE** 🔊 **COACH** *online for help with this subject.*   7.2.7

How Soil Forms

UNLOCK THE BIG ?

🗝 **What Is Soil?**
7.2.6, 7.NS.8

🗝 **How Do Living Things Affect Soil?**
7.2.6, 7.DP.10

my planet Diary

Life Beneath Your Feet

The soil beneath your feet may not look very interesting, but it's packed with life! Many microscopic organisms live in soil and affect the lives of other organisms. Some bacteria, like the *Pseudomonas* shown above, can protect plants from disease. Hundreds of thousands of soil mites can live in a single square meter of soil. And tiny worms called nematodes eat plants, bacteria, fungi, and even other nematodes!

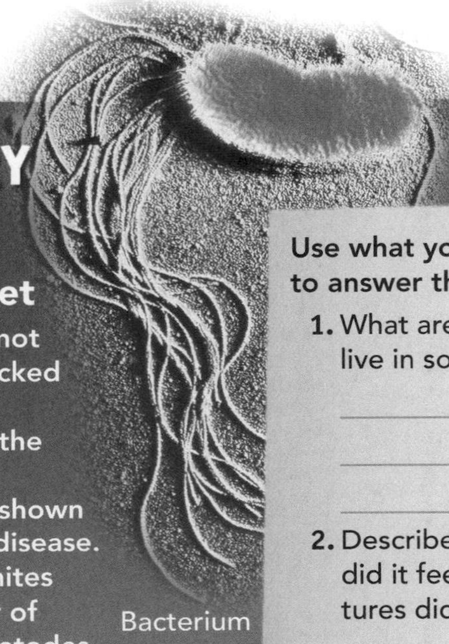

Bacterium

Nematode

Mite

FUN FACT

Use what you have read and your experiences to answer the questions below.

1. What are some examples of organisms that live in soil?

_____

_____

2. Describe soil you have seen or touched. What did it feel like? How did it smell? What creatures did you see in it?

_____

_____

_____

_____

▶ PLANET DIARY Go to Planet Diary to learn more about soil.

Lab zone® Do the Inquiry Warm-Up *What Is Soil?*

Vocabulary

- soil • bedrock • humus • fertility • loam
- pH scale • soil horizon • topsoil • subsoil
- decomposer

Skills

↩ Reading: Ask Questions

△ Inquiry: Form Operational Definitions

What Is Soil?

Have you ever seen a plant growing in a crack in a rock? It may look like the plant is growing on solid rock, but it isn't. Plants can only grow when soil begins to form in the cracks. **Soil** is the loose, weathered material on Earth's surface in which plants can grow.

Soil Composition 🔑 **Soil is a mixture of rock particles, minerals, decayed organic material, water, and air.** One of the main ingredients of soil comes from bedrock. **Bedrock** is the solid layer of rock beneath the soil. Once bedrock is exposed to air, water, and living things, it gradually weathers into smaller and smaller particles that are the most common components of soil.

The particles of rock in soil are classified by size as gravel, sand, silt, and clay. **Figure 1** shows the relative sizes of these particles. Together, gravel, sand, silt, and clay make up the portion of soil that comes from weathered rock.

The decayed organic material in soil is called humus. **Humus** (HYOO mus) is a dark-colored substance that forms as plant and animal remains decay. Humus helps create spaces in soil for air and water. Humus also contains nutrients that plants need.

FIGURE 1 ·······

Soil Particle Size

The particles shown here have been enlarged.

✏ **Graph** Mark where a 1.5-mm particle would fall on the graph. What type of particle is it? _____

7.NS.8

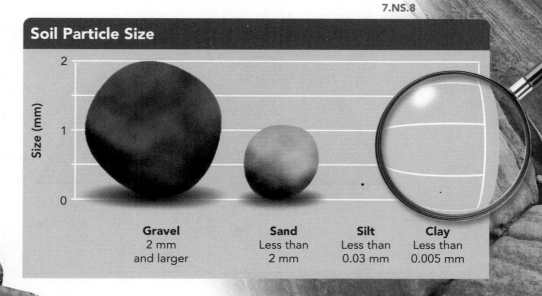

Soil Particle Size

Size (mm)

Gravel	Sand	Silt	Clay
2 mm and larger	Less than 2 mm	Less than 0.03 mm	Less than 0.005 mm

Vocabulary Suffixes How does adding the suffix *-ity* change the form of the word *fertile*?

_____

_____

_____

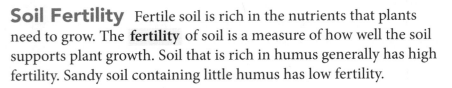

↻ **Ask Questions** Before you read the section Soil pH, write a question that you would like answered. Then write the answer.

_____

_____

_____

_____

Soil Fertility Fertile soil is rich in the nutrients that plants need to grow. The **fertility** of soil is a measure of how well the soil supports plant growth. Soil that is rich in humus generally has high fertility. Sandy soil containing little humus has low fertility.

Soil Texture Sandy soil feels coarse and grainy, but soil with lots of clay feels smooth and silky. These differences are differences in texture. Soil texture depends on the size of the soil particles.

Soil texture is important for plant growth. Soil that is mostly clay may hold too much water and not enough air. In contrast, sandy soil loses water quickly. Plants may die for lack of air or water. Soil that is made up of about equal parts of clay, sand, and silt is called **loam.** Loam is the best soil for growing most plants.

Soil pH Soil can be acidic or basic. Acidic substances react with some metals and turn blue litmus paper red. Basic substances feel slippery and turn red litmus paper blue. The **pH scale** measures acidity. A substance with a pH less than 4 is strongly acidic. A substance with a pH of 7 is neither acidic nor basic. (Pure water has a pH of 7.) A substance with a pH greater than 10 is strongly basic. Most garden plants grow best in soil with a pH between 6 and 7.5. Some soils can have a pH as low as 4, which is quite acidic.

apply it!

This diagram is called the soil texture triangle. To use the triangle, first find the percentages of silt, sand, and clay in a soil sample. Then locate each percentage on its side of the triangle. The point where the lines meet tells you the type of soil. (This example shows clay loam soil that is 40% silt, 30% clay, and 30% sand.)

❶ **Interpret Diagrams** What percentage of silty clay loam is silt? (*Hint:* Look at the corners of the silty clay loam area.)

_____

❷ **Interpret Diagrams** A soil sample has 20% silt, 10% clay, and 70% sand. What kind of soil is it? (*Hint:* Draw lines to find out.)

_____

❸ **Form Operational Definitions** How would you define silty clay soil?

_____

_____

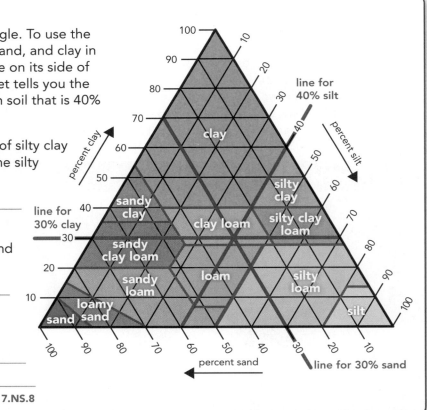

7.NS.8

The Process of Soil Formation 🔑 **Soil forms as rock is broken down by weathering and mixes with other materials on the surface.** Soil forms constantly wherever bedrock weathers. Soil formation continues over a long period of time.

Gradually, soil develops layers called horizons. A **soil horizon** is a layer of soil that differs in color, texture, and composition from the layers above or below it. **Figure 2** shows how scientists classify soil into three horizons.

C Horizon The C horizon forms as bedrock begins to weather. The rock breaks up into small particles.

A Horizon The A horizon is made up of **topsoil,** a crumbly, dark brown soil that is a mixture of humus, clay, and other minerals. Topsoil forms as plants add organic material to the soil, and plant roots weather pieces of rock.

B Horizon The B horizon, often called **subsoil,** usually consists of clay and other particles of rock, but little humus. It forms as rainwater washes these materials down from the A horizon.

FIGURE 2 ·······························
Soil Layers
✎ **Use the diagram to answer the questions.**

1. **Compare and Contrast** Which layer contains the most organic material?

   _____

2. [CHALLENGE] In what climates would you expect soil to form fastest? Why?

   _____

   _____

   _____

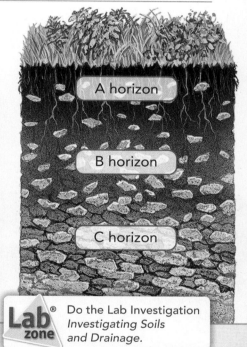

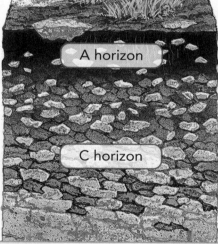

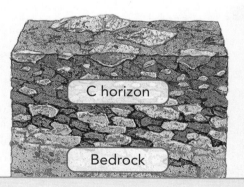

A horizon

B horizon

C horizon

C horizon

C horizon

Bedrock

Lab zone® Do the Lab Investigation *Investigating Soils and Drainage.*

🔑 Assess Your Understanding

1a. List What are three characteristics used to describe soil?

_____

7.2.6

b. Compare and Contrast How are the A, B, and C horizons different?

_____

_____

_____

_____

7.2.6

got it? ·······························

○ I get it! Now I know that soil forms from _____

_____

_____

○ I need extra help with _____

Go to **MY SCIENCE** 💬 **COACH** *online for help with this subject.* 7.2.6

Academic Standards for Science

7.2.6 Describe physical and chemical characteristics of soil layers and how they are influenced by the process of soil formation, including the action of bacteria, fungi, insects, and other organisms.
7.DP.10 Communicate the solution using drawings.

How Do Living Things Affect Soil?

Many organisms live in soil. **Some soil organisms make humus, the material that makes soil fertile. Other soil organisms mix the soil and make spaces in it for air and water.**

Forming Humus
Dead leaves, roots, and other plant materials contribute most of the organic remains that form humus. Humus forms in a process called decomposition. **Decomposers** are the organisms that break the remains of dead organisms into smaller pieces and digest them with chemicals. This material then mixes with the soil as humus. Soil decomposers include fungi (such as mushrooms), bacteria, worms, and other organisms.

Mixing the Soil
Earthworms and burrowing mammals mix humus with air and other materials in soil. As earthworms eat their way through the soil, they carry humus down to the subsoil and subsoil up to the surface. Mammals such as mice, moles, and prairie dogs break up hard, compacted soil and mix humus with it. Animal wastes contribute nutrients to the soil as well.

FIGURE 3 ·····························

Life in Soil
Interpret Diagrams Label the three soil horizons. Then label each organism *decomposer, burrower,* or *humus source.* Some organisms may get more than one label.

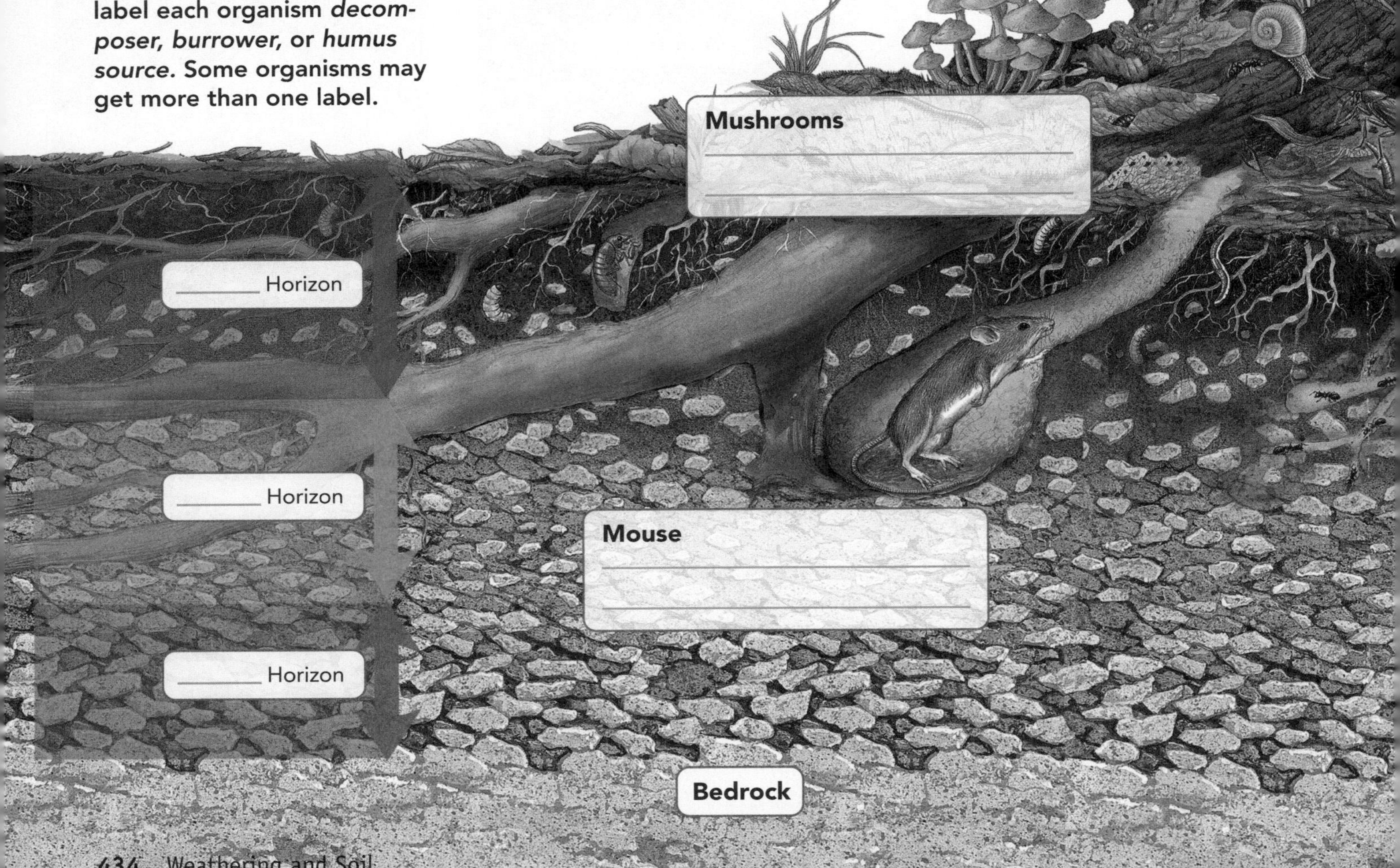

Mushrooms
_____
_____

_____ Horizon

_____ Horizon

_____ Horizon

Mouse
_____
_____

Bedrock

EXPLORE THE BIG ?

From Rock *to* Soil

What processes break down rock?

FIGURE 4 ·······

> INTERACTIVE ART   The illustrations show a rock and rich, fertile soil. In the remaining boxes, draw the steps that could change the rock into the soil. Label the processes in each drawing. Include at least two types of weathering.   7.DP.10

Dead leaves

Earthworm

Bacteria

Lab zone®   Do the Quick Lab *The Contents of Soil.*

🔑 Assess Your Understanding

2a. Identify Organisms contribute to soil formation by _____ and _____

7.2.6

b. Describe List two types of decomposers.

_____

7.2.6

c. ANSWER THE BIG ? What processes break down rock? Include the processes of soil formation in your answer.

_____
_____
_____
_____

7.2.6

got it? ·······

○ **I get it!** Now I know that living things affect soil by _____

○ **I need extra help with** _____

Go to MY SCIENCE ⓢ COACH online for help with this subject.   7.2.6

435

Indiana

LESSON

3 Soil Conservation

UNLOCK THE BIG **?**

🔑 **How Can Soil Lose Its Value?**
7.2.6

🔑 **How Can Soil Be Conserved?**
7.2.6

my planet diary
for **Indiana**

DISCOVERY

The Indiana Conservation Partnership

In the 1930s, poor farming techniques and a long, severe drought transformed the land of the Great Plains into a dry wasteland. The area most affected became known as the Dust Bowl.

The federal government worked to prevent further soil erosion in the country. It taught and promoted modern soil conservation techniques to local farmers and landowners. The Indiana Conservation Partnership (ICP) was established to help manage and preserve Indiana's natural resources. The ICP provides technical, financial, and educational assistance in the hopes of improving the quality of Indiana's land and water.

Read the information about the Dust Bowl and the Indiana Conservation Partnership. Then answer the questions below.

1. What were two causes of the Dust Bowl?

_____

_____

2. How does the ICP work to help prevent another event like the Dust Bowl?

_____

_____

_____

_____

_____

▶ PLANET DIARY Go to **Planet Diary** to learn more about how soil can be damaged.

 Do the Inquiry Warm-Up *How Can You Keep Soil From Washing Away?*

Vocabulary
- natural resource • soil conservation
- crop rotation • contour plowing
- conservation plowing

Skills
↻ **Reading:** Summarize
△ **Inquiry:** Observe

How Can Soil Lose Its Value?

Today, much of the area affected by the Dust Bowl is once again covered with farms. But the Dust Bowl was a reminder of how important soil is for humans.

The Value of Soil A **natural resource** is anything in the environment that humans use. Soil is one of Earth's most valuable natural resources because everything that lives on land, including humans, depends directly or indirectly on soil. Plants depend directly on the soil to live and grow. Humans and animals depend on plants—or on other animals that depend on plants—for food.

Fertile soil is valuable because there is a limited supply of it. Less than one eighth of the land on Earth has soils that are well suited for farming. Soil is also in limited supply because it takes a long time to form. It can take hundreds of years for just a few centimeters of soil to form.

FIGURE 1 ....
Prairie Grasses
Prairie soils like those found on the Great Plains are still among the most fertile in the world.

✎ **Make Generalizations** Based on the illustration below, how do you think prairie grasses protect soil?

_____

_____

Academic Standards for Science

7.2.6 Describe physical and chemical characteristics of soil layers and how they are influenced by the process of soil formation, including the action of bacteria, fungi, insects, and other organisms.

↻ **Summarize** Write two sentences to summarize the value of soil.

_____

_____

_____

_____

_____

_____

_____

_____

_____

_____

apply it!

The two photos show samples of different soils.

1 ⚠️ **Observe** List two visible differences between the two soil samples.

_____

_____

_____

_____

2 **CHALLENGE** Which sample would you predict is more fertile? (Sample A/Sample B)

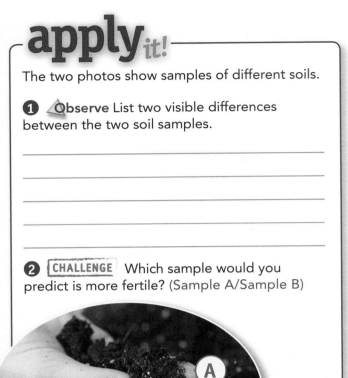

Soil Damage and Loss Human actions and changes in the environment can affect soil. 🔑 **The value of soil is reduced when soil loses its fertility or when topsoil is lost due to erosion.**

Loss of Fertility Soil can be damaged when it loses its fertility. This can happen through loss of moisture and nutrients. This type of soil damage occurred in large parts of the southern United States in the late 1800s, where cotton was the only crop. Cotton used up many nutrients in the soil, and those nutrients were not replaced.

Loss of Topsoil Whenever soil is exposed, water and wind can quickly erode it. Plant cover can protect soil from erosion in several ways. Plants break the force of falling rain, and plant roots hold the soil together.

Wind erosion is most likely to occur in areas where farming methods are not suited to dry conditions. For example, wind erosion contributed to the Dust Bowl on the Great Plains. Farmers plowed up the prairie grasses that held the soil together. Without roots to hold it, the soil blew away more easily.

Do the Quick Lab
Using It Up.

🔑 Assess Your Understanding

1a. Explain Why is soil valuable?

_____

_____

_____

7.2.6

b. Relate Cause and Effect How does wind erosion affect the value of soil?

_____

_____

_____

7.2.6

got it? ···

○ **I get it!** Now I know that soil can lose value when _____

_____

○ **I need extra help with** _____

Go to MY SCIENCE COACH online for help with this subject.

7.2.6

How Can Soil Be Conserved?

Today, many farmers use methods of soil conservation. **Soil conservation** is the management of soil to limit its destruction. 🔑 **Soil can be conserved through practices such as contour plowing, conservation plowing, and crop rotation.**

Changes in Crops Some crops, such as corn and cotton, take up large amounts of nutrients from the soil. Others, such as peanuts, alfalfa, and beans, help restore soil fertility. These plants, called legumes, have small lumps on their roots that contain nitrogen-fixing bacteria. These bacteria make the important nutrient nitrogen available in a form that plants can use.

In **crop rotation,** a farmer plants different crops in a field each year. One year, the farmer plants a crop such as corn or cotton. The next year, the farmer plants crops that use fewer soil nutrients, such as oats, barley, or rye. The year after that the farmer sows legumes to restore the nutrient supply.

Changes in Plowing In **contour plowing,** farmers plow their fields along the curves of a slope instead of in straight rows. This method helps slow the runoff of excess rainfall and prevents it from washing the soil away. In **conservation plowing,** dead weeds and stalks of the previous year's crop are plowed into the ground to help return soil nutrients, retain moisture, and hold soil in place.

Academic Standards for Science

7.2.6 Describe physical and chemical characteristics of soil layers and how they are influenced by the process of soil formation, including the action of bacteria, fungi, insects, and other organisms.

Nodules containing bacteria

FIGURE 2 ·······················

> REAL-WORLD INQUIRY

Farming Methods

Peanuts (above) are useful for crop rotation. The bacteria on their roots make nitrogen available. Contour plowing (left) is one way to conserve soil.

✏️ **Make Judgments** Which method would you recommend to a farmer who wanted to maintain soil fertility?

_____

_____

_____

_____

 Do the Quick Lab
Soil Conservation.

🔑 Assess Your Understanding

gotit? ···

○ **I get it!** Now I know that soil can be conserved by_____

_____

○ **I need extra help with** _____

Go to my science ⓢ coach *online for help with this subject.*

7.2.6

12 Study Guide

Processes of _____ and _____ break down rocks and carry them away. The broken rocks combine with _____ to make soil.

LESSON 1 Rocks and Weathering

7.2.7, 7.NS.1, 7.NS.8, 7.DP.9

🔑 Erosion works continuously to weather and carry away rocks at Earth's surface.

🔑 The natural agents of mechanical weathering include freezing and thawing, release of pressure, plant growth, actions of animals, and abrasion. The agents of chemical weathering include water, oxygen, carbon dioxide, living organisms, and acid rain.

🔑 The most important factors that determine the rate at which weathering occurs are the type of rock and the climate.

Vocabulary
• uniformitarianism • erosion • weathering • mechanical weathering
• chemical weathering • abrasion • frost wedging • oxidation • permeable

LESSON 2 How Soil Forms

7.2.6, 7.NS.8, 7.DP.10

🔑 Soil is a mixture of rock particles, minerals, decayed organic material, water, and air. Soil forms as rock is broken down by weathering and mixes with other materials on the surface.

🔑 Some soil organisms make humus, the material that makes soil fertile. Other soil organisms mix the soil and make spaces in it for air and water.

Vocabulary
• soil • bedrock • humus • fertility • loam • pH scale
• soil horizon • topsoil • subsoil • decomposer

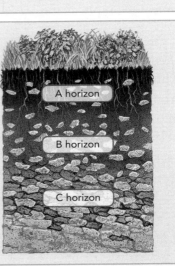

LESSON 3 Soil Conservation

7.2.6

🔑 The value of soil is reduced when soil loses its fertility and when topsoil is lost due to erosion.

🔑 Soil can be conserved through practices such as contour plowing, conservation plowing, and crop rotation.

Vocabulary
• natural resource • soil conservation • crop rotation
• contour plowing • conservation plowing

Review and Assessment

LESSON 1 Rocks and Weathering

1. The process that splits rock through freezing and thawing is called

- **a.** abrasion.
- **b.** dissolving.
- **c.** erosion.
- **d.** frost wedging.

7.2.7

2. Which of the following is caused by acid rain?

- **a.** abrasion
- **b.** dissolving of rock
- **c.** release of pressure
- **d.** oxidation

7.2.7

3. Classify Classify each of the following as mechanical or chemical weathering.

Cracks in a sidewalk next to a tree

_____

Limestone with holes like Swiss cheese

_____

A rock that slowly turns reddish brown

_____

7.2.7

4. Predict If mechanical weathering breaks a rock into pieces, how would this affect the rate at which the rock weathers chemically?

_____

_____

_____

7.2.7, 7.NS.1

5. Write About It A community group wants to build a monument in a city park. They want the monument to last for a long time. They ask you for advice on choosing long-lasting stone for the monument. Write a proposal explaining what factors would affect how long the monument would last.

7.2.7, 7.NS.2

LESSON 2 How Soil Forms

6. Soil that is made up of roughly equal parts of clay, sand, and silt is called

- **a.** loam.
- **b.** sod.
- **c.** subsoil.
- **d.** topsoil.

7.2.6

7. The decayed organic material in soil is called

- **a.** bedrock.
- **b.** humus.
- **c.** silt.
- **d.** subsoil.

7.2.6

8. Identify What are two roles living things play in soil formation?

_____

_____

7.2.6

Use the graph to answer Question 9.

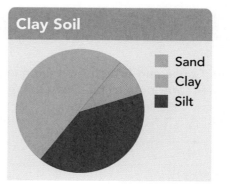

Clay Soil

- Sand
- Clay
- Silt

9. Pose Questions The graph shows a farmer's soil sample. What questions would the farmer need to answer before choosing whether to plant soybeans in this soil?

_____

_____

_____

_____

7.2.6, 7.NS.8

LESSON 3 **Soil Conservation**

10. Which technique returns nutrients to soil?

　a. chemical weathering

　b. contour plowing

　c. crop rotation

　d. wind erosion

7.2.6

11. What role do grasses play in conserving the soil of the prairies?

　a. holding the soil in place

　b. increasing wind erosion

　c. decreasing the amount of fertile soil

　d. making nitrogen available to plants

7.2.6

12. Draw Conclusions Why is soil important to people and to other living things?

_____

_____

_____

_____

_____

_____

7.2.6

13. Relate Cause and Effect How did human activities contribute to the Dust Bowl?

_____

_____

_____

_____

_____

7.2.6

14.  **Write About It** Write information for a pamphlet explaining to farmers why they should use conservation plowing and contour plowing. Explain how these methods would help conserve soil.

7.2.6

 What processes break down rock?

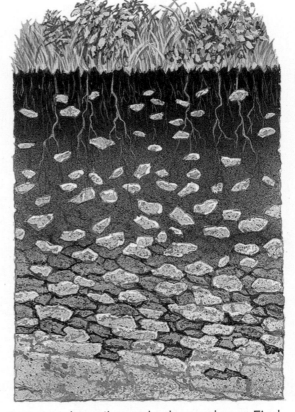

15. Examine the soil sample shown above. Find the A, B, and C horizons. Describe the processes that formed each layer of the soil. Remember to include examples of weathering in your description.

_____

_____

_____

_____

_____

_____

_____

_____

_____

_____

7.2.6

Indiana ISTEP+ Practice

Multiple Choice

Circle the letter of the correct answer.

1. Use the picture to answer the question.

   What **most likely** caused the weathering shown in the picture?

   A. abrasion   **B.** ice wedging

   C. plant growth   **D.** animal actions

   7.2.7

2. Fertile soil is an important natural resource because

   A. no new soil can be produced.

   B. everything that lives on land depends on soil.

   C. there is an unlimited supply of fertile soil.

   D. plants cannot grow in fertile soil.

   7.2.6

3. In which type of climate would a limestone monument weather **most** quickly?

   A. a cold, dry climate

   B. a hot, dry climate

   C. a cold, wet climate

   D. a hot, wet climate

   7.2.7

4. A farmer wants to reduce the amount of runoff in his fields. Which of the following methods would be **most** helpful?

   A. contour plowing

   B. conservation plowing

   C. crop rotation

   D. topsoil erosion

   7.2.6

Constructed Response

Write your answer to Question 5 on the lines below.

5. What is the **most** important role that burrowing animals play in the formation of soil?

   _____

   _____

   _____

   7.2.6

Extended Response

Use the diagram and your knowledge of science to answer the question. Write your answer on another piece of paper.

6. Examine the soil samples above. Describe the soil in each pot. Predict whether each soil would be good for growing most kinds of plants and explain your reasoning.

   7.2.6, 7.NS.1

SCIENCE MATTERS

Museum of Science

TECH & DESIGN

HASTA LA VISTA, REGULAR CONCRETE

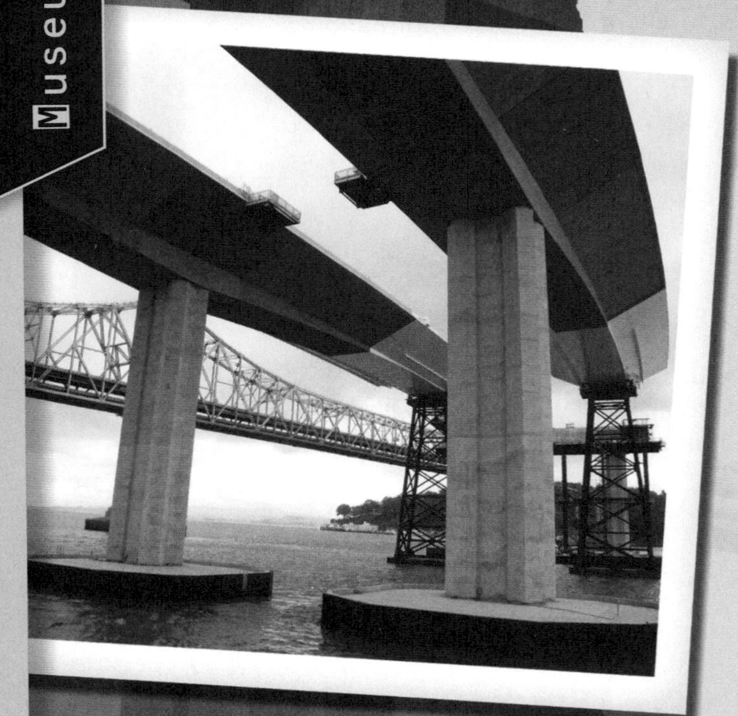

▲ The new fly-ash concrete bridge, beside the old metal bridge.

When engineers had to build a new elevated highway for the San Francisco–Oakland Bay Bridge, they had a lot of things to worry about. After all, if you're going to spend more than 1 billion dollars upgrading a bridge, you want to make sure it will be around for a long time!

The supports of the bridge needed to stand in salt water and mud. Chemicals called sulfates in salt water and soil can weather the concrete and weaken the structure. Sulfates also cause weathering by allowing salt crystals to form on the bridge. But when fly ash is mixed into concrete, it protects the concrete against the weathering effects of the sulfates. Fly ash is powder left behind after coal has been burned. This waste product is usually dumped in landfills.

The engineers of the huge concrete elevated highway used a mixture of concrete and fly ash to build the bridge supports. This improved concrete is helping the bridge to stand up to everything nature throws its way.

Analyze It **Identify how weathering has affected a local site, such as a bridge or a monument. Find out what materials were used to build the site, and research what other materials might better withstand weathering. Write a paragraph making the case for using these different materials in future building projects.**

7.NS.2

Museum of Science

THE Plant Doctor

Even as a young boy, George Washington Carver understood plants. Born into slavery in the 1860s, Carver spent his days studying plants. He observed that some plants needed a lot of sunlight and some needed very little. He experimented with mixtures of sand, soil, and clay to find out the kind of soil each plant needed. He knew so much about plants, neighbors called him the "plant doctor."

Carver received a master of science degree from Iowa State Agricultural College and began to teach and do research at Tuskegee Institute. Because Southern farmers grew only cotton, their soil was in poor condition and had started to erode. Carver taught farmers that crop rotation would enrich the soil. Many farmers found that the crops Carver suggested grew better in their soil, and that his methods made the soil healthier. Crop rotation is now a common farming technique.

Dr. Carver inspecting plants in a research greenhouse ▶

Research It Dr. Carver taught farmers in the South to plant peanuts, sweet potatoes, and soybeans. The success of these crops often left farmers with more than they could use or sell. Research the many uses discovered by Dr. Carver for one of these crops and present them in a poster.

7.2.6, 7.NS.2, 7.NS.11

WHAT RESHAPED THESE ROCKS?

THE BIG ?

What processes shape the surface of the land?

Smooth and colorful, the sandstone walls of Antelope Canyon look more like a sculpture than like natural rock. Located in Arizona, this slot canyon was carved by nature. From above, the opening of the canyon is so narrow that you can jump across. But be careful, some areas of the canyon are more than 30 meters deep!

Infer How could nature have carved these rocks?

_____

_____

_____

_____

_____

_____

> **UNTAMED SCIENCE** Watch the **Untamed Science** video to learn more about erosion and deposition.

Erosion and Deposition

Academic Standards for Science

7.2.6, 7.2.7, 7.NS.1, 7.NS.2, 7.NS.8, 7.NS.11

13 Getting Started

Check Your Understanding

1. **Background** Read the paragraph below and then answer the question.

> A giant **mass** of mud blocked the road after a storm. "How did it get there?" asked Gail. "During the storm, the nearby river rose really fast, so the **force** of the water pushed it there," said her dad. "Spring flooding is part of the natural **cycle** of the seasons."

Mass is an amount of matter that has an indefinite size and shape.

Force is the push or pull exerted on an object.

A **cycle** is a sequence of events that repeats over and over.

- Why does it take the force of fast-moving water to move a large mass of mud?

_____

_____

▶ **MY READING WEB** If you had trouble completing the question above, visit **My Reading Web** and type in *Erosion and Deposition.*

Vocabulary Skill

Word Origins Many science words come to English from other languages. By learning the meaning of a few common Latin roots, you can determine the meaning of new science words.

Latin Word	Meaning of Latin Word	Example
sedere	sit, settle	sediment, *n.* pieces of rock or soil moved by the process of erosion
flare	blow	deflation, *n.* the process by which wind removes surface materials

2. **Quick Check** Use the chart to answer the question.

- How does the Latin word *sedere* relate to the word *sediment*?

_____

_____

mass movement

flood plain

glacier

sand dune

Chapter Preview

LESSON 1
- erosion • sediment • deposition
- gravity • mass movement

↻ **Relate Text and Visuals**
△ **Infer**

LESSON 2
- runoff • rill • gully • stream
- tributary • flood plain • meander
- oxbow lake • delta • alluvial fan
- groundwater • stalactite
- stalagmite • karst topography

↻ **Identify Supporting Evidence**
△ **Develop Hypotheses**

LESSON 3
- glacier • continental glacier
- ice age • valley glacier
- plucking • till • moraine • kettle

↻ **Relate Cause and Effect**
△ **Draw Conclusions**

LESSON 4
- headland • beach
- longshore drift • spit

↻ **Summarize**
△ **Communicate**

LESSON 5
- deflation • sand dune • loess

↻ **Ask Questions**
△ **Predict**

▸ VOCAB FLASH CARDS For extra help with vocabulary, visit **Vocab Flash Cards** and type in *Erosion and Deposition.*

Mass Movement

🔑 **What Processes Wear Down and Build Up Earth's Surface?**
7.2.7

🔑 **What Are the Different Types of Mass Movement?**
7.2.7, 7.NS.8

MY PLANET DIARY

DISASTER

Mudflow Hits Town

In December 2007, severe storms hit the northwestern United States. These storms started landslides in the hills above Woodson, Oregon. When landslide debris dammed a creek in the hills, a deep lake formed. If the debris gave way, a mudflow could run downhill and damage the town.

Fortunately, a landowner called the Oregon Department of Forestry (ODF). People were quickly evacuated and a nearby highway was closed. It wasn't long before the pile of debris collapsed, allowing the water to escape. A large mudflow swept away homes, cars, and trees! But thanks to the ODF, no one was harmed.

Lab zone® Do the Inquiry Warm-Up *How Does Gravity Affect Materials on a Slope?*

Discuss the story with a classmate and answer the question.

What caused the mudflow?

_____

_____

_____

▶ **PLANET DIARY** Go to **Planet Diary** to learn more about mass movement.

Academic Standards for Science

7.2.7 Use geological features such as karst topography and glaciation to explain how large-scale physical processes have shaped the land.

What Processes Wear Down and Build Up Earth's Surface?

On a rainy day, you may have seen water carrying soil and gravel down a driveway. That's an example of **erosion**—the process by which natural forces move weathered rock and soil from one place to another. Gravity, moving water, glaciers, waves, and wind are all agents, or causes, of erosion.

Vocabulary

- erosion
- sediment
- deposition
- gravity
- mass movement

Skills

- Reading: Relate Text and Visuals
- Inquiry: Infer

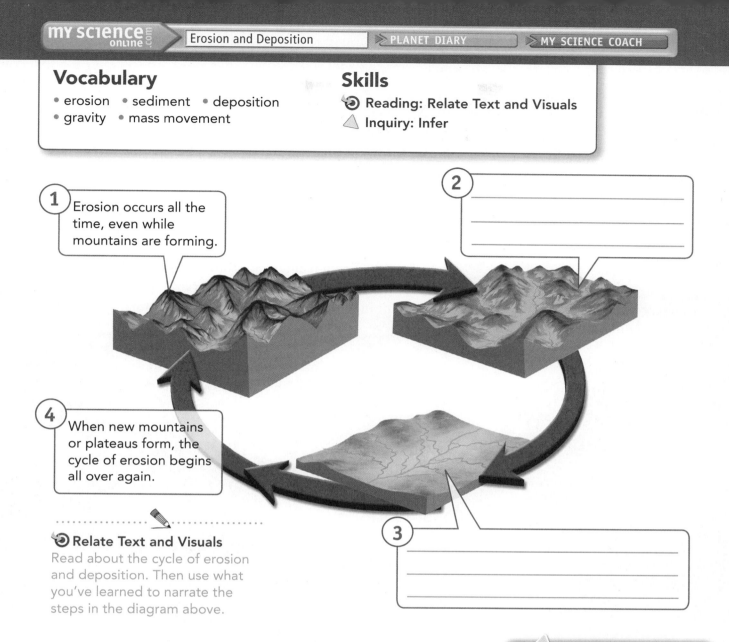

1 Erosion occurs all the time, even while mountains are forming.

2 _____

4 When new mountains or plateaus form, the cycle of erosion begins all over again.

3 _____

✎ Relate Text and Visuals

Read about the cycle of erosion and deposition. Then use what you've learned to narrate the steps in the diagram above.

The process of erosion moves material called **sediment.** Sediment may consist of pieces of rock or soil, or the remains of plants and animals. **Deposition** occurs where the agents of erosion deposit, or lay down, sediment. Deposition changes the shape of the land. You may have watched a playing child who picked up several toys, carried them across a room, and then put them down. This child was acting something like an agent of erosion and deposition.

🔑 **Weathering, erosion, and deposition act together in a cycle that wears down and builds up Earth's surface.** Erosion and deposition are at work everywhere on Earth. As a mountain wears down in one place, new landforms build up in other places. The cycle of erosion and deposition is never-ending.

Lab zone ® Do the Quick Lab *Weathering and Erosion.*

🔑 Assess Your Understanding

got it? ·····

○ **I get it!** Now I know the three major processes that shape Earth's surface are _____

_____

○ I need extra help with _____

Go to **my science** ⓢ **coach** *online for help with this subject.* **7.2.7**

What Are the Different Types of Mass Movement?

You're sitting on a bicycle at the top of a hill. With a slight push, you can coast down the hill. **Gravity** is the force that pulls you and your bike downward. It also moves rock and other materials downhill.

Gravity causes **mass movement,** any one of several processes that move sediment downhill. Mass movement can be rapid or slow. Erosion and deposition both take place during a mass movement event. 🔑 **The different types of mass movement include landslides, mudflows, slumps, and creep.**

FIGURE 1 ·······

▶ **INTERACTIVE ART** Mass Movement

✎ **Interpret Diagrams** Read about the types of mass movement. Then match each description with its corresponding diagram.

7.NS.8

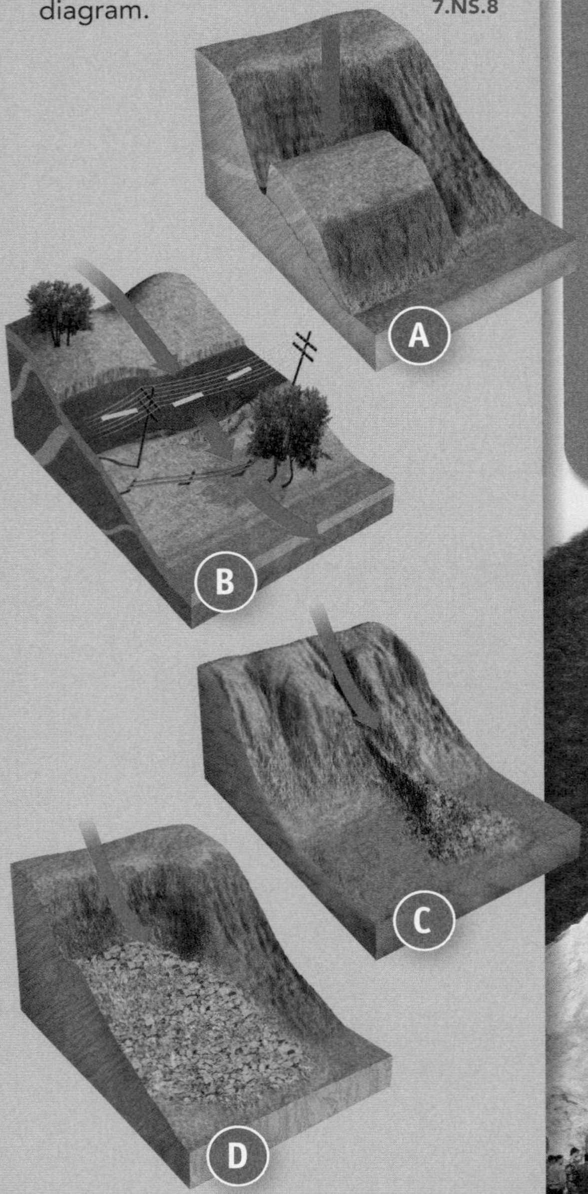

A

B

C

D

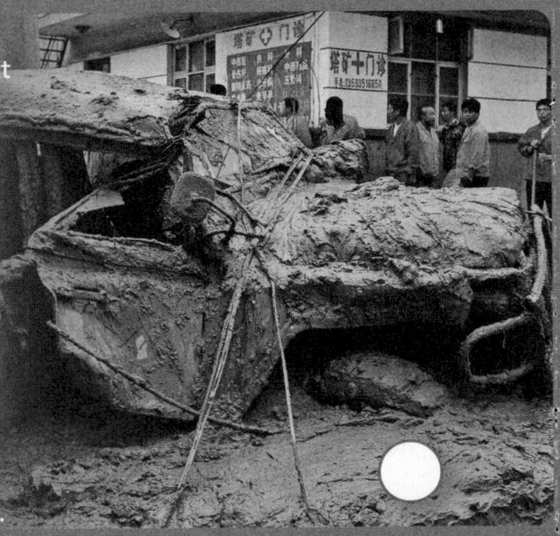

Mudflows A mudflow is the rapid downhill movement of a mixture of water, rock, and soil. The amount of water in a mudflow can be as high as 60 percent. Mudflows often occur after heavy rains in a normally dry area. In clay soils with a high water content, mudflows may occur even on very gentle slopes. Under certain conditions, clay soils suddenly behave as a liquid and begin to flow.

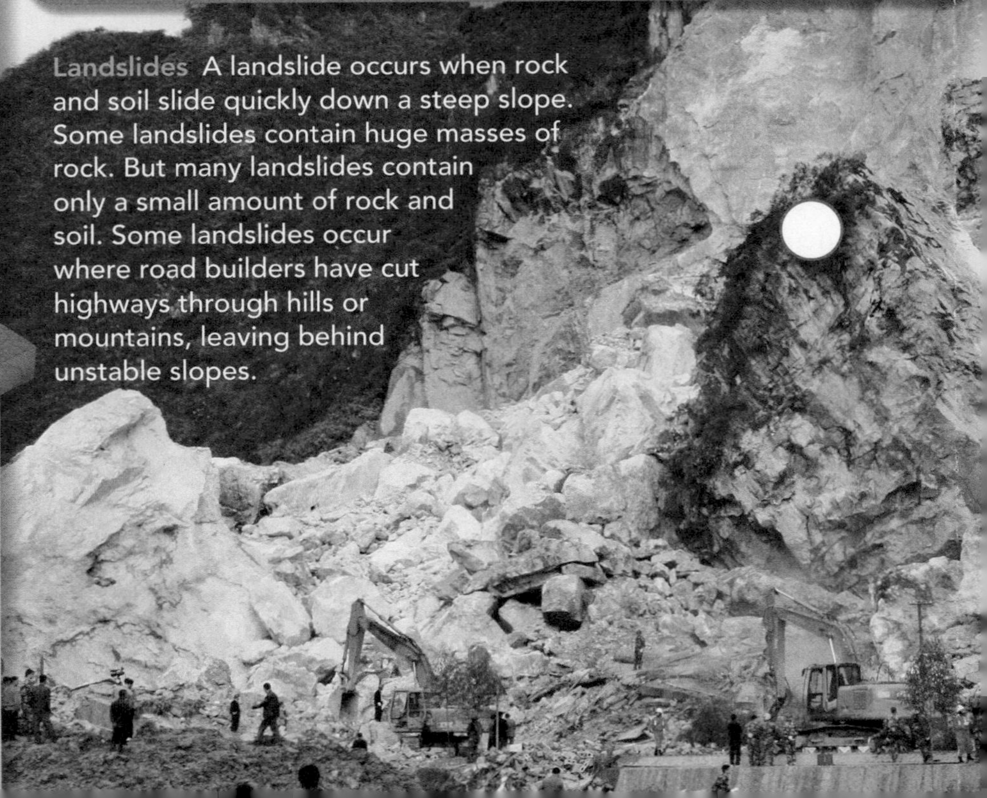

Landslides A landslide occurs when rock and soil slide quickly down a steep slope. Some landslides contain huge masses of rock. But many landslides contain only a small amount of rock and soil. Some landslides occur where road builders have cut highways through hills or mountains, leaving behind unstable slopes.

apply it!

Infer A fence runs across a steep hillside. The fence is tilted downhill and forms a curve rather than a straight line. What do you think happened?

_____

_____

_____

_____

7.NS.8

Slumps If you slump your shoulders, the entire upper part of your body drops down. In the type of mass movement known as slumps, a mass of rock and soil suddenly slips down a slope. Unlike a landslide, the material in a slump moves down in one large mass. It looks as if someone pulled the bottom out from under part of the slope. A slump often occurs when water soaks the bottom of soil that is rich in clay.

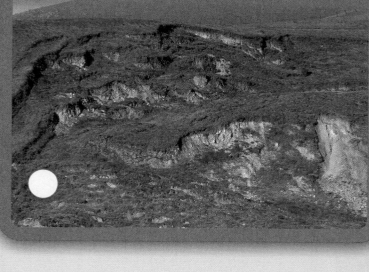

Creep Creep is the very slow downhill movement of rock and soil. It can even occur on gentle slopes. Creep often results from the freezing and thawing of water in cracked layers of rock beneath the soil. Like the movement of an hour hand on a clock, creep is so slow you can barely notice it. But you can see the effects of creep in vertical objects such as telephone poles and tree trunks. Creep may tilt these objects at unusual angles.

Lab **zone** Do the Lab Investigation *Sand Hills.*

🔑 Assess Your Understanding

1a. Review What is mass movement?

_____

_____

_____

7.2.7

b. Relate Cause and Effect What force causes all types of mass movement? Explain.

_____

_____

_____

7.2.7

got it? ....

○ **I get it!** Now I know that mass movement is the _____

_____

○ **I need extra help with** _____

Go to **MY SCIENCE** ⓢ **COACH** online for help with this subject.

7.2.7

Water Erosion

UNLOCK
THE BIG
?

🔑 **How Does Moving Water Cause Erosion?**
7.2.7, 7.NS.11

🔑 **What Land Features Are Formed by Water Erosion and Deposition?**
7.2.7, 7.NS.1, 7.NS.8, 7.NS.11

my PLaNeT DiaRY

FIELD TRIP

The Great Blue Hole

The boat leaves at 5:30 A.M. But you don't mind the early hour because it's the trip of a lifetime: a visit to the Great Blue Hole of Belize.

The Great Blue Hole is actually the remains of a cave formed by erosion. Several factors, including rising sea levels, caused the roof of the cave to collapse. This resulted in a natural depression called a sinkhole.

The Great Blue Hole is more than 300 meters wide and 125 meters deep. It's possibly the deepest and most massive sinkhole in the world. If you want to explore it, you have to scuba dive through the roof. It's an impressive example of what nature can accomplish over time!

> **Read the story. Then answer the question.**
> How was the Great Blue Hole formed?
> _____
> _____
> _____
>
> ⬭ PLANET DIARY Go to **Planet Diary** to learn more about water erosion.

Lab zone Do the Inquiry Warm-Up *How Does Moving Water Wear Away Rocks?*

Academic Standards for Science

7.2.7 Use geological features such as karst topography and glaciation to explain how large-scale physical processes have shaped the land.

7.NS.11 Communicate findings using charts and models.

How Does Moving Water Cause Erosion?

Erosion by water begins with a splash of rain. Some rainfall sinks into the ground. Some evaporates or is taken up by plants. The rest of the water runs off over the land surface. 🔑 **Moving water is the major agent of the erosion that has shaped Earth's land surface.**

Vocabulary
- runoff • rill • gully • stream • tributary
- flood plain • meander • oxbow lake • delta
- alluvial fan • groundwater • stalactite
- stalagmite • karst topography

Skills
Reading: Identify Supporting Evidence
Inquiry: Develop Hypotheses

Runoff As water moves over the land, it carries particles with it. This moving water is called **runoff.** When runoff flows in a thin layer over the land, it may cause a type of erosion called sheet erosion. The amount of runoff in an area depends on five main factors. The first factor is the amount of rain an area gets. A second factor is vegetation. Grasses, shrubs, and trees reduce runoff by absorbing water and holding soil in place. A third factor is the type of soil. Some types of soils absorb more water than others. A fourth factor is the shape of the land. Steeply sloped land has more runoff than flatter land. Finally, a fifth factor is how people use land. For example, a paved parking lot absorbs no water. All the rain that falls on it becomes runoff. Runoff also increases when farmers cut down crops, since this removes vegetation from the land.

Generally, more runoff means more erosion. In contrast, factors that reduce runoff will reduce erosion. Even though deserts have little rainfall they often have high runoff and erosion because they have few plants and thin soil. In wet areas, runoff and erosion may be low because there are more plants to help protect the soil.

Identify Supporting Evidence As you read the paragraph on the left, number each of the factors that affect runoff.

Factor	Example

FIGURE 1 ·····
Factors Affecting Runoff
Complete the task below.

1. **List** Record the five main factors affecting runoff.

2. **Identify** Using a specific location, such as a park, identify an example for each factor.

3. **Communicate** Explain to a partner what the runoff would be like at your location.

7.NS.11

Stream Formation Because of gravity, runoff and the material it contains flow downhill. As this water moves across the land, it runs together to form rills, gullies, and streams.

Rills and Gullies As runoff travels, it forms tiny grooves in the soil called **rills.** When many rills flow into one another, they grow larger, forming a gully. A **gully** is a large groove, or channel, in the soil that carries runoff after a rainstorm. As water flows through gullies, it moves soil and rocks with it, thus enlarging the gullies through erosion. Gullies only contain water during a rainstorm and for a short time after it rains.

Streams and Rivers Gullies join together to form a larger channel called a stream. A **stream** is a channel along which water is continually flowing down a slope. Unlike gullies, streams rarely dry up. Small streams are also called creeks or brooks. As streams flow together, they form larger and larger bodies of flowing water. A large stream is often called a river.

Tributaries A stream grows into a larger stream or river by receiving water from tributaries. A **tributary** is a stream or river that flows into a larger river. For example, the Missouri and Ohio rivers are tributaries of the Mississippi River. A drainage basin, or watershed, is the area from which a river and its tributaries collect their water.

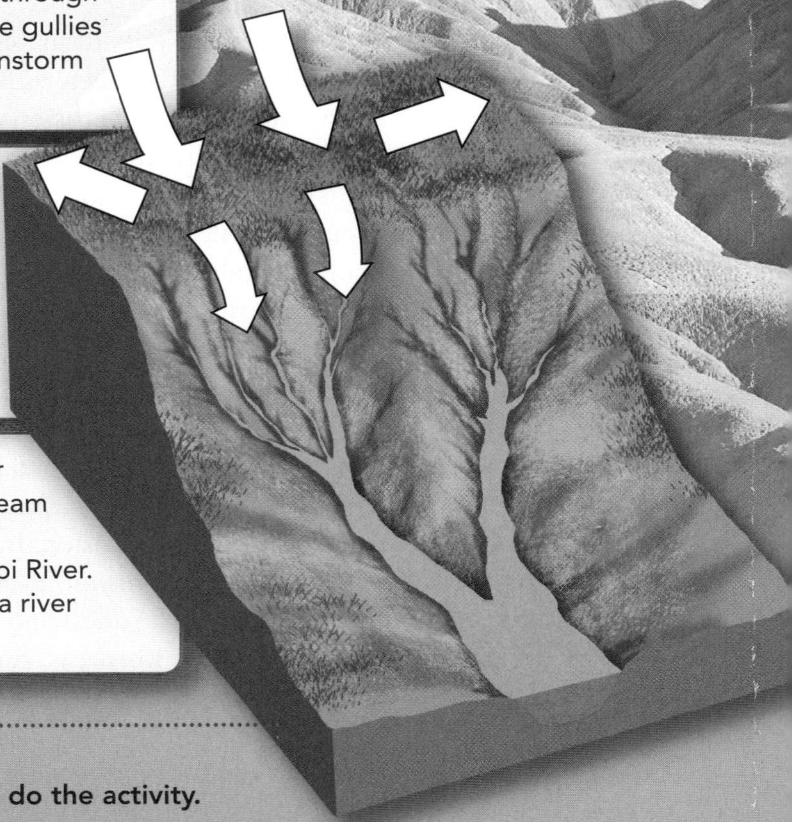

FIGURE 2
Stream Formation
✎ **Relate Text and Visuals** After you read, do the activity.
1. Shade in the arrows that indicate the direction of sheet erosion.
2. Circle the terms *rills, gully,* and *stream* in the text. Then draw a line from the word to examples of them in the picture.

Do the Quick Lab
Raindrops Falling.

🔑 Assess Your Understanding

1a. Review How does runoff affect the rate of erosion?

_____

_____

7.2.7

b. Sequence Put these in order of size from smallest to biggest: creek, rill, gully, river.

_____

_____

7.2.7

got it?

○ I get it! Now I know what runoff does: _____

_____

○ I need extra help with _____

Go to **MY SCIENCE ☁ COACH** online for help with this subject.

7.2.7

What Land Features Are Formed by Water Erosion and Deposition?

Walking in the woods in summer, you can hear the racing water of a river before you see the river itself. When you reach the river's banks, you see water rushing by. Sand and pebbles tumble along the river bottom. As it swirls downstream, the water also carries twigs, leaves, and bits of soil. In sheltered pools, insects skim the water's calm surface. Beneath the surface, a rainbow trout swims in the clear water. As the seasons change, so does the river. In winter, the surface of the river may freeze. But during spring, it may flood. Throughout the year, the river continues to erode Earth's surface.

Academic Standards for Science

7.2.7 Use geological features such as karst topography and glaciation to explain how large-scale physical processes have shaped the land.

7.NS.1 Make predictions and develop testable questions.

7.NS.8 Analyze data.

7.NS.11 Communicate findings using models.

FIGURE 3 ··

River Erosion

✎ **Interpret Photos** How does a river's ability to erode change with the seasons? (*Hint:* Look at how the amount of water changes during each season.)   **7.NS.8**

Spring   Summer   Fall   Winter

_____

_____

_____

_____

_____

Water Erosion Many rivers begin on steep mountain slopes. Near their source, these rivers can be fast-flowing and generally follow a straight, narrow course. The steep slopes along the river erode rapidly, resulting in a deep, V-shaped valley. As a river flows from the mountains to the sea, it forms many features. 🔑 **Through erosion, a river creates valleys, waterfalls, flood plains, meanders, and oxbow lakes.**

Waterfalls Waterfalls may occur where a river meets an area of rock that is very hard and erodes slowly. The river flows over this rock and then flows over softer rock downstream. Softer rock wears away faster than harder rock. Eventually a waterfall develops where the softer rock was removed. Areas of rough water called rapids also occur where a river tumbles over hard rock.

FIGURE 4
Waterfalls
✎ **Apply Concepts**
Where do you think the layers of hard and soft rock are located? Label the areas on the diagram to show your answer.

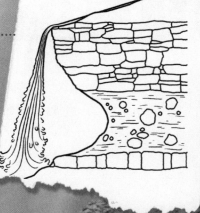

Flood Plain Lower down on its course, a river usually flows over more gently sloping land. The river spreads out and erodes the land, forming a wide river valley. The flat, wide area of land along a river is a **flood plain.** On a wide flood plain, the valley walls may be kilometers away from the river itself. A river often covers its flood plain when it overflows its banks during a flood. When the flood water finally retreats, it deposits sediment as new soil. This makes a river valley fertile.

Meanders A river often develops meanders where it flows through easily eroded rock or sediment. A **meander** is a looplike bend in the course of a river. As the river winds from side to side, it tends to erode the outer bank and deposit sediment on the inner bank of a bend. Over time, a meander becomes more curved.

Because of the sediment a river carries, it can erode a very wide flood plain. Along this part of a river's course, its channel may be deep and wide. The southern stretch of the Mississippi River meanders on a wide, gently sloping flood plain.

Oxbow Lakes Sometimes a meandering river forms a feature called an oxbow lake. As the photo below shows, an **oxbow lake** is a meander that has been cut off from the river. An oxbow lake may form when a river floods. During the flood, high water finds a straighter route downstream. As the flood waters fall, sediments dam up the ends of a meander, forming an oxbow lake.

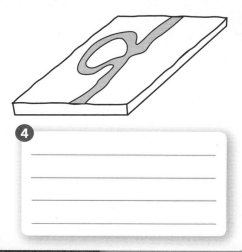

FIGURE 5 ·······················
Oxbow Lakes
A meander may gradually form an oxbow lake.

✎ **Make Models** Draw steps 2 and 4 to show how an oxbow lake forms and describe the last step.

7.NS.11

1 A small obstacle creates a slight bend in the river.

Outer edge

Inner edge

2 As water erodes the outer edge, the bend becomes bigger, forming a meander. Deposition occurs along the inner edge.

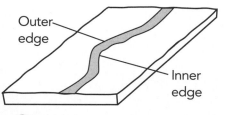

3 Gradually, the meander becomes more curved. The river breaks through and takes a new course.

4

_____

_____

_____

_____

Water Deposition

As water moves, it carries sediment with it. Any time moving water slows down, it drops, or deposits, some of the sediment. In this way, soil can be added to a river's flood plain. As the water slows down, large stones quit rolling and sliding. Fine particles fall to the river's bed as the river flows even more slowly. 🗝 **Deposition creates landforms such as alluvial fans and deltas.**

Deltas A river ends its journey when it flows into a still body of water, such as an ocean or a lake. Because the river water is no longer flowing downhill, the water slows down. At this point, the sediment in the water drops to the bottom. Sediment deposited where a river flows into an ocean or lake builds up a landform called a **delta.** Deltas can be a variety of shapes. Some are arc-shaped, others are triangle-shaped. The delta of the Mississippi River, shown here, is an example of a type of delta called a "bird's foot" delta.

Alluvial Fans Where a stream flows out of a steep, narrow mountain valley, the stream suddenly becomes wider and shallower. The water slows down. Here sediments are deposited in an alluvial fan. An **alluvial fan** is a wide, sloping deposit of sediment formed where a stream leaves a mountain range. As its name suggests, this deposit is shaped like a fan.

Key

Mississippi delta

LOUISIANA

MISSISSIPPI

TEXAS

Mississippi River

New Orleans

| 0 | 50 | 100 mi |
| 0 | 50 | 100 km |

Gulf of Mexico

FIGURE 6 ·······················
Deposits by Rivers
✏️ **Interpret Photos** Use the pictures above to describe the difference between an alluvial fan and a delta.

_____

_____

_____

_____

_____

_____

Rolling Through the Hills

What processes shape the surface of the land?

FIGURE 7 ··

▶ REAL-WORLD INQUIRY You're a tour guide in the area pictured below, and your tour group wants to learn more about some of the features they are seeing.

✏ Relate Evidence and Explanation Identify the two missing features on the image below. Then summarize what you would say about them to your tour group.

Waterfalls and Rapids Waterfalls and rapids are common where the river passes over harder rock.

V-Shaped Valley Near its source, the river flows through a deep, V-shaped valley. As the river flows, it cuts the valley deeper.

Tributary The river receives water and sediment from a tributary—a smaller river or stream that flows into it.

Oxbow Lake An oxbow lake is a meander cut off from the river by deposition of sediment.

Flood Plain A flood plain forms where the river's power of erosion widens its valley rather than deepening it.

Valley Widening As the river approaches sea level, it meanders more and develops a wider valley and broader flood plain.

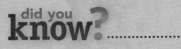

Groundwater Erosion

When rain falls and snow melts, not all of the water evaporates or becomes runoff. Some water soaks into the ground. There it fills the openings in the soil and trickles into cracks and spaces in layers of rock. **Groundwater** is the term geologists use for this underground water. Like running water on the surface, groundwater affects the shape of the land.

🔑 **Groundwater can cause erosion through a process of chemical weathering.** Rainwater is naturally acidic. In the atmosphere, water combines with carbon dioxide to form a weak acid called carbonic acid. Carbonic acid can break down limestone. Groundwater containing carbonic acid flows into any cracks in the limestone. Then some of the limestone dissolves and is carried away in a solution of water. This process gradually hollows out pockets in the rock. Over time, these pockets develop into large holes underground, called caves or caverns.

Cave Formations

The action of carbonic acid on limestone can also result in deposition. Inside limestone caves, deposits called stalactites and stalagmites often form. Water containing carbonic acid and calcium from limestone drips from a cave's roof. Carbon dioxide escapes from the solution, leaving behind a deposit of calcite. A deposit that hangs like an icicle from the roof of a cave is known as a **stalactite** (stuh LAK tyt). Slow dripping builds up a cone-shaped **stalagmite** (stuh LAG myt) from the cave floor.

FIGURE 8 ···
Groundwater Erosion and Deposition
✏️ **Explain** How do erosion and deposition shape caves? Take notes as you read. Then discuss with a classmate.　　7.NS.11

Process of Erosion	Process of Deposition

Karst Topography In rainy regions where there is a layer of limestone near the surface, groundwater erosion can significantly change the shape of the land. Streams are rare, because water easily sinks down into the weathered limestone. Deep valleys and caverns are common. If the roof of a cave collapses because of the erosion of the underlying limestone, the result is a depression called a sinkhole. This type of landscape is called **karst topography** after a region in Eastern Europe.

This sinkhole is in Russia's Perm region.

apply it!

Study the map and answer the questions below.

① Name three states in which you can find karst topography.

_____

② ⚠ **Develop Hypotheses** Why do you think karst topography occurs in these areas?

_____

_____

_____

Key

▮ Areas of karst topography

7.NS.1

Assess Your Understanding

2a. List Name two features of water erosion.

_____

7.2.7

b. **CHALLENGE** What is carbonic acid and how does it affect rock?

_____

_____

_____

7.2.7

c. **ANSWER THE BIG ?** What processes shape the surface of the land?

_____

_____

_____

_____

_____

7.2.7

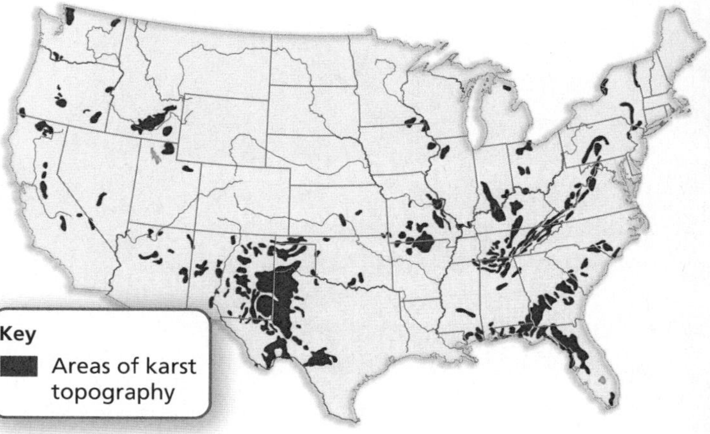

Lab zone® Do the Quick Lab *Erosion Cube.*

got it?

○ **I get it!** Now I know that features of erosion and deposition include _____

_____

○ **I need extra help with** _____

Go to **MY SCIENCE COACH** *online for help with this subject.*

7.2.7

Indiana
LESSON 3
Glacial Erosion

How Do Glaciers Form and Move?
7.2.7, 7.NS.8

How Do Glaciers Cause Erosion and Deposition?
7.2.7

my planet Diary *for* Indiana

Sculpting the Great Lakes

Imagine a large part of Indiana covered in ice! Most of the state was exactly that during the last Ice Age. For a great part of the last 2 million years, a period geologists call the Pleistocene epoch, Earth went through long periods of extreme cold. During the last Ice Age, which ended about 10,000 years ago, the northern two-thirds of Indiana was covered by huge, continent-sized sheets of ice.

These ice masses advanced as they grew larger and then receded as they melted. They scoured valleys and wore away the soft rock around them. The basins eventually filled with water when the glaciers melted, becoming the Great Lakes.

DISCOVERY

Extent of Glaciation
18,000 years before present

Indiana

Read the information about the formation of the Great Lakes. Then answer the question below.

1. How did the Great Lakes form?

_____

_____

_____

_____

_____

_____

> **PLANET DIARY** Go to **Planet Diary** to learn more about glacial erosion and deposition.

 Do the Inquiry Warm-Up *How Do Glaciers Change the Land?*

Vocabulary
- glacier
- continental glacier
- ice age
- valley glacier
- plucking
- till
- moraine
- kettle

Skills
↻ Reading: Relate Cause and Effect
△ Inquiry: Draw Conclusions

How Do Glaciers Form and Move?

On a boat trip off the coast of Alaska you sail by evergreen forests and snowcapped mountains. As you round a point of land, you see an amazing sight. A great mass of ice winds like a river between rows of mountains. This river of ice is a glacier. Geologists define a **glacier** as any large mass of ice that moves slowly over land. ⚿ **Glaciers can form only in an area where more snow falls than melts.** There are two kinds of glaciers—continental glaciers and valley glaciers.

Continental Glaciers A **continental glacier** is a glacier that covers much of a continent or large island. It can spread out over millions of square kilometers. Today, continental glaciers cover about 10 percent of Earth's land. They cover Antarctica and most of Greenland. ⚿ **Continental glaciers can flow in all directions as they move.** They spread out much as pancake batter spreads out in a frying pan. Many times in the past, continental glaciers have covered larger parts of Earth's surface. These times are known as **ice ages.** About 1 million years ago, continental glaciers covered nearly one third of Earth's land. The glaciers advanced and retreated, or melted back, several times. They most recently retreated about 10,000 years ago.

Academic Standards for Science

7.2.7 Use geological features such as karst topography and glaciation to explain how large-scale physical processes have shaped the land.
7.NS.8 Analyze data.

FIGURE 1 ·····················

Continental Glaciers
You're traveling across Antarctica from Point A to Point H on the route below. The cross section shows changes in the ice sheet along your journey.

✎ **Interpret Diagrams** What changes in elevation and ice depth will you encounter?

_____
_____
_____
_____
_____
_____
_____
_____
_____
_____

7.NS.8

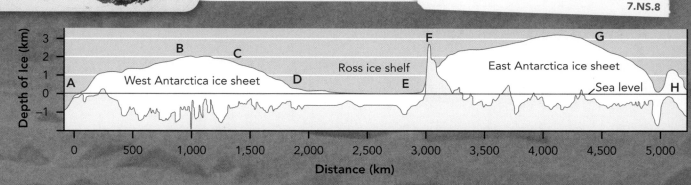

Valley Glaciers

A **valley glacier** is a long, narrow glacier that forms when snow and ice build up high in a mountain valley. The sides of mountains keep these glaciers from spreading out in all directions. Instead, they usually move down valleys that have already been cut by rivers. Valley glaciers are found on many high mountains. Although they are much smaller than continental glaciers, valley glaciers can be tens of kilometers long.

High in mountain valleys, temperatures rarely rise above freezing. Snow builds up year after year. The weight of more and more snow compacts the snow at the bottom into ice. 🔑 **Gravity constantly pulls a glacier downhill.** Once the layer of snow and ice is more than about 30 to 40 meters deep, the glacier begins to move.

Valley glaciers flow at a rate of a few centimeters to a few meters per day. But a valley glacier that surges, or slides quickly, can move as much as 6 kilometers in a year.

apply it!

When glaciers recede, they leave behind evidence of their existence.

7.NS.8

❶ Observe What was the landscape like before glaciers formed?

_____

_____

❷ ⚠ Draw Conclusions What did the glaciers do to the area?

_____

_____

_____

Before glaciers form   **After glaciers have melted**

 Do the Quick Lab *Surging Glaciers.*

🔑 Assess Your Understanding

got it? ....

○ **I get it!** Now I know that glaciers differ in how they move: _____

_____

○ **I need extra help with** _____

Go to MY SCIENCE 🔍 COACH *online for help with this subject.*

7.2.7

How Do Glaciers Cause Erosion and Deposition?

The movement of a glacier changes the land beneath it. Although glaciers work slowly, they are a major force of erosion. 🔑 **The two processes by which glaciers erode the land are plucking and abrasion.**

Glacial Erosion As a glacier flows over the land, it picks up rocks in a process called **plucking.** Beneath a glacier, the weight of the ice can break rocks apart. These rock fragments freeze to the bottom of the glacier. When the glacier moves, it carries the rocks with it, as shown in **Figure 2.** Plucking can move huge boulders.

Many rocks remain on the bottom of the glacier, and the glacier drags them across the land. This process, called abrasion, gouges and scratches the bedrock.

Academic Standards for Science

7.2.7 Use geological features such as karst topography and glaciation to explain how large-scale physical processes have shaped the land.

Bedrock

FIGURE 2 ·······················

Glacial Erosion

✎ **After you read about glaciers, do the activity.**

1. **Identify** Draw an arrow in the diagram above to show the direction the ice is moving.

2. **Explain** In your own words, describe the glacial erosion taking place in the diagram.

_____

_____

_____

_____

_____

_____

..............✏..............
⟳Relate Cause and Effect As you read, underline the cause of glacial deposition and circle the effects.

Glacial Deposition A glacier gathers a huge amount of rock and soil as it erodes the land in its path. 🔑 **When a glacier melts, it deposits the sediment it eroded from the land, creating various landforms.** These landforms remain for thousands of years after the glacier has melted. The mixture of sediments that a glacier deposits directly on the surface is called **till.** Till is made up of particles of many different sizes. Clay, silt, sand, gravel, and boulders can all be found in till.

The till deposited at the edges of a glacier forms a ridge called a **moraine.** A terminal moraine is the ridge of till at the farthest point reached by a glacier. Part of Long Island in New York is a terminal moraine from the continental glaciers of the last ice age.

Retreating glaciers also create features called kettles. A **kettle** is a small depression that forms when a chunk of ice is left in glacial till. When the ice melts, the kettle remains. The continental glacier of the last ice age left behind many kettles. Kettles often fill with water, forming small ponds or lakes called kettle lakes. Such lakes are common in areas such as Wisconsin, that were once covered with ice.

FIGURE 3 ....

▷**ART IN MOTION** Glacial Landforms

✏ **After you read, complete this activity.**

1. **Classify** Identify the features of erosion and deposition in the scene below. Record your answers in the boxes provided on the next page.

2. CHALLENGE Identify the feature in the photo on the next page. Describe how it formed.

Cirque A cirque is a bowl-shaped hollow eroded by a glacier.

Horn When glaciers carve away the sides of a mountain, the result is a horn, a sharpened peak.

Fiord A fiord forms when the level of the sea rises, filling a valley once cut by a glacier.

Arête An arête is a sharp ridge separating two cirques.

Glaciers have shaped the land in Denali National Park, Alaska.

Features of Erosion	Features of Deposition	Photo Feature

Glacial Lake Glaciers may leave behind large lakes in long basins.

U-Shaped Valley A flowing glacier scoops out a U-shaped valley.

Moraine A moraine forms where a glacier deposits a mound or a ridge.

Drumlin A drumlin is a long mound of till that is smoothed in the direction of the glacier's flow.

Kettle Lake A kettle lake forms when a depression left in till by melting ice fills with water.

Lab zone® Do the Quick Lab *Modeling Valleys.*

🔑 Assess Your Understanding

1a. Review How do glaciers erode by abrasion?

_____

_____

7.2.7

b. Describe How does a moraine form?

_____

_____

7.2.7

got it?..

○ **I get it!** Now I know that glaciers shape the landscape through the processes of _____

_____

_____

○ **I need extra help with** _____

_____

Go to 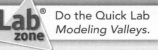 *online for help with this subject.* 7.2.7

Wave Erosion

🔑 How Do Waves Cause Erosion and Deposition?
7.2.7

UNLOCK
THE BIG
?

my planet diary

BLOG

Posted by: Lila

Location: Camden, Maine

I was returning home from an island picnic on our 24-foot motor boat, when the wind whipped up. The water in the bay became rough. The waves were splashing up the sides of the boat. Even though my dad slowed down, our boat slammed into wave after wave. My head hit the ceiling of the cabin, as I got bounced each time the boat hit a wave. Anything not strapped down slipped toward the back of the boat. It was scary!

After you read about Lila's trip, answer the question.

How did the waves affect Lila's boat ride?

_____

_____

_____

> PLANET DIARY Go to **Planet Diary** to learn more about wave erosion and deposition.

Lab zone Do the Inquiry Warm-Up *What Is Sand Made Of?*

Academic Standards for Science

7.2.7 Use geological features such as karst topography and glaciation to explain how large-scale physical processes have shaped the land.

How Do Waves Cause Erosion and Deposition?

The energy in waves comes from the wind. When the wind makes contact with the water some of its energy transfers to the water, forming waves. As a wave approaches land the water becomes shallower. The friction between the wave and the bottom causes the wave to slow down, and the water moves forward as the wave breaks. This forward-moving water provides the force that shapes the land along the shoreline.

Vocabulary
- headland • beach
- longshore drift • spit

Skills
- ⟳ Reading: Summarize
- △ Inquiry: Communicate

Erosion by Waves 🔑 **Waves shape the coast through erosion by breaking down rock and moving sand and other sediment.** One way waves erode the land is by impact. Large waves can hit rocks along the shore with great force. This energy in waves can break apart rocks. Over time, waves can make small cracks larger. Eventually, the waves cause pieces of rock to break off. Waves also erode by abrasion. As a wave approaches shallow water, it picks up sediment, including sand and gravel. This sediment is carried forward by the wave. When the wave hits land, the sediment wears away rock like sandpaper wearing away wood.

Waves coming to shore gradually change direction. The change in direction occurs as different parts of a wave begin to drag on the bottom. The waves in **Figure 1** change direction as they approach the shore. The energy of these waves is concentrated on headlands. A **headland** is a part of the shore that sticks out into the ocean. It is made of harder rock that resists erosion by the waves. But, over time, waves erode the headlands and even out the shoreline.

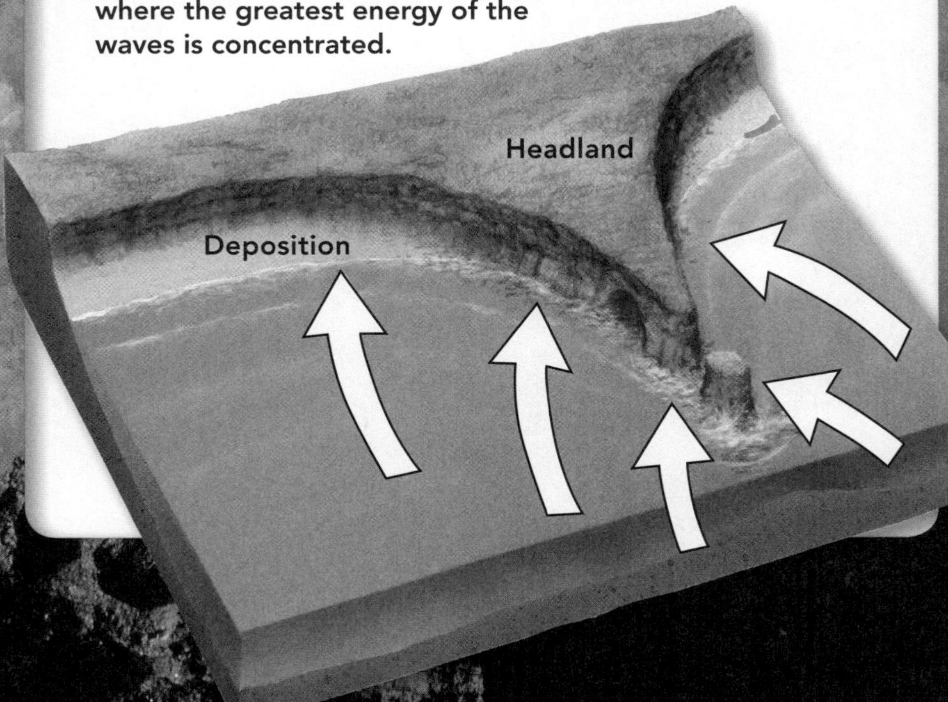

⟳ **Summarize** Read the text about wave erosion and explain how a wave erodes by abrasion.

_____
_____
_____
_____
_____

FIGURE 1 ·····························

Wave Erosion

✎ **Identify** Shade in the arrows that indicate where the greatest energy of the waves is concentrated.

Headland

Deposition

Landforms Created by Wave Erosion Think of an ax striking the trunk of a tree. The cut gets bigger and deeper with each strike of the blade. Finally the tree falls. In a similar way, ocean waves that hit a steep, rocky coast erode the base of the land there. Where the rock is softer, the waves erode the land faster. Over time the waves may erode a hollow area in the rock called a sea cave. Eventually, waves may erode the base of a cliff so much that the rock above collapses. The result is a wave-cut cliff. A sea arch is another feature of wave erosion that forms when waves erode a layer of softer rock that underlies a layer of harder rock. If an arch collapses, a pillar of rock called a sea stack may result.

Deposits by Waves Deposition occurs when waves slow down, causing the water to drop its sediment. 🔑 **Waves shape a coast when they deposit sediment, forming coastal features such as beaches, sandbars, barrier beaches, and spits.**

❶ Beaches A **beach** is an area of wave-washed sediment along a coast. The sediment deposited on beaches is usually sand. Most sand comes from rivers that carry eroded particles of rock to the ocean. Some beaches are made of small fragments of coral or seashells piled up by wave action. Florida has many such beaches.

Waves usually hit the beach at an angle, creating a current that runs parallel to the coast-line. As waves repeatedly hit the beach, some of the beach sediment moves down the beach with the current, in a process called **longshore drift.**

FIGURE 2 ··

> **INTERACTIVE ART** **The Changing Coast**

✎ **Apply Concepts** Use what you've learned about features of wave erosion and deposition to complete the activity.

1. Identify the landforms above. Label them in the spaces on the art.
2. Write an *E* or a *D* in each circle to indicate whether the landform was shaped by erosion or deposition.

② Sandbars and Barrier Beaches Incoming waves carrying sand may build up sandbars, long ridges of sand parallel to the shore. A barrier beach is similar to a sandbar. A barrier beach forms when storm waves pile up large amounts of sand above sea level, forming a long, narrow island parallel to the coast. Barrier beaches are found in many places along the Atlantic coast of the United States, such as the Outer Banks of North Carolina. People have built homes on many of these barrier beaches. But the storm waves that build up the beaches can also wash them away. Barrier beach communities must be prepared for the damage that hurricanes and other storms can bring.

apply it!

⚠️ **Communicate** How could a sea cave become a sea arch? Discuss with a classmate and write your conclusions below.

_____

_____

_____

_____

_____

Sediment

Longshore drift

③ Spits One result of longshore drift is the formation of a **spit.** A spit is a beach that projects like a finger out into the water. Spits form as a result of deposition by longshore drift. Spits occur where a headland or other obstacle interrupts longshore drift, or where the coast turns abruptly.

Lab zone® Do the Quick Lab *Shaping a Coastline.*

🔑 **Assess Your Understanding**

1a. Identify List two ways waves erode rock.

_____

7.2.7

b. List What are two features formed by wave depostion?

_____

_____

7.2.7

got it? ···

⚪ **I get it!** Now I know that waves shape the

coast by _____

_____

⚪ **I need extra help with** _____

Go to **MY SCIENCE** 🄢 **COACH** *online for help with this subject.* 7.2.7

Wind Erosion

🔑 **How Does Wind Cause Erosion and Deposition?**
7.2.7, 7.NS.1

my planet diary

Saving the Navajo Rangelands

How does wind erosion affect humans? You don't have to go far to find out. In the Southwest, sand dunes cover one third of Navajo Nation lands where sheep and cattle graze. Increasing drought is harming the plants that hold the dunes in place. As a result, the wind is moving the dunes on the Navajo rangelands. This makes it harder for living things to survive. Geologist Margaret Hiza Redsteer studies wind erosion. She left the Navajo Nation land to attend college, but she's come back to help. Recently, Dr. Redsteer met with Chinese scientists to learn how they stabilize dunes. Now, she'll use these methods to help slow erosion on the Navajo rangelands.

Lab zone Do the Inquiry Warm-Up *How Does Moving Air Affect Sediment?*

CAREERS

Read about Dr. Margaret Hiza Redsteer and answer the questions with a classmate.

1. Why are the dunes eroding on the Navajo land?

_____

_____

_____

2. Do you think it's important for scientists to problem solve together? Explain.

_____

_____

_____

_____

▶ **PLANET DIARY** Go to **Planet Diary** to learn more about wind erosion.

Academic Standards for Science

7.2.7 Use geological features such as karst topography and glaciation to explain how large-scale physical processes have shaped the land.

7.NS.1 Make predictions and develop testable questions.

How Does Wind Cause Erosion and Deposition?

Wind can be a powerful force in shaping the land in areas where there are few plants to hold the soil in place. In the east African nation of Eritrea, sandstorms like the one in the photo are common. Strong winds blowing over loose soil can reduce visibility.

Vocabulary
- deflation
- loess
- sand dune

Skills
- ↻ Reading: Ask Questions
- △ Inquiry: Predict

Deflation Wind causes erosion mainly by deflation. Geologists define **deflation** as the process by which wind removes surface materials. You can see the process of deflation in **Figure 1.** When wind blows over the land, it picks up the smallest particles of sediment, such as clay and silt. The stronger the wind, the larger the particles it can pick up. Slightly heavier particles, such as sand, might skip or bounce for a short distance. But sand soon falls back to the ground. Strong winds can roll heavier sediment particles over the ground. In deserts, deflation can sometimes create an area of rock fragments called *desert pavement.* There, wind has blown away the smaller sediment, leaving behind rocky materials.

Abrasion Abrasion by wind-carried sand can polish rock, but it causes relatively little erosion. Geologists think that most desert landforms are the result of weathering and water erosion.

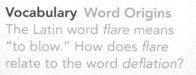

Vocabulary Word Origins
The Latin word *flare* means "to blow." How does *flare* relate to the word *deflation?*

_____

_____

_____

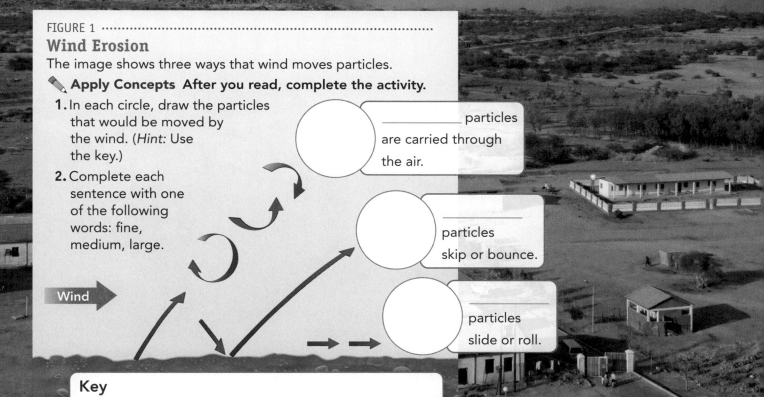

FIGURE 1 ·······
Wind Erosion
The image shows three ways that wind moves particles.

✏️ **Apply Concepts After you read, complete the activity.**

1. In each circle, draw the particles that would be moved by the wind. (*Hint:* Use the key.)

2. Complete each sentence with one of the following words: fine, medium, large.

Wind →

_____ particles are carried through the air.

_____ particles skip or bounce.

_____ particles slide or roll.

Key
- • Fine particle
- ☁ Medium particle
- ☁ Large particle

Ask Questions Read the headings on this page, then write down one question you have. After you read, try to answer your question.

_____

_____

_____

_____

FIGURE 2

Dune Formation
Draw Conclusions Why do these dunes have different shapes?

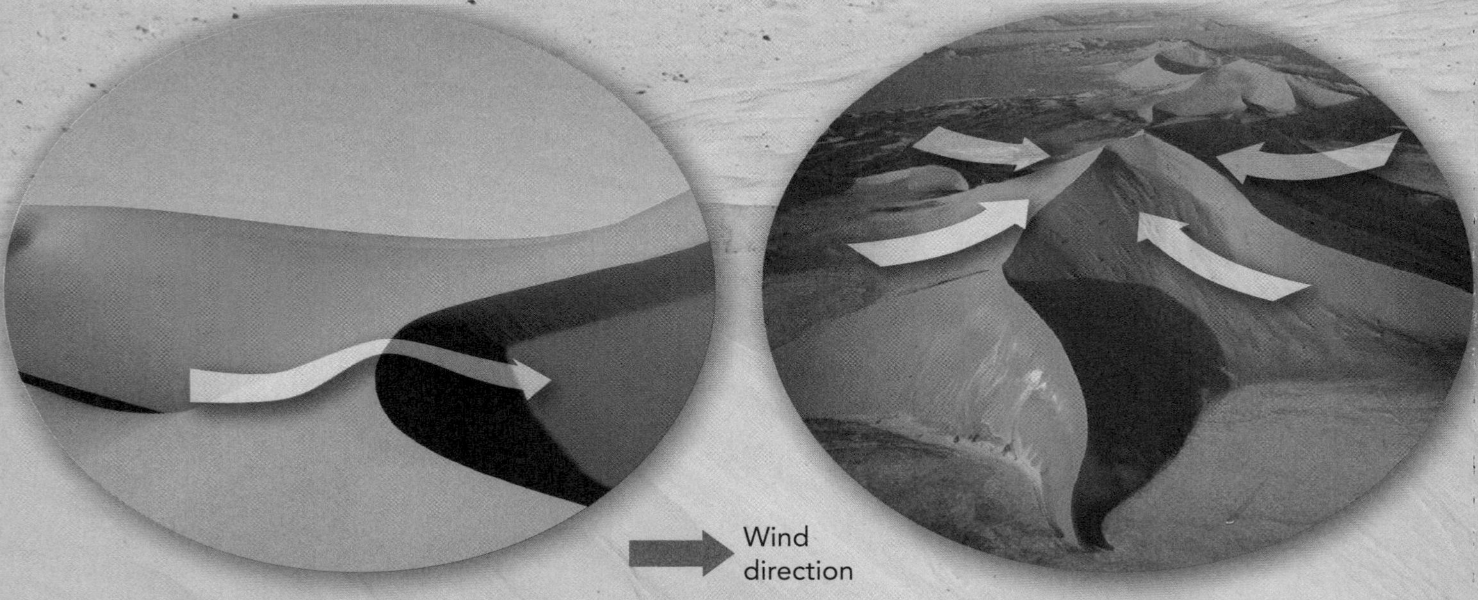

_____

_____

_____

_____

Deposits by Wind

All the sediment picked up by wind eventually falls to the ground. This happens when the wind slows down or an obstacle, such as a boulder or a clump of grass, traps the windblown sand sediment. **Wind erosion and deposition may form sand dunes and loess deposits.** When the wind meets an obstacle, the result is usually a deposit of windblown sand called a **sand dune.** The shape of sand dunes is determined by the direction of the wind, the amount of sand, and the presence of plants.

Sand Dunes You can see sand dunes on beaches and in deserts where wind-blown sediment has built up. Sand dunes come in many shapes and sizes. Some are long, with parallel ridges, while others are U-shaped. They can also be very small or very large. Some sand dunes in China are 500 meters high. Sand dunes move over time. Little by little, the sand shifts with the wind from one side of the dune to the other. Sometimes plants begin growing on a dune. Plant roots can help to anchor the dune in one place.

Loess Deposits Sediment that is smaller than sand, such as particles of clay and silt, is dropped far from its source in large deposits. This fine, wind-deposited sediment is **loess** (LOH es). There are large loess deposits in central China and in states such as Nebraska, South Dakota, Iowa, Missouri, and Illinois. Loess helps to form fertile soil. Many areas with thick loess deposits are valuable farmlands.

Crescent-shaped dunes

Wind direction

Star-shaped dunes

apply it!

Look at the photos and answer the questions with a classmate.

1 ⚠️ **Predict** Which dune do you think is likely to erode faster? Why?

_____

_____

_____

_____

7.NS.1

2 Why do you think plants grew on Dune B?

_____

_____

3 How could sand dunes be held in place to prevent them from drifting onto a parking lot?

_____

_____

_____

_____

Dune A

Dune B

Lab zone Do the Quick Lab *Desert Pavement.*

🔑 Assess Your Understanding

1a. Review What is deflation?

_____

_____

b. Relate Cause and Effect What causes wind to deposit sand or other sediment?

_____

_____

7.2.7

c. [CHALLENGE] In a desert, a soil mixture of sand and small rocks is exposed to wind erosion. How would the land surface change over time?

_____

_____

_____

_____

_____

7.2.7

got it? ....

○ **I get it!** Now I know that wind causes erosion through _____

○ **I need extra help with** _____

Go to **MY SCIENCE** Ⓢ **COACH** online for help with this subject.

7.2.7

13 Study Guide

REVIEW THE BIG ?

The surface of the land is shaped by the processes of erosion and deposition caused by

gravity, _____ , _____ , glaciers, and _____ .

LESSON 1 Mass Movement

7.2.7, 7.NS.8

🔑 Weathering, erosion, and deposition act together in a cycle that wears down and builds up Earth's surface.

🔑 The different types of mass movement include landslides, mudflows, slumps, and creep.

Vocabulary
• erosion • sediment • deposition
• gravity • mass movement

LESSON 2 Water Erosion

7.2.7, 7.NS.1, 7.NS.8, 7.NS.11

🔑 Moving water is the major agent of erosion that has shaped Earth's land surface. Groundwater erodes through chemical weathering.

🔑 Through erosion, a river forms valleys, waterfalls, flood plains, meanders, and oxbow lakes. Deposition forms alluvial fans and deltas.

Vocabulary
• runoff • rill • gully • stream • tributary
• flood plain • meander • oxbow lake
• delta • alluvial fan • groundwater
• stalactite • stalagmite • karst topography

LESSON 3 Glacial Erosion

7.2.7, 7.NS.8

🔑 Glaciers can form only in an area where more snow falls than melts.

🔑 Continental glaciers can flow in all directions as they move.

🔑 Gravity constantly pulls a glacier downhill.

🔑 Glaciers erode the land through plucking and abrasion. When a glacier melts, it deposits the sediment it eroded from the land.

Vocabulary
• glacier • continental glacier • ice age
• valley glacier • plucking • till • moraine • kettle

LESSON 4 Wave Erosion

7.2.7

🔑 Waves shape the coast through erosion by breaking down rock and moving sand and other sediment.

🔑 Waves shape a coast when they deposit sediment, forming coastal features such as beaches, sandbars, barrier beaches, and spits.

Vocabulary
• headland • beach
• longshore drift • spit

LESSON 5 Wind Erosion

7.2.7, 7.NS.1

🔑 Wind erosion and deposition may form sand dunes and loess deposits.

Vocabulary
• deflation
• sand dune
• loess

Review and Assessment

LESSON 1 Mass Movement

1. What is the process by which weathered rock, sediment, and soil are moved from place to place?

   a. runoff

   b. delta formation

   c. erosion

   d. longshore drift

   7.2.7

2. Freezing and thawing of water can cause creep, which is _____

_____

   7.2.7

3. Compare and Contrast How are landslides and mudflows similar? How are they different?

_____

_____

_____

_____

   7.2.7

4. Sequence Identify the steps in the erosion cycle. Explain why it has no beginning or end.

_____

_____

_____

_____

_____

   7.2.7

5. Relate Cause and Effect What type of mass movement is shown below? Explain.

_____

_____

   7.2.7

LESSON 2 Water Erosion

6. Which feature typically contains water only during a rainstorm and right after it rains?

   a. a river

   b. a rill

   c. a gully

   d. a stream

   7.2.7

7. Sediments are deposited in an alluvial fan because _____

_____

   7.2.7

8. Sequence Complete the flowchart about stream formation.

Stream Formation

Raindrops strike ground.

↓

Runoff forms.

↓

a._____

↓

b._____

↓

c._____

↓

d._____

   7.2.7

9. Make Judgments Your family looks at a new house right on a riverbank. Why might they hesitate to buy this house?

_____

_____

_____

_____

   7.2.7

10. **Write About It** Explain to visitors to your valley how the lake called *Oxbow Lake* formed. Use words and a drawing.

   7.2.7, 7.NS.11

LESSON 3 Glacial Erosion

11. What do you call a mass of rock and soil deposited directly by a glacier?

  a. kettle   **b.** till

  c. slump   **d.** loess

                                       7.2.7

12. When glaciers drag attached rocks across the land, they _____

_____

                                       7.2.7

13. Solve Problems You're in the mountains studying a valley glacier. What methods would you use to tell if it is advancing or retreating?

_____

_____

_____

_____

_____

                                       7.2.7

LESSON 4 Wave Erosion

14. What is a rocky part of the shore that sticks out in the ocean?

  a. spit   **b.** barrier beach

  c. rill   **d.** headland

                                       7.2.7

15. Waves change direction as they near shore because _____

_____

                                       7.2.7

16. Apply Concepts Under what conditions would you expect abrasion to cause the most erosion on a beach?

_____

_____

                                       7.2.7

17. **Write About It** You're walking on a beach and see a spit. Explain how a spit could have formed from a rocky headland.

                               7.2.7, 7.NS.1

LESSON 5 Wind Erosion

18. What do you call the erosion of sediment by wind?

  a. drifting   **b.** deposition

  c. plucking   **d.** deflation

                                       7.2.7

19. Compare and Contrast How is wind deflation different from wind abrasion?

_____

_____

_____

_____

_____

                                       7.2.7

20. Relate Cause and Effect How does a loess deposit form?

_____

_____

                                       7.2.7

APPLY THE BIG Q What processes shape the surface of the land?

21. Suppose you are a geologist traveling in a region that has limestone bedrock and plenty of rainfall. What features would you expect to find in this landscape? How do they form?

_____

_____

_____

_____

_____

_____

_____

_____

_____

                               7.2.7, 7.NS.1

Indiana ISTEP+ Practice

Multiple Choice

Circle the letter of the best answer.

1. The diagram shows a meander. Where would sediment likely be eroded to help form an oxbow?

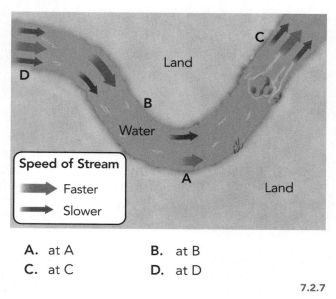

A. at A
B. at B
C. at C
D. at D

7.2.7

2. What is the slow, downhill mass movement of rock and soil caused by gravity?

A. creep
B. a glacier
C. a landslide
D. runoff

7.2.7

3. What is the name for a small depression created by the melting of a chunk of ice in glacial sediment?

A. till
B. kettle
C. moraine
D. spit

7.2.7

4. What "drifts" in longshore drift?

A. a chunk of glacier
B. a river's course
C. beach sediment
D. groundwater

7.2.7

Constructed Response

Write your answer to Question 5 on the lines below.

5. What is an alluvial fan?

_____

_____

_____

7.2.7

Extended Response

Use the diagram below and your knowledge of science to help you answer Question 6. Write your answer on a separate piece of paper.

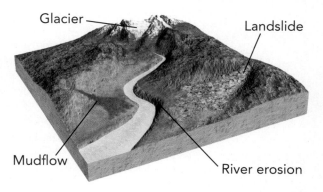

6. Describe how gravity affects the erosion of Earth's surface in mass movement, running water, and glaciers.

7.2.7

THE UNDERGROUND WORLD OF KARST

Muscatatuck Plateau

Mitchell Plateau

A dark and mysterious world hides beneath the green rolling hills along Indiana's border with Kentucky. It's a world of winding caves, cathedral-like caverns, sinkholes, and disappearing streams. Welcome to the Mitchell and Muscatatuck plateaus, Indiana's karst region!

Imagine thousands of years of rainwater pouring over ancient limestone. If you've ever examined limestone, you know how soft it is and how easily it dissolves in water. Think of how rainwater, combined with acidic carbon dioxide from the air, can erode limestone into interesting formations. If you could speed up time, you'd see winding drainage tunnels forming right before your very eyes.

If you're ready to embark on a caving adventure, you can enjoy it safely by bringing along specialized equipment. Walk softly and minimize your presence to preserve this unique environment. Trained guides with cave tours and exploring clubs help you learn more. So grab your gear and bring some adults to explore the world of karst!

Write About It Research one of Indiana's many cave systems. Write and illustrate a brief travel brochure persuading your classmates to visit the cave. Be sure to include an explanation of features, history, location, and ways to preserve it.

7.2.7, 7.NS.2, 7.NS.11

Any Way the Wind Blows

Mars is a pretty cool place. Gusts of wind blow frosty sand dunes around and cause strange streaks of sand and frost. When the Mars Rovers arrived on Mars in 2004, scientists at the National Aeronautics and Space Administration got their first chance to learn about wind and erosion on another planet. The rovers captured pictures of grains of Martian sand (called "blueberries" by the scientists) and of the patterns of dust and rock on the surface of Mars. From these pictures, scientists learned a lot about wind erosion.

By measuring these Martian blueberries and recording where they landed on the surface, scientists could estimate how strong Martian winds must be. Looking at the patterns of sand and bare rock, they could tell which directions the winds on Mars blow. Data showed that they blow from either the northwest or the southeast.

Scientists used all their measuring, counting, and other observations to design a computer model. The model can describe what happens to a planet's sandy surface when the wind starts blowing. By counting millions of blueberries on Mars, scientists are learning how to track wind erosion anywhere in the solar system!

Research It Dr. Douglas Jerolmack is a geophysicist who helped prove there is wind on Mars. Research Dr. Jerolmack's observations. Write a paragraph giving reasons why Dr. Jerolmack's scientific claims are considered to be valid (true).

7.2.6, 7.NS.2

▲ Scientists measured "blueberries"—grains of Martian sand and dust.

WHAT CAN YOU LEARN FROM A BUG?

How do scientists study Earth's past?

Long ago, a fly got stuck in resin from a tree. Today, that fly is a fossil that scientists can study. It's a clue to what Earth was like on the day the fly got stuck.
△ Develop Hypotheses **What do you think scientists can learn from fossils like this?**

▶ **UNTAMED SCIENCE** Watch the **Untamed Science** video to learn more about fossils.

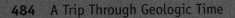

Indiana

CHAPTER 14

A Trip Through Geologic Time

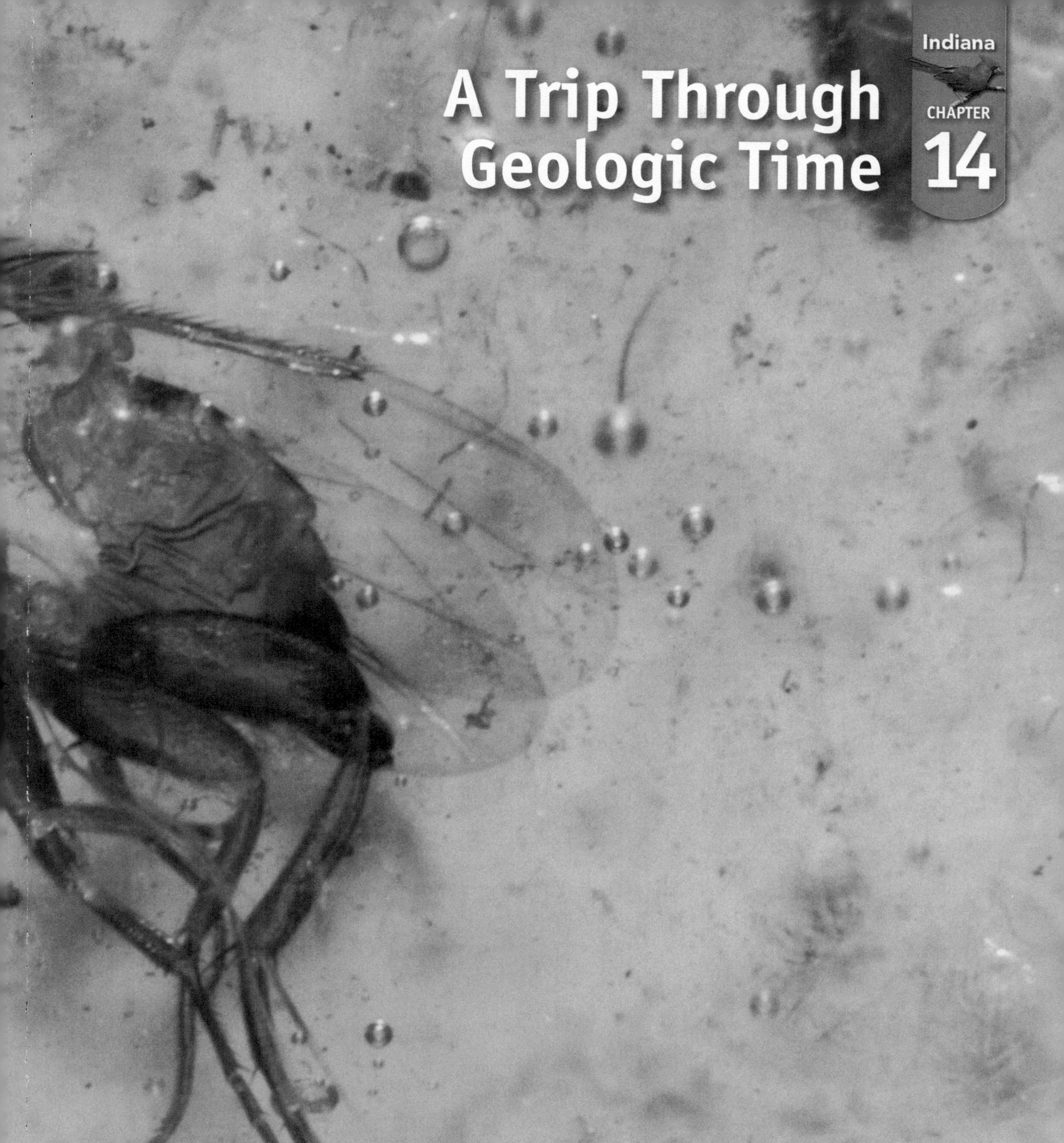

Academic Standards for Science

7.2, 7.2.3, 7.2.8, 7.NS.1, 7.NS.2, 7.NS.3, 7.NS.8, 7.NS.11

14 Getting Started

Check Your Understanding

1. **Background** Read the paragraph below and then answer the question.

Forces inside Earth move large pieces, or plates, of Earth's crust very slowly over long periods of time. These forces are explained by **plate tectonics.** Where these plates meet, volcanic eruptions can produce **igneous rocks.** Over time, rivers, wind, and ice can break down the rocks and carry **sediment** to new places.

> The theory of **plate tectonics** states that pieces of Earth's upper layers move slowly, carried by convection currents inside Earth.
>
> An **igneous rock** forms when melted material hardens inside Earth or on the surface.
>
> **Sediment** is made up of small pieces of rock and other material.

• How do volcanic eruptions produce rocks?

_____

_____

> **MY READING WEB** If you had trouble answering the question above, visit **My Reading Web** and type in *A Trip Through Geologic Time.*

Vocabulary Skill

Prefixes The root of a word is the part of the word that carries the basic meaning. A prefix is a word part placed in front of the root to change the meaning of the root or to form a new word. Look at the examples in the table below.

Prefix	Meaning	Example
in-	inside, inward	intrusion, *n.*
ex-	outside, outward	extrusion, *n.*
super-	over, above	superposition, *n.*

2. **Quick Check** The root *–trusion* means "pushing." What might *extrusion* mean?_____

fossil

intrusion

law of superposition

vertebrate

Chapter Preview

LESSON 1
- fossil • mold • cast
- petrified fossil • carbon film
- trace fossil • paleontologist
- evolution • extinct

↺ **Compare and Contrast**
△ **Pose Questions**

LESSON 2
- relative age • absolute age
- law of superposition • extrusion
- intrusion • fault • index fossil
- unconformity

↺ **Relate Text and Visuals**
△ **Infer**

LESSON 3
- geologic time scale • era
- period

↺ **Summarize**
△ **Make Models**

LESSON 4
- invertebrate • vertebrate
- amphibian • reptile
- mass extinction • mammal

↺ **Identify Supporting Evidence**
△ **Classify**

> **VOCAB FLASH CARDS** For extra help with vocabulary, visit **Vocab Flash Cards** and type in *A Trip Through Geologic Time.*

Fossils

UNLOCK THE BIG ?

🔑 **What Are Fossils?**
7.2.8

🔑 **What Are the Kinds of Fossils?**
7.2.8, 7.NS.1, 7.NS.8

🔑 **What Do Fossils Show?**
7.2.8, 7.NS.8

my planet diary *for* Indiana

FIELD TRIP

From Sea to Land

If you lived in Indiana 300 million to 500 million years ago, chances are your house would have been underwater. A shallow sea covered a large part of Laurentia, an ancient continent that would later become North America.

In western Indiana, near Crawfordsville, scientists have found fossils of marine organisms called crinoids. These discoveries have helped scientists reconstruct the prehistoric environment in and around Indiana, confirming the existence of an ancient sea.

Land
Shallow sea
Deep sea

LAURENTIA

Indiana

✎ **Communicate** Discuss the questions with a partner. Write your answers below.

1. What do the marine fossils tell scientists about the area that would become Indiana during the Paleozoic Era?

_____

_____

_____

2. What major natural force may have led to the change from shallow sea to dry land?

_____

_____

> PLANET DIARY Go to **Planet Diary** to learn more about fossils.

Lab zone® Do the Inquiry Warm-Up *What's in a Rock?*

Vocabulary
- fossil • mold • cast • petrified fossil • carbon film
- trace fossil • paleontologist • evolution • extinct

Skills
- ⤷ Reading: Compare and Contrast
- △ Inquiry: Pose Questions

What Are Fossils?

Fossils are the preserved remains or traces of living things.
🔑 **Most fossils form when living things die and are buried by sediment. The sediment slowly hardens into rock and preserves the shapes of the organisms.** Sediment is made up of rock particles or the remains of living things. Most fossils form from animals or plants that once lived in or near quiet water such as swamps, lakes, or shallow seas where sediment builds up. In **Figure 1,** you can see how a fossil might form.

When an organism dies, its soft parts often decay quickly or are eaten by animals. That is why only hard parts of an organism generally leave fossils. These hard parts include bones, shells, teeth, seeds, and woody stems. It is rare for the soft parts of an organism to become a fossil.

> 🔷 **Academic Standards for Science**
>
> **7.2.8** Compare and contrast fossils with living organisms in a given location to explain how earth processes have changed environments over time.

FIGURE 1 ······························

> INTERACTIVE ART **How a Fossil Forms**
A fossil may form when sediment quickly covers an organism's body.

An organism dies and sinks to the bottom of a lake.

The organism is covered by sediment.

✏️ **Sequence** What happens next?

_____

_____

 Do the Quick Lab
Sweet Fossils.

🔑 Assess Your Understanding

got it? ···

○ **I get it!** Now I know that fossils are_____

_____

○ **I need extra help with** _____

7.2.8 Compare and contrast fossils with living organisms in a given location to explain how earth processes have changed environments over time.

7.NS.1 Make predictions and develop testable questions based on research and prior knowledge.

7.NS.8 Analyze data and use it to identify patterns and make inferences.

Compare and Contrast How are carbon films and preserved remains different?

_____

_____

_____

_____

_____

_____

What Are the Kinds of Fossils?

Fossils found in rock include molds and casts, petrified fossils, carbon films, and trace fossils. Other fossils form when the remains of organisms are preserved in substances such as tar, amber, or ice. Look at examples of the kinds of fossils in **Figure 2.**

Molds and Casts The most common fossils are molds and casts. A **mold** is a hollow area in sediment in the shape of an organism or part of an organism. A mold forms when the organism is buried in sediment. Later, water may deposit minerals and sediment into a mold, forming a cast. A **cast** is a solid copy of the shape of an organism. Molds and casts can preserve fine details.

Petrified Fossils A fossil may form when the remains of an organism become petrified. The term _petrified_ means "turned into stone." **Petrified fossils** are fossils in which minerals replace all of an organism, or a part, such as a dinosaur bone. This can also happen to wood, such as tree trunks. Water carrying minerals seeps into spaces in the plant's cells. Over time, the water evaporates, leaving the minerals behind.

Carbon Films Another type of fossil is a **carbon film,** an extremely thin coating of carbon on rock. When sediment buries an organism, some gases escape from the sediment, leaving carbon behind. Eventually, only a thin film of carbon remains. This process can preserve the delicate parts of plant leaves and insects.

FIGURE 2 ·······························

Types of Fossils

In addition to petrified fossils, fossils may be molds and casts, carbon films, trace fossils, or preserved remains.

Classify Identify each fossil shown here by its type.

Raised Fern

This fossil shows the texture of a leaf. Fossil type:

_____

Fine Details

This fossil preserves a thin layer that shows the details of an ancient insect. Fossil type:

_____

Hollow Fern

Can you see the veins in this plant leaf? Fossil type:

_____

Where They Walked

This footprint shows how a dinosaur walked. Fossil type:

_____

apply it!

This fossil is of an ancient organism called *Archaeopteryx*. Study the photograph and then answer the questions.

1 What type of fossil is this?

_____

2 **Pose Questions** List two questions about the organism that studying this fossil could help you answer.

_____

_____

7.NS.1, 7.NS.8

Trace Fossils

Trace fossils provide evidence of the activities of ancient organisms. A fossilized footprint is one example. In such a fossil, a print is buried by sediment, which slowly becomes solid rock. Trails and burrows can also become trace fossils.

Preserved Remains

Some processes can preserve entire organisms. For example, some organisms become trapped in sticky tar or tree resin. When the resin hardens, it becomes a substance called amber. Freezing can also preserve remains.

Frozen in Time
Ice preserved even the fur and skin of this woolly mammoth for thousands of years. Fossil type:

_____

From Wood to Stone
Minerals replaced other materials inside this tree, producing the colors shown here. Fossil type:

_____

Do the Quick Lab
Modeling Trace Fossils.

Assess Your Understanding

1a. **Identify** A (mold/trace fossil) can form when sediment buries the hard part of an organism. 7.2.8

b. **Explain** A petrified fossil forms when _____ replace parts of a(n) _____ . 7.2.8

c. **Make Generalizations** What might you learn from a carbon film that you could not learn from a cast?

_____

_____

7.2.8

got it?

○ **I get it!** Now I know that the kinds of fossils are _____

_____

○ **I need extra help with** _____

Go to MY SCIENCE COACH online for help with this subject. 7.2.8

Academic Standards for Science

7.2.8 Compare and contrast fossils with living organisms in a given location to explain how earth processes have changed environments over time.

7.NS.8 Analyze data and use it to identify patterns and make inferences.

What Do Fossils Show?

Would you like to hunt for fossils all over the world? And what could you learn from them? Scientists who study fossils are called **paleontologists** (pay lee un TAHL uh jists). Together, all the information that paleontologists have gathered about past life is called the fossil record. 🔑 **The fossil record provides evidence about the history of life and past environments on Earth. The fossil record also shows how different groups of organisms have changed over time.**

Fossils and Past Environments Paleontologists use fossils to build up a picture of Earth's past environments. The fossils found in an area tell whether the area was a shallow bay, an ocean bottom, or a freshwater swamp.

Fossils also provide evidence about the past climate of a region. For example, coal has been found in Antarctica. But coal forms only from the remains of plants that grow in warm, swampy regions. The presence of coal shows that the climate of Antarctica was once much warmer than it is today. **Figure 3** shows another example of how fossils show change in an environment.

FIGURE 3 ························

> **INTERACTIVE ART** **Wyoming, 50 Million Years Ago**
Today, as you can see in the postcard, Wyoming has areas of dry plateaus. But 50 million years ago, the area was very different. ✎ **Infer** Identify the organism or kind of organism shown by fossils a, b, and c.
7.NS.8

Palms

a

b

c

Crocodilian

Bat

CHALLENGE What features of *Hyracotherium* show that it is related to horses?

_____

_____

_____

_____

7.NS.8

Gar

Change and the Fossil Record The fossil record also reveals changes in organisms. Older rocks contain fossils of simpler organisms. Younger rocks contain fossils of both simple and more complex organisms. In other words, the fossil record shows that life on Earth has evolved, or changed over time. **Evolution** is the change in living things over time.

The fossil record shows that millions of types of organisms have evolved. But many others, including the dinosaurs, have become extinct. A type of organism is **extinct** if it no longer exists and will never again live on Earth.

Scientists use fossils to reconstruct extinct organisms and determine how they may be related to living organisms. For example, the animals called *Hyracotherium* in **Figure 3** are related to modern horses.

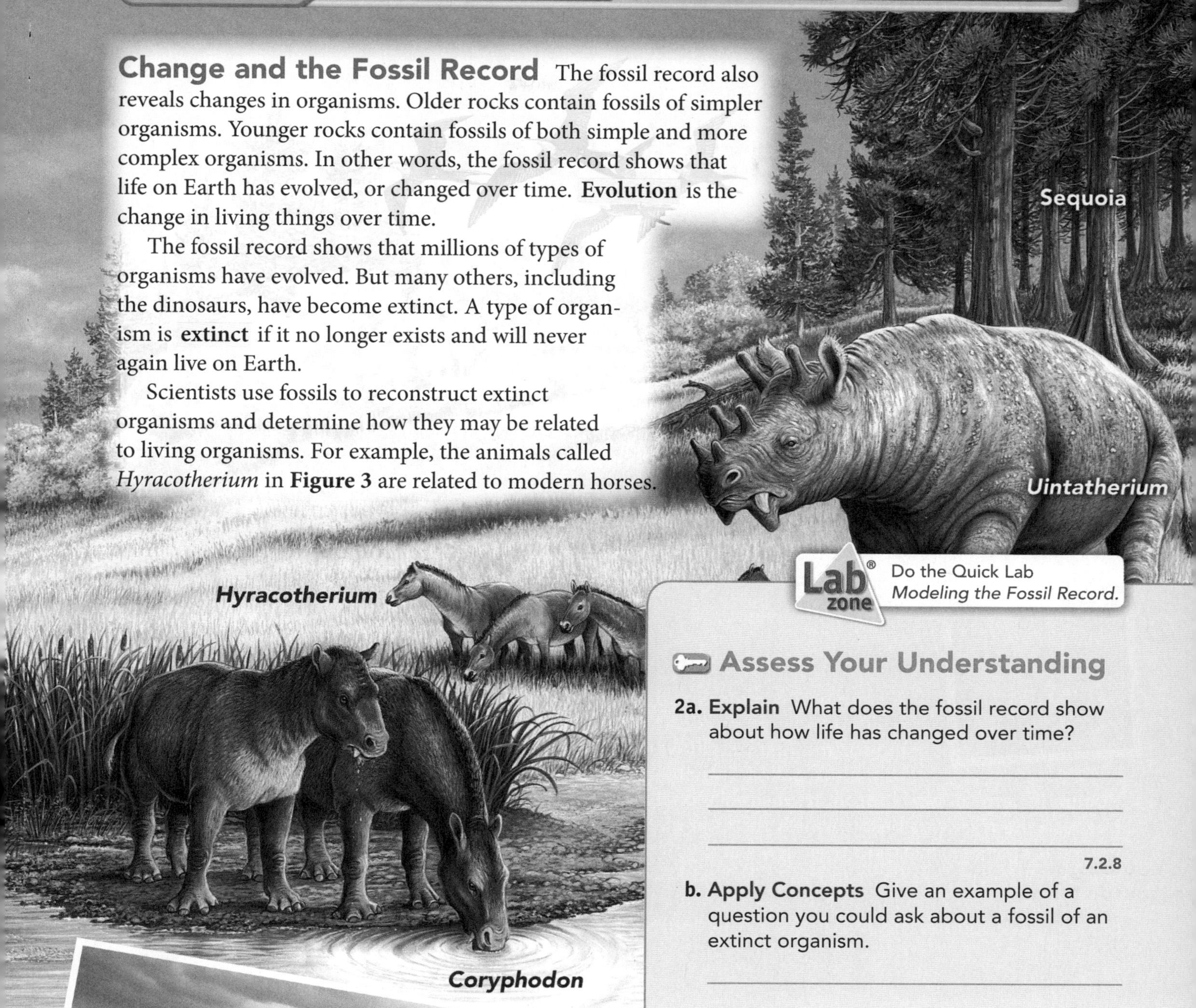

Sequoia

Uintatherium

Hyracotherium

Coryphodon

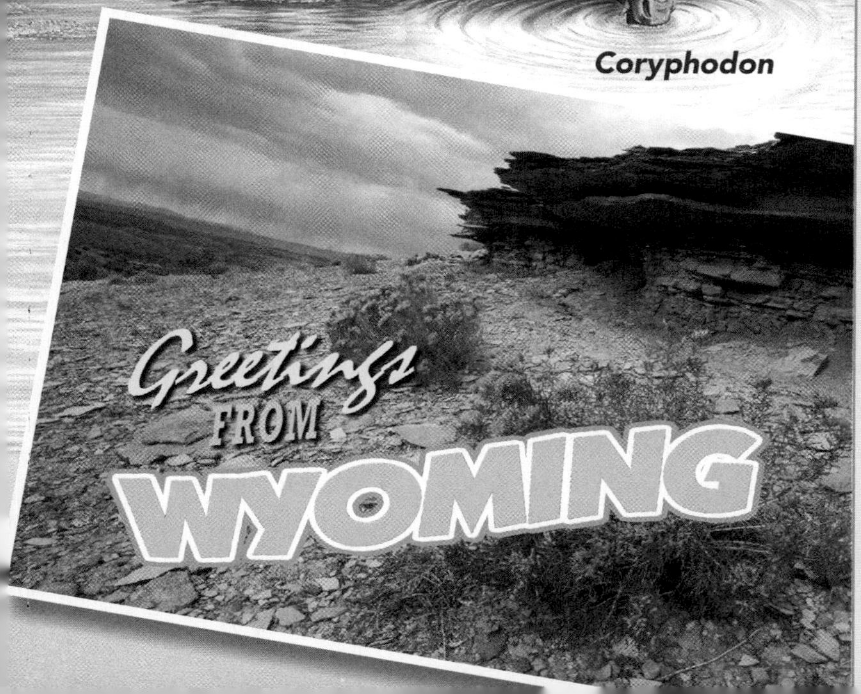

Greetings FROM **WYOMING**

Lab zone® Do the Quick Lab *Modeling the Fossil Record.*

🔑 Assess Your Understanding

2a. Explain What does the fossil record show about how life has changed over time?

_____

_____

_____

7.2.8

b. Apply Concepts Give an example of a question you could ask about a fossil of an extinct organism.

_____

_____

_____

7.2.8

got it? ● ● ● ● ● ● ● ● ● ● ● ● ● ● ● ● ● ● ●

○ **I get it!** Now I know that the fossil record shows _____

_____

_____

○ **I need extra help with** _____

Go to **MY SCIENCE** ⓢ **COACH** online for help with this subject. 7.2.8

The Relative Age of Rocks

🔑 **How Old Are Rock Layers?**
7.2, 7.NS.8

🔑 **How Can Rock Layers Change?**
7.2, 7.NS.8

MY PLANET DIARY

BLOG

Posted by Owen

Location Tacoma, WA

A couple of summers ago, my dad took me rock climbing for the first time. I went to a place called Frenchman Coulee in central Washington. It was really cool because the rock was basalt, which forms in giant pillars. It starts as lava, and then cools and you can see the different lava flows in the rock. Another cool thing is that Frenchman Coulee, which is a canyon, was gouged out by huge Ice Age floods.

✏️ **Communicate** Discuss the question below with a partner. Then answer it on your own.

How do you think scientists figure out the age of the basalt layers at Frenchman Coulee?

_____

_____

_____

_____

▶ PLANET DIARY Go to **Planet Diary** to learn more about the age of rock layers.

Lab ® Do the Inquiry Warm-Up
zone *Which Layer Is the Oldest?*

How Old Are Rock Layers?

If you found a fossil in a rock, you might start by asking, "What is it?" Your next question would probably be, "How old is it?" The first step is to find the age of the rock.

Relative and Absolute Age Geologists have two ways to express the age of a rock. The **relative age** of a rock is its age compared to the ages of other rocks. You have probably used the idea of relative age when comparing your age with someone else's. For example, if you say that you are older than your brother but younger than your sister, you are describing your relative age.

Academic Standards for Science

7.2 Core Standard Describe how earth processes have shaped the topography of the earth and have made it possible to measure geological time.

7.NS.8 Analyze data and use it to identify patterns and make inferences.

Vocabulary
- relative age • absolute age • law of superposition
- extrusion • intrusion • fault • index fossil
- unconformity

Skills
↻ Reading: Relate Text and Visuals
△ Inquiry: Infer

The relative age of a rock does not provide its absolute age. The **absolute age** of a rock is the number of years that have passed since the rock formed. It may be impossible to know a rock's absolute age exactly, so geologists often use both absolute and relative ages.

Rock Layers Fossils are most often found in layers of sedimentary rock. Geologists use the **law of superposition** to determine the relative ages of sedimentary rock layers. **According to the law of superposition, in undisturbed horizontal sedimentary rock layers the oldest layer is at the bottom. Each higher layer is younger than the layers below it.** The deeper you go, the older the rocks are.

Figure 1 shows rock layers in the Grand Canyon. Rock layers like these form a record of Earth's history. Scientists can study this record to understand how Earth and life on Earth have changed.

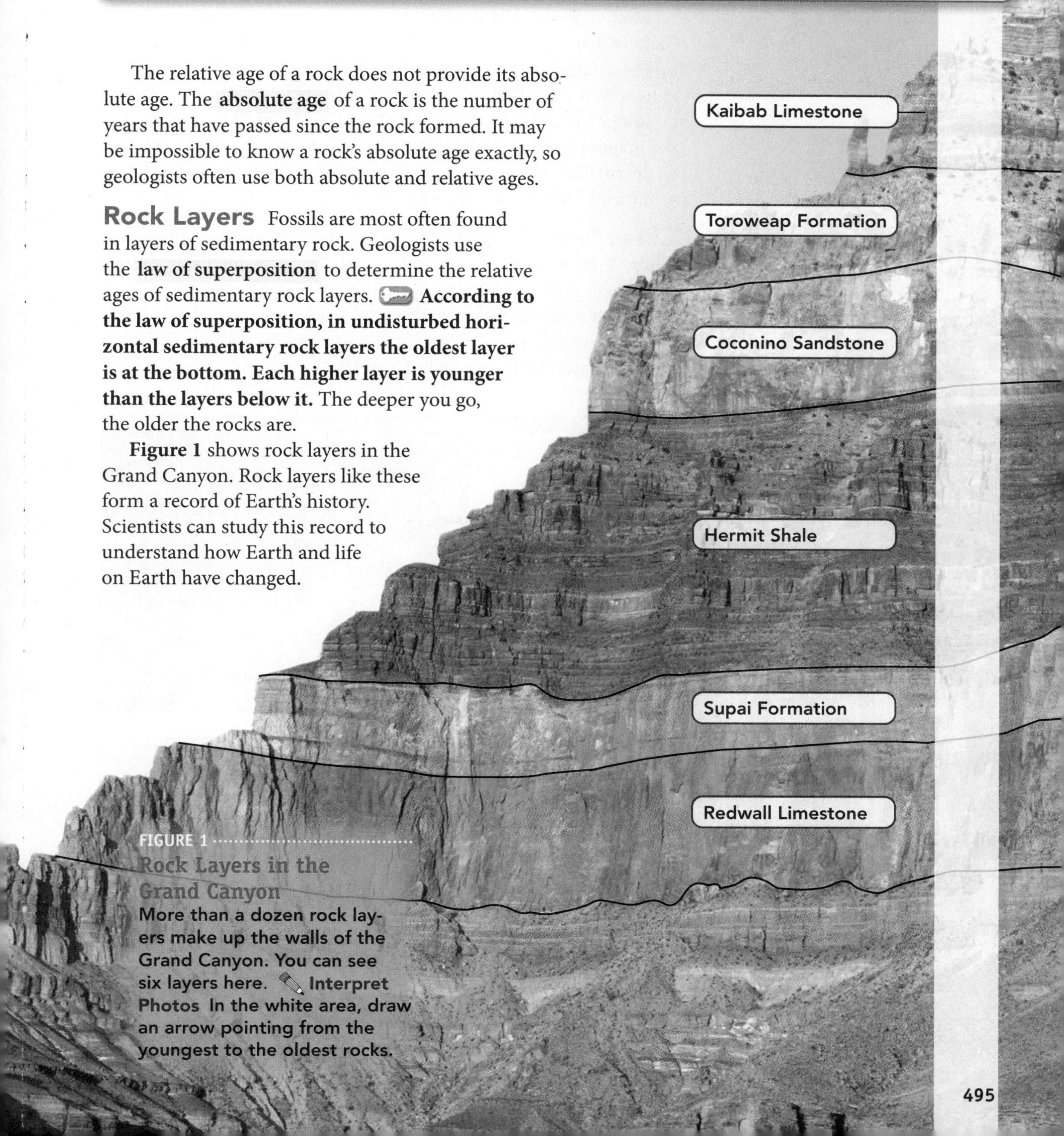

Kaibab Limestone

Toroweap Formation

Coconino Sandstone

Hermit Shale

Supai Formation

Redwall Limestone

FIGURE 1

Rock Layers in the Grand Canyon

More than a dozen rock layers make up the walls of the Grand Canyon. You can see six layers here. ✎ **Interpret Photos** In the white area, draw an arrow pointing from the youngest to the oldest rocks.

7.NS.8

Vocabulary Prefixes How does knowing the prefixes *in-* and *ex-* help you remember the difference between an intrusion and an extrusion?

_____

_____

_____

_____

_____

_____

_____

Clues From Igneous Rock There are other clues to the relative ages of rocks besides the position of rock layers. To determine relative age, geologists also study extrusions and intrusions of igneous rock, faults, and index fossils.

Molten material beneath Earth's surface is called magma. Magma that reaches the surface is called lava. Lava that hardens on the surface and forms igneous rock is called an **extrusion.** An extrusion is always younger than the rocks below it.

Magma may push into bodies of rock below the surface. There, the magma cools and hardens into a mass of igneous rock called an **intrusion.** An intrusion is always younger than the rock layers around and beneath it. **Figure 2** shows an intrusion.

Clues From Faults More clues come from the study of faults. A **fault** is a break in Earth's crust. Forces inside Earth cause movement of the rock on opposite sides of a fault.

A fault is always younger than the rock it cuts through. To determine the relative age of a fault, geologists find the relative age of the youngest layer cut by the fault. **Figure 3** shows a fault.

apply it!

The diagram below shows rock layers found at a site.

1 Circle the area on the diagram that shows an intrusion.

2 Shade the oldest layer on the diagram.

3 Infer What can you infer about the relative ages of areas B and E?

_____

_____

_____

_____

_____

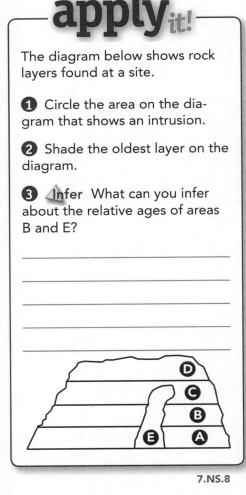

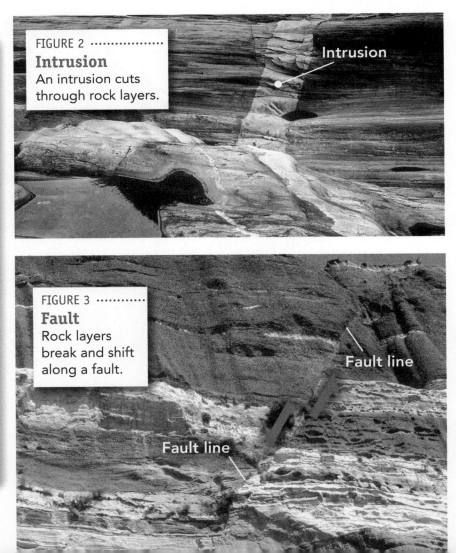

FIGURE 2 ....
Intrusion
An intrusion cuts through rock layers.

Intrusion

FIGURE 3 ....
Fault
Rock layers break and shift along a fault.

Fault line

Fault line

How Do Fossils Show Age?

To date rock layers, geologists first find the relative age of a layer of rock at one location. Then they can match layers in other locations to that layer.

Certain fossils, called index fossils, help geologists match rock layers. To be useful as an **index fossil**, a fossil must be widely distributed and represent an organism that existed for a geologically short period of time. 🔑 **Index fossils are useful because they tell the relative ages of the rock layers in which they occur.** Scientists infer that layers with matching index fossils are the same age.

You can use index fossils to match rock layers. Look at **Figure 4,** which shows rock layers from four different locations. Notice that two of the fossils are found in only one of these rock layers. These are the index fossils.

FIGURE 4 ⋯⋯⋯⋯⋯⋯⋯⋯⋯⋯⋯

> INTERACTIVE ART Index Fossils

Scientists use index fossils to match rock layers.

✎ **Interpret Diagrams** Label the layers to match the first area shown. Circle the fossil or fossils that you can use as index fossils. What can you infer about the history of Location 4? **7.NS.8**

_____

_____

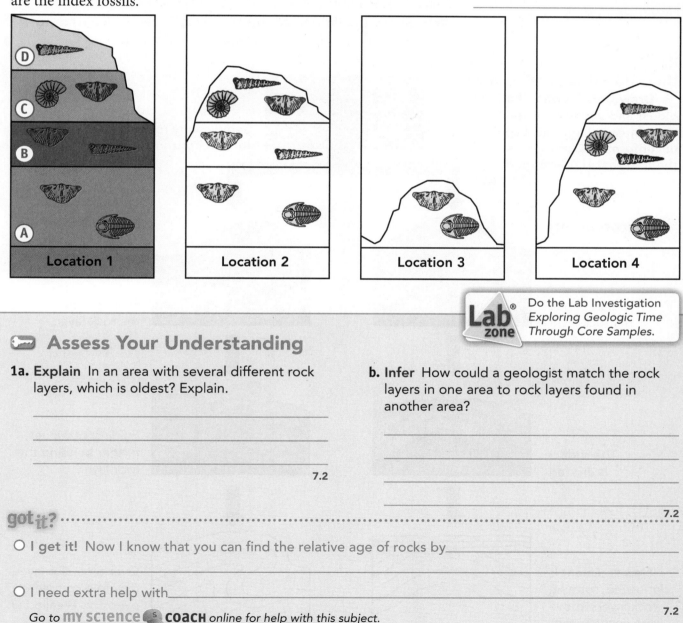

Location 1   Location 2   Location 3   Location 4

Lab® zone Do the Lab Investigation *Exploring Geologic Time Through Core Samples.*

🔑 Assess Your Understanding

1a. Explain In an area with several different rock layers, which is oldest? Explain.

_____

_____

_____

7.2

b. Infer How could a geologist match the rock layers in one area to rock layers found in another area?

_____

_____

_____

_____

7.2

got it? ⋯⋯⋯⋯⋯⋯⋯⋯⋯⋯⋯⋯⋯⋯⋯⋯⋯⋯⋯⋯⋯⋯ 7.2

○ **I get it!** Now I know that you can find the relative age of rocks by_____

_____

○ **I need extra help with**_____

Go to MY SCIENCE ⓢ COACH online for help with this subject.

7.2

Relate Text and Visuals
Underline the sentences that explain how the rock layers in **Figure 5** changed.

How Can Rock Layers Change?

The geologic record of sedimentary rock layers is not complete. In fact, most of Earth's geologic record has been lost to erosion. **Gaps in the geologic record and folding can change the position in which rock layers appear.** Motion along faults can also change how rock layers line up. These changes make it harder for scientists to reconstruct Earth's history. **Figure 5** shows how the order of rock layers may change.

Gaps in the Geologic Record When rock layers erode away, an older rock surface may be exposed. Then deposition begins again, building new rock layers. The surface where new rock layers meet a much older rock surface beneath them is called an unconformity. An **unconformity** is a gap in the geologic record. It shows where rock layers have been lost due to erosion.

FIGURE 5

Unconformities and Folding
Draw Conclusions Shade the oldest and youngest layers in the last two diagrams. Label the unconformity. Circle the part of the fold that is overturned.

7.NS.8

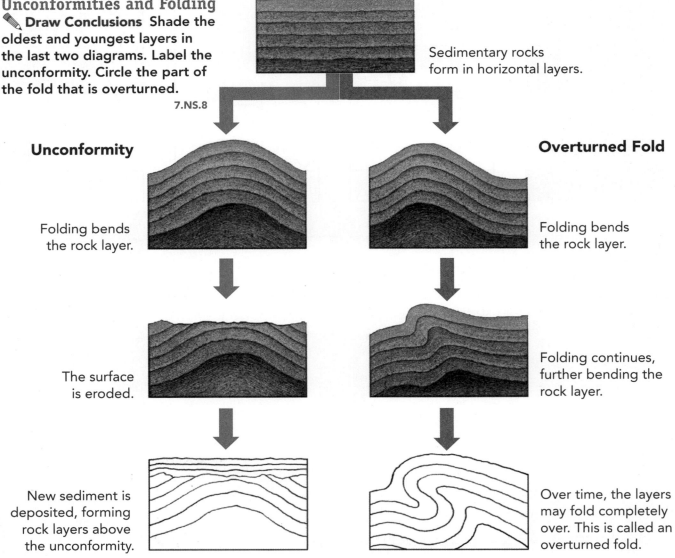

Sedimentary rocks form in horizontal layers.

Unconformity

Folding bends the rock layer.

The surface is eroded.

New sediment is deposited, forming rock layers above the unconformity.

Overturned Fold

Folding bends the rock layer.

Folding continues, further bending the rock layer.

Over time, the layers may fold completely over. This is called an overturned fold.

Folding Sometimes, forces inside Earth fold rock layers so much that the layers are turned over completely. In this case, the youngest rock layers may be on the bottom!

No one place holds a complete geologic record. Geologists compare rock layers in many places to piece together as complete a sequence as possible.

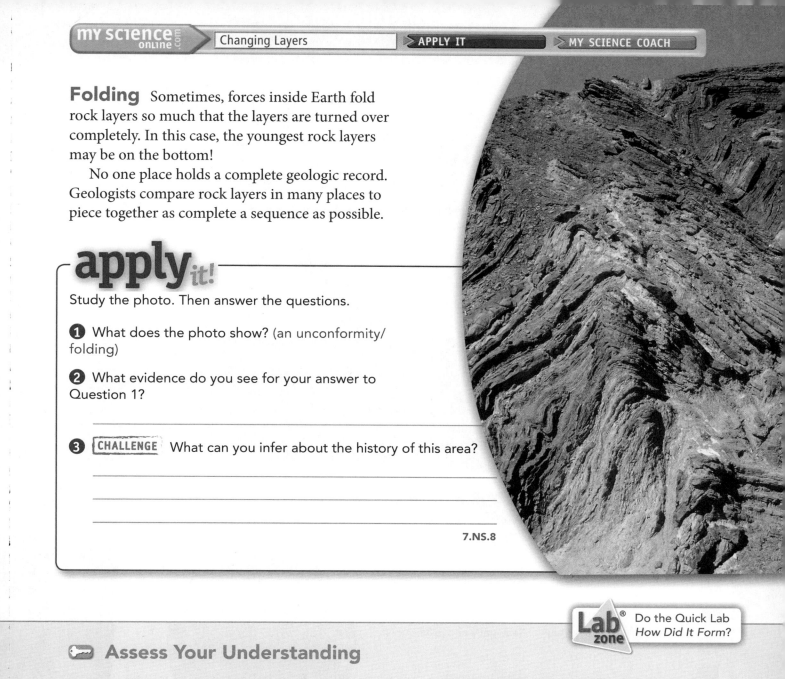

apply it!

Study the photo. Then answer the questions.

❶ What does the photo show? (an unconformity/ folding)

❷ What evidence do you see for your answer to Question 1?

_____

❸ **CHALLENGE** What can you infer about the history of this area?

_____

_____

_____

7.NS.8

Lab zone ® Do the Quick Lab *How Did It Form?*

🔑 Assess Your Understanding

2a. List Name two ways rock layers can change.

_____
7.2

b. Explain How does folding change rock layers?

_____

_____

_____
7.2

c. Draw Conclusions Two locations include a layer of rock with a particular index fossil. In one location, the layer occurs in a higher position than in the other. What can you conclude about the history of the two areas?

_____

_____

_____
7.2

got it? ....

○ **I get it!** Now I know that rock layers can change due to _____

_____

○ **I need extra help with** _____

Go to my science ⓢ **coach** *online for help with this subject.* **7.2**

The Geologic Time Scale

🗝 **What Is the Geologic Time Scale?**

7.2.3, 7.NS.3, 7.NS.8

my planet diary

SCIENCE STATS

Earth's History in a Day

Suppose you could squeeze all of Earth's 4.6-billion-year history into one 24-hour day. The table shows the times at which some major events would take place.

	Time	First Appearance
A	Midnight	Earth
B	3:00 A.M.	Rocks
C	4:00 A.M.	Bacteria
D	2:00 P.M.	Algae
E	8:30–9:00 P.M.	Seaweeds and jellyfish
F	10:00 P.M.	Land plants
G	10:50 P.M.	Dinosaurs
H	11:39 P.M.	Mammals
I	11:58:43 P.M.	Humans

Use the data in the table to answer these questions.

1. ✏ **Sequence** Write the letter for each event on the clock diagram.

2. Did anything surprise you about the data? If so, what?

_____

_____

▷ **PLANET DIARY** Go to **Planet Diary** to learn more about Earth's history.

Lab zone® Do the Inquiry Warm-Up *This Is Your Life!*

Vocabulary
- geologic time scale
- era • period

Skills
- Reading: Summarize
- Inquiry: Make Models

What Is the Geologic Time Scale?

When you speak of the past, what names do you use for different spans of time? You probably use names such as century, decade, year, month, week, and day. But these units aren't very helpful for thinking about much longer periods of time. Scientists needed to develop a way to talk about Earth's history.

🔑 **Because the time span of Earth's past is so great, geologists use the geologic time scale to show Earth's history.** The **geologic time scale** is a record of the geologic events and the evolution of life forms as shown in the fossil record.

Scientists first developed the geologic time scale by studying rock layers and index fossils worldwide. With this information, scientists placed Earth's rocks in order by relative age. Later, radioactive dating helped determine the absolute age of the divisions in the geologic time scale. **Figure 1** shows some of the earliest known rocks.

FIGURE 1 ....

Ancient Rocks
The Isua rocks in Greenland are among the oldest rocks on Earth. They formed after heat and pressure changed sedimentary rocks that formed under early oceans.

Academic Standards for Science

7.2.3 Characterize the immensity of geologic time and recognize that it is measured in eras and epochs.

7.NS.3 Collect quantitative data and use appropriate units to label numerical data.

7.NS.8 Analyze data and use it to identify patterns and make inferences based on these patterns.

✏️

🔄 **Summarize** Write two or three sentences to summarize the information on this page.

_____

_____

_____

_____

_____

_____

FIGURE 2 ·······························

The Geologic Time Scale

The divisions of the geologic time scale are used to date events in Earth's history.

✎ **Calculate** After you read the next page, calculate and fill in the duration of each period. Then use the time scale to identify the period in which each organism below lived.

7.NS.8

Organism: *Wiwaxia*
Age: about 500 million years
Period: _____

Organism: *Velociraptor*
Age: about 80 million years
Period: _____

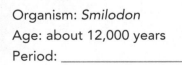

Organism: *Smilodon*
Age: about 12,000 years
Period: _____

PERIOD		MILLIONS OF YEARS AGO	DURATION (MILLIONS OF YEARS)
Cenozoic Era	QUATERNARY	1.8	
	NEOGENE	23	
	PALEOGENE	66	
Mesozoic Era	CRETACEOUS	146	
	JURASSIC	200	
	TRIASSIC	251	
Paleozoic Era	PERMIAN	299	
	CARBONIFEROUS	359	
	DEVONIAN	416	
	SILURIAN	444	
	ORDOVICIAN	488	
	CAMBRIAN	542	
Precambrian Time		4,600	

Dividing Geologic Time

As geologists studied the fossil record, they found major changes in life forms at certain times. They used these changes to mark where one unit of geologic time ends and the next begins. Therefore, the divisions of the geologic time scale depend on events in the history of life on Earth. **Figure 2** shows the major divisions of the geologic time scale.

Precambrian Time Geologic time begins with a long span of time called Precambrian Time (pree KAM bree un). Precambrian Time, which covers about 88 percent of Earth's history, ended 542 million years ago. Few fossils survive from this time period.

Eras Geologists divide the time between Precambrian Time and the present into three long units of time called **eras.** They are the Paleozoic Era, the Mesozoic Era, and the Cenozoic Era.

Periods Eras are subdivided into units of geologic time called **periods.** You can see in **Figure 2** that the Mesozoic Era includes three periods: the Triassic Period, the Jurassic Period, and the Cretaceous Period. The names of many of the geologic periods come from places around the world where geologists first described the rocks and fossils of that period. For example, the name *Cambrian* refers to Cambria, a Latin name for Wales.

Epochs The periods listed in **Figure 2** are subdivided into even smaller units of time called epochs. For example, the Neogene Period is divided into two epochs: the Miocene and the Pliocene. Epochs are generally between 5 and 50 millions years. The Holocene, the time in which we currently live, is the youngest epoch. It only goes back approximately 11,500 years in the past.

apply it!

Refer to the geologic time scale shown in **Figure 2** to answer the questions below. 7.NS.3

Suppose you want to make a model of the geologic time scale. You decide to use a scale of 1 cm = 1 million years.

1 Not counting Precambrian time, which era would take up the most space? _____

2 Make Models How long would the Mesozoic Era be in your model? _____

3 CHALLENGE Suppose you used a different scale: 1 m = 1 million years. What would be one advantage and one disadvantage of this scale?

_____

_____

_____

_____

_____

_____

Do the Quick Lab
Going Back in Time.

Assess Your Understanding

1a. Define The geologic time scale is a record of _____ and _____.
7.2.3

b. Sequence Number the following periods in order from earliest to latest.

Neogene _____   Jurassic _____

Quaternary _____   Triassic _____

Cretaceous _____   7.2.3

c. Draw Conclusions Refer to My Planet Diary and **Figure 2.** During which period did modern humans arise?

_____

7.2.3

got it? ....

○ I get it! Now I know that geologic time _____

_____

○ I need extra help with _____

Go to MY SCIENCE COACH online for help with this subject.

7.2.3

Eras of Earth's History

UNLOCK
THE BIG
?

🔑 **What Happened in the Paleozoic Era?**
7.2.3, 7.2.8

🔑 **What Happened in the Mesozoic Era?**
7.2.3, 7.2.8, 7.NS.8

🔑 **What Happened in the Cenozoic Era?**
7.2.3, 7.2.8, 7.NS.3

my pLaneT DiaRY

Mystery Metal

The rock layers in the photo hold evidence in one of the great mysteries of science: What killed the dinosaurs?

Find the thin, pale layer of rock marked by the ruler. This layer formed at the end of the Cretaceous period. It contains unusually high amounts of the metal iridium. At first, scientists could not explain the amount of iridium in this layer.

Iridium is more common in asteroids than on Earth. Many scientists now infer that an asteroid struck Earth. The impact threw dust into the air, blocking sunlight for years. About half the plant and animal species on Earth—including the dinosaurs—died out.

FUN FACT

Think about what you know about fossils and Earth's history as you answer these questions.

1. What have many scientists inferred from the iridium found at the Cretaceous boundary?

_____

_____

_____

2. What are some questions you have about the history of life on Earth?

_____

_____

_____

▶ PLANET DIARY Go to **Planet Diary** to learn more about mass extinctions.

Lab zone® Do the Inquiry Warm-Up *Dividing History.*

Vocabulary
- invertebrate
- vertebrate
- amphibian
- reptile
- mass extinction
- mammal

Skills
- Reading: Identify Supporting Evidence
- Inquiry: Classify

What Happened in the Paleozoic Era?

The extinction of the dinosaurs is one of the most famous events in Earth's history, but it is just one example of the changes that have taken place. Through most of Earth's history, the only living things were single-celled organisms.

Near the end of Precambrian time, more complex living things evolved. Feathery, plantlike organisms anchored themselves to the seafloor. Jellyfish-like organisms floated in the oceans. Scientists have found fossils of such organisms in Australia, Russia, China, and southern Africa. But a much greater variety of living things evolved during the next phase of geologic time—the Paleozoic Era.

The Cambrian Explosion During the Cambrian Period, life took a big leap forward. 🔑 **At the beginning of the Paleozoic Era, a great number of different kinds of organisms evolved. For the first time, many organisms had hard parts, including shells and outer skeletons.** Paleontologists call this event the Cambrian Explosion because so many new life forms appeared within a relatively short time.

Academic Standards for Science

7.2.3 Characterize the immensity of geologic time and recognize that it is measured in eras and epochs.

7.2.8 Compare and contrast fossils with living organisms in a given location to explain how earth processes have changed environments over time.

FIGURE 1 ·······························

Cambrian Life

The photo below shows a fossil of a Cambrian organism called *Anomalocaris*. The illustration shows one artist's idea of what *Anomalocaris* (the large organism) and other organisms looked like.

✏️ **Interpret Photos** What does the fossil tell you about what *Anomalocaris* looked like?

_____

_____

505

In the Ordovician Period, much of Indiana was covered by a glacial sea. In southeastern Indiana, in stone quarries and places where roads cut through the rock, you can see parts of the Ordovician sea bottom. The Ordovician sea was populated by many marine species, including nautiloids, ancestors of modern cephalopods.

FIGURE 2 ⋯⋯⋯⋯⋯⋯⋯⋯⋯⋯⋯⋯

Changing Landscapes

✎ **Summarize** Based on the text and illustrations, describe the organisms in each period and how they differed from those in the previous period.

Silurian _____

_____

_____

_____

_____

_____

Invertebrates Develop At this time, all animals lived in the sea. Many were animals without backbones, or **invertebrates.** Invertebrates such as jellyfish, worms, and sponges made their home in the Cambrian ocean.

Brachiopods and trilobites were also common in the Cambrian seas. Brachiopods resembled modern clams, but are only distantly related to them. Trilobites were a huge and varied group of arthropods (AR thru pahds), animals with jointed legs and many body segments.

New Organisms Arise
Invertebrates soon shared the seas with a new type of organism. During the Ordovician (awr duh VISH ee un) Period, the first vertebrates evolved. A **vertebrate** is an animal with a backbone. Jawless fishes with suckerlike mouths were the first vertebrates.

The First Land Plants Until the Silurian (sih LOOR ee un) Period, only one-celled organisms lived on the land. But during the Silurian Period, plants became abundant. These first, simple plants grew low to the ground in damp areas. By the Devonian Period (dih VOH nee un), plants that could grow in drier areas had evolved. Among these plants were the earliest ferns.

Early Fishes Both invertebrates and vertebrates lived in the Devonian seas. Even though the invertebrates were more numerous, the Devonian Period is often called the Age of Fishes. Every main group of fishes was present in the oceans at this time. Most fishes now had jaws, bony skeletons, and scales on their bodies. Sharks appeared in the late Devonian Period.

Silurian

Devonian

Animals Reach Land

The Devonian Period was also when animals began to spread widely on land. The first insects evolved during the Silurian Period, but vertebrates reached land during the Devonian. The first land vertebrates were lungfish with strong, muscular fins. The first amphibians evolved from these lungfish. An **amphibian** (am FIB ee un) is an animal that lives part of its life on land and part of its life in water.

The Carboniferous Period

Throughout the rest of the Paleozoic, other vertebrates evolved from amphibians. For example, small reptiles developed during the Carboniferous Period. **Reptiles** have scaly skin and lay eggs that have tough, leathery shells.

During the Carboniferous Period, winged insects evolved into many forms, including huge dragonflies and cockroaches. Giant ferns and cone-bearing plants formed vast swampy forests called coal forests. The remains of the coal-forest plants formed thick deposits of sediment that changed into coal over hundreds of millions of years.

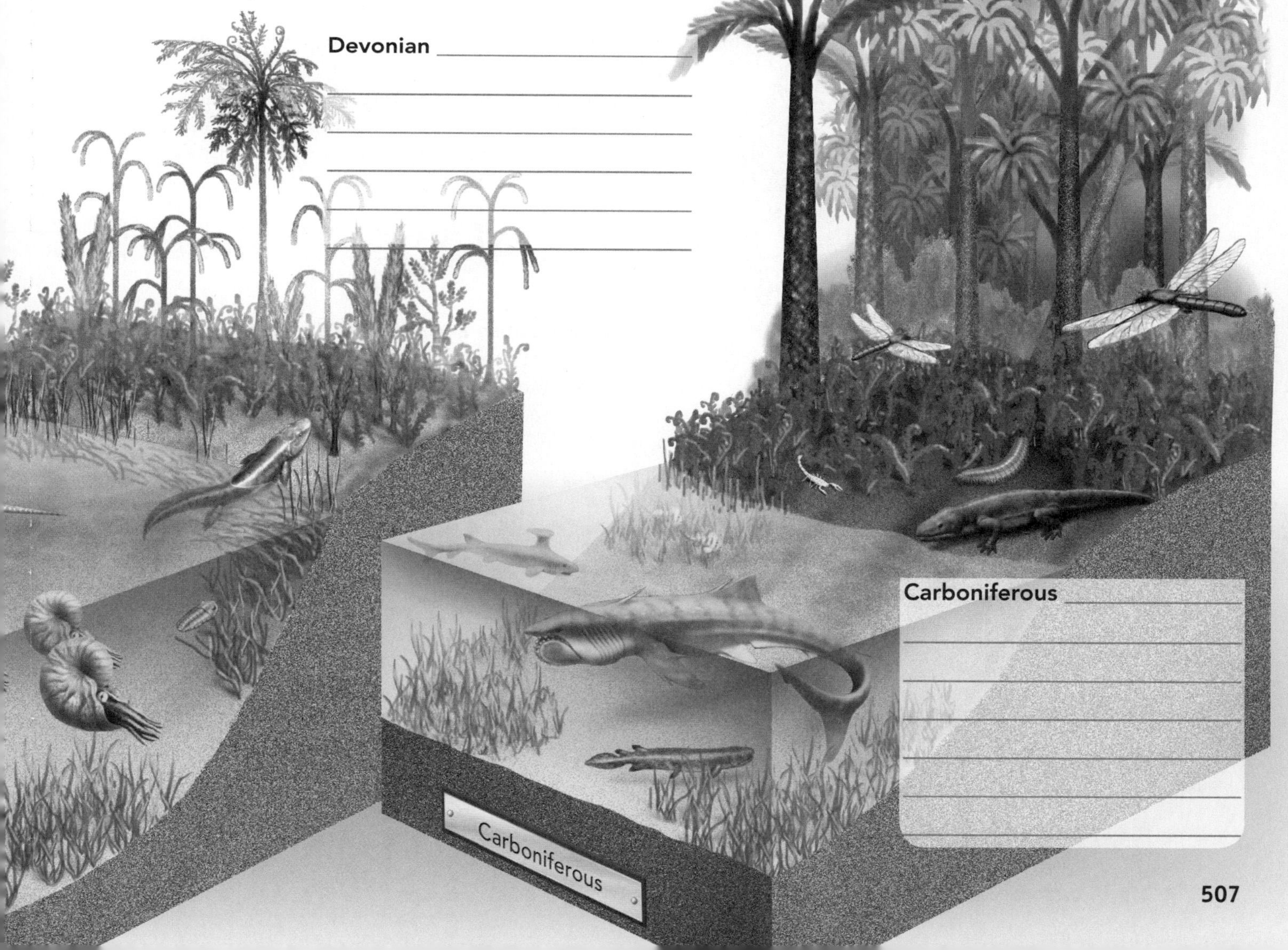

Identify Supporting Evidence Underline the evidence that supports the statement, "The Devonian Period was also when animals began to spread widely on land."

Devonian _____

Carboniferous _____

Carboniferous

What two effects did the formation of Pangaea have?

_____

_____

_____

_____

_____

Pangaea

During the Permian Period, between 299 and 250 million years ago, Earth's continents moved together to form a great landmass, or supercontinent, called Pangaea (pan JEE uh). The formation of Pangaea caused deserts to expand in the tropics. At the same time, sheets of ice covered land closer to the South Pole.

Mass Extinction At the end of the Permian Period, most species of life on Earth died out. This was a **mass extinction,** in which many types of living things became extinct at the same time. Scientists estimate that about 90 percent of all ocean species died out. So did about 70 percent of species on land. Even widespread organisms like trilobites became extinct.

Scientists aren't sure what caused this extinction. Some think an asteroid struck Earth, creating huge dust clouds. Massive volcanic eruptions spewed carbon dioxide and sulfur dioxide into the atmosphere. Temperatures all over Earth rose during this time, too. The amount of carbon dioxide in the oceans increased and the amount of oxygen declined, though scientists aren't sure why. All these factors may have contributed to the mass extinction.

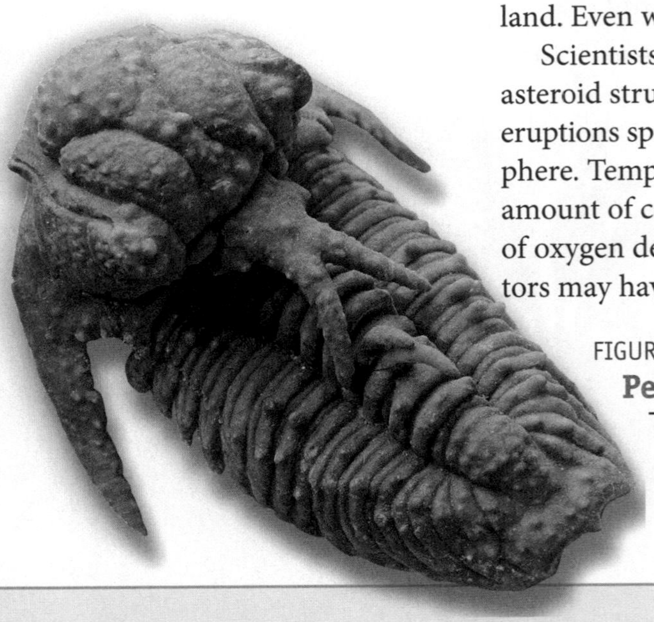

FIGURE 3 ⋯⋯⋯⋯⋯⋯⋯⋯⋯⋯⋯⋯⋯⋯⋯⋯

Permian Trilobite

Throughout the Paleozoic, trilobites such as this Permian example were one of the most successful groups of organisms. But no species of trilobites survived the Permian mass extinction.

Lab® zone Do the Quick Lab
Graphing the Fossil Record.

Assess Your Understanding

1a. List What are the periods of the Paleozoic Era?

_____

_____

_____

7.2.3, 7.2.8

b. Sequence Number the following organisms in order from earliest to latest appearance.

amphibians _____   jawless fishes _____

trilobites _____   bony fishes _____

7.2.3, 7.2.8

c. Relate Cause and Effect Name two possible causes of the mass extinction at the end of the Paleozoic.

_____

_____

_____

_____

_____

_____

7.2.3, 7.2.8

got it? ⋯⋯⋯⋯⋯⋯⋯⋯⋯⋯⋯⋯⋯⋯⋯⋯⋯⋯⋯⋯⋯⋯⋯⋯

○ **I get it!** Now I know that the main events in the Paleozoic Era were _____

_____

○ **I need extra help with** _____

Go to MY SCIENCE ⓢ COACH *online for help with this subject.*

7.2.3, 7.2.8

What Happened in the Mesozoic Era?

When you think of prehistoric life, do you think of dinosaurs? If so, you're thinking of the Mesozoic Era.

The Triassic Period Some living things managed to survive the Permian mass extinction. Plants and animals that survived included fish, insects, reptiles, and cone-bearing plants called conifers. 🔑 **Reptiles were so successful during the Mesozoic Era that this time is often called the Age of Reptiles.** The first dinosaurs appeared about 225 million years ago, during the Triassic (tri AS ik) Period.

Mammals also first appeared during the Triassic Period. A **mammal** is a vertebrate that can control its body temperature and feeds milk to its young. Mammals in the Triassic Period were very small, about the size of a mouse.

The Jurassic Period During the Jurassic Period (joo RAS ik), dinosaurs became common on land. Other kinds of reptiles evolved to live in the ocean and in the air. Scientists have identified several hundred different kinds of dinosaurs.

One of the first birds, called *Archaeopteryx*, appeared during the Jurassic Period. The name *Archaeopteryx* means "ancient winged one." Many paleontologists now think that birds evolved from dinosaurs.

Academic Standards for Science

7.2.3 Characterize the immensity of geologic time and recognize that it is measured in eras and epochs.

7.2.8 Compare and contrast fossils with living organisms in a given location to explain how earth processes have changed environments over time.

7.NS.8 Analyze data and use it to identify patterns and make inferences.

apply it!

The illustrations show a flying reptile called *Dimorphodon* and one of the earliest birds, *Archaeopteryx*.

1 Identify two features the two animals have in common.

_____

_____

2 Identify one major difference between the two animals.

_____

_____

3 🔺 Classify Which animal is *Archaeopteryx*? How do you know it is related to birds?

_____

_____

7.NS.8

509

FIGURE 4 ······························

The End of the Dinosaurs

Many scientists hypothesize that an asteroid hit Earth near the present-day Yucatán Peninsula, in southeastern Mexico.

✏️ CHALLENGE Write a short story summarizing the events shown in the illustration.

_____

_____

_____

_____

_____

_____

_____

_____

_____

_____

_____

7.NS.8

The Cretaceous Period Reptiles, including dinosaurs, were still widespread throughout the Cretaceous Period (krih TAY shus). Birds began to replace flying reptiles during this period. Their hollow bones made them better adapted to their environment than the flying reptiles, which became extinct.

Flowering plants first evolved during the Cretaceous. Unlike conifers, flowering plants produce seeds that are inside a fruit. The fruit helps the seeds spread.

Another Mass Extinction 🗝️ **At the close of the Cretaceous Period, about 65 million years ago, another mass extinction occurred. Scientists hypothesize that this mass extinction occurred when an asteroid from space struck Earth.** This mass extinction wiped out more than half of all plant and animal groups, including the dinosaurs.

When the asteroid hit Earth, the impact threw huge amounts of dust and water vapor into the atmosphere. Dust and heavy clouds blocked sunlight around the world for years. Without sunlight, plants died, and plant-eating animals starved. The dust later formed the iridium-rich rock layer you read about at the beginning of the lesson. Some scientists think that climate changes caused by increased volcanic activity also helped cause the mass extinction.

THE DEATH OF THE DINOSAURS
BY TERRY DACTYL

 Do the Quick Lab
Modeling an Asteroid Impact.

🗝️ Assess Your Understanding

got it? ···

○ I get it! Now I know that the main developments in the Mesozoic Era were _____

_____

○ I need extra help with _____

Go to MY SCIENCE ⑤ COACH online for help with this subject.   7.2.3, 7.2.8

What Happened in the Cenozoic Era?

During the Mesozoic Era, mammals had to compete with dinosaurs for food and places to live. **The extinction of dinosaurs created an opportunity for mammals. During the Cenozoic Era, mammals evolved to live in many different environments—on land, in water, and even in the air.**

The Paleogene and Neogene Periods During the Paleogene and Neogene periods, Earth's climates were generally warm and mild, though they generally cooled over time. In the oceans, mammals such as whales and dolphins evolved. On land, flowering plants, insects, and mammals flourished. Grasses first began to spread widely. Some mammals became very large, as did some birds.

The Quaternary Period Earth's climate cooled and warmed in cycles during the Quaternary Period, causing a series of ice ages. Thick glaciers covered parts of Europe and North America. The latest warm period began between 10,000 and 20,000 years ago. Over thousands of years, most of the glaciers melted.

In the oceans, algae, coral, mollusks, fish, and mammals thrived. Insects and birds shared the skies. Flowering plants and mammals such as bats, cats, dogs, cattle, and humans became common. The fossil record suggests that modern humans may have evolved as early as 190,000 years ago. By about 12,000 to 15,000 years ago, humans had migrated to every continent except Antarctica.

Academic Standards for Science

7.2.3 Characterize the immensity of geologic time and recognize that it is measured in eras and epochs.

7.2.8 Compare and contrast fossils with living organisms in a given location to explain how earth processes have changed environments over time.

7.NS.3 Collect quantitative data with appropriate tools or technologies and use appropriate units to label numerical data.

FIGURE 5 ·······················

Giant Mammals

Many giant mammals evolved in the Cenozoic Era. This *Megatherium* is related to the modern sloth shown to the right, but was up to six meters tall.

✎ **Measure** About how many times taller was *Megatherium* than a modern sloth? _____

7.NS.3

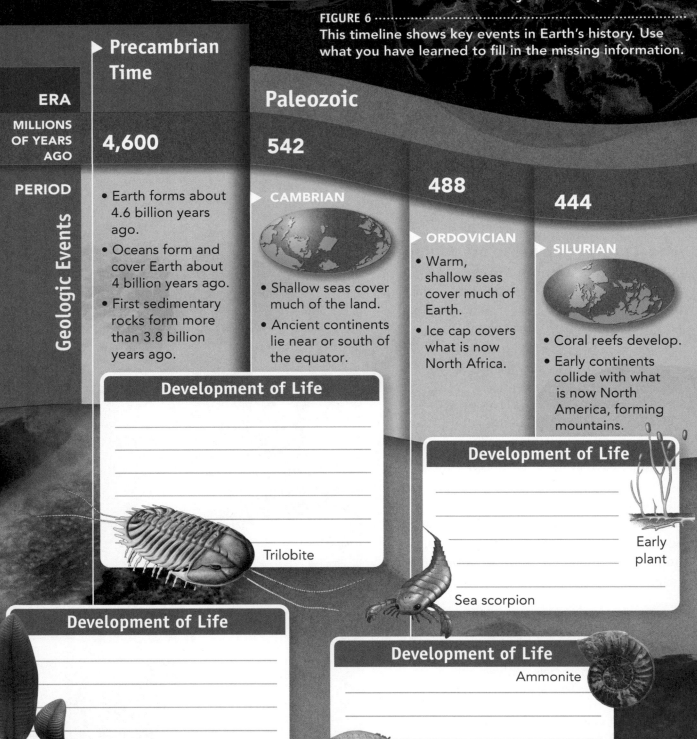

Geologic History

EXPLORE THE BIG ?

> ART IN MOTION   How do scientists study Earth's past?

FIGURE 6 ···
This timeline shows key events in Earth's history. Use
what you have learned to fill in the missing information.

ERA	Precambrian Time	Paleozoic		
MILLIONS OF YEARS AGO	4,600	542	488	444
PERIOD		CAMBRIAN	ORDOVICIAN	SILURIAN

Geologic Events

Precambrian Time (4,600)
- Earth forms about 4.6 billion years ago.
- Oceans form and cover Earth about 4 billion years ago.
- First sedimentary rocks form more than 3.8 billion years ago.

CAMBRIAN (542)
- Shallow seas cover much of the land.
- Ancient continents lie near or south of the equator.

ORDOVICIAN (488)
- Warm, shallow seas cover much of Earth.
- Ice cap covers what is now North Africa.

SILURIAN (444)
- Coral reefs develop.
- Early continents collide with what is now North America, forming mountains.

Development of Life
_____
_____
_____
_____

Trilobite

Development of Life
_____
_____
_____
_____

Sea scorpion

Early plant

Development of Life
_____
_____
_____
_____

Sea pen

Development of Life
_____
_____
_____
_____

Ammonite

Jawless fish

Giant dragonfly
(Carboniferous)

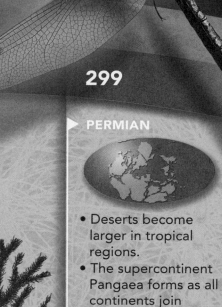

359

416

299

▶ **CARBONIFEROUS**

▶ **DEVONIAN**

• Early Appalachian Mountains form.
• North America and northern Europe lie in warm, tropical region.

▶ **PERMIAN**

• Seas rise and fall over what is now North America.

• Deserts become larger in tropical regions.
• The supercontinent Pangaea forms as all continents join together.

Development of Life

Club moss

Development of Life

Bony fish

Early amphibian

Development of Life

Dimetrodon

513

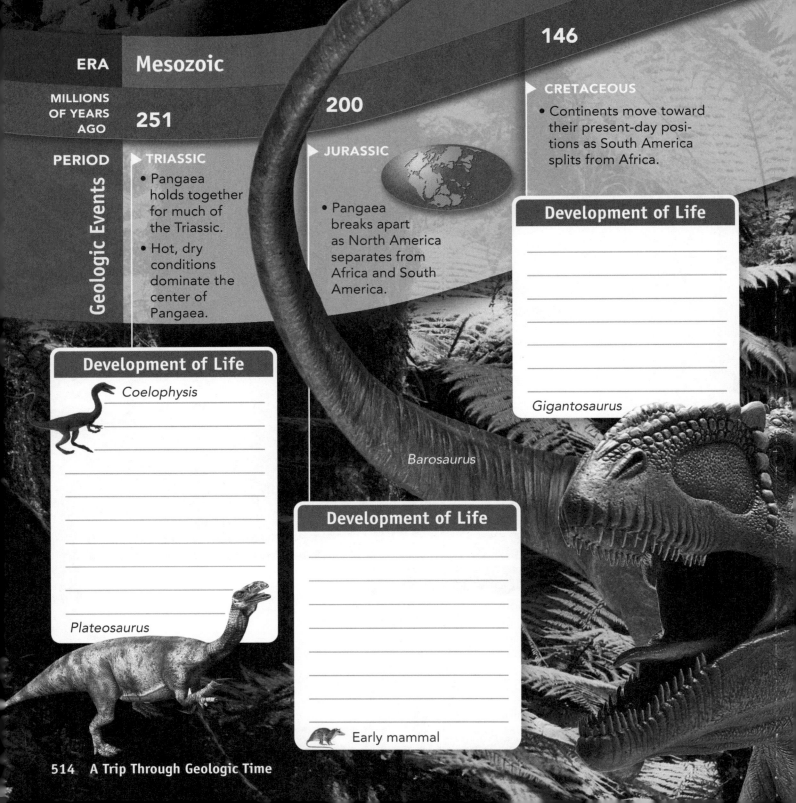

Geologic History

ERA	Mesozoic		146
MILLIONS OF YEARS AGO	251	200	

CRETACEOUS
- Continents move toward their present-day positions as South America splits from Africa.

| PERIOD | TRIASSIC | JURASSIC | |

Geologic Events

TRIASSIC
- Pangaea holds together for much of the Triassic.
- Hot, dry conditions dominate the center of Pangaea.

JURASSIC
- Pangaea breaks apart as North America separates from Africa and South America.

Development of Life

Coelophysis
_____
_____
_____
_____
_____
_____
_____
_____

Plateosaurus

Development of Life

_____
_____
_____
_____
_____
_____
_____

Early mammal

Development of Life

_____
_____
_____
_____
_____
_____

Gigantosaurus

Barosaurus

Cenozoic

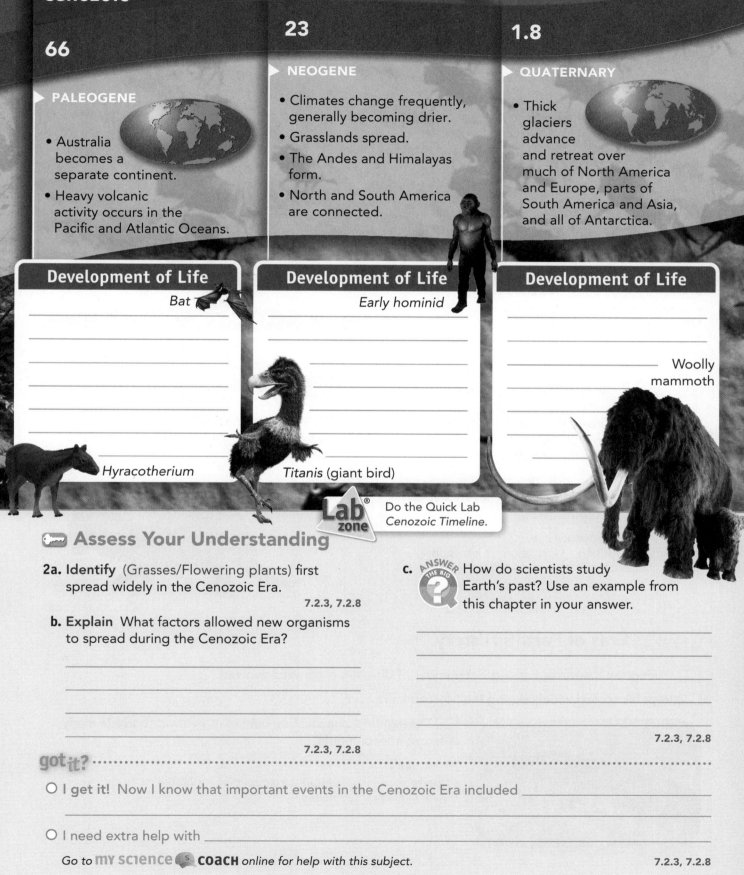

66

▶ **PALEOGENE**

- Australia becomes a separate continent.
- Heavy volcanic activity occurs in the Pacific and Atlantic Oceans.

23

▶ **NEOGENE**

- Climates change frequently, generally becoming drier.
- Grasslands spread.
- The Andes and Himalayas form.
- North and South America are connected.

1.8

▶ **QUATERNARY**

- Thick glaciers advance and retreat over much of North America and Europe, parts of South America and Asia, and all of Antarctica.

Development of Life

Bat

Hyracotherium

Development of Life

Early hominid

Titanis (giant bird)

Development of Life

Woolly mammoth

Lab zone Do the Quick Lab *Cenozoic Timeline.*

🔑 Assess Your Understanding

2a. Identify (Grasses/Flowering plants) first spread widely in the Cenozoic Era.

7.2.3, 7.2.8

b. Explain What factors allowed new organisms to spread during the Cenozoic Era?

_____

_____

_____

7.2.3, 7.2.8

c. **ANSWER THE BIG ?** How do scientists study Earth's past? Use an example from this chapter in your answer.

_____

_____

_____

_____

_____

7.2.3, 7.2.8

got it? ....

○ **I get it!** Now I know that important events in the Cenozoic Era included _____

_____

○ **I need extra help with** _____

Go to **MY SCIENCE** ˢ **COACH** online for help with this subject.

7.2.3, 7.2.8

Study Guide

Scientists study _____ in order to draw inferences about how _____ have changed over time.

LESSON 1 Fossils
7.2.8, 7.NS.1, 7.NS.8

🔑 Most fossils form when sediment hardens into rock, preserving the shapes of organisms.

🔑 Fossils include molds, casts, petrified fossils, carbon films, trace fossils, and preserved remains.

🔑 Fossils provide evidence about Earth's history.

Vocabulary
• fossil • mold • cast • petrified fossil
• carbon film • trace fossil • paleontologist
• evolution • extinct

LESSON 2 The Relative Age of Rocks
7.2, 7.NS.8

🔑 In horizontal sedimentary rock layers, the oldest layer is generally at the bottom. Each layer is younger than the layers below it.

🔑 Gaps in the geologic record and folding can change the position in which rock layers appear.

Vocabulary
• relative age • absolute age
• law of superposition • extrusion • intrusion
• fault • index fossil • unconformity

LESSON 3 The Geologic Time Scale
7.2.3, 7.NS.3, 7.NS.8

🔑 Because the time span of Earth's past is so great, geologists use the geologic time scale to show Earth's history.

Vocabulary
• geologic time scale
• era
• period

LESSON 4 Eras of Earth's History
7.2.3, 7.2.8, 7.NS.3, 7.NS.8

🔑 During the Paleozoic Era, a great number of different organisms evolved.

🔑 Reptiles spread widely during the Mesozoic Era.

🔑 During the Cenozoic Era, mammals evolved to live in many different environments.

Vocabulary
• invertebrate • vertebrate • amphibian • reptile
• mass extinction • mammal

Review and Assessment

LESSON 1 Fossils

1. A hollow area in sediment in the shape of all or part of an organism is called a

  a. mold.   **b.** cast.

  c. trace fossil.   **d.** carbon film.

                                     7.2.8

2. A series of dinosaur footprints in rock are an

  example of a(n) _____ fossil.

                                     7.2.8

3. Develop Hypotheses Which organism has a better chance of leaving a fossil: a jellyfish or a bony fish? Explain.

_____

_____

_____

                             7.2.8, 7.NS.1

Use the picture below to answer Questions 4–5.

4. Classify What type of fossil is shown?

_____

                                     7.2.8

5. Infer This fossil was found in a dry, mountainous area. What can you infer about how the area has changed over time?

_____

_____

_____

                                     7.2.8

6. 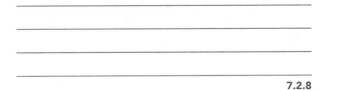 **Write About It** Suppose you are developing a museum exhibit about fossils. Write a guide for visitors to your exhibit explaining how fossils form and what scientists can learn from them.

                                     7.2.8

LESSON 2 The Relative Age of Rocks

7. A gap in the geologic record that occurs when sedimentary rocks cover an eroded surface is called a(n)

  a. intrusion.   **b.** unconformity.

  c. fault.   **d.** extrusion.

                                       7.2

8. A geologist finds an area of undisturbed

  sedimentary rock. The _____

  layer is most likely the oldest.

                                       7.2

9. Apply Concepts A geologist finds identical index fossils in a rock layer in the Grand Canyon in Arizona and in a rock layer in northern Utah, more than 675 kilometers away. What can she infer about the ages of the two rock layers?

_____

_____

                                       7.2

10. Explain Why do geologists sometimes use both relative and absolute age to describe rocks?

_____

_____

_____

_____

                                       7.2

11. Compare and Contrast Explain the difference between an intrusion and an extrusion.

_____

_____

_____

_____

_____

                                       7.2

12. A fault is always (older/younger) than the rock it cuts through.

                                       7.2

14 Review and Assessment

LESSON 3 **The Geologic Time Scale**

13. The geologic time scale is subdivided into

    a. relative ages.   **b.** absolute ages.

    c. unconformities.   **d.** eras, epochs, and periods.

                        7.2.3

14. Scientists developed the geologic time scale

by studying _____

_____

                        7.2.3

15. Sequence Which major division of geologic time came first?

_____

Which period of geologic time occurred most recently?

_____

                        7.2.3

16. An epoch is a (larger/smaller) than a period.

                        7.2.3

17. Calculate Using the diagram of the geologic time scale, find the length of each era in millions of years.

Cenozoic Era: _____ Mesozoic Era: _____

Paleozoic Era: _____

                7.2.3, 7.NS.8

18. Explain How do scientists decide when one unit of time begins and another ends?

_____

_____

_____

                        7.2.3

LESSON 4 **Eras of Earth's History**

19. The earliest multicelled organisms were

    a. invertebrates.   **b.** land plants.

    c. vertebrates.   **d.** bacteria.

                  7.2.3, 7.2.8

20. Explain How did Earth's environments change from the Neogene to the Quaternary Period?

_____

_____

                  7.2.3, 7.2.8

21. Evaluate Science in the Media If you see a movie in which early humans fight dinosaurs, how would you judge the scientific accuracy of that movie? Give reasons for your judgment.

_____

_____

_____

_____

_____

                  7.2.3, 7.2.8

How do scientists study Earth's past?

22. Look at the fossil below. What can you infer about the organism and its environment? Be sure to give evidence for your inferences.

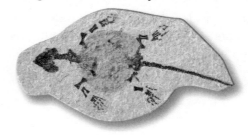

_____

_____

_____

_____

_____

_____

            7.2.3, 7.2.8, 7.NS.8

Indiana ISTEP+ Practice

Multiple Choice

Circle the letter of the correct answer.

1. Use the table to answer the question.

Geologic Time Scale	
Time Period	**Duration (Millions of Years)**
Cenozoic Era	66
Mesozoic Era	185
Paleozoic Era	291
Precambrian Time	about 4,058

A class is designing an outdoor model to show the geologic time scale from Precambrian Time through the present. If they use a scale of 1 m = 100 million years, how long will their model be?

A. 46,000 m   **B.** 460 m

C. 46 m   **D.** 4.6 m

7.2.3, 7.NS.8

2. A leaf falls into a shallow lake and is rapidly buried in the sediment. The sediment changes to rock over millions of years. Which type of fossil would *most likely* be formed?

A. carbon film

B. cast

C. preserved remains

D. trace fossil

7.2.3, 7.2.8

3. The extinction of the dinosaurs marks the end of which geologic period?

A. Precambrian

B. Carboniferous

C. Cretaceous

D. Neogene

7.2.8

4. Which of the following organisms lived during the Paleozoic Era?

A. dinosaurs

B. flowering plants

C. grasses

D. trilobites

7.2.8

Constructed Response

Write your answer to Question 5 on the lines below.

5. What are two major events characterizing the Quaternary Period?

_____

_____

_____

7.2.8

Extended Response

Use the diagram below and your knowledge of science to answer Question 6. Write your answer on a separate sheet of paper.

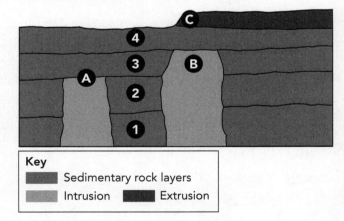

Key	
Sedimentary rock layers	
Intrusion	Extrusion

6. Write the order in which the rock areas shown formed. Justify your answer using evidence from the diagram.

7.2.3, 7.NS.8, 7.NS.11

PUTTING THE PUZZLE TOGETHER

Imagine you are putting together a puzzle, but you don't have all the pieces. That's the problem for scientists trying to determine exactly what an animal looked like. Paleontologists may find only some of the bones of a prehistoric animal. They may find bones from more than one of the same kind of animal.

Scientists build reconstructions of the animals based on the fossils they have and observations of living relatives of the animal. Computed tomography (CT) scans help scientists make virtual fossils. They start with the pieces they have and then fill in the rest of the puzzle virtually. For example, if the scientists have found a fossil of the right jaw bone, the computers are able to help them model the left jaw bone, and build virtual models of the entire head.

Bones tell a story that scientists can understand. It's much harder to figure out the size and shape of the muscles or the color of the animal. Different scientists will build slightly different reconstructions of the same kind of animal. Because so many pieces of the puzzle are missing, it may be impossible to have a perfectly accurate reconstruction. Because the organisms are extinct, scientists may never know for sure.

Write About It Research the different ways in which paleontologists have reconstructed *Tyrannosaurus rex*. Choose one change and explain how it differed from a previous reconstruction. Why did paleontologists think this was a good change?

7.NS.2

These scientists are studying a Messel snake fossil on a digital scanning system. ▶

Teen Finds Fossils

In early 2007, sixteen-year-old Sierra Sarti-Sweeney went for a walk at Boca Ciega Millenium Park in Seminole, Florida. She wanted to take some nature pictures. She did not expect to stumble on a mammoth!

During her walk, Sierra noticed bones in a stream bed. With her older brother, Sean, she brought the bones to local scientists. The bone Sierra found was the tooth of a prehistoric Columbian mammoth. Archaeologists say that the tooth and other fossils Sierra found could be as much as 100,000 years old!

Since Sierra's find, digging at the site has uncovered even more bones, including those from prehistoric camels, 2-meter turtles, and saber-toothed cats. According to scientists, the findings suggest that this part of Florida was once like the African savanna region.

For Sierra, the experience was exciting. She even had a call from a late-night television host. Finding the tooth confirmed Sierra's desire to be a zoologist and to keep looking at the world around her.

Design It Plan an exhibit of Sierra's findings. What would people want to know and see? Make a brochure advertising your exhibit and develop a presentation of the fossils found at Boca Ciega Millenium Park.

7.NS.11

FROZEN EVIDENCE

In the giant ice cap at the South Pole, a continuous record of snow exists reaching back more than 800,000 years. Scientists have drilled 3.2 kilometers down into the ice. From the cores they pull up, scientists learn about the temperature and the different gases in the air when each layer was formed.

These cores show that temperatures go up and down in cycles. Long ice ages (about 90,000 years) follow short warm periods (about 10,000 years). The climate record also shows that temperatures and amounts of carbon dioxide change together. If carbon dioxide levels rise, temperatures also rise.

Research It Find at least three sources that explain the ice cores project. Write an essay critiquing the explanations provided. Note any bias, misinformation, or missing information.

 7.NS.2, 7.NS.8

Researchers extract samples from the ice at the South Pole. ▲

HOW ARE YOU LIKE THIS CREATURE?

What are cells made of?

You sure don't see this sight when you look in the mirror! This deep-sea animal does not have skin, a mouth, or hair like yours. It's a young animal that lives in the Atlantic Ocean and may grow up to become a crab or shrimp. Yet you and this creature have more in common than you think.

△Infer **What might you have in common with this young sea animal?**

_____

_____

_____

_____

_____

> **UNTAMED SCIENCE** Watch the **Untamed Science** video to learn more about cells.

Cells and Human Body Systems

Academic Standards for Science

7.3.1, 7.3.2, 7.3.3, 7.3.4, 7.3.5, 7.3.6, 7.3.7,
7.NS.1–7.NS.3, 7.NS.8, 7.NS.11

CHAPTER

15 Getting Started

Check Your Understanding

1. Background Read the paragraph below and then answer the question.

You heard that a pinch of soil can contain millions of **organisms,** and you decide to check it out. Many organisms are too small to see with just your eyes, so you bring a hand **lens.** You see a few organisms, but you think you would see more with greater **magnification.**

An **organism** is a living thing.

A **lens** is a curved piece of glass or other transparent material that is used to bend light.

Magnification is the condition of things appearing larger than they are.

• How does a hand lens help you see more objects in the soil than you can see with just your eyes?

_____

_____

▶ MY READING WEB If you had trouble answering the question above, visit **My Reading Web** and type in *Cells and Human Body Systems.*

Vocabulary Skill

Prefixes Some words can be divided into parts. A root is the part of the word that carries the basic meaning. A prefix is a word part that is placed in front of the root to change the word's meaning. The prefixes below will help you understand some of the vocabulary in this chapter.

Prefix	Meaning	Example
chroma-	color	chromatin, *n.* the genetic material in the nucleus of a cell that can be colored with dyes
multi-	many	multicellular, *adj.* having many cells

2. Quick Check Circle the prefix in the boldface word below. What does the word tell you about the organisms?

• Fishes, insects, grasses, and trees are examples of **multicellular** organisms.

_____

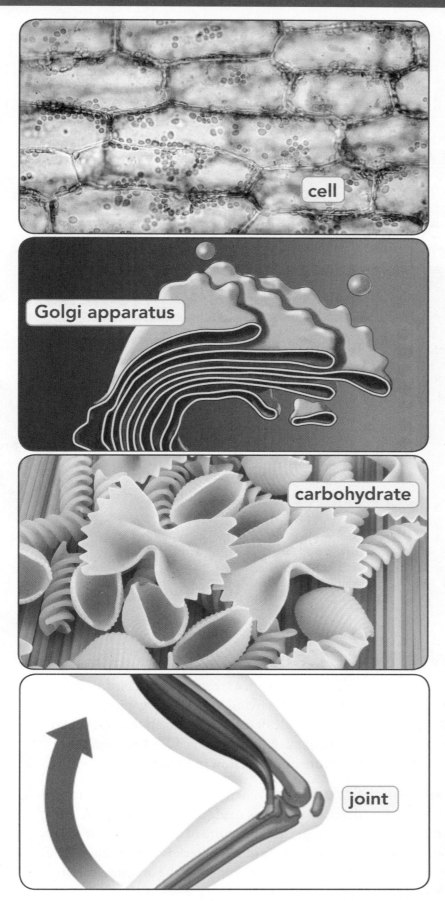

cell

Golgi apparatus

carbohydrate

joint

Chapter Preview

LESSON 1
* cell * microscope * cell theory
* Sequence △ Measure

LESSON 2
* cell wall * cell membrane
* nucleus * organelle * ribosome
* cytoplasm * mitochondria
* endoplasmic reticulum
* Golgi apparatus * vacuole
* chloroplast * lysosome
* multicellular * unicellular * tissue
* organ * organ system
* Identify the Main Idea
△ Make Models

LESSON 3
* element * compound
* carbohydrate * lipid * protein
* enzyme * nucleic acid * DNA
* double helix
* Compare and Contrast
△ Draw Conclusions

LESSON 4
* cell cycle * interphase
* replication * chromosome
* mitosis * cytokinesis
* Ask Questions
△ Interpret Data

LESSON 5
* differentiation * muscle tissue
* nervous tissue * connective tissue
* epithelial tissue
* Identify the Main Idea
△ Make Models

LESSON 6
* skeleton * skeletal muscle * joint
* nutrient * absorption * gland
* stimulus * response * hormone
* Summarize
△ Develop Hypotheses

> VOCAB FLASH CARDS For extra help
with vocabulary, visit **Vocab Flash
Cards** and type in *Cells and Human
Body Systems.*

Discovering Cells

UNLOCK
THE BIG
?

🔑 **What Are Cells?**
7.3.1

🔑 **What Is the Cell Theory?**
7.3.1

🔑 **How Do Microscopes Work?**
7.NS.1, 7.NS.3, 7.NS.8

my PLANET DiaRY

Life at First Sight

Anton van Leeuwenhoek was the first researcher to see bacteria under a microscope. In his journal, he described how he felt after discovering this new and unfamiliar form of life.

"For me . . . no more pleasant sight has met my eye than this of so many thousand of living creatures in one small drop of water."

VOICES FROM HISTORY

Read the quote, and answer the question below.

Why do you think Leeuwenhoek was so excited about what he saw?

_____

_____

▶ PLANET DIARY Go to **Planet Diary** to learn more about studying cells.

A modern view of bacteria similar to those seen by Leeuwenhoek

Lab zone Do the Inquiry Warm-Up *What Can You See?*

Academic Standards for Science

7.3.1 Explain that all living organisms are composed of one or more cells and that the many functions needed to sustain life are carried out within such cells.

What Are Cells?

What do you think a mushroom, a tree, a spider, a bird, and you have in common? All are living things, or organisms. Like all organisms, they are made of cells. **Cells** form the parts of an organism and carry out all of its functions. 🔑 **Cells are the basic units of structure and function in living things.**

Cells and Structure When you describe the structure of an object, you describe what it is made of and how its parts are put together. For example, the structure of a building depends on the way bricks, steel beams, or other materials are arranged. The structure of a living thing is determined by the amazing variety of ways its cells are put together.

Vocabulary

- cell
- microscope
- cell theory

Skills

↻ Reading: Sequence

△ Inquiry: Measure

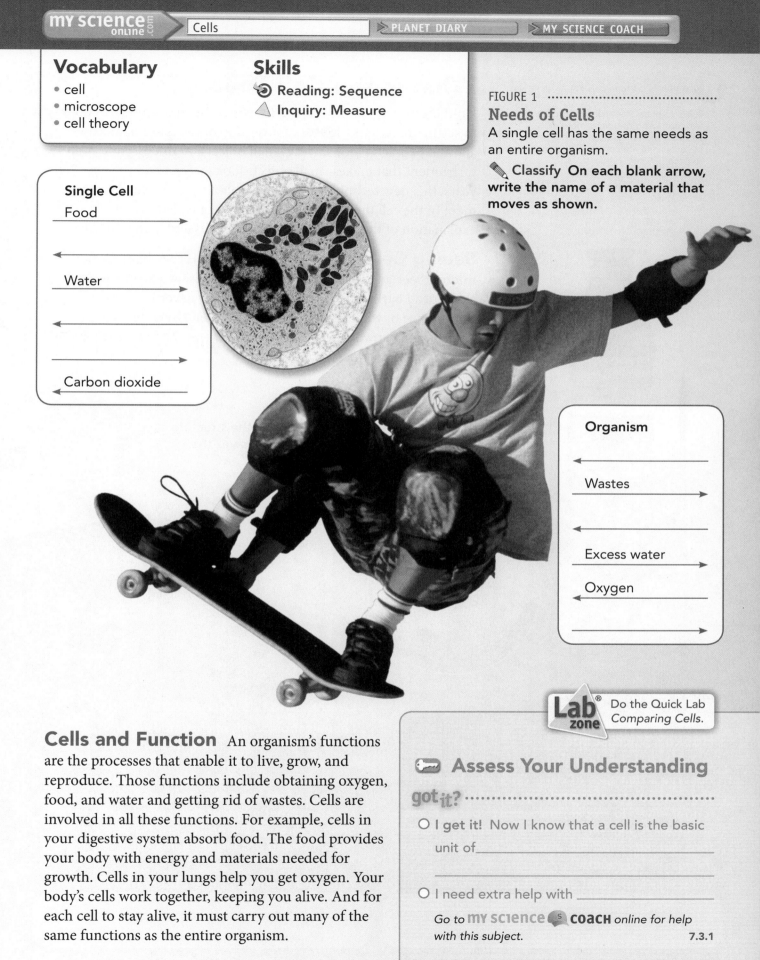

Single Cell

Food →

←

Water →

←

Carbon dioxide ←

FIGURE 1 ·····················

Needs of Cells

A single cell has the same needs as an entire organism.

✎ **Classify** On each blank arrow, write the name of a material that moves as shown.

Organism

←

Wastes →

←

Excess water →

Oxygen ←

→

Cells and Function An organism's functions are the processes that enable it to live, grow, and reproduce. Those functions include obtaining oxygen, food, and water and getting rid of wastes. Cells are involved in all these functions. For example, cells in your digestive system absorb food. The food provides your body with energy and materials needed for growth. Cells in your lungs help you get oxygen. Your body's cells work together, keeping you alive. And for each cell to stay alive, it must carry out many of the same functions as the entire organism.

Lab zone Do the Quick Lab *Comparing Cells.*

🔑 Assess Your Understanding

got it? ·····································

○ **I get it!** Now I know that a cell is the basic unit of_____

_____

○ **I need extra help with** _____

Go to **MY SCIENCE** 💬 **COACH** *online for help with this subject.*   7.3.1

527

What Is the Cell Theory?

Until the 1600s, no one knew cells existed because there was no way to see them. Around 1590, the invention of the first microscope allowed people to look at very small objects. A **microscope** is an instrument that makes small objects look larger. Over the next 200 years, this new technology revealed cells and led to the development of the cell theory. The **cell theory** is a widely accepted explanation of the relationship between cells and living things.

Seeing Cells English scientist Robert Hooke built his own microscopes and made drawings of what he saw when he looked at the dead bark of certain oak trees. Hooke never knew the importance of what he saw. A few years later, Dutch businessman Anton van Leeuwenhoek (LAY von hook) was the first to see living cells through his microscopes.

FIGURE 2 ···

Growth of the Cell Theory
The cell theory describes how cells relate to the structure and function of living things. ✎ **Review Answer the questions in the spaces provided.**

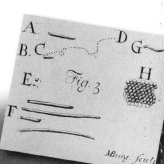

Drawing by Leeuwenhoek

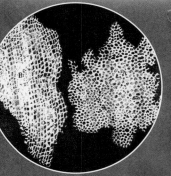

Hooke's drawing of cork

Hooke's Microscope

In 1663, Robert Hooke used his microscope to observe a thin slice of cork. Cork, the bark of the cork oak tree, is made up of cells that are no longer alive. To Hooke, the empty spaces in the cork looked like tiny rectangular rooms. Therefore, Hooke called the empty spaces cells, which means "small rooms."

What was important about Hooke's work?

Leeuwenhoek's Microscope

Leeuwenhoek built microscopes in his spare time. Around 1674, he looked at drops of lake water, scrapings from teeth and gums, and water from rain gutters. Leeuwenhoek was surprised to find a variety of one-celled organisms. He noted that many of them whirled, hopped, or shot through water like fast fish. He called these moving organisms animalcules, meaning "little animals."

What did Leeuwenhoek's observations reveal?

What the Cell Theory Says

Figure 2 highlights people who made key discoveries in the early study of cells. Their work and the work of many others led to the development of the cell theory. 🔑 **The cell theory states the following:**

- **All living things are composed of cells.**
- **Cells are the basic units of structure and function in living things.**
- **All cells are produced from other cells.**

Living things differ greatly from one another, but all are made of cells. The cell theory holds true for all living things, no matter how big or how small. Because cells are common to all living things, cells can provide clues about the functions that living things perform. And because all cells come from other cells, scientists can study cells to learn about growth and reproduction.

✏️ **Sequence** Fill in the circle next to the name of the person who was the first to see living cells through a microscope.

○ Matthias Schleiden
○ Robert Hooke
○ Anton van Leeuwenhoek
○ Rudolf Virchow
○ Theodor Schwann

Schleiden, Schwann, and Virchow

In 1838, using his own research and the research of others, Matthias Schleiden concluded that all plants are made of cells. A year later, Theodor Schwann reached the same conclusion about animals. In 1855, Rudolf Virchow proposed that new cells are formed only from cells that already exist. "All cells come from cells," wrote Virchow.

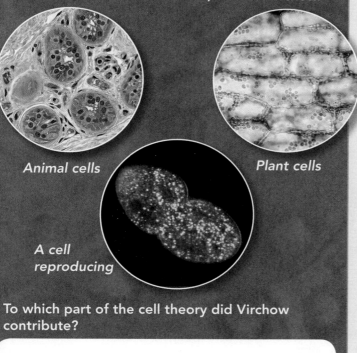

Animal cells

Plant cells

A cell reproducing

To which part of the cell theory did Virchow contribute?

_____

_____

Lab ® Do the Quick Lab
zone *Observing Cells.*

🔑 Assess Your Understanding

1a. Relate Cause and Effect Why would Hooke's discovery have been impossible without a microscope?

_____

_____

_____

7.3.1

b. Apply Concepts Use Virchow's ideas to explain why plastic plants and stuffed animals are not alive.

_____

_____

_____

_____

7.3.1

got it? ....

○ **I get it!** Now I know that the cell theory describes_____

_____

_____

○ **I need extra help with** _____

Go to **my science** ⓢ **coach** *online for help with this subject.*

7.3.1

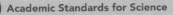
Vocabulary Prefixes The prefix *magni-* means "great" or "large." Underline all the words in the paragraph at the right that you can find with this prefix.

How Do Microscopes Work?

The cell theory could not have been developed without microscopes. **Some microscopes focus light through lenses to produce a magnified image, and other microscopes use beams of electrons.** Both light microscopes and electron microscopes do the same job in different ways. For a microscope to be useful, it must combine two important properties—magnification and resolution.

Magnification and Lenses Have you ever looked at something through spilled drops of water? If so, did the object appear larger? Magnification is the condition of things appearing larger than they are. Looking through a magnifying glass has the same result. A magnifying glass consists of a convex lens, which has a center that is thicker than its edge. When light passes through a convex lens and into your eye, the image you see is magnified. Magnification changes how you can see objects and reveals details you may not have known were there, as shown in **Figure 3**.

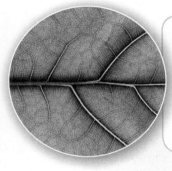

❶ Leaf; green color and veins

❷ _____

❸ _____

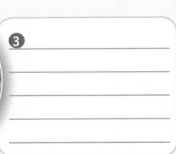

❹ _____

FIGURE 3 ·······································

Magnification

The images above have all been magnified, which makes them look unfamiliar. ✎ Infer On the lines, write what you think each photograph shows, and explain your reasoning. (One answer is completed for you.) 7.NS.8

530 Cells and Human Body Systems

Magnification With a Compound Microscope

Figure 4 shows a microscope that is similar to one you may use in your classroom. This type of instrument, called a compound microscope, magnifies the image using two lenses at once. One lens is fixed in the eyepiece. A second lens is chosen from a group of two or three lenses on the revolving nosepiece. Each of these lenses has a different magnifying power. By turning the nosepiece, you can select the lens you want. A glass slide on the stage holds the object to be viewed.

A compound microscope can magnify an object more than a single lens can. Light from a lamp (or reflecting off a mirror) passes through the object on the slide, the lower lens, and then the lens in the eyepiece. The total magnification of the object equals the magnifications of the two lenses multiplied together. For example, suppose the lower lens magnifies the object 10 times, and the eyepiece lens also magnifies the object 10 times. The total magnification of the microscope is 10×10, or 100 times, which is written as "100×."

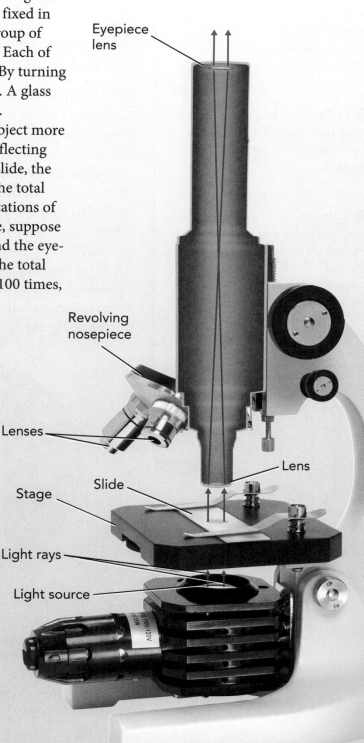

FIGURE 4 ·····················
＞VIRTUAL LAB A Compound Microscope

This microscope has a 10× lens in the eyepiece. The revolving nosepiece holds three different lenses: 4×, 10×, and 40×.

✎ **Complete these tasks.**

1. **Calculate** Calculate the three total magnifications possible for this microscope.

_____

_____

_____

2. **Predict** What would happen if the object on the slide were too thick for light to pass through it?

_____

_____

_____

7.NS.1, 7.NS.8

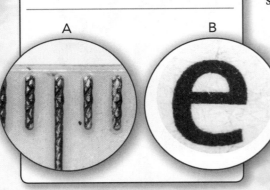
Measuring Microscopic Objects

When you see objects through a microscope, they look larger than they really are. How do you know their true size? One way is to use a metric ruler to measure the size of the circular field in millimeters as you see it through the microscope. Then you can estimate the size of the object you see by comparing it to the width of the field.

Resolution To create a useful image, a microscope must help you see the details of the object's structure clearly. The degree to which two separate structures that are close together can be distinguished is called resolution. Better resolution shows more details. For example, the colors of a newspaper photograph may appear to your eye to be solid patches of color. However, if you look at the colors through a microscope, you will see individual dots. You see the dots not only because they are magnified but also because the microscope improves resolution. In general, for light microscopes, resolution improves as magnification increases. Good resolution, as shown in **Figure 5,** makes it easier to study cells.

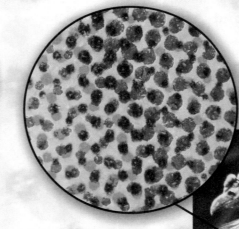

FIGURE 5 ················

Resolution

The images in colorful photographs actually consist of only a few ink colors in the form of dots.

🖋 **Interpret Photos** What color dots does improved resolution allow you to see?

_____
_____
_____

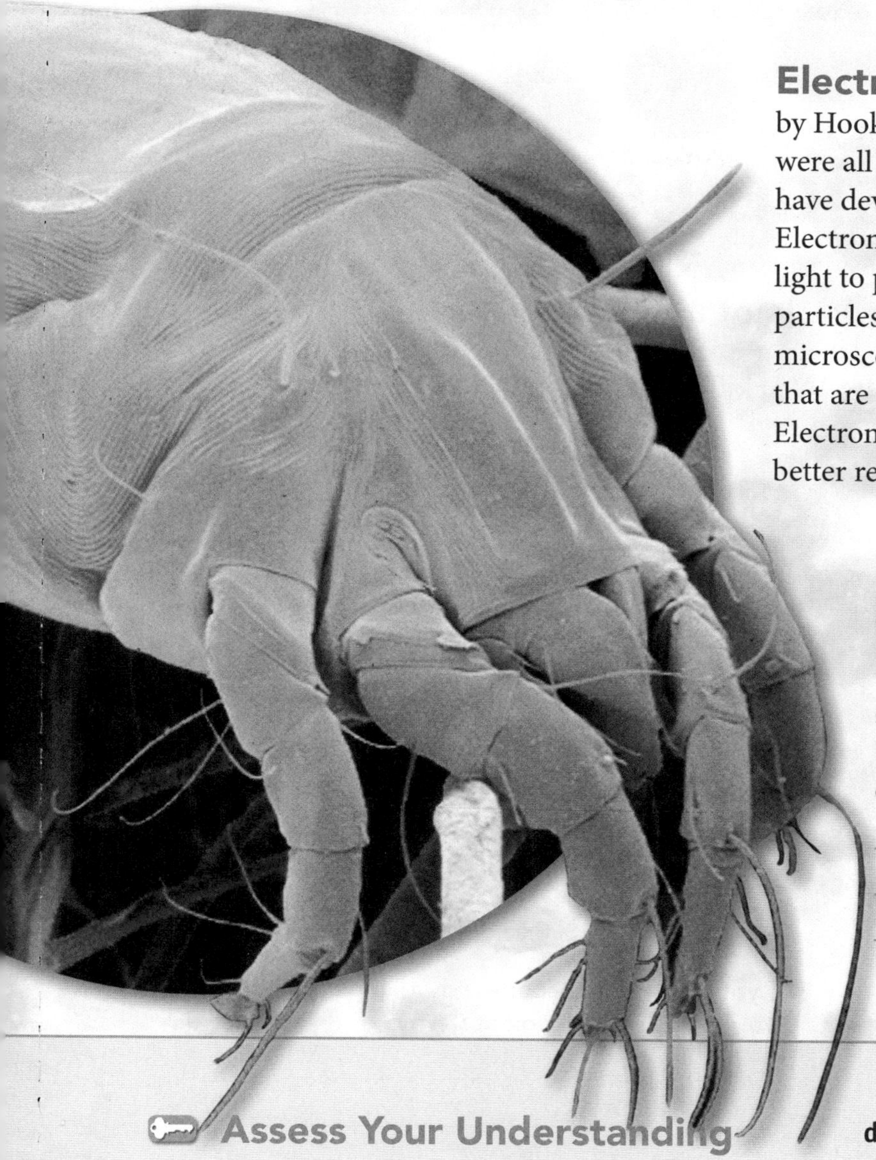

Electron Microscopes

The microscopes used by Hooke, Leeuwenhoek, and other early researchers were all light microscopes. Since the 1930s, scientists have developed several types of electron microscopes. Electron microscopes use a beam of electrons instead of light to produce a magnified image. (Electrons are tiny particles that are smaller than atoms.) By using electron microscopes, scientists can obtain pictures of objects that are too small to be seen with light microscopes. Electron microscopes allow higher magnification and better resolution than light microscopes.

FIGURE 6 ·······································

A Dust Mite

Dust mites live in everyone's homes. A colorized image made with an electron microscope reveals startling details of a mite's body.

✏ **Observe** List at least three details that you can see in the photo.

_____

_____

_____

_____

Lab zone® Do the Lab Investigation *Design and Build a Microscope.*

🔑 Assess Your Understanding

2a. Define Magnification makes objects look (smaller/larger) than they really are.

7.NS.3

b. Estimate The diameter of a microscope's field of view is estimated to be 0.9 mm. About how wide is an object that fills two thirds of the field? Circle your answer.

1.8 mm   0.6 mm   0.3 mm

7.NS.3

c. Compare and Contrast How are magnification and resolution different?

_____

_____

_____

_____

7.NS.3

d. Explain How do the characteristics of electron microscopes make them useful for studying cells?

_____

_____

_____

_____

_____

7.NS.3

got it? ·······································

○ **I get it!** Now I know that light microscopes work by_____

_____

○ **I need extra help with** _____

Go to **MY SCIENCE ⑤ COACH** *online for help with this subject*

7.NS.3

Looking Inside Cells

UNLOCK
THE BIG
?

🔑 **How Do the Parts of a Cell Work?**
7.3.3, 7.3.4, 7.NS.8

🔑 **How Do Cells Work Together in an Organism?**
7.3.5, 7.3.6, 7.NS.8

my planeT DiaRY

Glowing Globs

Do these cells look as if they're glowing? This photograph shows cells that have been stained with dyes that make cell structures easier to see. Scientists view such treated cells through a fluorescent microscope, which uses strong light to activate the dyes and make them glow. Here, each green area is a cell's nucleus, or control center. The yellow "fibers" form a kind of support structure for the cell.

Lab ® Do the Inquiry Warm-Up
zone *How Large Are Cells?*

TECHNOLOGY

Communicate Discuss these questions with a partner. Then write your answers below.

1. Why is staining useful when studying cells through a microscope?

_____

_____

2. If you had a microscope, what kinds of things would you like to look at? Why?

_____

_____

_____

▷ **PLANET DIARY** Go to **Planet Diary** to learn more about cell parts.

Vocabulary
- cell wall • cell membrane • nucleus • organelle
- ribosome • cytoplasm • mitochondria
- endoplasmic reticulum • Golgi apparatus • vacuole
- chloroplast • lysosome • multicellular • unicellular
- tissue • organ • organ system

Skills
- Reading: Identify the Main Idea
- Inquiry: Make Models

How Do the Parts of a Cell Work?

When you look at a cell through a microscope, you can usually see the outer edge of the cell. Sometimes you can also see smaller structures within the cell. **Each kind of cell structure has a different function within a cell.** In this lesson, you will read about the structures that plant and animal cells have in common. You will also read about some differences between the cells.

Cell Wall The **cell wall** is a rigid layer that surrounds the cells of plants and some other organisms. The cells of animals, in contrast, do not have cell walls. A plant's cell wall helps protect and support the cell. The cell wall is made mostly of a strong material called cellulose. Still, many materials, including water and oxygen, can pass through the cell wall easily.

Cell Membrane Think about how a window screen allows air to enter and leave a room but keeps insects out. One of the functions of the cell membrane is something like that of a screen. The **cell membrane** controls which substances pass into and out of a cell. Everything a cell needs, such as food particles, water, and oxygen, enters through the cell membrane. Waste products leave the same way. In addition, the cell membrane prevents harmful materials from entering the cell.

All cells have cell membranes. In plant cells, the cell membrane is just inside the cell wall. In cells without cell walls, the cell membrane forms the border between the cell and its environment.

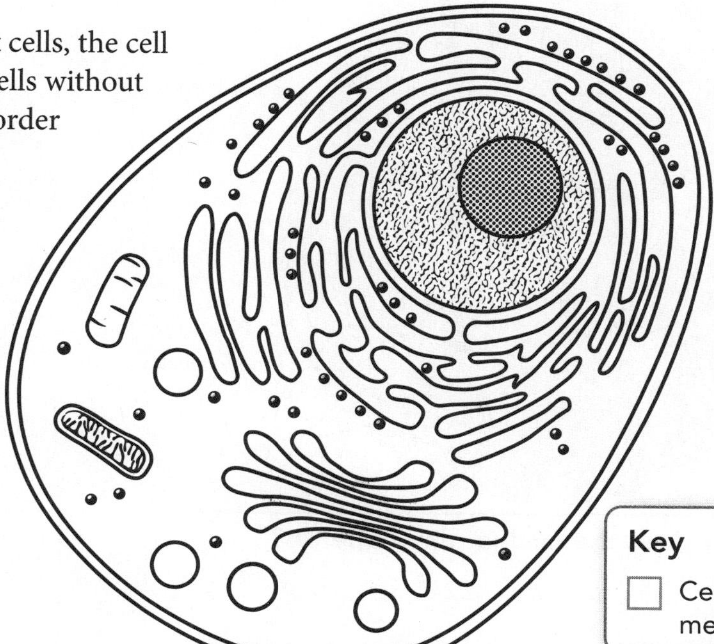

Academic Standards for Science

7.3.3 Explain that although the way cells function is similar in all living organisms, multicellular organisms also have specialized cells whose specialized functions are directly related to their structure.

7.3.4 Compare and contrast similarities and differences between specialized subcellular components within plant and animal cells, including organelles and cell walls that perform essential functions and give a cell its shape and structure.

7.NS.8 Analyze data, and use it to identify patterns and make inferences.

FIGURE 1 ·····················
A Typical Animal Cell
You will see this diagram of a cell again in this lesson.

✎ **Identify** Use a colored pencil to shade the cell membrane and fill in the box in the key.

Key

☐ Cell membrane

Nucleus

A cell doesn't have a brain, but it has something that functions in a similar way. A large oval structure called the **nucleus** (NOO klee us) acts as a cell's control center, directing all of the cell's activities. The nucleus is the largest of many tiny cell structures, called **organelles,** that carry out specific functions within a cell. Notice in **Figure 2** that the nucleus is surrounded by a membrane called the nuclear envelope. Materials pass in and out of the nucleus through pores in the nuclear envelope.

Chromatin

You may wonder how the nucleus "knows" how to direct the cell. Chromatin, thin strands of material that fill the nucleus, contains information for directing a cell's functions. For example, the instructions in the chromatin ensure that leaf cells grow and divide to form more leaf cells.

Nucleolus

Notice the small, round structure in the nucleus. This structure, the nucleolus, is where ribosomes are made. **Ribosomes** are small grain-shaped organelles that produce proteins. Proteins are important substances in cells.

FIGURE 2 ··

Organelles of a Cell

The structures of a cell look as different as their functions.

✎ **Complete each task.**

1. **Review** Answer the questions in the boxes.

2. **Relate Text and Visuals** In the diagram on the facing page, use different-colored pencils to color each structure and its matching box in the color key.   **7.NS.8**

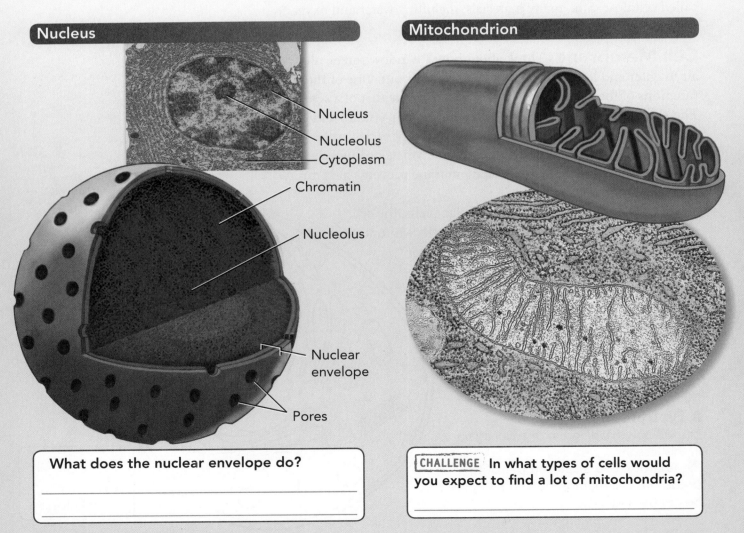

Nucleus

- Nucleus
- Nucleolus
- Cytoplasm
- Chromatin
- Nucleolus
- Nuclear envelope
- Pores

Mitochondrion

What does the nuclear envelope do?
_____
_____

CHALLENGE In what types of cells would you expect to find a lot of mitochondria?
_____

Organelles in the Cytoplasm Most of a cell consists of a thick, clear, gel-like fluid. The **cytoplasm** fills the region between the cell membrane and the nucleus. The fluid of the cytoplasm moves constantly within a cell, carrying along the nucleus and other organelles that have specific jobs.

Mitochondria Floating in the cytoplasm are rod-shaped structures that are nicknamed the "powerhouses" of a cell. Look again at **Figure 2. Mitochondria** (myt oh KAHN dree uh; singular *mitochondrion*) convert energy stored in food to energy the cell can use to live and function.

Endoplasmic Reticulum and Ribosomes In **Figure 2,** you can see what looks something like a maze of passageways. The **endoplasmic reticulum** (en doh PLAZ mik rih TIK yuh lum), often called the ER, is an organelle with a network of membranes that produces many substances. Ribosomes dot some parts of the ER, while other ribosomes float in the cytoplasm. The ER helps the attached ribosomes make proteins. These newly made proteins and other substances leave the ER and move to another organelle.

Vocabulary Prefixes The prefix *endo-* is Greek for "within." If the word part *plasm* refers to the "body" of the cell, what does the prefix *endo-* tell you about the endoplasmic reticulum?

_____

_____

Endoplasmic Reticulum and Ribosomes

Ribosomes

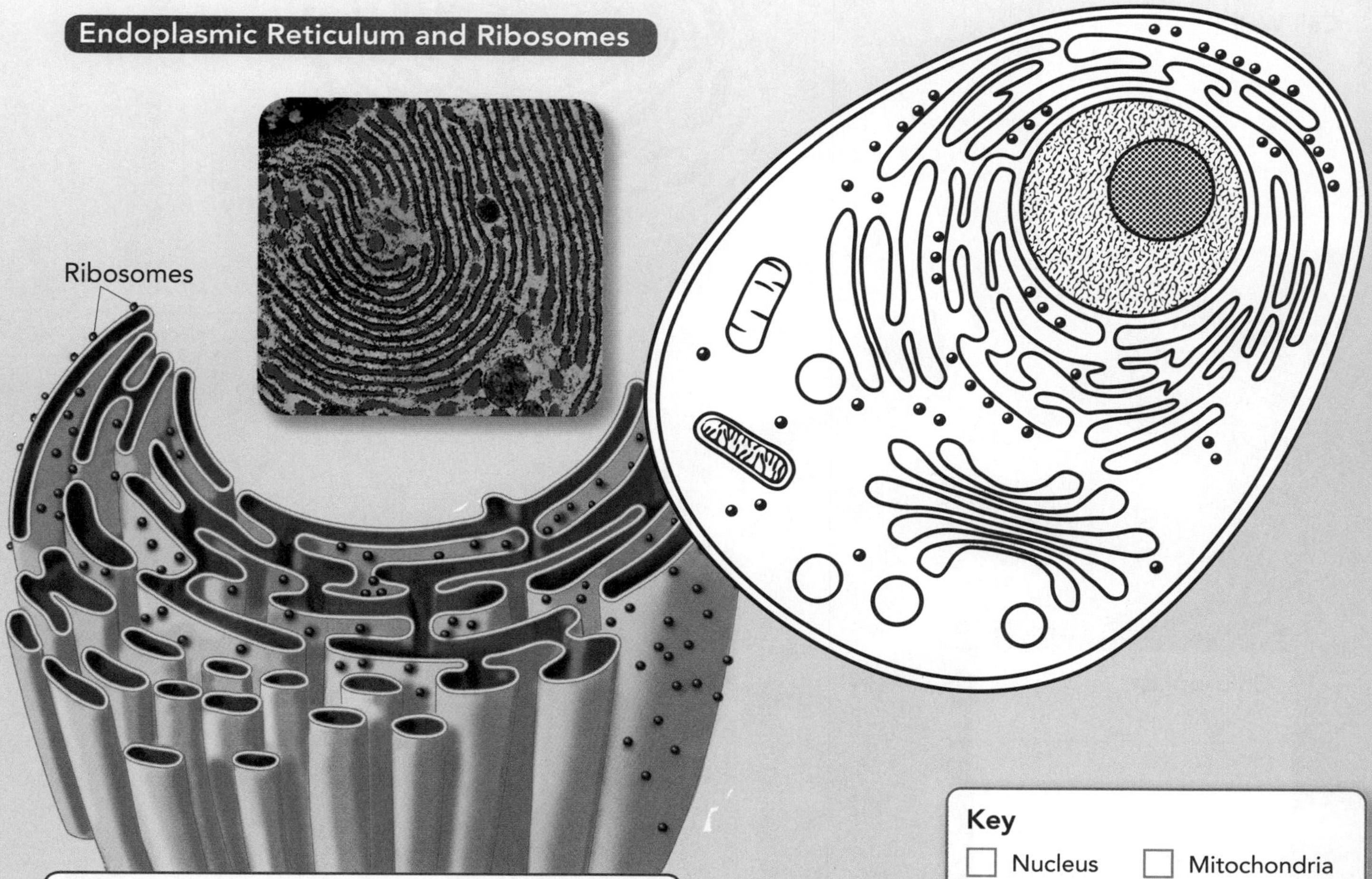

What do ribosomes do?

_____

Key

☐	Nucleus	☐ Mitochondria
☐	Nucleolus	☐ ER
☐	Cytoplasm	☐ Ribosomes

CELLS IN LIVING THINGS

What are cells made of?

FIGURE 3 ···

> INTERACTIVE ART These illustrations show typical structures found in plant and animal cells. Other living things share many of these structures, too. ✎ Describe **Describe the function of each structure in the boxes provided.**

7.NS.8

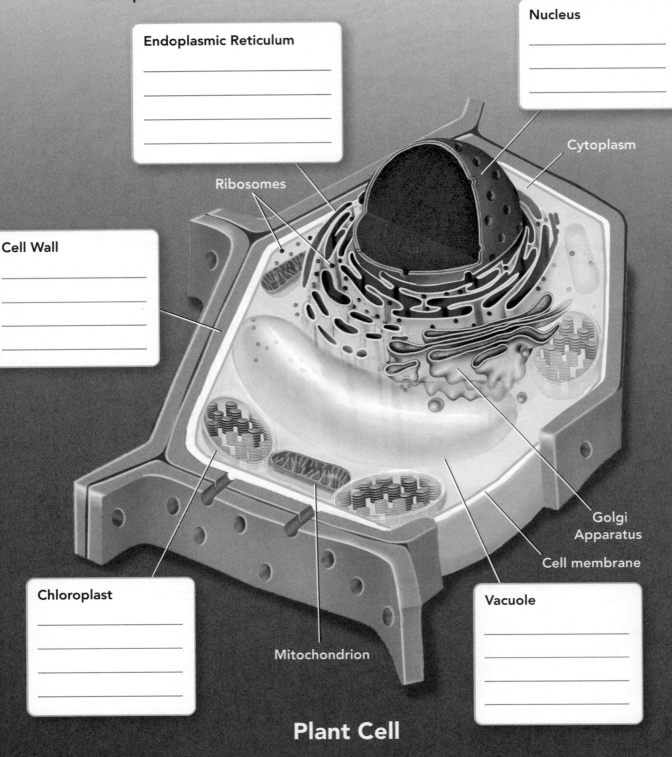

Endoplasmic Reticulum

_____
_____
_____

Nucleus

_____
_____
_____

Cytoplasm

Ribosomes

Cell Wall

_____
_____
_____

Golgi
Apparatus

Cell membrane

Chloroplast

_____
_____
_____

Vacuole

_____
_____
_____

Mitochondrion

Plant Cell

Check the box for each structure present in plant cells or animal cells.

Structure	Cell wall	Cell membrane	Cytoplasm	Nucleus	Mitochondria	Chloroplasts	Ribosomes	Endoplasmic reticulum	Vacuoles	Golgi apparatus	Lysosomes
Plant cells											
Animal cells											

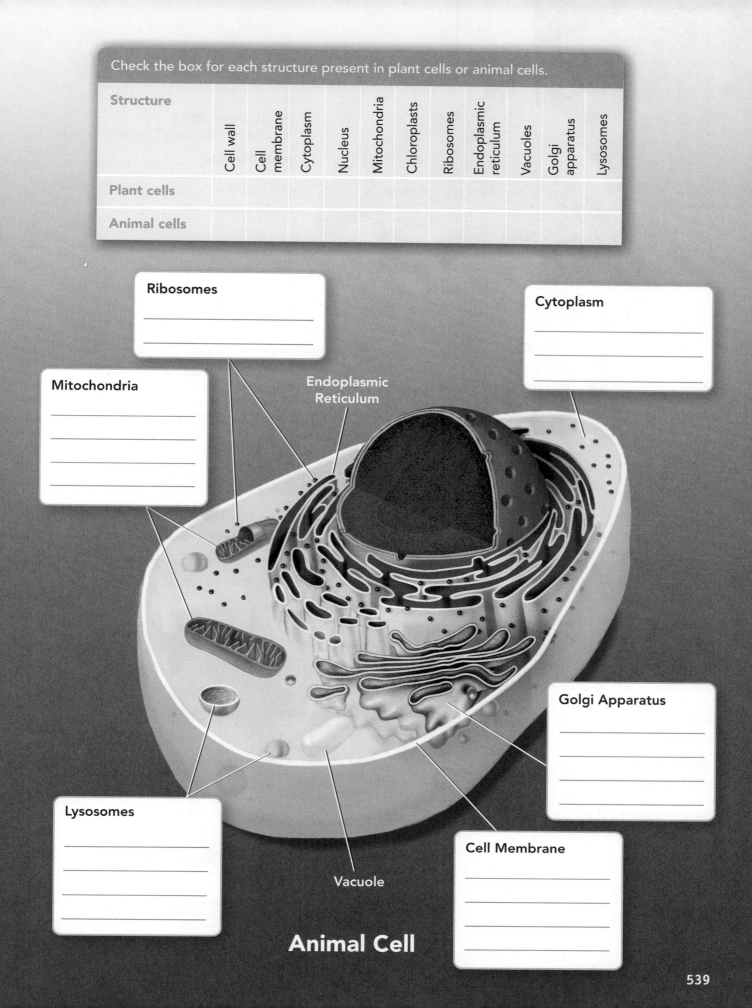

Ribosomes

Cytoplasm

Mitochondria

Endoplasmic Reticulum

Golgi Apparatus

Lysosomes

Cell Membrane

Vacuole

Animal Cell

FIGURE 4 ·····································
Golgi Apparatus

✏️ **Define** The Golgi apparatus is an

organelle that _____

and _____ materials

made in the _____

Golgi Apparatus As proteins leave the endoplasmic reticulum, they move to a structure that looks like the flattened sacs and tubes shown in **Figures 3 and 4.** This structure can be thought of as a cell's warehouse. The **Golgi apparatus** receives proteins and other newly formed materials from the ER, packages them, and distributes them to other parts of the cell or to the outside of the cell.

Vacuoles Plant cells often have one or more large, water-filled sacs floating in the cytoplasm. This type of sac, called a **vacuole** (VAK yoo ohl), stores water, food, or other materials needed by the cell. Vacuoles can also store waste products until the wastes are removed. Some animal cells do not have vacuoles, while others do.

apply it!

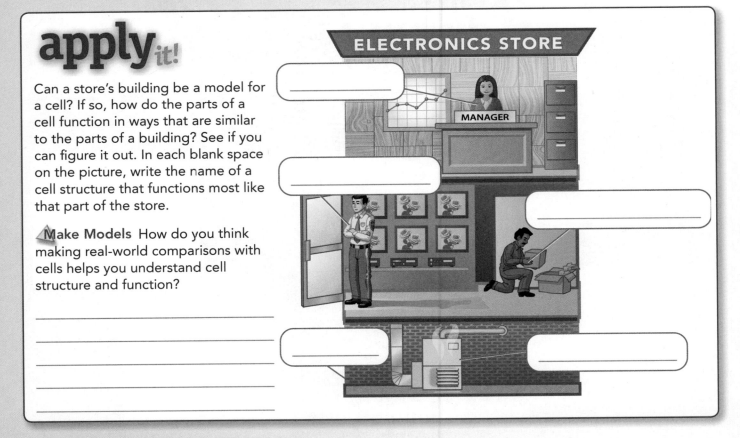

Can a store's building be a model for a cell? If so, how do the parts of a cell function in ways that are similar to the parts of a building? See if you can figure it out. In each blank space on the picture, write the name of a cell structure that functions most like that part of the store.

△ **Make Models** How do you think making real-world comparisons with cells helps you understand cell structure and function?

_____

_____

_____

_____

Chloroplasts A typical plant cell contains green structures, called chloroplasts, in the cytoplasm. A **chloroplast,** shown in **Figure 5,** captures energy from sunlight and changes it to a form of energy cells can use in making food. Animal cells don't have chloroplasts, but the cells of plants and some other organisms do. Chloroplasts make leaves green because leaf cells contain many chloroplasts.

Lysosomes Look again at the animal cell in **Figure 3**. Notice the saclike organelles, called **lysosomes** (LY suh sohmz), which contain substances that break down large food particles into smaller ones. Lysosomes also break down old cell parts and release the substances so they can be used again. You can think of lysosomes as a cell's recycling centers.

FIGURE 5 ···

A Chloroplast

✎ **Infer** In which part of a plant would you NOT expect to find cells with chloroplasts?

_____

_____

 Do the Quick Lab
Gelatin Cell Model.

🔑 Assess Your Understanding

1a. Interpret Tables Use the table you completed in **Figure 3** to summarize the differences between a plant cell and an animal cell.

_____

_____

_____

_____

7.3.4

b. Make Generalizations How are the functions of the endoplasmic reticulum and the Golgi apparatus related?

_____

_____

_____

_____

7.3.3

c. CHALLENGE A solar panel collects sunlight and converts it to heat or electrical energy. How is a solar panel similar to chloroplasts?

_____

_____

_____

_____

7.3.3, 7.3.4

d. ANSWER THE BIG **?** What are cells made of?

_____

_____

_____

_____

7.3.3, 7.3.4

got**it?** ···

○ **I get it!** Now I know that different kinds of organelles in a cell_____

○ **I need extra help with** _____

Go to MY SCIENCE ⓢ COACH *online for help with this subject.* 7.3.3, 7.3.4

Academic Standards for Science

7.3.5 Explain that all cells in multicellular organisms repeatedly divide to make more cells for growth and repair.

7.3.6 Explain that after fertilization, a small cluster of cells divides to form the basic tissues of an embryo which further develops into all the specialized tissues and organs within a multicellular organism.

7.NS.8 Analyze data, and use it to identify patterns and make inferences.

✍ Identify the Main Idea

Reread the paragraph about specialized cells. Then underline the phrases or sentences that describe the main ideas about specialized cells.

How Do Cells Work Together in an Organism?

Plants and animals (including you) are **multicellular,** which means "made of many cells." Single-celled organisms are called **unicellular.** In a multicellular organism, the cells often look quite different from one another. They also perform different functions.

Specialized Cells All cells in a multicellular organism must carry out key functions, such as getting oxygen, to remain alive. However, cells also may be specialized. That is, they perform specific functions that benefit the entire organism. These specialized cells share what can be called a "division of labor." One type of cell does one kind of job, while other types of cells do other jobs. For example, red blood cells carry oxygen to other cells that may be busy digesting your food. Just as specialized cells differ in function, they also differ in structure. **Figure 6** shows specialized cells from plants and animals. Each type of cell has a distinct shape. For example, a nerve cell has thin, fingerlike extensions that reach toward other cells. These structures help nerve cells transmit information from one part of your body to another. The nerve cell's shape wouldn't be helpful to a red blood cell.

FIGURE 6 ···

▷ **INTERACTIVE ART** **The Right Cell for the Job**
Many cells in plants and animals carry out specialized functions.
✍ **Draw Conclusions** Write the number of each kind of cell in the circle of the matching function.   7.NS.8

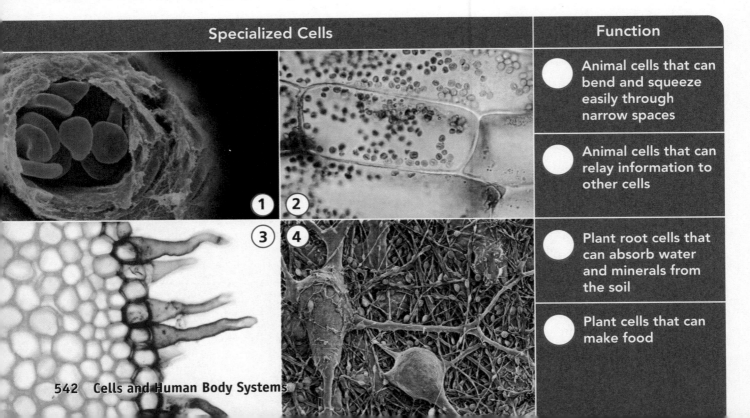

Specialized Cells	Function
① ② ③ ④	○ Animal cells that can bend and squeeze easily through narrow spaces
	○ Animal cells that can relay information to other cells
	○ Plant root cells that can absorb water and minerals from the soil
	○ Plant cells that can make food

Organization of Your Body

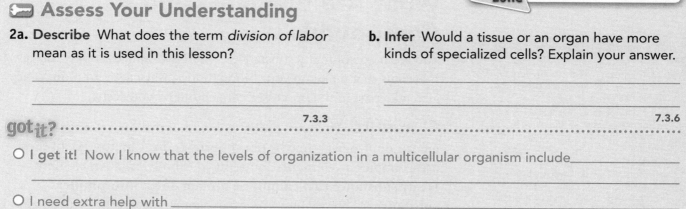

Cell ❯ Tissue ❯ Organ ❯ Organ system ❯ Organism

Organization of Your School

School

Cells Working Together A division of labor occurs among specialized cells in an organism. It also occurs at other levels of organization. 🔑 **In multicellular organisms, cells are organized into tissues, organs, and organ systems.** A **tissue** is a group of similar cells that work together to perform a specific function. For example, your brain is made mostly of nerve tissue, which consists of nerve cells that relay information to other parts of your body. An **organ,** such as your brain, is made of different kinds of tissues that function together. For example, the brain also has blood vessels that carry the blood that supplies oxygen to your brain cells. Your brain is part of your nervous system, which directs body activities and processes. An **organ system** is a group of organs that work together to perform a major function. As **Figure 7** shows, the level of organization in an organism becomes more complex from cell, to tissue, to organ, to organ systems.

FIGURE 7 ·······················
Levels of Organization
Living things are organized in levels of increasing complexity. Many nonliving things, like a school, have levels of organization, too.

✏ **Apply Concepts** On the lines above, write the levels of organization of your school building, from the simplest level, such as your desk, to the most complex.

 Do the Quick Lab
Tissues, Organs, Systems.

🔑 Assess Your Understanding

2a. Describe What does the term *division of labor* mean as it is used in this lesson?

_____

_____

7.3.3

b. Infer Would a tissue or an organ have more kinds of specialized cells? Explain your answer.

_____

_____

7.3.6

got it? ···

◯ **I get it!** Now I know that the levels of organization in a multicellular organism include_____

_____

◯ **I need extra help with** _____

Go to MY SCIENCE ⓢ COACH online for help with this subject.

7.3.5, 7.3.6

543

3 Chemical Compounds in Cells

UNLOCK THE BIG ?

🔑 **What Are Elements and Compounds?**
7.3.1, 7.3.2, 7.3.3

🔑 **What Compounds Do Cells Need?**
7.3.1, 7.3.2, 7.3.3, 7.NS.8

MY PLANET DIARY

Energy Backpacks

Some people think a camel's humps carry water. Not true! They actually store fat. A hump's fatty tissue supplies energy when the camel doesn't eat. When a camel has enough food, the hump remains hard and round. But when food is scarce, the hump gets smaller and may sag to the side. If the camel then gets more food, the hump can regain its full size and shape in about three or four months.

Communicate **Discuss this question with a group of classmates. Then write your answer below.**

How do you think the camel might be affected if it didn't have humps?

_____

_____

_____

▷ PLANET DIARY Go to **Planet Diary** to learn more about chemical compounds in cells.

Lab zone® Do the Inquiry Warm-Up *Detecting Starch.*

What Are Elements and Compounds?

You are made of many substances. These substances supply the raw materials that make up your blood, bones, muscles, and more. They also take part in the processes carried out by your cells.

Elements You have probably heard of carbon, hydrogen, oxygen, and nitrogen—maybe phosphorus and sulfur, too. All of these are examples of **elements** found in your body. 🔑 **An element is any substance that cannot be broken down into simpler substances.** The smallest unit of an element is a particle called an atom. Any single element is made up of only one kind of atom.

Academic Standards for Science

7.3.1 Explain that the many functions needed to sustain life are carried out within cells.

7.3.2 Understand that water is a major component within all cells and is required to carry out many cellular functions.

7.3.3 Explain that although the way cells function is similar in all living organisms, multicellular organisms also have specialized cells whose specialized functions are directly related to their structure.

544 Cells and Human Body Systems

Vocabulary

- element • compound • carbohydrate • lipid
- protein • enzyme • nucleic acid • DNA
- double helix

Skills

- Reading: Compare and Contrast
- Inquiry: Draw Conclusions

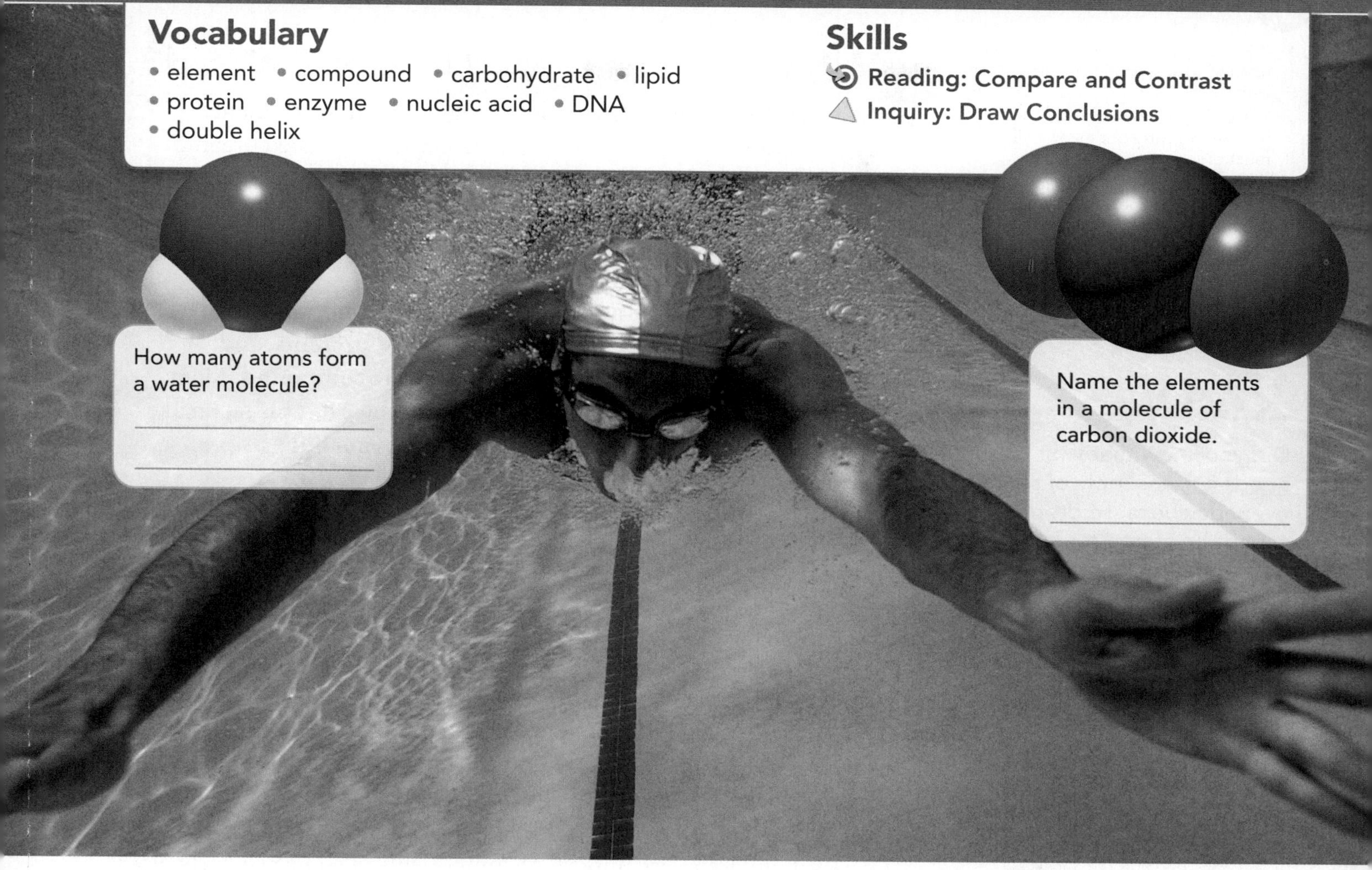

How many atoms form a water molecule?

_____

_____

Name the elements in a molecule of carbon dioxide.

_____

_____

Compounds

Carbon dioxide and water are examples of **compounds**. **Compounds form when two or more elements combine chemically.** Most elements in living things occur in the form of compounds. For example, carbon dioxide is a compound made up of the elements carbon and oxygen.

The smallest unit of many compounds is a molecule. A molecule of carbon dioxide consists of one carbon atom and two oxygen atoms. Compare the diagrams of the carbon dioxide molecule and the water molecule in **Figure 1**.

FIGURE 1 ·····································

Molecules and Compounds

Carbon dioxide, in the air exhaled from the swimmer's lungs, is a compound. So is water.

Interpret Diagrams Answer the questions in the boxes provided.

Do the Quick Lab
What Is a Compound?

Assess Your Understanding

got it? ···

○ **I get it!** Now I know that compounds form when _____

_____

○ **I need extra help with** _____

Go to **MY SCIENCE** ⓢ **COACH** *online for help with this subject.*

7.3.1, 7.3.2, 7.3.3

545

Academic Standards for Science

7.3.1 Explain that the many functions needed to sustain life are carried out within cells.

7.3.2 Understand that water is required to carry out many cellular functions.

7.3.3 Explain that multicellular organisms also have specialized cells whose specialized functions are directly related to their structure.

7.NS.8 Analyze data.

What Compounds Do Cells Need?

Many of the compounds in living things contain the element carbon. Most compounds that contain carbon are called organic compounds. Organic compounds that you may have heard of include nylon and polyester. Compounds that don't contain carbon are called inorganic compounds. Water and table salt are familiar examples of inorganic compounds.

Some important groups of organic compounds that living things need are carbohydrates, lipids, proteins, and nucleic acids. Water is a necessary inorganic compound. Many of these compounds are found in the foods you eat. This fact makes sense because the foods you eat come from living things.

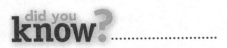

did you know?

Did you know that your body needs a new supply of proteins every day because protein cannot be stored for later use, as fat or carbohydrates can?

Carbohydrates

You have probably heard of sugars and starches. They are examples of **carbohydrates,** energy-rich organic compounds made of the elements carbon, hydrogen, and oxygen.

The food-making process in plants produces sugars. Fruits and some vegetables have a high sugar content. Sugar molecules can combine, forming larger molecules called starches, or complex carbohydrates. Plant cells store excess energy in molecules of starch. Many foods, such as potatoes, pasta, rice, and bread, come from plants and contain starch. When you eat these foods, your body breaks down the starch into glucose, a sugar your cells can use to get energy.

Carbohydrates are important components of some cell parts. For example, the cellulose found in the cell walls of plants is a type of carbohydrate. Carbohydrates are also found on cell membranes.

FIGURE 2

Energy-Rich Compounds

Cooked pasta served with olive oil, spices, and other ingredients makes an energy-packed meal.

Classify Label each food a starch or a lipid. Next to the label, write another example of a food that contains starch or lipids.

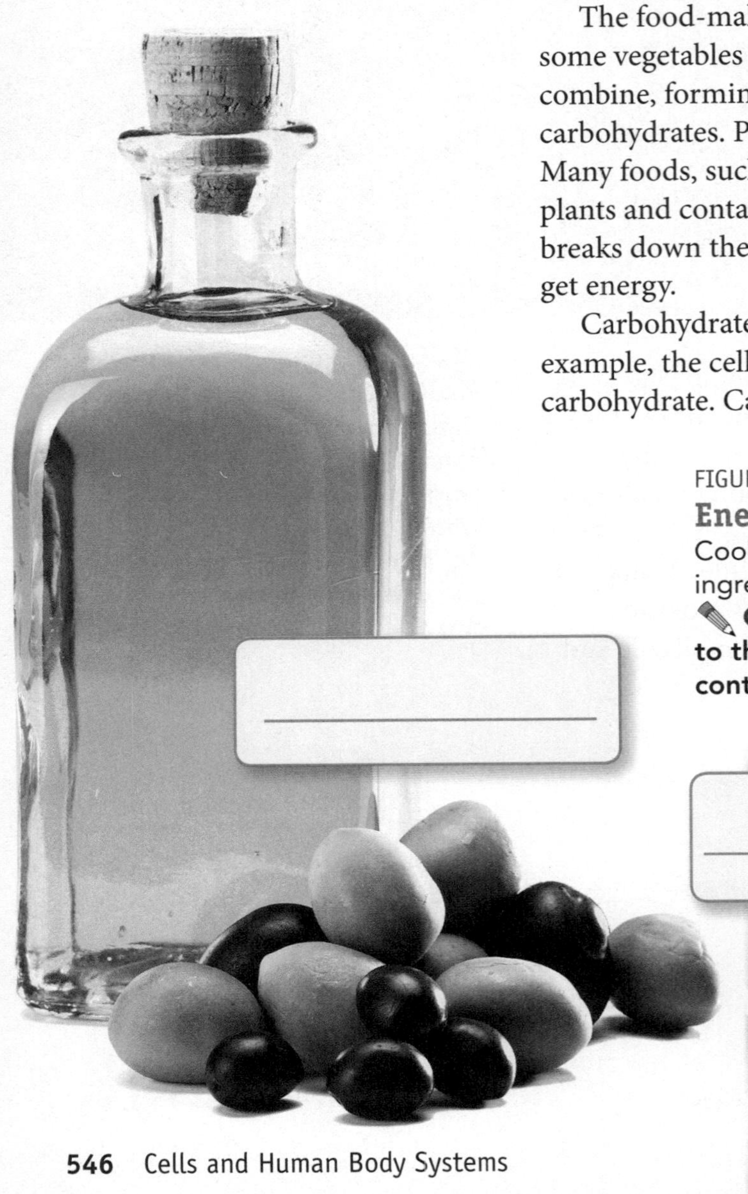

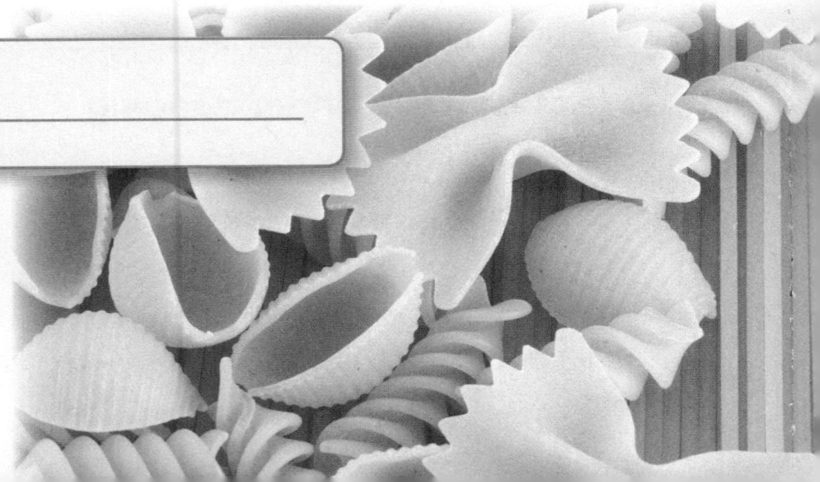

Lipids Have you ever seen a cook trim fat from a piece of meat before cooking it? The cook is trimming away one kind of lipid. **Lipids** are compounds that are made mostly of carbon and hydrogen and some oxygen. Cell membranes consist mainly of lipids.

Fats, oils, and waxes are all lipids. Gram for gram, fats and oils contain more energy than carbohydrates. Cells store energy from fats and oils for later use. For example, during winter, an inactive bear lives on the energy stored in its fat cells. Foods high in fats include whole milk, ice cream, and fried foods.

Proteins What do a bird's feathers, a spider's web, and a hamburger have in common? They consist mainly of proteins. **Proteins** are large organic molecules made of carbon, hydrogen, oxygen, nitrogen, and, in some cases, sulfur. Foods that are high in protein include meat, dairy products, fish, nuts, and beans.

Much of a cell's structure and function depends on proteins. Proteins form part of a cell's membrane. Proteins also make up parts of the organelles within a cell. A group of proteins known as **enzymes** speed up chemical reactions in living things. Without enzymes, the many chemical reactions that are necessary for life would take too long. For example, an enzyme in your saliva speeds up the digestion of starch. The starch breaks down into sugars while still in your mouth.

FIGURE 3
Proteins
A parrot's beak, feathers, and claws are made of proteins.

✏ **Apply Concepts** What part of your body most likely consists of proteins similar to those of a parrot's claws?

_____

_____

⟳ **Compare and Contrast**
As you read, complete the table below to compare carbohydrates, lipids, and proteins.

Type of Compound	Elements	Functions
Carbohydrate		
Lipid		
Protein		

FIGURE 4 ······························

DNA

Smaller molecules connect in specific patterns and sequences, forming DNA.

✎ **Interpret Diagrams** In the diagram below, identify the pattern of colors. Then color in the ones that are missing.

7.NS.8

Nucleic Acids

Nucleic acids are very long organic molecules. These molecules consist of carbon, oxygen, hydrogen, nitrogen, and phosphorus. Nucleic acids contain the instructions that cells need to carry out all the functions of life. Foods high in nucleic acids include red meat, shellfish, mushrooms, and peas.

One kind of nucleic acid is deoxyribonucleic acid (dee AHK see RY boh noo KLEE ik), or DNA. **DNA** is the genetic material that carries information about an organism and is passed from parent to offspring. This information directs a cell's functions. Most DNA is found in a cell's nucleus. The shape of a DNA molecule is described as a **double helix.** Imagine a rope ladder that's been twisted around a pole, and you'll have a mental picture of the double helix of DNA. The double helix forms from many small molecules connected together. The pattern and sequence in which these molecules connect make a kind of chemical code the cell can "read."

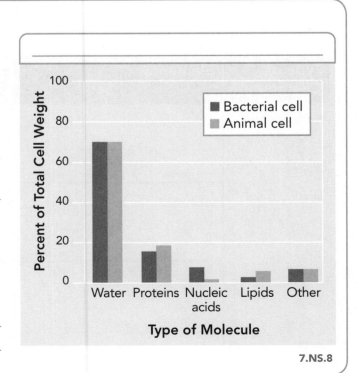

do the math!

Most cells contain the same compounds. The graph compares the percentages of some compounds found in a bacterial cell and in an animal cell. Write a title for the graph and answer the questions below.

❶ **Read Graphs** Put a check above the bar that shows the percentage of water in an animal cell. How does this number compare to the percentage of water in a bacterial cell?

❷ **Read Graphs** (Proteins/Nucleic acids) make up a larger percentage of an animal cell.

❸ **Draw Conclusions** In general, how do you think a bacterial cell and an animal cell compare in their chemical composition?

Percent of Total Cell Weight

100

80

60

40

20

0

■ Bacterial cell
■ Animal cell

Water Proteins Nucleic acids Lipids Other

Type of Molecule

7.NS.8

Water and the Properties of Cells

Water plays an important role in cells and determines many of their properties. Most chemical reactions in cells depend on substances that must be dissolved in water to react. For example, plant cells would not be able to convert the energy captured by chloroplasts into food without water.

As a liquid, water fills up cells so that they keep their sizes and shapes. A cell without water would be like a balloon without air! Think about how the leaves of a plant wilt when the plant needs water. Plant cells retain or lose their shape based on the amount of water in them. After you add water to the soil, the cells absorb the water, and the leaves perk up.

Another unique property of water is that it changes temperature slowly. This slow rise or fall in the temperature of water keeps cells from changing rapidly—a change that can be harmful to an organism.

Water is essential in transporting materials into cells. Substances dissolved in water bathe the cells in the fluids they need to function properly. Water also plays an important role in moving wastes out of the cells and the organism.

So the next time you take a drink of water, remember how you are helping your cells. All living things must take in the right amount of this unique liquid to remain healthy. Without water on our planet, life as we know it would not exist!

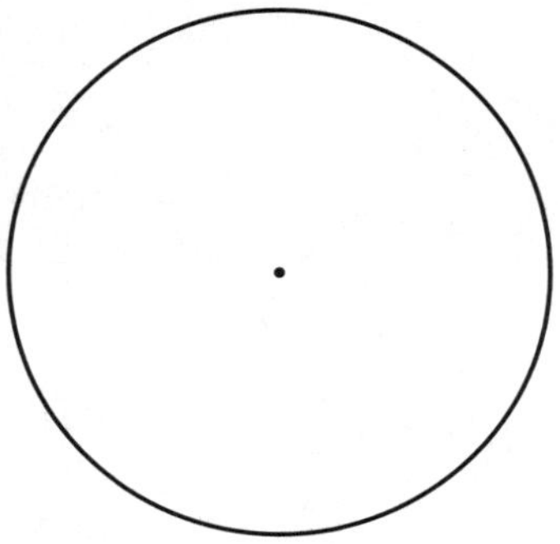

FIGURE 5 ···
Mostly Water

About two thirds of the human body is water. ✎ **Graph Complete and label the circle graph to show the percentage of water in your body.**

7.NS.8

 Do the Quick Lab
What's That Taste?

Assess Your Understanding

1a. Describe An organic compound that contains only the elements carbon, hydrogen, and oxygen is most likely (a carbohydrate/ a protein/DNA). Explain your answer.

_____

_____

_____

7.3.3

b. Classify Which groups of organic compounds found in living things are NOT energy rich?

_____

7.3.1, 7.3.3

c. Review What is the function of DNA?

_____

_____

_____

7.3.1, 7.3.3

d. CHALLENGE Describe ways a lack of water could affect cell functions.

_____

_____

_____

7.3.2

got**it?** ··

O **I get it!** Now I know that the important compounds in living things include _____

O **I need extra help with** _____

Go to MY SCIENCE COACH *online for help with this subject.*

7.3.1, 7.3.2, 7.3.3

Cell Division

UNLOCK THE BIG ?

🔑 **What Are the Functions of Cell Division?**
7.3.5

🔑 **What Happens During the Cell Cycle?**
7.3.5, 7.NS.8

my planet diary

Cycling On

How long do you think it takes a cell to grow and reproduce, that is, to complete one cell cycle? The answer depends on the type of cell and the organism. Some cells, such as the frog egg cells shown here, divide every 30 minutes, and others take as long as a year! The table below compares the length of different cell cycles.

Comparing Cell Cycles

Frog Egg Cells	Yeast Cells	Fruit Fly Wing Cells	Human Liver Cells
30 minutes	90 minutes	9–10 hours	Over 1 year

SCIENCE STATS

Interpret Data Use the table to help you answer the following questions.

1. Which type of cell completes a cell cycle fastest?

_____

2. With each cell cycle, two cells form from one cell. In three hours, how many cells could form from one frog egg cell?

_____

▶ **PLANET DIARY** Go to **Planet Diary** to learn more about cell division.

Lab®zone Do the Inquiry Warm-Up *What Are the Yeast Cells Doing?*

Academic Standards for Science

7.3.5 Explain that cells in multicellular organisms repeatedly divide to make more cells for growth and repair.

What Are the Functions of Cell Division?

How do tiny frog eggs become big frogs? Cell division allows organisms to grow larger. One cell splits into two, two into four, and so on, until a single cell becomes a multicellular organism.

How does a broken bone heal? Cell division produces new healthy bone cells that replace the damaged cells. Similarly, cell division can replace aging cells and those that die from disease.

Vocabulary
- cell cycle • interphase
- replication • chromosome
- mitosis • cytokinesis

Skills
◉ Reading: Ask Questions
△ Inquiry: Interpret Data

Growth and repair are two functions of cell division. A third function is reproduction. Some organisms reproduce simply through cell division. Many single-celled organisms, such as amoebas, reproduce this way. Other organisms can reproduce when cell division leads to the growth of new structures. For example, a cactus can grow new stems and roots. These structures can then break away from the parent plant and become a separate plant.

Most organisms reproduce when specialized cells from two different parents combine, forming a new cell. This cell then undergoes many divisions and grows into a new organism.

Cell division has more than one function in living things, as shown in **Figure 1**. 🗝 **Cell division allows organisms to grow, repair damaged structures, and reproduce.**

FIGURE 1 ·····························
Cell Division
Each photo represents at least one function of cell division.

✎ **Answer these questions.**

1. **Identify** Label each photo as
   (A) growth,
   (B) repair, or
   (C) reproduction.

2. **CHALLENGE** Which photo(s) represents more than one function and what are they?

_____

_____

Lab ® Do the Quick Lab
zone *Observing Mitosis.*

🗝 Assess Your Understanding

got it? ···

○ **I get it!** Now I know the functions of cell division are _____

○ **I need extra help with** _____

Go to **my science** ⁵ **coach** *online for help with this subject.*

Academic Standards for Science

7.3.5 Explain that cells in multicellular organisms repeatedly divide to make more cells for growth and repair.

7.NS.8 Analyze data.

What Happens During the Cell Cycle?

The regular sequence of growth and division that cells undergo is known as the **cell cycle**. **During the cell cycle, a cell grows, prepares for division, and divides into two new cells, which are called "daughter cells."** Each of the daughter cells then begins the cell cycle again. The cell cycle consists of three main stages: interphase, mitosis, and cytokinesis.

Stage 1: Interphase

The first stage of the cell cycle is **interphase.** This stage is the period before cell division. During interphase, the cell grows, makes a copy of its DNA, and prepares to divide into two cells.

Growing Early during interphase, a cell grows to its full size and produces the organelles it needs. For example, plant cells make more chloroplasts. And all cells make more ribosomes and mitochondria. Cells also make more enzymes, substances that speed up chemical reactions in living things.

Copying DNA Next, the cell makes an exact copy of the DNA in its nucleus in a process called **replication.** You may know that DNA holds all the information that a cell needs to carry out its functions. Within the nucleus, DNA and proteins form threadlike structures called **chromosomes.** At the end of replication, the cell contains two identical sets of chromosomes.

Preparing for Division Once the DNA has replicated, preparation for cell division begins. The cell produces structures that will help it to divide into two new cells. In animal cells, but not plant cells, a pair of centrioles is duplicated. You can see the centrioles in the cell in **Figure 2.** At the end of interphase, the cell is ready to divide.

FIGURE 2 ···

Interphase: Preparing to Divide
The changes in a cell during interphase prepare the cell for mitosis.

✎ **List** Make a list of the events that occur during interphase.

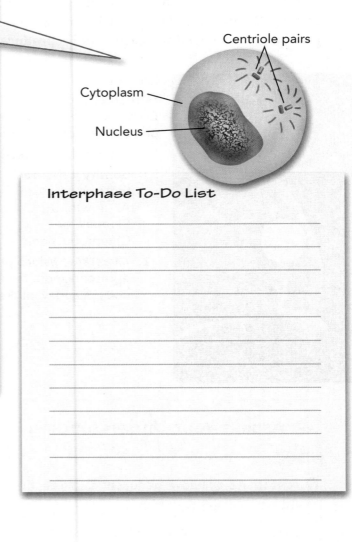

Centriole pairs

Cytoplasm

Nucleus

Interphase To-Do List

apply it!

When one cell splits in half during cell division, the result is two new cells. Each of those two cells can divide into two more, and so on.

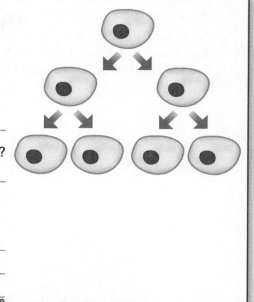

❶ **Calculate** How many cell divisions would it take to produce at least 1,000 cells from one cell?

_____

❷ **Describe** What happens to the number of cells after each division?

_____

❸ CHALLENGE Do you think all human cells divide at the same rate throughout life? Justify your answer.

_____

_____

_____

7.NS.8

Stage 2: Mitosis

Once interphase ends, the second stage of the cell cycle begins. During **mitosis** (my TOH sis), the cell's nucleus divides into two new nuclei and one set of DNA is distributed into each daughter cell.

Scientists divide mitosis into four parts, or phases: prophase, metaphase, anaphase, and telophase. During prophase, the chromosomes condense into shapes that can be seen under a microscope. In **Figure 3** you can see that a chromosome consists of two rod-like parts, called chromatids. Each chromatid is an exact copy of the other, containing identical DNA. A structure known as a centromere holds the chromatids together until they move apart later in mitosis. One copy of each chromatid will move into each daughter cell during the final phases of mitosis. When the chromatids separate they are called chromosomes again. Each cell then has a complete copy of DNA. **Figure 4** on the next page summarizes the events of mitosis.

FIGURE 3 ·····························

Mitosis: Prophase

Mitosis begins with prophase, which involves further changes to the cell.

✎ **Compare and Contrast** How does prophase look different from interphase?

_____

_____

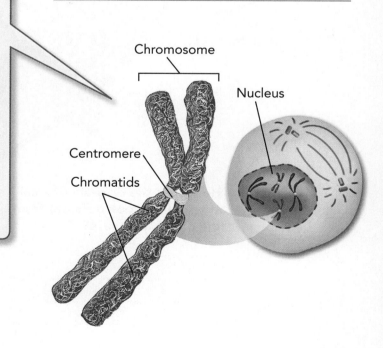

Chromosome

Nucleus

Centromere

Chromatids

FIGURE 4 ....

INTERACTIVE ART The Cell Cycle

Cells undergo an orderly sequence of events as they grow and divide. The photographs show cells of a developing whitefish.

✎ **Interpret Diagrams** Answer the questions and draw the missing parts of the stages in the spaces provided. 7.NS.8

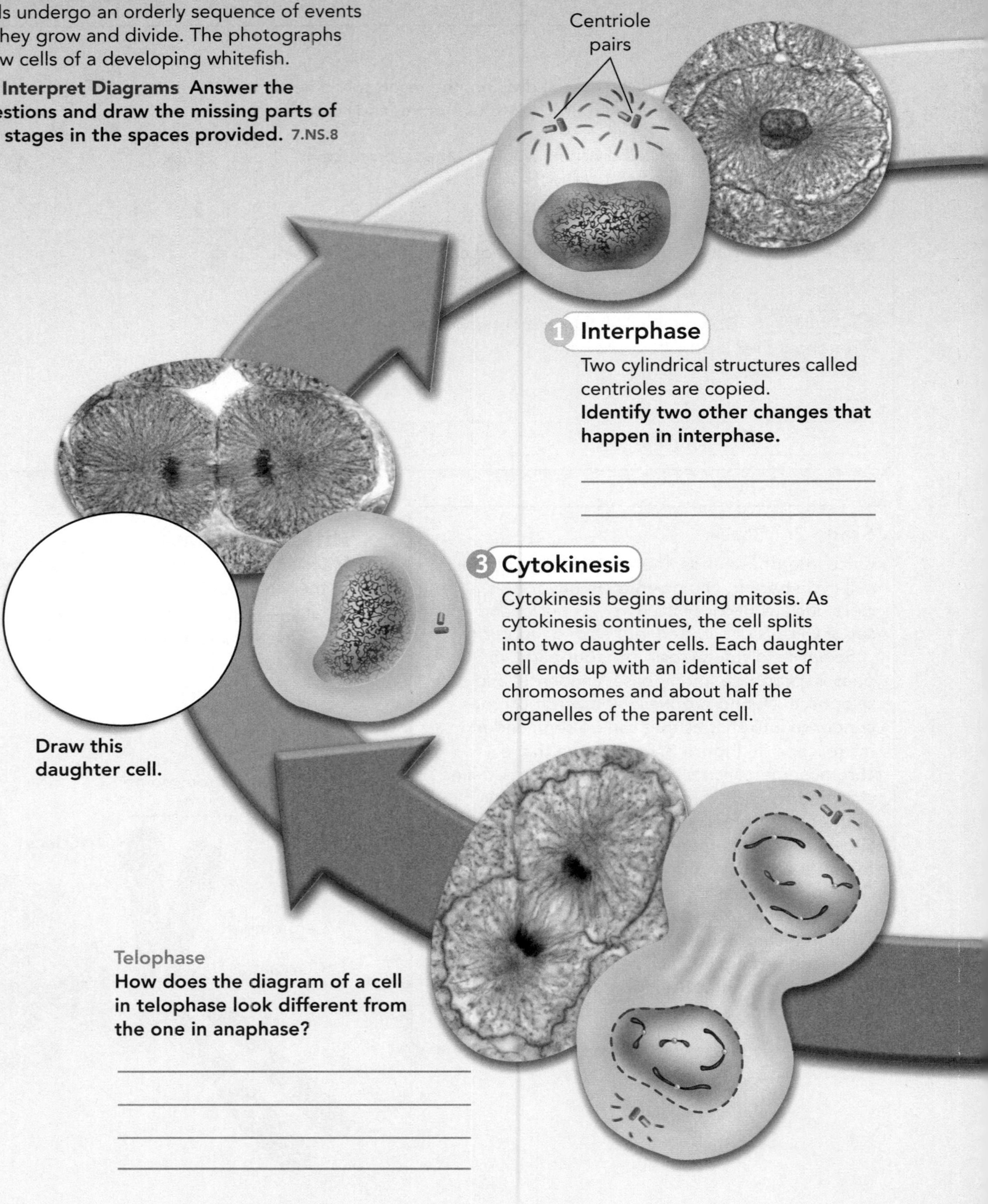

Centriole pairs

1 Interphase

Two cylindrical structures called centrioles are copied.
Identify two other changes that happen in interphase.

_____

_____

3 Cytokinesis

Cytokinesis begins during mitosis. As cytokinesis continues, the cell splits into two daughter cells. Each daughter cell ends up with an identical set of chromosomes and about half the organelles of the parent cell.

Draw this daughter cell.

Telophase
How does the diagram of a cell in telophase look different from the one in anaphase?

_____

_____

_____

_____

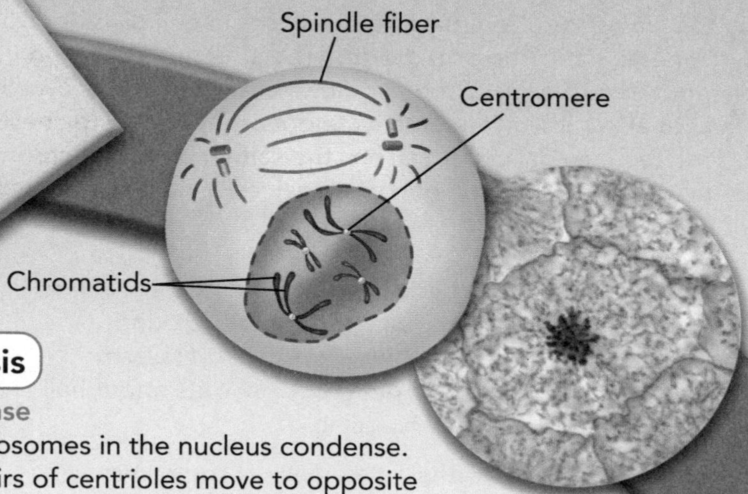

Spindle fiber

Centromere

Chromatids

2 Mitosis

Prophase
Chromosomes in the nucleus condense. The pairs of centrioles move to opposite sides of the nucleus. Spindle fibers form a bridge between the ends of the cell. The nuclear envelope breaks down.

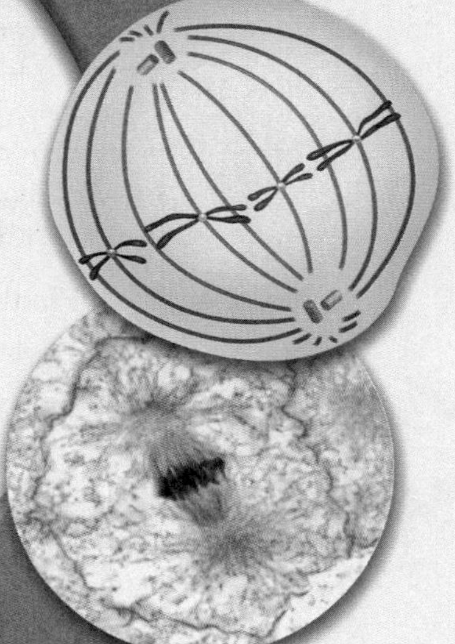

Metaphase
Each chromosome attaches to a spindle fiber at its centromere.
What is missing from the cell? What happened to the chromosomes?

_____

_____

_____

Anaphase
The centromere of each chromosome splits, pulling the chromatids apart. Each chromatid is now called a chromosome. These chromosomes are drawn by their spindle fibers to opposite ends of the cell. The cell stretches out.
Draw the missing structures.

did you know?

Certain bacteria divide only once every 100 years! Bacteria known as *Firmicutes* live in certain rocks that are found 3 kilometers below Earth's surface. The life functions of *Firmicutes* occur so slowly that it takes 100 years or more for them to store enough energy to split in two.

Stage 3: Cytokinesis

The final stage of the cell cycle, which is called **cytokinesis** (sy toh kih NEE sis), completes the process of cell division. During cytokinesis, the cytoplasm divides. The structures are then distributed into each of the two new cells. Cytokinesis usually starts at about the same time as telophase. When cytokinesis is complete, each daughter cell has the same number of chromosomes as the parent cell. At the end of cytokinesis, each cell enters interphase, and the cycle begins again.

Cytokinesis in Animal Cells During cytokinesis in animal cells, the cell membrane squeezes together around the middle of the cell, as shown here. The cytoplasm pinches into two cells. Each daughter cell gets about half of the organelles of the parent cell.

Cytokinesis in Plant Cells Cytokinesis is somewhat different in plant cells. A plant cell's rigid cell wall cannot squeeze together in the same way that a cell membrane can. Instead, a structure called a cell plate forms across the middle of the cell, as shown in **Figure 5.** The cell plate begins to form new cell membranes between the two daughter cells. New cell walls then form around the cell membranes.

Plant cells ▼   **Animal cells ▶**

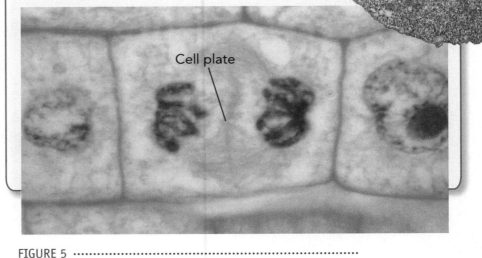

Cell plate

FIGURE 5 ·····························

Cytokinesis

Both plant and animal cells undergo cytokinesis.

Compare and Contrast How does cytokinesis differ in plant and animal cells?

_____

_____

_____

do the math! Analyzing Data

Length of a liver cell cycle

How long does it take for a cell to go through one cell cycle? It depends on the cell. Human liver cells generally reproduce less than once per year. At other times, they can complete one cell cycle in about 22 hours, as shown in the circle graph. Study the graph and answer the following questions.

1 **Read Graphs** What do the three curved arrows outside of the circle represent?

_____

_____

2 **Read Graphs** The wedge representing growth is in which stage of the cell cycle?

_____

3 **Interpret Data** About what percentage of the cell cycle is shown for DNA replication?

_____

4 **Interpret Data** What stage in the cell cycle takes the shortest amount of time? How do you know?

_____

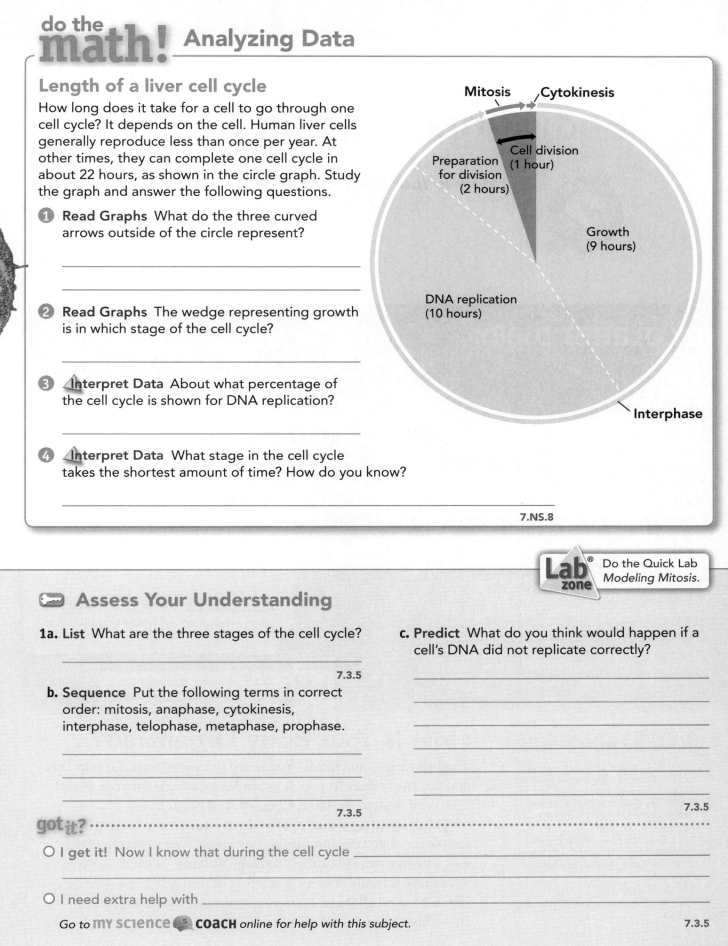

Mitosis   Cytokinesis

Cell division (1 hour)

Preparation for division (2 hours)

Growth (9 hours)

DNA replication (10 hours)

Interphase

7.NS.8

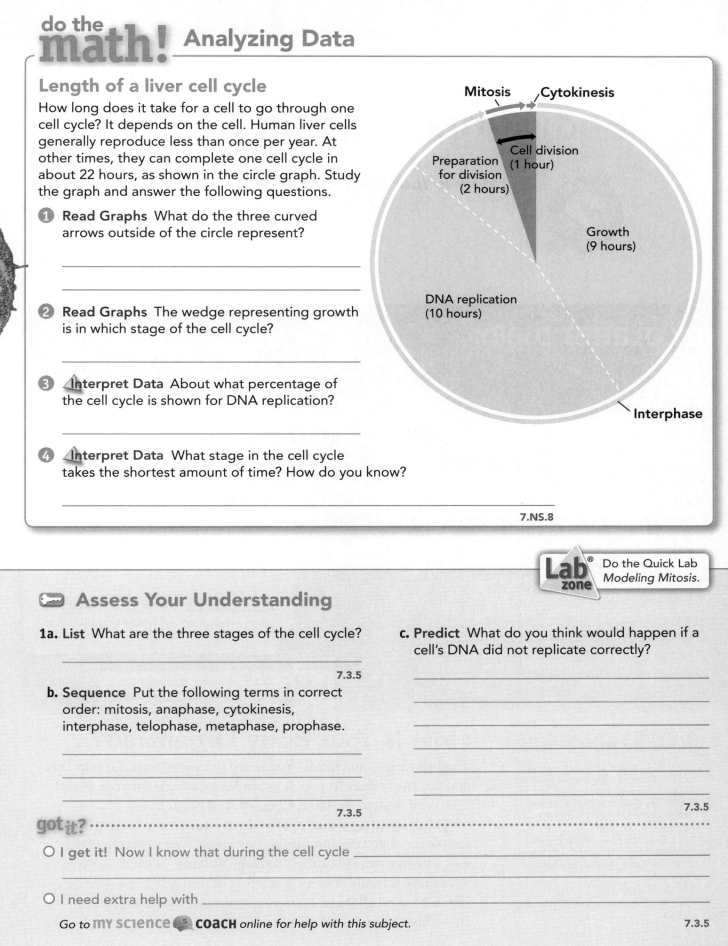
Lab zone® Do the Quick Lab Modeling Mitosis.

Assess Your Understanding

1a. List What are the three stages of the cell cycle?

_____

7.3.5

b. Sequence Put the following terms in correct order: mitosis, anaphase, cytokinesis, interphase, telophase, metaphase, prophase.

_____

_____

_____

7.3.5

c. Predict What do you think would happen if a cell's DNA did not replicate correctly?

_____

_____

_____

_____

_____

_____

7.3.5

got it? ....

○ **I get it!** Now I know that during the cell cycle _____

_____

○ **I need extra help with** _____

Go to MY SCIENCE COACH *online for help with this subject.*

7.3.5

Body Organization

🔑 **How Is Your Body Organized?**
7.3.6, 7.3.7, 7.NS.8, 7.NS.11

MY PLANET DIARY

CAREER

Medical Illustrator

Who made the colorful drawings of human body structures in this book? The drawings are the work of specialized artists called medical illustrators. These artists use their drawing skills and knowledge of human biology to make detailed images of body structures. Many artists draw images, such as the one on this page, using 3-D computer graphics. The work of medical illustrators appears in textbooks, journals, magazines, videos, computer learning programs, and many other places.

Communicate Answer the question below. Then discuss your answer with a partner.

Why do you think medical illustrations are important to the study of human biology?

_____

_____

_____

_____

> **PLANET DIARY** Go to **Planet Diary** to learn more about body organization.

Lab zone Do the Inquiry Warm-Up
How Is Your Body Organized?

Academic Standards for Science

7.3.6 Explain that after fertilization, a small cluster of cells divides to form the basic tissues of an embryo which further develops into all the specialized tissues and organs within a multicellular organism.

7.3.7 Describe how various organs and tissues serve the needs of cells for nutrient and oxygen delivery and waste removal.

7.NS.8 Analyze data.

7.NS.11 Communicate findings using models.

How Is Your Body Organized?

The bell rings—lunchtime! You hurry to the cafeteria, fill your tray, and pay the cashier. You look around the cafeteria for your friends. Then you walk to the table, sit down, and begin to eat.

Think about how many parts of your body were involved in the simple act of getting and eating your lunch. Every minute of the day, whether you are eating, studying, walking, or even sleeping, your body is busily at work. Each part of the body has a specific job to do. And all these different parts usually work together so smoothly that you don't even notice them.

Vocabulary
- differentiation • muscle tissue • nervous tissue
- connective tissue • epithelial tissue

Skills
- Reading: Identify the Main Idea
- Inquiry: Make Models

Levels of Organization The smooth functioning of your body is due partly to how the body is organized. **The levels of organization in the human body consist of cells, tissues, organs, and organ systems.** The smallest unit of organization is a cell. The next largest unit is a tissue, then an organ. Finally, an organ system is the largest unit of organization in an organism.

Cells A cell is the basic unit of structure and function in a living thing. Complex organisms are made up of many cells in the same way that your school is made up of many rooms. The human body contains about 100 trillion tiny cells. Most cells cannot be seen without a microscope.

Structures and Functions Almost all cells in the human body have the same basic structures, such as a nucleus, a cell membrane, and cytoplasm. Each of these structures has a specific job that keeps the cell functioning properly.

Cells carry on the processes that keep organisms alive. Inside cells, for example, molecules from digested food undergo changes that release energy that the cells can use. Cells also grow, reproduce, and get rid of the waste products that result from these activities.

Differentiation As you learned in the previous lesson, when a cell divides by mitosis, it produces two daughter cells with identical sets of chromosomes. So how do cells in multicellular organisms such as humans become different from one another? They do this through a process called differentiation. In differentiation, cells change in structure and become capable of carrying out specialized functions.

As **Figure 1** shows, after fertilization, cell division occurs rapidly in an embryo. When cells differentiate, they become organized. At first, cells of the same type group into tissues. Groups of tissues combine to form organs that carry out specific functions, such as the stomach or small intestines. Finally, different organs that work together form an organ system, such as your digestive system. And to think that all of this comes from one original cell!

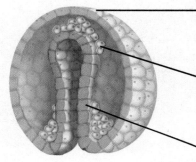

Outer Layer
Skin, nervous system, pituitary gland, salivary glands

Middle Layer
Heart, bones, muscles, kidneys, lymphatic system, testes, ovaries

Inner Layer
Pancreas, thyroid gland, liver, parts of the digestive system

Embryo With Three Layers

FIGURE 1 ·······························

Cell Differentiation
During the first week after fertilization, a human embryo forms from a hollow ball with three layers. Some of the structures that form from each layer are listed.

✎ **Interpret Diagrams** Which layer gives rise to the skeletal system?

_____

7.NS.8, 7.NS.11

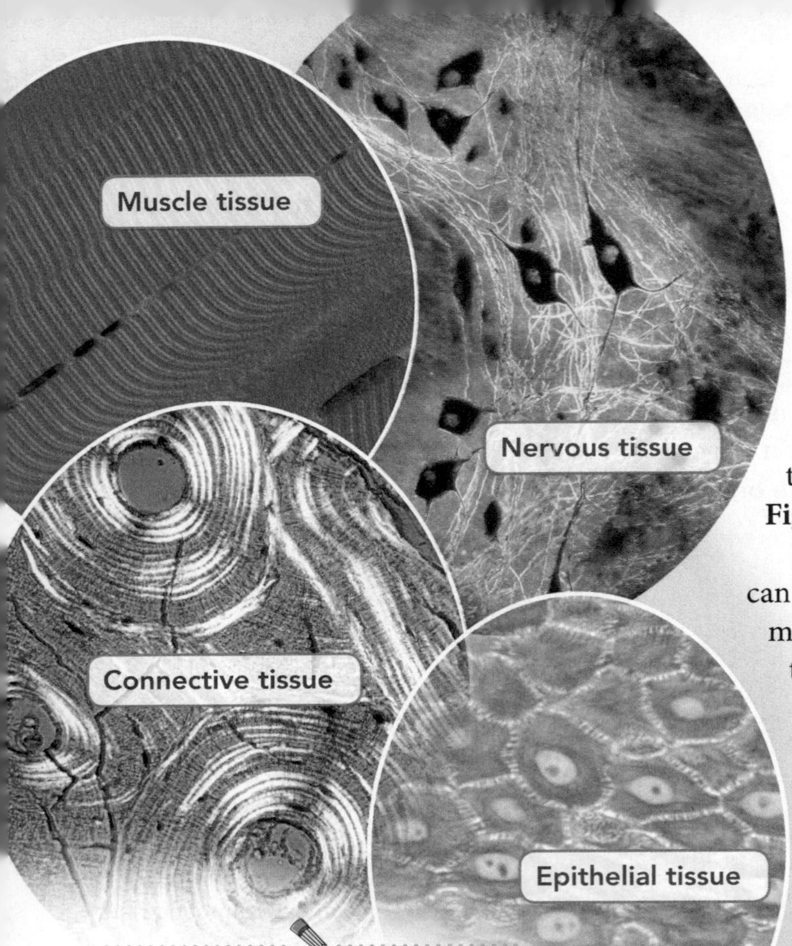

Muscle tissue

Nervous tissue

Connective tissue

Epithelial tissue

Tissues
The next largest unit of organization in your body is a tissue. A tissue is a group of similar cells that perform the same function. Your body contains several types of tissue. Four of these are muscle tissue, nervous tissue, connective tissue, and epithelial tissue. You can see examples in **Figure 2** at left.

Like the muscle cells that form it, **muscle tissue** can contract, or shorten. By doing so, muscle tissue makes parts of your body move. While muscle tissue carries out movement, **nervous tissue** directs and controls the process. Nervous tissue carries electrical messages back and forth between the brain and other parts of the body. Another type of tissue, **connective tissue,** provides support for your body and connects all its parts. Bone tissue and fat tissue are examples of connective tissue.

Epithelial tissue (ep uh THEE lee ul) covers the surfaces of your body, inside and out. Some epithelial tissue, such as your skin, protects the delicate structures that lie beneath it. The lining of your digestive system consists of epithelial tissue that allows you to digest and absorb the nutrients in your food.

Identify the Main Idea
Choose the best description of the structure and function of a tissue.

○ A group of different cells that have the same function

○ A group of similar cells that have different functions

○ A group of similar cells that have the same function

FIGURE 2
The Heart
The heart, like your other organs, is made of different kinds of tissues that have different functions.

✎ **Answer the following questions.**

1. **Relate Text and Visuals** In each box, fill in the kind of tissue that matches the function described.

2. CHALLENGE Pick one type of tissue shown and describe how the heart would be affected if the tissue did not function properly.

_____

_____

_____

_____

_____

provides strength and flexible support for muscle tissue and other structures inside and outside the heart.

Organs Your stomach, heart, brain, and lungs are all organs. An organ is a structure that is made up of different kinds of tissue. Like a tissue, an organ performs a specific job. The job of an organ, however, is usually more complex than that of a tissue. For example, the heart pumps blood through your body over and over again. The heart contains muscle, connective, and epithelial tissues. In addition, nervous tissue connects to the heart and helps control heart function. **Figure 2** shows a diagram of a human heart and describes how some of the heart's tissues work. Each type of tissue contributes in a different way to the organ's job of pumping blood.

_____
covers the inside surfaces of the heart and of the blood vessels that lead into and out of the heart.

_____
carries electrical messages from the brain to the heart but is not shown in this diagram.

_____
contracts, squeezing the heart so blood moves through the heart's chambers and then into blood vessels that lead to the body.

Books are a nonliving model of levels of organization. Find out how a book is organized.

STEP 1 **Observe** Examine this book to see how its chapters, lessons, and other parts are related.

STEP 2 **Make Models** Next, compare levels of organization in this book to those in the human body. Draw lines to show which part of this book best models a level in the body.

Organism — Lessons

Organ systems — Book

Organs — Words

Tissues — Chapters

Cells — Paragraphs

STEP 3 **Make Models** Where in the book model do you think this Apply It fits? What level of organization in the body does the Apply It represent?

_____

_____

_____

_____

_____

7.NS.11

561

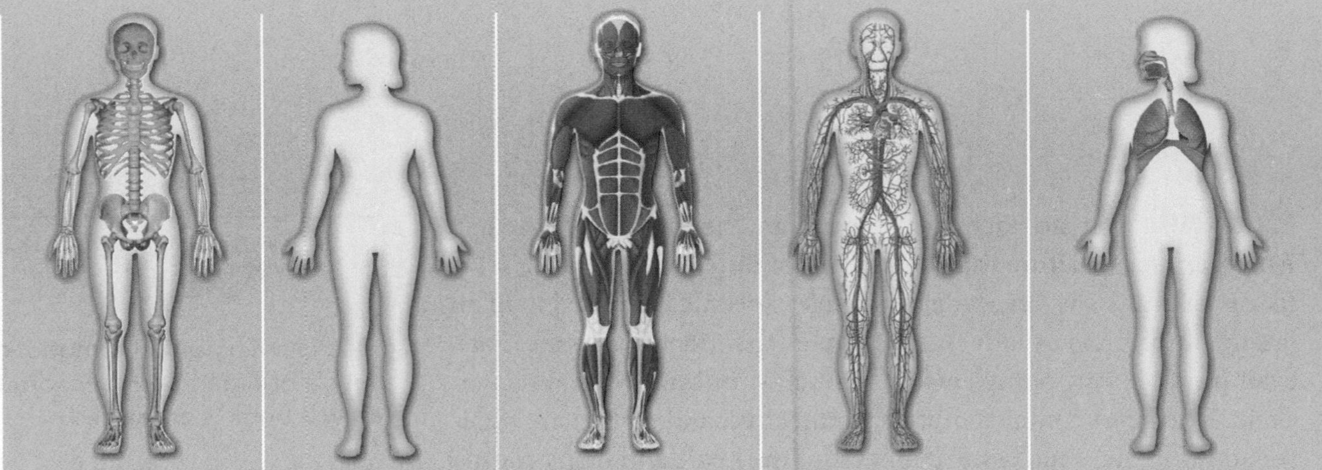

BODY SYSTEM					
	Skeletal System	Integumentary System	Muscular System	Circulatory System	Respiratory System
STRUCTURES	Bones, cartilage, ligaments, tendons	Skin, hair, nails, sweat glands, oil glands	Skeletal muscle, smooth muscle, cardiac muscle	Heart, blood vessels	Nose, pharynx, larynx, trachea, bronchi, lungs
FUNCTIONS	Supports body; protects internal organs; allows movement; stores minerals; produces blood cells	Guards against infection and injury; helps regulate body temperature	With skeletal system, produces movement; helps circulate blood and move food through the digestive system	Transports oxygen, nutrients, and wastes; fights infection; helps regulate body temperature	Brings in oxygen needed by cells; removes carbon dioxide from body

FIGURE 3 ·········

> INTERACTIVE ART **Body Systems**

✎ **Apply Concepts** Describe the levels of organization in a complex system. Write about a sports team, a supermarket, a digital audio player, or an orchestra. Or choose your own example.

_____
_____
_____
_____
_____
_____
_____
_____
_____
_____
_____

Systems Each organ in your body is part of an organ system, which is a group of organs that work together, carrying out major functions. For example, your heart is part of your circulatory system, which carries oxygen and other materials throughout your body. The circulatory system also includes blood vessels and blood. **Figure 3** shows most of the organ systems in the human body.

Organisms Starting with cells, the levels of organization in an organism become more and more complex. A tissue is more complex than a cell, an organ is more complex than a tissue, and so on. You, as an organism, are the next level of organization. And all organisms are part of levels of organization within the environment.

BODY SYSTEM	Digestive System	Excretory System	Nervous System	Endocrine System	Reproductive System
STRUCTURES	Mouth, esophagus, stomach, small intestine, liver, pancreas, large intestine, rectum	Skin, lungs, liver, kidneys, urinary bladder, urethra	Brain, spinal cord, nerves	Glands, such as the thyroid, pancreas, adrenals, ovaries, testes, and others	In males: testes, ducts, urethra, penis; in females: ovaries, ducts, uterus, vagina
FUNCTIONS	Breaks down food; absorbs nutrients; removes food wastes	Removes waste products from the body	Controls body's responses to changes in inside and outside environments	Controls growth, development, and energy processes; helps maintain homeostasis	Produces and delivers sex cells; in females, nurtures and protects developing embryo

Lab zone® Do the Quick Lab
Observing Cells and Tissues.

🗝 Assess Your Understanding

1a. Review How are cells, tissues, and organs related?

_____

_____

_____

7.3.6, 7.3.7

b. Infer What systems of the body are involved in preparing and eating a sandwich?

_____

_____

_____

7.3.7

c. Make Judgments How does learning about body systems help you make informed decisions about your health?

_____

_____

_____

_____

_____

_____

_____

7.3.7

got it? ....

○ **I get it!** Now I know that the body's levels of organization, from least complex to most complex, are

_____

○ I need extra help with _____

Go to MY SCIENCE Ⓢ COACH *online for help with this subject.*

7.3.7

563

System Interactions

UNLOCK THE BIG **?**

🔑 **How Do You Move?**
7.3.7, 7.NS.1

🔑 **Which Systems Move Materials in Your Body?**
7.3.7, 7.NS.1

🔑 **Which Systems Control Body Functions?**
7.3.7

my planet diary

Do you hear in color?

What color is the letter *b* or the roar of a tiger? You might not see colors when you hear sounds, but some people do. In people with synesthesia (sin us THEE zhuh), their senses overlap. Some people with synesthesia may taste a shape or hear music in colors. Others may hear a sound when they see motion. Even people without synesthesia experience some connections between their senses. You can explore how your own senses overlap in the first question on this page.

FUN FACTS

Communicate Answer the questions and then discuss your answers with a partner.

1. Look at the shapes below. One of them is called kiki and the other bouba. Which name do you think matches each shape?

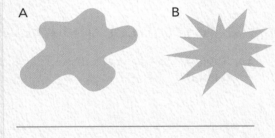

A   B

_____

_____

2. Most people call the rounded shape bouba and the pointed shape kiki. Why do you think that is?

_____

_____

_____

▶ PLANET DIARY Go to **Planet Diary** to learn more about how body systems interact.

Lab zone® Do the Inquiry Warm-Up
How Does Your Body Respond?

Vocabulary
- skeleton • skeletal muscle • joint • nutrient
- absorption • gland • stimulus • response • hormone

Skills
- Reading: Summarize
- Inquiry: Develop Hypotheses

How Do You Move?

Carefully coordinated movements let you thread a needle, ride a bicycle, brush your teeth, and dance. These movements—and all of your body's other movements—happen as a result of the interactions between body systems. Your muscular system is made up of all the muscles in your body. Your skeletal system, or **skeleton,** includes all the bones in your body. **Muscles and bones work together, making your body move. The nervous system tells your muscles when to act.**

Academic Standards for Science

7.3.7 Describe how various organs and tissues serve the needs of cells for nutrient and oxygen delivery and waste removal.

7.NS.1 Make predictions and develop testable questions.

Muscles and Bones

Skeletal muscles are attached to the bones of your skeleton and provide the force that moves your bones. Muscles contract and relax. When a muscle contracts, it shortens and pulls on the bones to which it is attached, as shown in **Figure 1.**

FIGURE 1 ....
Muscles Moving Bones
As this dancer's muscles pull on his leg bones, he can make rapid, skillful moves.

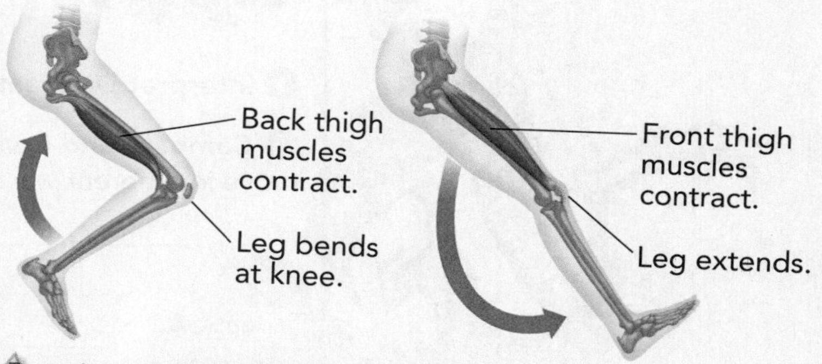

Back thigh muscles contract.

Leg bends at knee.

Front thigh muscles contract.

Leg extends.

△ Develop Hypotheses An octopus has no bones. Explain how you think it moves.

7.NS.1

_____

_____

_____

_____

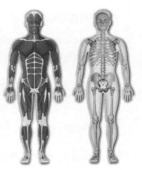

Bones and Joints

What happens when you wiggle your fingers or touch your toes? Even though your bones are rigid, your body can bend in many ways. Your skeleton bends at its joints. A **joint** is a place in the body where two bones come together. For example, your elbow and your shoulder are two joints that move when you raise your hand.

Making Movement Happen

Muscles make bones move at their joints. Try standing on one leg and bending the other leg at the knee. Hold that position. You can feel that you are using the muscles at the back of your thigh. Now straighten your leg. You can feel the muscles in the back of your leg relax, but the muscles in the front of your leg are at work. Your nervous system controls when and how your muscles act on your bones. You will read more about the nervous system later in this lesson.

------- Summarize In your own words, describe which of your systems work together when you write in this book.

_____

_____

_____

_____

apply it!

❶ **Interpret Diagrams** Circle three of the football player's joints.

❷ **Compare and Contrast** Describe how your shoulder and elbow move in different ways.

_____

_____

_____

❸ **CHALLENGE** From a standing position, bend down and grab your ankles. List six places or joints where your skeleton bends.

_____

_____

 Do the Lab Investigation
A Look Beneath the Skin.

🦴 Assess Your Understanding

got it? ....

○ **I get it!** Now I know that _____ and _____ work together to make the body move.

○ **I need extra help with** _____

Go to MY SCIENCE ⓢ COACH *online for help with this subject.*

7.3.7

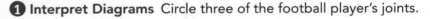

Which Systems Move Materials in Your Body?

The trillions of cells that make up your body need materials to function. Cells also produce wastes that must be removed. If the processes of moving these materials were made into a movie, your nervous system would be the director. The movie set would include the muscular and skeletal systems. And the main characters would be some of your other systems. **The circulatory, respiratory, digestive, and excretory systems play key roles in moving materials in your body.**

Academic Standards for Science

7.3.7 Describe how various organs and tissues serve the needs of cells for nutrient and oxygen delivery and waste removal.

7.NS.1 Make predictions.

Transporting Materials Your circulatory system includes your heart, blood vessels, and blood. Blood vessels are found throughout your body. Blood that flows through these vessels carries materials such as water, oxygen, and food to every cell, as shown in **Figure 2.** Materials that your cells must get rid of, such as carbon dioxide and other cell wastes, are also moved through the body in the blood.

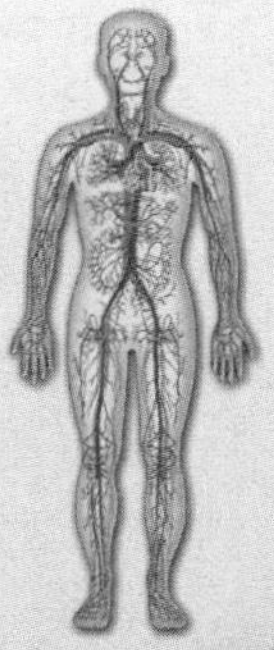

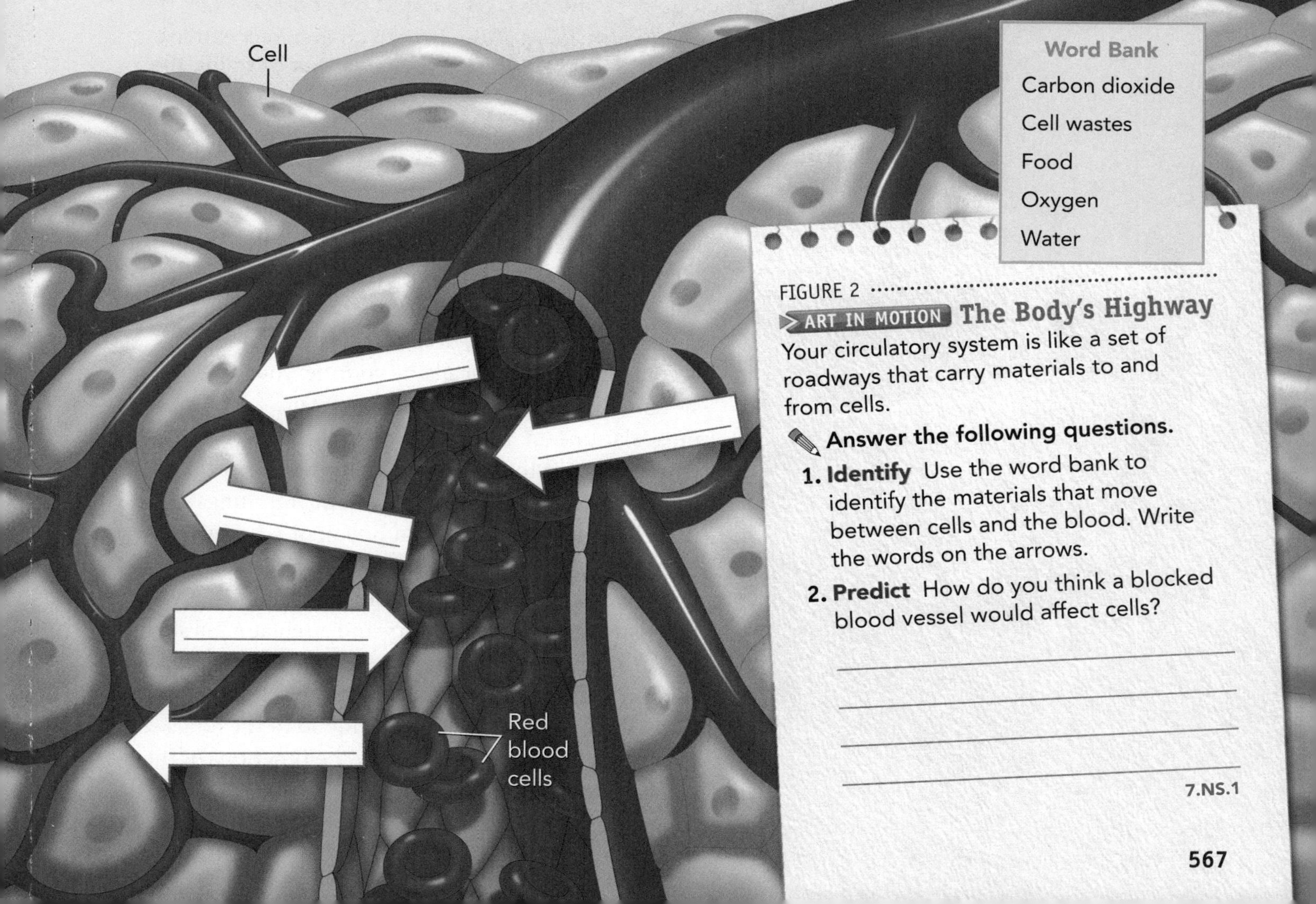

Blood vessel

Cell

Word Bank

Carbon dioxide

Cell wastes

Food

Oxygen

Water

FIGURE 2 ·········
> ART IN MOTION The Body's Highway
Your circulatory system is like a set of roadways that carry materials to and from cells.

✎ **Answer the following questions.**

1. **Identify** Use the word bank to identify the materials that move between cells and the blood. Write the words on the arrows.

2. **Predict** How do you think a blocked blood vessel would affect cells?

_____

_____

_____

_____

7.NS.1

Red blood cells

567

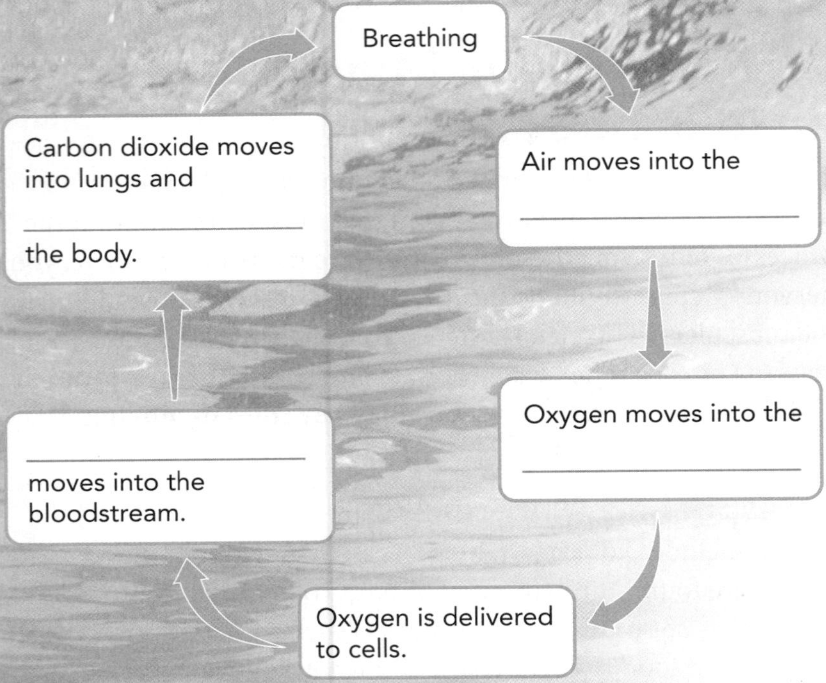

Breathing

Carbon dioxide moves into lungs and

_____

the body.

Air moves into the

_____

Oxygen moves into the

_____

_____ moves into the bloodstream.

Oxygen is delivered to cells.

FIGURE 3 ···

Something in the Air

About 21 percent of air is oxygen gas. The rest is mainly nitrogen gas and small amounts of other gases.

✏ **Sequence Read about breathing in and breathing out. Then complete the steps above that describe the functions of the respiratory system by filling in the missing terms in the boxes.**

Breathing In, Breathing Out

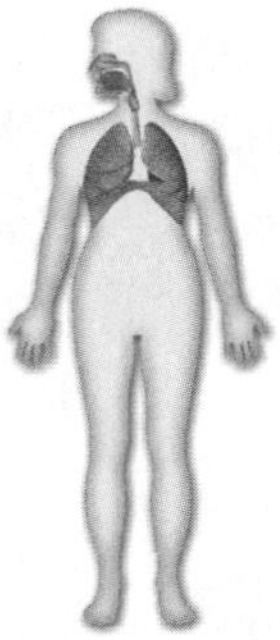

Can you imagine doing something more than 20,000 times a day? Without even realizing it, you already do. You breathe! You don't usually think about breathing, because this process is controlled automatically by your nervous system. Breathing also depends on your muscular system. Muscles in your chest cause your chest area to expand and compress. These changes make air move in and out of your lungs.

When you breathe in, that breath of air goes into your lungs, which are part of your respiratory system. Oxygen from the air moves from your lungs into your bloodstream. Your respiratory and circulatory systems work together, delivering oxygen to all your cells. Your cells give off carbon dioxide as a waste product. Carbon dioxide is carried in the blood to the lungs, where you breathe it out. Review the functions of the respiratory system in **Figure 3**.

Getting Food

Your respiratory system takes in oxygen, and your circulatory system delivers it to your cells. Oxygen is used in cells to release energy from sugar molecules that come from the food you eat. But how do sugar molecules get to your cells? Your digestive system helps to break down foods into sugars and other nutrient molecules that your body can use. A **nutrient** is a substance that you get from food and that your body needs to carry out processes, such as contracting muscles. Through a process called **absorption,** nutrients move from the digestive system into the bloodstream. The circulatory system then delivers the nutrients to all the cells in your body. In this way, your digestive system and circulatory system work together to get food to your cells.

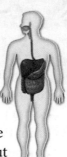

Moving Wastes

The excretory system eliminates wastes from your body. Your respiratory, circulatory, and digestive systems all have roles in the excretory system. You already read that carbon dioxide passes from the circulatory system into the respiratory system and leaves the body when you exhale. Other cellular wastes also pass into the blood. These wastes are filtered out of the blood by the kidneys. This process produces urine, which then carries the wastes out of your body. Materials that are not used by the digestive system leave the body as solid waste.

Vocabulary **Suffixes** The names of three body systems contain the suffix -*atory* or -*etory*, which both mean "of, or pertaining to." Circle the name of each of these systems once in the text on this page. Then underline sentences that describe what these systems do.

Do the Quick Lab
Working Together, Act I.

🔑 Assess Your Understanding

1a. List Name four body systems that are involved in getting oxygen to your cells.

_____

_____

7.3.7

b. Explain How is absorption an important function of the digestive system?

_____

_____

_____

7.3.7

c. Draw Conclusions How does the circulatory system help other systems function?

_____

_____

_____

_____

_____

_____

7.3.7

got it? ....

○ I get it! Now I know that materials are moved within my body by the _____

_____

○ I need extra help with _____

Go to MY SCIENCE ⓢ COACH *online for help with this subject.*

7.3.7

Academic Standards for Science

7.3.7 Describe how various organs and tissues serve the needs of cells for nutrient and oxygen delivery and waste removal.

did you **know?**

An optical illusion fools your brain about what you see. Are the horizontal lines in the picture below parallel to one another or slanted?

_____

_____

Which Systems Control Body Functions?

To function properly, each part of your body must be able to communicate with other parts of your body. For example, if you hear a phone ring, that message must be sent to your brain. Your brain then directs your muscles to move your bones so you can answer the phone. These actions are controlled by the nervous system, which is made up of the brain, spinal cord, and nerves. In your nervous system, information travels through nerve cells.

Other messages are sent by chemical signals that are produced by the endocrine system. The endocrine system is made up of organs called **glands** that release chemical signals directly into the bloodstream. For example, when you exercise, your endocrine system sends signals that make you perspire, or sweat. As sweat evaporates, it helps you cool down. **The nervous system and the endocrine system work together to control body functions.**

Nervous System Your eyes, ears, skin, nose, and taste buds send information about your environment to your nervous system. Your senses let you react to bright light, hot objects, and freshly baked cookies. A signal in the environment that makes you react is called a **stimulus** (plural *stimuli*). A **response** is what your body does in reaction to a stimulus. Responses are directed by your nervous system but often involve other body systems. For example, your muscular and skeletal systems help you reach for a cookie. And your digestive system releases saliva before the cookie even reaches your mouth.

FIGURE 4 ··

Stimulus and Response

Have you ever been startled by something unexpected?

✎ **Use the pictures to complete these tasks.**

1. **Sequence** Use numbers 1, 2, and 3 to put the pictures in order.

2. **Explain** Use the terms *stimulus* and *response* to explain what happened.

_____

_____

_____

_____

_____

apply it!

Among the drugs that affect the nervous system, caffeine is one of the most commonly used worldwide. Caffeine is found in coffee, tea, soda, other beverages, and even in chocolate.

1 Explain How does caffeine reach the brain after someone drinks a cup of coffee or tea? In your answer, be sure to identify the systems involved.

_____

_____

_____

2 Infer Caffeine is addictive, which means that the body can become physically dependent on the drug. Which body system do you think would be most involved in an addiction? Explain your answer.

_____

_____

_____

Endocrine System The chemical signals released by the endocrine system are called **hormones.** Hormones are transported through your body by the circulatory system. These chemicals affect many body processes. For example, one hormone interacts with the excretory system and the circulatory system to control the amount of water in the bloodstream. Another hormone interacts with the digestive system and the circulatory system to control the amount of sugar in the bloodstream. Hormones also affect the reproductive systems of both males and females.

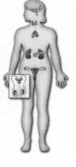

 Lab zone® Do the Quick Lab _Working Together, Act II._

🔑 Assess Your Understanding

2a. Compare and Contrast How are the nervous system and the endocrine system different?

_____

_____

_____

_____

7.3.7

b. Apply Concepts Describe an example of a stimulus and response that involves your sense of hearing.

_____

_____

_____

_____

7.3.7

got it? ....

○ **I get it!** Now I know that the _____ system and _____ system work together to _____

○ **I need extra help with** _____

_Go to_ **my science** 🔵ˢ **coach** _online for help with this subject._ 7.3.7

15 Study Guide

All living things are made of _____, which are the smallest units of _____

and _____

LESSON 1 Discovering Cells

7.3.1, 7.NS.1, 7.NS.3

🔑 Cells are the basic units of structure and function in living things.

🔑 All living things are composed of cells, and all cells come from other cells.

🔑 Some microscopes focus light through lenses to produce a magnified image, and other microscopes use beams of electrons.

Vocabulary
• cell • microscope • cell theory

LESSON 2 Looking Inside Cells

7.3.3, 7.3.4, 7.3.5, 7.3.6, 7.NS.8

🔑 Each kind of cell structure has a different function within a cell.

🔑 In multicellular organisms, cells are organized into tissues, organs, and organ systems.

Vocabulary
• cell wall • cell membrane • nucleus • organelle
• ribosome • cytoplasm • mitochondria
• endoplasmic reticulum • Golgi apparatus
• vacuole • chloroplast • lysosome
• multicellular • unicellular • tissue • organ
• organ system

LESSON 3 Chemical Compounds in Cells

7.3.1, 7.3.2, 7.3.3, 7.NS.8

🔑 Elements are the simplest substances. Compounds form when elements combine.

🔑 Important compounds in living things include carbohydrates, lipids, proteins, nucleic acids, and water.

Vocabulary
• element • compound • carbohydrate
• lipid • protein • enzyme
• nucleic acid • DNA • double helix

LESSON 4 Cell Division

7.3.5, 7.NS.8

🔑 Cell division allows organisms to grow, repair damaged structures, and reproduce.

🔑 During the cell cycle, a cell grows, prepares for division, and divides into two new cells, which are called "daughter cells."

Vocabulary
• cell cycle • interphase • replication
• chromosome • mitosis • cytokinesis

LESSON 5 Body Organization

7.3.7, 7.NS.8, 7.NS.11

🔑 The levels of organization in the human body consist of cells, tissues, organs, and organ systems.

Vocabulary
• differentiation • muscle tissue • nervous tissue
• connective tissue • epithelial tissue

LESSON 6 System Interactions

7.3.7, 7.NS.1

🔑 Muscles, bones, and nerves work together to make your body move.

🔑 The circulatory, respiratory, digestive, and excretory systems play key roles in moving materials in your body.

🔑 The nervous system and the endocrine system work together to control body functions.

Vocabulary
• skeleton • skeletal muscle • joint • nutrient
• absorption • gland • stimulus • response
• hormone

Review and Assessment

LESSON 1 Discovering Cells

1. Which tool could help you see a plant cell?

   a. a filter
   b. a microscope
   c. a microwave
   d. an electromagnet

   7.NS.3

2. The _____ states that all living things are made of cells.

   7.3.1

3. **Classify** Your cells take in oxygen, water, and food. What is one waste product that leaves your cells?

   _____

   _____

   7.3.1

LESSON 2 Looking Inside Cells

4. Which cellular structures are found in plant cells but NOT in animal cells?

   a. chloroplast and cell wall
   b. Golgi apparatus and vacuole
   c. mitochondrion and ribosome
   d. endoplasmic reticulum and nucleus

   7.3.4

5. **Interpret Diagrams** What is the function of the cell structure shown in purple in the cell at the right?

   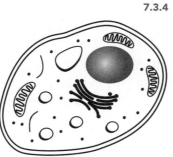

   _____

   _____

   _____

   _____

   7.3.3

6. **Write About It** Imagine you are a tour guide. You and the tour group have shrunk to the size of water molecules. You are now ready to start a tour of the cell! Write a narrative of your tour that you could give a new tour guide to use.

   7.3.3, 7.3.4, 7.NS.11

LESSON 3 Chemical Compounds in Cells

7. Which type of organic molecule is found primarily in a cell's nucleus?

   _____

   7.3.1, 7.3.3

8. **math!** The graph below shows the amounts of different compounds that make up an animal cell. What percentage of the total cell weight is made up of lipids?

   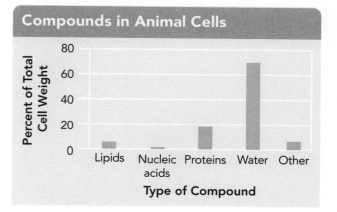

   Compounds in Animal Cells

   _____

   7.3.2, 7.NS.8

LESSON 4 Cell Division

9. During which phase of the cell cycle does DNA replication occur?

   a. mitosis
   b. division
   c. interphase
   d. cytokinesis

   7.3.5

10. During _____, a cell's nucleus divides into two new nuclei.

    7.3.5

11. **Make Generalizations** Why is cell division a necessary function of living things?

    _____

    _____

    _____

    7.3.5

573

15 Review and Assessment

Body Organization

12. Bone tissue and fat tissue are examples of

a. muscle tissue. b. nervous tissue.

c. epithelial tissue. d. connective tissue.

7.3.7

13. _____ is a process by which cells change in structure.

7.3.6

14. Sequence Use numbers 1 through 5 to label the diagrams below in order of smallest to largest levels of organization.

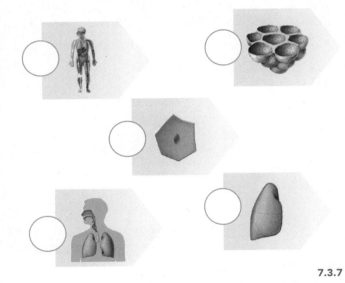

7.3.7

15. Compare and Contrast How is a tissue different from an organ? How are they similar?

_____

_____

_____

_____

_____

7.3.7

16. [Write About It] Scientists classify blood as connective tissue. On a separate paper, explain why you think blood is classified as a tissue.

7.3.7

System Interactions

17. Signals from the _____ make skeletal muscles move.

a. nervous system b. digestive system

c. respiratory system d. muscular system

7.3.7

18. Infer Your knee is called a hinge joint. What is another joint that works like a hinge?

_____

7.3.7

19. Apply Concepts Pick one material that is moved within the body by the organ systems. Describe which systems are involved and how they work together.

_____

_____

_____

_____

_____

7.3.7

 What are cells made of?

20. At right is a photograph of a multicellular plant called a primrose. List three conclusions you can make about the primrose as a living thing.

_____

_____

_____

_____

7.3.1, 7.3.2

Indiana ISTEP+ Practice

Multiple Choice

Circle the letter of the best answer.

1. Which term best fits the level of organization pictured in the diagram below?

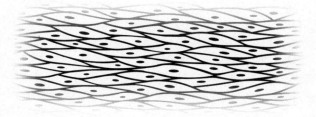

   A. organ
   B. tissue
   C. single cell
   D. organ system

   7.3.7

2. Which of the following types of cells have cell walls?
   A. plant cells   B. muscle cells
   C. blood cells   D. animal cells

   7.3.4

3. Which of the following is an example of an element?
   A. cell   B. water
   C. hydrogen   D. starch

   7.3.3

4. The cell membrane is made mostly of a double layer of molecules called
   A. lipids   B. proteins
   C. nucleic acids   D. carbohydrates

   7.3.3

Contructed Response

Write your answer to Question 5 on the lines below.

5. What is the result of cell division?

   _____

   _____

   7.3.5

Extended Response

Use the diagram below and your knowledge of cells to help you answer Question 6 on a separate sheet of paper.

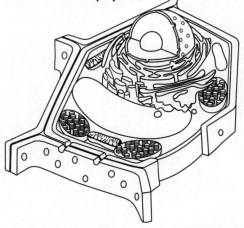

6. Identify this drawing as a plant cell or an animal cell. Justify your answer by describing how the structures of this cell compare to those of plant cells and animal cells.

   7.3.2

Technology and History

 ElectronEYES

▼ Looking through a TEM gives a close-up view of the cells of an onion.

The invention of the optical microscope around the year 1600 caused a revolution in science. For the first time, scientists were able to see the cells that make up living things. However, even the most modern optical microscopes that focus light through lenses to produce an enlarged image can magnify an object only about 1,000 times.

Beginning in the early 1930s, new kinds of microscopes have caused new revolutions in science. The electron microscope uses electrons, instead of light, to make very detailed images of specimens. Today, powerful microscopes can magnify images up to 1,000,000 times—enough to enable scientists to see individual atoms!

Scientists use three main types of very powerful microscopes:

Transmission Electron Microscope (TEM) A TEM focuses a beam of electrons so that they pass through a very thinly sliced specimen. They are very useful for studying the interior structures of cells.

▼ Samples of bread mold as captured by an SEM

Scanning Electron Microscope (SEM) An SEM uses an electron beam to scan the surface of the specimen. The electron beam excites the electrons on the object's surface. The excited electrons are used to make a three-dimensional image of the specimen.

Scanning Tunneling Microscope (STM) An STM works by passing an electrically charged probe very close to the surface of a specimen. As the probe passes over the specimen, the probe moves up and down to keep the current in the probe constant. The path of the probe is recorded and is used to create an image of the specimen's surface.

Design It Research to find images taken by electron or scanning tunneling microscopes. Create a gallery or slide presentation of amazing microscope images to share with your class. See if your classmates can guess what object is shown in each image!

7.NS.2, 7.NS.11

THE GENOGRAPHIC PROJECT

Have you ever wondered where your earliest ancestors came from? Archaeologists have worked for years to uncover evidence of ancient human migrations. They study the things people left behind, such as arrowheads, beads, and tools. Yet some of the most promising evidence is not found in archaeological sites. It is found in the cells that make up our bodies! The Genographic Project is a research project that uses DNA samples to help uncover the history of the human species.

Participants in the Genographic Project receive a kit that allows them to provide a DNA sample. To give a sample, participants use a cotton swab to gather cells from the inside of their cheek. This sample is mailed to a lab that analyzes the DNA contained in the cells. The DNA in the cells is compared with other DNA samples from around the world.

Then participants receive a report that describes the history of their earliest ancestors. The report includes a map that shows the migration route that these ancestors may have followed. Participants may choose to have their genetic information anonymously added to a genetic database. This database will help researchers build a very detailed map of ancient and modern human migration.

Explore It What has the Genographic Project discovered so far? Research the project, and create a map that shows what it has revealed about ancient human migration.

7.NS.2, 7.NS.3, 7.NS.8, 7.NS.11

▲ People who want to help the Genographic Project collect cells from their cheeks.

▲ Scientists trace ancestry by determining which individuals share specific genes or sequences of genes called genetic markers.

APPENDIX A

The Design Process

Engineers are people who use scientific and technological knowledge to solve practical problems. To design new products, engineers usually follow the process described here, even though they may not follow these steps in the same order each time.

Lab zone® Do the Indiana Design Project *Winding Up With Wind*

Identify a Need

Before engineers begin designing a new product, they must first identify the need they are trying to meet or the problem they want to solve. For example, suppose you are a member of a design team in a company that makes model cars. Your team has identified a need: a model car that is inexpensive and easy to assemble.

Research the Problem

Engineers often begin by gathering information that will help them with their new design. This research may include finding articles in books, magazines, or on the Internet. It may also involve talking to other engineers who have solved similar problems. Engineers often perform experiments related to the product they want to design.

For your model car, you could look at cars that are similar to the one you want to design. You might do research on the Internet. You could also test some materials to see whether they will work well in a model car.

Design a Solution

Brainstorm Ideas When engineers design new products, they usually work in teams. Design teams often hold brainstorming meetings in which any team member can contribute ideas. **Brainstorming** is a creative process in which one team member's suggestions often spark ideas in other group members. Brainstorming can lead to new approaches to solving a design problem.

Document the Process As the design team works, its members document, or keep a record of, the process. Having access to documentation enables others to repeat, or replicate, the process in the future. Design teams document their research sources, ideas, lists of materials, and so on because any part of the process may be a helpful resource later.

Identify Constraints During brainstorming, a design team may come up with several possible designs. To better focus their ideas, team members consider constraints. A **constraint** is a factor that limits a product design. Physical characteristics, such as the properties of materials used to make your model car, are constraints. Money and time are also constraints. If the materials in a product cost a lot or if the product takes a long time to make, the design may be impractical.

Make Trade-offs Design teams usually need to make trade-offs. In a **trade-off,** engineers give up one benefit of a proposed design in order to obtain another. In designing your model car, you might have to make trade-offs. For example, you might decide to give up the benefit of sturdiness in order to obtain the benefit of lower cost.

Select a Solution After considering the constraints and trade-offs of the possible designs, engineers then select one idea to develop further. That idea represents the solution that the team thinks best meets the need or solves the problem that was identified at the beginning of the process. The decision includes selecting the materials that will be used in the first attempt to build a product.

Create, Test, and Evaluate a Prototype

Once the team has chosen a design plan, the engineers build a prototype. A **prototype** is a working model used to test a design. Engineers evaluate the prototype to see whether it meets the goal. They must determine whether it works well, is easy to operate, is safe to use, and holds up to repeated use.

Part of the evaluation includes collecting data in the form of measurements. For example, think of your model car. Once you decide how to build your prototype, what would you want to know about it? You might want to measure how much baggage it could carry or how its shape affects its speed.

Troubleshoot and Redesign

Few prototypes work perfectly, which is why they need to be tested. Once a design team has tested a prototype, the members analyze the results and identify any problems. The team then tries to **troubleshoot,** or fix the design problems. Troubleshooting allows the team to redesign the prototype to improve on how well the solution meets the need.

Communicate the Solution

A team needs to communicate the final design to the people who will manufacture and use the product. To do this, teams may use sketches, detailed drawings, computer simulations, and word descriptions. The team may also present the evidence that was collected when the prototype was tested. This evidence may include mathematical representations, such as graphs and data tables, that support the choice for the final design.

Academic Standards for Science

The Design Process

7.DP.1 Identify a need or problem to be solved.

7.DP.2 Brainstorm potential solutions.

7.DP.3 Document the design throughout the entire design process so that it can be replicated in a portfolio/notebook with drawings including labels.

7.DP.4 Select a solution to the need or problem.

7.DP.5 Select the most appropriate materials to develop a solution that will meet the need.

7.DP.6 Create the solution through a prototype.

7.DP.7 Test and evaluate how well the solution meets the goal.

7.DP.8 Evaluate and test the design using measurement.

7.DP.9 Present evidence using mathematical representations (graphs, data tables).

7.DP.10 Communicate the solution including evidence using mathematical representations (graphs, data tables), drawings or prototypes.

7.DP.11 Redesign to improve the solution based on how well the solution meets the need.

Science, Engineering and Technology

7.4 Core Standard: Design and construct a device that converts energy from one form to another to perform work.

7.4.1 Understand that energy is the capacity to do work.

7.4.2 Explain that energy can be used to do work using many processes, for example generation of electricity by harnessing wind energy.

7.4.3 Explain that power is the rate that energy is converted from one form to another.

7.4.4 Explain that power systems are used to provide propulsion for engineered products and systems.

APPENDIX B

Common Minerals

Group 1: Metallic Luster, Mostly Dark-Colored

Mineral/ Formula	Hardness	Density (g/cm³)	Luster	Streak	Color	Other Properties/Remarks
Pyrite FeS_2	6–6.5	5.0	Metallic	Greenish, brownish black	Light yellow	Called "fool's gold," but harder than gold and very brittle
Magnetite Fe_3O_4	6	5.2	Metallic	Black	Iron black	Very magnetic; important iron ore; some varieties known as "lodestone"
Hematite Fe_2O_3	5.5–6.5	4.9–5.3	Metallic or earthy	Red or red brown	Reddish brown to black	Most important ore of iron; used as red pigment in paint
Pyrrhotite FeS	4	4.6	Metallic	Gray black	Brownish bronze	Less hard than pyrite; slightly magnetic
Sphalerite ZnS	3.5–4	3.9–4.1	Resinous	Brown to light yellow	Brown to yellow	Most important zinc ore
Chalcopyrite $CuFeS_2$	3.5–4	4.1–4.3	Metallic	Greenish black	Golden yellow, often tarnished	Most important copper ore; softer than pyrite and more yellow
Copper Cu	2.5–3	8.9	Metallic	Copper red	Copper red to black	Used in making electrical wires, coins, pipes
Gold Au	2.5–3	19.3	Metallic	Yellow	Rich yellow	High density; does not tarnish; used in jewelry, coins, dental fillings
Silver Ag	2.5–3	10.0–11.0	Metallic	Silver to light gray	Silver white (tarnishes)	Used in jewelry, coins, electrical wire, photography
Galena PbS	2.5	7.4–7.6	Metallic	Lead gray	Lead gray	Main ore of lead; used in shields against radiation
Graphite C	1–2	2.3	Metallic to dull	Black	Black	Feels greasy; very soft; used as pencil "lead" and as a lubricant

Group 2: Nonmetallic Luster, Mostly Dark-Colored

Mineral/ Formula	Hardness	Density (g/cm³)	Luster	Streak	Color	Other Properties/Remarks
Corundum Al_2O_3	9	3.9–4.1	Brilliant to glassy	White	Usually brown	Very hard; used as an abrasive; transparent crystals used as "ruby" (red) and "sapphire" (blue) gems
Garnet $(Ca,Mg,Fe)_3$ $(Al,Fe,Cr)_2$ $(SiO_4)_3$	7–7.5	3.5–4.3	Glassy to resinous	White, light brown	Red, brown, black, green	A group of minerals used in jewelry, as a birthstone, and as an abrasive
Olivine $(Mg,Fe)_2SiO_4$	6.5–7	3.3–3.4	Glassy	White or gray	Olive green	Found in igneous rocks; sometimes used as a gem
Augite $Ca(Mg,Fe,Al)$ $(Al,Si)_2O_6$	5–6	3.2–3.4	Glassy	Greenish gray	Dark green to black	Found in igneous rocks
Hornblende $NaCa_2$ $(Mg,Fe,Al)_5$ $(Si,Al)_8O_{22}(OH)_2$	5–6	3.0–3.4	Glassy, silky	White to gray	Dark green, brown, black	Found in igneous and metamorphic rocks

Group 2: Nonmetallic Luster, Mostly Dark-Colored

Mineral/Formula	Hardness	Density (g/cm³)	Luster	Streak	Color	Other Properties/Remarks
Apatite $Ca_5(PO_4)_3F$	5	3.1–3.2	Glassy	White	Green, brown, red, blue	Sometimes used as a gem; source of the phosphorus needed by plants. Found in bones.
Azurite $Cu_3(CO_3)_2(OH)_2$	3.5–4	3.8	Glassy to dull	Pale blue	Intense blue	Ore of copper; used as a gem
Biotite $K(Mg,Fe)_3$ $AlSiO_{10}(OH)_2$	2.5–3	2.8–3.4	Glassy or pearly	White to gray	Dark green, brown, or black	A type of mica; sometimes used as a lubricant
Serpentine $Mg_6Si_4O_{10}(OH)_8$	2–5	2.2–2.6	Greasy, waxy, silky	White	Usually green	Once used in insulation but found to cause cancer; used in fireproofing; can be in the form of asbestos
Bauxite Aluminum oxides	1–3	2.0–2.5	Dull to earthy	Colorless to gray	Brown, yellow, gray, white	Ore of aluminum, smells like clay when wet; a mixture, not strictly a mineral

Group 3: Nonmetallic Luster, Mostly Light-Colored

Mineral/Formula	Hardness	Density (g/cm³)	Luster	Streak	Color	Other Properties/Remarks
Diamond C	10	3.5	Brilliant	White	Colorless and varied	Hardest substance; used in jewelry, abrasives, cutting tools
Topaz $Al_2SiO_4(F,OH)_2$	8	3.5–3.6	Glassy	White	Straw yellow, pink, bluish	Valuable gem
Quartz SiO_2	7	2.6	Glassy, greasy	White	Colorless, white; any color when not pure	The second most abundant mineral; many varieties are gems (amethyst, jasper); used in making glass
Feldspar (K,Na,Ca) $AlSi_3O_8$	6	2.6	Glassy	Colorless, white	Colorless, white; various colors	As a family, the most abundant of all minerals; the feldspars make up over 60 percent of Earth's crust
Fluorite CaF_2	4	3.0–3.3	Glassy	Colorless	Purple, light green, yellow, bluish green	Some types are fluorescent (glow in ultraviolet light); used in making steel
Calcite $CaCO_3$	3	2.7	Glassy	White to grayish	Colorless, white	Easily scratched; bubbles in dilute hydrochloric acid; frequently fluorescent
Halite $NaCl$	2.5	2.1–2.6	Glassy	White	Colorless	Perfect cubic crystals; has salty taste
Gypsum $CaSO_4 \cdot 2H_2O$	2	2.3	Glassy, pearly	White	Colorless, white	Very soft; used in plaster of Paris; form known as alabaster used for statues
Sulfur S	2	2.0–2.1	Resinous to greasy	White	Yellow to brown	Used in medicines, in production of sulfuric acid, and in vulcanizing rubber
Talc $Mg_3Si_4O_{10}(OH)_2$	1	2.7–2.8	Pearly to greasy	White	Gray, white, greenish	Very soft; used in talcum powder; also called "soapstone"

A

abrasion The grinding away of rock by other rock particles carried in water, ice, or wind. (425)
abrasión Tipo de desgaste de la roca por otras partículas de roca transportadas por el agua, el viento o el hielo.

absolute age The age of a rock given as the number of years since the rock formed. (495)
edad absoluta Edad de una roca basada en el número de años de su formación.

absorption The process by which nutrient molecules pass through the wall of the digestive system into the blood. (569)
absorción Proceso en el cual las moléculas de nutrientes pasan a la sangre a través de las paredes del sistema digestivo.

acceleration The rate at which velocity changes. (96)
aceleración Ritmo al que cambia la velocidad.

accuracy How close a measurement is to the true or accepted value. (50)
exactitud Cuán cerca está una medida del valor verdadero o aceptado.

alluvial fan A wide, sloping deposit of sediment formed where a stream leaves a mountain range. (460)
abanico aluvial Depósito de sedimento ancho e inclinado que se forma donde un arroyo sale de una cordillera.

amphibian A vertebrate whose body temperature is determined by the temperature of its environment, and that lives its early life in water and its adult life on land. (507)
anfibio Animal vertebrado cuya temperatura corporal depende de la temperatura de su entorno, y que vive la primera etapa de su vida en el agua y su vida adulta en la tierra.

amplitude 1. The height of a transverse wave from the center to a crest or trough. **2.** The maximum distance the particles of a medium move away from their rest positions as a longitudinal wave passes through the medium. (197)
amplitud 1. Altura de una onda transversal desde el centro a una cresta o un valle. **2.** Máxima distancia del desvío de las partículas de un medio, desde sus posiciones de reposo, al ser atravesado por una onda longitudinal.

anomalous data Data that do not fit with the rest of a data set. (54)
datos anómalos Información que no encaja con los otros datos de un conjunto de datos.

antinode A point of maximum amplitude on a standing wave. (208)
antinodo Punto de máxima amplitud de una onda estacionaria.

asthenosphere The soft layer of the mantle on which the lithosphere floats. (284)
astenósfera Capa suave del manto en la que flota la litósfera.

atmosphere The relatively thin layer of gases that form Earth's outermost layer. (276)
atmósfera Capa de gases relativamente delgada que forma la capa exterior de la Tierra.

average speed The overall rate of speed at which an object moves; calculated by dividing the total distance an object travels by the total time. (90)
velocidad media Índice de velocidad general de un objeto en movimiento; se calcula dividiendo la distancia total recorrida por el tiempo total empleado.

B

basalt A dark, dense, igneous rock with a fine texture, found in oceanic crust. (283)
basalto Roca ígnea, oscura y densa, de textura lisa, que se encuentra en la corteza oceánica.

batholith A mass of rock formed when a large body of magma cools inside the crust. (411)
batolito Masa de roca formada cuando una gran masa de magma se enfría dentro de la corteza terrestre.

beach Wave-washed sediment along a coast. (472)
playa Sedimento depositado por las olas a lo largo de una costa.

bedrock Rock that makes up Earth's crust; also the solid rock layer beneath the soil. (431)
lecho rocoso Roca que compone la corteza terrestre; también, la capa sólida de roca debajo del suelo.

biomass fuel Fuel made from living things. (168)
combustible de biomasa Combustible creado a partir de seres vivos.

biosphere The parts of Earth that contain living organisms. (277)
biósfera Partes de la Tierra que contienen organismos vivos.

brainstorming A process in which group members freely suggest any creative solutions that come to mind. (578)
lluvia de ideas Proceso mediante el cual los miembros de un grupo sugieren libremente cualquier solución creativa que se les ocurre.

C

caldera The large hole at the top of a volcano formed when the roof of a volcano's magma chamber collapses. (407)
caldera Gran agujero en la parte superior de un volcán que se forma cuando la tapa de la cámara magmática de un volcán se desploma.

carbohydrate An energy-rich organic compound, such as a sugar or a starch, that is made of the elements carbon, hydrogen, and oxygen. (546)
carbohidrato Compuesto orgánico rico en energía, como un azúcar o almidón, formado por los elementos carbono, hidrógeno y oxígeno.

carbon film A type of fossil consisting of an extremely thin coating of carbon on rock. (490)
película de carbono Tipo de fósil que consiste en una capa de carbono extremadamente fina que recubre la roca.

cast A fossil that is a solid copy of an organism's shape, formed when minerals seep into a mold. (490)
vaciado Fósil que es una copia sólida de la forma de un organismo y que se forma cuando los minerales se filtran y crean un molde.

cell cycle The series of events in which a cell grows, prepares for division, and divides to form two daughter cells. (552)
ciclo celular Serie de sucesos en los que una célula crece, se prepara para dividirse y se divide para formar dos células hijas.

cell membrane A thin, flexible barrier that surrounds a cell and controls which substances pass into and out of a cell. (535)
membrana celular Barrera delgada y flexible alrededor de la célula, que controla lo que entra y sale de la célula.

cell theory A widely accepted explanation of the relationship between cells and living things. (528)
teoría celular Explicación ampliamente aceptada sobre la relación entre las células y los seres vivos.

cell wall A rigid supporting layer that surrounds the cells of plants and some other organisms. (535)
pared celular Capa fuerte de apoyo alrededor de las células de las plantas y algunos otros organismos.

cementation The process by which dissolved minerals crystallize and glue particles of sediment together into one mass. (323)
cementación Proceso mediante el cual minerales disueltos se cristalizan y forman una masa de partículas de sedimento.

chemical energy A form of potential energy that is stored in chemical bonds between atoms. (134)
energía química Forma de energía potencial almacenada en los enlaces químicos de los átomos.

chemical rock Sedimentary rock that forms when minerals crystallize from a solution. (326)
roca química Roca sedimentaria que se forma cuando los minerales de una solución se cristalizan.

chemical weathering The process that breaks down rock through chemical changes. (424)
desgaste químico Proceso que erosiona la roca mediante cambios químicos.

chloroplast An organelle in the cells of plants and some other organisms that captures energy from sunlight and changes it to an energy form that cells can use in making food. (541)
cloroplasto Orgánulo de las células vegetales y otros organismos que absorbe energía de la luz solar y la convierte en una forma de energía que las células pueden usar para producir alimentos.

chromosome A threadlike structure within a cell's nucleus that contains DNA that is passed from one generation to the next. (552)
cromosoma Estructura filamentosa en el núcleo celular que contiene el ADN que se transmite de una generación a la siguiente.

cinder cone A steep, cone-shaped hill or small mountain made of volcanic ash, cinders, and bombs piled up around a volcano's opening. (408)
cono de escoria Colina o pequeña montaña escarpada en forma de cono que se forma cuando ceniza volcánica, escoria y bombas se acumulan alrededor del cráter de un volcán.

classifying The process of grouping together items that are alike in some way. (8)
clasificar Proceso de agrupar objetos con algún tipo de semejanza.

clastic rock Sedimentary rock that forms when rock fragments are squeezed together under high pressure. (324)
roca clástica Roca sedimentaria que se forma cuando fragmentos de roca se unen bajo gran presión.

GLOSSARY

cleavage A mineral's ability to split easily along flat surfaces. (309)
exfoliación Facilidad con la que un mineral se divide en capas planas.

compaction The process by which sediments are pressed together under their own weight. (323)
compactación Proceso mediante el cual los sedimentos se unen por la presión de su propio peso.

complementary colors Any two colors that combine to form white light. (248)
colores complementarios Dos colores cualesquiera que se combinan para crear luz blanca.

composite volcano A tall, cone-shaped mountain in which layers of lava alternate with layers of ash and other volcanic materials. (408)
volcán compuesto Montaña alta en forma de cono en la que las capas de lava se alternan con capas de ceniza y otros materiales volcánicos.

compound A substance made of two or more elements chemically combined in a specific ratio, or proportion. (545)
compuesto Sustancia formada por dos o más elementos combinados químicamente en una razón o proporción específica.

compression 1. Stress that squeezes rock until it folds or breaks. 2. The part of a longitudinal wave where the particles of the medium are close together. (194)
compresión 1. Fuerza que oprime una roca hasta que se pliega o se rompe. 2. Parte de una onda longitudinal en la que las partículas del medio están muy próximas unas con otras.

concave lens A lens that is thinner in the center than at the edges. (261)
lente cóncava Lente que es más fina en el centro que en los extremos.

concave mirror A mirror with a surface that curves inward. (253)
espejo cóncavo Espejo cuya superficie se curva hacia dentro.

conduction The transfer of thermal energy from one particle of matter to another. (143, 289)
conducción Transferencia de energía térmica de una partícula de materia a otra.

connective tissue A body tissue that provides support for the body and connects all its parts. (560)
tejido conector Tejido del cuerpo que mantiene la estructura del cuerpo y une todas sus partes.

conservation plowing Soil conservation method in which weeds and dead stalks from the previous year's crop are plowed into the ground. (439)
arado de conservación Método de conservación de la tierra en el que las plantas y los tallos muertos de la cosecha del año anterior se dejan en la tierra al ararla.

constraint Any factor that limits a design. (578)
restricción Cualquier factor que limita un diseño.

constructive force Any natural process that builds up Earth's surface. (278)
fuerza constructiva Proceso natural que incrementa la superficie de la Tierra.

constructive interference The interference that occurs when two waves combine to make a wave with an amplitude larger than the amplitude of either of the individual waves. (206)
interferencia constructiva Interferencia que ocurre cuando se combinan ondas para crear una onda con una amplitud mayor a la de cualquiera de las ondas individuales.

continental drift The hypothesis that the continents slowly move across Earth's surface. (347)
deriva continental Hipótesis que sostiene que los continentes se desplazan lentamente sobre la superficie de la Tierra.

continental glacier A glacier that covers much of a continent or large island. (465)
glaciar continental Glaciar que cubre gran parte de un continente o una isla grande.

controlled experiment An experiment in which only one variable is manipulated at a time. (22)
experimento controlado Experimento en el cual sólo se manipula una variable a la vez.

contour plowing Plowing fields along the curves of a slope to prevent soil loss. (439)
arado en contorno Arar los campos siguiendo las curvas de una pendiente para evitar la pérdida del suelo.

control rod A cadmium rod used in a nuclear reactor to absorb neutrons from fission reactions. (172)
varilla de control Varilla de cadmio que se usa en un reactor nuclear para absorber los neutrones emitidos por reacciones de fisión.

convection The transfer of thermal energy by the movement of a fluid. (143, 289)
convección Transferencia de energía térmica por el movimiento de un líquido.

convection current The movement of a fluid, caused by differences in temperature, that transfers heat from one part of the fluid to another. (290)
corriente de convección Movimiento de un líquido ocasionado por diferencias de temperatura y que transfiere calor de un área del líquido a otra.

convergent boundary A plate boundary where two plates move toward each other. (357)
borde convergente Borde de una placa donde dos placas se deslizan una hacia la otra.

convex lens A lens that is thicker in the center than at the edges. (262)
lente convexa Lente que es más gruesa en el centro que en los extremos.

convex mirror A mirror with a surface that curves outward. (254)
espejo convexo Espejo cuya superficie se curva hacia fuera.

crater A bowl-shaped area that forms around a volcano's central opening. (399)
cráter Área en forma de tazón que se forma en la abertura central de un volcán.

crest The highest part of a transverse wave. (193)
cresta Parte más alta de una onda transversal.

crop rotation The planting of different crops in a field each year to maintain the soil's fertility. (439)
rotación de las cosechas Cultivo anual de cosechas diferentes en un campo para mantener la fertilidad del suelo.

crust The layer of rock that forms Earth's outer surface. (283)
corteza terrestre Capa de rocas que forma la superficie externa de la Tierra.

crystal A solid in which the atoms are arranged in a pattern that repeats again and again. (303)
cristal Cuerpo sólido en el que los átomos siguen un patrón que se repite una y otra vez.

crystallization The process by which atoms are arranged to form a material with a crystal structure. (310)
cristalización Proceso mediante el cual los átomos se distribuyen y forman materiales con estructura de cristal.

cultural bias An outlook influenced by the beliefs, social forms, and traits of a group. (13)
prejuicio cultural Opinión influenciada por las creencias, costumbres sociales y características de un grupo.

cytokinesis The final stage of the cell cycle, in which the cell's cytoplasm divides, distributing the organelles into each of the two new daughter cells. (556)
citocinesis Última etapa del ciclo celular en la que se divide el citoplasma y se reparten los orgánulos entre las dos células hijas nuevas.

cytoplasm The thick fluid region of a cell located inside the cell membrane (in prokaryotes) or between the cell membrane and nucleus (in eukaryotes). (537)
citoplasma Región celular de líquido espeso ubicada dentro de la membrana celular (en las procariotas) o entre la membrana celular y el núcleo (en las eucariotas).

D

data Facts, figures, and other evidence gathered through observations. (23)
dato Hechos, cifras u otra evidencia reunida por medio de observaciones.

decibel (dB) A unit used to compare the loudness of different sounds. (219)
decibelio (dB) Unidad usada para comparar el volumen de distintos sonidos.

decomposer An organism that gets energy by breaking down biotic wastes and dead organisms, and returns raw materials to the soil and water. (434)
descomponedor Organismo que obtiene energía al descomponer desechos bióticos y organismos muertos, y que devuelve materia prima al suelo y al agua.

deductive reasoning A way to explain things by starting with a general idea and then applying the idea to a specific observation. (15)
razonamiento deductivo Manera de explicar las cosas en la que se aplica una idea general a una observación específica.

deep-ocean trenches A deep valley along the ocean floor beneath which oceanic crust slowly sinks toward the mantle. (354)
fosa oceánica profunda Valle profundo a lo largo del suelo oceánico debajo del cual la corteza oceánica se hunde lentamente hacia el manto.

deflation The process by which wind removes surface materials. (475)
deflación Proceso por el cual el viento se lleva materiales de la superficie.

GLOSSARY

delta A landform made of sediment that is deposited where a river flows into an ocean or lake. (460)
delta Accidente geográfico formado por sedimento que se deposita en la desembocadura de un río a un océano o lago.

density The measurement of how much mass of a substance is contained in a given volume. (44)
densidad Medida de la masa de una sustancia que tiene un volumen dado.

deposition Process in which sediment is laid down in new locations. (323)
sedimentación Proceso por el cual los sedimentos se asientan en nuevos sitios.

destructive force Any natural process that tears down or wears away Earth's surface. (279)
fuerza destructiva Proceso natural que destruye o desgasta la superficie de la Tierra.

destructive interference The interference that occurs when two waves combine to make a wave with an amplitude smaller than the amplitude of either of the individual waves. (207)
interferencia destructiva Interferencia que ocurre cuando dos ondas se combinan para crear una onda con una amplitud menor a la de cualquiera de las ondas individuales.

diffraction The bending or spreading of waves as they move around a barrier or pass through an opening. (205)
difracción Desviación de las ondas al desplazarse alrededor de una barrera o atravesar una abertura.

diffuse reflection Reflection that occurs when parallel rays of light hit an uneven surface and all reflect at different angles. (251)
reflexión difusa Reflexión que ocurre cuando rayos de luz paralelos tocan una superficie rugos y se reflejan en diferentes ángulos.

dike A slab of volcanic rock formed when magma forces itself across rock layers. (410)
dique discordante Placa de roca volcánica formada cuando el magma se abre paso a través de las capas de roca.

distance The length of the path between two points. (87)
distancia Medida del espacio entre dos puntos.

divergent boundary A plate boundary where two plates move away from each other. (357)
borde divergente Borde de una placa donde dos placas se separan.

DNA Deoxyribonucleic acid; the genetic material that carries information about an organism and is passed from parent to offspring. (548)
ADN Ácido desoxirribonucleico; material genético que lleva información sobre un organismo y que se transmite de padres a hijos.

Doppler effect The change in frequency of a wave as its source moves in relation to an observer. (220)
efecto Doppler Cambio en la frecuencia de una onda a medida que la fuente se mueve en relación al observador.

dormant Not currently active but able to become active in the future (as with a volcano). (404)
inactivo Que no está activo en la actualidad pero puede ser activo en el futuro (como un volcán).

double helix The shape of a DNA molecule. (548)
doble hélice Forma de una molécula de ADN.

--------------------- E ---------------------

earthquake The shaking that results from the movement of rock beneath Earth's surface. (381)
terremoto Temblor que resulta del movimiento de la roca debajo de la superficie de la Tierra.

efficiency The percentage of input work that is converted to output work. (177)
eficacia Porcentaje de trabajo aportado que se convierte en trabajo producido.

electrical energy The energy of electric charges. (134)
energía eléctrica Energía de las cargas eléctricas.

electromagnetic energy The energy of light and other forms of radiation, which travels through space as waves. (134)
energía electromagnética Energía de la luz y otras formas de radiación, que viaja a través del espacio en forma de ondas.

electromagnetic radiation The energy transferred through space by electromagnetic waves. (233)
radiación electromagnétic Energía transferida a través del espacio por ondas electromagnéticas.

electromagnetic spectrum The complete range of electromagnetic waves placed in order of increasing frequency. (238)
espectro electromagnético Gama completa de ondas electromagnéticas organizadas de menor a mayor frecuencia.

electromagnetic wave **1.** A wave made up of a combination of a changing electric field and a changing magnetic field. **2.** A wave that can transfer electric and magnetic energy through a vacuum of space. (233)
onda electromagnética **1.** Onda formada por la combinación de un campo eléctrico cambiante y un campo magnético cambiante. **2.** Onda que puede transportar energía eléctrica y magnética a través del vacío del espacio.

element A pure substance that cannot be broken down into other substances by chemical or physical means. (544)
elemento Sustancia que no se puede descomponer en otras sustancias por medios químicos o físicos.

endoplasmic reticulum An organelle that forms a maze of passageways in which proteins and other materials are carried from one part of the cell to another. (537)
retículo endoplasmático Orgánulo que forma un laberinto de conductos que llevan proteínas y otros materiales de una parte de la célula a otra.

energy The ability to do work or cause change. (191)
energía Capacidad para realizar un trabajo o producir cambios.

energy conservation The practice of reducing energy use. (179)
conservación de energía Práctica de reducción del uso de energía.

energy transformation A change from one form of energy to another; also called an energy conversion. (134)
transformación de la energía Cambio de una forma de energía a otra; también se le llama conversión de energía.

enzyme A type of protein that speeds up a chemical reaction in a living thing. (547)
enzima Tipo de proteína que acelera una reacción química de un ser vivo.

epicenter The point on Earth's surface directly above an earthquake's focus. (382)
epicentro Punto de la superficie de la Tierra directamente sobre el foco de un terremoto.

epithelial tissue A body tissue that covers the interior and exterior surfaces of the body. (560)
tejido epitelial Tejido del cuerpo que cubre las superficies interiores y exteriores.

era One of the three long units of geologic time between the Precambrian and the present. (503)
era Cada una de las tres unidades largas del tiempo geológico entre el precámbrico y el presente.

erosion The process by which water, ice, wind, or gravity moves weathered particles of rock and soil. (323)
erosión Proceso por el cual el agua, el hielo, el viento o la gravedad desplazan partículas desgastadas de roca y suelo.

estimate An approximation of a number based on reasonable assumptions. (49)
estimación Aproximación de un número basada en conjeturas razonables.

ethics The study of principles about what is right and wrong, fair and unfair. (12)
ética Estudio de los principios de qué es lo bueno y lo malo, lo justo y lo injusto.

evaluating Comparing observations and data to reach a conclusion about them. (8)
evaluar Comparar observaciones y datos para llegar a una conclusión.

evolution Change over time; the process by which modern organisms have descended from ancient organisms. (493)
evolución Cambios a través del tiempo; proceso por el cual los organismos modernos se originaron a partir de organismos antiguos.

experimental bias A mistake in the design of an experiment that makes a particular result more likely. (13)
prejuicio experimental Error en el diseño de un experimento que aumenta la probabilidad de un resultado.

extinct Term used to describe a volcano that is no longer active and is unlikely to erupt again. (404)
extinto Término que describe un volcán que ya no es activo y es poco probable que vuelva a hacer erupción.

extrusion An igneous rock layer formed when lava flows onto Earth's surface and hardens. (496)
extrusión apa de roca ígnea formada cuando la lava fluye hacia la superficie de la Tierra y se endurece.

extrusive rock Igneous rock that forms from lava on Earth's surface. (319)
roca extrusiva Roca ígnea que se forma de la lava en la superficie de la Tierra.

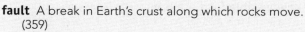

F

fault A break in Earth's crust along which rocks move. (359)
falla Fisura en la corteza terrestre a lo largo de la cual se desplazan las rocas.

GLOSSARY

feedback Output that changes a system or allows the system to adjust itself. (62)
retroalimentación Salida que cambia un sistema o permite que éste se ajuste.

fertility A measure of how well soil supports plant growth. (432)
fertilidad Medida de cuán apropiado es un suelo para estimular el crecimiento de las plantas.

field Any area outside of the laboratory. (72)
campo Cualquier área fuera del laboratorio.

flood plain The flat, wide area of land along a river. (458)
llanura de aluvión Área de tierra extensa y plana a lo largo de un río.

fluid friction Friction that occurs as an object moves through a fluid. (107)
fricción de fluido Fricción que ocurre cuando un cuerpo se mueve a través de un fluido.

focal point The point at which light rays parallel to the optical axis meet, or appear to meet, after being reflected (or refracted) by a mirror (or a lens). (253)
punto de enfoque Punto en el que se encuentran, o parecen encontrarse, los rayos de luz paralelos al eje óptico después de reflejarse (o refractarse) en un espejo (o lente).

focus The point beneath Earth's surface where rock first breaks under stress and causes an earthquake. (382)
foco Punto debajo de la superficie de la Tierra en el que la roca empieza a romperse debido a una gran fuerza y causa un terremoto.

foliated Term used to describe metamorphic rocks that have grains arranged in parallel layers or bands. (330)
foliación Término que describe las rocas metamórficas con granos dispuestos en capas paralelas o bandas.

force A push or pull exerted on an object. (101)
fuerza Empuje o atracción que se ejerce sobre un cuerpo.

fossil The preserved remains or traces of an organism that lived in the past. (348)
fósil Restos o vestigios conservados de un organismo que vivió en el pasado.

fossil fuel Coal, oil, or natural gas that forms over millions of years from the remains of ancient organisms; burned to release energy. (157)
combustible fósil Carbón, petróleo o gas natural que se forma a lo largo de millones de años a partir de los restos de organismos antiguos; se queman para liberar energía.

fracture The way a mineral looks when it breaks apart in an irregular way. (309)
fractura Apariencia de un mineral cuando se rompe de manera irregular.

frequency The number of complete waves that pass a given point in a certain amount of time. (198)
frecuencia Número de ondas completas que pasan por un punto dado en cierto tiempo.

friction The force that two surfaces exert on each other when they rub against each other. (105)
fricción Fuerza que dos superficies ejercen una sobre la otra al frotarse.

frost wedging Process that splits rock when water seeps into cracks, then freezes and expands. (425)
acuñado rocoso Proceso que separa las rocas cuando el agua se filtra entre grietas y luego se congela y expande.

fuel A substance that provides energy as the result of a chemical change. (157)
combustible Sustancia que libera energía como resultado de un cambio químico.

fuel rod A uranium rod that undergoes fission in a nuclear reactor. (172)
varilla de combustible Varilla de uranio que se somete a la fisión en un reactor nuclear.

G

gamma rays Electromagnetic waves with the shortest wavelengths and highest frequencies. (242)
rayos gamma Ondas electromagnéticas con la menor longitud de onda y la mayor frecuencia.

gasohol A mixture of gasoline and alcohol. (168)
gasohol Mezcla de gasolina y alcohol.

geode A hollow rock inside which mineral crystals have grown. (310)
geoda Roca hueca dentro de la que se forman cristales minerales.

geologic time scale A record of the geologic events and life forms in Earth's history. (501)
escala de tiempo geológico Registro de los sucesos geológicos y de las formas de vida en la historia de la Tierra.

geosphere The densest parts of Earth that include the crust, mantle, and core. (276)
geósfera Partes más densos de la Tierra que incluye la corteza, el manto y el núcleo.

geothermal energy The intense heat energy that comes from Earth's interior. (169)
energía geotérmica Energía intensa que proviene del interior de la Tierra.

glacier Any large mass of ice that moves slowly over land. (465)
glaciar Cualquier masa grande de hielo que se desplaza lentamente sobre la tierra.

gland An organ that produces and releases chemicals either through ducts or into the bloodstream. (570)
glándula Órgano que produce y libera sustancias químicas por los ductos o al torrente sanguíneo.

Golgi apparatus An organelle in a cell that receives proteins and other newly formed materials from the endoplasmic reticulum, packages them, and distributes them to other parts of the cell. (540)
aparato de Golgi Orgánulo de la célula que recibe, empaqueta y distribuye a otras partes de la célula las proteínas y otros materiales que se forman en el retículo endoplasmático.

grains The particles of minerals or other rocks that give a rock its texture. (316)
granos Partículas de minerales o de otras rocas que le dan textura a una roca.

granite A usually light-colored igneous rock that is found in continental crust. (283)
granito Roca generalmente de color claro que se encuentra en la corteza continental.

graph A picture of information from a data table; shows the relationship between variables. (57)
gráfica Representación visual de la información de una tabla de datos; muestra la relación entre las variables.

gravity The attractive force between objects; the force that moves objects downhill. (452)
gravedad Fuerza que atrae a los cuerpos entre sí; fuerza que mueve un cuerpo cuesta abajo.

groundwater Water that fills the cracks and spaces in underground soil and rock layers. (462)
aguas freáticas Agua que llena las grietas y huecos de las capas subterráneas de tierra y roca.

gully A large channel in soil that carries runoff after a rainstorm. (456)
barranco Canal grande en el suelo formado por corrientes de agua durante una tormenta de lluvia.

H

headland A part of the shore that sticks out into the ocean. (471)
promontorio Parte de la costa que se interna en el mar.

hertz (Hz) Unit of measurement for frequency. (198)
hercio (Hz) Unidad de medida de la frecuencia.

hormone A chemical that affects growth and development. (571)
hormona Sustancia química que afecta el crecimiento y el desarrollo.

hot spot An area where magma from deep within the mantle melts through the crust above it. (397)
punto caliente Área en la que el magma de las profundidades del manto atraviesa la corteza.

humus Dark-colored organic material in soil. (431)
humus Material orgánico de color oscuro del suelo.

hydrocarbon An organic compound that contains only carbon and hydrogen atoms. (157)
hidrocarburo Compuesto orgánico que contiene átomos de carbón e hidrógeno solamente.

hydroelectric power Electricity produced by the kinetic energy of water moving over a waterfall or dam. (167)
energía hidroeléctrica Electricidad producida a partir de la energía cinética del agua que baja por una catarata o presa.

hydrosphere The portion of Earth that consists of water in any of its forms, including oceans, glaciers, rivers, lakes, groundwater and water vapor. (276)
hidrósfera Parte de la Tierra formada por agua en cualquiera de sus formas, ya sea océanos, glaciares, ríos, lagos, agua subterránea y vapor de agua.

hypothesis A possible explanation for a set of observations or answer to a scientific question; must be testable. (20)
hipótesis Explicación posible de un conjunto de observaciones o respuesta a una pregunta científica; se debe poder poner a prueba.

I

ice age Time in Earth's history during which glaciers covered large parts of the surface. (465).
edad de hielo Período en la historia de la Tierra durante el cual gran parte de la superficie terrestre estaba cubierta por glaciares.

GLOSSARY

igneous rock A type of rock that forms from the cooling of molten rock at or below the surface. (317)
   roca ígnea Tipo de roca que se forma cuando se enfrían las rocas fundidas en la superficie o debajo de la superficie.

image A copy of an object formed by reflected or refracted rays of light. (251)
   imagen Copia de un objeto formado por rayos de luz que se reflejan y se refractan.

index fossil Fossils of widely distributed organisms that lived during a geologically short period. (497)
   fósil guía Fósiles de organismos altamente dispersos que vivieron durante un período geológico corto.

index of refraction A measure of the amount a ray of light bends when it passes from one medium to another. (258)
   índice de refracción Medida de la inclinación de un rayo de luz cuando pasa de un medio a otro.

inductive reasoning Using specific observations to make generalizations. (16)
   razonamiento inductivo Usar observaciones específicas para hacer generalizaciones.

inertia The tendency of an object to resist a change in motion. (113)
   inercia Tendencia de un cuerpo de resistirse a cambios de movimiento.

inferring The process of making an inference, an interpretation based on observations and prior knowledge. (6)
   inferir Proceso de hacer una inferencia; interpretación basada en observaciones y conocimientos previos.

infrared rays Electromagnetic waves with shorter wavelengths and higher frequencies than microwaves. (240)
   rayos infrarrojos Ondas electromagnéticas con longitudes de onda más cortas y frecuencias más altas que las microondas.

inner core A dense sphere of solid iron and nickel at the center of Earth. (285)
   núcleo interno Esfera densa de hierro y níquel que se encuentra en el centro de la Tierra.

inorganic Not formed from living things or the remains of living things. (303)
   inorgánico Que no está formado por seres vivos o por los restos de seres vivos.

input Material, energy, or information that goes into a system. (62)
   entrada Material, energía o informacion que se agrega a un sistema.

instantaneous speed The speed of an object at one instant of time. (91)
   velocidad instantánea Velocidad de un objeto en un instante del tiempo.

insulation Material that traps air to help block heat transfer between the air inside and outside of a building. (177)
   aislante Material que atrapa el aire para ayudar a bloquear el paso del calor del aire adentro y afuera de un edificio.

intensity The amount of energy per second carried through a unit area by a wave. (218)
   intensidad Cantidad de energía por segundo que transporta una onda a través de una unidad de área.

interference The interaction between waves that meet. (206)
   interferencia Interacción entre dos o más ondas que se encuentran.

International System of Units (SI) A system of units used by scientists to measure the properties of matter. (87)
   Sistema Internacional de Unidades (SI) Sistema de unidades que los científicos usan para medir las propiedades de la materia.

interphase The first stage of the cell cycle that takes place before cell division occurs, during which a cell grows and makes a copy of its DNA. (552)
   interfase Primera etapa del ciclo celular que ocurre antes de la división celular y durante la cual la célula crece y duplica su ADN.

intrusion An igneous rock layer formed when magma hardens beneath Earth's surface. (496)
   intrusión Capa de roca ígnea formada cuando el magma se endurece bajo la superficie de la Tierra.

intrusive rock Igneous rock that forms when magma hardens beneath Earth's surface. (319)
   roca intrusiva (o plutónica) Roca ígnea que se forma cuando el magma se endurece bajo la superficie de la Tierra.

invertebrate An animal without a backbone. (506)
   invertebrado Animal sin columna vertebral.

island arc A string of volcanoes that form as the result of subduction of one oceanic plate beneath a second oceanic plate. (396)
arco de islas Cadena de volcanes formados como resultado de la subducción de una placa oceánica debajo de una segunda placa oceánica.

J
---

joint A place in the body where two bones come together. (566)
articulación Lugar en el cuerpo en donde se unen dos huesos.

K
---

karst topography A region in which a layer of limestone close to the surface creates deep valleys, caverns, and sinkholes. (463)
topografía kárstica Región en la que una capa de piedra caliza cerca de la superficie crea valles hundidos, grutas y pozos.

kettle A small depression that forms when a chunk of ice is left in glacial till. (468)
marmita glacial Pequeña depresión formada cuando un trozo de hielo se asienta en arcilla glacial.

kinetic energy Energy that an object has due to its motion. (131)
energía cinética Energía que tiene un cuerpo debido a su movimiento.

L
---

lava Liquid magma that reaches the surface. (394)
lava Magma líquido que sale a la superficie.

lava flow The area covered by lava as it pours out of a volcano's vent. (399)
colada de lava Área cubierta de lava a medida que ésta sale por la chimenea del volcán.

law of conservation of energy The rule that energy cannot be created or destroyed. (140)
ley de conservación de la energía Regla que dice que la energía no se puede crear ni destruir.

law of superposition The geologic principle that states that in horizontal layers of sedimentary rock, each layer is older than the layer above it and younger than the layer below it. (495)
ley de la superposición Principio geológico que enuncia que, en las capas horizontales de las rocas sedimentarias, cada capa es más vieja que la capa superior y más joven que la capa inferior.

lens A curved piece of glass or other transparent material that is used to refract light. (261)
lente Trozo curvo de vidrio u otro material transparente que se usa para refractar la luz.

linear graph A line graph in which the data points yield a straight line. (58)
gráfica lineal Gráfica en la cual los puntos de los datos forman una línea recta.

lipid An energy-rich organic compound, such as a fat, oil, or wax, that is made of carbon, hydrogen, and oxygen. (547)
lípido Compuesto orgánico rico en energía, como una grasa, aceite o cera, formado por los elementos carbono, hidrógeno y oxígeno.

lithosphere A rigid layer made up of the uppermost part of the mantle and the crust. (284)
litósfera Capa rígida constituida por la parte superior del manto y la corteza.

loam Rich, fertile soil that is made up of about equal parts of clay, sand, and silt. (432)
marga Suelo rico y fértil formado por partes casi iguales de arcilla, arena y limo.

loess A wind-formed deposit made of fine particles of clay and silt. (476)
loes Depósito de partículas finas de arcilla y limo arrastradas por el viento.

longitudinal wave A wave that moves the medium in a direction parallel to the direction in which the wave travels. (194)
onda longitudinal Onda que mueve al medio en una dirección paralela a la dirección en la que se propaga la onda.

longshore drift The movement of water and sediment down a beach caused by waves coming in to shore at an angle. (472)
deriva litoral Movimiento de agua y sedimentos paralelo a una playa debido a la llegada de olas inclinadas respecto a la costa.

loudness Perception of the energy of a sound. (218)
volumen Percepción de la energía de un sonido.

luster The way a mineral reflects light from its surface. (305)
lustre Manera en la que un mineral refleja la luz en su superficie.

lysosome A cell organelle which contains chemicals that break down large food particles into smaller ones and that can be used by the rest of the cell. (541)
lisosoma Orgánulo de una célula, que tiene sustancias químicas que convierten partículas grandes de alimentos en partículas más pequeñas que el resto de la célula puede utilizar.

M

magma The molten mixture of rock-forming substances, gases, and water from the mantle. (394)
magma Mezcla fundida de las sustancias que forman las rocas, gases y agua, proveniente del manto.

magma chamber The pocket beneath a volcano where magma collects. (399)
cámara magmática Bolsa debajo de un volcán en la que está acumulado el magma.

magnitude The measurement of an earthquake's strength based on seismic waves and movement along faults. (384)
magnitud Medida de la fuerza de un sismo basada en las ondas sísmicas y en el movimiento que ocurre a lo largo de las fallas.

making models The process of creating representations of complex objects or processes. (9)
hacer modelos Proceso de crear representaciones de objetos o procesos complejos.

mammal A vertebrate whose body temperature is regulated by its internal heat, and that has skin covered with hair or fur and glands that produce milk to feed its young. (509)
mamífero Vertebrado cuya temperatura corporal es regulada por su calor interno, cuya piel está cubierta de pelo o pelaje y que tiene glándulas que producen leche para alimentar a sus crías.

manipulated variable The one factor that a scientist changes during an experiment; also called independent variable. (21)
variable manipulada Único factor que el científico cambia durante un experimento; también llamada variable independiente.

mantle The layer of hot, solid material between Earth's crust and core. (284)
manto Capa de material caliente y sólido entre la corteza terrestre y el núcleo.

mass A measure of how much matter is in an object. (41)
masa Medida de cuánta materia hay en un cuerpo.

mass extinction When many types of living things become extinct at the same time. (508)
extinción en masa Situación que ocurre cuando muchos tipos de seres vivos se extinguen al mismo tiempo.

mass movement Any one of several processes by which gravity moves sediment downhill. (452)
movimiento en masa Cualquiera de los procesos por los cuales la gravedad desplaza sedimentos cuesta abajo.

mean The numerical average of a set of data. (53)
media Promedio numérico de un conjunto de datos.

meander A looplike bend in the course of a river. (459)
meandro Curva muy pronunciada en el curso de un río.

mechanical energy Kinetic or potential energy associated with the motion or position of an object. (132)
energía mecánica Energía cinética o potencial asociada con el movimiento o la posición de un cuerpo.

mechanical wave A wave that requires a medium through which to travel. (191)
onda mecánica Onda que necesita un medio por el cual propagarse.

mechanical weathering The type of weathering in which rock is physically broken into smaller pieces. (424)
desgaste mecánico Tipo de desgaste en el cual una roca se rompe físicamente en trozos más pequeños.

median The middle number in a set of data. (53)
mediana Número del medio de un conjunto de datos.

medium The material through which a wave travels. (191)
medio Material a través del cual se propaga una onda.

meniscus The curved upper surface of a liquid in a column of liquid. (42)
menisco Superficie superior curva de un líquido en una columna de líquido.

metamorphic rock A type of rock that forms from an existing rock that is changed by heat, pressure, or chemical reactions. (317)
roca metamórfica Tipo de roca que se forma cuando una roca cambia por el calor, la presión o por reacciones químicas.

metric system A system of measurement based on the number 10. (39)
sistema métrico Sistema de medidas basado en el número 10.

microscope An instrument that makes small objects look larger. (528)
microscopio Instrumento que permite que los objetos pequeños se vean más grandes.

microwaves Electromagnetic waves that have shorter wavelengths and higher frequencies than radio waves. (239)
microondas Ondas electromagnéticas con longitudes de onda más cortas y frecuencias más altas que las ondas de radio.

mid-ocean ridge An undersea mountain chain where new ocean floor is produced; a divergent plate boundary under the ocean. (350)
cordillera oceánica central Cadena montañosa submarina donde se produce el nuevo suelo oceánico; borde de placa divergente bajo el océano.

mirage An image of a distant object caused by refraction of light as it travels through air of varying temperature. (260)
espejismo Imagen de un objeto distante causado por la refracción de la luz cuando viaja por el aire a temperaturas cambiantes.

mitochondria Rod-shaped organelles that convert energy in food molecules to energy the cell can use to carry out its functions. (537)
mitocondria Estructura celular con forma de bastón que transforma la energía de las moléculas de alimentos en energía que la célula puede usar para llevar a cabo sus funciones.

mitosis The second stage of the cell cycle during which the cell's nucleus divides into two new nuclei and one set of DNA is distributed into each daughter cell. (553)
mitosis Segunda etapa del ciclo celular, durante la cual se divide el núcleo de la célula en dos núcleos nuevos y el conjunto del ADN se reparte entre cada célula hija.

mode The number that appears most often in a list of numbers. (53)
moda Número que aparece con más frecuencia en una lista de números.

model A representation of a complex object or process, used to help people understand a concept that they cannot observe directly. (61)
modelo Representación de un objeto o proceso complejo que se usa para explicar un concepto que no se puede observar directamente.

Modified Mercalli scale A scale that rates the amount of shaking from an earthquake. (384)
escala modificada de Mercalli Escala que evalúa la intensidad del temblor de un terremoto.

Mohs hardness scale A scale ranking ten minerals from softest to hardest; used in testing the hardness of minerals. (306)
escala de dureza de Mohs Escala en la que se clasifican diez minerales del más blando al más duro; se usa para probar la dureza de los minerales.

mold A type of fossil that is a hollow area in sediment in the shape of an organism or part of an organism. (490)
molde Tipo de fósil que consiste en una depresión del sedimento que tiene la forma de un organismo o de parte de un organismo.

moment magnitude scale A scale that rates earthquakes by estimating the total energy released by an earthquake. (385)
escala de magnitud de momento Escala con la que se miden los sismos estimando la cantidad total de energía liberada por un terremoto.

moraine A ridge formed by the till deposited at the edge of a glacier. (468)
morrena Montículo formado por arcilla glaciárica depositada en el borde de un glaciar.

motion The state in which one object's distance from another is changing. (84)
movimiento Estado en el que la distancia entre un cuerpo y otro va cambiando.

multicellular Consisting of many cells. (542)
multicelular Que se compone de muchas células.

muscle tissue A body tissue that contracts, or shortens, making body parts move. (560)
tejido muscular Tejido del cuerpo que se contrae o encoge, y permite que se muevan las partes del cuerpo.

N

natural resource Anything naturally occuring in the environment that humans use. (437)
recurso natural Cualquier elemento natural en el medio ambiente que el ser humano usa.

nervous tissue A body tissue that carries electrical messages back and forth between the brain and other parts of the body. (560)
tejido nervioso Tejido del cuerpo que transporta impulsos eléctricos entre el cerebro y otras partes del cuerpo.

GLOSSARY

net force The overall force on an object when all the individual forces acting on it are added together. (102)
fuerza neta Fuerza total que se ejerce sobre un cuerpo cuando se suman las fuerzas individuales que actúan sobre él.

newton A unit of measure that equals the force required to accelerate 1 kilogram of mass at 1 meter per second per second. (101)
newton Unidad de medida equivalente a la fuerza necesaria para acelerar 1 kilogramo de masa a 1 metro por segundo cada segundo.

node A point of zero amplitude on a standing wave. (208)
nodo Punto de amplitud cero de una onda estacionaria.

nonlinear graph A line graph in which the data points do not fall along a straight line. (58)
gráfica no lineal Gráfica lineal en la que los puntos de datos no forman una línea recta.

normal fault A type of fault where the hanging wall slides downward; caused by tension in the crust. (374)
falla normal Tipo de falla en la cual el labio elevado o subyacente se desliza hacia abajo como resultado de la tensión de la corteza.

nuclear energy The potential energy stored in the nucleus of an atom. (134)
energía nuclear Energía potencial almacenada en el núcleo de un átomo.

nuclear fission The splitting of an atom's nucleus into two smaller nuclei and neutrons, releasing a large quantity of energy. (172)
fisión nuclear Separación del núcleo de un átomo en núcleos y neutrones más pequeños, en la cual se libera una gran cantidad de energía.

nucleic acid A very large organic molecule made of carbon, oxygen, hydrogen, nitrogen, and phosphorus, that contains the instructions cells need to carry out all the functions of life. (548)
ácido nucleico Molécula muy grande formada por carbono, oxígeno, hidrógeno y fósforo, que porta las instrucciones necesarias para que las células realicen todas las funciones vitales.

nucleus In cells, a large oval organelle that contains the cell's genetic material in the form of DNA and controls many of the cell's activities. (536)
núcleo En las células, orgánulo grande y ovalado que contiene el material genético de la célula en forma de ADN y que controla muchas de las funciones celulares.

nutrient Substances in food that provide the raw materials and energy needed for an organism to carry out its essential processes. (569)
nutriente Sustancias de los alimentos que dan el material y la energía que un organismo necesita para sus funciones vitales.

O

objective Describes the act of decision-making or drawing conclusions based on available evidence. (14)
objetivo Describe el acto de tomar una decisión o llegar a una conclusión basándose en la evidencia disponible.

observing The process of using one or more of your senses to gather information. (5)
observar Proceso de usar uno o más de tus sentidos para reunir información.

opaque A type of material that reflects or absorbs all of the light that strikes it. (245)
material opaco Material que refleja o absorbe toda la luz que llega a él.

optical axis An imaginary line that divides a mirror in half. (253)
eje óptico Recta imaginaria que divide un espejo por la mitad.

organ A body structure that is composed of different kinds of tissues that work together. (543)
órgano Estructura del cuerpo compuesta de distintos tipos de tejidos que trabajan conjuntamente.

organ system A group of organs that work together to perform a major function. (543)
sistema de órganos Grupo de órganos que trabajan juntos para realizar una función importante.

organelle A tiny cell structure that carries out a specific function within the cell. (536)
orgánulo Estructura celular diminuta que realiza una función específica dentro de la célula.

organic rock Sedimentary rock that forms from remains of organisms deposited in thick layers. (325)
roca orgánica Roca sedimentaria que se forma cuando los restos de organismos se depositan en capas gruesas.

outer core A layer of molten iron and nickel that surrounds the inner core of Earth. (285)
núcleo externo Capa de hierro y níquel fundidos que rodea el núcleo interno de la Tierra.

output Material, energy, result, or product that comes out of a system. (62)
salida Material, energía, resultado o producto que un sistema produce.

oxbow lake A meander cut off from a river. (459)
lago de recodo Meandro que ha quedado aislado de un río.

oxidation A chemical change in which a substance combines with oxygen, as when iron oxidizes, forming rust. (427)
oxidación Cambio químico en el cual una sustancia se combina con el oxígeno, como cuando el hierro se oxida, y produce herrumbre.

P

P wave A type of seismic wave that compresses and expands the ground. (383)
onda P Tipo de onda sísmica que comprime y expande el suelo.

paleontologist A scientist who studies fossils to learn about organisms that lived long ago. (492)
paleontólogo Científico que estudia fósiles para aprender acerca de los organismos que vivieron hace mucho tiempo.

Pangaea The name of the single landmass that began to break apart 200 million years ago and gave rise to today's continents. (347)
Pangea Nombre de la masa de tierra única que empezó a dividirse hace 200 millones de años y que le dio origen a los continentes actuales.

percent error A calculation used to determine how accurate, or close to the true value, an experimental value really is. (52)
error porcentual Cálculo usado para determinar cuán exacto, o cercano al valor verdadero, es realmente un valor experimental.

period One of the units of geologic time into which geologists divide eras. (503)
período Una de las unidades del tiempo geológico en las que los geólogos dividen las eras.

permeable Characteristic of a material that contains connected air spaces, or pores, that water can seep through easily. (428)
permeable Característica de un material que contiene diminutos espacios de aire, o poros, conectados por donde se puede filtrar el agua.

personal bias An outlook influenced by a person's likes and dislikes. (13)
prejuicio personal Perspectiva influenciada por las preferencias de un individuo.

petrochemical A compound made from oil. (161)
petroquímico Compuesto que se obtiene del petróleo.

pertrified fossil A fossil in which minerals replace all or part of an organism. (490)
fósil petrificado Fósil en el cual los minerales reemplazan todo el organismo o parte de él.

petroleum Liquid fossil fuel; oil. (160)
petróleo Combustible fósil líquido.

pH scale A range of values used to indicate how acidic or basic a substance is; expresses the concentration of hydrogen ions in a solution. (432)
escala de pH Rango de valores que se usa para indicar cuán ácida o básica es una sustancia; expresa la concentración de iones hidrógeno de una solución.

photoelectric effect The ejection of electrons from a substance when light is shined on it. (235)
efecto fotoeléctrico Expulsión de electrones de una sustancia al ser iluminada.

photon A tiny particle or packet of light energy. (235)
fotón Partícula diminuta o paquete de energía luminosa.

pigment A colored substance used to color other materials. (249)
pigmento Sustancia de color que se usa para teñir otros materiales.

pipe A long tube through which magma moves from the magma chamber to Earth's surface. (399)
chimenea Largo tubo por el que el magma sube desde la cámara magmática hasta la superficie de la tierra.

pitch A description of how a sound is perceived as high or low. (216)
tono Descripción de un sonido que se percibe como alto o bajo.

plane mirror A flat mirror that produces an upright, virtual image the same size as the object. (252)
espejo plano Espejo liso que produce una imagen virtual vertical del mismo tamaño que el objeto.

GLOSSARY

plate A section of the lithosphere that slowly moves over the asthenosphere, carrying pieces of continental and oceanic crust. (356)
placa Sección de la litósfera que se desplaza lentamente sobre la astenósfera y que se lleva consigo trozos de la corteza continental y de la oceánica.

plate tectonics The theory that pieces of Earth's lithosphere are in constant motion, driven by convection currents in the mantle. (357)
tectónica de placas Teoría según la cual las partes de la litósfera de la Tierra están en continuo movimiento, impulsadas por las corrientes de convección del manto.

plateau A large landform that has high elevation and a more or less level surface. (379)
meseta Accidente geográfico que tiene una elevación alta y cuya superficie está más o menos nivelada.

plucking The process by which a glacier picks up rocks as it flows over the land. (467)
extracción Proceso por el cual un glaciar arranca las rocas al fluir sobre la tierra.

polarized light Light that has been filtered so that all of its waves are parallel to each other. (234)
luz polarizada Luz que se ha filtrado de manera que sus ondas queden paralelas unas con otras.

potential energy The energy an object has because of its position; also the internal stored energy of an object, such as energy stored in chemical bonds. (131)
energía potencial Energía que tiene un cuerpo por su posición; también es la energía interna almacenada de un cuerpo, como la energía almacenada en los enlaces químicos.

precision How close a group of measurements are to each other. (50)
precisión Cuán cerca se encuentran un grupo de medidas.

predicting The process of forecasting what will happen in the future based on past experience or evidence. (7)
predecir Proceso de pronosticar lo que va a suceder en el futuro, basándose en evidencia o experiencias previas.

pressure The force pushing on a surface divided by the area of that surface. (282)
presión 1. Fuerza que actúa contra una superficie, dividida entre el área de esa superficie. **2.** Fuerza que actúa sobre las rocas y que cambia su forma o volumen.

primary color One of three colors that can be used to make any other color. (248)
color primario Uno de los tres colores que se pueden usar para hacer cualquier color.

process A sequence of actions in a system. (62)
proceso Secuencia de acciones en un sistema.

protein Large organic molecule made of carbon, hydrogen, oxygen, nitrogen, and sometimes sulfur. (547)
proteína Molécula orgánica grande compuesta de carbono, hidrógeno, oxígeno, nitrógeno y, a veces, azufre.

prototype A working model used to test a design. (578)
prototipo Modelo funcional usado para probar un diseño.

pyroclastic flow The flow of ash, cinders, bombs, and gases down the side of a volcano during an explosive eruption. (403)
flujo piroclástico Flujo de ceniza, escoria, bombas y gases que corre por las laderas de un volcán durante una erupción explosiva.

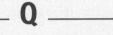

Q

qualitative observation An observation that deals with characteristics that cannot be expressed in numbers. (5)
observación cualitativa Observación que se centra en las características que no se pueden expresar con números.

quantitative observation An observation that deals with a number or amount. (5)
observación cuantitativa Observación que se centra en un número o cantidad.

R

radar A system that uses reflected radio waves to detect objects and measure their distance and speed. (239)
radar Sistema que usa ondas de radio reflejadas para detectar cuerpos y medir su distancia y velocidad.

radiation The transfer of energy by electromagnetic waves. (289)
radiación Transferencia de energía por medio de ondas magnéticas.

radio waves Electromagnetic waves with the longest wavelengths and lowest frequencies. (238)
ondas de radio Ondas electromagnéticas con las longitudes de onda más largas y las frecuencias más bajas.

range The difference between the greatest value and the least value in a set of data. (53)
rango Diferencia entre el mayor y el menor valor de un conjunto de datos.

rarefaction The part of a longitudinal wave where the particles of the medium are far apart. (194)
rarefacción Parte de una onda longitudinal donde las partículas del medio están muy apartadas entre sí.

ray A straight line used to represent a light wave. (250)
rayo Línea recta que se usa para representar una onda de luz.

reactor vessel The part of a nuclear reactor in which nuclear fission occurs. (172)
cuba de reactor Parte de un reactor nuclear donde ocurre la fisión.

real image An upside-down image formed where rays of light meet. (253)
imagen real Imagen invertida formada en el punto de encuentro de los rayos de luz.

reference point A place or object used for comparison to determine if an object is in motion. (85)
punto de referencia Lugar u objeto usado como medio de comparación para determinar si un objeto está en movimiento.

refinery A factory in which crude oil is heated and separated into fuels and other products. (161)
refinería Planta en la que el petróleo crudo se calienta y fracciona en combustibles y otros productos.

reflection The bouncing back of an object or a wave when it hits a surface through which it cannot pass. (203)
reflexión Rebote de un cuerpo o una onda al golpear una superficie que no puede atravesar.

refraction The bending of waves as they enter a new medium at an angle, caused by a change in speed. (204)
refracción Cambio de dirección de las ondas al entrar en un nuevo medio con un determinado ángulo, y a consecuencia de un cambio de velocidad.

regular reflection Reflection that occurs when parallel rays of light hit a smooth surface and all reflect at the same angle. (251)
reflexión regular Reflexión que ocurre cuando rayos de luz paralelos chocan contra una superficie lisa y se reflejan en el mismo ángulo.

relative age The age of a rock compared to the ages of other rocks. (494)
edad relativa Edad de una roca comparada con la edad de otras rocas.

replication The process by which a cell makes a copy of the DNA in its nucleus before cell division. (552)
replicación Proceso en el que la célula copia el ADN de su núcleo antes de la división celular.

reptile A vertebrate whose temperature is determined by the temperature of its environment, that has lungs and scaly skin, and that lays eggs on land. (507)
reptil Vertebrado cuya temperatura corporal es determinada por la temperatura de su medio ambiente, que tiene pulmones y piel escamosa y que pone huevos en la tierra.

resonance The increase in the amplitude of a vibration that occurs when external vibrations match an object's natural frequency. (209)
resonancia Aumento en la amplitud de vibración que ocurre cuando vibraciones externas corresponden con la frecuencia natural de un cuerpo.

responding variable The factor that changes as a result of changes to the manipulated, or independent, variable in an experiment; also called dependent variable. (21)
variable de respuesta Factor que cambia como resultado del cambio de la variable manipulada, o independiente, en un experimento; también llamada variable dependiente.

response An action or change in behavior that occurs as a result of a stimulus. (570)
respuesta Acción o cambio del comportamiento que ocurre como resultado de un estímulo.

reverse fault A type of fault where the hanging wall slides upward; caused by compression in the crust. (375)
falla inversa Tipo de falla en la cual el labio superior se desliza hacia arriba como resultado de compresión de la corteza.

ribosome A small grain-shaped organelle in the cytoplasm of a cell that produces proteins. (536)
ribosoma Orgánulo pequeño con forma de grano en el citoplasma de una célula que produce proteínas.

GLOSSARY

Richter scale A scale that rates an earthquake's magnitude based on the size of its seismic waves. (384)
escala de Richter Escala con la que se mide la magnitud de un terremoto según el tamaño de sus ondas sísmicas.

rift valley A deep valley that forms where two plates move apart. (359)
valle de fisura Valle profundo que se forma cuando dos placas se separan.

rill A tiny groove in soil made by flowing water. (456)
arroyo Pequeño surco en el suelo causado por el paso del agua.

Ring of Fire A major belt of volcanoes that rims the Pacific Ocean. (395)
Cinturón de Fuego Gran cadena de volcanes que rodea el océano Pacífico.

rock cycle A series of processes on the surface and inside Earth that slowly changes rocks from one kind to another. (332)
ciclo de la roca Serie de procesos en la superficie y dentro de la Tierra por medio del cual un tipo de roca se convierte lentamente en otro tipo.

rock-forming mineral Any of the common minerals that make up most of the rocks of Earth's crust. (315)
minerales formadores de rocas Uno de los minerales comunes de los que están compuestas la mayoría de las rocas de la corteza de la Tierra.

rolling friction Friction that occurs when an object rolls over a surface. (107)
fricción de rodamiento Fricción que ocurre cuando un cuerpo rueda sobre una superficie.

runoff Water that flows over the ground surface rather than soaking into the ground. (455)
escurrimiento Agua que fluye sobre la superficie en lugar de ser absorbida por el suelo.

S

S wave A type of seismic wave in which the shaking is perpendicular to the direction of the wave. (383)
onda S Tipo de onda sísmica que hace que el suelo se mueva en una dirección perpendicular a la onda.

safety symbols A sign used to alert you to possible sources of accidents in an investigation. (69)
símbolos de seguridad Señal de alerta sobre elementos que pueden causar accidentes durante una investigación.

sand dune A deposit of wind-blown sand. (476)
duna de arena Depósito de arena arrastrada por el viento.

science A way of learning about the natural world through observations and logical reasoning; leads to a body of knowledge. (5)
ciencia Estudio del mundo natural a través de observaciones y del razonamiento lógico; conduce a un conjunto de conocimientos.

scientific inquiry The ongoing process of discovery in science; the diverse ways in which scientists study the natural world and propose explanations based on evidence they gather.
indagación científica Proceso continuo de descubrimiento en la ciencia; diversidad de métodos con los que los científicos estudian el mundo natural y proponen explicaciones del mismo basadas en la evidencia que reúnen.

scientific law A statement that describes what scientists expect to happen every time under a particular set of conditions. (27)
ley científica Enunciado que describe lo que los científicos esperan que suceda cada vez que se da una serie de condiciones determinadas.

scientific theory A well-tested explanation for a wide range of observations or experimental results. (27)
teoría científica Explicación comprobada de una gran variedad de observaciones o resultados de experimentos.

sea-floor spreading Process by which molten material adds new oceanic crust to the ocean floor. (352)
despliegue del suelo oceánico Proceso mediante el cual la materia fundida añade nueva corteza oceánica al suelo oceánico.

secondary color Any color produced by combining equal amounts of any two primary colors. (248)
color secundario Color producido al combinar iguales cantidades de dos colores primarios cualesquiera.

sediment Small, solid pieces of material that come from rocks or the remains of organisms; earth materials deposited by erosion. (322)
sedimento Trozos pequeños y sólidos de materiales que provienen de las rocas o de los restos de organismos; materiales terrestres depositados por la erosión.

sedimentary rock Rock type that forms when particles from other rocks or the remains of plants and animals are pressed and cemented together. (317)
roca sedimentaria Tipo de roca que se forma a partir de la compactación y unión de partículas de otras rocas o restos de plantas y animales.

seismic wave Vibrations that travel through Earth carrying the energy released during an earthquake. (281)
ondas sísmicas Vibraciones que se desplazan por la Tierra, y que llevan la energía liberada durante un terremoto.

seismogram The record of an earthquake's seismic waves produced by a seismograph. (390)
sismograma Registro producido por un sismógrafo de las ondas sísmicas de un terremoto.

seismograph A device that records ground movements caused by seismic waves as they move through Earth. (384)
sismógrafo Aparato con el que se registran los movimientos del suelo ocasionados por las ondas sísmicas a medida que éstas se desplazan por la Tierra.

shearing Stress that pushes masses of rock in opposite directions, in a sideways movement. (373)
cizallamiento Fuerza que presiona masas de roca en sentidos opuestos, de lado a lado.

shield volcano A wide, gently sloping mountain made of layers of lava and formed by quiet eruptions. (409)
volcán en escudo Montaña ancha de pendientes suaves, compuesta por capas de lava y formada durante erupciones que no son violentas.

SI A system of units used by scientists to measure the properties of matter. (39)
SI Sistema de unidades que los científicos usan para medir las propiedades de la materia.

significant figures All the digits in a measurement that have been measured exactly, plus one digit whose value has been estimated. (50)
cifras significativas En una medida, todos los dígitos que se han medido con exactitud, más un dígito cuyo valor se ha estimado.

silica A material found in magma that is formed from the elements oxygen and silicon; it is the primary substance of Earth's crust and mantle. (400)
sílice Material presente en el magma, compuesto por los elementos oxígeno y silicio; es el componente más común de la corteza y el manto de la Tierra.

sill A slab of volcanic rock formed when magma squeezes between layers of rock. (410)
dique concordante Placa de roca volcánica formada cuando el magma queda comprimido entre capas de roca.

skeletal muscle A muscle that is attached to the bones of the skeleton and provides the force that moves the bones; also called striated muscle. (565)
músculo esquelético Músculo que está conectado a los huesos del esqueleto y que proporciona la fuerza que mueve los huesos; llamado también músculo estriado.

skeleton The inner framework made up of all the bones of the body. (565)
esqueleto Estructura interna compuesta de todos los huesos del cuerpo.

skepticism An attitude of doubt. (12)
escepticismo Actitud de duda.

sliding friction Friction that occurs when one solid surface slides over another. (106)
fricción de deslizamiento Fricción que ocurre cuando una superficie sólida se desliza sobre otra.

slope The steepness of a graph line; the ratio of the vertical change (the rise) to the horizontal change (the run). (94)
pendiente Inclinación de una gráfica lineal; la razón del cambio vertical (el ascenso) al cambio horizontal (el avance).

soil The loose, weathered material on Earth's surface in which plants can grow. (431)
suelo Material suelto y desgastado de la superficie terrestre donde crecen las plantas.

soil conservation The management of soil to limit its destruction. (439)
conservación del suelo Cuidado del suelo para limitar su destrucción.

soil horizon A layer of soil that differs in color and texture from the layers above or below it. (433)
horizonte de suelo Capa de suelo de color y textura diferentes a las capas que tiene encima o abajo.

solar energy Energy from the sun. (165)
energía solar Energía del Sol.

solution A mixture containing a solvent and at least one solute that has the same properties throughout; a mixture in which one substance is dissolved in another. (311)
solución Mezcla que contiene un solvente y al menos un soluto, y que tiene propiedades uniformes; mezcla en la que una sustancia se disuelve en otra.

speed The distance an object travels per unit of time. (89)
rapidez Distancia que viaja un objeto por unidad de tiempo.

GLOSSARY

spit A beach formed by longshore drift that projects like a finger out into the water. (473)
banco de arena Playa formada por la deriva litoral, que se proyecta como un dedo dentro del agua.

stalactite An icicle-like structure that hangs from the ceiling of a cavern. (462)
estalactita Estructura en forma de carámbano que cuelga del techo de una caverna.

stalagmite A columnlike form that grows upward from the floor of a cavern. (462)
estalagmita Estructura en forma de columna que crece hacia arriba desde el suelo de una caverna.

standing wave A wave that appears to stand in one place, even though it is two waves interfering as they pass through each other. (208)
onda estacionaria Onda que parece permanecer en un lugar, y que en realidad es la interferencia de dos ondas que se atraviesan.

static friction Friction that acts between objects that are not moving. (106)
fricción estática Fricción que actúa sobre los cuerpos que no están en movimiento.

stimulus Any change or signal in the environment that can make an organism react in some way. (570)
estímulo Cualquier cambio o señal del medio ambiente que puede causar una reacción en un organismo.

streak The color of a mineral's powder. (305)
raya Color del polvo de un mineral.

stream A channel through which water is continually flowing downhill. (456)
riachuelo Canal por el cual el agua fluye continuamente cuesta abajo.

stress A force that acts on rock to change its shape or volume. (372)
presión Fuerza que actúa sobre las rocas y que cambia su forma o volumen.

strike-slip fault A type of fault in which rocks on either side move past each other sideways with little up or down motion. (375)
falla transcurrente Tipo de falla en la cual las rocas a ambos lados se deslizan horizontalmente en sentidos opuestos, con poco desplazamiento hacia arriba o abajo.

subduction The process by which oceanic crust sinks beneath a deep-ocean trench and back into the mantle at a convergent plate boundary. (354)
subducción Proceso mediante el cual la corteza oceánica se hunde debajo de una fosa oceánica profunda y vuelve al manto por el borde de una placa convergente.

subjective Describes the influence of personal feelings on a decision or conclusion. (14)
subjetivo Describe la influencia de sentimientos personales sobre una decisión o conclusión.

subsoil The layer of soil below topsoil that has less plant and animal matter than topsoil and contains mostly clay and other minerals. (433)
subsuelo Capa de suelo debajo del suelo superior que tiene menos materia de plantas y animales que el suelo superior, y que principalmente contiene arcilla y otros minerales.

surface wave A type of seismic wave that forms when P waves and S waves reach Earth's surface. (383)
onda superficial Tipo de onda sísmica que se forma cuando las ondas P y las ondas S llegan a la superficie de la Tierra.

system A group of related parts that work together to perform a function or produce a result. (62)
sistema Grupo de partes relacionadas que trabajan conjuntamente para realizar una función o producir un resultado.

T
---

tension Stress that stretches rock so that it becomes thinner in the middle. (373)
tensión Fuerza que estira una roca, de modo que es más delgada en el centro.

texture The look and feel of a rock's surface, determined by the size, shape, and pattern of a rock's grains. (316)
textura Apariencia y sensación producida por la superficie de una roca, determinadas por el tamaño, la forma y el patrón de los granos de la roca.

thermal energy The total kinetic and potential energy of all the particles of an object. (134)
energía térmica Energía cinética y potencial total de las partículas de un cuerpo.

thermogram An image that shows regions of different temperatures in different colors. (240)
termograma Imagen que muestra regiones de distintas temperaturas con distintos colores.

till The sediments deposited directly by a glacier. (468)
marea La subida y bajada periódica del nivel de agua del océano.

tissue A group of similar cells that perform a specific function. (543)
tejido Grupo de células semejantes que realizan una función específica.

topsoil The crumbly, topmost layer of soil made up of clay and other minerals and humus (nutrients and decaying plant and animal matter). (433)
suelo superior Capa superior arenosa del suelo formada por arcilla, otros minerales y humus (nutrientes y materia orgánica de origen vegetal y animal).

trace fossil A type of fossil that provides evidence of the activities of ancient organisms. (491)
vestigios fósiles Tipo de fósil que presenta evidencia de las actividades de los organismos antiguos.

trade-off An exchange in which one benefit is given up in order to obtain another. (578)
sacrificar una cosa por otra Intercambio en el que se renuncia a un beneficio para obtener otro.

transform boundary A plate boundary where two plates move past each other in opposite directions. (357)
borde de transformación Borde de una placa donde dos placas se deslizan, en sentidos opuestos, y se pasan la una a la otra.

translucent A type of material that scatters light as it passes through. (245)
material traslúcido Material que dispersa la luz cuando ésta lo atraviesa.

transparent A type of material that transmits light without scattering it. (245)
material transparente Material que transmite luz sin dispersarla.

transverse wave A wave that moves the medium at right angles to the direction in which the wave travels. (193)
onda transversal Onda que desplaza a un medio perpendicularmente a la dirección en la que viaja la onda.

tributary A stream or river that flows into a larger river. (456)
afluente Río o arroyo que desemboca en un río más grande.

troubleshooting The process of analyzing a design problem and finding a way to fix it. (578)
solución de problemas Proceso por el cual se analiza un problema de diseño y se halla una forma de solucionarlo.

trough The lowest part of a transverse wave. (193)
valle Parte más baja de una onda transversal.

U
---

ultraviolet (radiation) rays Electromagnetic waves with wavelengths shorter than visible light but longer than X-rays. (241)
rayos (radiación) ultravioleta Ondas electromagnéticas con longitudes de onda más cortas que la luz visible pero mas largas que los rayos X.

unconformity A gap in the geologic record that shows where rock layers have been lost due to erosion. (498)
discordancia Interrupción en el récord geológico que muestra dónde las capas rocosas se han perdido a causa de la erosión.

unicellular Made of a single cell. (542)
unicelular Compuesto por una sola célula.

uniformitarianism The geologic principle that the same geologic processes that operate today operated in the past to change Earth's surface. (422)
uniformitarianismo Principio geológico que enuncia que los mismos procesos geológicos que cambian la superficie de la Tierra en la actualidad ocurrieron en el pasado.

V
---

vacuole A sac-like organelle that stores water, food, and other materials. (540)
vacuola Orgánulo en forma de bolsa que almacena agua, alimentos y otros materiales.

valley glacier A long, narrow glacier that forms when snow and ice build up in a mountain valley. (466)
glaciar de valle Glaciar largo y estrecho que se forma por la acumulación de hielo y nieve en el valle de una montaña.

variable A factor that can change in an experiment. (21)
variable Factor que puede cambiar en un experimento.

velocity Speed in a given direction. (92)
velocidad Rapidez en una dirección dada.

GLOSSARY

vein 1. A narrow deposit of a mineral that is sharply different from the surrounding rock. **2.** A blood vessel that carries blood back to the heart. (311)
vena 1. Placa delgada de un mineral que es marcadamente distinto a la roca que lo rodea. **2.** Vaso sanguíneo que transporta la sangre al corazón.

vent The opening through which molten rock and gas leave a volcano. (399)
ventiladero Abertura a través de la que la roca derretida y los gases salen de un volcán.

vertebrate An animal with a backbone. (506)
vertebrado Animal con columna vertebral.

vibration A repeated back-and-forth or up-and-down motion. (192)
vibración Movimiento repetido hacia delante y hacia atrás o hacia arriba y hacia abajo.

virtual image An upright image formed where rays of light appear to come from. (252)
imagen virtual Imagen vertical que se forma desde donde parecen provenir los rayos de luz.

visible light Electromagnetic radiation that can be seen with the unaided eye. (241)
luz visible Radiación electromagnética que se puede ver a simple vista.

volcanic neck A deposit of hardened magma in a volcano's pipe. (410)
cuello volcánico Depósito de magma solidificada en la chimenea de un volcán.

volcano A weak spot in the crust where magma has come to the surface. (394)
volcán Punto débil en la corteza por donde el magma escapa hacia la superficie.

volume The amount of space that matter occupies. (42)
volumen Cantidad de espacio que ocupa la materia.

W

wave A disturbance that transfers energy from place to place. (191)
onda Perturbación que transfiere energía de un lugar a otro.

wavelength The distance between two corresponding parts of a wave, such as the distance between two crests. (198)
longitud de onda Distancia entre dos partes correspondientes de una onda, por ejemplo la distancia entre dos crestas.

weathering The chemical and physical processes that break down rock and other substances. (323)
desgaste Procesos químicos y físicos que erosionan la roca y descomponen otras sustancias.

weight A measure of the force of gravity acting on an object. (41)
peso Medida de la fuerza de gravedad que actúa sobre un objeto.

X

X-rays Electromagnetic waves with wavelengths shorter than ultraviolet rays but longer than gamma rays. (242)
rayos X Ondas electromagnéticas con longitudes de onda más cortas que los rayos ultravioleta pero más largas que los rayos gamma.

INDEX

Page numbers for key terms are printed in **boldface** type.

INDEX

Page numbers for key terms are printed in **boldface** type.

INDEX

Page numbers for key terms are printed in **boldface** type.

INDEX

Page numbers for key terms are printed in **boldface** type.

INDEX

Page numbers for key terms are printed in **boldface** type.

ACKNOWLEDGMENTS

Staff Credits

The people who made up the *Interactive Science* team—representing composition services, core design digital and multimedia production services, digital product development, editorial, editorial services, manufacturing, and production—are listed below:

Jan Van Aarsen, Samah Abadir, Ernie Albanese, Chris Anton, Zareh Artinian, Bridget Binstock, Suzanne Biron, Niki Birbilis, MJ Black, Nancy Bolsover, Stacy Boyd, Jim Brady, Katherine Bryant, Michael Burstein, Pradeep Byram, Jessica Chase, Jonathan Cheney, Arthur Ciccone, Allison Cook-Bellistri, Rebecca Cottingham, AnnMarie Coyne, Bob Craton, Chris Deliee, Paul Delsignore, Michael Di Maria, Diane Dougherty, Kristen Ellis, Kelly Engel, Theresa Eugenio, Amanda Ferguson, Jorgensen Fernandez, Kathryn Fobert, Alicia Franke, Louise Gachet, Julia Gecha, Mark Geyer, Steve Gobbell, Paula Gogan-Porter, Jeffrey Gong, Sandra Graff, Robert M. Graham, Adam Groffman, Lynette Haggard, Christian Henry, Karen Holtzman, Susan Hutchinson, Sharon Inglis, Marian Jones, Sumy Joy, Sheila Kanitsch, Courtenay Kelley, Chris Kennedy, Toby Klang, Greg Lam, Russ Lappa, Margaret LaRaia, Ben Leveille, Thea Limpus, Charles Luey, Dotti Marshall, Kathy Martin, Robyn Matzke, John McClure, Mary Beth McDaniel, Krista McDonald, Tim McDonald, Rich McMahon, Cara McNally, Bernadette McQuilkin, Melinda Medina, Angelina Mendez, Maria Milczarek, Claudi Mimo, Mike Napieralski, Deborah Nicholls, Dave Nichols, William Oppenheimer, Jodi O'Rourke, Ameer Padshah, Lorie Park, Celio Pedrosa, Jonathan Penyack, Linda Zust Reddy, Jennifer Reichlin, Stephen Rider, Charlene Rimsa, Walter Rodriguez, Stephanie Rogers, Marcy Rose, Rashid Ross, Anne Rowsey, Logan Schmidt, Amanda Seldera, Laurel Smith, Nancy Smith, Ted Smykal, Emily Soltanoff, Cindy Strowman, Dee Sunday, Barry Tomack, Elizabeth Tustian, Patricia Valencia, Ana Sofia Villaveces, Stephanie Wallace, Amanda Watters, Christine Whitney, Brad Wiatr, Heidi Wilson, Heather Wright, Rachel Youdelman.

Photography

All otherwise unacknowledged photos are copyright © 2011 Pearson Education.

Cover, Front and Back
Ellen Skye/Photolibrary New York.

Front Matter
vi–vii fields, Alexey Stiop/Alamy; vii flag, Stacey Lynn Payne; vii cardinal, Tom Vezo/Peter Arnold Images/Photolibrary New York; viii, NASA Human Spaceflight Collection; ix, DAN GURAVICH/Science Source; x, Liane Cary/AGE Fotostock; xi, Nutscode/T Service/Photo Researchers, Inc.; xii, Greg Smith/Corbis; xiii, John Lund/Corbis; xiv, Don Carstens/Robertstock; xv, Whit Richardson/Getty Images; xvi, Matt Theilen/Getty Images; xvii, Peter Rowlands/PR Productions; xviii, Koji Sasahara/AP Images; xix, Kevin Schafer/Corbis; xx, Raimund Linke/Photolibrary New York; xxi, James L. Amos/Photo Researchers, Inc.; xxii, Solvin Zankl/Nature Picture Library; xxv laptop, iStockphoto; xxvii br, JupiterImages/Getty Images; xxviii laptop, iStockphoto; xxxii bl, Manoj Shah/The Image Bank/Getty Images; xxxii br, Randy Siner/AP Images; xxxiii l, Darryl Leniuk/Getty Images; xxxiii r, Stockbyte/Getty Images; xxxiv l, DEA/W. BUSS/De Agostini/Getty Images; xxxiv r, Image Source/Getty Images; xxxv l, John Cancalosi/Photo Researchers, Inc.; xxxv r, Thomas Deerinck, NCMIR/Science Source.

Chapter 1
Pages xxxvi–1 spread, NASA Human Spaceflight Collection; 3 m1, Ken Seet/Corbis; 3 b, Richard Haynes; 3 t, Michael Nichols/National Geographic Image Collection; 4 bkgrnd, Michael Nichols/National Geographic Image Collection; 5, Karl Ammann/Nature Picture Library; 6 b, Manoj Shah/The Image Bank/Getty Images; 6 t, Anup Shah/Nature Picture Library; 7, Christoph Becker/Nature Picture Library; 8 bkgrnd, Kennan Ward/Corbis; 9 tr, Rainer Raffalski/Alamy; 10 bkgrnd, Sarah Holmstrom/iStockphoto; 11 tl, Stephen Dalton/Photo Researchers, Inc.; 11 bl, Karin Lau/iStockphoto; 11 r, Kurt Lackovic/Alamy; 12 bkgrnd, Photo Network/Alamy; 14–15 bkgrnd, Ken Seet/Corbis; 15 mr, MBI/Alamy; 15 tr, Duncan Walker/iStockphoto; 16–17 spread, Stephen Dorey-Commercial/Alamy; 17 inset, Redmond Durrell/Alamy; 18 inset, Galileo Demonstrating the Law of Gravity of the Free Fall, detail of The Trial of Galileo (ca. 1839), Giuseppe Bezzuoli. Fresco. Museum of Physics and Natural History (Museo di Fisica e Storia Naturale), Florence, Italy; 19, Andy Sands/Nature Picture Library; 20, Richard Haynes; 21–22 t, Idamini/Alamy; 23–24, Idamini/Alamy; 25 b, Idamini/Alamy; 26 t, D. Hurst/Alamy; 26 m1, Don Carstens/Brand X Pictures/JupiterImages; 26 m2, Aartpack; 27, Photodisc/Getty Images; 28 t, Karl Ammann/Nature Picture Library; 28 b, Idamini/Alamy; 29, Stockdale Studios; 30, Image100/Corbis.

Chapter 1 Feature
Page 32, Académie des Sciences, Paris/Archives Charmet/The Bridgeman Art Library; 33, Tiago Estima/iStockphoto.

Chapter 2
Pages 34–35 spread, DAN GURAVICH/Science Source; 37 t, Chiyacat/Dreamstime; 37 m2, Image100/SuperStock; 38 r, Digital Vision/Alamy; 38 l, Philip Dowell/Dorling Kindersley; 38 inset, Anthony Mercieca/Photo Researchers, Inc.; 40, Richard Haynes; 41, Richard Haynes; 43 tr, Joe Traver/Time & Life Pictures/Getty Images; 44 t, Chiyacat/Dreamstime; 44 br, Terex/Dreamstime; 45, Ingots/Image Source Pink/JupiterImages; 48 bl, Simon Kwong/Reuters/Corbis; 48–49 spread, Michael S. Yamashita/Corbis; 49 inset, Kevin Fleming/Corbis; 51 bkgrnd, Robert Manella/Comstock/Corbis; 52 bl, Comstock Images/JupiterUnlimited; 52–53 bkgrnd, Reinhard Dirscherl/Ecoscene; 53 inset; Frank Greenaway/Dorling Kindersley; 54–55 bkgrnd, Chris Johnson/Alamy; 55 tr, NASA/Corbis; 56 b, Superclic/Alamy; 56 tr, Digital Vision/Alamy; 57 bl, Digital Vision/Alamy; 58 b, Image100 /SuperStock; 60 bkgrnd, Joseph Sohm/Visions of America/Corbis; 62 bkgrnd, PhotoStock-Israel/Alamy; 62 r, Bryan Whitney/Photonica/Getty Images; 63 bkgrnd, Kevin Foy/Alamy; 63 inset, Harris Shiffman/Shutterstock; 64–65 spread, Stephen Frink Collection/Alamy; 66–67 spread, James Balog/Aurora Photos; 68 tr, Martin Shields/Alamy; 68–69 b, William Philpott/AFP/Getty Images; 70 bm, Shattil & Rozinski/Nature Picture Library; 70, Richard Haynes; 71, Richard Haynes; 73, Corbis Super RF/Alamy; 74 tr, Richard Haynes; 76 l, Bedo/Dreamstime; 76 m, Dell/Dreamstime; 76 r, Pablo631/Dreamstime.

ACKNOWLEDGMENTS

Chapter 2 Feature
Page 78, JPL/NASA; 79, Andreas Gradin/Shutterstock.

Chapter 3
Pages 80–81, Brian Snyder/Reuters; 83 t, Mark Humphrey/ AP Images; 83m2, Darryl Leniuk/Getty Images; 83 b, David Wall/Lonely Planet Images/Zuma Press; 84 inset, Portrait of Nicolaus Copernicus (16th century). Pomeranian School. Oil on canvas. Nicolaus Copernicus Museum, Frombork, Poland/ Lauros/Giraudon/The Bridgeman Art Library International; 84 bkgrnd, Paul & Lindamarie Ambrose/Getty Images; 85 r, Grant Faint/Getty Images; 86 inset, Ingram Publishing/ SuperStock; 86 bkgrnd, Image 100/Corbis; 87 ml, Thepalmer/ iStockphoto; 88 bl, Jillian Bauer/Newhouse News Service/ Landov; 88 bkgrnd, Bill Ridder/The Paris News/AP Images; 88 tr, Liz O. Baylen/Washington Times/Zuma Press; 89 bl, John Walton/PA Photos/Landov; 90 b, Daniel Roland/AP Images; 90 inset, Adam Pretty/AP Images; 91, Andres Stapff/ Reuters/Landov; 92, Medford Taylor/National Geographic Stock; 93 bkgrnd, Google Earth Pro; 94 bkgrnd, Iconica/ Smith Collection/Getty Images; 96, Stephen Dalton/Science Source; 97 tr, IMAGEMORE Co.,Ltd./Getty; 97 br, Randy Siner/AP Images; 97 bl, The Laramie Boomerang/Barbara J. Perenic /AP Images; 99 bkgrnd, John Foxx/Stockbyte/Getty Images; 100, ColorBlind LLC/Blend Images/Photolibrary New York; 101, Mark Humphrey/AP Images; 105 br, Ron Sachs/ CNP/Newscom; 105 ml, Elena Elisseeva/Shutterstock; 105 m, Ian Wilson/Shutterstock; 105 mr, Jeff Whyte/iStockphoto; 108 t4, Dorling Kindersley; 108 t1, Steve Gorton/Dorling Kindersley; 108 t2, Dorling Kindersley; 108 t3, Clive Streeter/ Dorling Kindersley; 108–109 spread, Darryl Leniuk/Getty Images; 111 bkgrnd, NASA/JPL; 112 l, The Picture Desk/ Art Archive; 112–113 bkgrnd, David Wall/Lonely Planet Images/Zuma Press; 114 bkgrnd, David Trood/Getty Images; 115 bkgrnd, Andrea Raso/Lapresse/Zuma Press; 116 r, Grace Chiu/UPI; 116 l, Mark J. Terrill/AP Images; 117 b, Kim Kyung Hoon/Reuters; 117 tr, Steve Helber/AP Images; 123 br, Andrea Raso/Lapresse/Zuma Press.

Chapter 3 Feature
Page 124 bkgrnd, Rick Fischer/Masterfile; 124 inset, Car Culture/Corbis; 125 t, Colin Cuthbert/Photo Researchers, Inc.; 125 b, Harry Taylor/Dorling Kindersley.

Chapter 4
Pages 126–127 spread, Nutscode/T Service/Photo Researchers, Inc.; 129 b, Tips Italia/Photolibrary New York; 130–131 spread, Elena Elisseeva/Shutterstock; 132–133 spread, Dennis MacDonald/Alamy; 136 b, Bob Lyndall; 137, Christian Liewig/TempSport/Corbis; 138 b, Performance Image/Alamy; 138 t, James Schwabel/Alamy; 142, GRIN/ NASA; 143, Tips Italia/Photolibrary New York; 148, Don Bishop/The Travel Library/Photolibrary New York.

Chapter 4 Feature
Page 150, iStockphoto; 151, M. Brodie/Alamy.

Chapter 5
Pages 152–153 spread, Greg Smith/Corbis; 155 t, Kiyoshi Takahase Segundo/iStockphoto; 155 m1, Rosenfeld Images Ltd./Photo Researchers, Inc.; 155 m2, Ed Bock/Corbis;

155 b, Larry Dale Gordon/Getty Images; 156 inset, David R. Frazier Photolibrary, Inc.; 157 r, Kiyoshi Takahase Segundo/ iStockphoto; 157 bkgrnd, Phil Coale/AP Images; 158 br, Tim Wright/Corbis; 158–159 spread, Tim Wright/Corbis; 159 tl, Craig Aurness/Corbis; 159 t, Colin Keates/Dorling Kindersley, Courtesy of the Natural History Museum, London; 159 m, Andreas Einsiedel/Dorling Kindersley; 160–161 spread, ITAR-TASS/Grigory Sysoyev/Newscom; 161 bl, Misha Japaridze/ AP Images; 161 br, Konrad Wothe/Alamy; 162, Caro/Alamy; 164, Ethan Miller/Getty Images; 165 t, Rosenfeld Images Ltd./ Photo Researchers, Inc; 165 ml, Patrick Lynch/Alamy; 165 mr, Krys Bailey/Alamy; 165 bl, Voltaic Systems; 167, José Luis Gutiérrez/iStockphoto; 167 b, Jonah Manning/iStockphoto; 168 tl, Ed Bock/Corbis; 173 bkgrnd, Simeone Huber/Getty Images; 174 bkgrnd, Courtesy of Skip Baumhower/AP Images; 178 tl, Justin Sullivan/Getty Images; 179 tr, Larry Dale Gordon/Getty Images; 180 b, Rosenfeld Images Ltd./Photo Researchers, Inc; 180 t, Andreas Einsiedel/Dorling Kindersley; 181, Photo Library New York; 182, Photolibrary New York.

Chapter 5 Feature
Page 184 bkgrnd, Dburke/Alamy; 184 inset, David Pearson/ Alamy; 185 t, GlowImages/Alamy, 185 b, Amana Images inc/ Alamy.

Chapter 6
Pages 186–187 spread, John Lund/Corbis; 189 t, Sami Sarkis/Photographer's Choice/Getty Images; 189 m2, Richard Megna/Fundamental Photographs, NYC; 189 b, Richard Megna/Fundamental Photographs, NYC; 190 bkgrnd, Wen Zhenxiao/ChinaFotoPress/Zuma Press; 191, Adrian Lourie/ Alamy; 192 bkgrnd, Sami Sarkis/Photographer's Choice/ Getty Images; 194 br, Digital Vision/Alamy; 196 bkgrnd, Imagebroker/Alamy; 196 l, Kin Images/Getty Images; 196 m, Michael Durham/Nature Picture Library; 197 r, David Pu'u/ Corbis; 198–199 bkgrnd, Stockbyte/Getty Images; 200 inset, Moodboard/Corbis; 200 bkgrnd, Chad Baker/Digital Vision/ Getty Images; 201 bkgrnd, Walter Bibikow / Danita Delimont Inc./Alamy; 202 inset, Bettmann/Corbis; 202–203 bkgrnd, AP Images; 203 inset, Richard Megna/Fundamental Photographs, NYC; 204 tl, Matthias Kulka/Zefa/Corbis; 204 ml, Richard Megna/Fundamental Photographs, NYC; 204 mr, Nice One Productions/Corbis; 204 br, Richard Megna/Fundamental Photographs, NYC; 205 br, Richard Megna/Fundamental Photographs, NYC; 205 inset, Peter Steiner/Alamy; 206–207 bkgrnd, Yamado Taro/The Image Bank/Getty Images; 209, University of Washington Libraries; 210 bkgrnd, Digital Vision/Getty Images; 211, Ted S. Warren/AP Images; 213 bkgrnd, Andy King/AP Images; 214, Harrison H. Schmitt/ Johnson Space Center/NASA; 215, Jim Byrne/QA Photos; 216, Jean Frooms/iStockphoto; 217 l, Clive Barda/Arenapal; 217 r, Gregory Bull/AP Images; 218, Greg Baker/AP Images; 219, Caren Firouz/Reuters; 221 bkgrnd, Adam Hunger/AP Images.

Chapter 6 Feature
Page 226, Jason Verschoor/iStockphoto; 227 t, Chris Lemmens/iStockphoto; 227 b, Yevgen Timashov/iStockphoto.

Chapter 7

Pages 228–229 spread, Cloud Gate, Millennium Park, Chicago (2004), Anish Kapoor. Photo 2008 Kim Karpeles; **231 m1,** Corbis/Photolibrary New York; **231 t,** Glow Images/Photolibrary New York; **231 m2,** David R. Frazier Photolibrary, Inc./Alamy; **232 bkgrnd,** J. A. Kraulis/Masterfile; **234 bkgrnd,** Benjamin Rondel/Corbis; **235 tl,** Clive Streeter/Dorling Kindersley; **236 l,** Mode Images Limited/Alamy; **236 bkgrnd,** Arthur S. Aubry/Photodisc/Getty Images; **238–239 bkgrnd,** AbleStock/JupiterUnlimited; **239 t,** Dave L. Ryan/Photolibrary New York/AGE Fotostock; **240 l,** Joel Sartore/National Geographic/Getty Images; **240 r,** Nutscode/T Service/Photo Researchers, Inc.; **241 bkgrnd,** Goodshoot/Corbis; **241 br,** Tom Arne Hanslien/Alamy; **242 b,** Don Carstens/Robertstock; **243 bkgrnd,** Stocktrek Images, Inc./Alamy; **244,** Dennis Flaherty/Getty Images; **245,** Kevin Frayer/AP Images; **249,** Glow Images/Photolibrary New York; **251,** LOETSCHER CHLAUS/Alamy; **252,** Corbis/Photolibrary New York; **255 r,** age Fotostock/SuperStock; **256 bkgrnd,** Lawrence Lawry/Photo Researchers, Inc.; **259 bkgrnd,** AFP/AFP/Getty Images; **260,** David R. Frazier Photolibrary, Inc. / Alamy

Chapter 7 Feature

Page 268, Bart Nedobre/Alamy; **269 t bkgrnd,** Doug Steley C/Alamy; **269 t inset,** Tom McHugh/Photo Researchers, Inc.; **269 b,** Cornel Stefan Achirei/Alamy; **269 b inset,** Ed Reschke/Peter Arnold, Inc.

Chapter 8

Pages 270–271 spread, Whit Richardson/Getty Images; **273 t,** hecke61/Shutterstock; **273 b,** Rick Price/Nature Picture Library; **273 m,** Design Pics Inc./Alamy; **274 bkgrnd,** Michael Busselle/Getty Images; **275 b,** hecke61/Shutterstock; **276 ml,** InterNetwork Media/Getty Images; **276 bl,** Design Pics Inc./Alamy; **276 tl,** All Canada Photos/Alamy; **276–277 spread,** Marvin Dembinsky Photo Associates/Alamy; **277 inset,** Anna Yu/iStockphoto; **278 r,** Philip Dowell/Dorling Kindersley; **278 l,** Dietrich Rose/Zefa/Corbis; **279 m,** David Jordan/AP Images; **280 m,** Samuel B. Mukasa; **282 b,** Tracy Frankel/Getty Images; **283 bkgrnd,** Rick Price/Nature Picture Library; **283 m,** Harry Taylor/Royal Museum of Scotland, Edinburgh/Dorling Kindersley; **283 t,** NASA; **283 b,** Harry Taylor/Dorling Kindersley; **284 tl,** NASA; **285 tr,** NASA; **286–287 spread,** NASA; **288 m,** JupiterImages/Brand X/Alamy; **289 m,** Bloomimage/Corbis; **289 l,** Pancaketom/Dreamstime; **289 r,** INSADCO Photography/Alamy; **290 t,** Hall/Photocuisine/Corbis; **290 b,** TBK Media/Alamy; **291 tr,** NASA; **292 t,** Design Pics Inc./Alamy; **292 m,** NASA.

Chapter 8 Feature

Page 296 bkgrnd, Daniel Sambraus/Photo Researchers, Inc.; **296 b,** Courtesy of Michael Wysession; **297 t,** John McConnico/AP Images; **297 b,** Irochka/Fotolia.com.

Chapter 9

Pages 298–299 spread, Matt Theilen/Getty Images; **298 inset,** Loomis Dean/Time Life Pictures/Getty Images; **301 t,** Javier Trueba/MSF/Photo Researchers, Inc.; **301 m1,** Bill Brooks/Alamy; **301 m2,** Sandra vom Stein/iStockphoto; **302 r,** Linda Burgess/Dorling Kindersley; **302 l,** Linda Burgess/Dorling Kindersley; **303 l,** Rana Royalty Free/Alamy;

303 r, Arco Images GmbH/Alamy; **304 r,** Joel Arem/Photo Researchers, Inc.; **304 l,** Harry Taylor/Dorling Kindersley; **305 m1,** Colin Keates/Natural History Museum, London/Dorling Kindersley; **305 bl,** Breck P. Kent; **305 br,** Charles D. Winters/Photo Researchers, Inc.; **305 bm,** Breck P. Kent; **305 m2,** Russ Lappa; **305 t,** Breck P. Kent; **306 bl,** Colin Keates/Natural History Museum, London/Dorling Kindersley; **306 ml,** Colin Keates/Natural History Museum, London/Dorling Kindersley; **306 bm,** Colin Keates/Natural History Museum, London/Dorling Kindersley; **306 mr,** Colin Keates/Natural History Museum, London/Dorling Kindersley; **306 br,** Colin Keates/Natural History Museum, London/Dorling Kindersley; **306 tl,** JupiterImages/PIXLAND/Alamy; **307 bl,** Colin Keates/Natural History Museum, London/Dorling Kindersley; **307 ml,** Colin Keates/Natural History Museum, London/Dorling Kindersley; **307 bm,** Colin Keates/Natural History Museum, London/Dorling Kindersley; **307 mr,** Colin Keates/Natural History Museum, London/Dorling Kindersley; **307 br,** Dorling Kindersley; **308 tr,** Breck P. Kent; **308 bl,** Mark A Schneider/Science Source; **309 tr,** Chip Clark; **309 b,** Colin Keates/Natural History Museum, London/Dorling Kindersley; **309 m,** Biophoto Associates/Photo Researchers, Inc.; **310 b,** CLM/Shutterstock; **311 b,** Javier Trueba/MSF/Photo Researchers, Inc.; **311 cl,** Jane Burton/Bruce Coleman, Inc.; **311 cr,** John Cancalosi/Getty Images; **312 l,** Colin Keates/Natural History Museum, London/Dorling Kindersley; **312 r,** Gary Ombler/Oxford University Museum of Natural History/Dorling Kindersley; **314–315 spread,** Robert Glusic/Corbis; **315 t,** Breck P. Kent; **315 br,** Breck P. Kent; **315 bl,** George Whitely/Photo Researchers, Inc.; **315 m2,** Mark A. Schneider/Photo Researchers, Inc.; **316 tl,** Corbis/Photolibrary New York; **316 br,** Bill Brooks/Alamy; **316 ml,** Breck P. Kent; **316 tr,** Breck P. Kent; **316 mr,** Breck P. Kent; **316 r,** Breck P. Kent; **316 tm,** Breck P. Kent; **318 tr,** Jon Adamson/iStockphoto; **318 m,** Photo by Jiri Hermann/Courtesy Diavik Diamond Mines Inc.; **319 r,** Breck P. Kent; **319 b,** Breck P. Kent; **319 l,** Dirk Wiersma/Photo Researchers, Inc.; **320 tl,** Breck P. Kent; **321 bl,** Keith Levit/Alamy; **322 m,** Courtesy of Dr. Beverly Chiarulli; **324 ml,** Jeff Scovil; **324 bm,** John Shelton/Manuscripts, Special Collections, University Archives, University of Washington Libraries; **324 br,** Sandra vom Stein/iStockphoto; **324 tr,** Breck P. Kent; **324 bl,** Michael P. Gadomski/Photo Researchers, Inc.; **324 bm,** Lloyd Cluff/Corbis; **325 bl,** Andreas Einsiedel/Dorling Kindersley; **325 bkgrnd,** Martin Strmiska/Alamy; **325 bkgrnd,** Corbis Premium RF/Alamy; **325 br,** Breck P. Kent; **326 tr,** K-PHOTOS/Alamy; **327 m,** Daniel Dempster Photography/Alamy; **328 l,** Radius Images/Alamy; **328 t,** Sergey Peterman/Shutterstock; **329 b,** Phil Dombrowski; **330 mr,** Andrew J. Martinez/Photo Researchers, Inc.; **330 br,** Jeff Scovil; **331 tr,** Phooey/iStockphoto; **332 inset,** GlowImages/Alamy; **332 mr,** Adrian Page/Alamy; **333 b,** Kevin Fleming/Corbis; **334 tl,** Francois Gohier/Photo Researchers, Inc.; **334 bl,** Bern Petit/Breck P. Kent; **334 br,** Gregory G. Dimijian, M.D./Science Source; **334 tr,** Simon Fraser/Photo Researchers, Inc.; **336 br,** Kevin Fleming/Corbis; **336 l,** Breck P. Kent; **337 bl,** Don Nichols/iStockphoto; **338 tr,** Andrew J. Martinez/Photo Researchers, Inc.; **338 b,** Breck P. Kent; **338 tl,** Breck P. Kent.

ACKNOWLEDGMENTS

Chapter 9 Feature
Page 340, Loomis Dean/Time Life Pictures/Getty Images; **341,** Jane Stockman/Dorling Kindersley.

Chapter 10
Pages 342–343 spread, Peter Rowlands/PR Productions; **349 r,** Francois Gohier/Photo Researchers, Inc.; **350 m,** The Granger Collection, New York; **351 r,** Moodboard/Corbis; **352 t,** OAR/National Undersea Research Program/Photo Researchers, Inc.; **352 b,** Paul Zoeller/AP Images; **353 r,** Sandy Felsenthal/Corbis; **356 br,** Image Source/Getty Images; **358 bkgrnd,** Kristy-Anne Glubish/Design Pics/Corbis; **359 b,** Daniel Sambraus/Science Photo Library; **360 tl,** Blaine Harrington III/Corbis; **361 tl,** James Balog/Getty Images; **362 br,** Daniel Sambraus/Science Photo Library.

Chapter 10 Feature
Page 366, Emory Kristof/National Geographic Stock; **367 bkgrnd,** Carsten Peter/National Geographic Stock; **367 t,** Radius Images/Alamy.

Chapter 11
Pages 368–369 spread, Pata Roque/AP Images; **371 t,** Michael Nichols/Getty Images; **371 m,** D. Parker/Photo Researchers Inc.; **372 m,** vario images GmbH & Co. KG/Alamy; **374 l,** Fletcher & Baylis/Science Source; **374 r,** Marli Miller; **375 bl,** D. Parker/Photo Researchers Inc.; **376 spread,** Martin Bond/Photo Researchers, Inc.; **379 spread,** Michael Nichols/Getty Images; **380–381 spread,** AFP/Getty Images/Newscom; **384 bl,** Photo Japan/Alamy; **384 br,** Koji Sasahara/AP Images; **394 m,** George Steinmetz/Corbis; **398 m,** Karl Weatherly/Getty Images; **398 inset,** Colin Keates/Natural History Museum, London/Dorling Kindersley; **400 tl,** Rainer Albiez/iStockphoto; **400 b,** G. Brad Lewis/Omjalla Images; **401 b,** Stephen & Donna O'Meara/Getty Images; **401 t,** Rolf Schulten/imagebroker/Corbis; **402 t,** Pat and Tom Leeson/Photo Researchers, Inc.; **402 bl,** U.S. Geological Survey/Geologic Inquiries Group; **403 spread,** Alberto Garcia Photography; **405 l,** Courtesy of USGS; **406 bkgrnd,** Karen Kasmauski/Corbis; **407 m,** Justin Bailie/Aurora Photos/Corbis; **408 m,** Jeff Zenner/Shutterstock, Inc.; **408 b,** Rob Reichenfeld/Dorling Kindersley; **410 bkgrnd,** Danny Lehman/Corbis; **410 inset,** Eric & David Hosking/Photo Researchers, Inc.; **411 l,** Lee Foster/Alamy; **413 b,** Jewel Samad/AFP/Getty Images.

Chapter 11 Feature
Page 416 t, Arctic Images/Alamy; **416 b,** Bettmann/Corbis; **417 t,** Krafft/Explorer/Photo Researchers, Inc.; **417 b,** Tom Van Sant/Corbis.

Chapter 12
Pages 418–419 spread, Corbis/Kevin Schafer; **421 m,** PhotoAlto/Alamy; **421 b,** Stockbyte/SuperStock; **421 t,** Susan Rayfield/Photo Researchers, Inc.; **422 inset,** NASA/JPL/AP Images; **422 bkgrnd,** NASA/JPL/Cornell University/Zuma/Corbis; **423 bkgrnd,** Timothy Hearsum/Getty Images; **423 inset,** Adam Jones/Getty Images; **425 bl,** Susan Rayfield/Photo Researchers, Inc.; **425 tl,** Tom Till/Getty Images; **425 m,** Travel Ink/Alamy; **425 br,** Jim Nicholson/Alamy; **425 bkgrnd,** Alexander Benz/Corbis; **425 tr,** Fletcher & Baylis/Science Source; **426 t,** Bob Hammerstrom/The Nashua Telegraph/

Newscom; **426 m,** Jim Cole/AP Images; **427 inset,** Adam Hart-Davis/Photo Researchers, Inc.; **427 t,** John Elk III/Alamy; **429 r,** Nancy Smith/Pearson; **429 l,** Nancy Smith/Pearson; **429 t,** Nancy Smith/Pearson; **430 bkgrnd,** Vinicius Ramalho Tupinamba/iStockphoto; **430 inset,** Dr. Jeremy Burgess/Photo Researchers, Inc.; **430 t,** Dr. Tony Brain/Photo Researchers, Inc.; **431 br,** Micha Pawlitzki/Corbis; **431 bm,** Timurd/Dreamstime; **435 bkgrnd,** Andrew Bordwin/Beateworks/Corbis; **436 inset,** Ron Watts/Getty images; **436 bkgrnd,** Margaret Bourke-White(1954)/Time & Life Pictures/Getty Images; **437 b,** Glen Allison/Getty Images; **438 b,** Dino Ferretti/ANSA/Corbis; **438 t,** PhotoAlto/Alamy; **439 b,** Stockbyte/SuperStock; **439 inset,** Dr. Jeremy Burgess/Photo Researchers, Inc.; **439 t,** Westend61 GmbH/Alamy.

Chapter 12 Feature
Page 444 bkgrnd, Caryn Becker/Alamy; **444 m,** Caryn Becker/Alamy; **445,** Bettmann/Corbis.

Chapter 13
Pages 446–447 spread, Raimund Linke/Photolibrary New York; **449 m1,** Payne Anderson/Photolibrary New York; **449 m2,** Chris Jaksa/AGE Fotostock; **449 b,** George Steinmetz/Corbis; **450 m,** Rick Bowmer/AP Images; **452 t,** CNImaging/Photoshot/Newscom; **453 r,** paolo gislimberti/Alamy; **454 m,** Enrique Aguirre/Photolibrary New York; **456 spread,** Michael Just/age Fotostock; **457 l,** Gail Jankus/Photo Researchers, Inc.; **457 ml,** Gail Jankus/Photo Researchers, Inc.; **457 mr,** Gail Jankus/Photo Researchers, Inc.; **457 r,** Gail Jankus/Photo Researchers, Inc.; **458 l,** Darwin Wiggett/AGE Fotostock; **458 br,** Payne Anderson/Photolibrary New York; **458–459 t,** Roine Magnusson/Photolibrary New York; **459 br,** Aflo/Nature Picture Library; **460 l,** JPL/NGA/NASA; **460 r,** Marli Miller; **462 bkgrnd,** Chad Ehlers/Photolibrary New York; **462 tl,** Bernard Edmaier/Science Photo Library/Photo Researchers, Inc.; **463 tr,** Igor Katayev/ITAR-TASS/Landov; **464–465,** Arctos Images/Alamy; **466 tl,** Chris Jaksa/age Fotostock; **467 bkgrnd,** David Nunuk/age Fotostock; **469 t,** Adam Jones/Science Source; **470–471 spread,** Radius Images/Photolibrary New York; **474 m,** Photo courtesy Margaret Hiza Redsteer; **474–475 spread,** Andrew McConnell/Robert Harding World Imagery/Corbis; **476 l,** Patrick Poendl/Shutterstock; **476 r,** George Steinmetz/Corbis; **476–477 bkgrnd,** Ermin Gutenberger/iStockphoto; **477 l,** Richard and Ellen Thane/Science Source; **477 r,** Skip Brown/Getty Images; **478 br,** Andrew McConnell/Robert Harding World Imagery/Corbis; **478 m,** Adam Jones/Science Source.

Chapter 13 Feature
Page 482, Tony Campbell/iStockphoto; **483 both,** JPL/NASA.

Chapter 14
Pages 484–485 spread, Sinclair Stammers/Science Source; **487 t,** James L. Amos/Photo Researchers, Inc.; **487 m,** Michael Szoenyi/Photo Researchers, Inc.; **487 m2,** Dr. Marli Miller/Getty Images; **487 b,** Bedrock Studios/Dorling Kindersley; **488 inset,** The Natural History Museum/Alamy; **490 l,** Charles R. Belinky/Photo Researchers, Inc.; **490 tm,** Charles R. Belinky/Photo Researchers, Inc.; **490 bm,** Breck P. Kent; **490 r,** Travel Ink/Getty Images, Inc.; **491 bl,** Charlie Ott/Science Source; **491 m,** Dave King/Courtesy of the National Museum of Wales/Dorling

Kindersley; **491 t,** James L. Amos/Photo Researchers, Inc.; **492 l,** Courtesy of the Peabody Museum of Natural History, Yale University; **492 r,** Newscom; **493 b,** Phil Schermeister/Corbis; **495 spread,** Jeff Foott/Discovery Channel Images/Getty Images; **496 t,** Michael Szoenyi/Photo Researchers, Inc.; **496 b,** G. R. Roberts/Photo Researchers, Inc.; **499 tr,** Dr. Marli Miller/Getty Images; **500 rb,** Dave King/Dorling Kindersley; **500 t,** Gary Ombler/Robert L. Braun, modelmaker/Dorling Kindersley; **500 r,** Jeremy Walker/Science Photo Library/Photo Researchers; **500 l,** Gianni Tortoli/Photo Researchers, Inc.; **501 b,** James L. Amos/Corbis; **502 bl,** Colin Keates/Courtesy of the Natural History Museum, London/Dorling Kindersley; **502 ml,** Gary Ombler/Luis Rey, modelmaker/Dorling Kindersly; **502 tl,** Chase Studio/Photo Researchers, Inc.; **502 t,** Peter Johnson/Corbis; **502 m1,** Greg Vaughn/Alamy; **502 m2,** Georgette Douwma/Science Source; **502 br,** Gianni Tortoli/Photo Researchers, Inc.; **503 m,** R. Dolton/Alamy; **504 inset,** Francois Gohier/Photo Researchers, Inc.; **504 bkgrnd,** Mark Garlick/Photo Researchers, Inc.; **505 bl,** Alan Sirulnikoff/Photo Researchers, Inc.; **506 t,** Mark Hodson Stock Photography/Alamy; **508 l,** Sinclair Stammers/Photo Researchers, Inc.; **509 t,** Gary Ombler/Robert L. Braun, modelmaker/Dorling Kindersley; **509 b,** John Downs/Dorling Kindersley; **509 bkgrnd,** Jeremy Walker/Science Photo Library/Photo Researchers; **511 bl,** Harry Taylor/Courtesy of the Natural History Museum, London/Dorling Kindersley; **511 tr,** Jerry Young/Dorling Kindersley; **512 ml,** Chase Studio/Photo Researchers, Inc.; **512 t,** Colin Keates/Courtesy of the Natural History Museum, London/Dorling Kindersley; **512 mr,** Patrice Rossi Calkin; **512 m,** Publiphoto/Photo Researchers, Inc.; **512 bkgrnd,** Gianni Tortoli/Photo Researchers, Inc.; **512 bl,** Chase Studio/Photo Researchers, Inc.; **512 br,** Gary Meszaros/Alamy; **513 bkgrnd,** Greg Vaughn/Alamy; **513 m,** Harry Taylor/Courtesy of the Royal Museum of Scotland, Edinburgh/Dorling Kindersley; **513 bl,** Harry Taylor/Courtesy of the Royal Museum of Scotland, Edinburgh/Dorling Kindersley; **513 tr,** Steve Gorton/Courtesy of Oxford University Museum of Natural History/Dorling Kindersley; **513 tm,** Sheila Terry/Photo Researchers, Inc.; **513 br,** Bedrock Studios/Dorling Kindersley; **513 t,** Colin Keates/Courtesy of the Natural History Museum, London/Dorling Kindersley; **514 ml,** Gary Ombler/Gary Staab, modelmaker/Dorling Kindersley; **514 bl,** Bedrock Studios/Dorling Kindersley; **514 m,** Dave King/Jeremy Hunt at Centaur Studios, modelmaker/Dorling Kindersley; **514 bm,** Malcolm McGregor/Dorling Kindersley; **514 br,** Jon Hughes/Bedrock Studios/Dorling Kindersley; **514 bkgrnd,** Jeremy Walker/Science Photo Library/Photo Researchers; **514 tl,** Travel Ink/Getty Images, Inc.; **515 bkgrnd,** Peter Johnson/Corbis; **515 bl,** Harry Taylor/Courtesy of the Natural History Museum, London/Dorling Kindersley; **515 tm,** Bedrock Studios/Dorling Kindersley; **515 bm,** Jon Hughes/Bedrock Studios/Dorling Kindersley; **515 mr,** Javier Trueba/Madrid Scientific Films/Photo Researchers, Inc.; **515 br,** Dave King/Courtesy of the National Museum of Wales/Dorling Kindersley; **516 m,** Dave King/Dorling Kindersley; **516 t,** Phil Martin/PhotoEdit, Inc.; **516 b,** Alan Sirulnikoff/Photo Researchers, Inc.; **517 m,** Colin Keates/Dorling Kindersley; **518,** John Cancalosi/Photo Researchers, Inc.

Chapter 14 Feature
Page 520 t, Steppenwolf/Alamy; **520 b,** Jonathan Blair/Corbis; **521 tl,** Dorling Kindersley/Getty Images; **521 tr,** Colin Keates/Courtesy of the Natural History Museum, London/

Dorling Kindersley; **521 t bkgrnd,** Russell Sadur/Dorling Kindersley; **521 b bkgrnd,** Morton Beebe/Corbis; **521 inset,** Nick Cobbing/Alamy.

Chapter 15
Pages 522–523 spread, Solvin Zankl/Nature Picture Library; **525 m2,** Michael Rolands/iStockphoto; **526 m,** Biophoto Associates/Photo Researchers, Inc.; **527 bkgrnd,** Nils-Johan Norenlind/AGE Fotostock; **527 inset,** Steve Gschmeissner/Photo Researchers, Inc.; **528 tr,** Science Museum Library/Science and Society Picture Library; **528 l,** Dr. Cecil H. Fox/Photo Researchers, Inc.; **528 m,** Dr. Jeremy Burgess/Photo Researchers, Inc.; **528 br,** Dave King/Dorling Kindersley, Courtesy of The Science Museum, London; **529 l,** M. I. Walker/Photo Researchers, Inc.; **529 b,** John Walsh/Photo Researchers, Inc; **529 bkgrnd,** David Spears/Clouds Hill Imaging Ltd./Corbis; **530 tl,** Paul Taylor/Riser/Getty Images, Inc.; **530 tr,** TheRocky41/Shutterstock; **530 bl,** Wes Thompson/Corbis; **530 br,** Dorling Kindersley; **530 bm,** Millard H. Sharp/ Photo Researchers, Inc.; **532–533 spread,** A. Syred/Photo Researchers, Inc.; **534 m,** Dr. Torsten Wittmann/Photo Researchers, Inc.; **536 l,** Alfred Paskieka/Photo Researchers, Inc.; **536 r,** Bill Longcore/Photo Researchers, Inc.; **537 m,** CNRI/Photo Researchers, Inc./Photo Researchers, Inc.; **540 tl,** Photo Researchers, Inc.; **541 tr,** Biophoto Associates/Science Photo Library; **542 br,** Thomas Deerinck, NCMIR/Science Source; **542 tl,** Profs. P. Motta and S. Correr/Science Photo Library/Photo Researchers, Inc.; **542 tr,** Ed Reschke/Getty; **542 bl,** Biophoto Associates/Photo Researchers Inc.; **544 m,** Tierbild Okapia/Photo Researchers, Inc.; **545 t,** Digital Vision/Getty Images, Inc.; **546 br,** Michael Rolands/iStockphoto; **546 bl,** Dorling Kindersley; **547 tr,** Tstarr/Shutterstock; **550 inset,** George Grall/National Geographic Image Collection; **550 bkgrnd,** George Grall/National Geographic Image Collection; **551 r,** Eric Bean/Getty Images; **551 tr,** Michael Poliza/Getty; **551 l,** Helmut Gritscher/Peter Arnold, Inc.; **554 tr,** Ed Rescheke/Peter Arnold, Inc.; **554 br,** Ed Rescheke/Peter Arnold, Inc.; **554 m,** Ed Rescheke/Peter Arnold, Inc.; **555 t,** Ed Rescheke/Peter Arnold, Inc.; **555 m,** Ed Rescheke/Peter Arnold, Inc.; **555 b,** Ed Rescheke/Peter Arnold, Inc.; **556 t,** Dr. Gopal Murti/Photo Researchers, Inc.; **556 b,** Kent Wood/Getty; **558 m,** iStockphoto; **560 tr,** Innerspace Imaging/Photo Researchers, Inc.; **560 tl,** Michael Abbey/Science Source; **560 br,** Biophoto Associates/Photo Researchers, Inc.; **560 bl,** Manfred Kage/Peter Arnold, Inc.; **560–561 spread,** Dorling Kindersley; **564 l,** Lebedinski Vladislav/Shutterstock; **565 l,** Claro Cortes IV/Reuters/Corbis; **565 r,** Jeff Rotman/Nature Picture Library; **566 l,** Juice Images/Photolibrary New York; **568–569 spread,** Photodisc/Photolibrary New York; **570 l,** Dorling Kindersley; **571 t,** iStockphoto; **574 t,** Dorling Kindersley.

Chapter 15 Feature
Page 576 bkgrnd, Kim Taylor and Jane Burton/Dorling Kindersley; **576 t inset,** Kim Taylor and Jane Burton/Dorling Kindersley; **576 b inset,** David M. Phillips/Photo Researchers, Inc.; **577,** Martin Shields/Photo Researchers, Inc.

Appendix
Pages 578–579 foreground, Eckehard Schulz/AP Images; **bkgrnd,** Car Culture/Corbis.

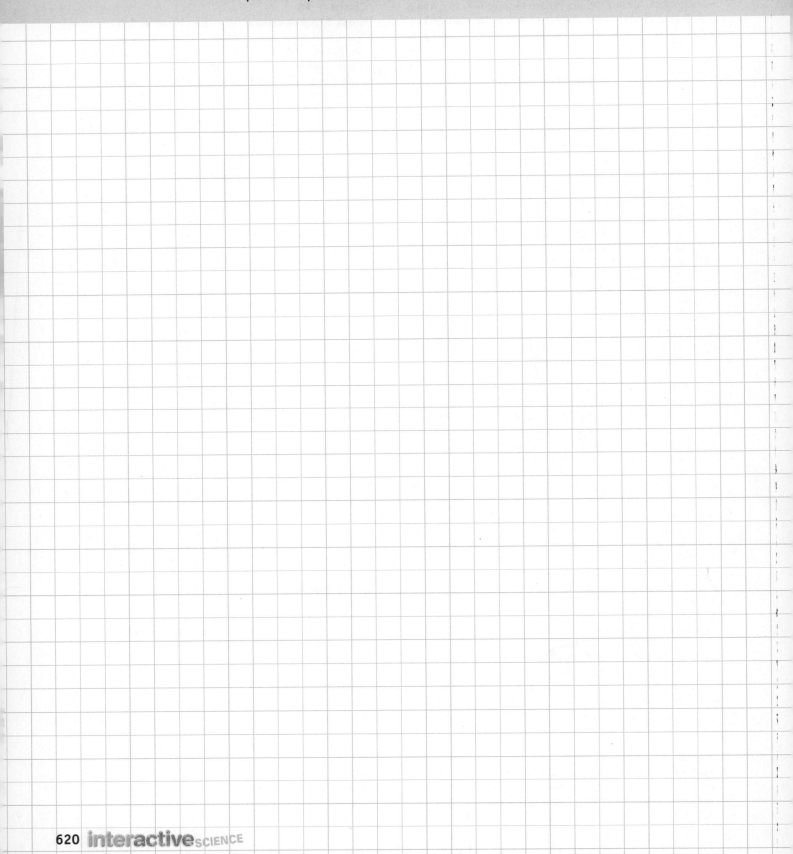